Register Now for
to Your E

SPRINGER PUBLISHING COMPANY
C🔺NNECT™

Your print purchase of *The Professional Practice of Rehabilitation Counseling, Second Edition,* **includes online access to the contents of your book**—increasing accessibility, portability, and searchability!

Access today at:

**http://connect.springerpub.com/content/book/978-0-8261-3893-4
or scan the QR code at the right with your smartphone
and enter the access code below.**

J05JSKFY

*Scan here for
quick access.*

If you are experiencing problems accessing the digital component of this product, please contact our customer service department at cs@springerpub.com

The online access with your print purchase is available at the publisher's discretion and may be removed at any time without notice.

Publisher's Note: New and used products purchased from third-party sellers are not guaranteed for quality, authenticity, or access to any included digital components.

LS

SPRINGER 🔺 PUBLISHING COMPANY

View all our products at springerpub.com

The Professional Practice of Rehabilitation Counseling

Vilia M. Tarvydas, PhD, CRC, is a professor emerita of Rehabilitation and Counselor Education and founding director of the Institute on Disabilities and Rehabilitation Ethics (I-DARE). She has worked in rehabilitation practice in traumatic brain injury and physical rehabilitation, and as a rehabilitation counselor educator for 40 years. Her scholarly works and national and international presentations have concentrated on the areas of ethics, ethical decision making, and professional governance and standards. She has published extensively in these areas, and, aside from this text, she is coauthor of *Counseling Ethics and Decision Making* (2016), a revised fourth edition of her earlier book, *Ethical and Professional Issues in Counseling*. Dr. Tarvydas has a career-long involvement in counseling professionalization, ethics, and credentialing. She served as chair of the Iowa Board of Behavioral Science Examiners, and its Disciplinary Committee. She served on the American Counseling Association (ACA) Licensure Committee for many years and more recently served on the Oversight Committee for the joint American Association of State Counseling Boards (AASCB)/ACA 20/20 Initiative. She also has had extensive experience in counselor certification, having served for 8 years with the Commission on Rehabilitation Counselor Certification (CRCC) as vice-chair and secretary, on the Examination and Research Committee, and as chair of the Ethics Committee. Dr. Tarvydas is a past president of three national professional organizations: the National Council on Rehabilitation Education (NCRE), the American Rehabilitation Counseling Association (ARCA), and the American Association of State Counseling Boards. She has been a member of the ACA Ethics Committee and the American Occupational Therapy Association's Judicial Council. She was a member of the ACA Taskforce on Revision of the Code of Ethics that produced the 2005 ACA Code of Ethics. She chaired the groups that developed the 1987 unified *Code of Professional Ethics for Rehabilitation Counselors* and served on the Task Force that drafted the 2002 CRCC Code of Professional Ethics. Most recently, she was the chair of the CRCC Task Force on Code Revision that produced the writing of the 2010 Code. She currently serves on the Council for Accreditation of Counseling and Related Educational Programs (CACREP) Board of Directors.

Michael T. Hartley, PhD, CRC, is an associate professor and coordinator of the rehabilitation and mental health specialization in the Counseling Program, Department of Disability and Psychoeducational Studies at the University of Arizona. His scholarly interests lie in the professionalization of rehabilitation counseling, including the application of ethical principles. Much of his work has targeted distributive justice issues and therefore his scholarship on ethical obligations has focused on the importance of promoting resilience and advocating against ableism or the preference for able-bodiedness. Dr. Hartley has collaborated on research grants and was the primary investigator on recent grant-funded research projects focused on developing innovative interventions to support resilience among military veterans with spinal cord injuries. He has also worked to support youth with disabilities during the school-to-work transition to increase resilience and decrease dropout. In the area of advocacy, he has been involved in leadership and research collaborations with Centers for Independent Living (CILs) to teach and empower individuals with disabilities to advocate for themselves. Rooted in the concept of self-advocacy, his research on advocacy has emphasized the use of digital technology as a way for individuals who have experienced marginalization to reclaim power and control over their environments. Finally, his research on salient ethical issues in contemporary rehabilitation counseling practice was used to guide recent revisions to the 2017 Commission on Rehabilitation Counselor Certification (CRCC) Code of Ethics, developed by a taskforce on which he served. Dr. Hartley is knowledgeable about the profession and professional practice of rehabilitation counseling, and is committed to defining and better preparing rehabilitation counselors to work ethically and effectively with persons with disabilities.

The Professional Practice of Rehabilitation Counseling

Second Edition

Editors

Vilia M. Tarvydas, PhD, CRC

Michael T. Hartley, PhD, CRC

SPRINGER PUBLISHING COMPANY

NEW YORK

Springer Publishing Company, LLC
11 West 42nd Street
New York, NY 10036
www.springerpub.com

Acquisitions Editor: Sheri W. Sussman
Compositor: Westchester Publishing Services

ISBN: 978-0-8261-3892-7
ebook ISBN: 978-0-8261-3893-4

Instructor's Materials: Qualified instructors may request supplements by emailing textbook@springerpub.com:
Instructor's Manual: 978-0-8261-3894-1
Instructor's Test Bank: 978-0-8261-3895-8
Instructor's PowerPoints: 978-0-8261-3896-5

17 18 19 20 21 / 5 4 3 2 1

The author and the publisher of this Work have made every effort to use sources believed to be reliable to provide information that is accurate and compatible with the standards generally accepted at the time of publication. The author and publisher shall not be liable for any special, consequential, or exemplary damages resulting, in whole or in part, from the readers' use of, or reliance on, the information contained in this book. The publisher has no responsibility for the persistence or accuracy of URLs for external or third-party Internet websites referred to in this publication and does not guarantee that any content on such websites is, or will remain, accurate or appropriate.

Library of Congress Cataloging-in-Publication Data

Names: Tarvydas, Vilia M., editor. | Hartley, Michael T., editor.
Title: The professional practice of rehabilitation counseling / editors, Vilia M. Tarvydas, Michael T. Hartley.
Description: Second edition. | New York, NY : Springer Publishing Company, LLC, [2018] | Includes bibliographical references and index.
Identifiers: LCCN 2017012065 | ISBN 9780826138927 (hard copy : alk. paper) | ISBN 9780826138934 (ebook) | ISBN 9780826138941 (instructors manual) | ISBN 9780826138958 (test bank) | ISBN 9780826138965 (Instructors PowerPoints)
Subjects: | MESH: Rehabilitation, Vocational—methods | Counseling—methods | Disabled Persons—rehabilitation | Professional Practice
Classification: LCC HD7255.5 | NLM WB 320 | DDC 362.4/0486—dc23
LC record available at https://lccn.loc.gov/2017012065

Contact us to receive discount rates on bulk purchases.
We can also customize our books to meet your needs.
For more information please contact: sales@springerpub.com

Printed in the United States of America by Gasch Printing.

Contents

Contributors

Mary Barros-Bailey, PhD, CRC, Bilingual Rehabilitation Counselor, Vocational Expert, and Life Care Planner, Intermountain Vocational Services, Inc., Boise, Idaho

Kevin Bengtson, MS, CRC, Doctoral Student, Department of Rehabilitation Psychology and Special Education, University of Wisconsin–Madison, Madison, Wisconsin

Susanne M. Bruyère, PhD, CRC, Professor of Disability Studies, Director of the K. Lisa Yang and Hock E. Tan Institute on Employment and Disability, ILR School, Cornell University, Ithaca, New York

Maggie K. Butler, MS, CRC, Doctoral Student, Department of Rehabilitation and Counselor Education, the University of Iowa, Iowa City, Iowa

Brenda Y. Cartwright, EdD, CRC, NCC, MHC, Professor, Department of Rehabilitation Counseling, School of Health Sciences, Winston-Salem State University, Winston-Salem, North Carolina

Fong Chan, PhD, CRC, Professor and Department Chair, Norman L. and Barbara M. Professor of Rehabilitation Psychology, Department of Rehabilitation Psychology and Special Education, University of Wisconsin-Madison, Madison, Wisconsin

Martha H. Chapin, PhD, CRC, CDMS, NCC, LPC, Professor, Director of the Rehabilitation Services Program, Department of Addictions and Rehabilitation Studies, College of Allied Health Sciences, East Carolina University, Greenville, North Carolina

Xiangli Chen, MS, Doctoral Student, Department of Rehabilitation Psychology and Special Education, University of Wisconsin–Madison, Madison, Wisconsin

Patrick Corrigan, PsyD, Distinguished Professor of Psychology, Department of Psychology, Lewis College of Human Sciences, Illinois Institute of Technology, Chicago, Illinois

R. Rocco Cottone, PhD, CFT, Professor, Division of Counseling of the Department of Education Sciences and Professional Programs, the University of Missouri—St. Louis, St. Louis, Missouri

Amanda B. Easton, PhD, CRC, LCPC, Assistant Professor of Practice, Department of Disability and Psychoeducational Studies, the University of Arizona, Tucson, Arizona

Noel Estrada-Hernández, PhD, CRC, Associate Professor and Program Coordinator of Rehabilitation and Mental Health Counseling, the University of Iowa, Iowa City, Iowa

Debra A. Harley, PhD, CRC, LPC, Professor, Department of Early Childhood, Special Education and Rehabilitation Counseling, the University of Kentucky, Lexington, Kentucky

Michael T. Hartley, PhD, CRC, Associate Professor and Coordinator of the Rehabilitation and Mental Health Specialization in the Counseling Program, Department of Disability and Psychoeducational Studies at the University of Arizona, Tucson, Arizona

James T. Herbert, PhD, CRC, LPC, Professor-in Charge, Rehabilitation and Human Services, Department of Educational Psychology, Counseling, and Special Education, Pennsylvania State University, University Park, Pennsylvania

Kanako Iwanaga, MS, Doctoral Student, Department of Rehabilitation Psychology and Special Education, University of Wisconsin–Madison, Madison, Wisconsin

Sara P. Johnston, PhD, CRC, Assistant Professor, Department of Clinical Counseling and Mental Health, Texas Tech University Health Sciences Center, Lubbock, Texas

Michael J. Leahy, PhD, CRC, LPC, University Distinguished Professor and Director, Office of Rehabilitation and Disability Studies, Department of Counseling, Educational Psychology and Special Education, Michigan State University, East Lansing, Michigan

Lisa Lopez Levers, PhD, CRC, NCC, LPCC, LPC, Professor, Department of Counseling, Psychology, and Special Education; and Rev. Francis Philben, C. S. Sp. Endowed Chair in African Studies, Duquesne University, Pittsburgh, Pennsylvania

William Ming Liu, PhD, Professor, Counseling Psychology Program, Department of Psychological and Quantitative Foundations, the University of Iowa, Iowa City, Iowa

Dennis R. Maki, PhD, CRC, NCC, LMHC, Professor Emeritus, Department of Rehabilitation and Counselor Education, the University of Iowa, Iowa City, Iowa

J. Barry Mascari, EdD, LPC, LCADC, Associate Professor, Chair of the Counselor Education Department, Nathan Weiss Graduate College, Kean University, Union, New Jersey

Henry McCarthy, PhD, CRC, LPC, Professor Emeritus, Department of Clinical Rehabilitation and Counseling, Louisiana State University Health Sciences Center, New Orleans, Louisiana

Elias Mpofu, PhD, DEd, CRC, Professor, Discipline of Rehabilitation Counseling Health Sciences, University of Sydney, Sydney, Australia

Ngonidzashe Mpofu, MCRC, Master Student, Department of Counselor Education, Rehabilitation Counseling and Educational Psychology, Pennsylvania State University, State College, Pennsylvania

Margaret A. Nosek, PhD, Executive Director, Center for Research on Women With Disabilities, Professor, Department of Physical Medicine and Rehabilitation, Senior Scientist, TIRR Memorial Hermann Rehabilitation and Research, Baylor College of Medicine, Houston, Texas

Deirdre O'Sullivan, PhD, CRC, Associate Professor, Department of Counselor Education, Counseling Psychology, and Rehabilitation Services, Pennsylvania State University, University Park, Pennsylvania

Vanessa M. Perry, PhD, CRC, Assistant Professor of Practice, Department of Disability and Psychoeducational Studies, the University of Arizona, Tucson, Arizona

Keisha G. Rogers, PhD, CRC, LCAS, LPC, Assistant Professor, Department of Rehabilitation Counseling, School of Health Sciences, Winston-Salem State University, Winston-Salem, North Carolina

Matthew C. Saleh, PhD, JD, Research Associate, K. Lisa Yang and Hock E. Tan Institute on Employment and Disability, ILR School, Cornell University, New York, New York

Linda R. Shaw, PhD, CRC, LMHC, Professor and Department Head, Department of Disability and Psychoeducational Studies at the University of Arizona, Tucson, Arizona

Susan G. Sherman, PhD, CRC, CPM, LPC, Assistant Professor, Director of Graduate Rehabilitation and Career Counseling Program, Coordinator of Certificate in Rehabilitation Counseling, Department of Addictions and Rehabilitation Studies, College of Allied Health Sciences, East Carolina University, Greenville, North Carolina

Keith Sofka, ATP (Retired), Caragonne and Associates, LLC, Assistive Technology Provider, Ajijic, Mexico

Mark A. Stebnicki, PhD, CRC, CCM, LPC, DCMHS, CCMC, Professor, Coordinator of the Military and Trauma Counseling (MTC) Certificate Program, Department of Addictions and Rehabilitation Studies, College of Allied Health Sciences, East Carolina University, Greenville, North Carolina

David R. Strauser, PhD, Professor, Work and Disability Research Lab, Department of Kinesiology and Community Health, University of Illinois at Urbana–Champaign, Champaign, Illinois

Vilia M. Tarvydas, PhD, CRC, Professor Emeritus, Faculty Director, I-SERVE, College of Education, Department of Rehabilitation and Counselor Education, the University of Iowa, Iowa City, Iowa

Rebecca L. Toporek, PhD, Associate Professor, Career Counseling Coordinator, Department of Counseling, San Francisco State University, San Francisco, California

Emre Umucu, MS, CRC, Assistant Professor, Department of Rehabilitation Sciences, College of Health Professionals, University of Texas at El Paso, El Paso, Texas

Alex W. K. Wong, PhD, DPhil, BSOT, Assistant Professor of Occupational Therapy and Neurology, Washington University School of Medicine, St. Louis, Missouri

Jia-Rung Wu, MS, Doctoral Student, Department of Rehabilitation Psychology and Special Education, University of Wisconsin–Madison, Madison, Wisconsin

Rana Yaghmaian, PhD, CRC, Assistant Professor, Clinical Rehabilitation Counseling Program Coordinator, Graduate School of Education, Portland State University, Portland, Oregon

Stephen A. Zanskas, PhD, CRC, LPC, Associate Professor & Concentration Coordinator, Rehabilitation & Clinical Rehabilitation Counseling, Co-Coordinator Ed.D. Counseling Program, Co-Director, Center for Rehabilitation & Employment Research, the University of Memphis, Memphis, Tennessee

Foreword

"The best way to find yourself is to lose yourself in the service of others."
—Mahatma Gandhi

Serve—serve proudly, ethically, professionally, and with an emphasis on empowerment—that is your mission after reading, reflecting on, and embracing the foundational and contemporary information eloquently presented in this textbook.

As a former recipient of rehabilitation counseling services, a former practicing rehabilitation counselor, and now a rehabilitation counselor educator and the president of the National Council on Rehabilitation Education (NCRE), I believe that the future for rehabilitation counseling is a positive one that will be highlighted by new opportunities, contributions, and advancements in the essential knowledge, attitudes, and skills for effective and ethical practice. The counseling profession recently reached yet another major milestone with the merger between the Council on Rehabilitation Education (CORE) and the Council for Accreditation of Counseling and Related Educational Programs (CACREP). As the president of NCRE, I have had the opportunity to discuss the CORE and CACREP merger with faculty and students, listening to concerns about the potential loss and abandonment of rehabilitation counseling concepts, values, and traditions. Like the many scholars who have written chapters in this textbook, my message has been to note the advantages of the merger. The possibilities are endless because rehabilitation counseling concepts of consumer empowerment, psychosocial rehabilitation, and the effect of disability in all aspects of life are vital to the future practice of all counselors, regardless of specialization. The merger has also reinforced the notion that **rehabilitation counselors are indeed counselors.**

With this in mind, I am honored to provide my reflection and commentary on the great work included in the present edition of *The Professional Practice of Rehabilitation Counseling.* Readers will find that the main pillars of the new edition of this text are the unification of the counseling profession and the full inclusion of individuals in less restrictive environments regardless of gender, race, socioeconomic status, religion, physical or mental abilities, or any other individual characteristic. The position adopted in this text does not call for the abandonment of the traditional practice of rehabilitation counseling and its emphasis on vocational, medical and psychosocial aspects of disability, case management, independent living, and assistive technology. Rather, the position adopted in this text integrates these traditional concepts within the framework of advocacy, empowerment, recovery, and the clinical counseling practices embraced by psychiatric rehabilitation and mental health professionals. The editors and their contributors have highlighted the need for rehabilitation educators, students, and rehabilitation counselors to embrace the concept of a **qualified rehabilitation counselor**. A qualified rehabilitation counselor is a professional who can effectively attend to the vocational and mental/emotional needs of individuals who historically have been challenged by the stigma and oppression that are caused by the disability experience. The end result is an integrated professional identity that honors the foundational concepts of our noble profession.

The present edition of *The Professional Practice of Rehabilitation Counseling* arrives at a critical moment in time with the CORE and CACREP merger. Our agenda as rehabilitation counselors must be to reexplore the contributions of the rehabilitation counseling scope of practice, research body, and knowledge domains of clinical rehabilitation counseling practice and the counseling profession more generally. This is an agenda that is consistent with the vision of many of our professional organizations, such as NCRE. It also requires the expansion of the rehabilitation counselor education curriculum to reflect contemporary professional requirements, competencies, and knowledge domains; the formulation of research agendas that focus on emerging issues and trends; and the development of professionals, leaders, and advocates who will advance the profession while meeting the needs of people with disabilities. To be sure, the chapters in this text have been conceptualized and written by forward-thinking individuals who represent the core values, knowledge base, and traditions of rehabilitation counseling as a specialty and with counseling as our profession. Many of these scholars and leaders have contributed significantly through their service to many counseling professional organizations (e.g., American Counseling Association [ACA], American Rehabilitation Counseling Association [ARCA], National Rehabilitation Association [NRA], National Rehabilitation Counseling Association [NRCA], and NCRE), credentialing bodies (e.g., CORE and CACREP), credentialing associations (Commission on Rehabilitation Counselor Certification [CRCC] and National Board for Certified Counselors [NBCC]), and licensure boards (e.g., American Association of State Counselor Licensure Boards [AASCB]), while at the same time making important scholarly contributions to the specialized knowledge base of rehabilitation counseling.

It is my firm belief that the present edition of *The Professional Practice of Rehabilitation Counseling* will crystallize the intersection of the traditional practice of rehabilitation counseling with emerging practice settings, such as behavioral and mental health. In doing so, this textbook will highlight the application of rehabilitation counseling concepts and techniques to the practice of mental health counseling, an increasingly common job function of rehabilitation counselors. Chapters included in this edition of the text present contemporary and seminal literature on the foundations of the rehabilitation counseling practice, including: an overview of private sector practice; information on the disability experience, with particular attention to family relations, disability rights, and disability issues from a global perspective; and a detailed account of perennial and emerging professional roles and competencies. Special attention is given to key aspects of practice, including advocacy and social justice, psychiatric rehabilitation, counseling and mental health issues, assessment, vocational and career development, case management, and ethics.

On a personal note, I knew Vilia Tarvydas as well as Dennis Maki, the previous editor of this textbook, while earning my doctoral degree at the University of Iowa. Their teachings, advice, mentorship, and collegiality are second only to my appreciation for their friendship. I also have had the pleasure of knowing Michael Hartley since we were fellow doctoral students at the University of Iowa. He is a strong researcher and colleague, and I look forward to his many contributions as a future leader in the field. A work of this magnitude requires the knowledge and expertise of many scholars, and I want to thank all the chapter contributors. It has been an honor to have read and followed their scholarly work, hoping one day to contribute and serve as significantly as they all have. Last but not least, in the spirit of Gandhi's life and reflection on service to others, I encourage all of the readers of this text to read, reflect, and consider the many ways to be of service to others. There is a continued need to promote a more welcoming and inclusive society by increasing opportunities and services for people with disabilities, thereby diminishing the *isms* that affect their everyday life.

Noel Estrada-Hernández, PhD, CRC
President, National Council on Rehabilitation Education, 2015–2016

Preface

We welcome you to the second edition of *The Professional Practice of Rehabilitation Counseling*, or more accurately, the fourth edition of this foundational text on rehabilitation counseling, titled in previous editions as the *Handbook of Rehabilitation Counseling* and *Rehabilitation Counseling: Profession and Practice*. The current title is the same as the third edition edited by Dennis Maki and Vilia Tarvydas, maintaining the structure and format of that edition, yet with new and most timely content to address more broadly psychiatric rehabilitation and the practice of mental health counseling as practiced by rehabilitation counselors. The opening chapter describes in detail the organization of the text and the content that has been included throughout subsequent chapters.

The information in this text has been developed by some of the strongest scholars in the field. The contributing authors are experts on their respective topics, and we are fortunate to have put together such as remarkable group of scholars. In each chapter, the authors have provided clear lines of inductive and deductive reasoning to provide clear takeaway points allowing us both to understand our past as well as look to the future. In doing so, our intent is to memorialize the history and philosophy of rehabilitation counseling, while simultaneously assimilating new research and knowledge from breakthroughs in neuroscience and pharmacology, innovations in digital communication and technology, and shifts in the economy and social milieu. In other words, without throwing out the baby with the bathwater, we fundamentally believe that the knowledge and tools used by rehabilitation counselors today should not be the same as 10 years ago.

It became apparent when we surveyed rehabilitation counselor educators and their students that there was a need for an updated introductory textbook in rehabilitation counseling. The professional practice of rehabilitation counseling is in a state of change, yet no versions of introductory texts have emerged that directly address the significant changes in the nature of practice since the last edition of this text in 2012. It is a daunting task to predict what will happen in the field moving forward, because of unprecedented changes. Although we do not claim to know the future, we believe a clear understanding of our history and philosophy will allow current and future students, educators, and practitioners to have a fairly good sense of a future for themselves as well as their clients.

Editing this text has been a remarkable journey, reassuring us that rehabilitation counselors will continue to have a wide range of professional opportunities because of their unique training, expertise, and emphasis on disability as a civil rights issue. With this in mind, we hope that readers will respond with excitement to imagining the futures that excellence in professional practice in rehabilitation counseling may bring them. We also hope that they will take to heart the knowledge and wisdom that our authors have sought to impart to them to guide them on this journey. We have been careful to make the content as accessible as possible for readers new to the field. For qualified instructors who adopt this text, we alert you to the very fine ancillaries to this book, including PowerPoint slides, learning activities, Internet resources, and a test item bank. Requests for these ancillaries can be made by e-mail (textbook@springerpub.com).

Vilia M. Tarvydas
Michael T. Hartley

Acknowledgments

A work such as this requires the support and hard work of many individuals. First and foremost, we are grateful to the chapter authors who found time to write these chapters amid their many other responsibilities and commitments. All of these authors have generously shared their wisdom and inspired us through their contributions to this text. Many of them have shared the struggles, work, and hopes for improving rehabilitation counseling with us over the years—and for that, all of us in rehabilitation counseling will be forever grateful. We also wish to thank Sheri W. Sussman, our editor at Springer Publishing Company, who was supportive in the face of looming deadlines, and the adroit editorial team helping us produce the highest-quality text possible.

It will become apparent when reading this text that the professionalization efforts of rehabilitation counseling are greater than any single individual. With this in mind, we would like to acknowledge the presidents of the National Council on Rehabilitation Education (NCRE), the National Rehabilitation Counseling Association (NRCA), and the American Rehabilitation Counseling Association (ARCA) for their leadership and outstanding contributions to the profession over the years. In addition to honoring these remarkable individuals, we hope to inspire our fellow professionals to follow in their footsteps and continue to guide the profession and practice of rehabilitation counseling through service and leadership.

As educators, we want to express our heartfelt gratitude to the countless students whose questions and interests have caused us to remain thoughtful and passionate about the improvement of the practice and professional evolution of rehabilitation counseling. Teaching is one of the most rewarding occupations imaginable when there is genuine care and respect between teachers and students. We hope we have been gracious enough to personally express our thanks to the many students we have worked with and learned from. It is one of the most rewarding aspects of being an educator.

A final acknowledgment is to our friends and family, who have motivated and sustained us to be thoughtful scholars, the book would not have been possible without your love and support.

PART I: INTRODUCTION

ONE

Rehabilitation Counseling: A Specialty Practice of the Counseling Profession

VILIA M. TARVYDAS, DENNIS R. MAKI, AND MICHAEL T. HARTLEY

The authors are honored to present the fourth edition of this introductory text on the professional practice of rehabilitation counseling. The timing of the current edition of this text could not be better. We are gratified to see that rehabilitation counseling has become an official *specialization* of the counseling profession with the merger between the two major accrediting bodies, the Council on Rehabilitation Education (CORE) and the Council for Accreditation of Counseling and Related Educational Programs (CACREP), completed on July 1, 2017. The merger was preceded by the formal acknowledgment of CORE as an affiliate of CACREP by the American Counseling Association (ACA) to support graduates of rehabilitation counseling education programs having access to state licensure as professional counselors through the CACREP accreditation in Clinical Rehabilitation Counseling. The merger represents an important step in the progression and professionalization of rehabilitation counseling. In other words, *rehabilitation counselors are counselors*. By this we mean that rehabilitation counseling does not meet the historical or sociological definition of a separate and distinct profession with its own unique accreditation and certification standards (Rothman, 1987). We, therefore, place rehabilitation counseling firmly within the profession of counseling and include information about the profession of counseling and rehabilitation counseling's relationship to it in this text, making a choice in the timeworn debate about whether rehabilitation counseling at its core is essentially counseling or case management (Patterson, 1957).

Rehabilitation counseling has evolved from its inception in federal legislation in the early 1900s to its current recognition as a specialization of the counseling profession (see Chapter 4). An initial focus on case management served a constructive purpose during the early years, given the historic link of rehabilitation counseling to the state-federal vocational rehabilitation (VR) system. At the same time, an overemphasis on rehabilitation counselors (RCs) as vocational RCs prioritized case management in its identity and credentials, and diverted attention from a natural link to the counseling profession (Emener & Cottone, 1989). Specializations are common when a profession is too broad for every practitioner to be sufficiently trained to provide high-quality services in all areas, yet the profession of counseling is unique because the specializations of rehabilitation counseling, school counseling, and community mental health counseling emerged separately until changes in our society and health care system required a more unified counseling profession in the 1990s (Myers, 1995). Today, the legal ability to practice counseling and to be reimbursed for the provision of counseling services has become increasingly contingent on the designation of counseling as a profession, including parallel mechanisms of accreditation, certification, and licensure across the counseling specialty areas.

Reflecting the evolution of rehabilitation counseling, the guiding framework for this text has been developed by the first two authors, as illustrated in the construction of the curriculum in the rehabilitation counseling program at the University of Iowa. The first two authors' scholarship and leadership of professional organizations has been instrumental in growing and operationalizing the scope of practice for rehabilitation counseling throughout the course of their careers. The third author has benefited greatly, both personally and professionally, from his relationship with the first two authors, including his formal studies as a doctoral student at the University of Iowa. The "Iowa Point of View" was introduced in the previous edition of this text to provide a clear context for readers to understand the viewpoint that rehabilitation counseling is a specialty practice of the counseling profession. The "Iowa Point of View" is the "conviction that counseling is the core profession with which rehabilitation counseling is linked" (Maki & Tarvydas, 2012, p. 5). This is a dialectical, not dichotomous, focus. It does not diminish the traditional practice of rehabilitation counseling that is heavily linked with vocational, case management, independent living, and psychosocial adjustment to disability; rather, it incorporates these traditions and strengthens our focus on advocacy, recovery, and clinical rehabilitation that have been more characteristic of psychiatric rehabilitation (see Chapter 20). As of this edition of this introductory text, it is no longer necessary to call this perspective the "Iowa Point of View" because it has become the national point of view with the merger between the accreditation bodies of CORE and CACREP.

REHABILITATION COUNSELING IS A SPECIALTY PRACTICE OF THE COUNSELING PROFESSION

On the face of it, the preceding statement about the national point of view would appear to be a simple, declarative sentence, and recent changes in the field have now made it so. Rehabilitation counseling has finally arrived as an official specialty practice of the counseling profession, and now additional questions have emerged, such as how the knowledge, skills, and attitudes of rehabilitation counseling complement those of mental health counseling, one of the fastest growing aspects of counseling and an expertise necessary for new graduates who will need to gain licensure and often employment opportunities in behavioral health contexts. With this in mind, we view psychiatric rehabilitation as a bridge to understand the intersection of traditional rehabilitation counseling with mental health and clinical rehabilitation in this introductory text.

Psychiatric rehabilitation emerged in the 1960s as a result of the deinstitutionalization movement whereby hundreds of thousands of individuals with significant psychiatric disabilities were "discharged from long-stay psychiatric hospitals into the community, and others were never institutionalized" (Mueser, 2016, p. vii). Highly pioneering, respected, and effective psychiatric rehabilitation programs and models such as that developed at Boston University by Dr. Bill Anthony and his colleagues evolved within the rehabilitation and recovery traditions (Anthony, Cohen, & Farkas, 1990). Anthony is clear that this psychiatric rehabilitation model was based on traditional rehabilitation counseling philosophies and practices. Indeed, RCs have served individuals with psychiatric disabilities within the VR system since the 1940s and contributed their advanced expertise to provide innovative treatment models to assist people with psychiatric disabilities to manage mental health symptoms as well as polysubstance abuse (Corrigan,

2016; Pratt, Gill, Barrett, & Roberts, 2014). Additionally, RCs have always found it in their mission to work with those people who experience the greatest stigma and biggest barriers to living their lives with a disability. At this point in our history, people with psychiatric disorders would certainly be the group most in need of professionals who carry this perspective and have the requisite skills to assist them (Corrigan & Lam, 2007). Therefore, RCs should be practitioners of mental health counseling, clinical rehabilitation, or psychiatric rehabilitation.

RCs work with "persons with physical, mental, developmental, cognitive, and emotional disabilities to achieve their personal, career, and independent living goals in the most integrated setting possible," according to the Commission on Rehabilitation Counselor Certification (CRCC, 2016, p. 1). Today, mental illness is a leading cause of disability in the United States and across the world (Murray & Lopez, 1996; McAlpine & Warner, 2002). In a special issue on psychiatric rehabilitation, Koch, Donnell Carey, and Lusk (2016) summarize the prevalence of mental illness in the United States as one in five (18.5%) adults, with approximately 10 million (4.2%) individuals in 2013 meeting the criteria for a serious mental illness (Substance Abuse and Mental Health Services Administration [SAMHSA], 2014). A **psychiatric disability** is when an individual with a serious mental illness is unable to perform major life activities in particular life contexts, such as work, community participation, and independent living (Sánchez, Rosenthal, Chan, Brooks, & Bezyak, 2016). With unemployment rates as high as 80% to 90% (Goldberg et al., 2001), it is not surprising that individuals with serious mental illness are the largest disability group served by state-federal VR, constituting 32.2% of the cases in a study by Rosenthal, Dalton, and Gervey (2007). At the same time, individuals with psychiatric disabilities have the lowest success rates in VR, with fewer than 15% obtaining competitive employment (Anthony, 1993). It is our firm belief that rehabilitation counseling practice must evolve and become better at addressing the vocational, independent living, and psychosocial needs of people with psychiatric disabilities, not only in the state-federal VR system (Lusk, Koch, & Paul, 2016) but also in our health care system, including the delivery of behavioral and mental health services (Sheehan & Lewicki, 2016).

As a unifying paradigm to consolidate VR, clinical rehabilitation, and mental health counseling, psychiatric rehabilitation is consistent with the overall philosophy and practice of rehabilitation counseling (Olney & Gill, 2016), especially the recovery-based focus on health and wellness (Swarbrick & Nemec, 2016). All counselors, regardless of specialization, emphasize a **wellness model of mental health** focused on client strengths and "a holistic view of wellness across many areas of life, including physical, emotional, mental, spiritual, relational, vocational, financial, and sexual realms" (Young & Cashwell, 2017, p. 8). At the same time, RCs have developed unique expertise to promote employment, independent living, and overall quality of life (QOL) related to living well with a disability (see Chapter 5). Therefore, RCs can play a significant role in the creation of a recovery-orientated behavioral health system as called for by the U.S. Surgeon General and SAMHSA (U.S. Department of Health and Human Services [DHHS], 1999, 2005).

Recovery is defined by Anthony (1993) as a "deeply personal process of changing one's attitudes, values, feelings, goals, skills, and/or roles. . . . Recovery involves the development of new meaning and purpose in one's life as one grows beyond the catastrophic effects of mental illness" (p. 15). Rather than focusing on a "cure" for mental health symptoms, a **recovery-orientated perspective** emphasizes "self-determination and such normal life pursuits as education, employment, sexuality, friendship, spirituality, and voluntary membership in faith and other kinds of communities beyond the limits of the disorder and of the mental health system" (Davidson, Tondora, Staeheli Lawless,

O'Connell, & Rowe, 2009, p. 11). Similar to how RCs work with individuals with spinal cord injury, recovery does not refer to the restoration of spinal cord function or ability to walk, but rather to the rights of individuals to "access and join in with those elements of community life the person chooses, and to be in control of his or her life and destiny, *even and especially while remaining disabled*" (Davidson et al., 2009, p. 15). Even when individuals continue to experience mental health symptoms, Davidson et al. denote "being *in* recovery" as containing and minimizing the disruptive impact of mental illness on an individual's personal, vocational, and independent living goals (2009, p. 11). Aligned with the core values of rehabilitation counseling, Deegan (1988) describes a recovery-orientated behavioral health system whereby individuals' mental illness does not "get rehabilitated" in the way that cars "get tuned up" or appliances "get repaired," but instead the focus is on "recovering a new sense of self and of purpose within and beyond the limits of the disability" (1988, p. 11). Ultimately concerned with empowerment and self-determination, the involvement of RCs in the delivery of behavioral and mental health services is an opportunity for people with psychiatric disabilities to be assisted by professionals who bring advanced knowledge, skills, and attitudes related to disability and a commitment to advocacy.

As noted by Jane Myers (2012), a leader of the counseling profession, rehabilitation counseling as a specialization of the profession of counseling "stands at the forefront in creating sustained positive change in the holistic wellbeing of persons with disabilities . . . to be effective advocates and change agents for themselves, their families, their communities and society" (p. xvi). RCs have a long history of partnering with the advocacy efforts of people with disabilities, and have specialized knowledge of disabilities, the lived disability experience, and the sociopolitical-environmental factors that impact people with disabilities (Jenkins, Patterson, & Szymanski, 1992; Leahy & Szymanski, 1995). However, in order to ethically assert our continued place in the practice of behavioral and mental health, RCs must have education and professional preparation standards that embrace and integrate all the necessary elements to practice responsibly and with skill and respect. For example, stronger attention to such areas as evidence-based practices and diagnosis and treatment of psychiatric disorders are necessary. The recent knowledge domain study (Leahy, Munzen, Saunders, & Strauser, 2009) in rehabilitation counseling indicated an increased need for preservice and continuing education in counseling, mental health, and substance abuse. It is our view that these topics have not been sufficiently addressed in rehabilitation counseling texts. Embracing the broadest scope of practice possible, the ideas and information contained in this text provide a necessary structuring of rehabilitation counseling around a clear point of view on its identity and credentials as a specialty practice of counseling.

With our counseling skills as well as disability and rehabilitation expertise, RCs also perform functions such as case management, advocacy, and consultation when working with our clients in achieving their individualized goals. Furthermore, some RCs provide assessment and forensic services and do not have clients, but rather evaluees (see Chapter 16). Yet, the fact that RCs do more than counsel does not compromise our primary affiliation with the counseling profession, nor does it diminish our other essential functions. In fact, to embrace our core identity as counselors is not incompatible with, or disrespectful to, the RCs who choose to work in areas of practice that are not titled counselor or are not primarily counseling in function. Therefore, we are proud to highlight the necessary knowledge, skills, and attitudes in this text whereby RCs may proudly announce: "I am a counselor who works with people who have disabilities"—whether the disability is mental illness, some other type of disability, or coexisting disabilities.

PROFESSIONAL CREDENTIALS

Credentialing has defined and regulated the professional practice of rehabilitation counseling in recent years (see Chapter 16). This text is predicated on creating the most robust practitioner: a licensed mental health or professional counselor with a certification in rehabilitation counseling. Thus, we advocate for the licensure of the counseling generalist and for certification of the rehabilitation specialist. It is our belief that RCs must have robust careers available to them, with access to all positions and work for which they are qualified; and the ability to experience new opportunities, mobility, and advancement throughout a long-term career. To maximize employment opportunities, RCs must understand accreditation, certification, and licensure as distinct forms of credentialing:

- **Accreditation** is a mechanism that educational institutions and programs voluntarily undergo to demonstrate quality assurance to students, professionals, and the general public that the education and training of professional counselors is consistent across the country. Accreditation guarantees that only graduates of accredited programs or those who can demonstrate completion/attainment of all accreditation standards are eligible for licensure and certification as professional counselors, and accreditation is regulated by professionals within the field. The recent merger between CORE and CACREP is important because graduation from an accredited educational program is increasingly associated with eligibility for certification and licensure.
- **Certification** is a process to ensure that an individual counselor has obtained the knowledge, attitudes, and skills to specialize and work in unique employment settings, with particular client populations, and/or implement specialized techniques. Certification is thus associated with employment in particular work settings. Certification standards are developed by senior members of the profession who wish to define and promote the necessary knowledge and skills for specialty practice, much like medical professions where medical doctors are licensed by their state to practice general medicine, yet apply for board certifications to demonstrate their expertise in a specialty field (e.g., allergist, cardiologist, endocrinologist). The certified rehabilitation counselor (CRC) certification is a critical credential to establish expertise in forensic rehabilitation counseling practice.
- **Licensure** is a governmentally sanctioned credential intended to protect the public safety by assuring that citizens are served by qualified providers of counseling services. Licensure is regulated by individual states; thus, individuals who are not licensed in a state may be prohibited from engaging in professional activities that include counseling if both the title of counseling and its practice are written into the licensure law. Licensure is important because it defines the legal ability to practice counseling, as well as to receive reimbursement from third-party insurance companies and private payers for the provision of counseling services. Although licensure laws may vary with respect to the title and practice of counseling, there is increasing parity as the licensed professional counselor (LPC) has become the most common title and practice legislation across the 50 states.

Highly regulated and supervised work environments have historically been exempt from state licensure and national certification requirements, including the state-federal VR system. However, it has become increasingly difficult to convince the public and other professionals that RCs employed in exempt settings are sufficiently trained to provide professional counseling services without state licensure and national certification requirements. As a comparison, consider that physicians who worked in hospitals were initially exempt from medical licensure, yet over time licensure became a requirement for all physicians regardless of setting (Remley, 2012). Similarly, licensure is likely to become a legal requirement to provide counseling services, and individual counselors will likely need to obtain licensure in order to document sufficient training and expertise to perform counseling-related job functions, such as diagnosis and treatment planning (Tarvydas, Hartley, & Gerald, 2015). It is therefore critical that RCs graduate from properly accredited educational programs, obtain certification, and continue to become licensed, especially if engaged in the provision of mental health and substance abuse counseling.

PROFESSIONAL IDENTITY

The underlying premise of this text is one of professional identity. The professional identity of an RC as a counselor has had wide formal endorsement by the major professional organizations and leaders in the field. As George Wright (1980) pointed out, "counseling is inherent in rehabilitation counseling: this is a nontransferable obligation of the rehabilitation counselor . . . the ultimate professional responsibility for the function of counseling cannot be delegated" (p. 55). More recently, the identity of RCs as counselors was formally endorsed in 2005 by professional organizations within the Rehabilitation Counseling Consortium (RCC), including (a) CORE, (b) CRCC, (c) American Rehabilitation Counselor Association (ARCA), (d) National Rehabilitation Counseling Association (NRCA), (e) National Council on Rehabilitation Education (NCRE), (f) Canadian Association of Rehabilitation Professionals (CARP), (g) International Association of Rehabilitation Professionals (IARP), and (h) American Deafness and Rehabilitation Association (ADARA). The following definition of **rehabilitation counseling** was established and adopted by these organizations:

> A rehabilitation counselor is a counselor who possesses the specialized knowledge, skills, and attitudes needed to collaborate in a professional relationship with persons with disabilities to achieve their personal, social, psychological, and vocational goals. (RCC, 2005)

Clearly supporting the identity of RCs as counselors, accreditation and certification standards in rehabilitation counseling have mirrored the standards of other counseling specializations over the last decade.

Since the early 2000s, the accreditation and certification standards of rehabilitation counseling have been recognized as having parity with their equivalents in general counseling by the ACA (Tarvydas, Leahy, & Zanskas, 2009). CORE was the first accreditation body in counseling, accrediting master's programs in rehabilitation counseling. With specialty standards covering rehabilitation and disability, the CORE accreditation standards were consistent with the general accreditation standards of CACREP leading up to the recent merger of the two organizations. Similarly, the CRCC was the first certification body in counseling, governing the CRC credential and the Certified Rehabilitation Counselor Examination (CRCE). As an entry-level exam for licensure in some states, the CRCE is viewed as equivalent to the National Counselor Examination (NCE), governed by the National Board for Certified Counselors (NBCC) and associated with the National Certified Counselor (NCC) credential. One part of the CRCE tests knowledge about general counseling, whereas the other part tests knowledge related to rehabilitation and disability. All candidates must pass both sections of the CRCE exam, requiring that master's programs in rehabilitation counseling prepare students in both counseling and rehabilitation competencies.

The driving force behind equivalent accreditation and certification has been the need for graduates of rehabilitation counseling education programs to be eligible for state licensure as professional counselors. Although rehabilitation counseling has contributed to the professionalization efforts of the counseling profession, the initial counselor licensure law in 1976 was advocated for by community mental health counselors. The Community Mental Health Act of 1963 legislated the creation of community mental health centers, shifting the focus of mental health services from institutions and into the community (Young & Cashwell, 2017). By the 1970s, "it was clear that counselors were providing services that we would now call mental health counseling" as a form of community-based care (Sheperis & Sheperis, 2015, p. 7). Counselor licensure laws emerged because of regulations by Medicare and Medicaid, as well as private health insurance, that required licensure for the reimbursement of mental health services. Advocating for counselor licensure, the American Mental Health Counselors Association (AMHCA) formed in 1976 with early ties to the American Rehabilitation Counseling Association (ARCA). Although licensure laws were slowly being passed by individual states, the Academy of Mental Health Certification approached the CRCC in the 1980s to consider the creation of a specialty certification in mental health counseling, which was not pursued at the time. Today, there appears to be more and more overlap between RCs and community mental health counselors in terms of clients served, employment settings, knowledge requirements, and counseling techniques. Additionally, if we consider it imperative for the field of rehabilitation counseling to address the needs of people with disabilities, rehabilitation counseling must be firm in continuing to pursue the education, credentials, and access to settings in which those with psychiatric disabilities are served. It could be argued that in our contemporary society people with psychiatric disabilities have great need for expert application of rehabilitation and recovery approaches (see Chapter 20). Due to attitudinal and policy barriers to services, jobs, housing, and other aspects of our society, it could be argued that people with psychiatric disabilities and those who have other disabilities that co-occur with them constitute a group most in need of assistance in achieving their goals for full inclusion in our society. Thus, the field should embrace new opportunities to provide expert assistance to this group.

With the merger between CORE and CACREP, a growing number of rehabilitation counseling programs have sought coaccreditation under Clinical Rehabilitation as well as Clinical Mental Health, a specialty CACREP accreditation created in 2009 (Newsome & Gladding, 2014). Furthermore, a joint CORE and CACREP task force led by RC was appointed in October 2016 to infuse rehabilitation and disability-related concepts into the training of all counselors regardless of specialization, in order to establish common knowledge requirements and improve services to individuals with disabilities.

In an effort to unify the various counseling specializations, the ARCA and other professional rehabilitation counseling organizations, including NRCA, CORE, and CACREP, were involved in the decade-long 20/20 Initiative ending in 2013 (Kaplan, Tarvydas, & Gladding, 2014). The 20/20 Initiative was organized by the ACA and the American Association of State Counseling Boards (AASCB) to facilitate the unification of the counseling profession and foster collaborative dialogue among the counseling constituency. The 20/20 Initiative required that all participating organizations endorse the following seven core principles of counseling:

1. Sharing a common professional identity is critical for counselors.
2. Presenting ourselves as a unified profession has multiple benefits.

3. Working together to improve the public perception of counseling and to advocate for professional issues will strengthen the profession.
4. Creating a portability system for licensure will benefit counselors and strengthen the counseling profession.
5. Expanding and promoting our research base is essential to the efficacy of professional counselors and to the public perception of the profession.
6. Focusing on students and prospective students is necessary to ensure the ongoing health of the counseling profession.
7. Promoting client welfare and advocating for the populations we serve is the primary focus of the counseling profession.

Efforts such as the 20/20 Initiative have been critical to the ability of RCs to be reimbursed by third-party health insurance for the provision of counseling services. Indeed, a driving force behind the 20/20 Initiative was a stronger collective voice on Capitol Hill to compete with the lobbying efforts of social work and psychology. The lobbying efforts of the counseling profession have resulted in legislation to assure Medicare reimbursement for counselors, the hiring of counselors into the Veterans Administration (VA), and increasing mental health counseling within elementary and secondary schools (ACA, 2016). Furthermore, the counseling profession has successfully lobbied to have counselors reimbursed for the provision of counseling services by the U.S. Department of Defense (DoD) under TRICARE health insurance services (Federal Register, 2014). The significance of TRICARE is that RCs can work with mental health centers, agencies, and organizations as well as the VA and veteran organizations as long as they obtain and maintain the necessary credentials. RCs can play a critical role in improving the delivery of counseling and rehabilitation services to all individuals with disabilities, especially those served in our behavioral and mental health care systems.

EMERGING TRENDS

It is an exciting time to be an RC. Rehabilitation counseling was recently rated as the 10th most meaningful job in America (Smith, 2015), as well as the highest-paid counseling specialization in a survey by ACA (2014), with an average annual salary of $53,561. Part of the reason for the higher salaries is the wide range of employment opportunities for RCs, including for-profit insurance and forensic settings. The types of people served by RCs, their residual assets and limitations that impact their QOL, and their successful integration into their responsibilities and communities has continued to expand in recent years (see chapters in Part III). As such, the parameters of the scope of practice of rehabilitation counseling are evolving to meet the changing needs of society and the individuals whom it serves, as reflected in the growth and diversity in employment opportunities and professional functions (see chapters in Part IV). Finally, a growing awareness and appreciation of individuals within the context of their culture, as well as the advances of technology and a broadening research base for best practices, require an increasingly broad set of professional competencies reflected in more intense preservice preparation and commitment to ongoing continuing education (see chapters in Part V). With this in mind, this text seeks to highlight the following emerging areas of importance while still providing the most up-to-date information about more traditional aspects of rehabilitation counseling practice.

Counselors were previously restricted from employment in **behavioral and mental health** settings because the prevention and intervention of mental illness such as anxiety or depression, as well as substance abuse and other addictions, were protected by the traditions and credentials of psychiatry and psychology. Yet, the scope of practice for counselors licensed as independent practitioners by counselor licensure laws now includes the legal ability to diagnose and treat mental health and substance abuse disorders. As a result, trends in counseling employment indicate job growth in behavioral and mental health settings, particularly with the expansion of services available to individuals following the signing of the Affordable Care Act. In fact, the U.S. Bureau of Labor Statistics (BLS, 2015a, 2015b) estimates that the field of rehabilitation counseling will grow by 9% between 2014 and 2024, and that the field of mental health counseling will add more than 31,400 jobs and grow more than 19% between 2014 and 2024. RCs also are being called upon to work with wounded veterans as they return from Iraq and Afghanistan toward their medical and vocational reintegration (Frain, Bishop, Tansey, Sanchez, & Wijngaarde, 2013). Today's veterans' "signature injuries" are cognitive and emotional injuries, calling upon those who serve them to add strong mental health counseling skills to serve those recovering from primarily traumatic brain injuries and psychiatric disorders (Isham et al., 2010). With this in mind, we have included a chapter on psychiatric rehabilitation in this introductory text to highlight the substantial evidence-based research supporting the effectiveness of psychosocial interventions provided by psychiatric rehabilitation practitioners.

The professional landscape of rehabilitation counseling has changed globally as well. More and more international students are studying rehabilitation counseling in the United States and returning to their home countries to educate and practice rehabilitation counseling. With an increased focus on international rehabilitation, the *International Classification of Functioning, Disability and Health* (ICF) model has become an essential complement to the *Diagnostic and Statistical Manual of Mental Disorders* (DSM). This edition of the textbook more robustly addresses the expansion of international rehabilitation, including an emphasis on the *ICF* model in the chapter on assessment. Further, a global perspective is infused throughout the chapters, especially in the chapter on disability in a global context.

Finally, new ethical standards have emerged to address roles and relationships with clients, professional responsibility and competence, and confidentiality and privacy because of economic and cultural shifts with respect to social media, health care legislation, and insurance practices. The CRCC recently released a new *Code of Professional Ethics for Rehabilitation Counselors*, effective January 1, 2017 (CRCC, 2017). The textbook overviews changes to the new CRCC *Code* related to social justice and cultural competence, technology and social media, mental health and trauma, and assessment and forensics, as well as comparing and contrasting these new changes to the CRCC *Code* with the new changes to the 2014 ACA *Code of Ethics*.

OVERVIEW OF BOOK

Intended Audience

This text is intended to be useful to a wide range of readers and can readily serve as a core textbook or resource to explain the history, development, and current practice of RCs within the context of the contemporary practice of counseling. Although most clearly useful to counselors-in-training in an introductory course, we think that those RCs at the doctoral level or already in practice interested in the field and its broader positioning and potential will find this text appealing.

Framework for the Text

With the evolution of society in our current environment and technology, there is a place for RCs in the delivery of behavioral health services. If they are not included, their absence is a loss of practice opportunities for its professionals and the clients they serve. The following are the underlying principles of this textbook:

- Rehabilitation counselor education (RCE) and practice should include a "hybridization" of the content in rehabilitation and mental health counseling to best serve the entire range of disabilities and co-occurring conditions common in practice and to reflect a truly holistic and inclusive point of view.
- RCE and practice should involve a developmental perspective relative to the client's needs throughout the life span.
- RCE and practice are best conducted from the framework of an ecological, transformative rehabilitation perspective that addresses the person–environment context of disability. Our practices seek to assist individuals with disabilities to adapt to the physical and attitudinal environments in which they live, work, learn, and recreate. Simultaneously, it assists these environments to accommodate these individuals.
- RCE and practice are best conducted from a culturally competent perspective that respects the individual differences, as well as the commonalities, of both the client and the counselor. This view includes both social justice and advocacy perspectives. Rehabilitation counseling must seek a better infusion of the sensibilities and "ways of knowing" about the disability experience within the discipline of disability studies. This field and the study of the various fine arts, social science, and humanities representations of disability and the sensibilities they portray must be taken as serious source material to expand the professional viewpoint that represents the traditional teachings of the field.
- The rehabilitation counseling philosophy views clients as decision makers in their own lives. This perspective is predicated on clients making meaning of their lives in their current circumstances. Making meaning requires informed consent; that is, being given accurate and complete information about the choices in a manner that is useful and tailored to the needs of the client. This is essential to the quality of the client's ability to make informed choices.

Features of the Text

New features have been added to assist both instructors and students in gaining full benefit from this volume. Learning objectives begin each chapter, and discussion questions are provided at the conclusion of each chapter to expand the understanding and relevance of the material covered in the text. Additionally, learning activities conclude each chapter, and the appendices have been updated and expanded to provide key reference materials. Of particular note is the inclusion of the newly revised CRCC 2017 *Code of Professional Ethics for Rehabilitation Counselors.*

Parts and Chapters

The Professional Practice of Rehabilitation Counseling consists of 22 chapters, which are divided into parts that emphasize different themes important to understanding both the people and the types of situations with which RCs work and the specific roles and skill sets that describe professional practice.

Part II: Foundations consists of basic information about the structure and professional practice of rehabilitation counseling. It is here that the evolution and vision of rehabilitation counseling as a specialty practice of the profession of counseling is emphasized and interpreted within the context of the merger of CORE and CACREP. This perspective is integrated within the important traditional aspects of the field's history, credentialing structures, and disability policy and laws, as well as a conceptual paradigm to undergird its practice. A new chapter has been added that explicitly sets forth these core frameworks. We have also added a focus on understanding how social justice and human development within the broader field of counseling relate to the important history and tradition of rehabilitation counseling.

Part III: People With Disability serves the important role of introducing the readers to the RC's most important partner in the counseling process: the person with a disability. The chapters are presented to situate the lives of people with disabilities by focusing on hierarchically arranged contexts in their lives—moving from individual, to family and intimate relationships, to the disability community, and finally to disability in global contexts. Care was taken to emphasize the experience, not only the facts, of disability, and to give particular attention to the voices of people with disabilities themselves through discussion of the disability community/disability rights perspective that is too often superficially treated.

In *Part IV: Professional Functions*, we return to a focus on the professional practice of rehabilitation counseling and introduce the new work in the field that sharpens the emphasis on evidence-based practices and research utilization in the field in the introduction to this part. Further chapters describe in more detail the specific functions that constitute the work of rehabilitation counseling: assessment, counseling, forensic and indirect services, clinical case management and case coordination, psychiatric rehabilitation, advocacy, and career development, vocational behavior, and work adjustment of individuals with disabilities. These core functions are masterfully presented by authorities who describe the core elements of each area. Taken together, the chapters in this part sketch out the broad parameters of the professional scope of practice in the robust field of rehabilitation counseling.

Part V: Professional Competencies introduces the competencies that provide the types of skills, knowledge, and attitudes that must infuse the practice of rehabilitation counseling because of their pervasive and overarching importance in all aspects of practice. The areas of ethics, ethical decision making, and cultural competency are widely acknowledged as major forces for professionalism and are considered at the outset of the part. The increased prominence of technology used in rehabilitation is a force for innovation and critical to maintaining current practice. Fittingly, in the last chapter of this part, clinical supervision is discussed, as it performs a critical translational and evaluative role in both the initial education and continual improvement of our professional colleagues.

REFERENCES

American Counseling Association. (2014). 2014 state of the profession: Counselor compensation. Retrieved from http://www.counseling.org

American Counseling Association. (2016). Government affairs. Retrieved from http://www.counseling.org

American Psychiatric Association. (2013). *Diagnostic and statistical manual of mental disorders* (5th ed.). Arlington, VA: American Psychiatric Publishing.

Anthony, W. A. (1993). Recovery from mental illness: The guiding vision of the mental health service system in the 1990s. *Psychosocial Rehabilitation Journal, 16*(4), 11–23. doi:10.1037/h0095655

Anthony, W. A., Cohen, M., & Farkas, M. (1990). *Psychiatric rehabilitation* (1st ed.). Boston, MA: Boston University, Center for Psychiatric Rehabilitation.

Commission on Rehabilitation Counselor Certification. (2016). Rehabilitation counseling. Retrieved from http://www.crccertification.com/pages/rehabilitation_counseling/30.php

Commission on Rehabilitation Counselor Certification. (2017). *Code of professional ethics for rehabilitation counselors.* Schaumburg, IL: Author.

Corrigan, P. W. (2016). *Principles and practice of psychiatric rehabilitation: An empirical approach* (2nd ed.). New York, NY: Guilford Press.

Corrigan, P. W., & Lam, C. (2007). Challenging the structural discrimination of psychiatric disabilities: Lessons learned from the American disability community. *Rehabilitation Education, 21*(1), 53–58.

Davidson, L., Tondora, J., Staeheli Lawless, M., O'Connell, M. J., & Rowe, M. (2009). *A practical guide to recovery-oriented practice.* New York, NY: Oxford University Press.

Deegan, P. E. (1988). Recovery: The lived experience of rehabilitation. *Psychosocial Rehabilitation Journal, 11,* 11–19.

Emener, W. G., & Cottone, R. R. (1989). Professionalization, deprofessionalization, and reprofessionalization of rehabilitation counseling according to criteria of the professions. *Journal of Counseling and Development, 67,* 576–581.

Federal Register. (2014). TRICARE certified mental health counselors. Retrieved from https://www.federalregister.gov

Frain, M., Bishop, M., Tansey, T., Sanchez, J., & Wijngaarde, F. (2013). Current knowledge and training needs of certified rehabilitation counselors to work effectively with veterans with disabilities. *Rehabilitation Research, Policy, and Education, 27,* 2–17.

Goldberg, R. W., Lucksted, A., McNary, S., Gold, J. M., Dixon, L., & Lehman, A. (2001). Correlates of long-term unemployment among inner-city adults with serious and persistent mental illness. *Psychiatric Services, 52*(1), 101–103.

Isham, G. J. (Chair), Basham, K. K., Busch, A. B., Cassimatis, N. E. G., Moxley, J. H. III., Pincus, H. A., . . . Tarvydas, V. M. (2010). *Provision of mental health services under TRICARE.* Washington, DC: Institute of Medicine, National Academies Press.

Jenkins, W., Patterson, J. B., & Szymanski, E. M. (1992). Philosophical, historic, and legislative aspects of the rehabilitation counseling profession. In R. M. Parker & E. M. Szymanski (Eds.), *Rehabilitation counseling: Basics and beyond* (2nd ed., pp. 1–41). Austin, TX: Pro-Ed.

Kaplan, D. M., Tarvydas, V. M., & Gladding, S. T. (2014). 20/20: A vision for the future of counseling: The new consensus definition of counseling. *Journal of Counseling and Development, 92,* 366–372. doi:10.1002/j.1556-6676.2014.00164x

Koch, L. C., Donnell Carey, C., & Lusk, S. L. (2016). Introduction to the special issue on psychiatric rehabilitation. *Rehabilitation Research, Policy, and Education, 30*(3), 198–203. doi:10.1891/2168-6653.30.3.198

Leahy, M. J., Munzen, P., Saunders, J. L., & Strauser, D. (2009). Essential knowledge domains underlying effective rehabilitation counseling practice. *Rehabilitation Counseling Bulletin, 52*(2), 95–106. doi:10.1177/0034355208323646

Leahy, M. J., & Szymanski, E. M. (1995). Rehabilitation counseling: Evolution and current status. *Journal of Counseling and Development, 74,* 163–166.

Lusk, S. L., Koch, L. C., & Paul, T. M. (2016). Recovery-oriented vocational rehabilitation services for individuals with co-occurring psychiatric disabilities and substance abuse disorders. *Rehabilitation Research, Policy, and Education, 30*(3), 243–258. doi:10.1891/2168-6653.30.3.243

Maki, D. R., & Tarvydas, V. M. (2012). Rehabilitation counseling: A specialty practice of the counseling profession. In D. R. Maki & V. M. Tarvydas (Eds.), *The professional practice of rehabilitation counseling* (pp. 3–16). New York, NY: Springer Publishing.

McAlpine, D. D., & Warner, L. (2002). Barriers to employment among persons with mental illness: A review of the literature. Newark, NJ: Center for Research on the Organization and Financing of Care for the Severely Mentally Ill, Institute for Health, Health Care Policy and Aging Research, Rutgers University. Retrieved from http://www.dri.illinois.edu/research/p01-04c/final_technical_report_p01-04c.pdf

Mueser, K. T. (2016). Foreword. In P. Corrigan (Ed.), *Principles and practice of psychiatric rehabilitation: An empirical approach* (2nd ed., pp. vii–viii). New York, NY: Guilford Press.

Murray, C. J. L., & Lopez, A. D. (Eds.). (1996). *The global burden of disease: A comprehensive assessment of mortality and disability from diseases, injuries, and risk factors in 1990 and projected to 2020.* Cambridge, MA: Harvard University Press.

Myers, J. E. (1995). Specialties in counseling: Rich heritage or force for fragmentation? *Journal of Counseling and Development, 74,* 115–116.

Myers, J. E. (2012). Foreword. In D. R. Maki & V. M. Tarvydas (Eds.), *The professional practice of rehabilitation counseling* (pp. xv–xvii). New York, NY: Springer Publishing.

Newsome, D. B., & Gladding, S. T. (2014). *Clinical mental health counseling in community and agency settings* (4th ed.). Upper Saddle River, NJ: Pearson.

Olney, M. F., & Gill, K. J. (2016). Can psychiatric rehabilitation be CORE to CORE? *Rehabilitation Research, Policy, and Education, 30*(3), 204–214. doi:10.1891/2168-6653.30.3.204

Patterson, C. H. (1957). Counselor or coordinator? *Journal of Rehabilitation, 25*(2), 9–10, 27–28.

Pratt, C. W., Gill, K. J., Barrett, N. M., & Roberts, M. M. (2014). *Psychiatric rehabilitation.* San Diego, CA: Academic Press.

Rehabilitation Counseling Consortium. (2005). *Rehabilitation counselor and rehabilitation counseling definitions.* Schaumburg, IL: Commission on Rehabilitation Counselor Certification.

Remley, T. P. (2012). Evolution of counseling and its specializations. In D. R. Maki & V. M. Tarvydas (Eds.), *The professional practice of rehabilitation counseling* (pp. 17–38). New York, NY: Springer Publishing.

Rosenthal, D. A., Dalton, J. A., & Gervey, R. (2007). Analyzing vocational outcomes of individuals with psychiatric disabilities who received state vocational rehabilitation services: A data mining approach. *International Journal of Social Psychiatry, 53,* 357–368. doi:10.1177/0020764006074555

Rothman, R. A. (1987). *Working: Sociological perspectives.* Englewood Cliffs, NJ: Prentice Hall.

Sánchez, J., Rosenthal, D. A., Chan, F., Brooks, J., & Bezyak, J. L. (2016). Relationships between World Health Organization *International Classification of Functioning, Disability and Health* constructs and participation in adults with severe mental illness. *Rehabilitation Research, Policy, and Education, 30*(3), 286–304. doi:10.1891/2168-6653.30.3.286

Sheehan, L., & Lewicki, T. (2016). Collaborative documentation in mental health: Applications to rehabilitation counseling. *Rehabilitation Research, Policy, and Education, 30*(3), 305–320. doi:10.1891/2168-6653 .30.3.305

Sheperis, D. S., & Sheperis, C. J. (2015). *Clinical mental health counseling: Fundamentals of applied practice.* Upper River Saddle, NJ: Pearson.

Smith, J. (2015, July 23). The 13 most meaningful jobs in America. *Business Insider.* Retrieved from http:// www.businessinsider.com/most-meaningful-jobs-in-america-2015-7

Substance Abuse and Mental Health Services Administration. (2014). Substance use and mental health estimates from the 2013 National Survey on Drug Use and Health: Overview of findings. Retrieved from http://www.samhsa.gov/data/sites/default/files/NSDUH-SR200-RecoveryMonth-2014/NSDUH-SR200 -RecoveryMonth-2014.htm

Swarbrick, M., & Nemec, P. B. (2016). Supporting the health and wellness of individuals with psychiatric disabilities. *Rehabilitation Research, Policy, and Education, 30*(3), 321–333. doi:10.1891/2168-6653.30.3.321

Tarvydas, V., Hartley, M. T., & Gerald, M. (2015). Professional credentialing. In M. Stebnicki and I. Marini (Eds.), *Professional counselors' desk reference* (2nd ed., pp. 17–22). New York, NY: Springer Publishing.

Tarvydas, V., Leahy, M. J., & Zanskas, S. A. (2009). Judgment deferred: Reappraisal of rehabilitation counseling movement toward licensure parity. *Rehabilitation Counseling Bulletin, 52,* 85–94. doi:10.1177/ 0034355208323951

U.S. Bureau of Labor Statistics. (2015a). Rehabilitation counselors. *Occupational outlook handbook.* Retrieved from https://www.bls.gov/ooh/community-and-social-service/rehabilitation-counselors.htm

U.S. Bureau of Labor Statistics. (2015b). Mental health counselors and marriage and family therapists. *Occupational outlook handbook.* Retrieved from https://www.bls.gov/ooh/community-and-social-service/mental -health-counselors-and-marriage-and-family-therapists.htm

U.S. Department of Health and Human Services. (1999). *Mental health: A report of the Surgeon General.* Rockville, MD: U.S. Department of Health and Human Services, Public Health Service, Office of the Surgeon General.

U.S. Department of Health and Human Services. (2005). *Transforming mental health care in America: Federal action agenda: First steps.* Rockville, MD: Substance Abuse and Mental Health Services Administration.

Wright, G. N. (1980) *Total rehabilitation.* Boston, MA: Little, Brown.

World Health Organization. (2001) *International classification of functioning, disability and health [ICF].* Geneva, Switzerland: Author.

Young, J. S., & Cashwell, C. S. (2017). *Clinical mental health counseling: Elements of effective practice.* Thousand Oaks, CA: Sage.

PART II: FOUNDATIONS

TWO

Rehabilitation Counseling Professional Competencies

MICHAEL J. LEAHY

LEARNING OBJECTIVES

After reading this chapter, you should be able to:

- Define the scope of practice for rehabilitation counseling and explain why this is important to the discipline.
- Understand how empirical research has provided an evidence-based foundation for the discipline in relation to role and function and knowledge requirements for effective practice.
- Explain how this knowledge about role and function and knowledge and skill requirements has been translated over the years within the discipline and beyond.

Underlying the practice of any discipline or professional specialty area is the delineation of specific knowledge and skill competencies required for effective service delivery. *Job analysis, role and function, professional competency, critical incident,* and *knowledge validation research* are all terms that describe a process whereby the professional practice of rehabilitation counseling has been systematically studied. These research efforts over the past five decades have identified and described the critical functions and tasks, or knowledge and skills, associated with the effective delivery of services to individuals with disabilities (Leahy, 2012). The findings from these research efforts also have been translated to empirically inform the discipline's scope of practice and professional identity, as well as the rehabilitation counseling preservice training curricula, academic accreditation standards, and practitioner certification at the national level.

Among the various professionals (e.g., physiatrists, psychologists, social workers, and medical case managers) who may provide services to individuals with disabilities during their individual rehabilitation processes, the rehabilitation counselor (RC) represents a unique professional, who plays a central role in the extra-medical phase of the rehabilitation process, for individuals with both acquired and congenital disabilities (Wright, 1980). Rehabilitation counseling emerged as a full-time occupation 96 years ago. Unlike the beginnings of other counseling specialties and health-related occupations, rehabilitation counseling was mandated as a specific work role through federal legislation (Smith-Fess Act of 1920), which established the public or state-federal rehabilitation program in this country. In the years following this landmark legislation, rehabilitation counseling practice in the public and private sectors evolved and expanded to provide a comprehensive array of vocational and independent living services to an ever-increasing adult population of people with a wide range of physical and mental disabilities (Leahy & Szymanski, 1995).

Although the occupational status of rehabilitation counseling was established in the 1920s, it was not until the mid-1950s, with the passage of the 1954 Vocational Rehabilitation Act Amendments, that the discipline embarked on a series of significant ongoing developments (e.g., establishing preservice education, professional associations, code of ethics, and regulation of practice) that have led, over time, to the professionalization of practice in this country, and to some extent internationally. Initially, RCs were a very heterogeneous group of practitioners in terms of educational background and professional competencies. Today, as a result of the professionalization process over the past 60 years, RCs represent a group of professionals with a much higher degree of commonality in relation to preservice preparation, practice, and professional identity than at any previous time in our professional history.

The purpose of this chapter is to review those aspects of the discipline that serve to both uniquely identify and provide the foundation for rehabilitation counseling practice in today's health and human services environment. Particular attention is devoted to discussion of the scope and research-based foundation of practice. This chapter provides a foundation for deeper understanding of the nature of rehabilitation counseling practice. Specific professional functions and competencies are presented in greater detail in Parts IV and V of this book.

SCOPE OF PRACTICE

Rehabilitation counseling has been described as a process in which the counselor works collaboratively with the client to understand existing problems, barriers, and potentials in order to facilitate the effective use of personal and environmental resources for career, personal, social, and community adjustment following disability (Jaques, 1970). In carrying out this multifaceted process, RCs must be prepared to assist individuals with disabilities in adapting to the environment, assist environments in accommodating the needs of the individual, and work toward the full participation of individuals in all aspects of society, with a particular focus on career aspirations (Szymanski, 1985).

Over the years, the fundamental role of the RC has evolved (Jaques, 1970; Rubin & Roessler, 1995; Wright, 1980), with the subsequent functions and required knowledge and skill competencies of the RC expanding as well. Regardless of variations in their practice settings and client populations, most RCs (a) assess needs, (b) establish a working alliance with the individual to develop goals and individualized plans to meet identified needs, and (c) provide or arrange for the therapeutic services and interventions (e.g., psychological, medical, social, behavioral) needed, including job placement and follow-up services. Throughout this individualized process, counseling skills are considered an essential component of all activities. It is the specialized knowledge of disabilities and of environmental factors that interact with disabilities, as well as the range of knowledge and skills required in addition to counseling, that differentiate RCs from social workers, other types of counselors (e.g., mental health counselors, school counselors, career counselors), and other rehabilitation practitioners (e.g., vocational evaluators, job placement specialists) in today's service delivery environments (Jenkins, Patterson, & Szymanski, 1992; Leahy & Szymanski, 1995).

Utilizing the long-standing tradition in rehabilitation counseling research of studying the role and functions of qualified practitioners, in 1994 the Commission on Rehabilitation Counselor Certification (CRCC) led a national professionalization initiative to develop the discipline's official scope of practice statement, which was adopted by all the major professional and regulatory organizations in rehabilitation counseling. This statement is consistent with available empirical research, and it was required to more explicitly identify the scope of practice for the public, clients of services, related professional groups, and regulatory bodies. The overall importance of this statement cannot be overstated. It stands as the official statement that describes the professional practice of the discipline across clinical practice settings and the specific techniques and modalities typically used to address the needs of the clients engaged in a working alliance with the RC. The official scope of practice statement for rehabilitation counseling reads as follows:

> Rehabilitation counseling is a systematic process that assists people with physical, mental, developmental, cognitive, and emotional disabilities to achieve their personal, career, and independent living goals in the most integrated setting possible through the application of the counseling process. The counseling process involves communication, goal setting, and beneficial growth or change through self-advocacy, psychological, vocational, social, and behavioral interventions. The specific techniques and modalities utilized within this rehabilitation counseling process may include, but are not limited to:
>
> assessment and appraisal;
> diagnosis and treatment planning;
> career (vocational) counseling;
> individual and group counseling treatment interventions focused on facilitating adjustments to the medical and psychosocial impact of disability;
> case management, referral, and service coordination;
> program evaluation and research;
> interventions to remove environmental, employment, and attitudinal barriers;
> consultation services among multiple parties and regulatory systems;
> job analysis, job development, and placement services, including assistance with employment and job accommodations; and
> the provision of consultation about, and access to, rehabilitation technology. (CRCC, 1994, pp. 1–2)

RESEARCH-BASED FOUNDATIONS OF PRACTICE

Over the past 50 years, through various research methods, an extensive body of knowledge has been acquired that has empirically identified the specific competencies and job functions important to the practice of rehabilitation counseling. This long-standing emphasis on the development and ongoing refinement of a research-based foundation has served to define and validate the rehabilitation counseling scope of practice. It also distinguishes it from other counseling specialties that are also seeking to define and validate their scope of professional practice. These research efforts have provided the discipline with evidence of construct validity of rehabilitation counseling knowledge and skill areas (Leahy, 2012; Leahy, Chan, Sung, & Kim, 2013; Szymanski, Leahy, & Linkowski, 1993).

Role and function approaches generally provide an empirically derived description of the functions and tasks associated with that role. However, the knowledge required to perform these functions is typically more indirectly assessed and inferred on the basis of the described functions and tasks. Roessler and Rubin (1992), in their review of major studies (Emener & Rubin, 1980; Leahy, Shapson, & Wright, 1987; Rubin et al., 1984), concluded that RCs have a diverse role requiring many skills if they are to effectively assist individuals with disabilities to improve the quality of their lives. They also concluded that the role of the RC could be fundamentally described as encompassing the following functions or job task areas: (a) assessment, (b) affective counseling, (c) vocational (career) counseling, (d) case management, and (e) job placement.

In the years that have passed since the knowledge validation and role and function study described earlier, service settings have continued to diversify and the delivery of services has continued to evolve, to address not only the changing needs of people with disabilities, but also to keep pace with advances in medicine, technology, and new knowledge generation and translation in practice settings. Recognizing and understanding these changes is important and consistent with credentialing requirements. Consequently, the CRCC regularly studies and reviews the test specifications used to guide the certification examination (Leahy, Muenzen, Saunders, & Strauser, 2009). As a result of the changes noted, the most recent study was undertaken by Leahy and colleagues (2013). It examined the functions and knowledge requirements of rehabilitation counseling practice in today's rapidly changing practice environments. The findings and specific data from this study were used by the CRCC to examine and set test specifications for future versions of the CRC examination, and to empirically define the nature of professional practice of rehabilitation counseling more generally. See Box 2.1 for a description of the three major job function domains and associated subdomains (Job Placement and Vocational Assessment and Career Counseling; and Counseling, Psychosocial Interventions, and Case Management; and Demand-Side Employment and Workers' Compensation and Forensic Services) that are important for rehabilitation counseling across clinical practice settings. **Domains** is the term used to describe areas of similar job function or knowledge. They tend to be broad areas of practice. The **subdomains** within each domain provide a more specific description of the professional tasks or knowledge and skill associated with the domain.

Conversely, knowledge validation and professional competency approaches provide an empirically derived description of the knowledge and skills associated with a particular role, but the actual functions and tasks are more indirectly assessed and inferred on the basis of the knowledge and skills needed by an individual to practice. Recent research by Leahy and colleagues (2013) provided empirical support that the following 10 knowledge domains represent the core knowledge and skill requirements of RCs across practice settings: (1) assessment, appraisal, and vocational evaluation; (2) job development, job placement, and career and lifestyle development; (3) vocational consultation and services for employers; (4) case management, professional roles and practices, and utilization of community resources; (5) foundations of counseling, professional orientation and ethical practice, theories, social and cultural issues, and human growth and development; (6) group and family counseling; (7) mental health counseling; (8) medical, functional, and psychosocial aspects of disabilities; (9) disability management; and (10) research, program evaluation, and evidence-based practice. A complete listing of the knowledge domains and subdomains from this study is provided in Box 2.2.

BOX 2.1 Job Functions Related to Rehabilitation Counseling

Job Placement and Vocational Assessment and Career Counseling

Job Placement

- Instruct clients in preparing for the job interview (e.g., job application, resumé preparation, attire, interviewing skills).
- Instruct clients in developing systematic job-search skills.
- Respond to employer biases and concerns regarding hiring people with disabilities.
- Inform clients of job openings suitable to their needs and abilities.
- Monitor clients' postemployment adjustment to determine the need for additional services.
- Provide prospective employers with appropriate information on clients' work skills and abilities.
- Use supportive counseling techniques to prepare clients for the stress of the job search.
- Use local resources to assist with placement (e.g., employer contacts, colleagues, state employment service).
- Develop mutually agreed-upon vocational counseling goals.
- Apply knowledge of assistive technology in job accommodation.
- Identify hidden job leads and customized jobs/employment opportunities.
- Provide information to help clients answer other individuals' questions, including employers, about their disabilities.
- Identify and arrange for functional or skill remediation services for clients' successful job placements.
- Understand the applications of current laws affecting the employment of individuals with disabilities.
- Discuss clients' vocational plans when they appear unrealistic.
- Recommend modifications of job tasks to accommodate clients' functional limitations.
- Determine the level of intervention necessary for job placement (e.g., job club, supported work, on-the-job training [OJT]).
- Counsel clients to select jobs consistent with their abilities, interests, and rehabilitation goals.
- Discuss with clients labor market conditions that may influence the feasibility of entering certain occupations.
- Identify educational and training requirements for specific jobs.
- Recommend occupational and/or educational materials for clients to explore vocational alternatives and choices.

Vocational Assessment and Career Counseling

- Integrate assessment data to describe clients' assets, limitations, and preferences for rehabilitation planning purposes.
- Make logical job, work area, or adjustment training recommendations based on comprehensive client assessment information.

(continued)

BOX 2.1 Job Functions Related to Rehabilitation Counseling (*continued*)

- Use behavioral observations to make inferences about work personality characteristics and adjustment.
- Counsel with clients regarding educational and vocational implications of test and interview information.
- Interpret diagnostic information (e.g., tests vocational and educational records, medical reports) to clients.
- Select evaluation instruments and strategies according to their appropriateness and usefulness for a particular client.
- Match clients' needs with job reinforcers and clients' aptitudes with job requirements.
- Identify clients' work personality characteristics to be observed through an on-the-job evaluation or simulated work situation.
- Administer appropriate standardized tests for assessment purposes.
- Assess clients' readiness for gainful employment.
- Assess the significance of clients' disabilities.
- Review medical information with clients to determine vocational implications of their functional limitations.

Occupational Information Analysis
- Classify local jobs using the *Dictionary of Occupational Titles (DOT)* and Occupational Information Network (O*Net) or other classification systems.
- Utilize occupational information such as the *DOT*, *Occupational Outlook Handbook (OOH)*, and other publications.
- Analyze the tasks of a job.
- Use computer-based assessment, counseling, and job-matching systems in the rehabilitation process.
- Apply labor market information influencing the task of locating, obtaining, and progressing in employment.
- Identify transferable work skills by analyzing clients' work history and functional assets and limitations.

Counseling, Psychosocial Interventions, and Case Management

Counseling

- Clarify for clients mutual expectations and the nature of the counseling relationship.
- Adjust counseling approaches or styles according to clients' cognitive and personality characteristics.
- Employ counseling techniques (e.g., reflection, interpretation, summarization) to facilitate client self-exploration.
- Identify one's own biases and weaknesses, which may affect the development of a healthy client relationship.
- Develop a therapeutic relationship characterized by empathy and positive regard for the client.

(continued)

BOX 2.1 Job Functions Related to Rehabilitation Counseling (*continued*)

- Identify social, economic, and environmental forces that may present barriers to a client's rehabilitation.
- Counsel clients to help them appreciate and emphasize their personal assets.
- Counsel with clients to identify emotional reactions to disability.
- Recognize psychological problems (e.g., depression, suicidal ideation) requiring consultation or referral.
- Assist clients in terminating counseling in a positive manner, thus enhancing their ability to function independently.
- Use assessment information to provide clients with insights into personal dynamics.
- Apply psychological and social theory to develop strategies for rehabilitation intervention.
- Work with clients to prepare rehabilitation plans with mutually agreed-upon interventions and goals.
- Confront clients with observations about inconsistencies between their goals and their behavior.

Psychosocial Interventions

- Counsel with clients using group methods for psychosocial and vocational adjustment problems.
- Provide psychological counseling to clients regarding sexuality and disability issues.
- Counsel with clients' families to provide information and support positive coping behaviors.
- Use behavioral techniques such as shaping, rehearsal, modeling, and contingency management.
- Explore clients' needs for individual, group, or family counseling.
- Assist clients in verbalizing specific behavioral goals for personal adjustment.
- Conduct group activities and programs such as job clubs, vocational exploration groups, or job-seeking skills groups.
- Supervise new counselors and/or practicum or internship students in rehabilitation counseling activities.
- Develop acceptable client work behavior through the use of behavioral techniques.
- Assist clients in understanding stress and in utilizing mechanisms for coping.
- Diagnose and identify treatment options for mental health issues.
- Participate with advocacy groups to promote rehabilitation programs.

Case Management

- Collaborate with other providers so that services are coordinated, appropriate, and timely.
- Coordinate activities of all agencies involved in a rehabilitation plan.
- Monitor client progress.

(continued)

BOX 2.1 Job Functions Related to Rehabilitation Counseling (*continued*)

- Attend team conferences.
- Explain the services and limitations of various community resources to clients.
- Establish meaningful working alliances with the clients served.
- Refer clients to appropriate specialists and/or for special services.
- Identify and challenge stereotypic views toward people with disabilities.
- Determine clients' ability to perform independent living activities.
- Obtain regular client feedback regarding the satisfaction with services delivered and suggestions for improvement.
- Assist clients to identify needs and request accommodations or supports to address functional limitations.
- Teach problem-solving skills to clients.
- Determine appropriate community services for clients' stated needs.

Demand-Side Employment and Workers' Compensation and Forensic Services

Demand-Side Employment

- Research and secure funding, community resources, and support needed for community reentry.
- Provide benefits counseling to Social Security beneficiaries seeking vocational rehabilitation (VR) services.
- Promote public awareness and legislative support of rehabilitation programs.
- Train clients' coworkers/supervisors regarding work and disability issues.
- Provide consultation to employers regarding accessibility and issues related to Americans with Disabilities Act (ADA) compliance.
- Evaluate and select facilities that provide specialized care services for clients.
- Market rehabilitation services to businesses and organizations.
- Act as an advocate for the client and family with third-party payers and service providers.
- Contact vendors in order to purchase adaptive/accommodative equipment.
- Negotiate financial responsibilities for client rehabilitation with the referral source and/or sponsor.
- Use social networking in the rehabilitation and placement process.
- Negotiate with employers or labor union representatives to reinstate/rehire an injured worker.
- Utilize demand-side employment strategies related to hiring, return to work, and retention.
- Conduct a review of the rehabilitation literature on a given topic or case problem to identify the research-based evidence of effectiveness of various treatment or intervention options.
- Make sound and timely financial decisions within the context of caseload management in your work setting.

(*continued*)

BOX 2.1 Job Functions Related to Rehabilitation Counseling (*continued*)

- Apply evidence-based research results to professional practice.
- Apply principles of rehabilitation legislation to daily practice.

Workers' Compensation and Forensic Services

- Understand insurance claims processing and professional responsibilities in workers' compensation.
- Provide expert opinion or testimony regarding employability and rehabilitation feasibility.
- Document all significant client vocational findings in a manner sufficient for legal testimony or records.
- Discuss return-to-work options with the employer.
- Conduct labor market analyses.
- Report to referral sources regarding progress of cases.
- Obtain a release for a return to work from the treating physician.
- Obtain written reports regarding client progress.

BOX 2.2 Rehabilitation Counseling Knowledge Domains and Subdomains

Assessment, Appraisal, and Vocational Evaluation

- The tests and evaluation techniques available for assessing clients' needs
- Psychometric concepts related to measurement
- Interpretation of assessment results for rehabilitation planning purposes
- Computer-based job-matching systems
- Computer-based and online assessment tools

Job Development, Job Placement, and Career and Lifestyle Development

- Theories of career development and work adjustment
- Vocational implications of functional limitations associated with disabilities
- Methods and techniques used to conduct labor market surveys
- Transferable skills analysis
- Occupational and labor market information
- Job analysis
- Ergonomics, job accommodations, and assistive technology
- Job readiness, including seeking and retention skills development
- Job placement and job development strategies

(*continued*)

BOX 2.2 Rehabilitation Counseling Knowledge Domains and Subdomains (*continued*)

- Job modification and restructuring techniques
- Demand-side employment issues related to hiring, return to work, and retention
- Services available from one-stop career centers

Vocational Consultation and Services for Employers

- The workplace culture, environment, and business terminology
- Marketing strategies and techniques for rehabilitation services
- Employer development for job placement
- Consultation process with employers related to management of disability issues in the workplace
- Educating employers on disability-related issues

Case Management, Professional Roles and Practices, and Utilization of Community Resources

- Principles of caseload management
- Case management tools
- The case management process, including case finding, planning, service coordination, referral to and utilization of other disciplines, and client advocacy
- Case recording and documentation
- Professional roles, functions, and relationships with other human services providers
- Techniques for working effectively in teams and across disciplines
- Health promotion and wellness concepts and strategies for people with chronic illness and disability
- The services available for a variety of rehabilitation populations, including people with multiple disabilities
- Techniques for working with individuals who have limited English proficiency
- Negotiation, mediation, and conflict resolution strategies
- Advocacy processes needed to address institutional and social barriers that impede access, equity, and success for clients
- Human resources practices, diversity in the workplace, and workplace supports for people with disabilities
- Programs and services for specialty populations
- Organizational structure of rehabilitation counseling practice settings
- Social Security programs, benefits, work incentives, and disincentives
- Services available through client advocacy programs
- Community resources and services for rehabilitation planning
- Supported employment strategies and services
- School-to-work transition for students with disabilities
- Financial resources for rehabilitation services
- Independent living services
- Health care benefits and delivery systems
- Laws and public policy affecting individuals with disabilities

(continued)

BOX 2.2 Rehabilitation Counseling Knowledge Domains and Subdomains (*continued*)

Foundations of Counseling, Professional Orientation and Ethical Practice, Theories, Social and Cultural Issues, and Human Growth and Development

- Individual counseling theories
- Individual counseling practices and interventions
- Human growth and development
- Societal issues, trends, and developments
- Diversity and multicultural counseling issues
- Theories and techniques of clinical supervision
- Clinical problem-solving and critical-thinking skills
- Internet-based counseling tools and resources
- Risk management and professional ethical standards
- Ethical decision-making models and processes

Group and Family Counseling

- Family counseling theories
- Family counseling practices and interventions
- Group counseling theories
- Group counseling practices and interventions

Mental Health Counseling

- Behavior and personality theory
- Techniques for individuals with psychological disabilities
- Dual diagnosis and the workplace
- Human sexuality and disability issues
- Substance abuse and treatment
- Treatment planning for clinical problems
- Knowledge of the current version of the *Diagnostic and Statistical Manual of Mental Disorders*

Medical, Functional, and Psychosocial Aspects of Disabilities

- Medical aspects and implications of various disabilities
- Medical terminology
- Rehabilitation terminology and concepts
- The psychosocial and cultural impact of disability on the individual
- The psychosocial and cultural impact of disability on the family
- Environmental and attitudinal barriers for individuals with disabilities
- The functional capacities of individuals with disabilities
- Implications of medications as they apply to individuals with disabilities
- Individual and family adjustment to disability
- Appropriate medical intervention resources
- Work conditioning or work hardening resources and strategies

(continued)

BOX 2.2 Rehabilitation Counseling Knowledge Domains and Subdomains (*continued*)

Disability Management

- Disability prevention and management strategies
- Managed care concepts
- Insurance programs
- Workers' compensation laws and practices
- Forensic rehabilitation

Research, Program Evaluation, and Evidence-Based Practice

- Historical and philosophical foundations of rehabilitation counseling
- Program evaluation procedures for assessing the effectiveness of rehabilitation services and outcomes
- Research databases for locating empirically validated interventions
- Rehabilitation research literature related to evidence-based practice
- Research methods and statistics
- Evidence-based practice and research utilization
- Evidence-based psychiatric rehabilitation practices
- Systematic review/meta-analysis

Evidence-Based Foundation of Practice

In terms of research utilization and knowledge translation, these empirically derived descriptions of the RC's role, function, and required knowledge and skill competencies have assisted the discipline in a number of important ways. First, they have helped in defining the professional identity of the RC by empirically defining the uniqueness of the discipline and by providing evidence in support of the construct validity of its knowledge base. Second, the descriptions have been extensively used in the development of preservice educational curricula in order to provide graduate training in areas of knowledge and skill critical to the practice of rehabilitation counseling across major employment settings. Third, the long-standing emphasis on a research-based foundation to practice has greatly contributed to the rehabilitation counseling field's leadership role in the establishment and ongoing refinement of graduate educational program accreditation through the Council on Rehabilitation Education (CORE), and individual practitioner certification through the CRCC. Finally, this body of knowledge has also been useful in identifying both the common professional ground (shared competency areas) with the profession of counseling in general, and the uniqueness of rehabilitation counseling among related rehabilitation disciplines (e.g., vocational evaluators, job placement specialists) and other counseling specialties (e.g., career counselors, school counselors, mental health counselors). This process of further definition in the area of occupational competence is a normal sequence in the professionalization process for any occupation seeking public recognition.

The results of this most recent study (Leahy et al., 2013) provide further empirical support for the description of the knowledge base underlying the practice of rehabilitation counseling. It also contributes further empirical evidence in relation to the content and construct validity of the knowledge domains identified in this replication and extension of the most recent study completed in 2009. Over the past 25 years, there have been four large-scale national research initiatives (Leahy et al., 2013; Leahy, Chan, & Saunders, 2003; Leahy, Muenzen, Saunders, & Strauser, 2009; Leahy, Szymanski, & Linkowski, 1993) that have identified and defined the specific competencies and job functions important to the practice of rehabilitation counseling and the achievement of positive outcomes with the clients they serve. These last three studies have sampled the same population of interest, and used parallel definitions of variables, research questions, and research instruments. Each successive replication and extension of this line of inquiry has added to the evidence-based foundation of practice (DePalma, 2002) in terms of underlying knowledge dimensions essential for effective rehabilitation counseling. These studies and prior research efforts (e.g., Berven, 1979; Emener & Rubin, 1980; Harrison & Lee, 1979; Jaques, 1959; Leahy et al., 1987; Muthard & Salomone, 1969; Rubin et al., 1984; Wright & Fraser, 1975) have provided the discipline with consistent empirically based evidence of an established and mature discipline that is able to respond appropriately to the evolutionary demands and pressures of a dynamic human service field (Leahy et al., 2013; Leahy, Rak, & Zanskas, 2016).

Knowledge Translation

A series of studies has been conducted to investigate the relationship between rehabilitation counselor education (RCE) and service delivery outcomes that has provided consistent support for the position that RCs, as qualified providers, need to obtain preservice training at the graduate level in rehabilitation counseling or a closely related field prior to practice. Studies of the New York (Szymanski & Parker, 1989), Wisconsin (Szymanski, 1991), Maryland (Szymanski & Danek, 1992), and Arkansas (Cook & Bolton, 1992) state VR agencies demonstrated that counselors with master's degrees in rehabilitation counseling achieved better outcomes with clients with severe disabilities than did RCs with unrelated master's or bachelor's degrees. In another group of studies, involving RCs from a variety of employment settings, preservice education was linked to the RCs, perceived (self-assessed) level of competency. Shapson, Wright, and Leahy (1987) and Szymanski, Linkowski, Leahy, Diamond, and Thoreson (1993) demonstrated that counselors with master's degrees in rehabilitation counseling perceived themselves to be more competent or better prepared in critical knowledge and skill areas of rehabilitation counseling than did counselors with unrelated preservice preparation (Leahy & Szymanski, 1995).

A majority of RCs still practice in the public, private, and not-for-profit rehabilitation sectors. However, more recently RCs have begun to practice in independent living centers, employee assistance programs, hospitals, clinics, mental health organizations, public school transition programs, and employer-based disability prevention and management programs. Although setting-based factors may affect the relative emphasis or importance of various RC functions or may introduce new specialized knowledge requirements for the RC, there remains a great deal of communality in the role and function among RCs regardless of practice setting (Leahy et al., 1987, 1993, 2003, 2009, 2013). One aspect that is often affected by these various settings is the specific job title used by the RC. Although the RC job title is used in the majority of settings, one can also find the use of the title *rehabilitation consultant* or *case manager* among today's RCs in practice. In addition, as one advances up the career ladder within these various settings, RCs can assume supervisory, management, and administrative roles within these various organizations.

Although the majority of RCs are viewed as generalists, another aspect of variation among practicing RCs is the degree to which they specialize their practice. One particularly useful model for viewing this issue was developed by DiMichael (1967), who suggested a two-way classification of horizontal and vertical specialization. In DiMichael's model, **horizontal specialization** refers to RCs who restrict or specialize their practice with a particular disability group (e.g., deaf, blind, head injury, substance abuse) that requires a significant amount of specialized knowledge or skill, specific to the type of disability. **Vertical specialization**, in contrast, occurs when RCs attend to only one function in the rehabilitation process (e.g., assessment or job placement) in their work with clients. Vocational evaluators and job placement specialists are examples of vertical specialists in this model.

The previous section on qualified providers does not imply that only RCs should provide rehabilitation services for people with disabilities. In fact, there are numerous related work roles that contribute to the rehabilitation process and complement the role and services provided by the RC. In addition to vocational evaluators and job placement specialists, who can assist the RC and client at critical stages in the rehabilitation process (assessment and job placement), other supportive resources could include physicians and physiatrists, physical and occupational therapists, psychologists, work adjustment trainers, job coaches, and various vocational training personnel. Quite often, a very critical aspect of the RC's role is the coordination of services provided by these various professionals within the context of a multidisciplinary team approach to effectively address the multifaceted needs of the client in the rehabilitation process.

CONCLUSION

Rehabilitation counseling is a professional discipline and specialty area of counseling. It has had a rich history of professionalization over the past 62 years. Although the occupation has been in existence for 96 years, we have witnessed significant growth and development of this specialty area of practice over the past few decades. Today, there are more RCs practicing in a variety of employment settings than at any time in our history, and the future market for these types of trained professionals looks excellent.

CONTENT REVIEW QUESTIONS

- What is the scope of practice and definition of rehabilitation counseling, as a specialty area of counseling practice?
- What are the basic roles and functions of the RC in practice?
- What types of knowledge and skill areas are required to practice effectively within the discipline?

REFERENCES

Berven, N. L. (1979). The role and function of the rehabilitation counselor revisited. *Rehabilitation Counseling Bulletin, 22*, 84–88.

Commission on Rehabilitation Counselor Certification. (1994). *CRCC certification guide*. Rolling Meadows, IL: Author.

Cook, D., & Bolton, B. (1992). Rehabilitation counselor education and case performance: An independent replication. *Rehabilitation Counseling Bulletin, 36*, 37–43.

DePalma, J. A. (2002). Proposing an evidence-based policy process. *Nursing Administration Quarterly, 26*(4), 55–61.

DiMichael, S. G. (1967). New directions and expectations in rehabilitation counseling. *Journal of Rehabilitation, 33*, 38–39.

Emener, W. G., & Rubin, S. E. (1980). Rehabilitation counselor roles and functions and sources of role strain. *Journal of Applied Rehabilitation Counseling, 11*, 57–69.

Harrison, D. K., & Lee, C. C. (1979). Rehabilitation counselor competencies. *Journal of Applied Rehabilitation Counseling, 10*, 135–141.

Jaques, M. E. (1959). *Critical counseling behavior in rehabilitation settings*. Iowa City: State University of Iowa, College of Education.

Jaques, M. E. (1970). *Rehabilitation counseling: Scope and services*. Boston, MA: Houghton Mifflin.

Jenkins, W., Patterson, J. B., & Szymanski, E. M. (1992). Philosophical, historic, and legislative aspects of the rehabilitation counseling profession. In R. M. Parker & E. M. Szymanski (Eds.), *Rehabilitation counseling: Basics and beyond* (2nd ed., pp. 27–55). Austin, TX: Pro-Ed.

Leahy, M. J. (2009). Prologue: Rehabilitation counseling credentialing: Research practice and the future of the profession. *Rehabilitation Counseling Bulletin, 52*(2), 67–68.

Leahy, M. J. (2012). Qualified providers of rehabilitation counseling services. In D.R. Maki & V. M. Tarvydas (Eds.), *The professional practice of rehabilitation counseling* (pp. 193–211). New York, NY: Springer Publishing.

Leahy, M. J., Chan, F., & Saunders, J. (2003). Job functions and knowledge requirements of certified rehabilitation counselors in the 21st century. *Rehabilitation Counseling Bulletin, 46*(2), 66–81.

Leahy, M. J., Chan, F., Sung, C., & Kim, M. (2013). Empirically derived test specifications for the CRC examination. *Rehabilitation Counseling Bulletin, 56*(4), 199–214.

Leahy, M. J., Muenzen, P., Saunders, J. L., & Strauser, D. (2009). Essential knowledge domains underlying effective rehabilitation counseling practice. *Rehabilitation Counseling Bulletin, 52*(2), 95–106.

Leahy, M. J., Rak, E., & Zanskas, S. A. (2016). A brief history of counseling and specialty areas of practice. In M. Stebnicki & I. Marini (Eds.), *Professional counselor's desk reference* (2nd ed., pp. 3–8). New York, NY: Springer Publishing.

Leahy, M. J., Shapson, P. R., & Wright, G. N. (1987). Rehabilitation practitioner competencies by role and setting. *Rehabilitation Counseling Bulletin, 31*, 119–131.

Leahy, M. J., & Szymanski, E. M. (1995). Rehabilitation counseling: Evolution and current status. *Journal of Counseling and Development, 74*, 163–166.

Leahy, M. J., Szymanski, E. M., & Linkowski, D. C. (1993). Knowledge importance in rehabilitation counseling. *Rehabilitation Counseling Bulletin, 37*, 130–145.

Muthard, J. E., & Salomone, P. (1969). The roles and functions of the rehabilitation counselor. *Rehabilitation Counseling Bulletin, 13*, 81–168.

Roessler, R. T., & Rubin, S. E. (1992). *Case management and rehabilitation counseling: Procedures and techniques* (2ed ed.). Austin, TX: Pro-Ed.

Rubin, S. E., Matkin, R. E., Ashley, J., Beardsley, M. M., May, V. R., Onstott, K., & Puckett, F. D. (1984). Roles and functions of certified rehabilitation counselors. *Rehabilitation Counseling Bulletin, 27*, 199–224.

Rubin, S. E., & Roessler R. T. (1995). *Foundations of the vocational rehabilitation process* (4th ed.). Austin, TX: Pro-Ed.

Shapson, P. R., Wright, G. N., & Leahy, M. J. (1987). Education and the attainment of rehabilitation competencies. *Rehabilitation Counseling Bulletin, 31*, 131–145.

Smith-Fess Act, Pub. L. No. 66-236 (1920).

Szymanski, E. M. (1985). Rehabilitation counseling: A profession with a vision, identity, and a future. *Rehabilitation Counseling Bulletin, 29*, 2–5.

Szymanski, E. M. (1991). The relationship of the level of rehabilitation counselor education to rehabilitation client outcome in the Wisconsin Division of Vocational Rehabilitation. *Rehabilitation Counseling Bulletin, 35*, 23–37.

Szymanski, E. M., & Danek, M. M. (1992). The relationship of rehabilitation counselor education to rehabilitation client outcome: A replication and extension. *Journal of Rehabilitation, 58*, 49–56.

Szymanski, E. M., Leahy, M. J., & Linkowski, D. C. (1993). Reported preparedness of certified counselors in rehabilitation counseling knowledge areas. *Rehabilitation Counseling Bulletin, 37*, 146–162.

Szymanski, E. M., Linkowski, D. C., Leahy, M. J., Diamond, E. E., & Thoreson, R. W. (1993). Validation of rehabilitation counseling accreditation and certification knowledge areas: Methodology and initial results. *Rehabilitation Counseling Bulletin, 37,* 109–122.

Szymanski, E. M., & Parker, R. M. (1989). Relationship of rehabilitation client outcome to level of rehabilitation counselor education. *Journal of Rehabilitation, 55,* 32–36.

Wright, G. N. (1980). *Total rehabilitation.* Boston, MA: Little, Brown.

Wright, G, N., & Fraser, R. T. (1975). *Task analysis for the evaluation, preparation, classification, and utilization of rehabilitation counselor track personnel* (Wisconsin Studies in Vocational Rehabilitation Monograph No. 22, Series 3). Madison: University of Wisconsin.

THREE

Professional Credentialing

STEPHEN A. ZANSKAS AND SUSAN G. SHERMAN

LEARNING OBJECTIVES

After reading this chapter, you should be able to:

- Identify the role of credentialing in expanding career opportunities for professional rehabilitation counselors (RCs).
- Distinguish the purposes of and the difference between accreditation, certification, and licensure.
- Identify the professional associations associated with rehabilitation counseling.
- Understand the challenges confronting RCs, including changes in the legislative foundation, licensure requirements, and behavioral health and third-party insurance reimbursement.

Rehabilitation counseling is a dynamic counseling specialization with a rich history that is experiencing tremendous growth and transition. The Bureau of Labor Statistics (BLS, 2015) projects that the employment of RCs will grow by 9% between 2014 and 2022, faster than average. However, this projection is conservative, as many RCs have worked under other job titles since the 1980s (Dew & Peters, 2002; Goodwin, 2006; Stebnicki, 2009). As employment opportunities have expanded, so too has the regulatory role of credentialing.

The good news is that RCs are accustomed to practicing in rapidly changing environments (Leahy, 2009; Leahy, Chan, Sung, & Kim, 2012; Stebnicki, 2009; Zanskas & Leahy, 2007). A variety of social and labor market trends have impacted rehabilitation counseling over the years with respect to practice, setting, and service delivery (Hershenson & McKenna, 1998; Leahy, Chan, & Saunders, 2003; McClanahan & Sligar, 2015; Stebnicki, 2009; Zanskas & Leahy, 2007). Recently, evolving knowledge and skill requirements, legislative changes, and behavioral health and insurance reimbursement are all having a significant impact on the credentialing and practice of rehabilitation counseling (Emener & Cottone, 1989; Hershenson & McKenna, 1998; Leahy et al., 2003, 2012; McClanahan & Sligar, 2015; Shaw, Leahy, Chan, & Catalano, 2006; Stebnicki, 2009; Tarvydas & Hartley, 2009; Zanskas & Leahy, 2007). Certainly, rehabilitation counseling has dealt with these forces of change in the past.

Today, the credentialing mechanisms of accreditation, certification, and licensure are as relevant to the process of professionalization of rehabilitation counseling as they were in 1989, as noted by Emener and Cottone (1989). It is an exciting time to enter a counseling profession that is rife with opportunity. However, RCs interested in maximizing their employment opportunities must understand professional credentialing. As our profession continues to mature, the requirements for professional credentialing will become both more restrictive and important for your ability to practice. **Credentialing** refers to the general process of establishing the minimum standards, qualifications, and/or requirements essential to professional counseling practice. The credentialing process serves two fundamental purposes, namely control of the profession and public recognition of the profession (Tarvydas, Leahy, & Zanskas, 2009). The purpose of this chapter is to assist RCs to understand professional credentialing and the factors influencing the practice of rehabilitation counseling. In order to accomplish this objective, the elements of accreditation, certification, and licensure as well as the role of professional associations and legislative changes are discussed. As credentialing continues to grow, it is imperative that RCs understand both the basics and newly emerging trends.

ACCREDITATION

Graduation from an accredited educational program is often the first step in obtaining professional credentials. **Accreditation** is a voluntary process of review that organizations or educational programs undergo to demonstrate the ability to meet predetermined criteria and standards. Rather than at the individual level, accreditation is at an institutional or organizational level. For instance, the Commission on Accreditation of Rehabilitation Facilities (CARF, 2016) is an accreditation body that accredits rehabilitation and human service agencies (Tarvydas, Hartley, & Gerald, 2015). Accreditation by CARF means that an agency has undergone an evaluation by an outside group of professionals to improve the quality of its services and meet recognized standards of care. Similarly, accreditation in higher education is an evaluation process whereby an academic program completes a self-study and an external peer review process, such as on-site visitors (Urofsky, 2013).

The purpose of accreditation in rehabilitation counseling is to guarantee that practitioners have obtained fundamental counseling skill and knowledge requirements prior to applying for certification and licensure (Tarvydas et al., 2015). According to the Council for Higher Education Accreditation (CHEA), accreditation in higher education is intended to "ensure that appropriate and effective teaching, support, assessment and learning resources are provided for students; that the learning opportunities provided are monitored; and that the provider considers how to improve them" (CHEA, n.d., p. 3). A benefit of graduating from an accredited educational program is that graduates are often automatically eligible "to apply for certification and licensure through curriculum equivalency provisions" (Tarvydas et al., 2015, p. 17). Graduates of nonaccredited programs may also be able to submit documentation to demonstrate the nonaccredited entity's completion of equivalent educational standards; however, it does not guarantee that the nonaccredited entity's educational standards will be accepted. There have been two historic accredititation bodies for counseling specializations: the Council on Rehabilitation Education (CORE) and the Council for Accreditation of Counseling and Related Educational Programs (CACREP; Erford, 2014).

Council on Rehabilitation Education (CORE)

Accreditation is the main way counselor education programs show that high-quality training is being done to prepare new counselors for the field. The primary accreditation body of rehabilitation counselor education (RCE) programs has been CORE. CORE has conducted systematic reviews of its standards to assure that they continued to be relevant and created a process for doing the reviews that has been firmly grounded in research (Leahy & Tansey, 2008). Historically, research has been the foundation of rehabilitation counseling practice (Berven, 1979; Emener & Rubin, 1980; Jaques, 1959; Leahy et al., 2003; Leahy, Muenzen, Saunders, & Strauser, 2009; Leahy, Shapson, & Wright, 1987; Leahy, Szymanski, & Linkowski, 1993; Muthard & Salamone, 1969; Wright & Fraser, 1975). Empirical knowledge validation, job analysis, professional competency, critical incident, and national role and function studies have contributed to our professional identity, informed our preservice training and graduate program curricula, and shaped accreditation standards (Leahy, 2012).

The impetus for CORE, as the first accreditation body in the counseling profession, emerged when a group of professionals in the field of rehabilitation counseling met in 1969. In 1972, CORE was formally established and incorporated. CORE at that time was made up of the following five rehabilitation professional organizations (CORE structure and function; CORE, n.d., para. 2):

- International Association of Rehabilitation Facilities, later renamed the American Rehabilitation Association
- Council of State Administrators of Vocational Rehabilitation (CSAVR)
- Council of Rehabilitation Counselor Educators, which later became the National Council on Rehabilitation Education (NCRE)
- American Rehabilitation Counseling Association (ARCA)
- National Rehabilitation Counseling Association (NRCA)

Throughout its history, the purpose of CORE, as outlined in its September 2010 bylaws, has been to "develop and promulgate standards for the accreditation of graduate RCE programs and undergraduate rehabilitation education programs and to assist in the development of standards for other academic-based rehabilitation programs." CORE is recognized by the CHEA and is a member of the Association of Specialized and Professional Accreditors (ASPA). CORE's structure was made up of a board of directors from rehabilitation-related organizations. Some of these organizations changed over time, but CORE continued to be made up of diverse rehabilitation organizations (Shaw & Kuehn, 2009). In 2013, CORE changed its board model after it was encouraged do so by the CHEA, its accreditation organization. The new board model was no longer comprised of individuals appointed by organizations. The new board structure is comprised of no more 12 and no less than nine at-large members, including public members who apply to serve on the board. The board sets policy direction and reviews the final accreditation decisions and issues the final report for each program reviewed since the last board meeting. CORE has an executive director and maintains a contract with the Commission on Rehabilitation Counselor Certification (CRCC) for office space and administrative support. CORE also maintains a global registry of international university programs to identify and collect information regarding university-based programs possessing common and broad-based educational standards regarding rehabilitation and disability education that are measurable cross-culturally and responsive to individual country needs.

CORE had both a commission on accreditation of graduate programs and an undergraduate program registry. CORE changed its commission structure in July 2008 to include accreditation of undergraduate programs. The Committee on Undergraduate

Education (CUE) became the Commission on Undergraduate Standards and Accreditation (CUSA). A few years later, the graduate and undergraduate commissions merged, going from two commissions to one commission for both graduate and undergraduate programs. CORE's Commission on Standards and Accreditation is the entity whose function it is to review self-studies from programs under review. That commission also reviews the site-visit documents from its site surveyors and issues a preliminary report making suggestions to the CORE board of directors on conditions and recommendations on the length of accreditation for the programs under review (Shaw & Kuehn, 2009).

In 2002, CORE voted to establish a task force to explore development of a written agreement with CACREP as a way to unify and promote the counseling profession. A task force was formed and a written memorandum of understanding (MOU) for merger was developed between the two organizations. In 2007, the CACREP board voted to accept the agreement, whereas the CORE board chose not to vote on the MOU due to concerns about CACREP's requirements for faculty and program credit hours (48 versus 60); thus, the merger failed. Efforts by the counseling profession to create a unified counseling professional group continued through groups such as the American Counseling Association's (ACA) 20/20 visioning committee. On July 12, 2013, CORE became a corporate affiliate of CACREP and began a process to administer both CORE's traditional RC standards and the clinical RC standards owned by CACREP (CORE, 2013). In 2014, each of the organizations elected a member to serve on the other's board of directors (CORE, 2014). The following year, in 2015, CORE and CACREP signed a plan of merger agreement. As outlined in CORE's press release dated July 20, 2015, the two organizations stated that their vision for a unified counseling profession was better realized through a merger of both organizations. On July 30, 2017, CORE will dissolve and on July 1, 2017, CACREP will carry on the mission of both organizations (CORE, 2015). In 2016, it was announced that RCE PhD programs would become eligible for accreditation under CACREP. CORE had not accredited doctoral programs previously.

Individuals and professional organizations in the rehabilitation counseling field have had diverse opinions on the merger. Although some organizations, such as the NCRE, went on record to support the merger in a July 31, 2015, resolution of the NCRE Board, other organizations and rehabilitation professionals had a mix of reactions. Today, many professionals in the field of rehabilitation are waiting to see how the merging of these two organizations will improve RCE and improve services to individuals with disabilities. It is of note that in the merger documents, CACREP has agreed to infuse disability awareness into its standards for all of its accredited programs. Once the merger takes place, undergraduate programs will no longer be able to apply for accreditation, but can remain on a registry under CACREP. CORE records will be retained by CACREP and housed in their offices.

Council for Accreditation of Counseling and Related Educational Programs (CACREP)

CACREP was originally established through a partnership between the Association for Counselor Education and Supervision (ACES) and the American Personnel and Guidance Association (now known as the ACA) in 1981. CACREP has accredited programs in a variety of counseling specializations, such as Addictions Counseling; Career Counseling; Marriage, Couple, and Family Counseling; School Counseling; Student Affairs and College Counseling; Clinical Mental Health Counseling; and School Counseling (CACREP, n.d.). CACREP has as its mission to promote the professional competence of counseling and related practitioners through (a) the development of preparation standards; (b) the encouragement of excellence in program development; and (c) the accreditation of professional preparation programs (CACREP, n.d.). CACREP accredits master and doctoral programs in counseling and its specialties that are offered by colleges and universities in the United States and throughout the world.

CACREP is an independent organization accredited by the CHEA, a national advocate and institutional voice for self-regulation of academic quality through accreditation. CACREP's board of directors is made up of 13 to 15 members. Of those members, eight must be counselor educators, at least two must be counseling practitioners, and at least two must be public. With the agreement of the merger between CACREP and CORE in 2015, CACREP agreed that two of its board members will represent the profession of rehabilitation counseling: one clinical rehabilitation and the other traditional rehabilitation.

CACREP undertakes a standards revision for its programs about every 8 years to improve its accredited programs and make sure its standards remain relevant. Programs under CACREP review are required to submit "comprehensive assessment plans and document assessment of student learning outcomes for the specific curricular standards" (Urofsky, 2013, p. 10). In addition to having around 600 accredited counseling and counseling specialty programs, CACREP maintains an International Registry of Counsellor Education Programs (IRCEP) that meets basic standards of program quality and assists in preparation for the accreditation process (Erford, 2014, p. 55). Once the CORE–CACREP merger is complete on July 1, 2017, CACREP will maintain a registry of undergraduate rehabilitation education programs.

Licensure portability has long been a goal of the counseling profession and advocated for by CACREP. In 2006, the American Association of State Counseling Boards (AASCB), an organization made up of state licensure boards, collaborated with the ACA to conduct a series of meetings over a number of years titled "20/20: A Vision for the Future of Counseling" (Bobby, 2013). This group worked on core principles common to the counseling profession, such as professional identity, unification of the profession, the definition of *counseling*, and a common set of counseling standards. Five years later, a common definition of what a *counselor* is was established. During that time, in 2007, an attempted merger between CORE and CACREP failed to materialize. In September 2010, the U.S. Veterans Administration (VA) approved a decision to recognize licensed professional counselors (LPCs) as those who graduate from a CACREP-accredited program and are qualified to work with clients who have mental health issues. In 2010, the Institute of Medicine (IOM, 2010) put forth a similar recommendation for those working with veterans in the TRICARE system in the U.S. Department of Defense (DoD). The IOM report suggested that all mental health counselors complete a 60-hour CACREP-accredited clinical mental health program.

On July 12, 2013, CORE became a corporate affiliate of CACREP and began to administer both CORE's traditional RC standards and the CACREP clinical RC standards. The following year, CORE and CACREP signed a plan of merger agreement. As outlined in the CORE–CACREP press release dated July 20, 2015, the organizations stated that their vision for a unified counseling profession was better realized through a merger of both the organizations. On July 30, 2017, CORE will dissolve and on July 1, 2017, CACREP will carry on the mission of both organizations (CORE, 2015). On that date, all CORE-accredited programs will become CACREP-accredited programs. The merger between CORE and CACREP, long sought by the ACA and its 20/20 task force, will seek to move the counseling profession forward by creating one counseling accreditation organization in the quest for a unified counseling profession.

CORE and CACREP Merger

The merger of CORE and CACREP represents an example of professionalization of the counseling profession. However, whenever professions strive to control who is allowed to enter or practice within their guild, others who believe they have equivalent training, education, and competencies are inherently excluded. The 2009 CACREP Standards established minimum standards for core faculty (Urofsky, Bobby, & Pope, 2009). First, the CACREP Standards required new faculty hired after July 1, 2013 to "have earned a doctoral degree in counselor education and supervision . . . preferably from a CACREP-accredited program, or have been employed as full-time faculty members in a counselor education program for a minimum of one full academic year before July 1, 2013" (2016, p. 6). Second, CACREP-accredited programs require that at least half of the credit hours taught during any calendar year must be taught by a minimum of three faculty members who identify as counselor educators (CACREP, 2016). These standards were intended to enhance the professionalization of the field of counseling by ensuring that the primary or "core" counselor education faculty possess a professional counseling identity.

CERTIFICATION

Certification is a voluntary credentialing process developed by a group in order to foster the group's professional identity. Certification protects the public from unqualified individuals and serves as a basis for assuring that counseling practitioners have the knowledge, skills, and experience necessary to practice nationally and in specialty practice settings. Certification in counseling is similar to that in other professions, "such as medical doctors, who are licensed by their state to practice general medicine, yet apply for board certifications to demonstrate their expertise in a specialty field (i.e., allergist, cardiologist, endocrinologist)" (Tarvydas et al., 2015, p. 18). Certification organizations hold their certificants accountable to written, peer-reviewed standards and have codes of ethics by which their certificants must abide. Certification is a voluntary process that is often critical to the hiring and selection of practitioners who wish to specialize, and, in certain practice settings, practitioners are required to hold particular certifications. Certification is not to be confused with licensure. Only licensure governs professional counseling practice in your respective states (Hosie, 1995). Certification bodies typically require continuing education, at various intervals, so that those who are certified can stay current in the field in order to maintain their certification. The two primary certification bodies in our field are the CRCC and the National Board for Counselor Certification (NBCC).

Commission on Rehabilitation Counselor Certification (CRCC)

The CRCC was incorporated in January 1974 and is the oldest established credentialing body in the counseling profession (Saunders, Barros-Bailey, Chapman, & Nunez, 2008). Currently, the CRCC has more than 17,000 certified rehabilitation counselors (CRCs) in the United States (CRCC, n.d.). The CRCC has created other CRC certifications and designations, including the CCRC, Certified Rehabilitation Counselor-Master Addictions Counselor (CRC-MAC), and Certified Rehabilitation Counselor-Clinical Supervisor (CRC-CS), all of which eventually became supported in maintenance mode only with no active applications being accepted.

Since 1980, the CRCC has been accredited by the National Commission for Certifying Agencies (NCCA). Until July 1, 2013, governance in the CRCC was provided by a

17-member board of directors: 15 of the board members were appointed by professional associations in the field of rehabilitation, in addition to one public member and one at-large member. Today, the board is comprised of four elected officers, one student director, one public member not affiliated with the profession of rehabilitation counseling, and six additional directors. The board composition changed in July 2013 so that all qualified individuals interested in director or committee positions could submit applications, through an annual call for applications; the applications are then vetted using a competency/constituency model to allow for the greatest diversity possible in directors and committee members, thus representing individuals in the field of rehabilitation.

Many activities of the CRCC are handled by standing committees. Prior to 2013, those committees were Executive, Appeals, Examination and Research, Standards and Credentials, Public Education and Information, and Ethics. Other ad hoc committees were added as the need arose. Committees were streamlined after 2013, and now consist of Executive, Ethics, Finance and Audit, Governance, and Standards and Exam. Ad hoc committees are still used for special assignments.

To be eligible to sit for the exam (Certified Rehabilitation Counselor Examination; CRCE), individuals must have a master's degree in rehabilitation counseling or a closely related field and supervision hours under a CRC. There are various categories under which individuals who seek certification can apply, and those categories have changed slightly over the years to assure that all qualified individuals, who meet the requirements, can sit for the exam. According to the CRCC website, the 175-item exam consists of questions across 10 knowledge domains, which are further defined into subdomains. One part of the exam tests counseling knowledge, whereas the other part of the exam tests the applicants' knowledge of rehabilitation and disability issues. In order to pass the exam, applicants must pass both sections of the exam. In 2008, the CRCC began offering its exam in a computer-based format. A number of university rehabilitation counseling programs now utilize the CRC exam as the comprehensive examination for their programs. The CRCE is used today as an option for state counselor licensure examination in roughly 16 states.

The CRCC *Code of Professional Ethics for Rehabilitation Counselors* was first developed in 1987 and has been revised about every 5 years since then. In July 2007, the CRCC developed a task force for the code revision process (Saunders et al., 2008). Once the code is drafted, it is then sent out for public comment. Once comments are collected by the task force, the code is again revised. The draft code must be agreed to and approved by the ethics committee. After the ethics committee finishes its work, the revised code goes to the board of directors for final approval.

To assist CRCs in staying involved with their profession, in 2015 to 2016 the CRCC created an online community. The CRCC community includes a networking platform it calls "Engage," which is open to those interested in the rehabilitation counseling profession. For CRC applicants and CRCs, the community offers two additional services. CRCC "Aspire" is an online job board that connects rehabilitation professionals to employers looking to hire qualified RCs. CRCC "e-university" is an online learning community where counselors can take courses for credit. The site allows counselors who complete the training modules to have their CE credits automatically uploaded to their individual CRCC continuing education file (CRCC, n.d.).

Over the years, the CRCC has been involved in the organizational development and administrative support of other rehabilitation-related certifications. Furthermore, the CRCC has maintained certifications from other organizations that are no longer offered. For instance, the Commission on Certification of Work Adjustment and Vocational Evaluation Services (CCWAVES), beginning in 1981, offered three active certifications, for Certified Vocational Evaluation (CVE) from 1981 to 2008, Certified Work Adjustment (CWA) from 1981 to 1990, and Certified Career Assessment Associates (CCAA) from 1997 to 2002. CCWAVES started in 1981 and used FRER for administrative services. CCWAVES stopped using FRER for administrative services in the early 1990's, when they left to obtain them from entities in California, Colorado, and Virginia before returning to FRER in 1999. They discontinued the active application/exam process for CVE in 2008 and dissolved on April 1, 2009, at which time the maintenance of credentials was turned over to the CRCC.

National Board for Certified Counselors (NBCC)

In 1982, the ACA created the NBCC. The NBCC is a not-for-profit, independent certification organization with more than 62,000 certified counselors in more than 40 countries (NBCC, 2016a). The NBCC describes its major functions as establishing and monitoring a national certification system, identifying those counselors who have obtained certification, and maintaining a register of those counselors (NBCC, 2016a).

The NBCC has a president, who is the chief executive officer, and a board of directors. The NBCC offers certification for the counseling profession, and the NBCC's examination, the National Counselor Examination (NCE), is widely used as the exam for state counselor licensure and the National Certified Counselor (NCC) credential. The NCE was first used in 1983. The NBCC is accredited by the NCCA. The NCE is a 200-item test used to assess the knowledge and abilities determined to be important for providing effective counseling (NBCC, 2016b). Once an individual passes the NCE, he or she becomes eligible for national certification in a number of specialty areas, including school counseling, clinical mental health and addictions counseling, and clinical supervision, each of which requires additional educational, experience, and examination requirements. The NBCC also has its own code of ethics, which governs the behavior of all nationally certified counselors (Erford, 2014).

The NBCC also administers the National Clinical Mental Health Counseling Examination (NCMHCE). The NCMHCE consists of 10 simulated clinical mental health counseling cases covering three content areas: assessment and diagnosis; counseling and psychotherapy; and administration, consultation, and supervision. Each simulation involves five to eight sections including both information-gathering and decision-making questions. The information-gathering sections assess the test taker's ability to gather appropriate clinical data required to evaluate a situation or to make a decision. Decision-making sections assess the test taker's ability to solve clinical problems by utilizing data to make judgments and decisions (NBCC, 2016a). The NCMHCE is another exam used for state licensure in some states, for the Certified Clinical Mental Health Counselor (CCMHC) national certification, and in the military health systems (NBCC, 2016b). As the profession continues to mature, we anticipate that the NCMHCE will become more influential in the regulation of the counseling field.

LICENSURE

Historically, the licensing of RCs has been perceived as crucial to our professionalization (Barros-Bailey, Benschoff, & Fisher, 2009; Brubaker, 1977; Cottone, 1985; Hardy, Luck, & Chandler, 1982; Leahy, 2002; Stebnicki, 2009; Tarvydas & Leahy, 1993; Tarvydas et al., 2009; Trolley & Cervoni, 1999). In fact, as early as 1977, Brubaker expressed that licensing requirements would professionalize our discipline. Despite this long-standing recognition of the importance of licensure, rehabilitation counseling, with few exceptions, was a late entrant into the counselor licensure movement (Tarvydas & Leahy, 1993; Tarvydas et al., 2009). This might be due in part to professional identity issues (e.g., are we counselors with a specialty in rehabilitation or rehabilitation specialists; Tarvydas & Leahy, 1993; Tarvydas et al., 2009). Employment setting provides another potential explanation for the apparent delayed participation in the counselor licensure movement. Specifically, federal or state employees are often exempted from licensure (ACA, 2016).

Professional licensing, as a form of public recognition, represents one of the hall-marks of professional legitimization (Rothman, 1987). Most importantly, the intent of state counselor licensing laws is to establish the minimum level of competence necessary to protect the public from harm (ACA, 2016; Tarvydas & Leahy, 1993; Tarvydas et al., 2009; Wheeler & Bertram, 2015). Presently, all 50 states, the District of Columbia, and Puerto Rico have passed statutes to regulate the title, practice, or title and practice of professional counselors (ACA, 2016; Wheeler & Bertram, 2015). Each of these 52 governmental bodies has established a regulatory board, often referred to as a professional counselor licensure board, with oversight over the profession of counseling within their jurisdiction. Regulatory boards are responsible for developing the rules and regulations governing the practice of professional counseling, issuing licenses, handling complaints made against a professional counselor's practice, and enforcing the laws (Tarvydas & Leahy, 1993; Tarvydas et al., 2009; Wheeler & Bertram, 2015). Ultimately, licensing boards define the scope of practice for a profession in their respective states (Stebnicki, 2009; Tarvydas & Leahy, 1993; Tarvydas et al., 2009; Wheeler & Bertram, 2015).

According to the AASCB (2015), the majority of states require a master's degree in counseling (although some accept degrees in a related field), a degree from an accredited university or program, completion of an examination, and on average 3,000 hours of post-masters experience. Most states also require new graduates to complete a 60-credit-hour counseling related graduate degree (ACA, 2016).

Despite progress toward uniformity, counselor licensing currently remains a confusing array of rules regulating the title, definition of counseling, scope of practice, educational requirements, and postgraduate supervision requirements (ACA, 2016; Mascari & Webber, 2013; Tarvydas & Leahy, 1993; Tarvydas et al., 2009; Wheeler & Bertram, 2015). These state-by-state differences, in conjunction with regulatory bodies' inconsistent recognition of other regulatory bodies' standards for licensure, have limited portability and counselor mobility (Kaplan, 2012).

States choose to regulate the title, practice, or both when developing licensure laws. **Title protection** establishes and restricts the use of specific titles for professional counselors who have met education, training, and experiential requirements (ACA, 2016; Tarvydas & Leahy 1993; Tarvydas et al., 2009; Wheeler & Bertram, 2015). According to ACA (2016), the most commonly used title is licensed professional counselor (LPC). Other commonly used titles include, licensed mental health counselor (LMHC), licensed clinical professional counselor (LCPC), licensed professional clinical counselor of mental health (LPCC), licensed clinical mental health counselor (LCMHC), and licensed mental health practitioner (LMHP). In the process of regulation, states generally move from title to practice, or a combination of title and practice, protection in order to provide greater protection to consumers. Presently, only six states have title-only protection (ACA, 2016).

Practice protection refers to licensure laws that prohibit individuals who have not obtained a license from performing the functions or scope of practice of a professional counselor in that state. Because practice protection extends to what a counselor actually does rather than the title of the counselor, it provides the most protection for consumers. For example, according to the ACA (2016), 32 states have both title and practice acts. Of the 32 states with title and practice acts, 27 states and the District of Columbia include career counseling in their scope of practice, and 12 of these states also include rehabilitation counseling in their scope of practice.

Each of the 52 regulatory boards requires licensure applicants to pass one or more comprehensive examinations regarding counseling practice. In addition, many states require applicants to pass jurisprudence examinations regarding the laws governing counseling practice in their respective state. According to the ACA (2016, p. 7), the following national examinations are among the most frequently required:

> NCE: Administered by the NBCC, this is the exam most commonly used by states in the credentialing process.
> NCMHCE: Also administered by the NBCC, this examination focuses more specifically on mental health practice, and is used by a number of states for licensure.
> CRCE: Administered by the CRCC, passage of this exam is also accepted in some states for meeting testing requirements for licensure.

The following states accept the CRC examination by rule or regulation: Arizona, California, District of Columbia, Illinois, Iowa, Michigan, North Carolina, Oregon, Pennsylvania, West Virginia, Wisconsin, and Wyoming. Alaska, Minnesota, and Tennessee accept the CRC examination through departmental policy (CRCC, n.d.).

License portability represents the single most important issue to LPCs. **Portability** refers to a licensed counselor's ability to relocate to other states and retain the privilege of practicing the profession. **Reciprocity**, an older term, refers to state regulatory boards recognizing and accepting an LPC's license obtained in another state. Many states have adopted an "equal or exceeds" standard regarding licensure. In other words, the majority of states will accept the applicant's license held and obtained in another state provided the standards of that state meet or exceed their state requirements.

Although some professional counseling associations have recommended shorter time frames, the AASCB issued a position statement in 2015 regarding portability standards:

> A fully-licensed counselor, who is licensed at the highest level of licensure available in his or her state, and who is in good standing with his or her licensure board, with no disciplinary record, and who has been in active practice for a minimum of five years post-receipt of licensure, and who has taken and passed the NCE or the NCMHCE, shall be eligible for licensure in a state to which he or she is establishing residence. The state to which the licensed counselor is moving may require a jurisprudence examination based on the rules and statutes of said state. An applicant who meets these criteria will be accepted for licensure without further review of education, supervision and experiential hours.

RCs pursuing careers as LPCs are advised to research the licensing requirements in their current state of residence and in any state to which they might consider relocating. Aspiring professional RCs are encouraged to discuss their career plans with faculty or other mentors and contact licensure boards in order to prepare for potential practice in another state. Even though the majority of professional RCs never plan on moving to another state, there are many reasons for relocation throughout a career and lifetime. In our mobile society, relocation is often unanticipated. Exercising personal due diligence, undertaking broad academic preparation, and engaging in dialogue with mentors will assist prospective professional RCs and established professionals to prepare for the complexities of practicing in another state.

REHABILITATION COUNSELING PROFESSIONAL ASSOCIATIONS

Rehabilitation counseling has a rich, diverse history of many different professional associations. As the field of rehabilitation counseling and counseling continues to unify, there may be increased pressure for the field's professional associations to do the same. Leadership within rehabilitation counseling professional associations will be looking ahead at the challenges and opportunities of maintaining membership and seeking out ways to attract new members in a 21st-century environment. In this section we provide the reader with an introduction to the various rehabilitation counseling associations.

National Rehabilitation Counseling Association (NRCA)

Founded in 1958, NRCA was a division of the National Rehabilitation Association (NRA) until the organizations parted ways in 2005. NRCA is the oldest professional organization serving RCs. As stated in its original constitution, the purpose of NRCA is to provide standards of professional conduct and performance for its members (Kirk & LaForge, 1995; Mundt, 1986). NRCA was involved in the professionalization of landmarks within the rehabilitation counseling profession. These included the establishment of the CRCC in 1974 with ARCA, CORE in 1972, the development of the first RC code of ethics along with ARCA and CRCC, and the original RC scope of practice statement. NRCA is comprised of a board of directors and has in its history been governed by a delegate assembly. On October 26, 2005, the NRA board of directors voted to withdraw divisional status for NRCA, then a division of the NRA, due to ongoing failure to comply with the NRA constitution and bylaws. This action was effective as of November 1, 2005. During that same time frame, at the annual conference of the NRA, the NRCA delegate assembly voted to sever ties with the NRA and become a fully independent association. As a professional association, NRCA seeks to improve RC effectiveness through professional meetings and conferences, supporting research in the field and providing to its members the *Journal of Applied Rehabilitation Counseling (JARC)*. In October 2016, NRCA sent an e-mail to its membership notifying them that NRCA would officially end all daily office operations as of October 27, 2016 (Sherman, personal communication, December 2016). NRCA is working with the NRA and its Rehabilitation Counselors and Educators Association (RCEA) division on a merger agreement as this chapter goes to press.

Rehabilitation Counselors and Educators Association (RCEA)

In 2006, after NRCA and the NRA broke ties with each other, the NRA board of directors developed a new division. The RCEA was developed to replace NRCA as a home for its counselors and educators. In the winter of 2007, the Rehabilitation Counselors and Educators Association's first journal came out. The journal continues to be a mix of gray matter (news and views) and peer-reviewed research and conceptual articles. As stated in its bylaws, the RCEA promotes, through its journal and training opportunities, continuing activities to ensure that those in the field of rehabilitation stay up to date about their profession. Public information, as well as continuing education, is recognized as a responsibility of a professional group. The national RCEA is organized to develop, improve, strengthen, and enhance professional standards and performance within the field of rehabilitation counseling. The RCEA is governed by a board of directors and continues to be a division of the NRA. As such, it falls under the constitution of the NRA. The RCEA has affiliated state chapters of its organization in many states in the United States.

American Rehabilitation Counseling Association (ARCA)

ARCA was founded in 1958 and is a division of the ACA. ARCA is governed by a board of directors. According to its website, ARCA's mission is to enhance the development of people with disabilities throughout the life span and to promote best practices in the rehabilitation counseling profession. ARCA's goal is to provide leadership that encourages excellence in rehabilitation counseling practice, research, consultation, and professional development (ARCA, n.d.). ARCA publishes a scholarly journal, the *Rehabilitation Counseling Bulletin*, in addition to its newsletter (Erford, 2014). ARCA bills itself as an organization of rehabilitation counseling practitioners, educators, and students who are concerned with improving the lives of people with disabilities. ARCA believes that RCs are counselors with specialized training and expertise in providing counseling and other services to people with disability. One of ARCA's primary goals is to increase public awareness of rehabilitation counseling and to extend its influence by encouraging members to become involved in the association's outreach and educational efforts. Other goals include helping members develop their leadership skills through participation in ARCA's organizational activities and to work with state officials to develop appropriate licensure requirements (ARCA, n.d.).

National Council on Rehabilitation Education (NCRE)

The NCRE was formed in 1955 as a professional organization for rehabilitation educators. The NCRE (n.d.) is governed by a board of directors that includes officers, regional representatives, and international representative and a student representative. The NCRE has a committee structure, including the Council of Past Presidents, nominations, membership, research, and awards. The purpose of the organization, according to its bylaws, is to "promote the improvement of supports and services available to individuals with disabilities and/or chronic illnesses through quality rehabilitation and research" (NCRE, n.d.). The NCRE hosts two conferences annually, a fall and a spring conference. The fall conference features representative from the Rehabilitation Services Administration (RSA) and is usually held in the greater District of Columbia area. The NCRE puts out a scholarly journal called *Rehabilitation Research, Policy, and Education*, in addition to its newsletter. The organization offers awards to recognize excellence in profession.

International Association of Rehabilitation Professionals (IARP)

The International Association of Rehabilitation Professionals (IARP) is a global association for professional in private rehabilitation. According to IARP's bylaws, its mission is "promoting effective interdisciplinary rehabilitation, disability management, and return-to-work services on behalf of people with disabilities and the economically disadvantaged; enhancing the competency of service providers; supporting innovation in related business development and management; and becoming the preeminent source for shaping public policy that affects private sector rehabilitation" (IARP, 2016). IARP is governed by a board of directors with representatives from different sections such as forensic, life care planning, rehabilitation and disability case management, social security, and vocational rehabilitation (VR) transition services. The IARP structure includes director positions for marketing/membership and education. IARP's paid staff includes directors in the following areas: executive, technology, meetings, and education. The office is located in Glenview, Illinois. IARP has state chapters located around the country. The organization hosts conferences and has online educational offerings. IARP has an awards and recognition program, job bank, and publications. IARP's official journal is *The Rehabilitation Professional*, known as *RehabPro*, and the *Journal of Life Care Planning (JLCP)* for members of that section (IARP, 2016). IARP hosts professional conferences geared to the private rehabilitation professional. IARP has a code of ethics for its members, which was last amended in December 2007. The organization has standards of practice for life care planners, case management, and vocational/placement.

COORDINATING ASSOCIATIONS: THE ALLIANCE, 20/20, AND THE REHABILITATION COUNSELING COALITION

Attempts to unify rehabilitation counseling began with the Alliance for Rehabilitation Counseling, originally formed by ARCA and NRCA in 1994 (Leahy & Tarvydas, 2001). Though considerable progress was made through the dedicated efforts of leaders in our field, the alliance dissolved in 2002 (Leahy, 2009).

The Commission on Rehabilitation Counseling facilitated the development of the Rehabilitation Counseling Consortium (RCC) in 2005 (Leahy, 2009). The consortium collaborates on credentialing and professional issues. In 2014, representatives of rehabilitation organizations met to address the future of the rehabilitation counseling profession. As a result of this dialogue, eight rehabilitation organizations established the Rehabilitation Counseling Coalition (2014) in order to renew strategic planning efforts and advance the profession. Member organizations include the American Board of Vocational Experts (ABVE), ARCA, CSAVR, IARP, National Association of Service Providers in Private Rehabilitation (NASPPR), the NCRE, the NRA, and the RCEA. Although well intended, the impact of this coalition remains uncertain.

The ACA and the AASCB sponsored the formation of "20/20: A Vision for the Future of Counseling," as a response to concerns about the counseling profession's lack of unity (Kaplan & Gladding, 2011). Thirty-one organizations worked toward unifying the profession between 2005 and 2013 (ACA, 2016). Originally, a confederation of 29 professional counseling organizations identified the following principles as necessary for advancing the profession: the importance of counselors sharing a professional identity, the need for a unified profession, professional advocacy and collaboration necessary to improve the perception of the counseling profession, the importance of licensure portability, a commitment to research, a focus on students, and an emphasis on client welfare and advocacy as necessary to strengthen the profession (Kaplan & Gladding, 2011). In 2010, 29 of the 31 delegates of 20/20 met and agreed upon the following definition of counseling: **Counseling** is a professional relationship that empowers diverse individuals, families, and groups to accomplish mental health, wellness, education, and career goals (Kaplan, Tarvydas, & Gladding, 2014). Although the development of a consensus definition of counseling in 2010 was hailed as a precedent-setting achievement, the 20/20 confederation was unable to reach a similar consensus regarding other issues and the confederation ended in 2013.

Over the years, there have been attempts to unify rehabilitation counseling professional organizations. ARCA and NRCA formed the Alliance for Rehabilitation Counseling in 1994. In 2005, NRCA withdrew from the NRA and in 2006, the NRA replaced NRCA with the RCEA. Subsequently, in October 2016, NRCA members voted to merge with the NRA and the RCEA, thereby unifying the field (personal communication, Angela Price, October 20, 2016). Today, there are fewer members of all associations, as membership numbers have continued to decline in the 21st century leading to potentially less political clout for the field (Leahy, Tarvydas, & Phillips, 2011).

LEGISLATIVE INFLUENCES

TRICARE

TRICARE is the military health care insurance system that covers 9.4 million beneficiaries (TRICARE, 2016). Beneficiaries of TRICARE include uniformed service members, retired service members, and their families. In 2006, the DoD reported to Congress that LPCs lacked uniform prepractice training, education, and experience standards to provide the level of care that the DoD mandates for its beneficiaries. Subsequently, in 2010, an IOM report regarding the Provision of Mental Health Services Under TRICARE recommended that licensed counselors graduating from CACREP-accredited programs in mental health counseling who had also passed the NCMHCE should be allowed to practice independently under TRICARE.

On July 17, 2014, the DoD published the Final Rule regarding the TRICARE category of Certified Mental Health Counselors (TCMHC; ACA, 2014). It was considered a precedent setting act in establishing national criteria for LPCs to receive third-party reimbursement. This was a key component in the ACA's effort to demonstrate parity among those providing mental health services. The Final Rule also established a 5-year (rather than 5-month) transition period for meeting education, examination, and supervised clinical practice criteria to January 1, 2017. The Final Rule allows LPCs who meet the following criteria to operate as independent practitioners under TRICARE:

1. Possess a master's degree or higher from a mental health counseling program accredited by CACREP and passage of the NCE for licensure and certification
2. Possess a master's degree or higher in counseling from a regionally accredited institution and passage of the NCMHCE

Another provision of the Final Rule allowed those LPCs in the Supervised Mental Health Counselor (SMHC) category to continue indefinitely. Only physicians may supervise or refer to an SMHC. As originally drafted, counselors in this category would have no longer been able to practice within TRICARE.

Advocacy by the ACA resulted in the insertion of a broad grand parenting clause that affords more LPCs time to meet the TRICARE transition requirements originally included in The Final Rule until 2027 (ACA, 2015). The amended language is part of the

House version of the 2016 National Defense Authorization Act (NDAA), the legislation that sets the policy and rules for the nation's armed forces. Passage of these revisions would enable an LPC who possesses a master's degree in counseling from an institution that is regionally accredited, or has accreditation from the CACREP, in a 48- or 60-credit hour program, that has been licensed and practiced in good standing for at least 5 years in his or her respective state to be certified as an independent practitioner.

Workforce Innovation and Opportunity Act (WIOA)

The passage of the Workforce Innovation and Opportunity Act (WIOA), which became public law in 2014, appeared to reverse the progress toward professionalization of RCs in the state-federal VR system. Master's degrees were mandated for RCs employed in the state-federal VR system in 1992. Despite this mandate, by 2004, 30% to 50% of all public VR counselors still did not have a graduate degree (Chan, 2003). Explanations for the difficulties that states had recruiting and retaining qualified counselors have ranged from salary disparities (Chan, 2003; Frain, Ferrin, Rosenthal, & Wampold, 2006; McClanahan & Sligar, 2015) to work environments that were incongruent with counselor preparation and expectations (Lustig & Strauser, 2008, 2009; Zanskas & Strohmer, 2010). Regardless of the explanation, according to the comments in the Workforce Investment Act VR Final Rule (34 C.F.R. Parts 361, 363, & 397 Stat. 982, 2016), prospective RCs are only required to have a bachelor's degree in a field closely related VR such as VR counseling, social work, psychology, disability studies, business administration, human resources, special education, supported employment, customized employment, or economics.

The rehabilitation counseling community responded to the apparent dimuntion of professional level standards for RCs in the state-federal VR system. According to the comments in the Workforce Investment Act VR Final Rule, "There is nothing in the Act or these final regulations to preclude a DSU from continuing to hire VR professionals and paraprofessionals that satisfy the higher standard" (2016, p. 162). The comments clarified that the intent of the rule was to establish minimum standards for all VR professionals and paraprofessionals, not just VR counselors. The Final Rule allows states flexibility in their hiring decisions, allowing the use of a national or state certification standard or the hiring of individuals who have at least a baccalaureate degree in a specified field of study plus 1 year of relevant experience, or a master's or doctoral degree in one of the fields specified. The rules explicitly express that hiring is a state issue and that the personnel standards described are separate and independent of each other. Prospective applicants are not required to meet both personnel standards.

CONCLUSION

Rehabilitation counseling is a specialty area of counseling that offers tremendous career and employment opportunities. Never before have RCs had access to so many employment settings. Rehabilitation counseling has a rich history with more than 60 years of preservice education, pioneering both academic program accreditation and national certification for practitioners in the counseling profession. However, the environment for RCs is undergoing momentous change and the discipline cannot remain viable resting upon past accomplishments. Although the creation of the clinical RC specialty increases licensing opportunities for graduates of the 60-credit hour degree programs, it also raises new questions about our professional identity. The myriad of professional associations contributes to the public's confusion, ability to recognize, and understanding of our discipline. It is a new era, and dynamic leadership is necessary to strategically navigate the intricacies of the future. Many of the founding visionaries who contributed to our professionalization are retiring. New leadership is required and this represents one of the biggest challenges for our discipline and opportunities for you as a professional.

CONTENT REVIEW QUESTIONS

- What is the overall purpose of credentialing? Define and give examples of accreditation, certification, and licensure.
- What are the similarities and differences between licensing and certification as distinct forms of credentialing?
- What are the differences between title and practice licensure laws?
- What is the primary certification body for rehabilitation counseling?
- What are examples of professional associations in rehabilitation counseling?
- How have professional associations been instrumental in the evolution of the rehabilitation counseling profession?
- What are the challenges and current legislative influences on contemporary rehabilitation counseling practice?

REFERENCES

American Association of State Counseling Boards. (2015). Position letter to state counseling boards on portability. Retrieved from http://www.aascb.org/aws/AASCB/pt/sp/licensure

American Counseling Association. (2014). *Final TRICARE rules more beneficial to Licensed Professional Counselors* [Press release]. Retrieved from http://www.counseling.org/news/news-release-archives/by-year/2014/2014/07/18/final-tricare-rules-more-beneficial-to-licensed-professional-counselors

American Counseling Association. (2015). *More LPCs to be included under new TRICARE language* [Press release]. Retrieved from http://www.counseling.org/news/updates/2015/05/12/more-lpcs-to-be-included-under-new-tricare-language

American Counseling Association, The Center for Counseling Practice, Policy and Research. (2016). *Licensure requirements for professional counselors: A state-by-state report 2016 edition.* The Center for Counseling Practice (Ed.). Alexandria, VA: Author.

American Rehabilitation Counseling Association. (n.d.). Website. Retrieved from http://www.arcaweb.org

Barros-Bailey, M., Benschoff, J. J., & Fischer, J. (2009). Rehabilitation counseling in the year 2011: Perceptions of rehabilitation counselors. *Rehabilitation Counseling Bulletin, 52*(2), 107–113.

Berven, N. L. (1979). The role and function of the rehabilitation counselor revisited. *Rehabilitation Counseling Bulletin, 22,* 84–88.

Bobby, C. L. (2013). The evolution of specialties in the CACREP standard. *Journal of Counseling and Development, 91*(1), 35–43.

Brubaker, D. R. (1977). Professionalization and rehabilitation counseling. *Journal of Applied Rehabilitation Counseling, 8,* 208–217.

Bureau of Labor Statistics, U.S. Department of Labor. (2015). Rehabilitation counselors. *Occupational outlook handbook.* Retrieved from https://www.bls.gov/ooh/community-and-social-service/rehabilitation-counselors.htm

Chan, T. (2003, October). *Evaluation study: Findings and usage.* Paper presented at the National Council on Rehabilitation Education/Rehabilitation Services Administration/Council of State Administrators of Vocational Rehabilitation Conference on Rehabilitation Education, Arlington, VA.

Commission on Accreditation of Rehabilitation Facilities. (2016). Website. Retrieved from http://www.carf.org

Commission on Rehabilitation Counselor Certification. (n.d.). Website. Retrieved from https://www.crccertification.com

Cottone, R. R. (1985). The need for counselor licensure: A rehabilitation counseling perspective. *Journal of Counseling and Development, 63*, 625–629.

Council for Accreditation of Counseling and Related Educational Programs. (n.d.). Vision and core values. Retrieved from http://www.cacrep.org/about-cacrep

Council for Accreditation of Counseling and Related Educational Programs. (2016). 2016 CACREP standards. Retrieved from www.cacrep.org/wp-content/uploads/2012/10/2016-CACREP-Standards.pdf

Council for Higher Education Accreditation. (n.d.). Principles. Retrieved from http://chea.org/userfiles/CIQG/Principles_Papers_Complete_web.pdf

Council on Rehabilitation Education. (n.d.). What is CORE: Structure and function. Retrieved from http://core-rehab.org/whatiscore

Council on Rehabilitation Education. (2013, July 31). *CORE press release* [Press release]. Chicago, IL: Author.

Council on Rehabilitation Education. (2014, October 15). *CACREP and its affiliate CORE move forward with accreditation reviews for clinical rehabilitation counseling programs* [Press release]. Chicago, IL: Author.

Council on Rehabilitation Education. (2015, July 20). *CORE/CACREP merger agreement signed* [Press release]. Chicago, IL: Author.

Dew, D. W., & Peters, S. (2002). Survey of master's level rehabilitation counselor programs: Relationship to public vocational rehabilitation recruitment and retention of state vocational rehabilitation counselors. *Rehabilitation Education, 16*, 61–65.

Emener, W. G., & Cottone, R. R. (1989). Professionalization, deprofessionalization, and reprofessionalization of rehabilitation counseling according to criteria of the professions. *Journal of Counseling and Development, 67*, 576–581.

Emener, W. G., & Rubin, S. E. (1980). Rehabilitation counselor roles and functions and sources of role strain. *Journal of Applied Rehabilitation Counseling, 11*, 57–69.

Erford, B. (2014). *Orientation to the counseling profession.* Upper Saddle River, NJ: Pearson.

Frain, M., Ferrin, J., Rosenthal, D., & Wampold, B. (2006). A meta-analysis of rehabilitation outcomes on education level of the counselor. *Journal of Rehabilitation, 72*(1), 10–18.

Goodwin, L. R. (2006). Rehabilitation counselor specialty areas offered by rehabilitation counselor education programs. *Rehabilitation Education, 20*, 133–135.

Hardy, R. E., Luck, R. S., & Chandler, A. L. (1982). Licensure of rehabilitation counselors and related issues: Results of a national survey. *Rehabilitation Counseling Bulletin, 25*, 157–161.

Hershenson, D. B., & McKenna, M. A. (1998). Trends affecting rehabilitation counselor education. *Rehabilitation Education, 12*, 277–288.

Hosie, T. W. (1995). Counseling specialties: A case of basic preparation rather than advanced specialization. *Journal of Counseling and Development, 74*(2), 177–180.

Institute of Medicine. (2010). Provision of mental health services under TRICARE. Retrieved from http://www.nap.edu/openbook.php?record_id=12813

International Association of Rehabilitation Professionals. (2016). Bylaws. Retrieved from http://www.rehabpro.org/about-iarp/bylaws

Jaques, M. E. (1959). *Critical counseling behavior in rehabilitation settings.* Iowa City: State University of Iowa, College of Education.

Kaplan, David (2012, January). *Licensure reciprocity: A critical public protection issue that needs action.* Paper presented at the American Association of State Counseling Boards Conference, Charleston, SC.

Kaplan, D. M., & Gladding, S. T. (2011). A vision for the future of counseling: The 20/20 principles for unifying and strengthening the profession. *Journal of Counseling and Development, 89*, 367–372.

Kaplan, D. M., Tarvydas, V. M., & Gladding, S. T. (2014). 20/20: A vision for the future of counseling: The new consensus definition of counseling. *Journal of Counseling and Development, 92*, 366–372.

Kirk, F., & LaForge, J. (1995). The National Rehabilitation Association. *The Journal of Rehabilitation, 61*(3), 47–50.

Leahy, M. J. (2002). Professionalism in rehabilitation counseling: A retrospective review. *Journal of Rehabilitation, 26*(2), 99–109.

Leahy, M. J. (2009). Rehabilitation counseling credentialing: Research, practice, and the future of the profession. *Rehabilitation Counseling Bulletin, 52*(2), 67–68. doi:10.1177/0034355208323647

Leahy, M. J. (2012). Qualified providers of rehabilitation counseling services. In D. R. Maki & V. M. Tarvydas (Eds.), *The professional practice of rehabilitation counseling* (pp. 193–211). New York, NY: Springer Publishing.

Leahy, M. J., Chan, F., & Saunders, J. L. (2003). Job functions and knowledge requirements of certified rehabilitation counselors in the 21st century. *Rehabilitation Counseling Bulletin, 46*(2), 66–81.

Leahy, M. J., Chan, F., Sung, C., & Kim, M. (2012). Empirically derived test specifications for the Certified Rehabilitation Counselor Examination. *Rehabilitation Counseling Bulletin, 56*(4), 199–214. doi:10.1177/0034355212469839

Leahy, M. J., Muenzen, P., Saunders, J. L., & Strauser, D. (2009). Essential knowledge domains underlying effective rehabilitation counseling practice. *Rehabilitation Counseling Bulletin, 52*(2), 95–106.

Leahy, M. J., Shapson, P. R., & Wright, G. N. (1987). Rehabilitation practitioner competencies by role and setting. *Rehabilitation Counseling Bulletin, 31,* 119–131.

Leahy, M. J., Szymanski, E. M., & Linkowski, D. C. (1993). Rehabilitation counseling: Evolution and current status. *Journal of Counseling and Development, 74,* 163–166.

Leahy, M. J., & Tansey, T. N. (2008). The impact of CORE standards across the rehabilitation educational continuum. *Rehabilitation Education, 22*(3 & 4), 217–226.

Leahy, M. J., & Tarvydas, V. (2001). Transforming our professional organizations: A first step toward the unification of the rehabilitation counseling profession. *Journal of Applied Rehabilitation Counseling, 32*(3), 3–8.

Leahy, M. J., Tarvydas, V. M., & Phillips, B. N. (2011). Rehabilitation counseling's Phoenix Project: Re-visiting the call for unification of the professional associations in rehabilitation counseling. *Rehabilitation Education, 25*(1–2), 5–14.

Lustig, D. C., & Strauser, D. R. (2008). The relationship between degree type, certification status, and years of employment on rehabilitation counseling tasks in state-federal vocational rehabilitation. *Rehabilitation Counseling Bulletin, 52,* 28–34.

Lustig, D. C., & Strauser, D. R. (2009). Rehabilitation counseling graduate students' preferences for employment: Agreement between actual and perceived job tasks of state-federal vocational rehabilitation counselors. *Rehabilitation Counseling Bulletin, 52,* 179–188.

Mascari, J. B., & Webber, J. (2013). CACREP accreditation: A solution to license portability and counselor identity problems. *Journal of Counseling and Development, 91,* 15–25.

McClanahan, M. L., & Sligar, S. R. (2015). Adapting to WIOA minimum education requirement for vocational rehabilitation counselors. *Journal of Rehabilitation, 81*(3), 3–8.

Mundt, P. (1986). The National Rehabilitation Counseling Association. *Journal of Rehabilitation, 52*(3), 51–53.

Muthard, J. E., & Salamone, P. (1969). The roles and functions of the rehabilitation counselor. *Rehabilitation Counseling Bulletin, 13,* 81–168.

National Board for Certified Counselors. (2016a). About NBCC. Retrieved from http://www.nbcc.org/footer/AboutNBCC

National Board for Certified Counselors. (2016b). *National counselor examination for licensure and certification* [NBCC comment]. Retrieved from http://www.nbcc.org/exam/nationalcounselorexaminationforlicensureandcertification

National Council on Rehabilitation Education. (n.d.). The National Council on Rehabilitation Education Overview. Retrieved from https://ncre.org/ncre-overview/bylaw

Rehabilitation Counseling Coalition. (2014). *Public announcement of the Rehabilitation Counseling Coalition (RCC)* [Press release]. Retrieved from http://rehabcea.org/article/rehabilitation-counseling-coalition-rcc-officially-announced

Rothman, R. A. (1987). *Working: Sociological perspectives.* Englewood Cliffs, NJ: Prentice Hall.

Saunders, J. L., Barros-Bailey, M., Chapman, C., & Nunez, P. (2008). Rehabilitation counselor certification: Moving forward. *Journal of Applied Rehabilitation Counseling, 39*(4), 12–18.

Shaw, L., & Kuehn, M. D. (2009). Rehabilitation counselor education accreditation, history, structure, and evolution. *Rehabilitation Counseling Bulletin, 52*(2), 69–76.

Shaw, L., Leahy, M. J., Chan, F., & Catalano, D. (2006). Contemporary issues facing rehabilitation counseling: A Delphi study of the perspectives of leaders of the discipline. *Rehabilitation Education, 20,* 163–178.

Stebnicki, M. A. (2009). A call for integral approaches in the professional identity of rehabilitation counseling: Three specialty areas, one profession. *Rehabilitation Counseling Bulletin, 52*(2), 133–137. doi:10.1177/0034355208324263

Tarvydas, V., & Hartley, M. T. (2009). What practitioners need to know about professional counseling. In M. Stebnicki & I. Marini (Eds.), *The professional counselor's desk reference* (pp. 27–38). New York, NY: Springer Publishing.

Tarvydas, V., Hartley, M. T., & Gerald, M. (2015). Professional credentialing. In M. Stebnicki & I. Marini (Eds.), *Professional counselors' desk reference* (2nd ed, pp. 17–22). New York, NY: Springer Publishing.

Tarvydas, V., & Leahy, M. J. (1993). Licensure in rehabilitation counseling: A critical incident in professionalization. *Rehabilitation Counseling Bulletin, 37*(2), 92–108.

Tarvydas, V., Leahy, M. J., & Zanskas, S. (2009). Judgment deferred: Reappraisal of rehabilitation counseling movement toward licensure parity. *Rehabilitation Counseling Bulletin, 52*(2), 85–94.

TRICARE. (2016). Facts and figures. Retrieved from http://www.tricare.mil/About/Facts?sc_database=web

Trolley, B. C., & Cervoni, A. B. (1999). New millennium employment reflections for rehabilitation counselors: A follow-up study. *Rehabilitation Education, 13*(4), 335–347.

Urofsky, R. I. (2013). The Council for Accreditation of Counseling and related educational programs: Promoting quality in counselor education. *Journal of Counseling and Development, 91*(1), 6–14.

Urofsky, R. I., Bobby, C., & Pope, V. (2009). The CACREP 2009 standards. *Counseling Today*, May, 68–69.

Wheeler, A. M., & Bertram, B. (2015). *The counselor and the law: A guide to legal and ethical practice* (7th ed.). Alexandria, VA: American Counseling Association.

Workforce Innovation and Opportunity Act, Pub. L. No. 113–128 (2014).

Workforce Investment Act. (2016). VR Final Rule, 34 C.F.R. pts. 361, 363, & 397 Stat. 982 (2016).

Wright, G. N., & Fraser, R. T. (1975). *Task analysis for the evaluation, preparation, classification, and utilization of rehabilitation counselor track personnel* (Wisconsin Studies in Vocational Rehabilitation Monograph No. 22, Series 3). Madison: University of Wisconsin.

Zanskas, S. A., & Leahy, M. (2007). Preparing rehabilitation counselors for private sector practice within a CORE accredited generalist educational model. *Rehabilitation Education, 21*(3), 205–218.

Zanskas, S. A., & Strohmer, D. (2010). Rehabilitation counselor work environment: Examining congruence with prototypic work personality. *Rehabilitation Counseling Bulletin, 53*(3), 143–152.

FOUR

History and Evolution of Counseling and Rehabilitation Counseling

LINDA R. SHAW AND J. BARRY MASCARI

LEARNING OBJECTIVES

After reading this chapter, you should be able to:

- Recognize the reasons that rehabilitation counseling developed separately from the other counseling specializations.
- Understand the reasons that leaders within the counseling profession believe that a unified profession of counseling is desirable.
- Trace the important events and actions in the development of both the counseling profession and the specialty practice of rehabilitation counseling.

COUNSELING: ONE PROFESSION WITH MANY SPECIALTIES OR MANY SPECIALTY PROFESSIONS?

The relationship of rehabilitation counseling to the larger profession of counseling has evolved in response to ongoing changes in the legislative, social, and business arenas. This chapter reviews the parallel histories of the counseling profession and the counseling specialty of rehabilitation counseling, and explores the changes that have affected this evolution over time. The primary focus is on rehabilitation counseling, bringing the reader up to the current merger of the Council for Accreditation of Counseling and Related Educational Programs (CACREP) and the Council on Rehabilitation Education (CORE) and its implications for rehabilitation counseling and the larger profession moving forward, starting with the earliest history.

COUNSELING: THE BEGINNING

In 1952, four small organizations, including the National Vocational Guidance Association (NVGA, founded in 1913), joined to form the American Personnel and Guidance Association (APGA), an earlier name for the American Counseling Association (ACA; Smith, 2004). Counseling's start as a group of separate organizations with special interests and work settings resulted in a history of ongoing struggles to maintain this confederation of groups with divergent purposes as one profession.

Rehabilitation counseling is one of those groups that has, at times, struggled to clearly identify itself as either a counseling specialty or as a separate profession. More recently, however, the momentum of the counselor licensure movement and the Institute of Medicine's (IOM, 2010) decision influenced rehabilitation counseling to clearly identify itself as a specialty within the profession of counseling.

The question of whether counseling is one profession with many specialties or many specialty professions has not been fully resolved. Remley (2012) noted, "Probably the most significant problem the counseling profession faces today is determining whether the profession will develop a strong identity as one united profession with a common philosophical foundation and knowledge base, or whether the specialties will emerge as the dominant force within counseling" (p. 3). Is a trend toward increased unity taking shape? Recent developments suggest that there is a clear trend toward unification.

COUNSELING: A HOUSE DIVIDED AGAINST ITSELF

Counselors were found mostly in school settings during the profession's early years, but over time other specialty counseling groups began to emerge and organize (Mascari, 2004). The growth of the counseling profession took a major turn when the first call for licensing of counselors was formally endorsed by APGA in 1975 and it established its licensure commission (Swanson, 1981). Passage of the first licensure laws was followed by the development of the National Academy of Certified Clinical Mental Health Counselors (NACCMHC) in 1979, which led to greater dialogue about developing self-imposed standards for the training and practice of the profession (Smith, 2004).

In 1987, the National Board for Certified Counselors (NBCC) became a recognized credentialing body for the counseling profession (Smith, 2004). Although licensing was the major focus of attention for the counseling profession, the work of NBCC played a critical role in shaping counseling's professional standards. Smith (2004), speaking of the National Certified Counselor (NCC) credential, said:

> this professional credential, as opposed to the practicing credential of licensure, determines what it is that counselors must know to be able to hold themselves out to the public as a professional counselor. It is a matter of identity and integrity for the profession. (p. 9)

With the counseling profession seeking licensure and public recognition, ACA's leadership became increasingly aware that some common standards were essential, and formed CACREP in 1981 (Akos & Galassi, 2004; Steinhauser & Bradley, 1983).

The early struggles of the counseling profession continued, despite the establishment of a code of ethics that may have been too generic to satisfy the various divisions of ACA. As a result, by 1995, seven of the 12 ACA specialty divisions had developed their own codes of ethics (Herlihy & Remley, 1995) in addition to those of the national certification boards, licensing boards, and ACA. Herlihy and Remley (1995) called for the development of a single code, suggesting that if the goal is to have the public understand what the counseling profession is all about and what the ethical requirements are, "that goal could be attained much more readily if only one set of ethical standards existed for the profession" (p. 132).

Struggles among the ACA divisions have contributed further to the splintering of counselor identity. Policy decisions by the Governing Council have had profound effects on ACA and counselor identity. Carol Neiman, ACA Associate Executive Director for

Membership and Meetings (personal communication, July 16, 2004), identified key events having an impact on ACA's decreased membership numbers. Neiman noted that ACA attempted to address issues related to the proliferation of identity through multiple divisions by convening the Millennium Commission to consider "governance issues." Since nothing ever resulted from the Commission, a loose identification of the divisions with the counseling profession as a whole continued, consistent with ACA's history since its founding. Neiman also identified the Governing Council's October 17 to 19, 1997 meeting amid threats by American Mental Health Counselors Association (AMHCA) and American School Counselor Association (ASCA) to disaffiliate as another important event. At that meeting, the Governing Council voted to allow members to join ACA without a division membership and for divisions to accept members without ACA membership. After taking effect on July 1, 1998, the percentage of individuals who hold membership in ACA without also belonging to a division has hovered between 70/30 and 75/25. Additionally, another policy change that may have hurt ACA's membership numbers was the Insurance Trust's dropping the requirement that to obtain professional liability insurance, the applicant must be an ACA member.

Gale and Austin (2003) predicted the future when they said that "trends of the past 30 years show that counselors seeking licensure has further fragmented the profession" (p. 4). They added, "These trends underscore the genuine possibility that unless professional counselors collectively define their profession, it will be divided by specialization and will be circumscribed by other professions" (p. 4).

Although ACA was established to represent all counselors in all specialties, it has not yet been successful in bringing all counselors together from the various specializations to work consistently toward common goals. At present, it appears unlikely that counselors who represent various specializations would unanimously agree to unify all of the various organizations and agencies that represent counselors. Instead, it appears that specialty counselor certification groups will continue to coexist with NBCC, and that not all counselors consider ACA to be the organization with which they have their primary affiliation.

EVOLUTION OF REHABILITATION COUNSELING

Influence of World War I

Most observers trace the beginnings of rehabilitation counseling to a series of federal laws, beginning with the Smith-Fess Act in 1920, that established the state-federal system of vocational rehabilitation (VR; Leahy & Szymanski, 1995). From its beginnings as a practical system for returning an unprecedented number of disabled World War I veterans to work, the state-federal system expanded its services and populations served to become the primary service provider for disabled adults. Originally envisioned as a retraining program, the field attracted teachers and vocational-technical personnel. As the multifaceted needs of individuals served became increasingly apparent, and as services and diagnoses broadened, a multidisciplinary approach was needed. Elliott and Leung (2004) observed that involvement by professionals representing a multitude of professional disciplines was needed, including medicine, special education, physical therapy, occupational therapy, vocational education, psychology, and others.

Rehabilitation Act Amendments of 1954

As the rehabilitation process increased in complexity, the need for coordination of different providers became apparent. By 1954, the Vocational Rehabilitation Act Amendments of 1954 had provided funds to higher education to train rehabilitation counselors (RCs). With this Act, an understanding of the type of individual needed to serve as the primary point of intervention within the VR program began to emerge. A counselor with knowledge and skills required to assist individuals in the process of psychological adaptation to disability (referred to at the time as *adjustment counseling*) was needed. Additionally, the counselor's role as coordinator of the many service providers in the VR process was emphasized, and the importance of the counselor as a case manager was recognized (Jenkins, Patterson, & Szymanski, 1998).

Finally, a thorough understanding of the world of work, vocational counseling, and vocational placement was essential in order to accomplish the primary goal of the agency: return to work. Many of the programs that emerged in response to the 1954 legislation were established within Colleges of Education, reflecting both the early roots of the field and the commonalities between the training needs of VR counselors and guidance (school) counselors. However, programs also appeared in psychology and allied health academic units, and the early rehabilitation educators were drawn from many different fields.

Rehabilitation Emerges as a Counseling Specialty

The values and beliefs underscoring the practice of rehabilitation counseling had its roots in the turn-of-the-century movements that emphasized a humanistic approach to assisting individuals in need, such as poor, destitute, and mentally ill people, as well as those with physical disabilities. With advances in medicine and the development of new theories for explaining and treating mental illnesses, these individuals began to be viewed as people who could be "rehabilitated" and even returned to productive activity. Frank Parsons was credited with beginning the vocational guidance movement in 1906 with the Vocational Bureau of Boston (Jones, 1994). Sales (2012) observed that Parsons ushered in the start of systematic vocational guidance and counseling in the United States, which was further shaped by Williamson's development of a comprehensive theory of counseling.

As Neukrug (1994) noted, the challenges of quickly returning veterans who had experienced both physical and psychological trauma to work were not well-served by longer term psychoanalytic approaches, and the need for shorter-term interventions that emphasized the individual's skills, abilities, and capacity for mental health emerged. Undoubtedly, this emphasis on developing briefer, more targeted approaches also sprang from the increasingly accepted role of the government in improving the care of these individuals. With public funds underwriting the cost of care, extended psychoanalytic treatment that emphasized pathology would not offer a practical or cost-effective approach. What was needed was focused, shorter-term approaches that used clients' abilities and could more quickly transform individuals into productive, contributing workers. This trend was further solidified with the passage of the Community Mental Health Act in 1963, shifting the emphasis from mental illness to mental health.

Gladding (1996) asserted that the proliferation of a multitude of new approaches to treatment drove an increased demand for counselors, including approaches reflected in the work of Bandura, Wolpe, Rogers, Glasser, Perls, Berne, and Frankl. These approaches viewed individuals as self-empowered change agents who were ready to access their emotions, thoughts, and behaviors, and able to harness their strengths to effect positive change. The new breed of theorists viewed individuals through a developmental lens, acknowledging that the human organism is not static but naturally changing and developing.

Behavioral health professionals who ascribed to these approaches began to identify themselves collectively as counselors, while at the same time having separate identities tied to the settings in which they worked and the populations they served. Remley and Herlihy (2010) identified four beliefs that they asserted are common to all counselors, regardless of their areas of specialty. These beliefs include (a) wellness models being the preferred approach, (b) an appreciation for the importance of understanding the developmental process, (c) a commitment to early intervention and prevention, and (d) a commitment to empowering people to exercise their power to identify and solve problems using their inherent strengths and abilities.

A Philosophy of Rehabilitation Counseling

Although these counseling beliefs are shared by RCs, additional beliefs that were more closely tied to their traditional practice settings and population evolved to guide their development and practice, as occurred within other counseling specialties. Elliott and Leung (2004) argued that rehabilitation counseling philosophy was heavily influenced by a group of psychologists interested in disability and rehabilitation that included a number of influential social psychologists. These individuals concluded that societal attitudes, discrimination, and stigma were major factors that prevented people with disabilities from participation and integration. This perspective represented a radical divergence from the traditional view of disability as an all-encompassing characteristic, responsible for the inability to actively engage in work, relationships, and typical adult roles. In this view, social and environmental change becomes a focus of intervention and the goal of counseling becomes not "fixing" or "adjusting" to disability. Instead, disability began to be viewed as a part of the natural diversity among people, and the goal became assisting the individual, through advocacy and empowerment, to effect positive change in the environment that would remove barriers to participation and integration, and to diminish the handicapping effects of the disability (Hahn, 1985). The social model of disability took root and maintains a prominent place in the guiding philosophy of RCs.

Although the field of rehabilitation counseling grew out of the professional traditions of many disciplines, special education was one of the most influential. Sharing an interest in disability, both special education and rehabilitation counseling espoused the value of **normalization**, a term coined by Nirje (1969) and later popularized by Wolfensberger (1972). This guiding principle declares that all people with disabilities should have access to patterns and conditions of everyday living that are as near as possible to the regular patterns and conditions of life that exist within society at large. Wolfensberger later introduced the term **social role valorization** to extend the concept of normalization to include the idea that one must devote oneself to the "creation, support and defense of valued social roles for people who are at risk of social devaluation," including people with disabilities (p. 234).

The concept of normalization became the bedrock of the deinstitutionalization movement for people with developmental disabilities in the 1970s, and normalization became a critical part of the guiding principles of RCs. Consumers of rehabilitation services demanded the right to more normalized lives, and a consumer-directed movement termed **independent living** took root in support of this goal. Rehabilitation counseling was influenced by these social developments and RCs' roles broadened to include the facilitation of participation in the community in ways that extended beyond the vocational realm (Kundu & Schiro-Geist, 2006; Wright, 1980).

The emphasis on advocacy and empowerment as a bedrock of rehabilitation counseling was fueled further by the civil rights fervor that swept the country in the 1960s. As a group stigmatized by the possession of a disability, and having been denied access to opportunity through exclusion and segregation, people with disabilities, along with many RCs, took up the demand for civil rights along with women and African Americans. In the **minority group model** of disability, disability is viewed from a sociopolitical perspective and asserts that disability is not a functional limitation that resides within an individual, but rather is a societal refusal to address the needs of a minority group that shares the common characteristic of disability (Hahn, 1985).

Although there was ample evidence that people with disabilities faced clear and widespread discrimination, the battle for protection from discrimination was fraught with difficulties. People with disabilities were not included as a protected category under the Civil Rights Act and did not receive specific protections from discrimination until later legislation, such as Sections 501 and 504 of the Rehabilitation Act of 1973, as amended, and the 1990 Americans with Disabilities Act and its subsequent 2008 Amendments. Although the formal inclusion of social justice as an elemental value of the counseling profession is a relatively recent occurrence, most RCs would argue that it has been a bedrock value of their field of practice for many decades.

Rehabilitation Counseling Within Counseling Profession's Growth

Counseling experienced rapid growth from the post–World War II career guidance movement, and had established counselor licensing in four states by the 1970s: Virginia, Arkansas, Alabama, and Texas (Wayne, 1982). Although several other specialty areas, such as school counseling and mental health counseling, have struggled with their identification as a specialty of counseling rather than a separate and distinct profession (Palmo, 1990; Pistole & Roberts, 2002; Sparks, 2008), perhaps no other field has maintained such a professional distance from the main body of counseling as has rehabilitation counseling, as a result of a combination of practical and historical reasons.

Rehabilitation counseling is not alone among the counseling specialty practice areas in having developed unique foundational values and structures. The APGA, the precursor to ACA, was originally formed from professional groups representing four different specialty areas and was seen as an umbrella professional organization (Myers, 1995). Since that time, the counseling profession has struggled to build a strong unified and centralized profession. The counseling literature is filled with warnings about the consequences of splintering and calls for unification, along with numerous examples of the fractures that have occurred during the journey to build a common identity (Gale & Austin, 2003; Gladding, 2008; Leahy, Rak, & Zanskas, 2009; Mellin, Hunt, & Nichols, 2011; Neukrug & Remley, 2009; Reiner, Dobmeier, & Hernandez, 2013; Sweeney, 1995).

In 1998, Chi Sigma Iota had convened a two-part multi-day meeting attended by representatives from ACA and seven divisions/organizations representing various areas of specialty practice (including ARCA), the Education Resources Information Center Clearinghouse on Counseling and Student Services (ERIC/CASS), NBCC, and the North Carolina Counseling Association. Out of that meeting, a set of six themes was developed, intended to facilitate the profession's efforts at self-advocacy (Kaplan & Gladding, 2011). The themes that emerged from these meetings, titled the *Counselor Advocacy Leadership Conferences*, are reprinted in whole in Box 4.1. Unfortunately, not much came from this event at that time; however, the themes were echoed in later attempts at achieving consensus around the profession's self-advocacy efforts.

> **BOX 4.1 Counselor Advocacy Leadership Conference Themes**
>
> 1. Counselor education graduate students should develop a clear identity as a professional counselor and take pride in this identity.
> 2. Associations representing professional counseling should work closely together to promote a common advocacy agenda.
> 3. Professional counselors should receive adequate compensation and be unrestricted in their ability to provide services within areas of competency.
> 4. Professional counseling should partner with sister professions on matters of mutual interest.
> 5. Professional counseling should promote rigorous research in the areas of client outcomes, counselor preparation, counselor preparation, counselor employment, and public awareness; seek out research grants and contracts; and promote the use of research by clients, professionals and legislators.
> 6. Professional counseling should advocate for optimal human development by promoting prevention and wellness.
>
> Chi Sigma Iota (n.d.)

CREDENTIALING AND PROFESSIONALIZATION OF COUNSELING

Linkowski and Szymanski (1993) described the early professionalization efforts of a small group of rehabilitation educators who came together in 1969 to discuss the need for national educational standards for the many new rehabilitation counseling education programs that had come into existence over the last decade. Two years later, CORE was formed and it was incorporated in 1972 as the national accreditation body for master's-level programs in rehabilitation counseling. In that same year, it applied for accreditation from the National Commission on Accrediting (NCA), which later became the Council on Post-Secondary Accreditation (COPA), now the Council for Higher Education Association (CHEA). In 1974, rehabilitation counseling became the first counseling field to achieve national accreditation by NCA.

During this same time period, efforts got underway to establish a credential that would "establish professional standards whereby individuals with disabilities, associated professionals, and the general public can evaluate the qualifications of individuals practicing rehabilitation counseling" (Leahy & Holt, 1993, p. 71). In 1969, a joint committee of the National Rehabilitation Counseling Association (NRCA) and the American Rehabilitation Counseling Association (ARCA) was formed to explore the possibility of the development of a national certification for RCs, resulting in the formation of the Commission on Rehabilitation Counselor Certification (CRCC) in 1974. Informed by the first RC roles and functions study (Muthard & Salamone, 1969), CORE developed a field review examination and process. During a grandfathering-in period, the test was refined, validated, and carefully researched. Leahy and Holt (1993) observed that within the 3-year period from 1973 to 1976, CRCC went from a fledgling organization to a healthy certification body with an effective and efficient certification process, a valid and well-researched examination, and more than 8,000 certified rehabilitation counselors (CRCs). The certification process in rehabilitation counseling developed independently, and certification for RCs predated that of CACREP, the other major counseling accreditation body.

Counseling Moves to Establish Standards

Although rehabilitation counseling had its own niche market in the rehabilitation programs that had been established legislatively, the counseling specialties other than school counselor suffered from lack of recognition and credentialing. Sweeney (1992) identified movements in counselor preparation standards dating back to the 1950s and 1960s, and the adoption and implementation of preparation standards by the Association for Counselor Education and Supervision (ACES) in 1973, which ultimately were endorsed by the American Association for Counseling and Development (AACD—formerly APGA, now ACA) in 1979. He added that the Standards for Entry Preparation of Counselors and Other Personnel-Services Specialists were given to APGA in 1977; however, they were not acted upon until 1979. Sweeney identified ACES as the initiator of the proposal that CACREP adopt a 1,000-hour internship and 60 credit-hour degree program in 1983, that would be implemented within 3 years.

The first call for licensing of counselors was formally endorsed by APGA in 1975 when it established its licensure commission (Swanson, 1981). By 1981, APGA took the formal step of establishing CACREP with ACES leadership (Sweeney, 1995). In hopes of establishing an accreditation body for other counseling specialties as well, assistance was sought from CORE, which willingly provided consultation and support for the efforts. However, by the time CACREP was formed, CORE was well established and accredited by COPA, and already engaged in its first accreditation standards revision. Consequently, the two organizations operated and developed independent of one another.

National certification of other counseling specialties followed, first in 1979 with the AMHCA establishing the NACCMHC (now administered by NBCC). With the drive toward recognition, ACA established NBCC in 1983 (Brooks & Gerstein, 1990). By 1985, NBCC had established its first specialty credential when it assumed the certification of career counselors (Bradley, 1995).

Cowger et al. (1991) recommended the development of a consensus definition that would resolve the definition of mental health counseling. Weikel and Palmo (1989) suggested that the term *clinical mental health counseling* be reserved for clinical practice in medical and private practice settings. Wilcoxon (1990) proposed that the term "community mental health counseling" be used for practice in community mental health agencies. Sherrard and Fong (1991) urged reaching consensual agreement on the terms in order to eliminate confusion by other professionals and the public. Anderson (1992) identified, among five forces influencing the counseling profession, a wave of state-by-state licensing laws and national emphasis on counselor professionalism. By 1993, more than half of the states had some form of counselor licensing, and the term or title used to designate the licensed counselor became an important and concerning issue in counseling.

Rehabilitation Counseling's Continued Professionalization

The rehabilitation counseling field grew rapidly and made significant strides toward increased professionalization through the 1970s and 1980s with the development of a code of ethics and scope of practice, development of a strong research foundation, and healthy accreditation and certification bodies (Leahy & Tarvydas, 2001). The 1970s brought a dramatic expansion in the career opportunities for RCs. Changes in worker's compensation laws began mandating rehabilitation services, and private rehabilitation companies sprang up to meet this need (Lynch, 1983; Lynch, Lynch, & Beck, 1998; Lynch & Terrence, 1992; Matkin, 1995). The unique combined skill set of RCs in counseling, disability, and work created new opportunities in the private sector, including disability management and forensic evaluation and consultation in social security, worker's compensation, and personal injury litigation; however, its separation from the mainstream accreditation and certification activity within the larger counseling world came at a cost.

The professional organizations representing RCs give a glimpse into the identity confusion that consumed untoward amounts of effort and attention. RCs were, and still are, represented by multiple professional organizations whose affiliations were amazingly diverse. These organizations included the ARCA, which was a division of the AACD, now the ACA, suggesting a primary identification with other counseling fields; the NCRA, which was at this time a division of the National Rehabilitation Association (NRA), an organization comprised of counselors, vocational evaluators, and other professionals involved in VR; the National Association of Rehabilitation Professionals in the Private Sector (NARPPS), now the International Association of Rehabilitation Professionals (IARP), which consisted largely of RCs and nurses employed in private sector rehabilitation and case management; and the National Council on Rehabilitation Education (NCRE), an organization representing RC educators. NCRE maintained a close relationship with the Rehabilitation Services Administration (RSA) of the Department of Education that funded both the state-federal VR program and training grants that the programs relied on to help fund their students and populate their programs.

The lack of coherent professional identity represented by the splintering of the field among multiple professional associations first identified by Emener and Cottone (1989) was described by Leahy and Tarvydas (2001) as having made rehabilitation counseling "vulnerable to the whims of legislative bodies, the encroachment of other professional groups who have recently discovered disability issues, and increasingly to state-level regulatory bodies who control the practice of counseling and related activities" (p. 3).

Licensure and Advocacy

The impact of these legislative and regulatory bodies was about to hit the rehabilitation counseling field with hurricane force in the form of the expansion of counselor licensure laws and the access provided to third-party payers by licensure and independent practice. Sweeney (1991) reported that the counseling profession began to mobilize around the imperative to develop licensure for counselors in 1973 when the Southern Association for Counselor Education and Supervision (SACES) established the first counselor licensure committee. Sweeney reported that a year later the Board of Directors of APGA (now ACA) adopted a position paper titled "Counselor Licensure Position Statement," setting an agenda of establishing licensure as a primary goal for the organization. Bradley (1995) chronicled the rapid spread of counselor licensure laws through the late 1970s and 1980s, noting that by 1994, 41 states and the District of Columbia had counselor licensure laws. By 2009, California became the 50th and final state to pass its counselor licensure law. Lawson (2016) traced the roots of the counselor licensure movement to the threat posed by the psychology profession to exclude anyone from licensure who did not possess a doctoral degree in psychology. This policy meant that master's-level counselors who previously had been able to become licensed and had been practicing for years suddenly were being sued for practicing psychology without a license (Kress & Barrio-Minton, 2015).

Given that the process of achieving licensure in all 50 states took more than 30 years, why then the analogy to the hurricane for RCs? The weather patterns certainly were apparent and had been for some time. First, rehabilitation counseling had become isolated from the mainstream of counseling professional activity. They were simply not "at the table" as the threats of exclusion from licensure were developing. Second, most RCs were initially not much affected by the licensure movement. The state-federal program was still the largest employer of RCs and most states had exempted themselves from the licensure requirement for VR counselors employed in the state agencies. Many other RCs worked in the Veterans Benefits Administration's Vocational Rehabilitation and Employment (VRE) program, or in the private sector, primarily doing case management or forensic work, both work settings that required CRCs, but not licensure.

Groups such as ACA and AMHCA were more active in lobbying for licensure and had more direct vested interests that shaped the content of the laws. Not surprisingly, many laws passed cited the CACREP requirements as the educational requirements for becoming licensed. In some states, CACREP was mentioned by name; in others, although a person could become licensed without having graduated from a CACREP-accredited program, the requirements paralleled the CACREP requirements. AMHCA was an active partner in the counselor licensure movement and in some states, such as Florida, the requirements more closely resembled the CACREP specialty standards in mental health counseling. In most states, the National Counselor Examination (NCE), or the National Clinical Mental Health Counseling Examination (NCMHCE), both now administered by NBCC, were adopted as the state licensure examinations. Although the CRCC's examination was accepted as an alternative examination for licensure in some states, the number of states with this option never rivaled that number achieved by the NBCC examination adoptions.

Interestingly, most RCs had always seen themselves as counselors who worked with individuals with mental health issues. Disability was broadly construed and psychiatric disabilities were simply considered to be another category of disability that they had been working with for many years. However, the CORE curricular requirements did not stress diagnosis or the acquisition of expertise in treating mental health disabilities over any other type of disability. Additionally, as the number of specialists involved in VR expanded, the need for case management became a larger and larger part of the role of the RC working in state VR agencies. Many RCs were well trained and had a good deal of experience in mental health, and even often carried specialty mental health caseloads, but typically, when a client in the state-federal VR program needed a diagnosis, the RC would tend to refer out to a psychologist who would provide both the diagnosis and, if needed, ongoing psychotherapy.

As the scope of practice for RCs expanded, a fair number of counselors also had moved into mental health settings, since they had the necessary training and experience. As the licensure movement took root, many CORE-accredited programs began to revise their curricula to prepare their graduates for licensure; however, previous graduates of CORE-accredited programs and students in states that specified graduation from a CACREP-accredited program or included rigid curricular requirements based on CACREP curricular standards found that they were experiencing difficulty in becoming licensed. Opportunities once open to RCs began to close to them. In many cases, the rehabilitation counseling field realized too late that licensure was rapidly becoming the gateway to a career in counseling, and that rehabilitation counseling students' and graduates' career options were narrowing rapidly. RCs were trying to sort out what had happened and make a late entry into the state licensure discussion (Tarvydas & Leahy, 1993). At the same time ACA, AMHCA, CACREP, and the American Association of State Counseling Boards (AASCB), an organization made up of state licensing board representatives, already were working on national **portability** standards that would allow counselors to move from state to state, as well as a national credentials registry. Concern spread in the rehabilitation counseling community about whether they would again be overlooked.

Qualitative responses by CRCs on the 2006 Job Analysis Survey reflected a growing concern for greater recognition of RCs (Barros-Bailey, Benshoff, & Fisher, 2009). Also, in an earlier Delphi study, Shaw, Leahy, Chan, and Catalano (2006) queried leaders in rehabilitation about their concerns, and they identified licensure and public/professional recognition as priority issues. There was earlier participation by rehabilitation counseling organizations in the licensure movement in the late 1980s and 1990s licensure efforts by ARCA and NCRE. However, RCs resumed participation in AASCB meetings with leadership from CRCC, and sought input into new state laws and those undergoing revision. They achieved some modest success, with CRCC credentials and the CRCC exam finding their way into some state laws; however, they often found the door closed to them for a variety of reasons.

Tarvydas, Leahy, and Zanskas (2009) noted three major obstacles to rehabilitation efforts to gain access to licensure for RCs, including "(a) widespread lack of awareness, interest, and/or accurate information about counselor licensure among [RCs]; (b) some backlash from those counseling professionalization movement activists who had experienced awkward, agitated, or ill-informed contacts from RCs; and (c) substantive, structural problems in the counselor licensure movement's ability to understand and interpret the fit between rehabilitation counseling and the general profession of counseling as it is represented within the professional cornerstones of accreditation, certification and ethical standards" (p. 87). It was not unusual at this time to hear counselors and licensure board members questioning whether RCs were a part of the counseling profession, or whether they were a separate profession. RCs understood the need to settle that question among themselves in order to communicate this position clearly to licensure boards and to their sister counseling organizations.

Consequently, in 2005 a group titled the Rehabilitation Counseling Consortium (RCC), comprised of the leadership of ARCA, NRCA, IARP, the American Deafness and Rehabilitation Association (ADARA), the Canadian Association of Rehabilitation Professionals (CARP), CRCC, and CORE came together and developed a call to action. The group committed itself to ensuring that "rehabilitation counselors have access to the credentials to practice in employment settings for which they are qualified" (Shaw & Kuehn, 2009, p. 73). Out of that group came a definition of rehabilitation counseling, endorsed by all of the member organizations, that left no doubt as to the field's identification of RCs as counselors practicing in the specialty area of rehabilitation counseling. This definition stated "a rehabilitation counselor is a counselor who possesses the specialized knowledge, skills, and attitudes needed to collaborate in a professional relationship with persons with disabilities to achieve their personal, social, psychological, and vocational goals" (Maki & Tarvydas, 2012, p. 4).

As Leahy and Tarvydas (2001) had noted previously, RCs' chances of being accommodated once the laws were already in place depended on their ability to be seen as professional counselors, and the perception of external constituencies such as legislators and insurance companies that the field was unified and qualified to practice as counselors. There was no doubt that the field had an uphill climb before it, given the reality that

RCs still had separate credentialing bodies and professional organizations, and different academic standards.

RAPPROACHEMENT AND ACCREDITATION

Following a special meeting between CRCC, NBCC, CORE, and CACREP held in 2005, the leadership of CORE and CACREP began to explore the possibility of merging. This action came out of an acknowledgment that the two organizations shared many common goals, and that unifying the two organizations would strengthen both organizations and the entire counseling profession (Shaw & Kuehn, 2009). Glenn (2006) described the rationale for the merger as being "to strengthen both organizations as they combine resources to be responsive to the needs of their membership and the students served by those programs" (p. 71). A joint task force was formed to develop a merger document to be voted on by each of the respective boards. After several years of work to develop a merger agreement, the full boards were asked to vote on the agreement. Although the CACREP board unanimously voted for the merger, the CORE board declined to take a vote. It was felt that the degree of controversy generated by two standards in the CACREP-revised standards would result in a narrow defeat for the merger, and CORE wished to leave the door open for further negotiations. The standards of concern involved an increase in the number of core faculty required for accredited programs, and a requirement that after 2013 all *new* faculty teaching in the program would need to be graduates of a counselor education program (Kennedy, 2007). Despite a long grandfathering-in period, a number of the CORE board members had serious concerns that these requirements might create substantial harm to many programs. It was clear that without further negotiations, the merger would not pass the CORE board. Although both organizations committed to continued collaboration where their interests coincided in the future, the merger did not move forward at that time. However, the stage was set for a later effort that would prove more successful.

Drive for Unity

Rehabilitation counseling certainly was not the only outlier in the desire to unify the profession. Since the earliest days of ACA's precursors, the primary identification of various specialties as being counselors was tenuous. Additionally, a definition of counseling that was acceptable to all proved elusive. As the counseling profession entered the licensure arena and began to engage in earnest self-advocacy, the need to speak as a unified professional body and to achieve a shared identity was brought into sharp relief. Myers, Sweeney, and White (2002) called for a national plan for advocacy, noting that the effectiveness of such a plan "depends on achieving consensus concerning professional identity, promoting a positive public image, establishing effective intraprofessional and interprofessional collaboration, and obtaining the participation of each counselor in advocacy activities" (p. 394).

As noted earlier, the call for unification was certainly not new. The literature is filled with the struggles of the profession to achieve unity and calls to bring counselors together in a shared collective identity (Hanna & Bemak, 1997; Mascari & Webber, 2013; Smith, 2001). The difficulty that the profession experienced communicating with one voice in its advocacy for licensure and third-party reimbursement had become critical, and the profession began to take action to effect change. Reiner et al. (2013) summed up the predominant sentiment with their exhortation that "collaboration among counselors for the development of a single coherent message is necessary for advocacy efforts aimed at congressional Medicare leaders, managed care organizations, state licensing boards, and allied professions" (p. 174).

Mascari (2004) interviewed leaders of the counseling profession to identify issues they thought were important. In order, those issues were: (a) counselor identity, (b) portability, (c) variance in state licensing requirements, (d) psychologists' attempts to restrict diagnosis and testing in counselor practice, and (e) use of certified clinical supervisors. Mascari concluded that it is time that the counseling profession speak with a more unified voice, similar to those offered by NASW and APA. It was seen as imperative that a summit of all the major divisions and affiliates described in this study be convened for the purpose of providing a future direction for the profession. Mascari added that AASCB could provide leadership by encouraging state boards to move toward common licensing standards that would improve professional identity and make portability more feasible. In order for this goal to be accomplished, ACA, CACREP, NBCC, and ACES would have to agree in some formal way. He proposed convening a summit of the leadership of the aforementioned groups for the sole purpose of developing a document with vision toward common standards to improve the sense of professional identity and license portability.

Mascari and Webber (2013) described an informal discussion that took place in 2005 at the AASCB annual meeting among the AASCB presidential team of Jim Wilson, Charles Gagnon, and Barry Mascari; ACA's President Sam Gladding; and ACA Chief Professional Officer David Kaplan, at which mutual concerns about fragmenting counselor identity and threats to licensure portability were shared. Following a formal memorandum from AASCB President Wilson, the AASCB and ACA presidential teams met at the 2006 ACA conference in Atlanta and agreed to cohost a summit addressing counselor identity and licensing-related issues almost 20 years after the first attempt to hold a credentialing summit.

The result was an initiative that would last 8 years and involve 31 professional counseling organizations. This initiative would work to "unify the profession by developing a strategic plan for optimal positioning of the counseling profession in the year 2020" (Kaplan & Gladding, 2011, p. 367). An oversight committee was established to guide the effort, referred to as "20/20: A Vision for the Future of Counseling" (the 20/20 Initiative). Kaplan and Gladding (2011) reported that these individuals determined that they would operate by consensus, requiring a 90% vote for approval of any ideas emerging from the group; and they identified 30 organizations to invite as participants. These organizations represented a broad swath of the counseling profession and included ARCA, CRCC, and CORE. At a later date in the group's work, NRCA also joined the initiative. All of the invitees accepted and were asked to name a delegate. The delegates were to set priorities, determine the content and products of the group, and have complete control over the direction of the group, with the oversight committee limiting itself to assisting with process issues. Delegates were to have equal voting power, and would take any concept that reached consensus among the 20/20 organizations back to their appointing organization for endorsement (Kaplan & Gladding, 2011).

The first major product of the organization was "The 20/20 Principles for Unifying and Strengthening the Profession" (Kaplan & Gladding, 2011) approved by consensus, and endorsed by all but one (97%) of the organizations, reprinted in full in Box 4.2. The 20/20 Initiative originally was intended to be a 2-year project focused on developing a strategic direction for the future of the profession. However, it was decided that the

BOX 4.2 Consensus Issues for Advancing the Future of Counseling

I. Strengthening identity
   a. The counseling profession should develop a paradigm that identifies the core commonalities of the profession.
   b. The counseling profession should identify the body of core knowledge and skills shared by all counselors.
   c. Counselor education programs should reflect a philosophy that unifies professional counselors who share a body of core knowledge and skills.
   d. The counseling profession should reinforce for students that we are a single profession composed of counselors with specialized areas of training.
   e. The accreditation of counseling programs must reflect one identity.

II. Presenting ourselves as one profession
   a. The counseling profession should investigate the best structure for the future of counseling.
   b. The counseling profession should create a common counselor identification that would also allow for additional designations of special interests and specialties.
   c. While being unified, the counseling profession should respect counseling specialties.

III. Improving public perception/recognition and advocating for professional issues
   a. The counseling profession should develop a clear definition of counseling for the public.
   b. The counseling profession should present a stronger, more defined voice at the state and federal levels.
   c. The counseling profession should promote one licensure title across the different states.
   d. The counseling profession should work to educate the insurance industry about who we are, what we do, and the outcomes associated with counseling interventions.

IV. Creating licensure portability
   a. The counseling profession should establish common counselor preparation standards that unify both the CACREP and CORE standards into a single training model.

V. Expanding and promoting the research base of professional counseling
   a. The counseling profession should encourage interest in research by practitioners and students.
   b. The counseling profession should emphasize both qualitative and quantitative outcome research. At this time, many "best practices" are dictated to counselors by other mental health professions.

VI. Focusing on students and prospective students
   a. The counseling profession should more actively work with undergraduates and undergraduate programs.
   b. The counseling profession should promote mentor–practicum–internship relationships.
   c. The counseling profession should endorse/require student involvement in professional counseling associations.

(continued)

BOX 4.2 Consensus Issues for Advancing the Future of Counseling (*continued*)

VII. Promoting client welfare and advocacy
   a. The counseling profession should offer ongoing education and training for counselors on client and student advocacy.
   b. The counseling profession should identify one advocacy project that would be completed annually within a selected community as a way to strengthen our counseling identity, present ourselves as one profession, and improve public perception.
   c. The counseling profession should promote optimum health and wellness for those served as the ultimate goals of all counseling interventions.
   d. The counseling profession should encourage evidence-based, ethical practice as the foundation for counselors in training and professional counselors' interventions across settings and populations served.

CACREP, Council for Accreditation of Counseling and Related Educational Programs; CORE, Council on Rehabilitation Education.

Source: Kaplan & Gladding. Page 371. Retrieved from https://www.counseling.org/docs/licensure/principles-for-unifying-and-strengthening-the-profession.pdf?sfvrsn=0

---

group would continue in order to begin to address some of the more difficult areas on which consensus had proved problematic in the past. It was determined that the three areas of priority for the group were: (a) develop a clear definition of counseling for the public; (b) promote one licensure title across the different states; and (c) identify the body of core knowledge and skills shared by all counselors. Ultimately, the 20/20 Initiative was successful in achieving a definition which stated that counseling is a professional relationship that empowers diverse individuals, families, and groups to accomplish mental health, wellness, education, and career goals. It also agreed on the licensure title of licensed professional counselor (LPC), but was unable to agree on a specific educational/accreditation standard (Kaplan, Tarvydas, & Gladding, 2014; Lawson, 2016). Although the subcommittee working on this task had recommended that the CACREP standards become the educational model, it became clear that the group would not be able to reach consensus in this area. Instead, the delegates passed a resolution affirming the value of having a single accreditation body.

MERGER

A few events that occurred during the 20/20 Initiative process added a sense of urgency to the need for closure on defining educational standards. In 2006, the U.S. Department of Defense (DoD) convened a working group to address the need to ensure qualified assistance to service members in need of behavioral health services. The DoD's report to Congress stated that "the absence of a national homogenous standard curriculum to guide the training of LPCs fails to meet beneficiaries' expectations for the national, uniform quality care that is the Department's mandate" (Mascari & Webber, 2013, p. 18).

Several years later, in 2010, the IOM published a report, based on a comprehensive review conducted on counselor training, accreditation, and licensing standards, that highlighted the wide variation in the curricula of counseling training programs. The report recommended that only licensed counselors graduating from CACREP-accredited programs who passed the NCMHCE should be allowed independent practice privileges within TRICARE insurance programs. These study recommendations eventually influenced the requirements for counselors' access to DoD and Veterans Administration (VA) jobs. The report caused a ripple in the counseling world, as this standard would exclude many graduates of counseling programs, including CORE-accredited programs with a long history of treating veterans with disabilities. The TRICARE report seemed to many to be a harbinger of things to come. In a keynote address to the AASCB delegates, Mascari (2012) advised that "because TRICARE has established a national standard on which the profession itself could not agree, 'the portability train may have left the station' and the profession needs to move quickly to get on board" (Mascari, 2012, p. 22).

Following the disbanding of the 20/20 Initiative, CORE and CACREP continued to engage in advocacy efforts separately, but also continued to explore potential future avenues for collaboration. During the final 20/20 Initiative meeting, it was revealed that CACREP had developed a set of standards for a clinical RC specialty accreditation, but had not yet put them to use. CORE proposed a consortium model to CACREP, and CACREP offered a counterproposal for a merger, but under a different set of terms; further attempts at negotiation were unsuccessful (Evenson, Nunez, & Lane, 2013). Nevertheless, discussions continued and in July 2013, CACREP and CORE issued a joint announcement that they had signed an affiliation agreement, whereby CORE would become an affiliate of CACREP. The opportunities afforded to CORE-accredited programs were described in a jointly issued statement:

> CORE and CACREP have entered into a new relationship with CORE becoming a corporate affiliate of CACREP. As part of this agreement, CACREP and CORE have further agreed to develop a joint process that will allow RC programs to become dually accredited as both a Clinical Rehabilitation Counseling (ClRC) program and a CMHC program. As part of the process, CORE will implement CACREP's Clinical Rehabilitation Counseling Standards and determine which currently accredited RC programs meet these standards as a prerequisite for seeking dual accreditation as a CACREP accredited CMHC program. Programs that successfully complete the conversion process will be dually accredited as both Clinical Rehabilitation Counseling and Clinical Mental Health Counseling programs. (CORE, n.d., p. 1)

Disappointment at the perception that one important task undertaken by the 20/20 Initiative had not been completed led ACES to appoint a task force charged to study the issue and make recommendations regarding educational requirements. The task force was engaged in this work when the affiliation agreement was announced. The ACES executive council quickly approved and released a position paper recommending model language to licensure boards that set the educational standards for LPCs. This language included "graduation from a clinically-focused counselor preparation program accredited by CACREP or an approved affiliate of CACREP (e.g., CORE)" (ACES, 2014).

As the process of conversion unfolded, the two organizations found that juggling different processes and procedures was unwieldy. The two organizations concluded that a merger might be in the best interests of the students served by both organizations. Finally, on July 20, 2015, the two organizations signed an agreement with a merger planned for June 30, 2017. The agreement noted that "the benefits to the profession and the public have been of paramount importance as CACREP and CORE entered into merger discussions. Recognizing the prevalence of disability in our society, both organizations have agreed that counselors will be better prepared to meet the needs of all clients if there is a unified set of standards that can be supported by the counseling profession" (CORE, 2015).

CURRENT ISSUES AND FUTURE DIRECTIONS

The CORE–CACREP merger is a notable accomplishment and a significant moment in the move toward unity in the counseling profession. Most recently, a conversion process for doctoral program accreditation is underway, as CORE has never accredited doctoral programs. Also, CACREP and CORE appointed a task force to review the CACREP standards and recommend the inclusion of disability-specific language and content throughout the CACREP standards (CORE, 2016). There remain many questions and anxieties for rehabilitation counseling education programs and their students as the merger unfolds. What will the new standards look like? What is the difference between an RC and a clinical RC? What are the implications of the two different rehabilitation counseling program accreditations for licensure and/or third-party payment, and what should my program pursue? Will they both be around in 10 years? How can I get my doctoral program CACREP accredited? What will happen when dual accreditation disappears? What will it be like to have CACREP as my accreditor? Will they "get" rehabilitation counseling? How will RCs be involved in standards revision and program review? How do we protect the vocational emphasis of our specialty area given the infusion of new content in the Clinical Rehabilitation Counseling (ClRC) accreditation? How can we unify and engage our professional associations to carry forward the work of advocacy for the specialty of rehabilitation counseling? The answers to these and other questions are likely to unfold over the coming months. It is hoped that such anxieties will begin to subside.

The challenges to the counseling profession as a whole certainly have not disappeared, but perhaps we are a bit better equipped to address them at this juncture. Such challenges include the ongoing problems of portability, effective advocacy with regulatory bodies and third-party payers, the need to produce quality outcomes research and to improve our record of securing external funding for evidence-based research, and others. A review of the consensus issues listed in Box 4.2 shows that even then, there is a full agenda. These issues are the work of the near future for the profession. If the profession can tackle this agenda with a shared commitment, perseverance, respect, and inclusiveness, and—always—with our clients' interests in the forefront of everything we undertake, there is every reason to be optimistic.

Brian McMahon (2009) expounded on the challenges facing the field of rehabilitation counseling at that time and drew a conclusion that described the future of the field as he saw it:

> I envision the redevelopment of rehabilitation counseling as a genuine, assertive, proactive and unified profession that few of us could anticipate. After all, there is no mission more honorable than restoring dignity to human lives. I believe this will happen, but educators must return to leadership positions, research must be invigorated, the profession must be organized and cross-disability organizations must be engaged. (p. 123)

CONCLUSION

In summary, the identity of rehabilitation counseling has evolved from that of a separate profession that has elements in common with other counseling fields to a clear identification as being a counseling specialization within the larger profession of counseling. This evolution is not unique to the counseling specializations, but was complicated and made more challenging by a separate set of credentialing bodies and different professional circumstances. The merger of CORE and CACREP creates a unique opportunity for the profession to redefine itself as a unified whole. If the opportunity is to be realized, the profession still has work ahead of it. The challenges should prove achievable; however, if undertaken with commitment, mutual respect, and due consideration for the concerns and well-being of all counseling stakeholders, especially those whom we serve.

CONTENT REVIEW QUESTIONS

- Why did rehabilitation counseling develop separate professional organizations, including separate certification and accreditation bodies?
- What factors have resulted in the lack of agreement among counseling divisions about whether they are specialties within the profession of counseling or whether they are separate professions?
- How did the licensure movement lead to actions to promote unification of the counseling profession?
- What were the events leading up to and serving as an impetus for the merger between CORE and CACREP?

REFERENCES

Akos, P., & Galassi, J. P. (2004). Middle and high school transitions as viewed by students, parents, and teachers. *Professional School Counseling, 7*(4), 212–221.

Anderson, D. (1992). A case of standards of counseling practice. *Journal of Counseling & Development, 71*, 22–26.

Association for Counselor Education and Supervision. (2014). ACES document on educational standards. Retrieved from http://www.acesonline.net/news/aces-document-educational-standards

Barros-Bailey, M., Benshoff, J. J., & Fisher, J. (2009). Rehabilitation counseling in the year 2011: Perceptions of certified rehabilitation counselors. *Rehabilitation Counseling Bulletin, 52*(2), 107–113.

Bradley, L. (1995). Certification and licensure issues. *Journal of Counseling and Development, 74*(2), 185.

Brooks, D. K., & Gerstein, L. H. (1990). Counselor credentialing and interprofessional collaboration. *Journal of Counseling and Development, 68*, 477–485.

Chi Sigma Iota. (n.d.). Counselor advocacy leadership conferences I & II. Retrieved from http://www.csi-net.org/?CPALC

Council on Rehabilitation Education. (n.d.). Policy document: Converting a CORE accredited rehabilitation counseling program to a dually accredited clinical rehabilitation counseling and clinical mental health counseling program. Retrieved from http://www.core-rehab.org/Files/Doc/PDF/Conversion%20Policy%20of%20RC%20to%20ClRC_CMHC%2010.6.13.pdf

Council on Rehabilitation Education. (2015). For immediate release. Retrieved from http://www.core-rehab.org/Files/Doc/PDF/WhatsNewPDFs/Press%20Release-7.20.15.pdf

Council on Rehabilitation Education. (2016, October 26). CACREP and CORE appoint a 4-member task force to explore the infusion of disability concepts into CACREP standards. Retrieved from http://dev.cacrep.org/news/cacrep-core-press-release-october-2016

Cowger, E. L., Hinkle, J. S., DeRidder, L. M., & Erik, R. R. (1991). CACREP community counseling programs: Present status and implications for the future. *Journal of Mental Health Counseling, 13*, 172–186.

Elliott, T. R., & Leung, P. (2005). Vocational rehabilitation: History and practice. In W. B. Walsh & M. L. Savickas (Eds.), *Handbook of vocational psychology: Theory, research, and practice* (3rd ed., pp. 319–343). Mahwah, NJ: Erlbaum.

Emener, W. G., & Cottone, R. R. (1989). Professionalization, deprofessionalization, and reprofessionalization of rehabilitation counseling according to criteria of professions. *Journal of Counseling and Development, 67,* 576–581.

Evenson, T., Nunez, P., & Lane, F. (2012, October 29–30). CORE response to the 20/20 commission's request that CORE and CACREP consider forming a unified accreditation body. Presentation at the annual NCRE/RSA/VSAVR conference, Washington, DC.

Gale, A. U., & Austin, B. D. (2003). Professionalism's challenges to professional counselors' collective identity. *Journal of Counseling and Development, 81,* 3–9.

Gladding, S. T. (1996). *Counseling: A comprehensive profession* (3rd ed.) Englewood Cliffs, NJ: Merrill.

Gladding, S. T. (2008). *Counseling: A comprehensive profession* (6th ed.). Upper Saddle River, NJ: Prentice Hall.

Glenn, M. K. (2006). A rehabilitation educator's perspective on merging accreditation resources. *Rehabilitation Education, 20,* 71–78.

Hahn, H. (1985). Toward a politics of disability: Definitions, disciplines, and policies. *The Social Science Journal, 22*(4), 87–105.

Hanna, F. J., & Bemak, F. (1997). The quest for identity in the counseling profession. *Counselor Education and Supervision, 36,* 196–204.

Herlihy, B., & Remley, T. P. (1995). Unified ethical standards: A challenge for professionalism. *Journal of Counseling and Development, 74,* 130–133.

Institute of Medicine. (2010). Provision of mental health counseling services under TRICARE. Retrieved from http://www.nap.edu/openbook.php?record_id=12813

Jenkins, W. M., Patterson, J. B., & Szymanski, E. M. (1998). Philosophical, historical and legislative aspects of the rehabilitation counseling profession. In R. M. Parker & E. M. Szymanski (Eds.), *Rehabilitation counseling: Basics and beyond* (3rd ed., pp. 1–40). Austin, TX: Pro-Ed.

Jones, L. K. (1994). Frank Parsons' contribution to career counseling. *Journal of Career Development, 20*(4), 287–294.

Kaplan, D. M., & Gladding, S. T. (2011). A vision for the future of counseling: The 20/20 principles for unifying and strengthening the profession. *Journal of Counseling and Development, 89,* 367–372.

Kaplan, D. M., Tarvydas, V. M., & Gladding, S. T. (2014). 20/20: A vision for the future of counseling: The new consensus definition of counseling. *Journal of Counseling and Development, 92,* 366–372.

Kennedy, A. (2007). CORE, CACREP merger falls short. *Counseling Today, 50*(5), 16.

Kress, V. E., & Barrio-Minton, C. A. (2015). Thomas J. Sweeney: A visionary leader and advocate for the counseling profession. *Journal of Counseling and Development, 93,* 114–118.

Kundu, M., & Schiro-Geist, C. (2006) Legislative aspects of rehabilitation. In P. Leung, C. Flowers, W. Talley, & P. Sanderson (Eds.), *Multicultural issues in rehabilitation and allied health* (pp. 17–43). Osage Beach, MO: Aspen Professional Services.

Lawson, G. (2016). On being a profession: A historical perspective on counselor licensure and accreditation. *Journal of Counselor Leadership and Advocacy, 3*(2), 71–84. doi:10.1080/2326716X.2016.1169955

Leahy, M. J., & Holt, E. (1993). Certification in rehabilitation counseling: History and process. *Rehabilitation Counseling Bulletin, 37*(2), 71–80.

Leahy, M. J., Rak, E., & Zanskas, S. A. (2009). A brief history of counseling and specialty areas of practice. In I. Marini & M. A. Stebnicki (Eds.). *The professional counselor's desk reference* (pp. 3–13). New York, NY: Springer Publishing.

Leahy, M. J., & Szymanski, E. M. (1995). Rehabilitation counseling: Evolution and current status. *Journal of Counseling and Development, 74,* 163–166.

Leahy, M. J., & Tarvydas, V. M. (2001). Transforming our professional organizations: A first step toward the unification of the rehabilitation counseling profession. *Journal of Applied Rehabilitation Counseling, 32*(3), 3–8.

Linkowski, D. C., & Szymanski, E. M. (1993). Accreditation in rehabilitation counseling: Historical and current context and process. *Rehabilitation Counseling Bulletin, 37*(2), 81–91.

Lynch, R. K. (1983). The vocational expert. *Rehabilitation Counseling Bulletin, 27*(1), 18–25.

Lynch, R. K., & Terrence, M. (1982). Rehabilitation counseling in the private sector: A training needs survey. *Journal of Rehabilitation, 48*(3), 51.

Maki, D. R., & Tarvydas, V. M. (2012). Rehabilitation counseling: A specialty practice of the counseling profession. In D. R. Maki & V. M. Tarvydas (Eds.), *The professional practice of rehabilitation counseling* (pp. 3–13). New York, NY: Springer Publishing.

Mascari, J. B. (2004). *The relationship between counselor licensing standards and violations: A mixed method-ological review* (Doctoral dissertation). Available from ProQuest Dissertations and Theses database. (UMI No. 3148764)

Mascari, J. B. (2012, January). *Can the success of counselor licensing spoil the profession: Licensing portability-addressing the need for common standards and accreditation.* Keynote address presented at the meeting of the American Association of State Counseling Boards, Charleston, SC.

Mascari, J. B., & Webber, J. (2013). CACREP accreditation: A solution to licensure portability and coun-selor identity problems. *Journal of Counseling and Development, 91*(1), 15–25.

Matkin, R. (1995). Private sector rehabilitation. In S. Rubin & R. Roessler (Eds.), *Foundations of the voca-tional rehabilitation process* (4th ed., pp. 375–439). Austin, TX: Pro-Ed.

McMahon, B. T. (2009). One veteran counselor's take on the future of rehabilitation counseling. *Rehabilita-tion Counseling Bulletin, 52*(2), 120–123.

Mellin, E. A., Hunt, B., & Nichols, L. M. (2011). Counselor professional identity: Findings and implications for counseling and interprofessional collaboration. *Journal of Counseling and Development, 89*, 140–147.

Muthard, J. E., & Salamone, P. R. (1969). The roles and functions of the rehabilitation counselor [Special issue]. *Rehabilitation Counseling Bulletin, 13*, 81–168.

Myers, J. E. (1995). Specialties in counseling: Rich heritage or force for fragmentation? *Journal of Counseling and Development, 74*, 115–116.

Myers, J. E., Sweeney, T. J., & White, V. E. (2002). Advocacy for cousneling and counselors: A professional imperative. *Journal of Counseling and Development, 80*(4), 394–402.

Neukrug, E. (1994). *Theory, practice and trends in human services: An overview of an emerging profession.* Pacific Grove, CA: Brooks/Cole.

Neukrug, E., & Remley, T. P. (2009). Key historical events in professional identity and ethics. In American Counseling Association (Ed.), *The ACA encyclopedia of counseling* (pp. 411–413). Alexandria, VA: Ameri-can Counseling Association.

Nirje, B. (1985). The basis and logic of the normalization principle. *Australian and New Zealand Journal of Developmental Disabilities, 11*(2), 65–68.

Palmo, A. J. (1990). Mental health counseling: Definitely a profession unto itself. *Counselor Education and Supervision, 30*(2), 114–119.

Pistole, M., & Roberts, A. (2002). Mental health counseling: Toward resolving identity confusion. *Journal of Mental Health Counseling, 24*(1), 1–19.

Reiner, S. M., Dobmeier, R. A., & Hernandez, T. J. (2013). Perceived impact of professional counselor iden-tity: An exploratory study. *Journal of Counseling and Development, 91*(2), 174–183.

Remley, T. P. (2012). Evolution of counseling specialties. In D. R. Maki & V. M. Tarvydas (Eds.), *The profes-sional practice of rehabilitation counseling* (pp. 17–38). New York, NY: Springer Publishing.

Remley, T. P., & Herlihy, B. (2010). *Ethical, legal and professional issues in counseling* (3rd ed). Upper Saddle River, NJ: Merrill.

Sales, A. P. (2012). History of rehabilitation counseling. In D. R. Maki & V. M. Tarvydas (Eds.), *The profes-sional practice of rehabilitation counseling* (pp. 39–60), New York, NY: Springer Publishing.

Shaw, L. R., & Kuehn, M. D. (2009). Rehabilitation counselor education accreditation: History, structure, and evolution. *Rehabilitation Counseling Bulletin, 52*, 69–76.

Shaw, L. R., Leahy, M. J., Chan, F., & Catalano, D. (2006). Contemporary issues facing rehabilitation coun-seling. *Rehabilitation Education, 20*(3), 163–178.

Sherrard, P. A. D., & Fong, M. L. (1991). Mental health counselor training: Which model should prevail? *Journal of Mental Health Counseling, 13*, 204–209.

Smith, H. (2001). Professional identity for counselors. In D. C. Locke, J. E. Myers, & E. L. Herr (Eds.), *The handbook of counseling* (pp. 569–579). Thousand Oaks, CA: Sage.

Smith, H. (2004). The counseling profession: Reflections and projections. In G. W. Waltz & R. Yep (Eds.), *VISTAS perspectives on counseling.* (pp. 7–14) Alexandria, VA: American Counseling Association. Retrieved from http://www.counseling.org/knowledge-center/vistas/by-subject2/vistas-perspectives/docs/default-source/vistas/vistas_2004_2

Sparks, E. (2008). Column on school counselors earns large, varied response. *Counseling Today, 50*(11), 4.

Steinhauser, L., & Bradley, R. (1983). Accreditation of counselor education programs. *Counselor Education and Supervision, 23*, 89–108. doi:10.1002/j.1556-6978.1990.tb01176.x

Swanson, J. L. (1981). Moving toward counselor licensure: A statewide survey. *Personnel and Guidance Jour-nal, 60*, 78–79.

Sweeney, T. J. (1991). Counselor credentialing: Purpose and origin. In E. O. Bradley (Ed.), *Credentialing in counseling* (pp. 1–12). Alexandria, VA: American Association for Counseling and Development.

Sweeney, T. J. (1992). CACREP: Precursors, promises, and prospects. *Journal of Counseling and Development*, *70*, 667–671.

Sweeney, T. J. (1995). Accreditation, credentialing, professionalization: The role of specialties. *Journal of Counseling and Development*, *74*(2), 117–125.

Tarvydas, V. M., & Leahy, M. J. (1993). Licensure in rehabilitation counseling: A critical incident in professionalization. *Rehabilitation Counseling Bulletin*, *37*(2), 92–108.

Tarvydas, V. M., Leahy, M. J., & Zanskas, S. A. (2009). Judgment deferred: Reappraisal of rehabilitation counseling movement toward licensure parity. *Rehabilitation Counseling Bulletin*, *52*(2), 85–94.

Wayne, G. (1982). An examination of selected statutory licensing requirements for psychologists in the U.S. *Personnel and Guidance Journal*, *60*(7), 420–426.

Weikel, W. J., & Palmo, A. J. (1989). The evolution and practice of mental health counseling. *Journal of Mental Health Counseling*, *11*, 7–25.

Wilcoxon, S. A. (1990). Community mental health counseling: An option for the CACREP dichotomy. *Counselor Education and Supervision*, *30*, 26–37.

Wolfensberger, W. (1972). *The principle of normalization in human services*. Toronto, ON, Canada: National Institute on Mental Retardation.

Wolfensberger, W. (1983). Social role valorization: A proposed new term for the principle of normalization. *Mental Retardation*, *21*(6), 234–239.

Wright, G. (1980). *Total rehabilitation*. Boston, MA: Little, Brown.

FIVE

Concepts and Models

HENRY McCARTHY

LEARNING OBJECTIVES

After reading this chapter, you should be able to:

- List and describe fundamental philosophical values that characterize rehabilitation counselors (RCs) and how they approach their work.
- Name and explain different models of disability that analyze how disability has been perceived and interpreted in society.
- Express basic understanding of how the various concepts and perspectives presented affect the practice of rehabilitation counseling.

Rehabilitation counseling concepts and models have evolved progressively over the last century. Actually, one could say that the tasks and motivations that describe rehabilitation counseling are as old as when human nature developed to the point where people responded with a compassionate heart and helpful resources to a stranger who was injured or otherwise in need of assistance or accommodation to get back in action. Just about a century ago was the start of what has grown into our current system of service programs, followed by the formation of the profession we know as rehabilitation counseling. We have a rich legacy of groundbreaking accomplishments that have enabled the exciting activities with which we are currently engaged and blossoming opportunities for the future. Readers will notice that some of the references in this chapter are not recent, and a few are not the latest edition of that publication. This choice was purposeful, in order to recognize both cutting-edge applications and classic insights on perennial issues. The older citations offer a longer vantage point and highlight the historical context of the concepts and models presented. These ideas are still shaping the field as new knowledge develops. The majority of the observations and recommendations in this chapter apply to all counselors because the specialty of rehabilitation counseling is an integral part of the counseling profession.

This chapter is designed in three main sections. The first one describes fundamental philosophical values that characterize RCs and how they approach their work. The next section delineates four traditional models or conceptual frameworks of disability. They explain different ways that disability as a stimulus or personal characteristic—and people who have a disability—have been perceived and treated in society, from early civilizations to today. The third section presents four unconventional models of disability.

These are much less known, discussed, and represented in the implicit expectations and dedicated programs that society has developed in its response to disability. Indeed, the unconventional models were created largely as part of a consciousness and movement to change the ways disability is dealt with by society. All of the chapter's contents are woven together to describe the complex and evolving context within which the practice of rehabilitation counseling operates. Please take the "clay" of the accumulated knowledge that is presented in this chapter and shape it for your best understanding and eventual application as a rehabilitation counseling practitioner and advocate.

THE VALUES AND PERSPECTIVES UNDERGIRDING REHABILITATION COUNSELING

Values are crucial to informing our identity and guiding our behavior as individuals, groups, and organizations. Making values explicit to the public and real in our efforts to live by them should be an ongoing process that reinforces the meaningfulness of the values. Reflecting and acting on our values also serve as methods of professional self-monitoring and continued improvement. Beatrice Wright is a groundbreaking scholar whose insights and writings have been among the most prominent influences on the profession of rehabilitation counseling, especially with respect to its value base. Over the course of several years, starting with B. A. Wright (1959), she articulated several guidelines for rehabilitation practitioners that have endured as part of our profession's guiding conscience and ethical compass. The final list of 20 "value-laden beliefs and principles" explained in B. A. Wright's (1983) book have been reprinted in several sources. One of them is McCarthy (2011), which included an interview with Wright wherein she emphasized the ongoing need for professionals to review, critique, adapt, and embrace values in rehabilitation counseling practice, as illustrated in the following quote:

> Professionals preparing for certification should be given a list of values that have special significance for rehabilitation. . . . At the oral certification examination, candidates could be asked if there are any values that could be added or omitted and to explain their view, as a way of ensuring serious consideration of values. Each Board could revise the value-laden beliefs and principles based on suggestions made by candidates. (p. 77)

Contemporary rehabilitation counseling has benefited greatly from the progressive thinking and teaching of not only Wright, but also Jaques (1970), Rubin and Roessler (1978), Bowe (1978, 1980), G. Wright (1980), DeLoach and Greer (1981), and Chubon (1994). Many of their contributions are still incisive and germane today. The following section explains five core values of rehabilitation counseling and their underlying concepts and strategies.

Person–Environment Interaction

Beatrice Wright and other theorists and researchers who contributed to the early development of rehabilitation counseling were influenced by the field theory of Kurt Lewin (1936), a social psychologist who postulated the functional formula, $B = f (P \times E)$. That is, Lewin argued that in order to understand human behavior (B), we need to realize that it is a function (f) of the interaction (x) between aspects of the person (P) and forces in the surrounding context or environment (E). This interactionist proposition seems like common sense today, but it was avant-garde at that time when behavior was believed to be determined predominantly by the abilities, emotions, genes, motives, and vulnerabilities that existed within the person. For detailed explanations of how the early rehabilitation scholars (e.g., R. Barker, T. Dembo, G. Leviton, B. Wright) applied field theory's interest in environmental factors to conceptualizing the experience of disability, see Dunn (2015), Livneh, Bishop, and Anctil (2014), and McCarthy (2011, 2014).

The environment has been important in other theories about the consequences of having a disability. Vash and Crewe (2004) discussed how the disability experience is likely to be affected by various aspects of the environment that they classified into two spheres: the **cultural context** (including societal attitudes, technological developments, and political philosophies such as free enterprise versus socialist economies); and the **immediate environment** (including family characteristics, regional differences, and residence in home versus institutional settings). There are also notable examples of applied research in career development, work adjustment, and mental health that have focused on the fit between person and environment (e.g., Lofquist & Dawis, 1969, 1991; Moos, 1974). Thus, RCs are more likely than many of their counterparts in other human service disciplines to be more attentive to the influences of the environment—both its resources and its barriers. Nonetheless, the attention given to the environment is still not equal to the focus on the person. There continues to be a strong bias toward assessing and trying to change the person, to the comparative neglect of investigating and manipulating the environment, as explained by Groomes and Olsheski (2002), B. A. Wright and Lopez (2005), and McCarthy (2014).

Strengths-Based Practice

An **asset-oriented approach** (e.g., Atkins, 1988) or **strengths-based orientation** (e.g., Galassi & Akos, 2007) of uncovering and exploiting the positive aspects in both the person and the situation is the widely endorsed current expectation for RCs. Today, taking a purposefully positive approach is fairly common in social science, as reflected in the overwhelming popularity of the positive psychology movement (Chou et al., 2013) and wellness programs. However, there continues to be a tension between positive psychology and modern medicine. A prominent characteristic of the medical professions is focusing primarily or exclusively on the pathology or the problem, in order to prevent or cure disease with military aggressiveness. This is revealed in Western medicine's goals, such as "conquering cancer" or "wiping out polio." These are important, laudable goals. However, the zeal that drives the problem-oriented approach in medicine to treat disability tends to direct insufficient attention to the positive elements in the person and context. Rehabilitation counseling has for many decades espoused: (a) an optimistic perspective on the achievable potential of people with disabilities to lead satisfying and successful lives; (b) a focus on building up the skills and potential that remain after the changes that were brought on by a chronic illness, injury, or other significant loss; and (c) an emphasis on utilizing the client's situation and broader environment for supportive resources. Early explanations of the **coping attitude and behavior** demonstrated by people with disabilities were described by Dembo, Leviton, and Wright (1956/1975). Today, coping is often referred to by the term **resilience**: "the process of, capacity for, or outcome of successful adaptation despite challenging or threatening circumstances" (Masten, Best, & Garmezy, 1990, p. 426). Although it is widely accepted intellectually, taking such an approach requires persistent attention because of what has been called the **fundamental negative bias** by B. A. Wright (1988). She explained with many eye-opening examples how this tendency in the way humans process information leads to giving more attention and weight to salient negative stimuli, such as the stigma and misfortune often associated with a disability. With similar arguments about unconscious reactions to disability, Hahn (1993) cogently hypothesized that two major contributors to strained interaction (and eventual negative attitudes) are stimulated when able-bodied people encounter a person with a visible disability. These apprehensions are **aesthetic anxiety** (discomfort at being close to disfigured appearance) and **existential anxiety** (unconscious threat felt to one's own safety or existence by seeing disability and associating it with accidents and trauma). RCs may easily and inadvertently underestimate the ability of people with disabilities, unless they consciously apply a strengths-based approach.

Holistic Perspective

Because of its dedication to clients' long-term integration into community life, rehabilitation counseling has adopted a multidimensional **holistic approach** to assessing clients and addressing their concerns. Depending on the client's preferred focus and possible limitations set by the service agency, an appropriate rehabilitation counseling assessment could explore many aspects of the person's life, including the following domains (each exemplified with a few representative dimensions):

- Vocational (career aspirations, work history, volunteer experience)
- Social (family roles, support networks, community participation)
- Psychological (attitudes, perceptions, affect)
- Disability-related (capacities affected, accommodations used, personal coping strategies)
- Cognitive (communication skills, academic performance, problem-solving style)
- Health-related (insurance coverage, medications, wellness practices)
- Sexual (level of technical information, current satisfaction, safety-related concerns)
- Recreational (exercise routines, hobbies, access to community venues)
- Cultural/spiritual (important values, cultural identity, sense of hope)

Not all domains will generate issues the individual client wishes to address or resources that can be marshaled to fulfill desired goals. At times, the needs of the client may be beyond the scope of a single agency and a referral is necessary. Nonetheless, the larger point is that the RC demonstrates a broad interest in the client's comprehensive **quality of life (QOL)** and the factors that might complicate or facilitate the client's goals and the counseling process (e.g., Bishop, 2005; Fabian, 1991; Livneh, 2016). In many ways, RCs work to enhance resilience to cope with crises and daily stressors that emerge, and promote subjective QOL of their clients. QOL is a multidimensional wellness goal that is certainly well advanced by the wide variety of direct services, applied research, and social advocacy provided by contemporary rehabilitation counseling (e.g., Bishop, Chapin, & Miller, 2008; Hartley, 2011). It is also well served by the profession's evolved approach and commitment to its improvement and impact through theory development, meaningfully rigorous research, and evidence-based practice (e.g., Chan, Tarvydas, Blalock, Strauser, & Atkins, 2009; Tarvydas, Addy, & Fleming, 2010).

A holistic approach in rehabilitation counseling is similar to the conceptual developments referred to in counseling as the **wellness model**. A popular version is the wheel of wellness model developed by Witmer and Sweeney (1992) and Myers and Sweeney (2008). It defined *wellness* as "a way of life oriented toward optimal health and well-being in which body, mind, and spirit are integrated by the individual to live more fully within the human and natural community" (Myers, Sweeney, & Witmer, 2000, p. 252). Nested concentric circles compose the model's graphic representation of five proposed "life tasks"

(Spirituality, Self-Direction, Work and Leisure, Friendship, Love). The spokes of the wheel identify 12 "subtasks" that include various patterns of behavior and methods of adjustment, such as problem solving and creativity, sense of humor, nutrition, self-care, and cultural identity. The wellness model is quite widely embraced among the current frameworks for counseling. Its content and process are clearly holistic, affirmative, and interactive.

Collaborative and Interdisciplinary Partnerships

As early as the original edition of her classic book, B. A. Wright (1960, pp. 345–363) proposed and explained the necessity of counselors' collaborating with *clients as comanagers* of their rehabilitation plan. At the time, that was a revolutionary recommendation to advance. Currently, that philosophy of *actively involving stakeholders in activities that affect their health and welfare* is infused in most human services. Some well-established procedures formalize and ensure the solicitation of clients' input and continuing contributions to their process of habilitation (acquiring knowledge and life skills as a developmental process) or rehabilitation (relearning lost skills or developing compensatory strategies after the onset of disability). One such process is the **Individualized Educational Plan (IEP)**. This document is created annually for students with a disability in primary and secondary schools, if they are eligible for accommodations and support services. The team that discusses, determines, and implements the needed services includes the student, parent or advocate, and the school staff directly involved such as teacher(s) and the counselor. The counterpart document developed collaboratively by each new client in many vocational rehabilitation (VR) programs and her or his counselor is the **Individualized Plan for Employment (IPE)**. Clients not only discuss and sign the plan, but are also expected to write down their input in their own words. Hershenson (2015) has proposed and delineated the essential contents of an analogous instrument for the senior stage of life, the **Individualized Plan for Retirement (IPR)**.

The **interdisciplinary team** has been a primary model for the delivery of comprehensive rehabilitation services, especially in large clinical settings. RCs employed in hospitals and clinics coordinate with physiatrists (medical doctors specializing in physical medicine and rehabilitation), psychiatrists, neurologists, orthopedists, nurses, psychologists, occupational therapists, physical therapists, and speech-language therapists. The expectation of effective **interprofessional collaboration** has recently been reinforced in employment settings and preservice training programs by institutional and educational accreditation standards. RCs who work in vocational programs have an essential partner in employers, sometimes called the "second client." By providing training, paid jobs and work experience, local businesses and industries fulfill the occupational goals of the clients. In addition, employers have their own needs which many RCs are qualified to satisfy. The needs of **employers as rehabilitation's corporate clients** include assistance and consultation on topics such as (a) determining appropriate physical and procedural accommodations for their employees who require them (new hires as well as long-term employees with recently acquired functional limitations); (b) developing policies and procedures to ensure compliance with applicable laws governing nondiscrimination in employment; and (c) staff training on disability diversity, stress management, and strategies for optimizing safety and wellness in the workplace. Similarly, RCs employed in the private sector and workers' compensation system provide direct vocational services to a variety of clientele: (a) case management of workers with acquired disabilities; (b) expert testimony for court systems; and (c) detailed life care plans for attorneys representing catastrophically injured clients. All these professionals who advise, consult, or collaborate with RCs are important colleagues in the rehabilitation process. Nevertheless, the primary partner should be the individual client seeking our services.

Promotion of Dignity and Human Rights

Two significant indicators of the social disparities experienced by the disability community are persistently higher unemployment rates and lower rates of graduation from high school and beyond. Higher rates of poverty and social isolation are additional indices of the second-class citizenship experienced by many people with disabilities. To redress these problems of inequity of opportunity in our society, it is important that counselors contribute to facilitating improvements in these social indicators reflective of discrimination against and unfulfilled potential of people with disabilities. To reinforce recollection of the main empowerment strategies recommended, this author captured a variety of practical interventions in the following **five strategic A's** (awareness, accessibility, accommodation, advocacy, asking before acting).

Awareness

It is often said that recognizing a problem is halfway to creating the solution; certainly, it is an essential first step in the process. Therefore, a fundamental approach that RCs must take is to develop their own awareness of important issues in the disability community and educating others to achieve that awareness. Essential to developing a thorough awareness of more subtle forms of inequity against people with disabilities is an understanding of the concept of **ableism**. Like institutional racism and sexism, ableism refers to a form of systemic discrimination against people with functional and aesthetic differences due to disability. It is called ableism because it establishes performance requirements not on individual needs but on a single standard based on able-bodied capabilities. It is systemic because it has become pervasive throughout our social system. Because it is so ingrained and taken for granted in society's norms, the evidence of ableism can only be revealed by questioning and deconstructing the assumed validity of relevant practices and performance standards set by the dominant, able-bodied majority. This involves (a) *becoming informed, observant, and sensitive* to what is going on in your organization and community that prevents fair and equal treatment of people with disabilities; (b) honestly examining existing policies, attitudes, assumptions, expectations, or requirements that everything should be done the "normal" or usual way; and (c) remembering that not all barriers are concrete and visible, so it is necessary to look broadly and reflect deeply on possible problems with the status quo and to think creatively for solutions.

Accessibility

The term *accessibility* is used in regular conversation to refer to how easy it is to enter and move about a location or to obtain, use, and experience something. It has acquired heightened applicability to rehabilitation counseling since we have become more aware and concerned that many settings or experiences are not easily (or not at all) approachable or available to people with disabilities. When raised awareness reveals situations of disparity in need of change, it is important to investigate what the possible contributing factors are. Careful analysis of the aspects of the situation and listening to the complaints of those who have been marginalized or excluded should help identify whether there are *physical, procedural, or attitudinal barriers* that prevent or complicate access and full participation. Are there features of the natural or built environment that constitute physical barriers? Are there requirements in the process of participation that create procedural barriers? Are there assumptions or beliefs held by gatekeepers or peers in the situation that communicate attitudinal barriers that make some people feel unwelcome, mistreated, or denied equal opportunity? Reducing these barriers requires honesty about oneself and listening to the marginalized group, as well as commitment and creativity, in order to assess and then increase accessibility as appropriate. Most architectural or environmental features that promote access and convenience for people with disabilities actually improve those functional criteria for the general public as well. Ramps and automatic doors, for example, help all of us when we are transporting heavy loads or pushing a baby carriage. Technology that allows us to give information by voice or by touching a screen is generally easier and faster than writing or typing. The term **universal design** refers to intentionally creating such characteristics and choices that will maximize all people's access to and interface with environments, equipment, or experiences (e.g., Iwarsson & Ståhl, 2003; Null, 2014).

Accommodation

There is considerable overlap both in concept and in practical examples between accessibility and accommodation. Both are used to increase inclusion of people with disabilities. Accommodation has a few different definitions in its singular and plural forms. Its major meaning for rehabilitation counseling purposes was determined when it was written into the regulations for the nondiscrimination sections of the Rehabilitation Act of 1973 and the Americans with Disabilities Act (ADA) (1990). It was recommended as a principal strategy for reducing the discrimination by exclusion that people with disabilities experienced, particularly in employment and education. It consists of a variety of strategies that substitute or compensate for the different or limited abilities of people with disabilities. Examples include (a) modifying the setting, procedures, or schedule for performing work, academic, or leisure tasks, such as individualized work breaks or telecommuting options; (b) providing adaptive equipment or resources, such as screen-reading software or sign language interpreters; and (c) substituting alternatives for accomplishing requirements, such as allowing a job coach to train a new employee on site or offering a low-distraction testing environment. Although the rationale for both of these laws is to redress the inequities of opportunity experienced by people with disabilities, the lawmakers also recognized that in many situations, there is a mix of legitimate and possibly noncompatible needs (at the personal, group, and organizational level) that must be considered. Therefore, the regulations to these laws use the qualified phrase **reasonable accommodation.** Thus, a limit was set on the extensiveness of adjustments and modifications that a responsible organization such as a business or school should be expected to provide to a qualified individual with a disability. The term *reasonable* was purposefully not delineated by any list of specific examples or by a formula. Rather, the laws and regulations provide some guidance and criteria to be considered when accommodation requests are individually negotiated and determined. Two main criteria for assessing the reasonableness of requested or projected accommodations are (a) **business necessity**, which examines the extent to which the desired accommodation comports with or does not detract from the purpose of the organization; and (b) the projected cost–benefit consequences of various ways of achieving the requested accommodation, to ensure that implementing it would not impose **undue hardship** on the responsible organization.

Advocacy

One ongoing strategy that should be used by all RCs, other counselors, and, indeed, any person wanting to make meaningful change is doing advocacy and promoting self-advocacy by those directly affected. This in itself is a multimodal way of approaching change where it is needed. Three types of advocacy are (a) **individual advocacy** to empower a particular person; (b) **self-advocacy** when one is fighting a cause on behalf of oneself or one's community; and (c) **systems advocacy** to generate improvement on an institutional or societal level (such as effecting a policy change that benefits a class of people). *Advocacy* comes from Latin words meaning to speak up or use your voice to advance a cause. Accordingly, many modes of advocacy have to do with verbal communication: giving talks to educate stakeholders about an injustice; writing letters to controlling authorities; lobbying legislators; creating public service announcements; and participating in a boycott or protest march. Other ways of promoting a message or cause are to conduct research; solicit resources and supporters; monitor enforcement of equal-opportunity laws; and sponsor demonstration projects. These actions can serve to validate the need or instigate the change. Many other means of effecting advocacy can also be chosen to fit with the agenda and the preferred style of the advocate or self-advocate. Kiselica and Robinson (2001) discussed several qualities and skills that characterize people who are well suited to be advocates. These include ability to maintain a multisystems perspective; ability to use individual, group, and organizational change strategies; willingness to compromise; awareness of the impact of your personality on others; and ability to adjust your style in order to be an effective change agent. Internationally, both the declaration and protection of **human rights** are major sociopolitical goals pushed by advocates for women, children, and other marginalized sectors of society. This includes people with disabilities, as articulated in the 2006 United Nations (UN) Convention on the Rights of Persons with Disabilities (CRPD). Umeasiegbu, Bishop, and Mpofu (2013) provided informative analyses of this policy document and its relationship with counterpart laws in the United States and several other countries.

Within American academia, **social justice** has become the contemporary term to refer to the domain of issues and corresponding counseling and advocacy strategies focused on human rights. The goal is to reduce the impact of deprivation, discrimination, and oppression in the lives of clients and in the communities where they reside by eliminating the root causes and manifestations of the injustices. This agenda is relatively new for our profession and ought to be more fully infused into our curricula and ethical codes. That effort will require searching self-reflection and serious analysis and critique of our professional practices. Harley, Alston, and Middleton (2007, p. 44) cogently recommended that we:

> provide students with opportunities to critically examine the power dynamics of the rehabilitation counseling approach to service and to identify new ways of entering into a reciprocal relationship in the community (Rice & Pollack, 2000). Both teaching and learning about social justice are not destinations . . . they are processes of continuous growth and understanding.

Asking Before Acting

To be truly effective and ethical in pursuing social justice or any of the other missions of rehabilitation counseling, it is essential to approach the process with humility and to do the work collaboratively. This recommendation to check on the acceptability and validity of the perceptions and motivations that drive our helping behavior is an ongoing responsibility. Most directly, this can be done by getting input and feedback from the least powerful stakeholders who are most affected. The following examples refer back to the other "A-strategies" described in this section:

- Often a new awareness about an issue emerges from a powerful personal experience or an influential reading. When this happens, *ask affected stakeholders* what they think about the issue and why.
- Before constructing or retrofitting structures to achieve accessibility, invite a few people with different types of limitations to experience the site as is or to review the plan as designed, to give recommendations and priorities about features that would ensure access for them, *before the job is started.*
- When initiating a service relationship with consumers, make sure to invite them, preferably in a written document that is distributed or displayed, to make suggestions at any point in the process about accommodations to a disability that would enhance their participation in the program.
- Consult with concerned stakeholders about your ideas for engaging in an advocacy effort. Listen to their experiences and desires. Ask how you might partner with them on the journey to expand their personal sense of empowerment or to improve a cause for social justice in the community. The work of creating equal opportunity and full participation with dignity for all is not easy, but it can be effective and meaningful if it is carried out collaboratively with persistence and hopefulness.

TRADITIONAL MODELS OF HOW DISABILITY HAS BEEN PERCEIVED AND INTERPRETED IN SOCIETY

This section explains four different models that describe how people from ancient times to the present day have perceived disability. The models in this section are presented in the order in which they emerged historically; the later ones are more multifaceted; and they vary in their acceptability as useful conceptual frameworks. However, they all have some contemporary relevance to the experience of disability and the provision of rehabilitation services. Overall, these models represent the perspectives of the outsider or professional or scholar—looking out at disability and observing its interactions with the world. Although they are consistently called the **models of disability**, all of them discussed in this and the next section are descriptive and do not propose testable hypotheses that translate into verifiable outcomes, as the more predictive models in the physical sciences do (McLaren, 1998). Rather, the main value of these models is to examine critically how diverse perspectives on the origin and meaning of disability shape personal, professional, organizational, and societal responses to people who have, or are perceived to have, a disability. The reader should also understand that the presentations of the various conceptual models are not meant as an evaluation of specific programs, such as services that have the same label as the model (e.g., life-saving *medical* procedures or career-enhancing *vocational* services).

The Moral Model

The moral interpretation of disability is represented by a diverse accumulation of beliefs (whether explicitly expressed or unconsciously internalized), most of which are rooted in traditional thinking in some cultures and religions. The **moral model** views *disability as a symbolic attribute of the person* that demands an explanation. If the disability is perceived positively, then the individual is revered as blessed with special powers. For example, this was the case with certain people who were blind in ancient Greek and Roman civilizations, where it was deduced that because they could not see in the physical world, they were believed to have keen powers to "see" in the metaphysical realm. Therefore, they were brought into the inner sanctum of the emperor to serve as advisers and predictors of the future. Even today, it is not uncommon for people to believe that people who are blind inherently have alternate sensory powers, rather than understanding that greater reliance on and increased practice using nonvisual cues can strengthen other sensory modalities. Much more frequently, disabilities were reacted to with fear, stigmatization, ostracism, or death by infanticide. Typically, it was assumed that the disability was an outward sign that evil had befallen the family or sin had been committed. In different cultures or circumstances, the person blamed was either the person bearing the disability, the mother or both parents, or some ancestor.

The moral model is no longer a mainstream interpretation of disability as it was in past centuries. Indeed, such beliefs may seem so superstitious in today's scientific knowledge environment that they are considered nonexistent. But "primitive" beliefs can remain subliminally implanted in the depths of cultural consciousness and can result in imposition of stigma and shame, which are often internalized by people on whom such are imposed, however subtly. Some recent examples of these misconceptions include that HIV, the virus that causes AIDS, emerged as punishment for "choosing the gay lifestyle" over heterosexuality; and that people with biochemically based psychiatric disorders are "possessed by evil spirits." Psychiatric and behavioral conditions are more often stigmatized and considered the person's fault, compared to orthopedic and sensory disabilities. Perhaps the best descriptions of the contemporary intellectual (and more secular) version of this moral model are given in books by Susan Sontag (1978, 1989). She criticized some current perspectives on disease and the metaphorical language used in discussing its origins (especially cancer and the AIDS "plague"). Her discussions demonstrate how this metaphorical language is rooted in and reinforces the phenomenon of **blaming the victim** by shaming the character of those who acquire the disease.

The Medical Model

The conceptual framework known as the **medical model** is arguably the most dominant and culturally infused of those we will discuss. The medical model views disability as contained within the person as a result of an **organic impairment** in the body that is probed and prodded for diagnostic and treatment purposes. The role of the medical professional is to cure the disabling condition or reduce it to the closest approximation of "within normal limits." The person with a disability is expected to be compliant and unquestioning. On the macro level, the miracles of modern medicine have resulted in tremendous strides in saving lives, extending the life span, and increasing the level of residual function after the onset of a host of diseases, injuries, and congenital abnormalities. Medically, individuals with a significantly disabling condition are likely to agree that they are better off due to medical science. Psychosocially, however, the process of having a person single-mindedly **focus on "fixing"** something that is a permanent part of your identity and adapted lifestyle can have negative and lasting side effects. This can be true regardless of how good the professional's intention is and beneficial (functionally or cosmetically) the outcome is. Many people born with a disability that required extensive treatments feel that the medical improvement came to them at a high psychological price in terms of depleted sense of self-worth, loss of dignity, and being treated by others as abnormal. For this reason, the medical model has also been called the "individual pathology" or "personal defect" model because it disparages disability, in both indirect and explicit ways, rather than seeing disability as part of the spectrum of human variation. Additional concerns about the negative impact of the dominance of the medical model on psychotherapeutic practices are cogently and succinctly summarized by Vash (2004).

Another particularly problematic assumption of the medical model is that the credentialed expertise of the professional is more valid and important than the preferences, direct experience, and learned lessons of the person with a disability. This creates a tension between the *perspectives of the outsider versus the insider* (who personally experiences both the challenges and the growth opportunities from disability). Marshak and Seligman (1993, especially pp. 1–19) and B. A. Wright (1983, 1988; B. A. Wright & Lopez, 2005) provide many explanations of undesirable effects of the discrepancies between the experiential worlds of consumers and providers. Despite better sensitivity training of health care professionals and more assertiveness among clients than in the past, their inherent differences in power that get reinforced by the medical model can distance professionals from understanding what is going on inside the client, cognitively and emotionally. Discrepancies in perceptions and priorities can negatively affect the therapeutic process and outcome, thus demanding that professionals engage in honest reflection and self-monitoring to address the often-covert conflicts (B. A. Wright, 1987). For further critique and examples of the paradoxical negative impact of the helping professions, interested readers are referred to Schriner and Scotch (2001), Scotch (1988), and Szymanski and Trueba (1994).

The Labor-Market Economic Model

The basic tenet of the **labor-market economic model** is that inability to work defines one as disabled. This tenet presents a conundrum, because many people who have a disability are either successfully employed or know that they are capable of working. Thus, there is no simple, direct relationship between disability and employability. This model's main strategy is to rely on primarily medical assessments to determine the existence, extent, and projected time span of a disability and its limiting impact on a person's functional capacity to perform work tasks. Thus, some scholars call it the **functional limitations model** or **vocational model**. Based on the data from the medical/vocational evaluation or functional capacity assessment, a person is determined to be fully or partially capable of working, or defined as disabled and provided disability income to replace the lost or unrealized income from a job. Usually, if disability income is approved, so is government-subsidized health insurance (Medicare or Medicaid), because in the United States most people obtain health insurance as a benefit of their job, although this has recently begun to change.

Despite the value of their intended purpose, some regulatory features of disability benefits programs have created problems. First, the system has developed too rigid a diagnostic dichotomy: one can versus cannot work. In reality, most human characteristics are more differentiated along a continuum of capacities. It would have been wiser practice for disability determinations to be made by assessing actual work performance more adequately and creatively—including samples of behavior when assistive devices, accommodating strategies, or worksite modifications were used that could eliminate or reduce the impact of the specific functional limitation(s) associated with a particular disability.

Second, for people with disabilities who have ongoing needs for medical treatments and/ or personal attendant services that are provided by a single package of government-subsidized disability benefits, the system creates a difficult motivational dilemma called a **financial disincentive to work**. Many such beneficiaries are eager to work for a salary and give up the income portion of their benefit, but they cannot afford to lose certain medical benefits and long-term attendant services that are not covered by any employer's health insurance plan.

The Ecological Model

Comprised of domains of interdependent components, the **ecological model** is a multi-dimensional and more humanistic expansion of the medical model. Engel (1977, 1980) and others called it the **bio-psycho-social (BPS) model** because they saw illness as a function of more than an impaired body (the biological component). They recognized the integral importance of additional factors that contributed to disease or dysfunction— and to its remediation. These included an array of individual psychological characteristics (e.g., feelings, preferences, beliefs, compliance behaviors), as well as various social factors. The latter can encompass variables ranging from the closely surrounding context to broad societal forces. An inherent characteristic of the BPS model is an appreciation that the various components are interconnected in ways that can change as the person develops and responds to new experiences. Thus, the model depicts a system of relevant variables that not only interact with but also mutually influence each other. Accordingly, **systems model** is another term used by some authors (e.g., Cottone, 1987) to refer to this framework. Although some authors in psychology (e.g., Bronfenbrenner, 1979; Moos, 1979) and rehabilitation counseling (e.g., Hershenson, 1998; Szymanski, 1998) have used the term *ecological* in their publication titles and explanations of this conceptual perspective, it is not yet a common descriptor in our field. Nonetheless, we prefer the label *ecological model* because we believe it more clearly emphasizes the dynamic, interconnected web of influence of the components on each other and on the synthesized outcome.

Another reason why we prefer the more concise term *ecological* for this model is that it has continued to expand, as various authors argue for the specification of new components. Those who have added a *cultural* component and critique to the BPS model include Molina (1983); Jackson, Antonucci, and Brown (2003); and Hatala (2012). There is also a growing movement of scholars and practitioners who argue for incorporating the *spiritual* dimension of clients' lives and concerns in any holistic approach to counseling (Bruno, 1999; McCarthy, 1995, 2007; Mijares, 2014; Nosek & Hughes, 2001; Stebnicki, 2016; Vash, 1994). In 2009, the Association for Spiritual, Ethical, and Religious Values in Counseling developed and approved a list of spirituality competencies for counselors (www.counseling.org/knowledge-center/competencies). If these advancements were to become broadly accepted, we would then be using the cumbersome term, the *bio-psycho-social-cultural-spiritual model*.

The ecological model is the most popular and pervasive in current clinical and research endeavors. A prime example of this point is the *International Classification of Functioning, Disability and Health* (ICF; World Health Organization, 2001; also see Chapter 12 in this book and Peterson, 2016). *ICF* is the product of a global effort to devise a universal system for measuring the impact of disability on a person (the clinical application) and, more frequently, on a national or regional population (the public health research application). One notable quality of the *ICF* is that it conceptualizes the constructs of *disability* and *health* not as a dichotomy but as a continuum. Another is that it provides a multidimensional structure for categories of personal and environmental variables, each with multiple components and levels. However, a close examination of the substructure of this assessment tool does expose a definite preponderance of personal function and disability variables, compared to its identification of potentially influential environmental variables (McCarthy, 2014, pp. 4–5). For a more balanced application of the *ICF* and the ecological model, readers should review Millington's (2016) excellent explanation of the paradigm of **community-based rehabilitation (CBR)**.

UNCONVENTIONAL MODELS THAT ARE CHANGING HOW THE DISABILITY EXPERIENCE IS UNDERSTOOD AND APPRECIATED

This section explains four newer models that propose alternative interpretations and responses to the stimuli that disabilities represent. The models in this section are also presented in historical order. However, because they have rather recently emerged, the later ones have not benefited from as much time in the marketplace of ideas to be developed and discussed. In large measure, these models represent the perspectives of the insiders to the disability experience or innovators, as they look out at the world and its interface with disability, and work to reformulate that relationship.

The Social Model

Perhaps the most dramatic shift in thinking about disability over the past 50 years is represented by the **social model** of disability. This viewpoint strongly opposes the medical model's narrow and oppressive definition of disability as a problem within the person and the consequent solution as correcting or changing the person with a disability. From the social model perspective, the problem is not paralyzed legs but environments, buildings, and transportation systems that are not accessible to wheelchairs. The problem is not the inability of a person to see, hear, or stand for extended periods of time. It is the discriminatory refusal of people in the workplace to allow those with disabilities to perform the job duties in an accommodated way and with the assistive devices that enable them.

At least as early as Barker (1948), there were scholarly propositions suggestive of the social model of disability, noting a "minority parallel" with regard to biased preconceptions of and unjust discrimination against people with disabilities similar to what happens from racism against ethnic groups. Thus, some scholars refer to this framework as the **minority model**. However, it was the **independent living (IL) movement** about two decades later that became the powerful impetus for demonstrating this paradigm shift in analyzing disability. The leaders of the IL movement demonstrated that they were not "confined to a wheelchair" (an erroneous phrase often used to describe people who actively use wheelchairs as their regular mode of mobility). Rather, they were confined by unnecessary physical barriers and social policies or expectations that kept them in the parental homes where they were raised or in the nursing homes where they were placed, secluded from mainstream life. Readers are strongly encouraged to learn about the IL movement and the movers and shakers who started and further fueled it. The most extensive source is the Oral Histories/Archives project on Disability Rights and Independent Living Movement (www.bancroft.berkeley.edu/collections/drilm/index.html). Other informative and interesting accounts include Charlton (1998), Davis (2015), Fleischer and

Zames (2011), McCarthy (2003), McMahon and Shaw (2000), and Pelka (2012). Inspired by the wave of civil rights movements in the 1960s and 1970s by African American, feminist, and gay activists, early disability rights self-advocates forged their own liberation agenda and successes. Accordingly, we believe a clearer descriptor for the perspective known as the social model is the **self-determination philosophy** of the IL movement or the **civil rights model** of disability. Others choose to highlight the social power dynamics of this model and call it the politics of disability (e.g., Hahn, 1985; Stubbins, 1988) or the **sociopolitical model** (e.g., Smart & Smart, 2006).

The Disability Culture Model

An often-unacknowledged alternative in the collection of conceptual frameworks is the **disability pride and culture model**. There are lots of similarities in the perspectives of those who embrace this model and those who assert the civil rights model. Differences are primarily in (a) how and when the models developed historically and (b) their chosen emphases. At the risk of reducing the contrasts to a few phrases, one could say that the construct of **disability culture** emerged from ideological, psychological, and sociological discourse in academia and the arts, starting around 1990. Significant references and resources on disability culture include Brown (2003), Linton (1998), and Riddell and Watson (2003). By comparison, the rights model grew out of political engagement and "in the streets" activism for pragmatic changes in social policy and community access, starting in the 1960s with the IL movement. Perusing the following two selected websites will also help readers grasp the commonalities and differences between disability culture organizations (e.g., www.instituteondisabilityculture.org) and disability rights organizations (e.g., www.adapt.org). The academic discipline of **disability studies** and its flagship organization, the Society for Disability Studies (www.disstudies.org), are the main engines of scholarship and mentoring that have successfully promoted both of these models of disability.

Putnam (2005) hypothesized that **disability pride** is one component of **disability identity**; and that it consists of four affective–cognitive elements. These are (a) "claiming" disability (a term that contrasts with the typical therapeutic goal of "accepting" one's disability); (b) seeing impairments as a natural part of the human condition; (c) believing disability is not inherently negative, although it is frequently interpreted so; and (d) experiencing disability as creating the consciousness of a cultural minority group. She explains feelings of disability pride in these ways (Putnam, 2005, p. 191):

> [they] run counter to social and cultural beliefs that disability is tragedy and that persons with physical or mental disabilities would rather not be who they are . . . identify as part of a collective group of individuals who have both struggled within and contributed to the development of their home nation.

Actually, there are three distinguishable subpopulations of the disability pride model that share fundamental commonalities but usually operate within their own networks. One is composed primarily of people with obvious physical disabilities. For them, wheelchair access and accommodations for blindness have been major issues; assertive personalities and communication skills have been their notable strengths. This group is predominant among the trailblazers and current participants in the IL movement and adapted competitive sports such as the Paralympics. There are several publications that reflect this community's perspectives and agendas. Prominent among them is the monthly magazine, *New Mobility,* that publishes provocative and pragmatic articles. A second group is the **Deaf culture**, made up of people whose primary language is American Sign Language (ASL). (Note that deaf is the common adjective and diagnostic label for a significant hearing impairment, whereas Deaf with a capital "D" refers to the subgroup of that population who psychosocially self-identify with that culture.) Their disability is hidden, so these people do not have the experience of immediate reactions of being avoided, stared at, or given unwanted help that many people with visible physical disabilities have to handle. Instead, they experience significant isolation from mainstream culture because ability to communicate fluently in ASL among the nondeaf population is very rare.

People with chronic mental illness or past psychiatric histories comprise the third group. Typically, they do not encounter the physical or communication barriers just described. However, they bear the brunt of the deepest discrimination from the general population, in the form of **social stigma**, fearful rejection, and unreasonable or cruel treatment, even in allegedly therapeutic institutions. Schrader, Jones, and Shattell (2013) explained the evolution in self-advocacy priorities of this segment of the disability pride community, which they refer to as the consumer/survivor/ex-patient (c/s/x) movement:

> articulate a broader culture of madness . . . have emphasized the connections between madness and art, theater, spirituality, and a valuable sensitivity to individual and collective pain . . . supports interventions that target the social exclusion, poverty, trauma, and grief that contribute to distress and block positive adaptation. (pp. 62–63)

The Technology Model

Technology has had and will continue to have a significant influence on those in both developed and developing countries in many domains of their daily life. Increasingly, its impact on the disability experience has been even greater. Indeed, some predict it may ultimately lead to the dissolution of physical disability as a functional classification. Yet discourse about technology and disability has rarely risen to the level of conceptually organizing the viewpoints and strategies associated with perceiving disability as an intriguing engineering opportunity into a unique **technology model** of disability. Nonetheless, this perspective does have a very respected evidence base in the innovative research and product development conducted in the fields of assistive technology (e.g., Lenker & Paquet, 2003) and rehabilitation engineering (see www.resna.org). In an unpublished presentation, Susan Daniels (2009) contrasted three paradigms for understanding disability that she labeled as (a) individual defect, (b) human rights, and (c) eco-tech models. The first two were her renditions of the medical model and social model, respectively. The third could be considered an alternative version of the ecological model, but it was delineated distinctively enough around technology to warrant designation and explanation here as its own model of disability. She presented her comparisons cogently and succinctly by posing and answering the following questions. Because the other two models have already been discussed, only her answer captions to the defining questions for the eco-tech model are given (in parentheses) to explain the main ideas and implications of the technology model.

- Where is the problem? (The interface between individuals and the environment)
- What is the source of the problem? (Lack of fit between the variation in human capabilities and the requirements in the environment)
- How is the solution defined? (Modification of the interface to achieve a better fit)

- What solution strategies are used? (Improvements in technology, integrated delivery systems, knowledge transfer, market research, and systems design)
- How does society benefit? (More effective and efficient performance; more individual choice and control)
- Who are the experts? (Engineers, technologists, designers, manufacturers, users)
- What are the consequences for the individual? (Identification with the engineer role; motivation to create high-performance scenarios)

Her brief answers to the last, telling question highlight the different impact for people with disabilities when these conceptual models are applied in daily living. For the eco-tech model, the consequences are energizing. They contrast sharply with the disempowering consequences Daniels listed for the individual-defect model: internalization of a deviant role; acceptance of inferior status; endless effort to overcome in order to be socially acceptable.

The topic of technology related to people with disabilities is discussed more fully in Chapter 21. Here, we conclude our explanation of the technology model with the example of one practical assessment instrument that has been developed to optimize the use and effectiveness of assistive technology for people with disabilities. The website for the Matching Person and Technology (MPT) Assessment Process (www.matchingperso nandtechnology.com/index.html) provides a wealth of information on this approach, its various tools, and published evaluation research. It was developed by Marcia Scherer and several colleagues. MPT has a definite mission to collaborate with the user in all phases of the processes of assessment, selection, training, and adoption of assistive technology. Due attention is given to psychological, physical, and technical factors of potential influence (Scherer & Craddock, 2002). For example, MPT measures characteristics of the milieu, the attitudinal and physical characteristics of the multifaceted environment where the technology will be used, as well as personal preferences and capacities of the user. Another strength of this resource is its diversity of applications to the needs of consumers with either physical or mental disabilities and related to many performance domains, such as education, employment, and IL (Kirsch & Scherer, 2009).

The Consumer Economic Model

Perceiving people with disabilities as a growing market niche heretofore disregarded or unimagined by the retail industry is the premise of the **consumer economic model**. This is a perspective that has been discussed not in the counseling or rehabilitation literature, but to date almost exclusively in the media of a sector of the disability community. One good, brief explanation is provided in a blog posted (January 16, 2012) on the Audio Accessibility website (www.audio-accessibility.com/news/2012/01/economic-model-of -disability). Rather than starting with a focus on reducing the disadvantages of disability as a medical problem or functional deficit or stigmatized status deserving of legislative protection from unjust treatment, this perspective begins with positive expectations about people with disabilities. It positions these individuals as typical, active adults: consumers in search of better products, having money to spend, wanting to go on vacation, bringing along their friends and family. Furthermore, it openly acknowledges that by effectively responding to the purchase desires and consumer needs of people with disabilities, business and industry also benefit. This is true not only in terms of their increased revenue, but also in terms of learning ways of becoming a more inclusive and responsive business. In contrast, the mission of traditional human service organizations is assumed and expressed to be only serving the good of the client. Indeed, this is enshrined in the primary **ethical principle of beneficence** (i.e., to do good) that counselors and other helping professionals are obligated to follow. Certainly, service organizations provide benefits to many clients on a daily basis. However, these helping organizations and the practitioners who staff them also gain advantages from their professional work—financially, psychologically, and socially. Interested readers are referred to Szymanski, Parker, and Patterson (2012, pp. 375–381) for a thought-provoking presentation on this dilemma of the formal, bureaucratic relationship between professionals and clients in the "business of disability."

The expressed goal of the consumer-economic model is to create an inclusive culture through appealing to the growing population of people with disabilities and their loved ones as a competitive advantage in the marketplace. The proponents of this perspective rely on the principles of universal design, economic integration through market forces, and facilitated participation in all domains of living as the strategies for achieving **social inclusion**. People with disabilities are targeted as one of the groups of humanity to be included; therefore, they should be cultivated as desired consumers. Although its conceptual framework and mission are broader, this model to date has been primarily applied to the tourism and recreation business, which is an obvious launch pad for an approach that is based on the design of environments and products for universal access. The following description (Travability, 2011, pp. 3–4) capsulizes how the proponents of this model distinguish their marketing approach from the enforcement strategy of the civil rights model of disability:

> The shortcoming of the social model is that change has been driven as compliance . . . seen as a cost that society demands of a business . . . driven by social expectations and translated by rule makers. At that point it . . . just becomes another problem for organizations . . . and is handed across to their risk management departments.

Relatively recently, like other groups (e.g., ethnic and sexual minorities) that have been misrepresented or ignored, the disability community has begun to gain more attention and gradual understanding from the corporate sector. Accordingly, whereas once the voices and interests of people with disabilities were restricted to small-scale publications or organizations dedicated specifically to expressing their message or advancing their agendas, they are now beginning to be recognized in the mainstream media and marketplace (Rucker, 2016). This change is progress, albeit slow. Furthermore, as the disability community becomes more acknowledged by corporations, it is crucial that they not treat this sector as a single entity. It is a diverse population, with many intragroup differences in priorities and preferences.

CONCLUSION

This chapter delineated the quite straightforward value-based orientations of rehabilitation counseling. It also presented a diversity of conceptual frameworks that have shaped the complex context of societal expectations and structures within which RCs and people with disabilities work together. Part of the complexity uncovered was the contrast between traditional and unconventional models for understanding disability on both personal and societal levels. The following analysis of the goal of "independence" is designed not just to exemplify this difference, but also to suggest how each perspective has some pieces of "the truth" and reality of achieving the goal. The Functional Independence Measurement (FIM) system is a well-developed clinical and research tool commonly used to assess the current functioning of patients with physical disabilities in hospital rehabilitation programs (Uniform Data System for Medical Rehabilitation, 1997; www.rehabmeasures.org/lists/rehabmeasures/dispform.aspx?id=889). The tool is used to record therapeutic progress and to justify requests to health insurers to pay for further treatments by allied health staff, who complete the FIM form. It measures how independently the people with a disability can perform activities of daily living (ADLs) such as bathing, dressing, toileting, talking, and walking. The rating scale for each activity ranges from 1 (total assistance) to 7 (complete independence). The instructions for assigning someone a score of 7 read: "All of the tasks making up the activity are typically performed safely, without modification, assistive devices, or aids, and within a reasonable amount of time; no helper required." By this criterion, most people with disabilities would never reach independence. Actually, no person could be classified as independent in the activity of watching TV (if it were on the form!) because we all use the assistive device of a remote control—we just don't think of it in that way. An interesting alternative to the stringent FIM criteria is the broad concept of independence expressed by people with disabilities who endorse the philosophy of the IL movement: "independence, to them, does not imply being able to survive without the help of other people or assistive devices; it simply means **freedom of decision making and the power of self-determination**" (Vash, 1981, pp. 38–39). As an example, consider people with high-level quadriplegia (i.e., having no control of all four limbs). FIMs would categorize them as having "complete dependence" because they require "total assistance." However, if they embrace the IL ideology, the same people would define themselves (and could be understood by others) as independent, because they are in charge of the personal assistants whom they hire or manage. They are in control of the people and equipment that they use to accomplish their ADLs, go where they want to go, and do what they choose to do, when they desire.

Recommended references to help readers further grasp the potential implications of viewing disability issues from different conceptual frameworks include the following: Smart and Smart (2006), which focuses on counseling practice; Buntinx and Schalock (2010), which provides useful insights regarding the interpretation of intellectual disability; and Olkin (2016). The latter author's recommendations for **disability-affirmative therapy** are useful and needed because, "[a]s most therapists cannot become truly culturally competent in disability, they need to be culturally aware, informed, and receptive" (p. 222).

The following quote is a powerful message with which to conclude our discussion of these conceptual models—the diverse ways that disability has been interpreted and managed by society, often to the disregard and detriment of the insiders who actually experience disability day in and day out. Although the authors were speaking specifically about psychiatric survivors, the advice is an apt caveat for all counselors working with people who have any unusual differences and stigmatized characteristics. Schrader et al. (2013) recommend that human service professionals:

> suspend their assumptions about . . . clients' experiences (i.e., assumptions of disease, distress, and impairment), opening up both parties to deeper explorations of the desirable but neglected aspects of clients' experiences and personhood. Clinicians need to be aware of the impact that their own explanatory frameworks may have . . . [and] endeavor to facilitate individualized processes of meaning-making. (p. 63)

We encourage you to continue exploring the yin and yang of theory and practice, questioning and applying conceptual models to guide your mutual learning and collaborative work with people with disabilities and colleagues, now and in the future.

CONTENT REVIEW QUESTIONS

- Summarize the similarities and differences among the five strategic A's (awareness, accessibility, accommodation, advocacy, and asking before acting) for promoting equal opportunity and inclusion for people with disabilities in all spheres of society.
- Select the model of disability that best matches your own thinking and explain five reasons why.
- Review the section on the technology model and the set of questions that Daniels (2009) posed and answered to describe that model. Choose one of the other models of disability presented and answer each of the eight questions with respect to your chosen model.

REFERENCES

Atkins, B. (1988). An asset-oriented approach to cross-cultural issues: Blacks in rehabilitation. *Journal of Applied Rehabilitation Counseling, 19*(4), 45–49.

Barker, R. G. (1948). The social psychology of physical disability. *Journal of Social Issues, 4,* 28–35.

Bishop, M. (2005). Quality of life and psychosocial adaptation to chronic illness and disability: Preliminary analysis of a conceptual and theoretical synthesis. *Rehabilitation Counseling Bulletin, 48*(4), 219–231.

Bishop, M., Chapin, M. H., & Miller, S. (2008). Quality of life assessment in the measurement of rehabilitation outcome. *Journal of Rehabilitation, 74*(2), 45–55.

Bowe, F. G. (1978). *Handicapping America: Barriers to disabled people.* New York, NY: Harper & Row.

Bowe, F. G. (1980). *Rehabilitating America: Toward independence for disabled and elderly people.* New York, NY: HarperCollins.

Bronfenbrenner, U. (1979). *The ecology of human development: Experiments by nature and design.* Cambridge, MA: Harvard University Press.

Brown, S. E. (2003). *Movie stars and sensuous scars: Essays on the journey from disability shame to disability pride.* New York, NY: iUniverse, Inc.

Bruno, R. (1999, November). Buddhism plus disability: One "step" closer to Nirvana. *New Mobility, 10,* 32–37. Retrieved from http://www.angelfire.com/electronic/awakening101/ada-buddhism.html

Buntinx, W. H. E., & Schalock, R. L. (2010). Models of disability, quality of life, and individualized supports: Implications for professional practice in intellectual disability. *Journal of Policy and Practice in Intellectual Disabilities, 7*(4), 283–294.

Chan, F., Tarvydas, V., Blalock, K., Strauser, D., & Atkins, B. J. (2009). Unifying and elevating rehabilitation counseling through model-driven, diversity-sensitive evidence-based practice. *Rehabilitation Counseling Bulletin, 52*(2), 114–119.

Charlton, J. (1998). *Nothing about us without us: Disability oppression and empowerment.* Berkeley: University of California Press.

Chou, C. C., Chan, F., Chan, J. Y. C., Phillips, B., Ditchman, N., & Kaseroff, A. (2013). Positive psychology theory, research, and practice: A primer for rehabilitation counseling professionals. *Rehabilitation Research, Policy, and Education, 27*(3), 131–153.

Chubon, R. A. (1994). *Social and psychological foundations of rehabilitation.* Springfield, IL: Charles C. Thomas.

Cottone, R. R. (1987). A systemic theory of vocational rehabilitation. *Rehabilitation Counseling Bulletin, 30,* 167–176.

Daniels, S. (2009, October 24). Paradigms of disability. Workshop presented at the Louisiana State University Health Sciences Center, New Orleans, LA.

Davis, L. J. (2015). *Enabling acts: The hidden story of how the Americans with Disabilities Act gave the largest US minority its rights.* Boston, MA: Beacon Press.

DeLoach, C., & Greer, B. G. (1981). *Adjustment to severe physical disability: A metamorphosis.* New York, NY: McGraw-Hill.

Dembo, T., Leviton, G., & Wright, B. A. (1956). Adjustment to misfortune: A problem of social psychological rehabilitation. *Artificial Limbs*, 3(2), 4–62. [Reprinted in *Rehabilitation Psychology* (1975), 22, 1–100.]

Dunn, D. (2015). *The social psychology of disability*. New York, NY: Oxford University Press.

Engel, G. L. (1977, April 8). The need for a new medical model: A challenge to biomedicine. *Science*, 196, 129–136.

Engel, G. L. (1980). The clinical application of the biopsychosocial model. *American Journal of Psychiatry*, 137(5), 535–544.

Fabian, E. (1991). Using quality of life indicators in rehabilitation program evaluation. *Rehabilitation Counseling Bulletin*, 34(4), 344–356.

Fleischer, D., & Zames, F. (2011). *The disability rights movement: From charity to confrontation*. Philadelphia, PA: Temple University Press.

Galassi, J. P., & Akos, P. (2007). *Strengths-based school counseling: Promoting student development and achievement*. Mahwah, NJ: Lawrence Erlbaum.

Groomes, D. A. G., & Olsheski, J. (2002). Continued exploration of the psychosocial adaptation to disability research frontier: Possible new directions. *Rehabilitation Education*, 16(2), 213–226.

Hahn, H. (1985). Toward a politics of disability: Definitions, disciplines, and policies. *Social Science Journal*, 22(4), 87–105.

Hahn, H. (1993). The political implications of disability definitions and data. *Journal of Disability Policy Studies*, 4(2), 41–52.

Harley, D. A., Alston, R. J., & Middleton, R. A. (2007). Infusing social justice into rehabilitation education: Making a case for curricula refinement. *Rehabilitation Education*, 21(1), 41–52.

Hartley, M. T. (2011). Examining the relationships between resilience, mental health, and academic persistence in undergraduate college students. *Journal of American College Health*, 59(7), 596–604.

Hatala, A. R. (2012). The status of the "biopsychosocial" model in health psychology: Towards an integrated approach and a critique of cultural conceptions. *Open Journal of Medical Psychology*, 1, 51–62.

Hershenson, D. (1998). Systemic, ecological model for rehabilitation counseling. *Rehabilitation Counseling Bulletin*, 42(1), 40–50.

Hershenson, D. (2015). The individual plan for retirement: A missing part of plan development with older consumers. *Rehabilitation Counseling Bulletin*, 59(1), 9–17.

Iwarsson, S., & Ståhl, A. (2003). Accessibility, usability and universal design—positioning and definition of concepts describing person-environment relationships. *Disability and Rehabilitation*, 25(2), 57–66.

Jackson, J. S., Antonucci, T. C., & Brown, E. (2003). A cultural lens on biopsychosocial models of aging. In P. Costa & I. Siegler (Eds.), *Recent advances in psychology and aging* (pp. 221–241). Greenwich, CT: JAI Press.

Jaques, M. E. (1970). Rehabilitation counseling: Scope and services. Boston, MA: Houghton Mifflin.

Kirsch, N. L., & Scherer, M. J. (2009). Assistive technology for cognition and behavior. In R.G. Frank, M. Rosenthal, & B. Caplan (Eds.), *Handbook of rehabilitation psychology* (2nd ed., pp. 273–284). Washington, DC: American Psychological Association.

Kiselica, M., & Robinson, M. (2001). Bringing advocacy counseling to life: The history, issues, and human dramas of social justice work in counseling. *Journal of Counseling and Development*, 79(4), 387–397.

Lenker, J. A., & Paquet, V. L. (2003). A review of conceptual models for assistive technology outcomes research and practice. *Assistive Technology*, 15(1), 1–15.

Lewin, K. (1936). *Principles of topological psychology*. New York, NY: McGraw-Hill.

Linton, S. (1998). *Claiming disability: Knowledge and identity*. New York: New York University Press.

Livneh, H. (2016). Quality of life and coping with chronic illness and disability: A temporal perspective. *Rehabilitation Counseling Bulletin*, 59(2), 67–83.

Livneh, H., Bishop, M., & Anctil, T. (2014). Modern models of psychosocial adaptation to chronic illness and disability as viewed through the prism of Lewin's field theory: A comparative review. *Rehabilitation Research, Policy, and Education*, 28(3), 126–142.

Lofquist, L. H., & Dawis, R. V. (1969). *Adjustment to work: A psychological view of man's problems in a work-oriented society*. East Norwalk, CT: Appleton-Century-Crofts.

Lofquist, L. H., & Dawis, R. V. (1991). *Essentials of person-environment-correspondence counseling*. Minneapolis: University of Minnesota Press.

Marshak, L. E., & Seligman, M. (1993). *Counseling persons with physical disabilities: Theoretical and clinical perspectives*. Austin, TX: Pro-Ed.

Masten, A. S., Best, K. M., & Garmezy, N. (1990). Resilience and development: Contributions from the study of children who overcome adversity. *Development and Psychopathology*, 2, 425–444.

McCarthy, H. (1995). Understanding and reversing rehabilitation counseling's neglect of spirituality. *Rehabilitation Education*, 9(2–3), 187–199.

McCarthy, H. (2003). The disability rights movement: Experiences and perspectives of selected leaders in the disability community. *Rehabilitation Counseling Bulletin, 46*(4), 209–223.

McCarthy, H. (2007). Incorporating spirituality into rehabilitation counseling and coping with disability. In O. Morgan (Ed.), *Counseling and spirituality: Views from the profession* (pp. 202–229). Boston, MA: Lahaska Press, Houghton Mifflin.

McCarthy, H. (2011). A modest Festschrift and insider perspective on Beatrice Wright's contributions to rehabilitation theory and practice. *Rehabilitation Counseling Bulletin, 54*(2), 67–81.

McCarthy, H. (2014). Cultivating our roots and extending our branches: Appreciating and marketing rehabilitation theory and research. *Rehabilitation Counseling Bulletin, 57*(2), 67–79.

McLaren, N. (1998). A critical review of the biopsychosocial model. *Australian and New Zealand Journal of Psychiatry, 32*(1), 86–92.

McMahon, B. T., & Shaw, L. (2000). *Enabling lives: Biographies of six prominent Americans with disabilities.* Boca Raton, FL: CRC Press.

Mijares, S. G. (2014). *Modern psychology and ancient wisdom: Psychological healing practices from the world's religious traditions* (2nd ed.). New York, NY: Routledge, Taylor & Francis.

Millington, M. J. (2016). Community-based rehabilitation: Context for counseling. In I. Marini & M. Stebnicki (Eds.), *The professional counselor's desk reference* (pp. 111–116). New York, NY: Springer Publishing.

Molina, J. A. (1983). Understanding the biopsychosocial model. *International Journal of Psychiatry in Medicine, 13,* 29–36.

Moos, R. H. (1974). *Evaluating treatment environments: A social-ecological approach.* New York, NY: Wiley-Interscience.

Moos, R. H. (1979). Social–ecological perspectives on health. In G. C. Stone, F. Cohen, & N. E. Adler (Eds.), *Health psychology: A handbook* (pp. 259–275). San Francisco, CA: Jossey-Bass.

Myers, J. E., & Sweeney, T. J. (2008). Wellness counseling: The evidence base for practice. *Journal of Counseling and Development, 86*(4), 482–493.

Myers, J. E., Sweeney, T. J., & Witmer, J. M. (2000). The wheel of wellness, counseling for wellness: A holistic model for treatment planning. *Journal of Counseling and Development, 78*(3), 251–266.

Nosek, M., & Hughes, R. (2001). Psychospiritual aspects of sense of self in women with physical disabilities. *Journal of Rehabilitation, 67*(1), 20–25.

Null, R. L. (2014). *Universal design: Principles and models.* Boca Raton, FL: CRC Press.

Olkin, R. (2016). Disability-affirmative therapy. In I. Marini & M. Stebnicki (Eds.), *The professional counselor's desk reference* (pp. 215–223). New York, NY: Springer Publishing Company.

Pelka, F. (2012). *What we have done: An oral history of the disability rights movement.* Amherst: University of Massachusetts Press.

Peterson, D. B. (2016). The international classification of functioning, disability & health: Applications for professional counseling. In I. Marini & M. Stebnicki (Eds.), *The Professional counselor's desk reference* (2nd ed., pp. 329–336). New York, NY: Springer Publishing.

Putnam, M. (2005). Conceptualizing disability: Developing a framework for political disability identity. *Journal of Disability Policy Studies, 16*(3), 188–198.

Rice, K., & Pollack, S. (2000). Developing a critical pedagogy of service learning: Preparing self-reflective, culturally aware, and responsive community participants. In C. O'Grady (Ed.), *Integrating service learning and multicultural education in colleges and universities* (pp. 115–134). Mahwah, NJ: Lawrence Erlbaum.

Riddell, S., & Watson, N. (2003). *Disability, culture and identity.* New York, NY: Routledge, Taylor & Francis.

Rubin, S., & Roessler, R. (1978). *Foundations of the vocational rehabilitation process.* Baltimore, MD: University Park Press.

Rucker, A. (2016, April). Is ad land really changing? *New Mobility, 27,* 26–31.

Scherer, M., & Craddock, G. (2002). The assessment of assistive technology outcomes, effects and costs. *Technology and Disability, 14*(3), 125–131.

Schrader, S., Jones, N., & Shattell, M. (2013). Mad pride: Reflections on sociopolitical identity and mental diversity in the context of culturally competent psychiatric care. *Issues in Mental Health Nursing, 34,* 62–64.

Schriner, K., & Scotch, R. K. (2001). Disability and institutional change: A human variation perspective on overcoming oppression. *Journal of Disability Policy Studies, 12*(2), 100–106.

Scotch, R. K. (1988). Disability as the basis for a social movement: Advocacy and the politics of definition. *Journal of Social Issues, 44,* 159–172.

Smart, J. F., & Smart, D. W. (2006). Models of disability: Implications for the counseling profession. *Journal of Counseling and Development, 84*(1), 29–40.

Sontag, S. (1978). *Illness as metaphor.* New York, NY: Farrar, Straus & Giroux.

Sontag, S. (1989). *AIDS and its metaphors*. New York, NY: Farrar, Straus & Giroux.

Stebnicki, M. (2016). Integrative approaches in counseling and psychotherapy: Foundations of mind, body, and spirit. In I. Marini & M. A. Stebnicki (Eds.), *The Professional counselor's desk reference* (2nd ed., pp. 593–604). New York, NY: Springer Publishing.

Stubbins, J. (1988). The politics of disability. In H. E. Yuker (Ed.), *Attitudes toward persons with disabilities* (pp. 22–32). New York, NY: Springer Publishing.

Szymanski, E. (1998). Career development, school-to-work transition, and diversity: An ecological approach. In F. Rusch & J. Chadsey (Eds.), *Beyond high school: Transition from school to work* (pp. 127–145). Belmont, CA: Wadsworth.

Szymanski, E., Parker, R. M., & Patterson, J. B. (2012). Beyond the basics: The sociopolitical context of rehabilitation counseling practice. In R. M. Parker & J. B. Patterson (Eds.), *Rehabilitation counseling: Basics and beyond* (5th ed., pp. 369–384). Austin, TX: Pro-Ed.

Szymanski, E., & Trueba, H. T. (1994). Castification of people with disabilities: Potential disempowering aspects of classification in disability services. *Journal of Rehabilitation, 60*(3), 12–20.

Tarvydas, V., Addy, A., & Fleming, A. (2010). Reconciling evidence-based research practice with rehabilitation philosophy, ethics and practice: From dichotomy to dialectic. *Rehabilitation Education, 24*(3–4), 191–204.

Travability. (2011). Occasional Paper No. 4: An economic model of disability. Retrieved from http://travability.travel/Articles/economic_model_3.pdf

Umeasiegbu, V. I., Bishop, M., & Mpofu, E. (2013). The conventional and unconventional about disability conventions: A reflective analysis of United Nations Convention on the Rights of Persons with Disabilities. *Rehabilitation Research, Policy, and Education, 27*(1), 58–72.

Uniform Data System for Medical Rehabilitation. (1997). *Guide for the use of the uniform data set for medical rehabilitation, Version 5.0*. Buffalo: State University of New York at Buffalo Research Foundation.

Vash, C. L. (1994). *Personality and adversity: Psychospiritual aspects of rehabilitation*. New York, NY: Springer Publishing.

Vash, C. L. (2004). Viewing disability through differing lenses: Medical political, and psychological. *Rehabilitation Counseling Bulletin, 47*(4), 247–250.

Vash, C. L., & Crewe, N. M. (2004). *Psychology of disability* (2nd ed.). New York, NY: Springer Publishing.

Witmer, J. M., & Sweeney, T. J. (1992). A holistic model for wellness and prevention over the life span. *Journal of Counseling and Development, 71*(2), 140–148.

World Health Organization. (2001). *ICF: International classification of functioning, disability, and health*. Geneva, Switzerland: Author.

Wright, B. A. (Ed.). (1959). *Psychology and rehabilitation*. Washington, DC: American Psychological Association.

Wright, B. A. (1960). *Physical disability: A psychological approach*. New York, NY: Harper & Row.

Wright, B. A. (1983). *Physical disability: A psychosocial approach*. New York, NY: Harper & Row.

Wright, B. A. (1987). Human dignity and professional self-monitoring. *Journal of Applied Rehabilitation Counseling, 18*(4), 12–14.

Wright, B. A. (1988). Attitudes and the fundamental negative bias: Conditions and corrections. In H. E. Yuker (Ed.), *Attitudes toward persons with disabilities* (pp. 3–21). New York, NY: Springer Publishing.

Wright, B. A., & Lopez, S. J. (2005). Widening the diagnostic focus: A case for including human strengths and environmental resources. In C. R. Snyder & S. J. Lopez (Eds.), *Handbook of positive psychology* (pp. 26–44). New York, NY: Oxford University Press.

Wright, G. (1980). *Total rehabilitation*. Boston, MA: Little, Brown.

SIX

Disability Policy and Law

SUSANNE M. BRUYÈRE AND MATTHEW C. SALEH

LEARNING OBJECTIVES

After reading this chapter, you should be able to:

- Recognize the array of laws that govern and impact the provision of vocational rehabilitation (VR) services.
- Understand the specific provisions of laws related to improved employment outcomes for people with disabilities.
- Consider the implications of this legislation for VR counseling, practice, training, and research.

Although counseling focuses on the one-on-one relationship between the counselor and the client, services are provided within a context of state and national legislation and regulation that can have a significant influence. As well as being motivators for both service provider and recipient, service availability and outcomes are governed and influenced by a myriad of individual intersecting laws. The purpose of this chapter is to identify a selection of these laws, discuss their provisions, and know why these might be of interest to counselors—particularly those providing services to people with disabilities. Implications for the counseling profession, specifically the specialization of rehabilitation counseling, are presented as well. Employment is the focus in this chapter, as work is a means to economic and social independence, as well as to enhanced personal self-confidence and community participation. Access to employment for people with disabilities is a significant key to building a more inclusive society, one that not only contributes to an individual's economic self-sufficiency, but also enables that individual to have a higher quality of life (QOL).

Because improved employment outcomes are a primary focus of rehabilitation counseling, this chapter concentrates on laws that support and intersect with employment for people with disabilities. This is a worthy focus, as people with disabilities remain significantly disadvantaged in the employment arena. The ability to work and earn a living is an important contributing factor to individual overall QOL and economic independence, and many of the laws discussed in this chapter are designed to protect and increase opportunities for meaningful and safe employment. People with disabilities experience half the employment participation rates of those without disabilities. In 2014, an estimated 34.6% of noninstitutionalized working-age (21–64) people with a disability—regardless of gender, race, ethnicity, or education level—were employed, compared to 77.6% of those without disabilities (Erickson, Lee, & von Schrader, 2016). This translates to significant economic disparities: In 2014, the median annual income for households with at least one working-age person with a disability was $40,200, compared to $64,100 for households that do not have any person with disability (Erickson et al., 2016). Lower median household income translates to a significantly higher percentage of people with disabilities in the United States living below the poverty line (28.1% compared to 12.2% of those without disabilities) (Erickson et al., 2016).

The following laws have been selected for discussion in this chapter because of their relevance to employment and people with disabilities and therefore of importance to rehabilitation counseling practice: the Rehabilitation Act of 1973 as amended, the Americans with Disabilities Act (ADA) of 1990 as amended, the Family and Medical Leave Act (FMLA), the Uniformed Services Employment and Reemployment Rights Act (USERRA), Vietnam Era Veterans Readjustment Assistance Act (VEVRAA), the Workforce Innovation and Opportunity Act (WIOA) of 2014 and its predecessor the Workforce Investment Act (WIA) of 1998, the Ticket to Work and Work Incentives Improvement Act (TWWIIA), workers' compensation laws, the Health Insurance Portability and Accountability Act (HIPAA), the Genetic Information Nondiscrimination Act (GINA), and the Patient Protection and Affordable Care Act of 2010 (ACA).

These laws span more than 40 years, including important recent developments. Readers will learn about workplace disability nondiscrimination requirements in both public and private work settings, disability disclosure and confidentiality issues in employment, specific employment protections afforded to veterans with disabilities, service delivery systems, and emerging issues such as genetic testing and health care considerations as they intersect with VR systems.

OVERVIEW OF SELECT DISABILITY LAWS

Rehabilitation Act of 1973

Vocational Rehabilitation

Title I of the Rehabilitation Act, as modified by the 1992 and 1998 amendments and by the WIOA of 2014, deals with the state-federal VR system, which provides employment support to individuals with disabilities. The goal of this federal law is to assist states with the operation of "comprehensive, coordinated, effective, efficient, and accountable" VR programs (29 U.S.C. § 720(a)(2)). These programs involve both public and private sector services, including vocational assessment, career counseling, job training, job development and placement, assistive technology, supported employment, and follow-along services. In the event that state resources are not sufficient to serve all eligible parties, the Rehabilitation Act mandates that states first provide services to those individuals with the most significant disabilities. Although state VR agencies have discretion in determining which conditions constitute **most significant disabilities**, this term generally refers to individuals with "a severe physical or mental impairment that seriously limits one or more functional capacities (such as mobility, communication, self-care, self-direction, interpersonal skills, work tolerance, or work skills) . . . whose vocational rehabilitation can be expected to require multiple [VR] services over an extended period of time" (34 C.F.R. § 361.5(c)(30)).

Every year, the state and federal VR program serves approximately 1.2 million individuals with disabilities and places approximately 230,000 consumers into competitive employment (Rehabilitation Services Administration, 2016). The funding for the VR service delivery system was more than $3.7 billion in federal fiscal year 2013 (Institute on Disability, 2015).

The 2014 WIOA amendments to Title I of the Rehabilitation Act included the replacement of the preference for preparing people with disabilities for "gainful employment" with a preference for "competitive integrated employment" (§ 100(a)(2)). Under the new definitions implemented by WIOA, all individuals with disabilities are presumed to be employable. Placement in a competitive integrated employment setting at a prevailing wage rate for at least 90 days is considered a successful final outcome in the Act.

Previously, certain uncompensated vocational outcomes, including homemaker and unpaid family worker, were accepted as legitimate VR closures for individuals deemed unable to seek competitive employment. The new final regulations for WIOA have eliminated uncompensated employment as a successful outcome for state VR systems, and place significant limitations on the payment of subminimum wages to workers with disabilities (U.S. Department of Education, 2014, 2016). In place of such outcomes, the Final Rule incorporated additional new outcome targets involving supported and customized employment alternatives into the definition of VR employment outcomes.

Other important amendments included initiatives to further integrate VR programs and workforce development systems, common outcomes measures across VR programs to ensure accountability, new focus on "transition" VR services for youth with disabilities, and efforts to allocate program funding toward "21st-century" work-based learning needs. WIOA introduced accountability measures for programs covered under the Act, including accountability measures related to the program participant rates of unsubsidized employment, median earnings, postsecondary credentials and secondary diplomas, participation in skills training programs leading to postsecondary credential or employment, and core program effectiveness in serving employers (§ 116(a)(2)).

Employment Discrimination

Title V of the Rehabilitation Act of 1973 is the precursor to modern disability law as codified in the ADA, prohibiting discrimination against people with disabilities in the federal employment sector (Rubin & Roessler, 2001). Here, we discuss a few of the sections in Title V, which prohibit employment discrimination by federal agencies, contractors, and programs. The topic of nondiscrimination in private employment will be covered in the subsequent sections discussing Title I of the ADA. The Rehabilitation Act's standards for determining what constitutes employment discrimination mirror those of the ADA, and are discussed at length in the next section.

Section 501 of the Rehabilitation Act requires affirmative action and nondiscrimination by executive branch agencies. Section 503 requires the same for federal contractors and subcontractors, applying generally to federal contracts of $10,000 or more, whereas contractors with 50 or more employees and contracts of $50,000 or more are required to implement compliant affirmative action programs. Section 504 prohibits exclusion, discrimination, and/or denial of benefits in activities or programs receiving federal financial assistance or administered by an executive agency (including duty to accommodate, program accessibility, effective communication mediums, and accessible new construction and alterations). Section 508 provides accessibility standards and guidelines for federal agencies in the development, procurement, maintenance, and use of electronic and information technologies. Although Title V of the Rehabilitation Act is important for prohibiting discrimination on the basis of disability by the federal government, federal contractors, and recipients of federal financial assistance, it also served as a valuable model for Title II of the ADA, which extended these protections to state- and local government-funded programs.

In August 2013, new final regulations were released for Section 503 of the Rehabilitation Act, establishing a nationwide "aspirational goal" of 7% for federal contractors and subcontractors hiring people with disabilities. Although not a quota, the new goal requires appropriate outreach and recruitment activities, along with data collection, reporting, and accountability measures for demonstrating effective outreach activities (Rudstam et al., 2014). The new 503 regulations coincided with new rules for the VEVRAA, which similarly set an annual hiring benchmark of 8% for hiring veterans in disability categories, adjusted for regional and industry-specific workforce demographics. VEVRAA and other veteran employment legislation are discussed later in this chapter.

To aid affirmative action, the 503 regulations require contractors to invite applicants to self-identify as having a disability during the pre- and postoffer phases, using a standardized U.S. Department of Labor (DOL), Office of Federal Contract Compliance Programs (OFCCP, 2016) form. Self-identification must be completely voluntary and no penalty may be imposed for nondisclosure. All records of disclosure must remain confidential and separate from other personnel records. Moreover, disclosure information may not be used for hiring, promotion, or termination decisions, but rather is for the sole purpose of aggregate assessment of employer outreach, recruitment, employment, and accessibility efforts. The U.S. Equal Employment Opportunity Commission (EEOC) released specific guidance clarifying that this "invitation to self-identify" does not violate the ADA's restrictions on pre- and postoffer medical inquiries so long as it is used for affirmative action rather than hiring and employment decisions (EEOC, 2015).

Despite the new regulatory framework, disability disclosure remains a complex issue for employers and employees alike: common barriers to employee self-identification include perceived risk of being fired, losing health care benefits, limiting promotion opportunities, unsupportive management, and risk of being treated or viewed differently by coworkers and supervisors (von Schrader, Malzer, & Bruyère, 2013).

Americans With Disabilities Act of 1990

The ADA is the seminal piece of federal legislation addressing disability in the workplace. While passing the ADA in 1990, the U.S. Congress called attention to the fact that approximately 43 million Americans had one or more physical or mental disabilities, a number that was expected only to escalate as the age of the U.S. population continued to increase (42 U.S.C. § 12101). By 2010, this figure had risen to an estimated 56.7 million people—19% of the total U.S. population (U.S. Census Bureau, 2012). The ADA reached out to the millions of Americans working in nonfederal employment and extended to them the protections enjoyed by federal employees.

Definition of Disability

Title I of the ADA provides that no covered employer shall discriminate against a qualified individual with a disability on the basis of his or her disability with respect to job application procedures, hiring, advancement, compensation, job training, or other privileges of employment. The definition of **disability** in the ADA mirrors that contained in the Rehabilitation Act: "(1) a physical or mental impairment that substantially limits one or more of the major life activities of such individual, (2) a record of such an impairment, or (3) being regarded as having such an impairment" (42 U.S.C. § 12102(1)).

Regarding the phrase **major life activities**, the ADA specifically includes functions such as caring for oneself, performing manual tasks, walking, seeing, hearing, breathing, speaking, learning, reading, concentrating, communicating, and thinking. A major life activity also includes the operation of a major bodily function, such as the functions of the immune system, normal cell growth, and the functions of the respiratory, circulatory, endocrine, or neurological systems—to name a few examples (42 U.S.C. § 12102). The ADA Amendments Act (ADAAA) broadened the definition of "major life activities" in a number of ways, including adding the **major bodily functions** category, providing a nonexhaustive list of both major life activities and major bodily functions, and prohibiting consideration of the ameliorative effects of **mitigating measures** (e.g., medication, assistive technologies) in determining whether an individual meets the definition of disability under the law (U.S. Department of Labor, Office of Federal Contract Compliance Programs, 2016). The one exception to the "mitigating measures" rule is the use of eyeglasses or contact lenses, the ameliorative effects of which may be considered.

In order for an impairment to qualify as an ADA disability, it must substantially limit a major life activity or bodily function, meaning that the individual is unable to perform—or is significantly limited in the ability to perform—the function or activity as compared with an average person in the general population. One cannot consider mitigating measures when determining whether an impairment substantially limits a major life activity. Thus, an individual who ameliorates the effects of his or her impairment with medication, and as a result experiences few symptoms of the impairment while taking the medication, would nevertheless have an ADA disability if, among other things, the impairment substantially limits a major life activity or bodily function in its unmitigated state.

The definition of disability under the ADA initially proved problematic, with the U.S. Supreme Court issuing a series of opinions that dramatically changed the way the ADA is interpreted and who qualified as a person with a disability under the Act, limiting the broad meaning intended by the legislature (National Council on Disability, 2004). In response to the Court's limitations, Congress passed the ADAAA of 2008, which explicitly rejected the narrow judicial constructions of the ADA in favor of the broad coverage that was the original intent of the Act (EEOC, 2008). Although the ADAAA retained the basic definition of disability from the ADA, it specifically overturned judicial holdings that narrowed the definition of disability and overemphasized the effect of mitigating measures such as medications or assistive devices in determining whether an individual meets the definition of having a disability (EEOC, 2011).

Subsequent empirical analysis of ADAAA litigation outcomes found that summary judgments for employers on the basis of a lack of disability status were down significantly since the passage of the ADAAA (Befort, 2013). However, the study also demonstrated that an increase in rulings that an individual is not "qualified for" employment had occurred since passage of the ADAAA, seeming to indicate that judicial unease with disability discrimination and with reasonable accommodation claims persist nonetheless (Befort, 2013).

Determining Who Is Qualified to Work

In addition to having a disability as defined, individuals must be **otherwise qualified** for the position in question—with or without reasonable accommodation. If an applicant or employee cannot perform an essential function of the job, even with reasonable accommodation, then the ADA does not apply and the individual in question is not protected against discrimination. In other words, the ADA does not obligate employers to hire, promote, or provide any other privilege of employment to an individual who simply cannot perform the essential functions of the job. Nevertheless, this requirement protects the employee or applicant against an employer that might otherwise screen out individuals with disabilities based on stereotypes regarding those persons' abilities. Ideally, if employers base their employment decisions on the essential functions of the job rather than marginalized ones, they should be able to determine whether or not an individual is truly qualified for the position at issue.

Essential functions are those that are not marginal tasks. A job function may be essential if (a) the position exists solely for the performance of such function, (b) there are a limited number of employees available among whom the job function can be distributed and shared, or (c) the function is highly specialized and the employee was hired specifically because of his or her expertise.

Reasonable Accommodation

Provided that an individual who is otherwise qualified for a position has a mental or physical impairment that substantially limits a major life activity, then the ADA obligates the employer to reasonably accommodate him or her (42 U.S.C. § 12112). An employer therefore engages in **unlawful discrimination** if (a) the employer fails to provide reasonable accommodation to a qualified individual with a disability, and (b) that failure denies the applicant or employee an employment opportunity.

A **reasonable accommodation** is any modification or adjustment to a job, employment practice, or work environment that makes it possible for a qualified individual with a disability to participate in the job application process, perform the essential functions of a job, and/or enjoy benefits and privileges of employment equal to those enjoyed by similarly situated employees without disabilities (EEOC, 2002). Examples of reasonable accommodations include job restructuring, workspace modification, modifying work schedules or instituting flexible work schedules, providing adaptive or assistive equipment, and modifying the job application process or company policies.

Generally, the applicant or employee bears the burden of notifying the employer of the need for accommodation, whether in writing or in the course of conversation. In some circumstances, however, the employer should initiate the process of determining a reasonable accommodation. Specifically, employers should inquire whether an accommodation is necessary when they know that the employee's or applicant's disability exists, and know or have reason to know that the disability is causing problems in the workplace and that it also is preventing the employee or applicant from requesting any accommodation.

The ADAAA and its accompanying regulations reaffirmed that the duty to provide reasonable accommodations applies to only two of the **three qualifying prongs** for meeting the definition of disability ("actual" or "record of" disability, but not "regarded as" having a disability; EEOC, 2011). Under the "regarded as" prong, an employee may be perceived by an employer as having a disability even where there is no actual qualifying impairment or "record of" that employee having a disability. Although being "regarded as" indicates a disability that meets the ADA definition of disability, the accompanying protections apply primarily to issues of employment discrimination (e.g., failure to hire, termination, failure to promote, harassment, and so forth). An employee who meets the definition of disability under the "regarded as" prong is entitled to ADA protections but is usually not entitled to reasonable accommodations under the Act (EEOC, 2011).

Undue Hardship

The duty of an employer to provide reasonable accommodation is limited by the doctrine of **undue hardship**, which means significant difficulty or expense to the employer (42 U.S.C. § 12112). When determining whether a proposed accommodation would constitute an undue hardship, the employer examines factors such as its financial resources, its size, and the impact that the proposed accommodation would have on the operation of the facility. As one might imagine, employers often identify cost as the source of undue hardship (Olsheski & Schelat, 2003, p. 64). When this is the case, the employer should grant the employee or applicant the option of contributing the burdensome portion of that accommodation cost. This arrangement preserves the employment opportunity for the employee or applicant while bringing the employer's cost of accommodation within a reasonable price range.

Input from rehabilitation counseling professionals can be an integral part of the accommodation process. "The most successful accommodations are not developed when the employer operates independently of all others. Rather, they tend to be the product of the efforts of many individuals, including supervisors, union officials, health care workers, rehabilitation counseling professionals, occupational therapists, physical therapists, and ergonomists, among others" (Olsheski & Schelat, 2003, p. 65). Ideally, the accommodation process is one of give and take among the employer, the employee or applicant, and the relevant professionals. If there is more than one potential reasonable accommodation, the employer may select which one to implement.

Direct Threat

The ADA does allow an employer to exclude from employment any individual who poses a "direct threat" to workplace safety or to health (42 U.S.C. § 12113(b)). A **direct threat** is a significant, as opposed to slightly increased, risk of substantial harm to the health or safety of the individual or others that cannot be eliminated or reduced by reasonable accommodation (EEOC, 1997). This determination depends on an assessment of the present ability of the employee or applicant to perform job functions, taking into account reasonable medical opinion based on the best available medical knowledge or other objective evidence. The employer should consider the following factors and apply them equally to all employees and applicants, regardless of disability, when determining the presence of a direct threat: (a) the duration of the risk, (b) the nature and severity of the potential harm, (c) the likelihood that the potential harm will occur, and (d) the imminence of the potential harm (EEOC, 1997).

Medical Testing

The ADA limits the use of pre- and postemployment medical examinations and inquiries as an additional means of preventing employers from basing employment decisions on disability-related stereotypes (42 U.S.C. § 12111). During the initial application stage, an employer may ask any applicant about his or her professional qualifications for the job and/or ability to perform the essential functions of the job, but may not ask any questions regarding the applicant's health, medical history, or history of workers' compensation claims (Rubin & Roessler, 2001). For example, questions with respect to the number of days an applicant was absent in a prior job due to illness or whether the applicant is taking any prescription medication would be prohibited. In addition, no medical examination of any kind is allowed during the preemployment stage. Examinations that are not medical, per se, such as the measurement of an applicant's performance of relevant physical criteria would be allowed, provided that medical measurements such as blood pressure and heart rate are not obtained during or after such test (Rubin & Roessler, 2001).

Acknowledging that it is not always easy to determine whether an examination or inquiry is *medical*, the U.S. EEOC provided guidance outlining certain considerations in making this determination, including whether it is administered by, or has results interpreted by, a health care professional or someone trained by a health care professional; it is given in a medical setting or uses medical equipment; it is designed to reveal an impairment to physical or mental health; the employer is trying to determine the applicant's physical or mental health or impairments; it is invasive (e.g., drawing of blood, urine, or breath); it measures an applicant's physiological responses to performing the task (EEOC, n.d.-b).

Once the employer has extended an offer of employment to the applicant, however, the employer may condition such offer upon a medical exam or responses to medical inquiries, provided that such exams or inquiries are required for all entering candidates in that job category. If the employer screens out an applicant due to the presence of a disability, it must show that such decision was "job-related and consistent with business necessity" (42 U.S.C. § 12112(d)). The ADA provides that employers must keep any employee medical information or medical histories that it receives in separate medical files and treat all such information as a confidential medical record (42 U.S.C. § 12112; EEOC, n.d.-a). More than 10 million workers sign authorizations every year, before the commencement of their employment, for the release of medical records (Rothstein & Talbott, 2007).

It is useful to note that the GINA of 2008, discussed later in this chapter, provides additional prohibitions against medical inquiries by employers (such as requests for family medical history), and prohibits employers from requesting, requiring, or purchasing medical records or personal/family medical data (§ 202(a)–(b)) (EEOC, 2013).

Corresponding state disability law

Although Title I of the ADA applies only to employers having 15 or more employees, disability nondiscrimination legislation enacted by states may be more expansive. For example, New York (N.Y. Exec. Law § 292), California (Cal. Gov. Code § 12926), and other states have passed disability nondiscrimination legislation applicable to employers having fewer than 15 employees. Therefore, individuals who would be unable to file a claim against an employer under the ADA due to the small size of the employer's business should determine whether their claim is nevertheless viable under state law. Rehabilitation counselors (RCs) should familiarize themselves with the disability laws that are applicable in the states in which they practice.

Accommodating Individuals With Psychiatric Disabilities

The prevalence of mental disorder in the United States is quite high: In any given year, approximately one in four Americans is affected by a mental disorder, or about 61.5 million people (National Alliance on Mental Illness [NAMI], 2013; National Institutes of Health, n.d). The labor force participation rate of individuals with mental health disabilities has consistently lagged behind not only that of employees without disabilities, but also that of all employees with a disability in general. According to the 2002 National Health Interview Survey (NHIS) data, the employment rate of people aged 25 to 61 with mental illness was 37.1%—lower than that of people with physical impairments (43.8%) and those with sensory impairments (58.6%). A more recent analysis estimated an approximately 80% unemployment rate for Americans with mental health disabilities (NAMI, 2014). For comparison, in 2013 the employment rate for working-age people (21–65) with "any disability" was 34.5%, whereas the rate for people without any disability was 76.8% (Erickson et al., 2016). Not surprisingly, the workplace accommodation of individuals with psychiatric disabilities presents unique issues and leads to unique problems that merit separate discussion.

The ADA accommodation process encourages employers and employees to share information with each another. The employer has the right to request information regarding the nature of that disability so that it may make an informed decision regarding the accommodation request. Because psychiatric disabilities are often invisible or episodic, the employer may need to ask more questions and/or require reasonable documentation in order to determine an appropriate accommodation. Employees are encouraged to communicate with their employer in order to assist the employer in selecting the most effective accommodation. These forces, which strongly favor the disclosure of information regarding a psychiatric disability, run counter to an opposing force: the stigma of having a psychiatric disability. That stigma could cause the employer to assume, often incorrectly, that the individual with a psychiatric disability poses a significant risk to the health and safety of other individuals in the workplace, due in part to stereotypical beliefs about the association of psychiatric disability and violent behavior (Rubin & Roessler, 2001).

Some of the legal complexities related to preventing workplace discrimination for individuals with mental health disabilities include the episodic nature of many mental health conditions, the frequently shifting professional consensus on what constitutes a mental health condition, and the legal inconsistencies in the duty to accommodate where employers are unaware of the existence of a disability (Kaminer, 2016). Faced with the stigma of psychiatric disability, some rehabilitation counseling professionals have advised clients against disclosing prior hospitalizations to employers (Campbell, 1994). This would prevent an employee from obtaining ADA accommodation, however, because employers need not provide any accommodation for individuals with disabilities of which the employer is unaware (42 U.S.C. § 12112).

In contrast, the ADA confidentiality provisions forestall employers from sharing any information regarding an employee's psychiatric condition with fellow workers. If coworkers question the employer about an individual with a psychiatric disability, employers may not disclose that they are providing a reasonable accommodation to any particular individual, and they should state instead that they are "acting for legitimate business reasons or in compliance with federal law" (EEOC, 1997). In that respect, an employee need not be concerned that the opinion of his or her coworkers will be influenced by knowledge of his or her psychiatric condition.

Family and Medical Leave Act

The FMLA (29 U.S.C. §§ 2601–2654), which went into effect in 1993, allows eligible employees up to 12 weeks of leave for family or medical reasons during any 12-month period. Its purpose is different from that of the ADA, in that the FMLA seeks to provide reasonable leave opportunities for all eligible employees, rather than focusing on creating equal employment opportunities for qualified employees (Lipnic & DeCamp, 2007). An employee may have a condition, however, that qualifies him or her for FMLA leave, and leave may be a reasonable accommodation under the ADA. As such, rehabilitation counseling professionals must strive to understand both the manner in which these two statutes overlap and the manner in which they appear, at times, to conflict.

The FMLA applies to fewer employers than the ADA—only those employers with 50 or more employees rather than 15 or more. It specifically allows 12 weeks of unpaid leave for any one or more of the following reasons: the birth of a child; the care of a newborn child; the placement of a child with the employee through adoption or foster care and the care of such child; the care of the employee's spouse, son, daughter, or parent with a serious health condition; or a serious health condition of the employee that causes the employee to be incapable of performing one or more of the essential functions of his or her job. The FMLA also allows 26 weeks of unpaid leave for employee's next of kin who is a member of the Armed Forces (including the National Guard or Reserves) or, in some cases, a veteran who is undergoing medical treatment, recuperation, or therapy; is otherwise in outpatient status; or is otherwise on the temporary disability retired list for a serious injury or illness.

FMLA **serious health conditions** are illnesses, injuries, impairments, or physical or mental conditions that involve inpatient care or continuing treatment by a health care provider. FMLA serious health conditions and ADA disabilities are not mutually exclusive categories. If an employee must visit a doctor twice and stay out of work for 4 days due to an illness, the FMLA applies (Postol, 2002). By contrast, a condition must normally be long term and substantially limiting with respect to a major life activity to constitute an ADA disability (Postol, 2002). Although under the ADA an employer has no obligation to provide an accommodation if it would impose an "undue burden," such is not the case with FMLA leave.

An employer who desires to know the medical reason behind the requested leave may, in accordance with the FMLA, request evidence of the employee's "serious health condition" by means of an FMLA certification form (U.S. Department of Labor, 2009a). This form seeks information pertaining solely to the health condition that is the basis for the leave request. ADA medical inquiries are limited by a different standard—that is, the inquiry must be job related and consistent with business necessity. The EEOC has noted that an employer medical inquiry using the FMLA certification form will not violate the ADA medical inquiry standard (EEOC, 2000). Regardless, a more recent study has revealed employer problems in this area, as some employers grant FMLA requests that they deem to be of questionable reliability without additional inquiry out of fear of violating employee rights under the ADA (Lipnic & DeCamp, 2007).

Many issues also have arisen with respect to the option of light-duty work. Under the FMLA, an employer may offer light-duty work as an option in lieu of or in addition to leave, but may not compel the employee to select light-duty work. Some employers may perceive this as an obstacle to the employee's return to work. If the employee selects a light-duty option, the time spent doing that work does not count against his or her FLMA leave entitlement (Lipnic & DeCamp, 2007). In contrast, under the ADA, an employer may offer light-duty work as a reasonable accommodation for an injured worker who is returning to work. Any employee who accepts such accommodation, and who also possesses rights under the FMLA with respect to a serious health condition, reserves the FMLA right to be restored to the same or an equivalent position to that which he or she held at the commencement of the leave period.

The FMLA was amended in 2008 to clarify the rights of military personnel and their families to take and use FMLA leave (U.S. Department of Labor, 2009b). The new regulations specifically incorporated additional military family leave entitlements, including up to 26 weeks of leave during a 12-month period to care for a covered service member recovering from a serious injury or illness incurred in the line of duty on active duty

(U.S. Department of Labor, 2009b). In 2013, additional regulations were issued clarifying that the definition of a "serious injury or illness" was expanded to include injuries or illnesses existing before the beginning of active duty, but aggravated during military service (U.S. Department of Labor, Wages and Hours Division, 2013).

Veterans Employment Legislation

Veterans have enjoyed reemployment rights since the creation of the Selective Training and Service Act of 1940. In 1994, however, the U.S. Congress passed the USERRA, which is now the principal statute dealing with the employment and reemployment of members of the uniformed services (38 U.S.C. §§ 4301–4334). Although many provisions of USERRA are similar to those that were included in the 1940 law (Quinn, 2005), USERRA provides broader coverage in order to encourage noncareer service in the military by minimizing disadvantages to civilian careers, minimizing the disruption of the lives of service members and their employers' businesses by facilitating prompt job reinstatement, and reducing discrimination on the basis of service in the military (38 U.S.C. § 4301(a)).

More specifically, USERRA requires that employers must give employees time off from work for active military duty, prohibits employers from discriminating against employees or applicants based on military service, and provides that employers must reinstate their employees returning from up to 5 years of leave for service in the uniformed services—subject to certain limitations. Employers must also restore all benefits to their returning service members, treating time spent on leave as time worked. Finally, employers cannot fire returning service members without good cause for up to 1 year after their return from active duty.

USERRA is applicable to every employer, whether private or public. Even foreign businesses incorporated abroad must comply with USERRA if a U.S. employer controls the foreign business. With respect to veterans, those who separate from a uniformed service under other than honorable conditions will not be eligible for USERRA privileges and protections.

According to the U.S. Bureau of Labor Statistics (BLS, 2016), in August 2015 approximately 4.3 million veterans had a service-related disability, including 33% of Gulf War Era II Veterans, and about 20% of all veterans. Despite legislative efforts to support and promote the employment and reemployment of American veterans via USERRA, veterans have experienced unemployment rates close to those of nonveterans in recent years (U.S. Department of Labor, 2010). This may be due, in part, to the inadequate knowledge of USERRA on the part of the employers, the employees, or both (U.S. General Accounting Office, 2005). Rehabilitation counseling professionals should be aware of the expansive protections available to veterans under USERRA in order to best advise clients and employers regarding the rights of veterans with disabilities.

In 2010, Congress passed the Veterans Benefits Act, which provided additional benefits and programs aimed at enhancing employment opportunities and small business programs, among other initiatives, and clarified USERRA's prohibition of wage discrimination against veterans.

Additionally, the VEVRAA prohibits federal contractors and subcontractors from engaging in employment discrimination against protected veterans, and requires affirmative action steps in the recruitment, hiring, promotion, and retention of veterans. In August 2013, the U.S. DOL published new regulations for VEVRAA. Although VEVRAA provisions previously applied to all federal contracts and subcontracts of $25,000 or more, the new regulations updated the rule, so it now applies only to contracts of $100,000 or more. The new regulations require federal contractors to establish annual hiring benchmarks for protected veterans using benchmark data provided by the OFCCP's "Benchmark Database" (https://ofccp.dol-esa.gov/errd/VEVRAA.jsp). Under the new regulations, contractors must invite applicants to self-identify as protected veterans at the preoffer and postoffer phases.

Workforce Investment Act (1998) and Workforce Innovation and Opportunity Act (2014)

Although the WIOA of 2014 overrides its predecessor, the WIA of 1998, it is important to provide an overview of WIA for context.

WIA was a continuation and improvement of the VR services portion of the Rehabilitation Act. The goal of WIA was to require states to coordinate federally funded employment and training services, including those in Title V of the Rehabilitation Act, into a single, comprehensive, **One-Stop System** (U.S. General Accounting Office, 2003), thereby creating a new and improved workforce investment system.

WIA was designed to streamline the old system, in which parties sought services from a variety of sources in what could be a costly and confusing process (Hager & Sheldon, 2001). Instead, WIA designated 17 categories of programs as mandatory partners with the One-Stop System, including Veterans Employment and Training Services, adult literacy programs, Department of Housing and Urban Development-administered employment and training, and U.S. DOL-administered employment training for migrant workers, Native Americans, youths, and dislocated workers.

Any person who could demonstrate a physical, mental, or learning disability that creates a substantial impediment to his or her ability to work was eligible for WIA services. People qualified to receive Social Security Income or Social Security Disability Insurance (SSDI) were presumed to be eligible, provided that they sought WIA services for the purpose of obtaining employment (Hager & Sheldon, 2001). Similar to requirements under the Rehabilitation Act, VR agencies were required to provide services according to an order of selection if agency resources were inadequate to serve every individual seeking employment.

The role of the VR agency is to assist individuals with disabilities in making informed choices with respect to their desired employment outcomes and the services necessary to achieve such goal. VR agencies assist eligible individuals in developing a written Individualized Plan for Employment (IPE).

A VR agency may deny services to any individual whom it deems cannot benefit from them. WIA mandated a presumption that individuals with disabilities are capable of employment, but a VR agency may rebut that presumption if it shows by clear and convincing evidence that the individual cannot benefit from services. To this point, the VR agency must provide the individual with trial work experiences of "sufficient variety and over a sufficient length of time to determine" whether the individual may benefit from services (29 U.S.C. § 722(a)(2)(B)).

WIA faced challenges in achieving the complete integration of the workforce investment systems that existed prior to WIA (under the Rehabilitation Act) and the One-Stop system. For example, both systems continued to maintain separate administrations, and in some states, the systems are located in completely separate state agencies (Bruyère, VanLooy, & Golden, 2010). Part of the challenge arose from the fact that WIA attempted to integrate VR—a specialized field—into the broader workforce development system. In 2002, the Social Security Administration (SSA) and the U.S. DOL jointly launched their **Disability Program Navigator**, a resource aimed at connecting individuals with disabilities to appropriate VR services (www.doleta.gov/disability/new_dpn_grants.cfm).

Then, in July 2014, the WIOA was signed into law, and took effect a year later on July 1, 2015. As a reauthorization of the WIA, WIOA supersedes the WIA and WIA's amendments to the Rehabilitation Act, aiming to help job seekers access education, training, and support services necessary for success in the 21st-century labor market, while matching employers with skilled workers needed for global economic competition (U.S. Department of Labor, Employment and Training Administration, 2015). Importantly, WIOA takes steps to further align and integrate state VR programs with other core programs of the workforce development system, through unified strategic planning, common performance accountability measures, and one-stop delivery.

Efforts to streamline the workforce development system include (a) implementing common outcome measures for federal workforce programs, including six performance indicators for adults and six for youth served under the Rehabilitation Act; (b) smaller, more strategic state/local workforce development boards; (c) integration of intake, case management, evaluation, and reporting systems; and (d) elimination of the sequence of services to allow local boards to meet each unique individual's needs. Local boards are empowered under the Act to customize services for region-specific workforce needs. As described later, WIOA supports access to real-world education and workforce development opportunities for job seekers in the system (e.g., work based learning, incumbent worker, customized training, pay-for-performance contracts).

WIOA improves services to youth with disabilities by increasing opportunities for this population to practice workplace skills, exercise self-determination in career interests, and obtain work-based experience. At least 15% of federal program funds for VR agencies must now be set aside for preemployment transition services to students with disabilities. WIOA's job-driven programs emphasize employer engagement in matching employers with skilled individuals, including through a wider array of work-based learning opportunities under the VR program (e.g., apprenticeships and internships; Employer Assistance and Resource Network, 2014). As discussed previously in the Rehabilitation Act section of this chapter, new final regulations in 2016 updated the definition of VR outcomes in WIOA Title IV (programs authorized by the Rehabilitation Act), finalizing a shift from "gainful employment" to "competitive integrated employment" for people with disabilities, and specifying that "customized employment" constitutes a valid employment outcome.

The new **competitive integrated employment** terminology reflects the federal government's shift toward emphasizing integrated employment opportunities and pay that is commensurate with that of workers without disabilities in similar occupations, with similar training, experience, and skills (Title IV, § 404(5)). The Office of Disability Employment Policy (ODEP) recently described this shift, which it characterized as states "mov[ing] forward to implement policies that focus on integrated, community-based employment earning at or above the minimum wage as the first option for individuals with intellectual and other developmental disabilities . . . [in] employment first states, sheltered employment with subminimum wages and nonwork 'day activities' are no longer acceptable employment outcomes" (U.S. Department of Labor, 2009a). The final regulations specify common performance accountability measures for core state workforce development systems, and place substantial new restrictions on subminimum wage employment outcomes.

Ticket to Work and Work Incentives Improvement Act (TWWIIA)

The TWWIIA (Pub. L. No. 106-170, 113 Stat. 1860), enacted in 1999, was designed to provide beneficiaries and recipients of Supplemental Security Income (SSI, SSDI, or both) the incentives and supports that they need to prepare for, attach to, or advance in work. It also expanded options for continuing health care coverage benefits during recipients' transition to work and eliminating the disincentive to work for recipients of SSI or SSDI cash benefits that arose when such individuals lost their eligibility to receive benefits due to participation in work activities.

The Ticket-to-Work and Self-Sufficiency Program, found in Subtitle A of Title I of the TWWIIA, replaced the Social Security Administration's (SSA's) existing VR system with an outcome-based, market-driven program. It created a system in which all eligible beneficiaries receive a **Ticket to Work**: a voucher that the beneficiary may deposit with a service provider (otherwise known as an **Employment Network** [EN]) in order to receive employment services, which may include case management, work incentives planning, supported employment, career planning, career plan development, vocational assessment, job training, and other services like those available under state and federal VR programs discussed earlier (42 U.S.C. § 1320b-19(e)(5)).

The Ticket Program is purely voluntary on the part of the beneficiary. The beneficiary may decide whether to use the Ticket, may select a desirable EN from among an array of choices, and may at any time retrieve the Ticket from the EN if he or she feels that the EN's employment services are not adequate.

Service providers, either private or public organizations, that provide employment support services to assist an SSA beneficiary or recipient in preparing for, obtaining, or remaining at work may elect to become ENs. A state VR agency may be part of numerous ENs in any given state, but the statute requires each EN to be part of an agreement with a VR before referring a beneficiary to the designated state VR agency. ENs may also choose the preferred system of payment for services, either (a) outcome payments for those months in which the beneficiaries do not receive benefits due to work activity (up to 60 months), or (b) reduced outcome payments in addition to payments for helping the beneficiary achieve certain employment milestones. VRs have the additional option of electing to receive payment under a cost-reimbursement option.

Initial studies of the success of the Ticket Program following its rollout revealed low participation rates among potential beneficiaries due to an inadequate and inefficient payment system and the lack of adequate marketing, incentive, technical assistance, and training (Ticket to Work and Work Incentives Advisory Panel, 2004; Stapleton et al., 2008). In response to these findings, the SSA revised the Ticket Program regulations with the goal of improving program participation rates. The revisions took effect in late 2008, and included additional financial incentives for community service providers to participate in the program. One type of new financial incentive is **milestone payments**, payments triggered earlier in the employment process, for part-time and lower-paying outcomes, and based on gross earnings (rather than reduced by the value of SSA work incentives received by the beneficiary). In recognizing that disability beneficiaries need longer-term employment supports as they move toward self-sufficiency, the new regulations also established the **Partnership Plus** option, which allows participants served under the traditional cost-reimbursement program with state VR programs to continue access to individualized employment services through an EN, following their case closure with the state VR program.

Early empirical analyses provide only limited evidence of improved participant outcomes following the 2008 revisions: while the number of participating EN providers and program participants has increased, and while benchmark data for benefits forgone and termination of benefits for work have gone up, such benchmarks pertain to Ticket to Work (TTW) participants and nonparticipants alike, leaving questions as to the long-term efficacy of the revisions (Livermore, Hoffman, & Bardos, 2012; Schimmel, Stapleton, Mann, & Phelps, 2013).

Title II of TWWIIA governs the provision of health care services to workers with disabilities. This section of the law attempted to reduce the disincentives to employment for people with disabilities posed by the threat of loss of health care benefits by encouraging states to improve access to health care coverage available under Medicaid (Goodman & Livermore, 2004). Under this provision, new optional eligibility groups are established, creating two new Medicaid Buy-In eligibility categories, and also extending the period of premium-free Medicare Part A eligibility and requiring protection for certain individuals with Medigap. The U.S. Department of Health and Human Services (DHHS), through the U.S. Centers for Medicare and Medicaid Services, administers the health care provisions.

Workers' Compensation

Workers' compensation programs, which exist in each of the 50 states, the District of Columbia, and the U.S. territories, provide protections for employers and employees with respect to work-related injuries. Additional related federal laws are the Federal Coal Mine Health and Safety Act, the Longshore and Harbor Workers' Compensation Act, and the Federal Employers' Liability Act. Rehabilitation counseling professionals will regularly interact with these laws, as they impact the return-to-work process for most individuals with disabilities.

Prior to the development of workers' compensation laws, employees on the one hand had little recourse against employers in the event of a work-related injury, and many faced destitution resulting from occupational injuries or diseases. On the other hand, with respect to the few cases in which injured employees succeeded in suing their employers for negligence, employers faced the prospect of being ordered to pay injured employees large sums, and were thus subjected to unpredictable financial risk.

Workers' compensation remedies these two problems. First, it created a "no-fault approach" to occupational injury and disease, in which a worker would be eligible for disability benefits if he or she could show that the injury or disease was work related. Second, workers' compensation statutes limited employer liability by insulating them from negligence suits, provided that the employers paid for the no-fault workers' compensation benefits prescribed by statute (Spieler & Burton, 1998). The benefits available under workers' compensation law include medical care, disability payments, rehabilitation services, survivor benefits, and funeral expenses. In addition, benefits for temporary incapacity, scarring, and permanent impairment of specific body parts are typically included. The job and benefit protections available under the FMLA and, to an extent, under the ADA, are not available under workers' compensation law.

Initially, workers' compensation laws did not focus on returning injured workers to the workplace. A remarkable shift in workers' compensation law occurred during the latter half of the 20th century. These changes brought an increased focus on disability management and return-to-work options, and thus brought the goals of workers' compensation more closely in line with those of state and federal disability discrimination law (Spieler & Burton, 1998). The distinctive philosophies underlying workers' compensation and disability discrimination law give rise to somewhat conflicting perspectives of individuals with disabilities and their interaction with the workplace. Although the ADA focuses on the removal of barriers to employment through accommodations in the workplace, workers' compensation views impairments as causing work limitations. Thus, workers' compensation laws may require an employee to emphasize the limitations caused by his or her disability in order to be eligible for benefits, but those very statements may, at the same time, be detrimental to an ADA accommodation request (Geaney, 2004).

Rehabilitation counseling professionals may better assist individuals with disabilities and their employers if they possess a solid understanding of workers' compensation laws and the manner in which they interact with ADA and FMLA protections. Specific areas of concern include (a) whether an injured worker also qualifies as having an ADA disability or has a serious medical condition under the FMLA; (b) how the ADA rules regarding medical inquiries impact an applicant with a history of occupational injury or disease; (c) whether an employee with a history of occupational injury or disease poses a direct threat to himself or herself or coworkers under the ADA; (d) ADA accommodations available to individuals injured in the workplace, including the development of light-duty positions; and (e) the impact of exclusive remedy provisions under workers' compensation laws on an employee's rights under other disability statutes (EEOC, 1996). Although an employer bears the ultimate responsibility of determining whether an employee is ready to return to work, the employer may seek the advice of an RC or other specialist in order to understand an employee's specific functional limitations or abilities when returning to work.

Health Insurance Portability and Accountability Act

HIPAA (42 U.S.C. §§ 1320d–1320d-8) governs disclosure of medical information by covered entities. A **covered entity** is a health plan, health care provider, or health care clearinghouse. Based on this definition, employers generally do not qualify as covered entities under HIPAA. Thus, HIPAA rules would not apply to any "**return-to-work notes—** medical information provided to substantiate requests for employee benefits such as short-term disability, long-term disability, FMLA requirements, job accommodation requests, or medical information for compliance with ADA" (DiBenedetto, 2005). The confidentiality of the medical information in such records would remain protected, however, by the confidentiality rules contained within the ADA and FMLA, as previously mentioned.

The greater impact of HIPAA on the practice of rehabilitation counseling, however, involves the situation in which an occupational health provider qualifies as a health care provider or business affiliate under HIPAA. The regulations implementing HIPAA broadly define **health care provider** as one who "furnishes, bills, or is paid for health care in the normal course of business" (45 C.F.R. § 160.103). Health care

> means care, services, or supplies related to the health of an individual. Health care includes, but is not limited to, the following: (1) Preventive, diagnostic, therapeutic, rehabilitative, maintenance, or palliative care, and counseling, service, assessment, or procedure with respect to the physical or mental condition, or functional status, of an individual or that affects the structure or function of the body and (2) Sale or dispensing of a drug, device, equipment, or other item in accordance with a prescription. (45 C.F.R. § 160.103)

All covered entities must comply with HIPAA's Privacy Rule (Standards of Privacy for Individually Identifiable Health Information, 45 C.F.R. pt. 160 and subpts. A and E of pt. 164) in order to safeguard individually identifiable medical information (referred to as **protected health information** or PHI) that it handles or transmits. Generally, the covered entity may provide PHI to the individual to whom it belongs and may use such information for its own treatment, payment, and health care operations. Otherwise, covered entities may use PHI only as required by law or with the written authorization of the individual to whom it belongs.

HIPAA further requires that covered entities tailor their uses and disclosures of PHI, other than those to the subject individual or with his or her authorization, so that it uses or discloses only the minimum amount of information necessary to meet the purpose of that use or disclosure (45 C.F.R. § 164.502).

Interestingly, the Privacy Rule contains a direct reference to **psychotherapy notes**, which it defines as:

> notes recorded (in any medium) by a health care provider who is a mental health professional documenting or analyzing the contents of conversation during a private counseling session or a group, joint, or family counseling session and that are separated from the rest of the individual's medical record. Psychotherapy notes exclude medication prescription and monitoring, counseling session start and stop times, the modalities and frequencies of treatment furnished, results of clinical tests, and any summary of the following items: Diagnosis, functional status, the treatment plan, symptoms, prognosis, and progress to date. (45 C.F.R. § 160.501)

The **Privacy Rule** provides that covered entities must obtain the subject individual's permission to use or disclose psychotherapy notes except when using such notes for the treatment of that individual or for other specified circumstances generally pertaining to the training of the covered entity, the need to protect the health or safety of that individual or others in the community, or where necessitated by law (45 C.F.R. § 160.508(a)(2)). The Privacy Rule applies with general uniformity to all PHI, but special protections are afforded to psychotherapy notes because of their potential to contain particularly sensitive information and the fact that they are not typically used in treatment, payment, or health care operations (U.S. Department of Health and Human Services, 2014). This is why, with few exceptions (e.g., reporting of abuse and "duty to warn"), covered entities are required to obtain the patient's authorization prior to a disclosure of psychotherapy notes for any reason (45 C.F.R. § 164.508(a)(2)).

HIPAA also contains a **Security Rule** (Security Standards for the Protection of Electronic Protected Health Information, 45 C.F.R. pt. 160 and subpts. A and C of pt. 164), which sets forth the standards to which covered entities must adhere in order to maintain the confidentiality and integrity of PHI that is stored or transferred electronically. After a covered entity identifies any potential risks to its PHI, it must then adopt appropriate administrative, physical, and technical safeguards.

Business associates also are drawn within the umbrella of HIPAA legislation. HIPAA defines a **business associate** as a person or entity that provides services to a covered entity or performs functions or activities for a covered entity that involve the use or disclosure of PHI (45 C.F.R. § 160.103). The concept of a business associate was developed to prevent covered entities from shirking their responsibilities under HIPAA by simply outsourcing certain aspects of their businesses to noncovered entities. Under the HIPAA Privacy Rule, covered entities may release certain PHI to a business associate only if they obtain the business associate's written assurance that it will safeguard the PHI and assist the covered entity in complying with the Privacy Rule (45 C.F.R. § 164.502(e)).

Most recently, the Health Information Technology for Economic and Clinical Health (HITECH) Act (42 U.S.C. § 17921 *et seq.*) updates HIPAA obligations by requiring both business associates and covered entities to notify an individual if the confidentiality or integrity of that individual's PHI has been compromised. The HITECH Act also extends the application of many of the HIPAA privacy and security regulations that originally applied only to covered entities to business associates as well. As of the date of this publication, although the Office of Civil Rights (OCR) of the U.S. DHHS had not yet enacted the final rules implementing the HITECH Act, the interim rules were in full force and effect.

In conclusion, any individual planning to practice in the area of rehabilitation counseling or counseling in general must become educated regarding HIPAA in order to determine the extent to which he or she must comply with its rules and regulations. For those who are unsure whether they fall within the scope of HIPAA, they may certainly choose, nevertheless, to voluntarily implement the practices described in the Privacy Rule and the Security Rule as a means of protecting the privacy of their clients and maintaining the confidentiality of information to which they have access.

Patient Protection and Affordable Care Act of 2010

The 2010 Patient Protection and Affordable Care Act (ACA) refers to two pieces of legislation: the ACA (Pub. L. No. 111–148) and the Health Care and Education Reconciliation Act (Pub. L. No. 111–152). In combination, these statutes seek to enhance health care security in the United States through efforts to expand coverage, hold insurance companies accountable, increase consumer choice, lower health care costs, and improve the overall quality of care (U.S. Department of Health and Human Services, 2010). Commentators have noted that the ACA represents the most extensive regulatory and legal changes to the U.S. health care system since the passage of Medicare and Medicaid in 1965 (Manchikanti, Caraway, Parr, Fellows, & Hirsch, 2011). In June 2012, the U.S. Supreme Court upheld all provisions of the ACA except for the mandated expansion of Medicaid eligibility for low-income adults by state governments; as to this latter, the Court held that states opting out of the Medicaid expansion could not be penalized by a loss of federal funding to their existing Medicaid programs. Many states have nevertheless opted into the Medicaid expansion, with the most recent tally being 32 states opting in (including Washington, DC) and 19 opting out (Kaiser Family Foundation, 2016).

One persistent issue facing state VR agencies is how to manage and maximize state and federal funding to pay for services and supports (including health-related services). The ACA implements substantial new potential funding sources for such services, and contains important provisions that increase access to private health insurance, such as removing preexisting conditions from insurance eligibility determinations and expanding eligibility for the receipt of health care through Medicaid programs, depending on states' willingness to participate (Silverstein, 2012). Essential health benefits—including rehabilitative and habilitative services—may therefore be more readily available to VR service recipients as a result of the ACA.

Because individuals with disabilities tend to have lower rates of employment, and lower rates of employer-sponsored health insurance, health care and health insurance issues intersect heavily with the VR context (Croft & Parish, 2012). The ACA directly impacts access to health care by expanding Medicaid eligibility criteria, setting aside additional federal funds for states opting to expand their Medicaid programs to allow coverage of adults under 65 with income up to 133% of the federal poverty level, as well as children at that income level (U.S. Centers for Medicare and Medicaid Services, 2015). Therefore, for states that have opted in to the Medicaid expansion, free or low-cost health coverage is available to people with incomes below a certain threshold, regardless of disability, financial resources, family status, and other designations that would previously have been factored into eligibility determinations (U.S. Centers for Medicare and Medicaid Services, 2015). Finally, the ACA provides the option for state-level expansion of community VR services such as vocational supports and case management, allowing participating states to offer such services through their regular state Medicaid plans without seeking a waiver, for individuals with incomes up to 300% of the maximum SSI payment and who also have a high level of need (Croft & Parish, 2012).

Genetic Information Nondiscrimination Act

Enacted in 2008, GINA prohibits employers from discharging, refusing to hire, or making other decisions related to the terms and privileges of employment based on an employee's genetic information (42 U.S.C. § 200ff-1). GINA also bars employers from using genetic information to classify employees in such a way as to decrease their employment opportunities or to otherwise negatively affect their employment status. GINA was passed in response to mounting fears among Americans that employers could discriminate against them based on the improper use of genetic information. Such fears inhibited the use of genetic testing and raised issues regarding the viability of finding willing subjects for future genetic research (Appelbaum, 2010).

The definition of **genetic information** in GINA is broad enough that it covers genetic tests performed both on an employee/applicant and on his or her family members because the test results of family members could adversely affect the employee/applicant's risk status. In the absence of a formal genetic test, a family medical history may, in and of itself, constitute genetic information if it reveals the presence of genetically linked diseases among family members. Medical providers and health professionals should therefore omit both types of information when responding to an employer's request for medical information or documentation.

Regardless of efforts by health professionals to redact or omit genetic information contained in records that are being provided to employers, family medical information may be interspersed throughout the records and therefore be challenging to completely remove ("Are you compliant with genetic screening law?", 2010). Questions abound regarding whether medical providers and health professionals have "the time, inclination, or even ability to carefully redact genetic information from patient records," particularly with the increasing prevalence of electronic health record systems (Hoffman, 2010). Even assuming that medical providers and health professionals do have adequate time and ability to redact genetic information from records, it may be best for medical professionals to heed the recent warning of Marcia Scott, MD, affiliated with the Department of Psychiatry at Harvard Medical School: "because a family history is a necessary part of any evaluation, we all need to be aware that the pen and computer have become dangerous instruments" (Scott, 2010). When questions regarding genetic testing arise, health professionals should ensure that their patients/clients are aware of GINA and understand its protections (Appelbaum, 2010).

There is no overlap in coverage between GINA and the FMLA. Instead, GINA specifically excludes from its coverage any family medical history that an employer requests or requires in order to comply with the FMLA.

IMPLICATIONS FOR COUNSELING PRACTICE

Many rehabilitation counseling professionals work within the state VR service delivery system governed by the Rehabilitation Act, and are likely knowledgeable about these services. However, for those who are employed outside this system, being knowledgeable about available services for referral purposes is imperative, as is knowledge of the interface with other workforce development systems afforded by the WIA. Similarly, for those providing services to Social Security recipients, veterans, or those impacted by an occupational injury, awareness of TWWIIA, USERRA, VEVRAA, and workers' compensation laws is a necessity. Without this knowledge, counselors will not be able to direct their clients to the services for which they are eligible, or guide their vocational choices in light of available benefits that may affect decisions about income-earning capacity and benefits eligibility.

The purpose of this chapter is to provide a broad overview of select pieces of legislation that impact employment of people with disabilities, either through creation and implementation of employment services for people with disabilities or through protection of their employment rights. In the remainder of this chapter, the implications of these laws for rehabilitation and general counseling practice, training, and research are discussed.

The laws described here have implications for counseling practice in that they govern the provision of VR services and provide protections against workplace discrimination for both applicants and employees with disabilities. However, the summarized legislation and regulations are important to all counselors, even outside the VR context, who work with individuals with disabilities. Counseling professionals providing employment services to people with disabilities should know that these laws exist, be very familiar with the services they make available, and be knowledgeable about the rights and protections that people with disabilities are afforded in the employment process.

Support of employment disability nondiscrimination policy and practice is a part of every rehabilitation counseling professional's role. The opportunity to execute this responsibility comes daily, in moving people toward the employment application process and in coaching them on ways to maximize their employment retention and advancement. In addition, counselors have a role that they can provide in informing employers and workplace agents such as human resources (HR) professionals about the provisions of these laws and how these regulations should inform the design of disability-inclusive workplace HR policies and practices.

Doing this effectively requires that practitioners be knowledgeable about the protections against discrimination and the requirements of accommodations (including leaves) provided by the ADA, FMLA, workers' compensation laws, and newly emerging laws such as GINA. They should also be aware of common HR practices around these laws and related practices (Erickson, von Schrader, Bruyère, VanLooy, & Matteson, 2014). Coaching on disclosure issues can also be informed by knowledge of the confidentiality requirements of these laws, as well as the related provisions afforded by HIPAA. Finally, knowledge of the intersection between the new health care and community services provisions of the ACA can prove essential for VR practitioners, who deal on a daily basis with a population that has historically struggled to gain adequate access to health care and community services. These issues may be even more complex to navigate for those with psychiatric disabilities, where disclosure can be a particularly challenging issue, so heightened attention to the implications for this population is imperative.

COUNSELING PROFESSIONAL EDUCATION

The importance of being knowledgeable about these laws for effective rehabilitation counseling service delivery has been already presented. It is imperative that information about these laws be an expected part of core coursework requirements in counselor preparation. Inclusion in select related courses, such as those on legislation related to people with disabilities, is most appropriate. But, in addition, this information is also relevant to courses such as rehabilitation counseling scope of practice; history, systems, and philosophy of rehabilitation; disability benefits systems; employer consultation and disability prevention; workplace culture and environment; and vocational consultation and job placement strategies.

Perhaps not as obvious, however, are the implications of this knowledge for the preparation of counselors in fulfilling their professional roles as workplace educators and policy advocates. Not only rehabilitation clients, but the employers who hire them, as well as policy makers at the local and state level, must be informed about the provisions for employment disability nondiscrimination, confidentiality of medical information, access to employment services, application process and workplace accommodation, and other rights that these laws provide. Rehabilitation counseling professionals have a role to play in this community education process. Providing information to the **demand side** of the employment equation—that is, viewing things from the perspective of employers— to address HR strategists and build a convincing business case for employers will be vital (Barrington, Bruyère, & Waelder, 2014). Likewise, knowledge of how these laws are being interpreted and implemented by HR managers and hiring committees should become a part of preservice training (Nazarov & von Schrader, 2014). Only if HR students and practitioners are informed, as part of their preservice and postgraduate educational processes, about the laws and roles they can play will these outcomes be realized in their professional practices.

NEEDED RELATED RESEARCH

Finally, there is a significant need for rehabilitation counseling researchers to become partners in policy formulation and evaluation efforts (Nazarov, Erickson, & Bruyère, 2014). Far too often, this discipline is all but absent from policy discourse when such laws are being formulated. RCs' disciplinary preparation and field-based practice experiences make them exceedingly valuable potential allies in this process, as well as in the evaluation of these laws once implemented. Rehabilitation education should provide students the necessary information to be able to maximally utilize these laws to support effective rehabilitation counseling service delivery. They must also convey in this educational process the responsibility that future rehabilitation counseling practitioners have to be on-the-ground policy advocates and policy analysts.

As discussed in the overview of particular laws, in many cases the impact of these laws on increasing employment outcomes for people with disabilities is as yet unknown or unclear. Rehabilitation counseling researchers are needed who are able to work alongside economists, policy analysts, and others in determining the impact of WIOA, TWWIIA, and workers' compensation legislation in improving initial hiring and the return to work for people with disabilities. Similarly, RCs should be applying their unique analytical lens in determining whether employment disability nondiscrimination and accommodation provisions are currently designed in a way to minimize marginalization and maximize inclusion. They also should commit to seeking publishing outlets outside their field, to share their findings beyond the rehabilitation community with other participants in the employment process (Karpur, VanLooy, & Bruyère, 2014). It is a tremendous opportunity for these specialized professionals to contribute in the policy arena.

CONCLUSION

Counseling often focuses on the one-on-one relationship between the counselor and the client; however, state and federal legislation protects the legal rights of individuals with disabilities in our society. With this in mind, this chapter focused on the legislation most relevant to the employment and civil rights of people with disabilities. Laws and legislation are significant to promote a more inclusive society, one that not only contributes to an individual's economic self-sufficiency, but also enables that individual to have a higher QOL.

CONTENT REVIEW QUESTIONS

- How does the Vocational Rehabilitation Act of 1973 as amended assist states with the operation of comprehensive, coordinated, and effective VR services?
- What effect did WIOA's amendments to the Rehabilitation Act have on the types of employment outcomes that are permitted in state VR programs?
- What are the specific provisions of the ADA of 1990 as they relate to employer requirements to make reasonable accommodation for an applicant or employee with a disability?
- How might the requirements of the ADA and the FMLA intersect?
- Why should rehabilitation professionals be familiar with the provisions of the USERRA and the VEVRAA?
- What might be the strengths and weaknesses of the provision of services to people with disabilities through the workforce development system provided for under WIOA?
- Which challenges to employment faced by Social Security beneficiaries was the TWWIIA designed to address?
- How might the ADA and the provisions of state workers' compensation laws intersect?
- What are the rehabilitation counseling practice implications of HIPAA, GINA, and the ACA?

ACKNOWLEDGMENTS

The authors were supported in preparation of this manuscript by a grant from the National Institute on Disability, Independent Living, and Rehabilitation Research (NIDILRR), a center within the Administration for Community Living (ACL), DHHS, to the K. Lisa Yang and Hock E. Tan Institute on Employment and Disability at Cornell University ILR School for a Rehabilitation Research and Training Center (RRTC) on Employer Practices Related to Employment Outcomes for Individuals with Disabilities, Susanne M. Bruyère, Project Director (Grant 90RT5010-01-00).

The authors would like to acknowledge the work of Beth Reiter, coauthor of a prior version of this chapter, and the editorial assistance of Sara VanLooy, administrative/research assistant with the Yang-Tan Institute at Cornell University.

REFERENCES

Appelbaum, P. S. (2010). Law & psychiatry: Genetic discrimination in mental disorders: The impact of the Genetic Information Nondiscrimination Act. *Psychiatric Services, 61,* 338–340.

Are you compliant with genetic screening law? (2010, May 1). *Occupational Health Management.* Retrieved from https://www.ahcmedia.com/articles/19028-are-you-compliant-with-genetic-screening-law

Barrington, L., Bruyère, S., & Waelder, M. (2014). Employer practices in improving employment outcomes for people with disabilities: A trans-disciplinary and employer-inclusive research approach. *Journal of Rehabilitation Research, Policy and Education, 28*(4), 208–224.

Befort, S. F. (2013). An empirical analysis of case outcomes under the ADA Amendments Act. *Washington and Lee Law Review, 70,* 2027–2071.

Bruyère, S., VanLooy, S., & Golden, T. (2010). Legislation and rehabilitation professionals. In S. Flanagan, H. Zaretsky, & A. Moroz (Eds.), *Medical aspects of disability: A handbook for the rehabilitation professional* (4th ed., pp. 669–686). New York, NY: Springer Publishing.

Campbell, J. (1994). Unintended consequences in public policy: Persons with psychiatric disabilities and the Americans with Disabilities Act. *Policy Studies Journal, 22,* 133.

Council of State Administrators of Vocational Rehabilitation. (n.d.). *Public vocational rehabilitation program fact sheet.* Retrieved from https://www2.ed.gov/policy/speced/guid/rsa/im/1999/im-99-21.doc

Croft, B., & Parish, S. L. (2012). Care integration in the Patient Protection and Affordable Care Act: Implications for behavioral health. *Administration and Policy in Mental Health and Mental Health Services Research, 40,* 258–263.

DiBenedetto, D. V. (2005). HIPAA not always is applicable to occ-health. *Occupational Health Management.* Retrieved from https://www.ahcmedia.com/articles/84802-hipaa-not-always-is-applicable-to-occ-health

Employer Assistance and Resource Network. (2014). Workforce Innovation and Opportunity Act of 2014 (WIOA). Retrieved from http://askearn.org/refdesk/Disability_Laws/WIOA

Erickson, W., Lee, C., & von Schrader, S. (2016). *Disability statistics from the 2014 American Community Survey (ACS).* Ithaca, NY: Cornell University Yang Tan Institute. Retrieved from http://www.disabilitystatistics.org

Erickson, W., von Schrader, S., Bruyère, S., VanLooy, S., & Matteson, D. (2014). Disability-inclusive employer practices and hiring of individuals with disabilities. *Journal of Rehabilitation Research, Policy and Education, 28*(4), 309–328.

Geaney, J. (2004). The relationship of workers' compensation to the Americans with Disabilities Act and Family and Medical Leave Act. *Clinics in Occupational and Environmental Medicine, 4,* 273–293.

Goodman, N., & Livermore, G. (2004, July 28). The effectiveness of Medicaid Buy-In programs in promoting the employment of people with disabilities. Briefing paper prepared for the Ticket to Work and Work Incentives Advisory Panel of the Social Security Administration. Retrieved from https://www.scribd.com/document/1947561/Social-Security-Buy-in-20paper-20Goodman-Livermore-20072804r

Hager, R. M., & Sheldon, J. R. (2001). State and federal vocational rehabilitation programs: Services and supports to assist individuals with disabilities in preparing for, attaching to, and advancing in employment. Retrieved from http://digitalcommons.ilr.cornell.edu/cgi/viewcontent.cgi?article=1218&context=edicollect

Hoffman, S. (2010). Employing E-health: The impact of electronic health records on the workplace. *Kansas Journal of Law and Public Policy, 19,* 409.

Institute on Disability. (2015). *2015 annual disability statistics compendium.* Durham, NH: Institute on Disability. Retrieved from http://disabilitycompendium.org

Kaiser Family Foundation. (2016). Status of state action on the Medicaid expansion decision. Retrieved from http://kff.org/health-reform/state-indicator/state-activity-around-expanding-medicaid-under-the-affordable-care-act

Kaminer, D. N. (2016). Mentally ill employees in the workplace: Does the ADA Amendments Act provide adequate protection? *Health Matrix, 26,* 205–254.

Karpur, A., VanLooy, S., & Bruyère, S. (2014). Employer practices for employment of people with disabilities: A literature scoping review. *Journal of Rehabilitation Research, Policy and Education, 28*(4), 225–241.

Lipnic, V. A., & DeCamp, P. (2007). *Family and Medical Leave Act regulations: A report on the Department of Labor's request for information.* Washington, DC: U.S. Department of Labor. Retrieved from http://digitalcommons.ilr.cornell.edu/key_workplace/315

Livermore, G. A., Hoffman, D., & Bardos, M. (2012, September 24). *Ticket to work participant characteristics and outcomes under the revised regulations.* Washington, DC: Mathematica Policy Research Institute.

Manchikanti, L., Caraway, D., Parr, A. T., Fellows, B., & Hirsch, J. A. (2011). Patient Protection and Affordable Care Act of 2010: Reforming the health care reform for the new decade. *Pain Physician, 14,* 35–67.

National Alliance on Mental Illness. (2013). *Mental illness: Facts and numbers.* Arlington, VA: Author. Retrieved from http://www2.nami.org/factsheets/mentalillness_factsheet.pdf

National Alliance on Mental Illness. (2014). *Road to recovery: Employment and mental illness.* Arlington, VA: Author. Retrieved from http://www.nami.org/work

National Council on Disability. (2004). Righting the Americans with Disabilities Act. Washington, DC: Author. Retrieved from http://www.ncd.gov/publications/2004/Dec12004

National Institutes of Health, National Institute of Mental Health. (n.d.). Statistics: Any disorder among adults. Retrieved from https://www.nimh.nih.gov/health/statistics/prevalence/any-mental-illness-ami -among-us-adults.shtml

Nazarov, Z., Erickson, W., & Bruyère, S. (2014). Rehabilitation related research on disability and employer practices using individual-based national and administrative data sets. *Journal of Rehabilitation Research, Policy and Education, 28*(4), 242–263.

Nazarov, Z., & von Schrader, S. (2014). Comparison of employer factors in disability and other employment discrimination charges. *Journal of Rehabilitation Research, Policy and Education, 28*(4), 291–308.

Olsheski, J., & Schelat, R. (2003). Reasonable job accommodations for people with psychiatric disabilities. In D. Moxley & J. Finch (Eds.), *Sourcebook of rehabilitation and mental health practice* (pp. 61–76). New York, NY: Kluwer Academic Publishers.

Postol, L. (2002). Sailing the employment law Bermuda Triangle. *Labor Lawyer, 18*, 165–192.

Quinn, M. (2005). Uniformed Services Employment and Reemployment Rights Act (USERRA)—broad in protections, inadequate in scope. *University of Pennsylvania Journal of Labor & Employment, 8*, 237.

Rehabilitation Services Administration. (2016). Frequently asked questions. Retrieved from https://rsa.ed .gov/faqs.cfm

Rothstein, M. A., & Talbott, M. K. (2007). Compelled authorizations for disclosure of health records: Magnitude and implications. *American Journal of Bioethics, 7*, 38–40.

Rubin, S. E., & Roessler, R. T. (Eds.). (2001). *Foundations of the vocational rehabilitation process.* Austin, TX: Pro-Ed.

Rudstam, H., Golden, T. P., Strobel Gower, W., Switzer, E., Bruyère, S. M., & VanLooy, S. A. (2014). Leveraging new rules to advance new opportunities: Implications of the Rehabilitation Act Section 503 new rules for employment service providers. *Journal of Vocational Rehabilitation, 41*(3), 193–208. doi:10.3233/JVR -140713

Schimmel, J., Stapleton, D., Mann, D. R., & Phelps, D. (2013, July 25). *Participant and provider outcomes since the inception of ticket to work and the effects of the 2008 regulatory changes.* Washington, DC: Mathematica Policy Research Institute.

Scott, M. (2010). Letter: Family history and GINA. *Psychiatric Services, 61*, 634.

Silverstein, B. (2012). *Funding health-related VR services: The potential impact of the Affordable Care Act on the use of private health insurance and Medicaid to pay for health-related VR services.* Boston, MA: Institute for Community Inclusion.

Spieler, E. A., & Burton, J. F. (1998). Compensation for disabled workers: Workers' compensation. In T. Thomason, J. Burton, & D. Hyatt (Eds.), *New approaches to disability in the workplace* (pp. 205–244). Madison, WI: Industrial Relations Research Association.

Stapleton, D., Livermore, G., Thornton, C., O'Day, B., Weathers, R., Harrison, K., . . . Wright, D. (2008, September). *Ticket to work at the crossroads: A solid foundation with an uncertain future.* (Report submitted to the Social Security Administration Office of Disability and Income Support Programs). Washington, DC: Mathematica Policy Research Institute. Retrieved from https://www.ssa.gov/disabilityresearch/ ttw4/TTW_Rpt4_508_vol1r.pdf

Ticket to Work and Work Incentives Advisory Panel. (2004). *The crisis in EN participation: A blueprint for action.* Washington, DC: Social Security Administration.

U.S. Bureau of Labor Statistics. (2016). Employment situation of veterans summary. Retrieved from http:// www.bls.gov/news.release/vet.nr0.htm

U.S. Census Bureau. (2012). Nearly 1 in 5 people have a disability in the U.S. Census Bureau reports. Retrieved from https://www.census.gov/newsroom/releases/archives/miscellaneous/cb12-134.html

U.S. Centers for Medicare and Medicaid Services. (2015). Medicaid expansion & what it means for you. Retrieved from https://www.healthcare.gov/medicaid-chip/medicaid-expansion-and-you

U.S. Department of Education. (2014). The Workforce Innovation and Opportunity Act: Overview of Title IV: Amendments to the Rehabilitation Act of 1973. Retrieved from https://www2.ed.gov/about/offices/ list/osers/rsa/publications/wioa-changes-to-rehab-act.pdf

U.S. Department of Education. (2016, June 30). Final regulation: State vocational rehabilitation services program; State supported employment services program; limitations on use of subminimum wage. Retrieved from http://www2.ed.gov/about/offices/list/osers/rsa/wioa-vr-final-rule.pdf

U.S. Department of Health and Human Services. (2010). Patient Protection and Affordable Care Act: requirements for group health plans and health insurance issuers under the Patient Protection and Affordable Care Act relating to preexisting condition exclusions, lifetime and annual limits, rescissions, and patient protections. *Federal Register, 75*, 37187–37241.

U.S. Department of Health and Human Services. (2014). HIPAA privacy rule and sharing information related to mental health. Retrieved from http://www.hhs.gov/hipaa/for-professionals/special-topics/mental-health

U.S. Department of Labor. (2009a). *Frequently asked questions and answers about the revisions to the Family and Medical Leave Act.* Washington, DC: Author. Retrieved from http://www.dol.gov/whd/fmla/finalrule/ NonMilitaryFAQs.pdf

U.S. Department of Labor. (2009b). *Military family leave provisions of the FMLA (Family and Medical Leave Act): Frequently asked questions and answers.* Washington, DC: Author. Retrieved from http://www.dol .gov/whd/fmla/finalrule/MilitaryFAQs.pdf

U.S. Department of Labor. (2010). Bureau of labor statistics, economic news release: Employment situation of veterans—2009. Retrieved from http://www.bls.gov/news.release/vet.nr0.htm

U.S. Department of Labor, Employment and Training Administration. (2015). Obama administration seeks public comment on proposed rules to implement the Workforce Innovation and Opportunity Act. Retrieved from https://www.dol.gov/newsroom/releases/eta/eta20150691

U.S. Department of Labor Office of Federal Contract Compliance Programs. (2016). The ADA Amendments Act of 2008: Frequently asked questions. Retrieved from https://www.dol.gov/ofccp/regs/compliance/ faqs/ADAfaqs.htm

U.S. Department of Labor, Wage and Hour Division. (2013). Side-by-side comparison of current/final regulations. https://www.dol.gov/whd/fmla/finalrule/comparison.htm

U.S. Equal Employment Opportunity Commission. (n.d.-a). Facts about the Americans with Disabilities Act. Retrieved from http://www.eeoc.gov/facts/fs-ada.html

U.S. Equal Employment Opportunity Commission. (n.d.-b). ADA enforcement guidance: Preemployment disability-related questions and medical examinations. Retrieved from https://www.eeoc.gov/policy/ docs/medfin5.pdf

U.S. Equal Employment Opportunity Commission. (1996). *EEOC enforcement guidance: Workers' compensation and the ADA.* (No. 915.002). Retrieved from https://www.eeoc.gov/policy/html

U.S. Equal Employment Opportunity Commission. (1997, March 25). *Enforcement guidance on the Americans with Disabilities Act and psychiatric disabilities* (No. 915.002). Retrieved from https://www.eeoc.gov/ policy/docs/psych.html

U.S. Equal Employment Opportunity Commission. (2000, July 27). *Enforcement guidance: Disability-related inquiries and medical examinations of employees under the Americans with Disabilities Act* (No. 915.002). Retrieved from https://www.eeoc.gov/policy/docs/guidance-inquiries.html

U.S. Equal Employment Opportunity Commission. (2002). Enforcement guidance on reasonable accommodation and undue hardship under the Americans with Disabilities Act. Retrieved from https://www .eeoc.gov//policy/docs/accommodation.html#privileges

U.S. Equal Employment Opportunity Commission. (2008). Notice concerning the Americans with Disabilities Act (ADA) Amendments Act of 2008. Retrieved from http://www.eeoc.gov/ada/amendments_ notice.html

U.S. Equal Employment Opportunity Commission. (2011). Questions and answers on the final rule implementing the ADA Amendments Act of 2008. Retrieved from http://www.eeoc.gov/laws/regulations/ada_ qa_final_rule.cfm

U.S. Equal Employment Opportunity Commission. (2013). Press release: Fabricut to pay $50,000 to settle EEOC disability and genetic information discrimination lawsuit. Retrieved from https://www.eeoc.gov/ eeoc/newsroom/release/5-7-13b.cfm

U.S. Equal Employment Opportunity Commission. (2015). EEOC opinion on invitation to self-identify. Retrieved from https://www.dol.gov/ofccp/regs/compliance/sec503/Self_ID_Forms/OLC_letter_to_OFCCP _8-8-2013_508c.pdf

U.S. General Accounting Office. (2003). Workforce Investment Act: One-stop centers implemented strategies to strengthen services and partnerships, but more research and information sharing is needed. Retrieved from http://www.gao.gov/new.items/d03725.pdf

U.S. General Accounting Office. (2005). Military personnel: Federal management of service member employment rights can be further improved. Retrieved from http://www.gao.gov/new.items/d0660.pdf

von Schrader, S., Malzer, V., & Bruyère, S. (2013). Perspectives on disability disclosure: The importance of employer practices and workplace climate. *Employee Responsibilities and Rights Journal, 26,* 237–255. http://link.springer.com/article/10.1007/s10672-013-9227-9#page-1

PART III: PEOPLE WITH DISABILITIES

SEVEN

The Person With a Disability

MARGARET A. NOSEK

LEARNING OBJECTIVES

After reading this chapter, you should be able to:

- Recognize life as a process of constant change and adjustment for people with disabilities.
- Understand differences between medical models of disability and psychosocial models of disability.
- Identify environmental and psychosocial influences on relationships of individuals with disabilities.
- Explain how people with disabilities can achieve and maintain optimal health and functioning.
- Recognize the current health care systems in the United States and review alternative ways to improve weaknesses of the health care system.

Through the eyes of the individual, disability looks quite different from what has been taught in most textbooks. First, the traditional model for the academic understanding of disability has been medical and not psychosocial. Second, if you have had personal experience with disability yourself or in a close family member, you know that it is dynamic in nature and holistic in a way that is difficult to understand when your understanding of disability is from a distance. Third, the notion of coping has traditionally been regarded as a positive strategy, whereas for people with disabilities it could be both positive and negative. Fourth, the effect of disability on relationships is personal and intimate, and the adoption of a rights-bearing, positive attitude is often difficult to obtain or maintain. Fifth, individuals' efforts to maintain health and wellness in the context of disability do not always mean complying with medical advice. Sixth, public policies related to health care and social services, more often than not, reflect the arcane image of disability that is fueling the current rebellion. These are just a few of the topics that are discussed in this chapter in an attempt to convey to rehabilitation counselors (RCs) what it means to live with disability.

Disability is a universal phenomenon and few people recognize it as such. As an exercise, try to think of one person you know who does *not* have a disability. A career-changing memory comes to my mind. In the early 1980s, as I was working for my mentor, the father of the Americans with Disabilities Act (ADA), Justin W. Dart Jr., I helped him organize one of his famous parties as a lakeside fundraiser for the Austin (Texas) Resource Center for Independent Living. At the end of the event, he asked everyone present who had a disability to gather in one area for a group photo. Those with obvious disabilities, such as wheelchair users like Justin and myself, were the first to move toward the designated spot near the lake. Everyone else looked around rather awkwardly before another brave few walked over. Then the catcalls started—"Hey Bill, you have diabetes, don't you?" "Maria, I was in the same class as you and I know you got some tutoring because you still couldn't write in the fifth grade!" "Those glasses are mighty thick, Lupe." Eventually, everyone was over by the lake!

It would be surprising if you could think of anyone who does not have some type of chronic or disabling condition. We live in times that seem designed to produce disability—from accidents (industrial, traffic, or sports), pollution, never-ending wars, or unaffordable health insurance (Nosek, 2016). Disability can come into a life at any point and by any means. We now understand the genetic origins of some congenital conditions that may manifest at birth or not until later in life, such as my disability, spinal muscular atrophy. Problems with pregnancy, prenatal care, or the birthing process result more and more in babies with intellectual impairment, cerebral palsy, or other severe malformations of multiple organs, yet these children are able to survive thanks to advances in neonatal care and technology. Despite all the safety inventions and increased awareness, human beings seem to thrive on risk. This tendency, combined with the weakening of industrial safety standards, has led to an increasing rate of disability from work-related injury, such as back problems, spinal cord injury, brain injury, and amputations. Arthritis and fibromyalgia are just two conditions that have a gradual onset in early or middle adulthood, often associated with environmental and lifestyle factors, and affect women more than men. Lifestyle factors also can result in hearing and vision impairment; for example, listening to loud music (especially through earphones) or staring at a computer screen for untold hours. And finally, mental illness, which is one of the most common and yet mostly invisible disabilities, is often incapacitating for individuals and families. Although many types of mental illness, such as schizophrenia and severe depression, result from chemical imbalances in the brain, other types can be associated with a lifestyle of excess use of alcohol and drugs (both prescribed and otherwise), an inability to deal with rapid social change, disruption of support systems, and, most of all, stress.

No matter how or when disability has its onset, the impact is life altering. It can affect individuals in all four dimensions of health—biological, psychological, social, and spiritual—to varying degrees depending upon environmental and lifestyle factors and how well medical care and support systems align to match the individual's needs. The following two examples will illustrate this fact more clearly.

Gerald had worked as the manager of a small chain of restaurants for 12 years since graduating from high school. Driving home after closing up late one evening with more than the usual exhaustion, he failed to see an 18-wheel truck that had stalled around a bend in the road. The impact crushed both of his legs. After 5 months in the hospital and numerous surgeries, he was sent home with both legs amputated, one above the knee and one below the knee, chronic back pain, and a bill of more than $100,000 that his insurance did not cover. The pain medications left him in a constantly groggy and irritable state that eventually became clinical depression. He had no desire to return to work and was eventually told by the restaurant owner that he should apply for Social Security Disability Insurance (SSDI). However, his application was rejected. He started to drink and that put even more stress on his wife. She filed for divorce and was granted custody of their two young children and possession of their house. Gerald became homeless. After many months on the street, he discovered a resourcefulness that he did not know he had, inventing a cooking pot out of discarded cans and a way to arrange cardboard boxes to maximize warmth during the winter. He was able to survive and even found joy in teaching some of the other homeless people how to use his inventions. A street medicine doctor from the homeless clinic got to know him and invited him to serve on its board of directors. This was a turning point for Gerald that eventually led to full-time employment for him as a counselor at the clinic.

Laurel's experience with disability came on gradually. As a flight attendant for a major airline, she found it harder and harder to read the passenger manifest even with over-the-counter reading glasses. She finally made an appointment with an ophthalmologist through her health maintenance organization and found that she had a degenerative, incurable eye disease called retinitis pigmentosa. She was devastated by this news and was afraid to share it with her employer and family. When she finally got up the nerve, she was surprised to see that her supervisor at the airline was able to refer her to many different resources both within the company and in their home-base community. The first person with whom she talked was the company's coordinator for the ADA, who had also been trained as an RC. He told her about the company's policy of retraining employees with degenerative conditions for new positions that would take advantage of their other skills, before they were totally unable to deal with their current job. He also linked her up with a support group of people with visual impairments. The depression and fear she had been experiencing gradually diminished and she gained confidence and strength from the new friends she made in the support group. She is now working as branch manager in the reservations department of the airline and accesses her computer using a screen reading device with audio output that the company provided.

These personal stories show that although disability poses challenges in all dimensions of health and well-being, its effect on productivity and quality of life (QOL) is determined mostly by attitudes, and the availability and adaptability of environmental resources. In the example of Gerald, the health care system repaired his body but devastated his personal and financial life. At every turn he found dead ends and no one helped. The one supportive resource that opened for him was the key to regaining his self-esteem and status in the community. Laurel was much luckier in beginning her career with an extraordinarily progressive company that had a high level of awareness and understanding about tapping the potential of people with disabilities by offering them flexibility and supportive resources. These two examples illustrate extremes of how individuals and society can respond to disability, and they correspond to two very different paradigms referred to as the medical and the psychosocial models of disability.

MEDICAL VERSUS PSYCHOSOCIAL MODELS OF DISABILITY

An entire issue of the medical journal the *Lancet* in 2009 was dedicated to discussing the medical model of disability, which emphasizes an individual's physical or mental deficit, and the social model of disability, which highlights the barriers and prejudices that exclude people with disabilities from fully engaging in society and accessing appropriate health care ("Disability: Beyond the medical model," 2009). Most of us who live with disabilities suffer (and I use that word advisedly) not nearly as much from the disability itself as from millennia of negative perceptions surrounding it. The history of people with disabilities and society's response to them has been documented by several prominent historians who themselves had disabilities; among them are Steven E. Brown (2011), Paul K. Longmore (2003), Harlan Hahn (Hahn & Belt, 2004), and Hugh Gallagher (1995). All cite examples throughout Western history of disability as a sign of sin and suffering, being outcast, the object of pity, and most of all repulsion and fear. It was perceived as a great step forward when an attitude of charitable giving and protection toward people with mental and physical impairments was adopted in the Industrial Age. From this spectrum of attitudes that either put us high on a pedestal or stomped us beneath society's collective feet emerged the **medical model**. This paradigm established disability as a source of the problem that resides within the individual; a deficiency or abnormality, a negative that must, by any means, be eliminated, neutralized, or at least hidden from view. The starting point is when disability is diagnosed and labeled, and then becomes the focus of attention. The primary remedy for this problem is cure or normalization, most often delivered from the hands of a medical or educational professional. It follows that segregation and specialized attention are the most efficient and, therefore, the best means for delivering curative therapies and programs. The industry of rehabilitation services that arose from this paradigm included long-term rehabilitation centers in remote locations (e.g., Warm Springs, Georgia, and Gonzalez, Texas) and vocational training centers that focus on preparing people for placement in sheltered workshops (e.g., Goodwill Industries and the Salvation Army). Parallel with this development were efforts emerging from the wars of the early 20th century. Mentally and physically injured soldiers were given government funds, state-of-the-art medical treatment, prosthetic devices, and work training, so that they could return to society as productive citizens.

In the 1960s, a new paradigm of disability emerged called the **social model** (DeJong, 1979; Oliver, 1990; Union of the Physically Impaired Against Segregation [UPIAS], 1976). The social model regards disability as a difference within the range of human variation. Conditions causing impairments are in themselves neutral, but lead to disabilities when there is a dysfunctional interaction between the individual and society, or the environments that societies create. The source of the problem, therefore, resides in society, not within the individual, and it is the society's responsibility to become more inclusive and accommodating toward people with emotional, cognitive, physical, or sensory impairments. The agent of remedy is anyone who seeks to improve the response of society (e.g., families, friends, educators, employers, public services providers, or health care professionals) to the ordinary and extraordinary needs of people with disabilities. In the social model, individuals are valued for their humanity and potential to be threads in the fabric of society, and the differences they bring to their sphere of influence are valued as a source of enrichment.

When disability enters an individual's life, whether by gradual onset, sudden onset, or through the normal processes of aging, there is a point of decision about whether to follow and internalize the medical paradigm or social paradigm. Too often, the only information available to individuals and their families, friends, teachers, clergy, and health care providers is the traditional negative, isolationist medical model that places the "blame" on the individual. Negative messages are pervasive—"You shouldn't have been driving/drinking/playing/living so dangerously," "Don't expect to be able to work/love/have sex/do what you used to do anymore," "You should have listened to me when I told you a long time ago to go see a doctor/get some help/try harder." All these messages put responsibility on the individual for both causing and curing the condition. They also diminish any sense of responsibility on the part of the observer to change or address effective solutions to problems that may arise. By preserving distance, with the observer above and the disabled individual below, these attitudes do little more than perpetuate the archaic stigma and failure traditionally associated with disability.

The more current and progressive attitude toward disability, as illustrated in Laurel's example, accepts and deals with new limitations in function by spreading responsibility between the individual and everyone and everything within that person's circle.

A willingness to change and try new approaches to maintaining or even improving their way of doing things that matter characterizes the more positive and productive attitude toward disability. Amazing progress has been made not only in medicine to minimize the effects of disabling conditions, but also in the education of rehabilitation professionals, including psychologists, physical therapists, occupational therapists, and RCs, on how to use techniques that will help individuals adopt a positive attitude, learn the skills they need to maintain their roles in society, and preserve the relationships that offer them support and QOL.

DISABILITY AS DYNAMIC AND HOLISTIC

Living with disability is a process of constant change and constant adjustment, a process that is difficult to measure and categorize. There exists a dynamic tension between the response to disability by the person, and the response to a person's disability by an external observer (Schwartz, Andresen, Nosek, & Krahn, 2007). Albrecht and Devlieger (1999) described a "disability paradox" and addressed the question: "Why do many people with serious and persistent disabilities report that they experience a good or excellent QOL when to most external observers these people seem to live an undesirable daily existence?" (p. 977). In recognizing this phenomenon, Albrecht and Devlieger initiated a dialogue that raises central questions: (1) What constitutes QOL and health-related quality of life (HRQOL)? (2) Whose perceptions are most important in measuring HRQOL? (3) What appraisal framework influences those perceptions? (4) How do those perceptions vary over time and circumstances?

As an example, the experience of spinal cord injury by a person we will refer to as Juanita will help clarify this dynamic and holistic approach to disability. At the age of 18, a motor vehicle collision left her with complete C6 and C7 tetraplegia. Juanita spent 2 months in a comprehensive medical rehabilitation center where she regained mobility by using a motorized wheelchair and strength in her arms as she learned how to transfer using a transfer board and to access a keyboard by using a pointing device attached to her hand and forearm. After discharge, she experienced more difficulty with psychological adjustment than with physical functioning and found significant changes in how her family and friends responded to her and, indeed, how she viewed herself. Most difficult was reestablishing her relationship with her boyfriend. Realizing that he could never be able to regard her as anything but pitiable, she broke off their relationship. Juanita entered college as planned, and, despite having to learn the limits of her physical abilities and energy, she graduated, married, and secured a well-paying job. After the birth of her first child, she took some time off but returned to full-time employment after becoming comfortable with the adaptations that facilitated motherhood. Life was good for the following two decades, but then her self-image and understanding of her roles were challenged once again as symptoms of aging appeared. She was more likely to experience pressure ulcers than earlier in her life. For 4 months, she had to go on short-term disability leave from her work for surgery, and then to rebuild her strength and stamina. Because work plus homemaking had become more exhausting, she began considering the possibility of early retirement or applying for long-term disability benefits. The possible effects of her decision on her health and functioning and on the well-being of her family and their economic stability were distressing.

From a rehabilitation perspective, five distinct phases of life are discernable for Juanita: preinjury, immediate postinjury, intermediate postinjury, long-term postinjury, and aging.

Before her injury, she had strong relationships with and support from her parents, a positive self-image, and good grades; she was very active in her circle of friends and her community and had a lot of hope for the future. Immediate postinjury was dominated by dealing with the physical trauma and fears about the future. Everything about her physical body, from the way she moved to the way she had to care for it, had changed. Although the social workers at the rehabilitation hospital wanted to talk with her about sexuality, she was more interested in figuring out how she was going to help her boyfriend adjust to her new physical limitations and then get on with her life plan. The phase when she saw significant return of physical and psychosocial functioning for independence in her daily activities was intermediate postinjury, in which Juanita adjusted to these changes and prepared for her future. She recognized and accepted the fact that although she did things differently from others, she still fulfilled the roles of wage earner, wife, mother, and friend, and she cherished her ability to contribute to her family and society. Long-term postinjury was a period of relative stability, but the onset of aging symptoms initiated a new phase of change and adjustment. Some of her initial fears returned as she experienced menopause and had to make adjustments to more changes in her body. Comparing measures of HRQOL in each of these phases of Juanita's life could well be more like comparing measures of five different people. This constant change in physical and general life circumstances is even more dynamic for people with disabilities compared to most of their peers in the general population, and demands a corresponding change in the psychological and social processes that enable them to maintain positive self-esteem and fulfillment of their roles in family and community.

This process of continual reassessment and adjustment is called **response shift**. The most severe disabling conditions, such as blindness, stroke, neuromuscular disorders, amputation, traumatic brain injury, Parkinson's disease, or high-level spinal cord injury, are often referred to by others with terms like suffering, tragedy, catastrophe, and the end of life-worth-living. This outlook rarely reflects the perception of the individual experiencing such conditions. Those who hold negative and limiting attitudes toward disability often exert an undue influence and render a disservice to these individuals by forcing them to internalize these perceptions. The degree to which individuals and families have developed the capacity to adjust to any new circumstances will determine how they respond to disability.

COPING AS POSITIVE AND NEGATIVE

Coping refers to how we respond to adversity and to the distress that results (Carver & Connor-Smith, 2010). In the early days of RC training, coping was generally regarded as a positive phenomenon, synonymous with accommodating, adjusting, continuing the battle, pulling yourself up, managing, and other concepts from the rugged West. Research over the past 20 years has expanded this limited understanding by illuminating an equally important negative side to coping such that it is now divided into strategies or styles. How we cope can depend on many factors, including age, gender, personality, experience, intellectual ability, cognitive style, severity of stress, and how much time has passed since the stressful event (Carver & Connor-Smith, 2010).

Coping styles have been categorized in many different ways according to the focus and the method used: for example, problem focused or emotion focused (Lazarus & Folkman, 1984), engagement versus disengagement (Roth & Cohen, 1986), cognition or behavior (Moos & Billings, 1982), and internalizing or externalizing (Lengua &

Stormshak, 2000). According to Moos and Holahan (2003, p. 1391), these are often combined into four categories:

- Cognitive coping—logical analysis, positive reappraisal, paying attention to one aspect of the situation at a time, drawing on past experiences, mentally rehearsing alternative actions and their probable consequences, accepting but restructuring a situation to find something favorable
- Behavioral coping—seeking guidance and support and taking action to deal directly with a situation
- Cognitive avoidance coping—minimizing or denying the seriousness of a situation, accepting it as it is
- Behavioral avoidance coping—seeking alternative rewards, replacing losses by becoming involved in new activities, openly venting one's feelings of anger and frustration, acting impulsively, doing something risky

Hanoch Livneh has produced a body of literature on coping and disability in which he refers to five psychosocial reactions: anxiety, depression, anger, denial, and positive adjustment (Livneh & Antonak, 1997; Livneh & Martz, 2007). Anxiety reflects a negative regard for the past and fear of the future. A depressive orientation focuses on personal loss and failures, and is characterized by pessimism, hopelessness, and helplessness. Anger can be expressed within a wide range of social contexts. Feelings of frustration, perceptions of being mistreated, discounted, or invalidated as a person, and observational learning of aggressive acts have been found to be at the root of aggressive behaviors. Denial typically is viewed as either a conscious or an unconscious act of loosely linked efforts to mitigate distressing thoughts that remind the person of his or her condition, its long-term implications, emotional vulnerability, uncertain future, and even accelerated mortality. Positive adjustment is cognitive acceptance marked by increased insight into one's strength and limitations (Martz, 2004).

The literature has very little to teach us, however, about coping with other aspects of the disability experience beyond personal adjustment. Institutionalized social exclusion, discrimination, stigma, and devaluation are part of the disability reality, as is the social tendency to look the other way when people with disabilities are subjected to emotional, physical, sexual, or disability-related abuse. How individuals transcend these negative social tendencies to acquire positive, well-balanced self-images is not addressed in the literature on coping. Because most studies have been conducted on people with traumatic or adult-onset disabilities, we know little about how coping styles develop for those who grow up knowing only a self-determined sense of "normal." Denial is regarded by some as a maladaptive way of dealing with disability, and yet many people with disabilities use denial as a way to survive. Only by ignoring chronic pain, for example, or choosing to suppress acknowledgment of their distinctive appearance or manner of functioning are some people with disabilities able to maintain their sense of coherence and wholeness.

The grassroots independent living movement (see Hartley's discussion of the independent living movement in Chapter 9) has brought to light the importance of peer role modeling and peer counseling, borrowed from its predecessors in the feminist and the civil rights movements. By talking with others who face similar or even greater disability-related barriers and psychosocial challenges, individuals can gain confidence and new ideas about coping strategies, daily functioning, self-image, and more effective ways of relating to other people and the world around them.

EFFECT OF DISABILITY ON RELATIONSHIPS

People with disabilities often have more difficulty in finding partners and forming personal relationships leading to intimacy than people without disabilities. Chronic illness and disability tend to remove individuals from "accustomed personal, social, and sexual interactions, changing the entire life pattern. . . . Feelings of self-worth and attractiveness are threatened at a time when need for intimacy and belonging is greatest, causing a sense of loneliness and isolation" (Glass & Padrone, 1978, p. 44). The whole approach to sexuality and disability has been subject to the medical model discussed earlier, with the emphasis on "performing," a distinctly male phenomenon, and little attention paid to the development of relationships or sexual satisfaction (Tepper, 2000). Although the medical model limited sexuality and disability to issues of mechanics, social stigma has made it taboo. For women especially, eugenics has added the notion of "should not" to assumptions of "cannot" when it comes to pregnancy (Rintala et al., 1997; Waxman, 1994).

Psychosocial factors such as self-concept, self-esteem, desirability as a sexual partner, emotional status, independence, and social skills occasionally are discussed in relation to sexuality, but seldom studied empirically. One notable exception (Rintala et al., 1997) compared women with physical disabilities to women without disabilities and found that women with disabilities were less satisfied with their dating frequency, perceived more constraints on attracting dating partners, and perceived more societal and personal barriers to dating. In addition, women whose disabilities occurred before their first date were older at the time of their first date than women who were either not disabled or disabled after their first date. Higher self-esteem was associated with more satisfaction with dating. Within the last decade, "our understanding of individual sexuality has broadened such that we can acknowledge that one's sexual development is a multidimensional process and includes the basic needs of being liked and accepted, displaying and receiving affection, feeling valued and attractive, and sharing thoughts and feelings" (Esmail, Darry, Walter, & Knupp, 2010, p. 1149).

Expectations and opportunities have a lot to do with social and sexual development and opportunities, on both the positive and the negative sides. Children growing up with disabling conditions are often excluded from the mainstream school environment despite legislation prohibiting this except in the most severe cases, which makes them disadvantaged in learning about social role expectations and the rules of social engagement. Overprotective attitudes of family and medical professionals that can take the form of excessive assistance, recommendations to avoid activities, constant vigilance, constant reminders of self-care, and being overly deferential also serve to limit the exposure of children and adolescents with disabilities to normalized social expectations and can result in significantly lower happiness, self-esteem, perceived popularity, self-consciousness, and higher levels of anxiety (Blum, Resnick, Nelson, & St. Germaine, 1991). These sociocultural barriers can be more disabling than the impairment itself. It would be nice to be able to say that among people with disabilities, those who are expected to marry will marry. However, no studies have been conducted on the positive aspects of social expectations.

We know that disparities exist in opportunities for dating and rates of marriage from studies of specific disability samples and subpopulations, but population-based statistics are very difficult to find. One study examined data from the 1994 to 1995 national health interview survey and found a significant difference in rates of marriage among women with no functional limitations (63%), women with one or two functional limitations (55%), and women with three or more functional limitations (48%), even after adjusting for age (Chevarley, Thierry, Gill, Ryerson, & Nosek, 2006). It is generally understood that more men than women abandon marriages when their spouse becomes ill or disabled

(Sandowski, 1989). Men are more likely than women to have their spouses meet their needs for personal assistance whether disability has its onset before or after the intimate relationship has been established—a consequence of the caregiving role generally ascribed to women.

Opportunities to have an active dating life are limited by environmental barriers as much as psychosocial barriers. The classic notion of going out to eat with a significant other, for example, requires accessible transportation and affordable restaurants, two precious commodities for many people with disabilities (Taylor, Krane, & Orkis, 2010). Privacy is often at odds with the need for personal assistance (Earle, 1999). Internalized stereotypes of asexuality make some people with disabilities suspicious of why anyone would be attracted to them (Rintala et al., 1997). There is also the issue of having to explain, especially about assistive devices (Rintala et al., 1997) or when the disabling condition is not visible (Esmail et al., 2010).

Ending unhealthy relationships often is very difficult for people with disabilities. One woman who used a wheelchair spoke about her abusive partner by saying, "I think that was one reason why it sort of kept going or held on for so long was that even though I was trying to let it go, there was a large part of me that was saying, even though this is bad, this is all you have, the feeling that I wasn't good enough to get anybody else ever. This was my one and only shot." There are many ways that people with disabilities experience abuse: through emotional manipulation and belittlement, physical maltreatment, forced sexual activity, and withholding necessary equipment, medications, and assistance (Nosek, Foley, Hughes, & Howland, 2001). Compared to women without disabilities, women with disabilities are more likely to experience physical and sexual violence (Brownridge, 2006; Martin et al., 2006; Powers et al., 2002; Smith, 2008), increased severity of violence (Brownridge, 2006; Nannini, 2006; Nosek, Howland, & Hughes, 2001), multiple forms of violence (Curry, Powers, Oschwald, & Saxton, 2004; Martin et al., 2006; Nosek, Howland, & Hughes, 2001), and longer duration of violence (Nosek, Howland, & Hughes, 2001). Although not as well studied as violence against women with disabilities, violence against men with disabilities has been shown to be a serious problem (Cohen, Forte, DuMont, Hyman, & Romans, 2006; Marchetti & McCartney, 1990; Powers et al., 2008; Saxton et al., 2006). There is an emerging body of literature on interventions to help people with disabilities learn to identify abuse and plan for their safety (Powers, Hughes, & Lund, 2009).

Thankfully, with the emergence of the Internet as a communication, educational, and networking tool, resources are expanding rapidly for people with disabilities and the professionals who serve them to learn about healthy sexuality (e.g., www.disaboom.com/marriage-and-disability; www.sexualhealth.com/channel/view/disability-illness).

HEALTH AND WELLNESS IN THE CONTEXT OF DISABILITY

The notion that people with disabilities could achieve optimal health, in all of its physical, psychological, and social dimensions, is relatively new in wellness research. This realization gained momentum with the rise of the independent living movement in the mid-1970s, in which people with disabilities demanded acknowledgment of their civil rights and expected to exert control over their lives. Although still far behind the search for cures, the health of people with disabilities is a topic of growing interest and it is beginning to be the focus of federal research funds. As a result, we now have an embryonic body of literature and the beginnings of discussions about how disability puts to the test wellness theory, research, and practice (Nosek, 2005).

Health and wellness in the context of disability have many unique aspects that are not generally known or understood by medical or mental health professionals. These unique aspects interrelate in a complex web of factors that affect the ability of individuals with disabilities to achieve and maintain optimal health and functioning. Consider the case of a 54-year-old woman named Melinda who had polio as a child and functions with a motorized wheelchair and a variety of adaptive devices. For all of her work life, she has never had the opportunity to use the bathroom during the workday. She lives in an apartment complex that has a shared attendant program, but the attendants are not allowed to leave the premises to provide services. Even if she had not been raised with the expectation that she should be totally self-sufficient, or at least give the appearance of such, and even if she could find someone at the hospital where she works to help her at lunchtime, her wheelchair is too large to fit into the stalls of the public restrooms there. As a result, she has had to train her bladder to retain substantial amounts of urine and restrict her fluid intake to a minimum. Although this solution was uncomfortable, it was not a serious problem until recently. She now gets frequent urinary tract infections and is beginning to have some incontinence. Melinda's internist has no idea how she could change her living and working situation to be more conducive to health, so she prescribed antibiotics to get her through until the next occurrence.

The presentation of this real-life scenario could go on to include the effect of her managed care plan on getting needed prescriptions from her primary care physician, the restrictions it places on seeing specialists, the limitations it forces on her behaviors and planned activities, the impact this problem has on her self-image, the complicating effects that adaptive equipment (wheelchair, seat cushion) or the lack thereof (including an effective female urinal) has on the problem, and the numerous other health problems that stem from frequent urinary tract infections (e.g., yeast infections, antibiotic resistance, skin breakdowns, and lowered immunity to other bacterial and viral infections). The solution to this individual's health problems would require massive changes in policies governing the financing and delivery of health care services, rehabilitation services, social support services, and the research and development of adaptive equipment. Her health might also be improved if disability- and gender-sensitive health promotion education and intervention programs were available to her, perhaps something with peer interaction and information about her potential to improve her health. And so the litmus test for wellness theory, research, and practice becomes the question of how effectively it meets the needs of people with disabilities.

People with disabilities face the effects of the increased risk of developing health conditions that often accompany disability, the stresses that result from living in a society that imposes many limitations and stereotypes on people with disabilities, and the pervasive environmental barriers that restrict socialization and participation in the community. Nevertheless, some people with physical disabilities live in a state of vibrant health and, moreover, are able to maintain equilibrium whenever threats to their well-being arise.

Understanding that the process of living with disability carries with it a plethora of risks for additional health problems makes it difficult to imagine how a person with a disability could achieve and maintain wellness. To make sense of this, we must hold all preconceptions at bay and examine disability as one component of the context within which we all live. *It is largely society and our environment that make disability a disadvantage.* Consider the three-legged cat, functional in every way and even content, that is an object of pity only in the eyes of some humans. Even with progressively disabling conditions, achieving and maintaining wellness is associated most closely with resilience, perseverance, and creative problem solving, among other survival traits. The investigation of wellness in the context of disability, therefore, demands an understanding of the ingredients in this complex recipe.

We talk about a **model of health and wellness** that includes (1) physical or biological health, including general health status, body mass index, vitality, pain, functional limitations, chronic conditions, and secondary conditions; (2) psychological health, including general mental health, life satisfaction, perceived well-being, and self-esteem; (3) social health, including intimacy, social connectedness, social functioning, and social integration; and (4) spiritual health, including transcendence, meaning or purpose in life, optimism, and self-understanding (Nosek, 2005).

At the foundation of this model lies the intricate web of **contextual factors** that can have a very different configuration for people with disabilities. The contextual factors that are of interest in our research are either internal to the individual or external in the environment and cannot be easily changed, but some of them can be modified through management strategies. These factors include health history, disability characteristics, demographics, relationships, values and beliefs, life experiences, and environmental resources. The category of environmental resources encompasses many aspects of the micro-, meso-, exo-, and macro-systems in which people with disabilities live, including access to financial resources; education level; the built and natural environments; technology; information from the print and broadcast media and the Internet; instrumental social support and services; and access to health care services.

It is the challenge of each individual to adopt health-promoting behaviors to the extent his or her disability allows. Here, too, perceptions and stereotypes play an important role. Just because someone has significant impairment in their ability to walk does not mean that he or she cannot exercise. Whether or not an individual has a disability, behaviors such as smoking, excessive drinking of alcohol, and use of illegal drugs and other substances are self-destructive activities. Physical inactivity and obesity are quite prevalent among people with all types of disabilities, and often have more negative effects on their health than for people in the general population. Unfortunately, little is known about the types of activity and diet that would be most beneficial for people with specific types of disabilities. Adopting health-promoting behaviors also includes behaviors that specifically relate to disability management, such as medication management, personal assistance management, prevention of secondary conditions, and maintenance of assistive devices.

Maintaining health and wellness for individuals with any type of disabling condition is a complex balancing act affecting every dimension of living. It is no wonder, then, that stress and exhaustion can result from trying to maintain this balance, leaving little energy left over to hold down a paid job or be involved in family and community activities. Another Catch-22 situation that many people with disabilities face is the policy and political decision the United States has taken to link work and access to health care insurance, a decision that has left people with disabilities subject to work disincentives and health care apartheid (Nosek, 2010).

HEALTH CARE REFORM

There are essentially two ways to access to health care in the United States. The first is by having private health insurance purchased from a for-profit health insurance company by your employer, yourself, or a family member. The second is by being eligible for Medicare or government-funded programs, most commonly Medicaid, the Veterans

Health Administration, or the Indian Health Service. Eligibility for Medicare is automatic when you turn age 65 without regard to your income or work status, and there is no waiting period for receiving this benefit. If you are under age 65 and have worked and accumulated sufficient points in the Social Security system before you develop or acquire a disabling condition that prevents you from working, you can apply for SSDI, which includes Medicare. This process, however, demands that you have unequivocal medical evidence that you are too disabled to work. It may take years of submitting and resubmitting paperwork, and many people are forced to hire a lawyer to navigate the system of disability determination on their behalf. Once eligibility is obtained, there is a 2-year waiting period before you have access to health care insurance through Medicare.

Access to health care is automatically available for veterans through the Veterans Health Administration and for members or descendants of a federally recognized American Indian or Alaska Native Tribe through the Indian Health Service. Eligibility for Supplemental Security Income (SSI) and Medicaid, however, is totally dependent upon income. Each state determines income eligibility as a percentage (in most states 133%) of the federal poverty limit (Centers for Medicare and Medicaid Services, 2017a), which is based on a formula established by the U.S. Department of Health and Human Services (DHHS) that combines the amount of income received and the number of people who are supported by that income. For an individual with no dependents, the 2017 poverty level was $12,060 per year or $1,005 per month; for a family of four, it was $24,600 per year or $2,050 per month (limits are higher for Alaska and Hawaii; HealthCare.gov, 2017). The eligible income level for Medicaid in most states in 2017 was $1,336.65 per month for an individual and $2,726.50 per month for a family of four. There are also limits on the amount of resources that are available to the individual, such as bank accounts, real property, or other items that can be sold for cash (Centers for Medicare and Medicaid Services, 2017a). Medicaid benefits are only available to those who are U.S. citizens or lawfully admitted immigrants.

In addition to having limited income, individuals can be eligible for Medicaid if they are blind, children or adults with other disabilities or serious chronic health conditions, women who are pregnant, or people older than 65. Eligibility for Medicaid by an adult or child also brings with it eligibility for food stamps, housing assistance, personal assistance (attendant care) services, and other benefit programs that vary by state. For children growing up with health care coverage and other eligibilities through Medicaid, the burden is heavy to achieve an independent lifestyle or obtain work yielding an income and access to health insurance that would be sufficient to offset the monetary value of these benefits. This is referred to as the *work disincentive.*

The U.S. Congress attempted to remove some of these work disincentives by enacting the Ticket to Work and Work Incentives Improvement Act (TWWIIA) in 1999. Under this law, individuals who receive SSI or SSDI develop a plan to achieve self-sufficiency that can involve receiving vocational training, advanced education, or a trial work period during which they can maintain their benefits and access to health care coverage. At the end of their training or trial work period, cash benefits are terminated and eligibility for Medicaid or Medicare ends. If a plan to achieve self-sufficiency is not successful, individuals may continue to earn a salary up to a certain limit and still receive SSI or SSDI and Medicaid or Medicare coverage.

Once Medicaid-eligible children with disabilities reach adulthood, they risk losing all of their benefits if they marry, because their spouse's income and resources are considered in determining their continued eligibility. This is referred to as the *marriage penalty.* Parents can also jeopardize the Medicaid eligibility of their adult children with disabilities by writing them into their will without certain safeguards. They can establish some degree of security for their Medicaid-eligible child only by setting up a tightly regulated trust fund for any inherited funds or property.

The unfortunate truth about Medicaid-funded health care is that it is most often substandard. Reimbursement rates for medical providers are extremely low, causing the majority to refuse services to people who have Medicaid coverage. Only a little more than half of physicians (53%) reported that their practices were accepting all or most new Medicaid patients in 2008 (Boukus, Cassil, & O'Malley, 2009). Waiting times are extraordinarily long for getting an appointment with a provider who accepts Medicaid or with a county-funded community clinic or hospital, often coming well after initial symptoms have escalated into a serious illness. For this reason, many people with disabilities seek care for otherwise preventable conditions in the emergency room of a county hospital where service is guaranteed and more immediate, though much more expensive for taxpayers than if they had timely access to a primary care provider. This system of delivering health care at varying levels of quality depending upon an individual's income and type of health insurance is, in effect, healthcare apartheid (Nosek, 2010).

The Patient Protection and Affordable Care Act of 2010 (ACA) requires states to expand their Medicaid program by 2014 to include people with incomes that are a greater percentage above the federal poverty limit (Centers for Medicare and Medicaid Services, 2017b). The political drama surrounding this act resulted in 19 states opting out of the Medicaid expansion (Kaiser Family Foundation, 2017). Unknown to many members of the public is the fact that in most states Medicaid is funded 60% by the federal government and 40% by the state, and that the majority of these funds go toward maintaining older and younger people with disabilities in nursing homes. By not expanding Medicaid, these 19 predominantly southern states are losing a substantial amount of federal matching money, thereby increasing the tax burden on its own citizens.

Medicaid programs prevent indigent individuals and families from being totally without access to health care services, but they come at the price of individual freedom. Their strict income and resource eligibility requirements force people to maintain a state of impoverishment and reduce the incentive for finding work. The health care available with Medicaid coverage does not match the quality available with private health insurance in terms of choice of provider and waiting times for service. Medicaid-eligible individuals are limited in their freedom to marry or accept gifts from family without risk of losing critical life-sustaining services. In most states, it is difficult to obtain Medicaid-funded home-based services, creating the constant threat of institutionalization for many people with disabilities or age-related functional limitations.

An organization of activist people with disabilities called ADAPT (www.adapt.org) is dedicated to creating a priority on home-based services over institutionalization for people with disabilities. Through its nationwide advocacy, Community Living Assistance Services and Supports Act has been introduced to Congress and included in the Patient Protection and Affordable Care Act as Title VIII (Community Living Assistance Services and Supports Act, Title VIII of the Patient Protection and Affordable Care Act, 2010). This is a consumer-funded provision, whereby a designated amount determined by age is deducted monthly from an individual's paycheck. After an investment period of 5 years, funds can be deducted up to $75 per day when a disability-related need for in-home services arises. The provision is not available for those who are not working.

In the current economic climate with the skyrocketing costs of health care, more and more employers are eliminating health care benefits. This decline in coverage, combined with high unemployment rates, is creating a rapidly growing population of working-age people who are uninsured. The price of health care insurance, even with the state and federal health insurance exchanges in place under the Affordable Care Act, after considering the very high rates of deductibles and out of pocket expenses is generally unaffordable. Many people with disabling conditions also fall into this category if they are too disabled to work but not disabled enough to qualify for Medicaid or Medicare. Although the ACA prohibits exclusions, higher rates, and coverage caps for people with preexisting conditions, there is political pressure to force states to re-establish high-risk pools that offer coverage at a high price with limited benefits. It is, sadly, a no-win situation.

Efforts are underway by activists in Physicians for a National Health Program (www.PNHP.org) and Health Care Now (www.healthcare-now.org) to achieve more comprehensive health care reform. The Affordable Care Act, though opening new opportunities for coverage for some, essentially reinforces the existing system of high-priced health care insurance offered by for-profit corporations to those who are working or have the resources to purchase their own coverage. It relies on Medicaid and other government subsidies to provide what is generally regarded as substandard care for those who have significantly limited income and resources. In the rest of the industrialized world, single-payer health care systems predominate, in which necessary care is available to everyone with minimal or no out-of-pocket expenses. The "single-payer" in these cases is either the government or a not-for-profit insurance company. By expanding the risk pool to include everyone regardless of their age, health status, or work status, these systems are able to reduce health care costs while ensuring access to everyone. The profit motive in the United States has unfortunately taken priority over health care freedom for everyone.

CONCLUSION

Living with disability is complicated and can be overwhelming. RCs can also feel overwhelmed by the complex systems that have been set up to help people with disabilities achieve optimal health and social integration. At some point, everyone has to make the decision to keep up the fight, accept things as they are, or succumb to defeat. There will be days when all three of these can be experienced simultaneously. Many of us who work in the field of rehabilitation and also experience disability personally in our daily lives know that the fight can be positive, acceptance can be a victory, and defeat must be reframed so that it is consistent with striving for wholeness. By understanding that complexity can also bring richness and opportunity, we can gain strength to continue working toward positive change in our personal lives and in the context within which we live.

CONTENT REVIEW QUESTIONS

- Explain the difference between the medical and psychosocial models of disability.
- What are the limitations of current studies about the experience of coping with disability? How can these limitations be improved?
- Identify significant psychosocial and environmental barriers that limit opportunities of individuals with disabilities to have an active dating life.
- What is meant by contextual factors? How can contextual factors be used in understanding health and wellness of people with disabilities?
- What are the limitations of the health care systems available to the public? Explain societal efforts to improve the system.
- What are the major changes and challenges that people living with disabilities may experience?

REFERENCES

Albrecht, G. L., & Devlieger, P. J. (1999). The disability paradox: High quality of life against all odds. *Social Science and Medicine, 48,* 977–988.

Blum, R. W., Resnick, M. D., Nelson, R., & St. Germaine, A. (1991). Family and peer issues among adolescents with spina bifida and cerebral palsy. *Pediatrics, 20,* 280–285.

Boukus, E., Cassil, A., & O'Malley, A. S. (2009). *A snapshot of U.S. physicians: Key findings from the 2008 health tracking study physician survey* (Center for Studying Health System Change Data Bulletin No. 35.) Washington, DC: Center for Studying Health System Change. Retrieved from http://www.hschange.com/CONTENT/1078/#top

Brown, S. E. (2011). *Surprised to be standing: A spiritual journey.* Honolulu, HI: Healing Light.

Brownridge, D. A. (2006). Partner violence against women with disabilities: Prevalence, risk, and explanations. *Violence Against Women, 12,* 805–822.

Carver, C. S., & Connor-Smith, J. (2010). Personality and coping. *Annual Review Psychology, 61,* 679–704.

Centers for Medicare and Medicaid Services. (2017a). Medicaid eligibility. Retrieved from https://www.medicaid.gov/medicaid/eligibility/index.html

Centers for Medicare and Medicaid Services. (2017b). Affordable Care Act. Retrieved from https://www.medicaid.gov/affordable-care-act/index.html

Chevarley, F., Thierry, J. M., Gill, C. J., Ryerson, A. B., & Nosek, M. A. (2006). Health, preventive health care, and health care access among women with disabilities in the 1994–1995 National Health Interview Survey. *Women's Health Issues, 16*(6), 297–312.

Cohen, M. M., Forte, T., DuMont, J., Hyman, I., & Romans, S. (2006). Adding insult to injury: Intimate partner violence among women and men reporting activity limitations. *Annals of Epidemiology, 16,* 644–651.

Community Living Assistance Services and Supports Act, Title VIII of the Patient Protection and Affordable Care Act, Pub. L No. 111–148, 124 Stat. 119 (2010).

Curry, M. A., Powers, L. E., Oschwald, M., & Saxton, M. (2004). Development and testing of an abuse screening tool for women with disabilities. *Journal of Aggression, Maltreatment and Trauma, 8*(4), 123–141.

DeJong, G. (1979). Independent living: From social movement to analytic paradigm. *Archives of Physical Medicine and Rehabilitation, 60,* 435–446.

Disability: Beyond the medical model. (2009). Special issue editorial. *Lancet, 374*(9704), 1793.

Earle, S. (1999). Facilitated sex and the concept of sexual need: Disabled students and their personal assistants. *Disability and Society, 14,* 309–323.

Esmail, S., Darry, K., Walter, A., & Knupp, H. (2010). Attitudes and perceptions towards disability and sexuality. *Disability and Rehabilitation, 32*(14), 1148–1155.

Gallagher, H. G. (1995). *By trust betrayed: Patients, physicians, and the license to kill in the Third Reich.* St. Petersburg, FL: Vandamere Press.

Glass, D. D., & Padrone, F. J. (1978). Sexual adjustment in the handicapped. *Journal of Rehabilitation, 44*(1), 43–47.

Hahn, H. D., & Belt, T. L. (2004). Disability identity and attitudes toward cure in a sample of disabled activists. *Journal of Health and Social Behaviour, 45*(4), 453–464.

HealthCare.gov. (2017). Federal poverty level (FPL). Retrieved from https://www.healthcare.gov/glossary/federal-poverty-level-FPL

Kaiser Family Foundation. (2017). Current status of the Medicaid expansion decision. Retrieved from http://kff.org/health-reform/slide/current-status-of-the-medicaid-expansion-decision

Lazarus, R. S., & Folkman, S. (1984). *Stress, appraisal, and coping.* New York, NY: Springer Publishing.

Lengua, L. J., & Stormshak, E. A. (2000). Gender, gender roles, and personality: Gender differences in the prediction of coping and psychological symptoms. *Sex Roles, 43*(11/12), 787–820.

Livneh, H., & Antonak, R. F. (1997). *Psychosocial adaptation to chronic illness and disability.* Gaithersburg, MD: Aspen.

Livneh, H., & Martz, E. (2007). Reactions to diabetes and their relationship to time orientation. *International Journal of Rehabilitation Research, 30*(2), 127–136.

Longmore, P. K. (2003). *Why I burned my book and other essays on disability.* Philadelphia, PA: Temple University Press.

Marchetti, A. G., & McCartney, J. R. (1990). Abuse of persons with mental retardation: Characteristics of the abused, the abusers, and the informers. *Mental Retardation, 28*(6), 367–371.

Martin, S. L., Ray, N., Sotres-Alvarez, D., Kupper, L. L., Moracco, K. E., Dickens, P. A., . . . Gizlice, Z. (2006). Physical and sexual assault of women with disabilities. *Violence Against Women, 12,* 823–837.

Martz, E. (2004). Reactions of adaptation to disability as predictors of future time orientation among individuals with spinal cord injuries. *Rehabilitation Counseling Bulletin, 47,* 86–95.

Moos, R. H., & Billings, A. G. (1982). Conceptualizing and measuring coping resources and processes. In L. Goldberg & S. Breznitz (Eds.), *Handbook of stress: Theoretical and clinical aspects* (pp. 212–230). New York, NY: Free Press.

Moos, R. H., & Holahan, C. J. (2003). Dispositional and contextual perspectives on coping: Toward an integrative framework. *Journal of Clinical Psychology, 59,* 1387–1403.

Nannini, A. (2006). Sexual assault patterns among women with and without disabilities seeking survivor services. *Women's Health Issues, 16*(6), 372–379.

Nosek, M. A. (2005). Wellness in the context of disability. In J. Myers & T. Sweeney (Eds.), *Counseling for wellness: Theory, research, and practice* (pp. 257–302). Alexandria, VA: American Counseling Association.

Nosek, M. A. (2010). Healthcare apartheid and quality of life for people with disabilities. *Quality of Life Research, 19*(4), 609–610.

Nosek, M. A. (2016). Health disparities and equity: The intersection of disability, health, and sociodemographic characteristics among women. In S. E. Miles-Cohen & C. Signore (Eds.), *Eliminating inequities for women with disabilities: An agenda for health and wellness* (pp. 13–38). Washington, DC: American Psychological Association.

Nosek, M. A., Foley, C. C., Hughes, R. B., & Howland, C. A. (2001). Vulnerabilities for abuse among women with disabilities. *Sexuality and Disability, 19*(3), 177–190.

Nosek, M. A., Howland, C. A., & Hughes, R. B. (2001). The investigation of abuse and women with disabilities: Going beyond assumptions. *Violence Against Women, 7*(4), 477–499.

Oliver, M. (1990). *The individual and social models of disability.* Paper presented at Joint Workshop of the Living Options Group and the research unit of the Royal College of Physicians on People with Established Locomotor Disabilities in Hospitals, London, UK. Retrieved from http://www.leeds.ac.uk/disability-studies/archiveuk/Oliver/in%20soc%20dis.pdf

Patient Protection and Affordable Care Act, Pub. L. No. 111–148, 124 Stat. 119 (2010).

Powers, L. E., Curry, M. A., McNeff, E., Saxton, M., Powers, J., & Oswchald, M. M. (2008). End the silence: A survey of the abuse experiences of men with disabilities. *Journal of Rehabilitation, 7*(4), 41–53.

Powers, L. E., Curry, M. A., Oschwald, M., Maley, S., Saxton, M., & Eckels, K. (2002). Barriers and strategies in addressing abuse: A survey of disabled women's experiences. *Journal of Rehabilitation, 68*(1), 4–13.

Powers, L. E., Hughes, R. B., & Lund, E. M. (2009). *Interpersonal violence and women with disabilities: A research update.* Harrisburg, PA: National Resource Center on Domestic Violence/Pennsylvania Coalition Against Domestic Violence. Retrieved from http://www.vawnet.org

Rintala, D. H., Howland, C. A., Nosek, M. A., Bennett, J. L., Young, M. E., Foley, C. C., . . . Chanpong, G. (1997). Dating issues for women with physical disabilities. *Sexuality and Disability, 15*(4), 219–242.

Roth, S., & Cohen, L. J. (1986). Approach, avoidance, and coping with stress. *American Psychologist, 41,* 813–819.

Sandowski, C. L. (1989). *Sexual concerns when illness or disability strikes.* Springfield, IL: Charles C. Thomas.

Saxton, M., McNeff, E., Powers, L. E., Curry, M. A., Limont, M., & Benson, J. (2006). We are all little John Waynes: A study of disabled men's experiences of abuse by personal assistants. *Journal of Rehabilitation, 72*(4), 3–13.

Schwartz, C. E., Andresen, E. M., Nosek, M. A., & Krahn, G. L. (2007). Response shift theory: Important implications for measuring quality of life in people with disability. *Archives of Physical Medicine and Rehabilitation, 88*(4), 529–536.

Smith, D. L. (2008). Disability, gender and intimate partner violence: Relationships from the behavioral risk factor surveillance system. *Sexuality and Disability, 26*(1), 15–28.

Taylor, H., Krane, D., & Orkis, K. (2010). *The ADA, 20 years later: Kessler Foundation/NOD survey of Americans with disabilities.* New York, NY: Harris Interactive.

Tepper, M. S. (2000). Sexuality and disability: The missing discourse of pleasure. *Sexuality and Disability, 18,* 283–290.

Ticket to Work and Work Incentives Improvement Act, Pub. L. No. 106–170, 113 Stat. 1860–1951 (1999).

Union of the Physically Impaired Against Segregation. (1976). *Fundamental principles of disability.* London, UK: Author.

Waxman, B. F. (1994). Up against eugenics: Disabled women's challenge to receive reproductive health services. *Sexuality and Disability, 12*(2), 155–171.

EIGHT

Family and Relationship Issues

R. ROCCO COTTONE

LEARNING OBJECTIVES

After reading this chapter, you should be able to:

- Provide a historical backdrop related to the psychomedical framework of traditional vocational rehabilitation (VR) as compared to the emerging systemic-relational view of the rehabilitation process.
- Recognize the influence of relationships on the rehabilitation process, on the client, and within the family or social system of significance.
- Present a perspective of clients as embedded within the network of relationships and the rehabilitation counselor (RC) as a social agent facilitating interface of client and rehabilitation systems.
- Reconceptualize the rehabilitation process as a social process.
- Describe the role and influence of the family system in rehabilitation.
- Describe the adaptation process of families addressing disabilities, including defining the caregiver stages of adjustment.
- Outline the effect of disability on the family and on caregivers.
- Address family members' roles and possible disruption of family routines during the rehabilitation process.
- Describe family dynamics related to job placement or community living.
- Argue that the role of the RC is that of family advocate who encourages rehabilitation counseling training in family therapy and social systems theory.
- Address educational and competency issues of RCs related to family intervention.

Rehabilitation does not occur in a vacuum. Many people are involved in the rehabilitation process, including family members of the individual with a disability and any number of friends, acquaintances, and professionals. A relational perspective embraces the involvement of others in a person's rehabilitation; it is critical especially for understanding the experience of rehabilitation for individuals with disabilities and their families. There have been recent efforts to recognize the importance of family and relationship issues in rehabilitation counseling (Millington & Marini, 2015a). However, rehabilitation counseling is a counseling specialty that has been closely and historically aligned with the nonrelational psychomedical paradigm of mental health services (Cottone & Emener, 1990). The psychomedical paradigm of mental health services is a framework for conceptualizing client problems. It is also a framework for identification and implementation of methods of problem solving. The focus of the psychomedical paradigm is the individual person—the person with a diagnosed medical condition. The individual is viewed as an independent focus of treatment (Cottone & Emener, 1990). Prior to the late 1970s and early 1980s, RCs focused on individual clients, serving them outside of family or other larger influential social systems. Clients were viewed as individuals (somewhat isolated from their social contexts) with problems that derived from their physical and mental conditions. Disability was first and foremost a matter of limitations deriving from a medical problem. Historically, until recently, little emphasis was placed on identifying, researching, or treating social factors that affected a client's adaptation (Millington, Jenkins, & Cottone, 2015). Millington et al. (2015), lamenting the medical orientation of rehabilitation counseling, stated:

> The medical model has no active role for the family. . . . When the science is reductive, the social network is invisible and the issues of family are not recognized. For all the good intent, the medical model falls short for all rehabilitation professions, but particularly for rehabilitation counseling. (pp. 4–5)

The social systems or relational model of rehabilitation intervention is just beginning to get focused attention in the field, although there have been divergent and persistent calls for recognition of family and relational issues affecting both clients and the profession. In other words, the social systems model is relational in nature, and is interactive, because it is concerned with the influence of other individuals in the rehabilitation process, even to the degree to which systems of relationships (organizations, families, groups) are analyzed and addressed in the rehabilitation process.

Because, historically, rehabilitation counseling was closely associated with vocational issues, many of the early rehabilitation assessment and intervention methods were consistent with the vocational trait-factor movement (Kosciulek, 1993; Kosciulek & DeVinney, 2004), an approach that emphasized methods for fitting the peg (client) into the best hole (job). The trait-factor approach dates back to Parsons (1909) and the vocational choice movement. Trait-factorism held that a client could be viewed as having characteristics (in a classic psychological and physical sense). Matching the client's positive and negative characteristics to a job and a work context was thought to be the best and easiest way to find a place for the client to work and to earn a living. Clients could thereby become productive members of society.

Rehabilitation counseling, based on trait-factor philosophy and grounded in the psychomedical paradigm, was a conglomeration of methods that were used to assess and to treat clients. For example, vocational assessment focused on identifying traits. Psychological traits (such as intelligence, aptitudes, and interests) and physical skills (such as finger dexterity, speed of processing, physical mobility, and strength) were identified, assessed, and matched to jobs in the marketplace. In the late 1970s and early 1980s, some theoreticians began to identify and to challenge the trait-factor or psychomedical framework, arguing that such a framework was less than ideal for addressing issues associated with disability. Notably, the psychosocial movement in rehabilitation, as best represented by the work of Wright (1983) and Stubbins (1977), began to recognize and conceptualize the social (along with the psychological) aspects of disability. Stubbins (1984) further challenged the status quo, as he was the first to argue for a more social systemic understanding of disability. Stubbins argued for expanding the definition of VR to include "social systems factors" (p. 375).

Soon after the call by Stubbins (1984) for a systemic understanding of the rehabilitation process, the first comprehensive theory of VR was developed to challenge the historical psychomedical framework of rehabilitation counseling. Cottone (1987) developed his systemic theory of VR. The impetus for the development of this theory was the recognition that family issues were influential in the success of rehabilitation efforts, but they were largely ignored in rehabilitation programming. In those days, the individual written rehabilitation plan used in the state-federal program had no place to address family-relevant issues. Cottone, an RC with training in family therapy, began to realize that family involvement was crucial to rehabilitation success, and that family factors were related to or could be predictive of rehabilitation outcomes (Cottone, Handelsman, & Walters, 1986). Other authors and theorists also expressed the need to address family issues in rehabilitation (e.g., Power & Dell Orto, 1986). The client's family system began to be viewed as a network of relationships that was influential in the rehabilitation process. Cottone also took the position that the rehabilitation system could be conceptualized as a network of relationships, and that counselors could be viewed as social agents who were conduits for the larger social factors addressed at the interface between the counselor and the client being served in the state-federal or any rehabilitation service delivery system. From a purely relational viewpoint, the counselor–client relationship was crucial, because it represented a linkage of two systems: the client's system and the rehabilitation service delivery system. Rehabilitation outcomes could then be viewed as predictable based on the ease of interface of involved systems (Cottone, 1987; Cottone & Cottone, 1986; Cottone, Grelle, & Wilson, 1988). If a client came from a supportive family, showed social capacity, and could communicate in a healthy way, there was likely a place that could be found for that person to work, regardless of skills or abilities. In contrast, a client connected to an unhealthy family or other system (e.g., the drug culture) showing poor social skills, (e.g., poor grooming and unusual interaction) and poor communication skills would likely be expelled from the rehabilitation program, even if the client had some, work-related skill (Cottone & Cottone, 1986; Cottone et al., 1988). Expulsion from the program typically occurred as (a) case closure when the client was socially deficient and a poor risk, or (b) case closure after the client was put through a number of remediation measures (evaluation or personal adjustment programs) that acted more like social screening programs than rehabilitation interventions (Cottone & Cottone, 1986; Cottone et al., 1988). Those clients who survived screening were able to show some social capacity; those who did not fit socially (e.g., those who broke the rules) were clearly identified and prevented from receiving further services. It could be argued that too little rehabilitation and remediation and too much screening were occurring. Cottone et al. (1988) concluded that in cases of nonphysical disabilities (e.g., emotional, intellectual, or behavioral disabilities), vocational evaluators were making decisions about clients using data that were primarily social and interpersonal in making recommendations about client readiness for employment. The authors further concluded that:

> Psychological evidence, allegedly gathered for employability decision making, appears to play a lesser role. The results of this study bring into question the nature of the vocational evaluation process as presently conceived within a psychomedical framework. (p. 50)

In effect, the state-federal VR system could be viewed as a social mechanism for screening the socially deviant from entry into the work world.

Reconceptualizing the rehabilitation process as a social process requires rehabilitation professionals to at least acknowledge the influence of family and other relevant social systems on rehabilitation outcomes. Even if RCs do not adopt a purely social perspective, as recommended by Cottone's (1987) systemic theory of VR, they must acknowledge the influence of relational systems on the outcomes of rehabilitation programming, or they will blindly provide services always identifying failure as an individual client problem (e.g., poor motivation). Consider that a client who appears poorly motivated in the rehabilitation system might be the most motivated drug pusher on the street. Motivation, from a relational standpoint, is always viewed in context.

Family relationships and family dynamics will play a major role in the rehabilitation process and rehabilitation outcomes. Adaptation to disability is not just an individual issue. Families, too, adjust to disability, and the dynamics of the family may be significantly influenced by the presence of a mental or physical condition or some combination of conditions that affect family members as well as the individual with the disability. This chapter fully acknowledges the influence of relational factors in the rehabilitation process, but focuses primarily on the effect of disability from the perspective of the family. Adaptation to both disability and the rehabilitation process is also addressed.

THE FAMILY AS A SYSTEM

A system is a network of relationships—a "set of elements standing in interaction" (von Bertalanffy, 1968). Relationships (the interactions between people) are the focus of systems theory (Cottone, 1992). A system of three people is three relationships. A system of four people is six relationships (see Figure 8.1), and a system of five people is 10 relationships (see Figure 8.2).

The relationships are viewed as the crucial elements in a system. For a family of four in which one individual has a disability, each member is in relationship with each other. Each relationship is influenced by the disability. Although all family members experience the presence of the disability in the family through relationships, in some families parents may be the primary caregivers. In families with an absent parent, siblings may be significantly involved in daily activities with family members with disabilities. Spouses or partners of adults with disabilities are often involved. The interaction among family or household members around the disability is important to note, as the family not only has a history of adjustment dynamically to the presence of the disability, but also will have to adjust to changes in the family routine around the client's rehabilitation.

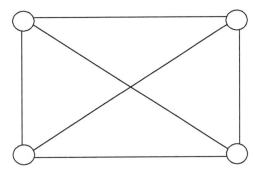

Figure 8.1 A system of four people is six relationships—each line represents a relationship; each circle represents a person.

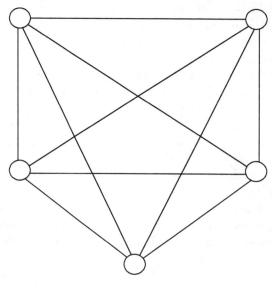

Figure 8.2 A system of five people is 10 relationships—each line represents a relationship; each circle represents a person.

FAMILY ADAPTATION TO DISABILITY

The Importance of Family

Millington and Marini (2015b) made the case that "family is the touchstone of client identity, a source of client power, and the core of the client's social support network" (p. 87). If there is an intact family system (whether the family is nuclear, extended, biological, blended, or culturally defined), and the family is involved with the individual with a disability, then most likely there has been significant family adaptation to the disability itself. Some disabilities are **congenital** (e.g., inherited conditions evident at birth) and they have been with the family since the beginning of the individual's life with a disability. Other disabilities are **acquired**, such as those that result from trauma (e.g., physical injury and traumatic brain injury). Some are **developmental** or reveal themselves at different stages (e.g., intellectual impairment). Some are **progressive**, which means that typically they are inherited but they worsen with time; in these instances, the individual may have had some normal developmental period (e.g., certain muscular dystrophies, arthritis, and dementia). Regardless of the type or onset of a condition, the intact family system must adjust. Family members must adapt to the disease process (if there is one) and to the personal limitations that exist or develop over time (see Box 8.1).

BOX 8.1 A Personal Experience

The reader should know that I have a child with a disability, and I have experienced family adjustment to disability in my own family and by observing the adjustments of my clients to their concerns. My son, Torre, now 20 years old, was diagnosed at age 2 with

---

(continued)

BOX 8.1 A Personal Experience (*continued*)

Duchenne muscular dystrophy, a genetic disorder that is fatal, usually taking young boys around the age of 20. The moment of diagnosis was one of the most powerful moments affecting my life, my wife's life, and the lives of my other children. Torre's condition is genetic and progressive. He had several early years of normal development. Now he is in a wheelchair and needs near total assistance with most daily activities. He still has partial use of his hands, so he can still use a computer mouse and drive his wheelchair with a joystick. He cannot support his own weight and he is not strong enough to turn in bed. As his condition has progressed, the family has had to adjust. The adjustment in this case was slow and followed the course of the disease. Each of us has had to learn to accommodate our needs to ensure that Torre's needs were met. It sounds burdensome at some level, but because Torre is a lovable and loved young man, in many ways it is a pleasure to be with him and to assist him. My wife and I have made a commitment to provide him and the other children with a rich and full life. Although there has been commitment to someone we love, it is also clear that sometimes relationships are strained and our lifestyles have been affected. Since Torre's diagnosis, I have worked extensively with individuals and families facing muscular dystrophy, and for those families that stay together, the process appears similar.

Family Challenges

Unfortunately, not all families faced with debilitating disease or impairment stay together. Sometimes, parents of children with disabilities divorce or abandon their children. Anecdotally, divorce rates among parents of children with disabilities have been estimated (often unreliably) to be as high as 80%. Divorce creates a complicated circumstance for remaining caregivers, as their share of the "load" increases with the lower number of committed caregivers. Generally, the percentage of children with disabilities in single-parent households exceeds the percentage of children without disabilities. Regardless of the presence and commitment of one or both parents, or of spouses or partners of individuals with disabilities, families of individuals with disabilities need help. Extended family members sometimes become involved. Sometimes, loving friends make special efforts to assist families in need. Reporting in a 1996 published survey, Burke (2008) indicated that "[t]he need for help and assistance in the families surveyed was overwhelming; over 60 percent of families indicated this need" (p. 48). Siblings often take a caregiver role; Burke indicated that parents reported that siblings of a child with a disability were involved directly in care 75% of the time (one study reported involvement as high as 80%). Some families are able to afford assistance or to obtain government assistance to hire others to care for, to watch over, or to supervise the individual with the disability. The greater the network of support, the greater the likelihood that the individual with the disability will find meaning in life and will seek and cooperate with means of rehabilitation. Even with support, families of individuals with disabilities face similar challenges. Case-Smith (2007) reported that parenting a child with a chronic medical condition was associated with several challenges, including (a) managing and scheduling caregiver responsibilities, (b) feeling the burden of "always having to be there," (c) experiencing negative effects on the caregiver's outside career trajectory/plans, (d) addressing compromises in dealing with external service providers (e.g., schools, pharmacies, insurance companies, and resource and rehabilitation agencies), (e) maintaining a social life outside the home, and (f) maintaining a self-identity.

Family Caregivers and Stages of Caregiver Adjustment

Committed parents tend to be incredible caregivers, often sacrificing their own needs for the needs of their children. But it is also the case that when the disability is acquired in adulthood, spouses and loving partners often accept the caregiver role. With serious disabilities, totally debilitating conditions such as amyotrophic lateral sclerosis or Huntington's disease (fatal disorders with serious downward health trajectories sometimes with death looming within a matter of years), or for conditions that permanently negatively affect a family member (e.g., brain damage and quadriplegia), the toll on caregivers can be serious. Millington and Marini (2015b) stated: "Family care is characterized by deep emotions, shared history, shared intimacy, and reciprocity. It is qualitatively different from the formal care of professionals, even where the service is the same. Caring is networked in the family system and orchestrated in its delivery through every family role" (pp. 88–89).

Debilitating progressive diseases or serious permanent loss of function are some of the most difficult situations for families to face (Frain et al., 2015). Caregivers in these circumstances appear to go through some predictable **stages**. First, upon diagnosis of the loved one, there is a sincere commitment to the love and care of the affected individual. Caregivers embrace the client and they formally commit to be there for the client, no matter what is faced. This is the *commitment stage.* The second stage is the *resource identification stage,* as the caregiver and family members collect resources (both personal and other resources) in order to make a difficult situation tolerable. There is much activity in this stage as the caregiver begins to identify resources, other helpers, family supports, community and church assistance, support from associations of others faced with similar circumstances, and financial supports (in the form of government assistance for rehabilitation or disability benefits). The third stage is the *plateau stage,* where often well-intended others begin to withdraw support and caregivers begin to face daily routines with limited assistance and limited or depleted resources. The fourth stage is the *exhaustion stage.* At this stage, caregivers begin to recognize that they cannot do it all—that they are overwhelmed even with the support they receive from others. They begin to feel neglected themselves and feel that their own needs are not being met. Anger may begin to set in, and they begin to ask, "Why?" They are often faced with their own career stressors, management of a home or other family members, household issues, financial issues, and lack of sleep. The fifth stage is the *confusion stage.* Caregivers actually find themselves wishing it were over, which is frightening to them, because in some cases that would mean that their loved one would be gone. They cannot see the end. They feel a sense of hopelessness. They also feel the competing interest of self and loved one. They begin to feel real loss in their own lives, while at the same time recognizing the loss experienced by the loved one. They are torn and do not feel that they have a way out. The sixth stage is the *recommitment stage.* This typically comes near the end of the life of the affected individual, at a point of near permanent stabilization, or at the end of the caregiver's formal commitment. Caregivers appear to rally at this stage, drawing on all their remaining resources as they recommit to the care and well-being of the individual with the disability. They are then committed until the end. Counseling through this process is crucial, as both the disability-affected individual and the caregiver face very serious social, physical, and psychological challenges.

If clients are lucky enough to stabilize and to have the capacity to work or to live independently, then family members and caregivers will face a transition when rehabilitation services become available.

FAMILY ADAPTATION TO THE REHABILITATION PROCESS

Routines in families with an individual with a disability appear to be fairly structured. Roles also appear to emerge over time and with experience. Consider transportation as an example. An individual in a wheelchair may be pushed by one member to a vehicle, then assisted by another to enter the car or to operate a lift or ramp, and then secured in the vehicle by another family member. So, something as typical as transportation often calls for a clear separation of roles and responsibilities in family accommodation to the unique requirements of transporting an individual in a wheelchair. Family members tend to fall into these roles as the family learns to address the limitations of the individual with the disability. These roles tend to crystallize and, at best, make life a little more predictable and orderly. At worst, the roles may become rigid and unyielding. Rehabilitation efforts always call for change, and family routines typically will be disrupted.

When a counselor develops a rehabilitation plan with a client, it is always wise to explore how the client's routine will change, and how family members will be required to adjust. The more resistant the family members are to change, the more likely it is that rehabilitation efforts will fail. For example, requiring a client to attend a workshop for training, when in the past the family's routine was established around the client staying at home, is a major change. In this case, the family members will have to adjust to what can be a burdensome task in adhering to a new schedule. In family systems theory, a change in routine may be interpreted as a disruption in the family **homeostasis**, the dynamic equilibrium of family interactions around the routines that have been well established in the home (Goldenberg & Goldenberg, 2008). Technically, it disrupts the homeostatic **set point**—the rules for family operation—just like leaving the door open on a very hot day disrupts the temperature in an air-conditioned home with a set point of 72°F. Disruption of a routine is equivalent to pushing the family to establish new family rules and requiring new family roles to emerge around the new rules. Classic systems theory teaches that family homeostasis tends toward stability, not change; there are often relationship dynamics that tend to work to reestablish the equilibrium (Bertalanffy, 1968). Counselors must be alert to such factors and they must not simply identify the client as "the culprit" if problems arise related to issues such as attendance, punctuality, and full engagement in the rehabilitation process. The client's apparent "resistance" may be the evidence of systemic dynamics designed to reassert the family's homeostatic process—to reestablish or maintain the old and once functional rules and roles.

Counselors would be wise to adopt a **family practice model** of rehabilitation (Lewis, 2015). A family practice model involves the counselor anticipating, planning, and participating in full family involvement in the rehabilitation process. Clients should not just be provided services with the expectation that an intact family system will not be affected or involved. Building the family into the process is recommended, so that the family is not left to its own means of addressing the "rough spots" along the way.

FAMILY ADAPTATION TO JOB PLACEMENT AND COMMUNITY LIVING

Dosa, White, and Schuyler (2007) stated that "in 2004, employment rates for the 14 million U.S. adults who have a disability (7.9% of adults age 18–64) were substantially lower than for adults who do not have a disability (19% versus 77%)" (p. 615). Dosa et al. went on to report a poverty rate of 28% for individuals with disabilities, versus 9% for individuals without disabilities. Certainly, VR professionals have a very important role in assisting individuals with disabilities in job training, development, and placement.

The family is an economic unit, and for those individuals with disabilities in a position to support (or to help to support) a family, employment is very important. In many cases, the moment of first meaningful employment, or a return to meaningful employment, will be welcomed by family members, especially when the family has been deprived of adequate resources, perhaps due to the disability. Therefore, motivated work-capable clients in a healthy support system will tend to appreciate work opportunity, as gainful employment may mean establishment of (or a return to) a better family life. Work may also prove to be personally fulfilling for the individual with the disability and lead to increased social connections, as in American society, workers are valued as productive members of society. For such clients, it will appear that the family is rallying around final rehabilitation efforts, and job placement and retention will be cause for celebration.

For individuals who do not appear motivated to find employment, even after extensive rehabilitation programming, it is incumbent upon the RC to assess the systemic dynamics that may be affecting what appears to be the client's poor motivation. **Motivation**, from a systemic perspective, is a reflection of activity within the social matrix; it is not inside the personality of the client. It is too easy to simply label a client as unmotivated and to close a demanding rehabilitation case. Often there are social factors, family dynamics, or other factors that may be pivotal to successful job placement and job retention. For example, the family may be losing Social Security benefits (either supplemental Security Income [SSI] or Social Security Disability Insurance [SSDI]), which may affect the financial stability of the household significantly, or temporary benefits may be lost (e.g., worker's compensation). The employment of one family member may affect the employment or routines of another family member adversely, for example, when the family has limited means of transportation and vehicle sharing is required. Alternatively, the absence of the individual with a disability in the home may create a void in the lives of those who have been actively involved in caregiving in the home, creating some role confusion. All these factors may be influential at the point of job placement. When family dynamics appear to interfere with the final stages of job placement, then the astute counselor must be willing to analyze possible relational pressures and to address those concerns in a way that will facilitate the final stages of worker placement.

It is often surprising to early career rehabilitation professionals when everything looks positive for employment after an otherwise successful rehabilitation program, and then something happens at the end of a rehabilitation program that appears to sabotage the job placement effort. Those kinds of experiences, especially when families are involved, may indicate the failure of the RC to take into account, address, or ameliorate systemic dynamics inconsistent with successful rehabilitation and employment of the individual with the disability.

Similar dynamics may operate when community living is a goal. Removal of the client from the household of a family of origin will significantly affect relationships in the household. Counselors must be alert to family dynamics when household members appear to resist a client's independence. Just like the empty nest syndrome that most couples experience when the last child leaves the household, families with an individual with a disability experience a change in routine and roles when a formerly dependent person is transitioned to a new living or working situation. It is important for RCs to be sensitive and responsive. RCs can help ensure smooth transitions, and their role as family counselors or family advocates is never clearer than at these times.

COUNSELING FAMILIES OF INDIVIDUALS WITH DISABILITIES

Is there a valuable role for RCs as family therapists for families of individuals with disabilities? Generally, family health and adaptation have played secondary roles in the rehabilitation process. The focus, consistent with the psychomedical paradigm, has been the well-being and adaptation of the person with the disability. But RCs are mental health professionals, and to ignore or to neglect the needs of the family is to view the client in isolation. This focus is potentially at the expense of rehabilitation goals or to the detriment of family members closely involved with the client.

Kosciulek (2004) has argued that the impact of disability is "at least as great for families as for the affected person, and family members are often more distressed than the person with the disability" (p. 264). He further stated, "family members themselves are a high-risk group for physical, emotional, and social difficulties. Families require help in their own right and not only as a by-product of the counseling or rehabilitation process with the family member with the disability" (p. 264). But how much help can RCs offer? Most RCs do not have adequate training to do marital and family therapy. It takes more than a course on systems theory and a course on family counseling to work competently and ethically with families. Counselors who have an interest in focusing on family issues must seek additional comprehensive training through coursework, continuing education, and supervised experience under the watchful eye of a trained family therapist. This expectation is asking much, because it constitutes additional specialty training for already highly trained specialists in counseling.

Short of cross-training to a second specialty, it is incumbent on rehabilitation counseling generalists to acquaint themselves with the systemic paradigm of mental health services. The systemic paradigm focuses exclusively on defining the nature of problems and solutions as imbedded in relationships. At its extreme, it is mutually exclusive to the psychomedical paradigm at the foundation of rehabilitation programs, which focuses on the individual client and individual stakeholders in the rehabilitation process. You cannot see people and focus on relationships at the same time. It is like the classic Gestalt diagram of the vase and the two twin faces—you see the vase if you focus on the middle of the diagram, but you see the twins if you look to one side (see Figure 8.3).

Systems theory focuses on the middle between two people (like looking at the vase). It does not focus on people—their traits, abilities, interests, or skills. It looks at each person as fitting within some context. **Good fit** means finding a special place within some social network; **bad fit** means the person will appear out of sync with other individuals within a social network. Counselors ideally facilitate good fit for the client in some healthy social context. The systemic framework requires counselors to be mindful of how relationships affect mental health and especially the specific behaviors of the client within the family and larger systemic contexts. It helps counselors see the big picture.

Figure 8.3 The Gestalt diagram—two twins facing each other versus a vase.

One way that RCs can begin to acquaint themselves with relational influences on the rehabilitation process is first to acknowledge the influence of relationships on their own adaptation. This exercise is usually fairly easy, because most counselors will readily admit that the times they have felt most unhealthy mentally were the times that they were enmeshed in relationships that were unhealthy. If one is in a healthy, loving network, it is easy to feel and act comfortably. Recognizing this fact is an easy first step. Then, it is important for the RCs to acquaint themselves with some literature on family adaptation and/or stress when faced with a member with a disability.

Some theorists have likened the family reaction to the diagnosis of a child with a disability to the bereavement process (e.g., Cobb & Warner, 1999). After the initial shock of the diagnosis, families may go through a period of denial, anger, and bargaining until some level of coping is achieved. The message in such analyses is that the adaptation process is not easy.

Related to connecting theory to practice, Kosciulek, McCubbin, and McCubbin's (1993) "Resiliency Model of Family Stress, Adjustment, and Adaptation" is a good place for RCs to start. This model is built on prior works that addressed: "(a) Illness and disability as potential family stressors, (b) family resistance resources (e.g., economic, psychological), (c) the family's appraisal of a disability, and (d) coping patterns designed to protect the family from breakdown and facilitate adjustment to disability" (Kosciulek, 2004, p. 265). By recognizing family reactions to disability, RCs can begin to conceptualize means to address such stress in a way that facilitates the family's adaptation to the rehabilitation process. Although rehabilitation may represent hope to families that their loved ones will achieve some level of independence, it still represents change. Where there is relationship change, all parties connected to the web of involved relations are affected, for better or for worse. The more resistance that is met by rehabilitation efforts within families, the more likely there will be dramatic adjustments necessary to accommodate changes; in those cases, family intervention would be important.

If an RC is not trained to provide family therapy interventions, then it is incumbent on the RC to refer families to appropriately trained professionals who will understand and work within the context of the rehabilitation programs. Many not-for-profit agencies provide family counseling services for little or no charge, and sometimes there are special considerations given to families with a member affected by a disabling condition. Knowing and developing family treatment resources should be a normal part of any RC's job when family issues are addressed in the rehabilitation process.

Typically, family therapy occurs with all household members present, or as many as will participate. Usually, it is acceptable to have up to five or six family members in a session. More than five or six participants become unwieldy and may challenge even the most skilled family therapist (because there 10 relationships interacting in a family of five). Thus, maintaining some control of the sessions becomes difficult when more relationships are present in the session.

Family counselors typically will analyze the relationship dynamics during sessions, viewing problems primarily within their social contexts (Goldenberg & Goldenberg, 2008; Nichols, 2006). They tend to be less interested in the individual behaviors, traits, or abilities of clients, and more interested in interactional patterns that have developed around specific family activities. Family therapists have many names for the patterns of interaction observed during sessions, such as "enmeshed," "disengaged," "symmetrical," "escalating," and "complementary" relationships. Each pattern has predictable consequences for individuals involved in the pattern. The intention of family counseling for rehabilitation clients typically is to strengthen family relationships and interactions that are supportive or facilitative of the natural transition experienced by successful rehabilitation clients.

Classic systems interventions always involve at least two people. Consider a family where parents have had to be extensively involved in their child's care. The child now is a young adult and is participating in a rehabilitation program. Thus, a family counselor might address how a mother and father of a young adult rehabilitation client might spend their time together or alone (in a healthy way) while the rehabilitation client is outside the home involved in rehabilitation programs. In this case, the intent would be to strengthen the marital bond, so that one or both parents do not become or remain enmeshed with the adult child rehabilitation client, potentially in a way that may interfere with the rehabilitation program. The astute family counselor, then, is always addressing relational dynamics and will intervene where it might seem tangential to the classically psycho-medically trained counselor.

There are a number of family therapy theories or approaches that may be used by a trained family therapist (see Gladding, 2007; Goldenberg & Goldenberg, 2008). Entire college graduate courses are offered surveying the well-known family therapy approaches of people such as Virginia Satir, Murray Bowen, Carl Whitaker, Salvador Minuchin, Jay Haley, Nathan Ackerman, and others. RCs should at least acquaint themselves with the major family therapy theorists so that they may speak and act intelligently on these matters when working closely with a family therapist. In fact, the Council for Accreditation of Counseling and Related Educational Programs (CACREP) standards for accreditation of educational programs for counselors require some basic introduction to family dynamics and interventions.

Ideally, family therapy will be viewed as a support for rehabilitation efforts. It may be adjunctive, but the effects may be very positive in those cases where there is active family involvement in the lives of family members with disabilities. From a purist systems perspective, involving family in the rehabilitation process is crucial to rehabilitation success and to the long-term healthy adaptation of clients.

Identifying a qualified family therapist is as easy as assessing their credentials. Those who are trained typically in counselor education programs will likely affiliate with the

International Association for Marriage and Family Counseling (IAMFC), which is a division of the American Counseling Association (ACA). The IAMFC has actively pursued establishment of a viable, credible, and valuable credential in family therapy, and members of the IAMFC have established the National Credentialing Academy (NCA) for certified family therapists (CFTs). The NCA has established standard coursework and experience requirements for mental health professionals to qualify as a CFT. RCs interested in seeking training in family counseling would do well to contact the NCA for information and standards for certification. The older, more established American Association for Marriage and Family Therapy (AAMFT) has set requirements for what they define as "clinical membership," which constitutes a certification of sorts. The AAMFT's standards are high, and there has been some tension between the AAMFT and the ACA, as the AAMFT has abandoned the use of the title "counselor," and some AAMFT members have argued that counseling and family therapy are separate professions. The ACA has taken the position that marriage and family counseling is a counseling "specialty." So, in a sense, there are two professional organizations vying for the allegiance of those who would identify themselves as marriage and family counselors/therapists. Regardless, if a family counselor is a CFT or a clinical member of the AAMFT, it is likely that he or she has met stringent training and supervision requirements in the areas of couples, marital, and family treatment.

CONCLUSION

This chapter has addressed relationship and family issues in rehabilitation counseling. Although rehabilitation counseling theory and practice have been closely and historically aligned with the psychomedical paradigm of mental health services, rehabilitation theoreticians and practitioners are now recognizing the influence of relationships on the rehabilitation process. The influence of relationships in rehabilitation may be reflective of the rehabilitation system itself, and the role the rehabilitation system plays within the larger free enterprise system in American society. It may also reflect the influence of intact family systems that may directly influence the behavior of clients being served by rehabilitation systems. A systemic theory of VR, the first comprehensive and coherent theory of VR to challenge the traditional rehabilitation model, addresses the relationship interface of clients and rehabilitation systems in conceptualizing and providing rehabilitation services and programs. The systemic perspective represents a call for recognition of relationship influences on the behavior of clients and professionals. It may act as an impetus for RCs to educate themselves on the relational way of viewing clients in the context of rehabilitation programs.

For clients with intact families, recognition of the influence of the family on the individual with a disability is important. Also, RCs must be sensitive to the adjustment of the family to (a) the disability, (b) rehabilitation efforts, and (c) job placement and community living. Some families may be more resilient facing disability; others may struggle. Some families adjust more easily to rehabilitation programs and goals; others may be resistant. By understanding family dynamics and the challenges faced by family members, RCs may be able to conceptualize the social and systems factors that may potentially affect rehabilitation outcomes, including job placement.

RCs should be educated about social systems theory and family therapy. Although cross-training in family therapy would be ideal, RCs must at least be willing to obtain continuing education and appropriate training to identify relationship factors impinging on the rehabilitation process. In cases where family or other relationship factors negatively affect the client, RCs must be able to intervene or to seek, to recommend, or to engage appropriate family relationship treatment. Both the families and the individuals with disabilities deserve no less.

CONTENT REVIEW QUESTIONS

- How does social systems theory reconceptualize the rehabilitation process?
- What is the family role in the rehabilitation process?
- What is the role of the RC addressing family issues during the rehabilitation process?
- How is the family affected by the rehabilitation process?
- How is the rehabilitation process affected by family dynamics?

REFERENCES

Burke, P. (2008). *Disability and impairment: Working with children and families.* Philadelphia, PA: Jessica Kingsley.

Case-Smith, J. (2007). Parenting a child with a chronic medical condition. In A. E. Dell Orto & P. W. Power (Eds.), *The psychological and social impact of illness and disability* (5th ed., pp. 310–328). New York, NY: Springer Publishing.

Cobb, H. C., & Warner, P. (1999). Counseling and psychotherapy with children and adolescents with disabilities. In H. T. Prout & D. T. Brown (Eds.), *Counseling and psychotherapy with children and adolescents: Theory and practice for school and clinical settings* (3rd ed., pp. 401–426). New York, NY: Wiley.

Cottone, R. R. (1987). A systemic theory of vocational rehabilitation. *Rehabilitation Counseling Bulletin, 30,* 167–176.

Cottone, R. R. (1992). *Theories and paradigms of counseling and psychotherapy.* Needham Heights, MA: Allyn & Bacon.

Cottone, R. R., & Cottone, L. P. (1986). A systemic analysis of vocational evaluation in the state-federal rehabilitation system. *Vocational Evaluation and Work Adjustment Bulletin, 19,* 47–54.

Cottone, R. R., & Emener, W. G. (1990). The psychomedical paradigm of vocational rehabilitation and its alternatives. *Rehabilitation Counseling Bulletin, 34,* 91–102.

Cottone, R. R., Grelle, M., & Wilson, W. C. (1988). The accuracy of systemic versus psychological evidence in judging vocational evaluator recommendations: A preliminary test of a systemic theory of vocational rehabilitation. *Journal of Rehabilitation, 54,* 45–52.

Cottone, R. R., Handelsman, M. M., & Walters, N. (1986). Understanding the influence of family systems on the rehabilitation process. *Journal of Applied Rehabilitation Counseling, 17,* 37–40.

Dosa, N. P., White, P. H., & Schuyler, V. (2007). Future expectations: Transition from adolescence to adulthood. In M. L. Batshaw, L. Pellegrino, & N. J. Roizen (Eds.), *Children with disabilities* (6th ed., pp. 613–622). Baltimore, MD: Paul H. Brookes.

Frain, M., Bishop, M., Frain, J., Frain, J. Tansey, T., & Tschopp, M. K. (2015). The family role in progressive illness. In M. J. Millington & I. Marini (Eds.), *Families in rehabilitation counseling: A community based rehabilitation approach* (pp. 171–191). New York, NY: Springer Publishing.

Gladding, S. T. (2007). *Family therapy: History, theory, and practice* (4th ed.). Upper Saddle River, NJ: Pearson/Merrill Prentice Hall.

Goldenberg, H., & Goldenberg, I. (2008). *Family therapy: An overview* (7th ed.). Belmont, CA: Thomson Brooks/Cole.

Kosciulek, J. F. (1993). Advances in trait-and-factor theory: A person x environment fit approach to rehabilitation counseling. *Journal of Applied Rehabilitation Counseling, 24*(2), 11–14.

Kosciulek, J. F. (2004). Family counseling. In F. Chan, N. L. Berven, & K. R. Thomas (Eds.), *Counseling theories and techniques for rehabilitation health professionals* (pp. 264–281). New York, NY: Springer Publishing.

Kosciulek, J. F., & DeVinney, D. J. (2004). The trait-factor approach. In F. Chan, N. L. Berven, & K. R. Thomas (Eds.), *Counseling theories and techniques for rehabilitation health professionals* (pp. 211–223). New York, NY: Springer Publishing.

Kosciulek, J. F., McCubbin, M. A., & McCubbin, H. I. (1993). A theoretical framework for family adaptation to head injury. *Journal of Rehabilitation, 59*(3), 40–45.

Lewis, T. (2015). Managing the rehabilitation environment around families. In M. J. Millington & I. Marini (Eds.), *Families in rehabilitation counseling: A community-based rehabilitation approach* (pp. 267–283). New York, NY: Springer Publishing.

Millington, M. J., Jenkins, B. C., & Cottone, R. R. (2015). Finding the family in rehabilitation counseling. In M. J. Millington & I. Marini (Eds.), *Families in rehabilitation counseling: A community-based rehabilitation approach* (pp. 1–20). New York, NY: Springer Publishing.

Millington, M. J., & Marini, I. (2015a). *Families in rehabilitatation counseling: A community-based rehabilitation approach*. New York, NY: Springer Publishing.

Millington, M. J., & Marini, I. (2015b). Family care and support. In M. J. Millington & I. Marini (Eds.), *Families in rehabilitation counseling: A community-based rehabilitation approach* (pp. 87–107). New York, NY: Springer Publishing.

Nichols, M. P. (2006). *Family therapy: Concepts and methods*. Boston, MA: Pearson/Allyn & Bacon.

Parsons, F. (1909). *Choosing a vocation*. Boston, MA: Houghton-Mifflin.

Power, P. W., & Dell Orto, A. E. (1986). Families, illness and disability: The roles of the rehabilitation counselor. *Journal of Applied Rehabilitation Counseling, 17*(2), 41–44.

Stubbins, J. (Ed.). (1977). *Social and psychological aspects of disability*. Austin, TX: Pro-Ed.

Stubbins, J. (1984). Vocational rehabilitation as social science. *Rehabilitation Literature, 45*, 375–380.

von Bertalanffy, L. (1968). *General systems theory: Foundations, development, applications*. New York, NY: George Braziller.

Wright, B. A. (1983). *Physical disability—A psychosocial approach*. New York, NY: Harper & Row.

NINE

The Disability Rights Community

MICHAEL T. HARTLEY

LEARNING OBJECTIVES

After reading this chapter, you should be able to:

- Review the history of the independent living movement, disability studies, and disability culture.
- Understand the fight for disability rights within the context of a larger cultural movement.
- Identify the core tenets of the independent living movement and corresponding services provided by Centers for Independent Living (CIL).
- Consider the emergence of the academic field of disability studies as a sociopolitical critique of the dominant cultural discourse of disability.
- Reflect on the power of disability culture as championing complex identities of people with disabilities.

Rehabilitation counselors (RCs) work with "persons with physical, mental, developmental, cognitive, and emotional disabilities to achieve their personal, career, and independent living goals in the most integrated setting possible" (Commission on Rehabilitation Counselor Certification [CRCC], 2016, p. 1). In other words, rehabilitation counseling involves supporting people with disabilities to function well in different environments (Maki & Tarvydas, 2012; Parker & Patterson, 2011; Rubin & Roessler, 2008; Sales, 2007). In rehabilitation counseling, a successful outcome is not the result of working with the individual alone, but rather of understanding the reciprocal interaction between the individual and his or her environment (Hershenson, 1998; Kosciulek, 1993; Lofquist & Dawis, 1969; Maki, McCracken, Pape, & Scofield, 1979). Over the years, rehabilitation counseling has been an important mechanism for offsetting social and economic disadvantage through legislation and policy making (Bruyère, 2000; Chubon, 1992; Kilbury, Benshoff, & Rubin, 1992), and the Disability Rights community can partner with the functional efforts of rehabilitation counseling to promote a more inclusive society by increasing opportunities and services for people with disabilities.

In rehabilitation counseling practice, there are three models that construct disability from three different points of view: (a) the medical or disease model, (b) the functional limitations or economic model, and (c) the sociopolitical or minority model, also known as the social model (Smart, 2004, 2015), as posited by the Disability Rights community (Shakespeare & Watson, 1997). In contrast to the medical model focus on pathology and cure, the social model views disability as a social, political, intellectual, and ideological issue (Albrecht, Seelman, & Bury, 2001; Davis, 2013; Longmore, 2003). What is more, although issues of access and accessibility are often addressed by the functional limitations model, rarely do interventions target social policies; "in reality, societal prejudice is rarely considered" (Smart, 2004, p. 39). The social model is thus distinct from the medical and functional limitations models because of its critique of the social prejudice of **ableism**, defined as discrimination against people with disabilities and preference for able-bodiedness (Carluccio & Patterson, 2001; Hahn, 1991). As noted by Weber, a disability activist, ableism creates a societal meta-narrative whereby "society perceives disabled persons to be damaged, defective, and less socially marketable than non-disabled persons," in essence causing "pain because it convinces us that there is something fundamentally wrong with us, that we are not acceptable as we are" (cited in Haller, 2010, p. iii). Aligned with the Disability Rights community, the focus of the social model in rehabilitation counseling centers on "anti-discrimination legislation, independent living and other responses to the social oppression" experienced by people with disabilities (Shakespeare, 2013, p. 216).

In many ways, rehabilitation counseling practice borders the medical community and the Disability Rights community, and "rehabilitation counselors are in a position to situate the medical and social model perspectives as mutually constitutive, rather than oppositional" (Tarvydas et al., 2012, p. 242). RCs have a long history of listening to and partnering with people with disabilities and thus are in a unique position among the disciplines of medicine and counseling (Jenkins, Patterson, & Szymanski, 1992; Leahy, Chan, & Saunders, 2003; Leahy, Muenzen, Saunders, & Strauser, 2009; Leahy & Szymanski, 1995). Although RCs must be knowledgeable and adept at synthesizing medical information, the overarching goal is to promote empowerment and self-determination from a social model perspective (Bolton & Brookings, 1998; Frain, Tschopp, & Bishop, 2009; Kosciulek, 2005). Rather than being entrenched in the social model perspective, RCs have the ability to traverse borders and mediate viewpoints that are often in opposition. In rehabilitation counseling practice, contact zones (Pratt, 1991) where the medical and Disability Rights communities intersect are an important place for student learning. *Contact zones* are social spaces where the perspectives of subordinate cultural groups often resist or even mediate dominant beliefs.

Psychiatric rehabilitation represents one such important contact zone (Pratt, 1991), where rehabilitation counseling practice borders the perspectives of the medical community and the Disability Rights community. The goal of psychiatric rehabilitation is not to *cure* mental illness, but rather to help individuals learn how to manage their mental health symptoms, "including understanding the nature and treatment of their mental illness" (Corrigan, 2016, p. 133). As such, psychiatric rehabilitation is based on the medical categorization of the *Diagnostic and Statistical Manual of Mental Disorders* (5th ed.; *DSM-5*; American Psychiatric Association, 2013) yet, a successful outcome is the social negotiation of **recovery** and **hope** within the context of an individual's life (Davidson, Tondora, Staeheli Lawless, O'Connell, & Rowe, 2009). Without being a contradiction, psychiatric rehabilitation seeks to minimize the disruptive effects of mental health symptoms, while also embracing depression, anxiety, delusions, and hallucinations as part of the *normal* human experience. Regardless of the type of disability, the larger takeaway message is that RCs must be well versed in medical understandings of disability and social conceptions of disability as a social and civil rights issue, as advocated for by the Disability Rights community.

The Disability Rights community is an assemblage of diverse disability-specific groups with parallel histories that have coalesced into a larger "sense of disability as collectively shared status and experience" (Longmore & Umansky, 2001, pp. 4–5), but the

Disability Rights community has never been homogeneous or monolithic (Barnartt & Scotch, 2001; Longmore, 2003; Longmore & Umansky, 2001). Viewed through the social model lens, the histories of disability-specific groups are distinct yet similarly characterized by experiences of cultural devaluation (Longmore, 2003; Longmore & Umansky, 2001; Scotch, 1988). From a sociological perspective, the Disability Rights community is a group of people who have a common goal of disability activism, even though there may be conflict between various factions of people within the community (Frazer, 1999; Hoggett, 1997).

Disability activism has existed for centuries; however, until the 1970s, there was never a broad-based Disability Rights community in the United States. Rather, "disability groups typically formed around disability-specific categories," often competing for scarce material resources (Longmore, 2003, p. 109). Since the 18th century, the Deaf community has campaigned to protect sign as an authentic language, seeking political and economic support for signing schools in Europe and America, including Gallaudet University (Baynton, 1996; Lane, 1984). As early as the 1940s, the Blind community rallied to form a political lobby in the United States (Koestler, 1975; Matson, 1990). Countless other disability-specific groups, such as individuals with physical disabilities (Byrom, 2001; Longmore & Goldberger, 2003), cognitive and learning disabilities (Noll & Trent, 2004; Trent, 1994), and psychiatric disabilities (Beers, 1908; Porter, 1989) have fought long and hard for inclusion in education, employment, and community living. Of course, disability-specific organizations, political interests, and agendas have remained (Longmore, 2003). Yet, since the 1970s there has been a collective view, expressing that individuals with disabilities should have a say in health care policies and practices, best captured by Charlton (1998) in the phrase: "Nothing About Us, Without Us" (p. 3).

Perhaps one of the most important moments was April 5, 1977 (Longmore, 2003; Shapiro, 1994), when the American Coalition of Citizens with Disabilities (ACCD) organized simultaneous protests in nine cities across the United States, including Denver, New York, and San Francisco, to demand implementation of Section 504 of the 1973 Rehabilitation Act (Barnartt & Scotch, 2001; Longmore, 2003). Captured in the YouTube documentary *Power of Section 504* (www.youtube.com/watch?v=SyWcCuVta7M), scholars have noted that it was during these protests that cross-disability identification first emerged, representing a critical transformation in the consciousness of people with disabilities (Barnartt, 1996; Charlton, 1998; Longmore, 1995, 2003). Longmore (2003), quoting San Francisco-activist Mary Jane Owen, noted that "People went into that building with some kind of idealism, but they didn't have much knowledge of other disabilities. Up to that point, we had blind organizations, organizations for deaf people, for wheelchair users, for people with spina bifida, or people with mental retardation" (p. 110). As with other social justice movements, such as the women's movement and the gay and lesbian movement, the fight for equal employment, greater political participation, and better community services represented the platform for a larger cultural movement (Campbell & Oliver, 1996; Longmore, 2003; Oliver, 1990).

With this in mind, RCs need to understand the rich history of the Disability Rights community to become effective practitioners. Indeed, even well-intentioned rehabilitation professionals can inadvertently contribute to the perceptions of people with disabilities as diseased, broken, and in need of fixing if they act without an understanding of this perspective, as embraced by the Disability Rights community (Baker, 2009; Bricher, 2000; Conyers, 2003; Donoghue, 2003; Illich, Zola, McKnight, Caplan, & Shaiken, 2005). Understanding the Disability Rights community will prepare practitioners to situate disability within sociopolitical contexts and thus be more empathetic and respectful of people with disabilities (Conyers, 2003). This chapter discusses some of the complexities of the Disability Rights community, including the emergence of the independent living movement, disability studies, and disability culture, in order to prepare practitioners to locate rehabilitation within the broader experience of disability.

INDEPENDENT LIVING MOVEMENT

Independent living, as a concept, emerged out of the 1959 deinstitutionalization movement, in which millions of individuals with disabilities were released from institutions and others were never institutionalized (DeJong, 1979; Longmore, 2003; Nosek, Zhu, & Howland, 1992; Switzer, 2003). As both a philosophy and an approach to disability rights, independent living is a movement to promote community integration and inclusion as well as the self-determination of individuals with disabilities in society. The Rehabilitation Services Administration (RSA) funded the first Center for Independent Living in the 1960s (using the acronym CIL or ILC) because of the social and political activism of students with physical disabilities in Berkeley, California (DeJong, 1979; Nosek et al., 1992; Switzer, 2003). Forced to live in a hospital infirmary because there was no accessible student housing, a group of students with disabilities led by Roberts exerted their right to participate in society and attend college during a time when very few people with significant physical disabilities lived independently in the community, let alone attended college (Shapiro, 1993). Roberts's self-advocacy efforts were a catalyst for the independent living movement because he demanded inclusion in mainstream university life (Shapiro, 1994; Switzer, 2003). Initially funded to serve college students, CILs quickly shifted to serving nonstudents, and centers were created in large urban environments such as Boston and Houston (DeJong, 1979; Longmore, 2003; Switzer, 2003).

Designed by activists, CILs were an important training ground for political and social activism, including participation in the April 5, 1977, protests demanding implementation of the Rehabilitation Act Amendments of 1973 (Longmore, 2003; Switzer, 2003). Yet, in the 1980s, in response to conservative political threats to withdraw funding, CILs began to emphasize individual services over large-scale activism (Longmore, 2003; Varela, 2001). As a consequence, those who believed that large-scale activism was the way to create societal change left CILs and formed groups that were not dependent on governmental funding, such as the American Disabled for Adaptive Public Transportation (ADAPT; Johnson, 2003; Longmore, 2003; Scotch, 1988). In the 1980s, with the exodus of many activists and increased government oversight, CILs were increasingly run by professionals without disabilities (Longmore, 2003; Nosek et al., 1992). In response to complaints from the Disability Rights community, the 1986 Amendments to the Rehabilitation Act of 1973 required that 51% of CIL staff and board of directors consist of people with disabilities (Longmore, 2003; Nosek et al., 1992). Today, CILs must be run by people with disabilities and as a result, many CILs have returned to social and political activism while also providing individual services (Longmore, 2003).

Imbedded within local communities, CILs are a critical resource to support the local needs of people with disabilities to live independently. CILs provide information and referral for accessible housing, transportation, and community services, such as personal care assistants and sign language interpreters (Frieden, 2001; Richards & Smith, n.d.). Furthermore, using a peer-based self-help model, they provide counseling and independent skill training to help people with disabilities become more independent (Cole, 2001; Saxton, 2001; Shreve, 1991). Finally, CILs provide advocacy to promote a dominant culture that is more welcoming and inclusive for people with disabilities. Distinct from other services, rather than providing direct services to the individual, CIL advocacy confronts inaccessible environments and negative social attitudes toward disability, which from a social model perspective serve to "exaggerate disability and even construct disability" (Smart, 2004, p. 42). CILs provide two types of advocacy: individual and large-scale social and political advocacy (Richards & Smith, n.d.). **Individual advocacy** supports the self-determination of individuals to obtain necessary support services from other community agencies, such as state-federal vocational rehabilitation (VR; Zola, 2001). **Social and political advocacy** is broader, advocating, for instance, for accessible housing and transportation in society to help a wide range of people with disabilities (Varela, 2001). Although all CILs in the United States are legally mandated to provide all these services, not all CILs have the same resources. Each one is unique in terms of funding, staff, and the local communities served (Frieden, 2001; Nosek et al., 1992). In addition, different services may be more or less important in different communities, and CILs are designed to be responsive to the needs of local communities. For instance, rural communities often struggle with lack of transportation; as a result, rural CILs may be particularly focused on providing accessible transportation (Schwab, 2001).

More than just services, it is important to understand the underlying philosophy of CILs. A basic premise of CILs is that people with disabilities are experts on living with their disabilities (Crewe & Zola, 2001; DeJong, 1979; Nosek et al., 1992; Switzer, 2003). Unlike other rehabilitation services, CILs are run by people with disabilities who themselves have been successful in establishing independent lives (DeJong, 1979; Nosek et al., 1992; Switzer, 2003). Most traditional rehabilitation programs were built on the medical model of service delivery; CILs were the first to use the social model of disability to help individuals with disabilities achieve and maintain independent lifestyles (Crewe & Zola, 2001; DeJong, 1979; Nosek et al., 1992). Thus, CILs were revolutionary in defining disability as primarily a social (rather than a medical) issue, and are a unique and important development in service delivery (DeJong, 1979; Longmore, 2003; Switzer, 2003). Early leaders of CILs were primarily individuals with physical disabilities (McCarthy, 2003), yet the underlying philosophy of independent living has been fundamental to the advocacy efforts of many other disability groups.

The Mad Pride movement emerged in the 1970s, named to signify the need for the "reversal of standard pathological connotations with madness" (B. Lewis, 2013, p. 115). Mad Pride has had its own historic leaders, such as Elizabeth Packard (1868) and Clifford Beers (1908), yet the movement as it is known today emerged from the self-advocacy efforts of Leonard Frank (see Farber, 1993) and Judi Chamberlin (1977). In the early 2000s, leaders of the independent living and Mad Pride movements advocated alongside one another to oppose the selection of Dr. Satel (2000) to the New Freedom Commission because of her outspoken position in favor of involuntary commitment and treatment laws as well as the discontinuation of peer-run programs. At the center of the debate was the 1999 *Olmstead* Supreme Court decision that upheld the "integration mandate" of the 1990 Americans with Disabilities Act (ADA, 1990), requiring that states expand the infrastructure and funds to support the full inclusion of individuals with disabilities in the community (Davidson et al., 2009, p. 2). Arguing against "diagnostic labeling and treatment—which all too often come in the form of forced or manipulated hospitalizations, restraints, seclusions, and medication" (B. Lewis, 2013, p. 116), the protesters wanted to raise awareness of the disproportionally low funding of mental health services: States were spending 30% *less* on mental health in 1997 than they did in 1955 when accounting for inflation (Bernstein, 2001; Davidson et al., 2009).

Dart, an early leader of the independent living movement, spoke about the issue of *No Forced Treatments Ever* for individuals with psychiatric disabilities (B. Lewis, 2013; Oakes, 2002) because it violated the principle of "Nothing About Us, Without Us" (Charlton, 1998, p. 3). The collaborative advocacy efforts of the independent living and Mad Pride activists persuaded the New Freedom Commission that the "mental health system is fundamentally broken, that it needs extensive overhaul (not just piecemeal reform), and that mental health services must be consumer and family centered, that modern psychiatry overemphasizes reductionist biomedical approaches, and consumers must be protected from unjust incarceration and the use of seclusion and restraints" (B. Lewis, 2013, p. 127). The larger argument is that the civil rights of individuals with mental illness must be protected at all times, "even and especially while remaining disabled" (Davidson et al., 2009, p. 15).

There are clear benefits to understanding the independent living movement emphasis on disability as a civil rights issue. Perhaps the most significant benefit is to advance a more inclusive and welcoming society for individuals with disabilities (Crewe & Zola, 2001; DeJong, 1979; Nosek et al., 1992). With increasingly high caseloads and limited resources, many RCs do not have the time or resources to work with clients to explore the effects of environmental factors on their experience of disability. If RCs do not have the time or resources, referrals to CILs and/or other consumer-run organizations, such as the Critical Psychiatric Network (www.criticalpsychiatry.co.uk) and Mind Freedom (www.mindfreedom.com) may promote the self-advocacy efforts of individuals with disabilities (Hartley, Johnson, & Tarvydas, 2015). Like other self-help movements, consumer-run programs provide a safe haven for individuals with disabilities to express themselves, offering a place to share experiences and realize that they are not alone (Saxton, 2001; Shreve, 1991; Zola, 2001). Furthermore, consumer-run programs have been a powerful voice in confronting inaccessible environments and negative social attitudes toward disability. RCs share a value on advocacy, social justice, and independent living. In fact, RCs who have personal experience with disability may want to pursue careers with consumer-run organizations. Similar to other work settings, interested RCs should consult relevant organizations, such as the National Council on Independent Living (2010), Association of Programs for Rural Independent Living (2010), and RI International (www.riinternational.com).

DISABILITY STUDIES

Although the independent living movement has greatly informed the Disability Rights community, it is also important to understand the field of **disability studies**, which offers a sociopolitical critique of the dominant cultural discourse of disability (Albrecht et al., 2001; Barnes, Oliver, & Barton, 2002; Davis, 2013; Linton, 1998). As an academic field of inquiry, the field of disability studies has come a long way in a short time (Cushing & Smith, 2009; Davis, 2013). Prior to the 1980s, "academic interest in disability was confined almost exclusively to conventional, individualistic medical explanations" (Barnes et al., 2002, p. 3). Initially based in the United Kingdom, by the 1980s disability studies courses were being taught in the United States, and the first American disability studies journal, *Disability Studies Quarterly*, was published by the Society for Disability Studies (Barnes et al., 2002; Davis, 2013). The initial disability studies movement was rooted in the social sciences, especially sociology; however, in the late 1980s, there was a shift toward a humanities approach of cultural reevaluation (Barnes et al., 2002; Davis, 2013; Linton, 1998). Going beyond a critique of the social forces of oppression that shaped the lives of people with disabilities, the goal became to assemble a collective body of knowledge that "places disability in a political, social, and cultural context, that theorizes and historicizes deafness or blindness or disability in similarly complex ways to the way race, class, and gender have been theorized" (Davis, 2006, p. xvi).

The number of disability studies programs and courses exploded in the 1990s and 2000s (Barnes et al., 2002; Cushing & Smith, 2009; Davis, 2013; Linton, 1998). Yet many of the courses and degrees remained in the social sciences and allied health fields, though this was incongruent with the social model of disability (Cushing & Smith, 2009; Linton, 1998). Although some argued that health care professionals were listening to a disability studies perspective, others were concerned that the field was being diluted and influenced by medical perspectives (Cushing & Smith, 2009; Linton, 1998). To distinguish disability studies programs rooted in the social model of disability, RCs should be able to recognize humanities-based language, curriculum, and worldview; a social model paradigm will emphasize power relations and subjectivity. As with other cultural identity studies, a second wave of disability studies scholars moved to postmodern theories, allowing for the complexity of multiple and shifting identities and differentiating the experiences of disabilities for men and women, middle-class White and nondominant minority communities, and heterosexual and lesbian, gay, bisexual, and transgender people (Davis, 2013; McRuer, 2006; Siebers, 2008; Snyder & Mitchell, 2006). Davis (2013) wrote that in the same way recent scholarship on race has turned its attention to whiteness and intersectionality, disability studies has shifted to focus less on "the construction of disability as on the construction of normalcy" because "the *problem* is not the person with disabilities; the problem is the way that normalcy is constructed to create the *problem* of the disabled person" (p. 1). Similar to other cultural studies, disability studies advances a critique of language use that depends upon defining some groups of people as normal contrasted against the abnormal. This pattern establishes how people with disabilities are defined as different or *othered*. Relatedly, the term *essentialized* refers to discourse practices that reduce a group of people who are different into a single salient trait rather than viewing the full complexity of an individual. The basic tenets of disability studies extend from and contribute to the Disability Rights community.

The primary mission of disability studies is to examine the meaning of disability through an analysis of the experiences of people with disabilities in social, political, and cultural contexts (Barnes et al., 2002; Davis, 2013; Gill, 1995; Linton, 1998). Disability studies challenges the notion of disability as primarily a medical category studied and treated by specialists in fields such as rehabilitation counseling that often reinforce the positioning of people with disabilities as abnormal (Davis, 2013; Linton, 1998). Indeed, disability studies scholars have argued that the ways in which disability is discussed provide a lens to see how disability is understood within our larger society. For instance, scholars have noted how disability has been used to justify inequality for people with disabilities and other groups of people, including women, African Americans, and immigrants (Baynton, 2001, 2013; Block, Balcazar, & Keys, 2001). Women, for instance, were considered inferior physically, intellectually, and psychologically and were not considered worthy of citizenship or equal employment until the Women's suffrage movement (Baynton, 2001, 2013; Block et al., 2001). Furthermore, a common mid–19th-century justification of slavery in the United States was that African Americans lacked sufficient intelligence to participate on an equal basis in society (Baynton, 2013; Block et al., 2001). In fact, a fictional mental illness termed drapetomania was used to explain the reason African American slaves wanted to escape slavery. Extending back to early immigration policies in the United States, traces of eugenics can be found in anti-immigration debates describing immigrants as "feeble-minded and prone to mental illness" (Baynton, 2001, p. 20). In all of these cases, disability has been used to justify unequal treatment.

There are three important aspects of the positioning of people with disabilities as abnormal. First, at the root of reframing disability is the use of language (Davis, 2013; Linton, 1998). Disability studies recognizes the underlying messages conveyed through language as a discourse system and thus shifts from medical discourse to discourses on disability as a social, political, intellectual, and ideological issue. Words such as *confined* to a wheelchair or *suffering* from mental illness represent a conceptual link to discourse of disability as deviance and thus mischaracterize disability as something that is inherently bad. Second, popular media have reinforced disability stereotypes, which have described people with disabilities as "pitiable and pathetic, objects of violence, sinister and evil, a curiosity, super-cripple, objects of ridicule, their own worst enemy, a burden, sexually abnormal, incapable of participating fully in community life, and normal life" (Barnes & Mercer, 2001, p. 519). Disability studies scholars have critiqued the effects of popular media on the perception of disability, especially Hollywood films glorifying assisted suicide, such as *Whose Life Is it Anyway?* (Badham, 1981), *The Sea Inside* (Amenábar, 2004), *Million Dollar Baby* (Eastwood, 2004), and *You Before Me* (Sharrock, 2016). The concern is that these films perpetuate **existential anxiety** (i.e., fear of the fragility of the nondisabled person's own body) and **aesthetic anxiety** (i.e., fear of appearances that look different), while discounting the high quality of life (QOL) experienced by many individuals with severe disabilities (Hahn, 1988). Third, extending from language and themes, the underlying cultural narratives of what it means to have a disability are being reexamined from a postmodern perspective (McRuer, 2006; Siebers, 2008; Tremain, 2006). In response to Hollywood films glorifying assisted suicide, the group *Not Dead Yet* (n.d.) has questioned the dominant cultural narrative of who has worth in our society (Johnson, 2003; Longmore, 2003). Extending from the 1930s theme of mercy killings, there are still dominant cultural messages regarding QOL and disability (Brockley, 2001). Without a critical understanding of a disability studies critique of dominant cultural narratives about disability, an individual may mistakenly believe it will be impossible to live a fulfilling life with a severe disability and that a mercy killing is preferable. Rather than transforming society through protests and legislation, disability studies seeks to change society through critical analysis of meanings that are taken for granted.

Rehabilitation counselors can benefit from the disability studies critique of disability as a disease or ailment (Albrecht et al., 2001; Barnes et al., 2002; Davis, 2013; Linton, 1998). Until recently, hospitals and institutions were used to warehouse individuals with disabilities in deplorable conditions (Goffman, 1961; Grob, 1994) as evident as recently as the 1972 expose of the Willowbrook State School (www.geraldo.com/page/willowbrook). RCs work with people with disabilities in hospitals, clinics, nursing homes, and behavioral health agencies. As frontline service providers, RCs can have a major impact on how agency policies and practices are implemented. Unfortunately, the medical model of disability makes it difficult to communicate with clients and therefore makes doing jobs in health care more challenging (Baker, 2009; Bricher, 2000; Conyers, 2003; Donoghue, 2003). For instance, an individual with a disability is likely to become suspicious and resentful if a counselor only sees the individual as a *patient* while ignoring the person's other life roles, such as child, parent, romantic partner, worker, student, and so on (Baker, 2009; Bricher, 2000; Conyers, 2003; Donoghue, 2003). With respect to mental health, there is a need to embrace the embodiment of mental difference without perpetuating **mentalist** beliefs (Price, 2013), a form of ableism "directed against people who are perceived as not having all of their mental faculties intact—people considered, for example to be mad, irrational, or insane" (Davidson et al., 2009, p. 24). Regardless of the type of disability, the development of a therapeutic relationship and working alliance are critical to rehabilitation practice (Lustig, Strauser, Rice, & Rucker, 2002; Stuntzner & Hartley, 2014); an RC who understands both medical and social aspects of disability will be able to more effectively communicate with and situate an individual's experiences, values, and attitudes in social, political, and cultural contexts.

DISABILITY CULTURE

Stemming from the sociopolitical critique of disability studies and the services and philosophies of the independent living movement, **disability culture** is best understood as a social movement that champions "a sense of common identity and interests that unite disabled people and separate them from their nondisabled counterparts" (Barnes & Mercer, 2001, p. 522). Beginning in the late 1980s, advocates of disability culture pointed to the need for a politicized identity for people with disabilities that resisted the marginalizing narratives of the dominant culture (Barnes & Mercer, 2001; Brannon, 1995; S. E. Brown, 2001; Gill, 1995; Hirsch, 1995; Johnson, 1987; Longmore, 1995). With the disability studies shift toward the humanities, disability culture was a response to the widespread cultural devaluation of people with disabilities (Brannon, 1995; S. E. Brown, 2001; Gill, 1995; Hirsch, 1995; Johnson, 1987; Longmore, 1995). For instance, during the 19th and 20th centuries, U.S. legislation, commonly known as the "Ugly Laws," restricted the public appearance of individuals with physical disabilities because they were considered offensive and frightening (Schweik, 2008). In contrast to the eugenics view that people with disabilities were biologically inferior, disability culture is a "lived interrogation" of the idea that disability is primarily a medical condition. The essence of disability culture is the celebration of the lived experience of disability as uniquely beautiful and shaped by a person's particular social and cultural identity (Barnes & Mercer, 2001; Conyers, 2003; Ingstad & Whyte, 1995; Snyder & Mitchell, 2006). Perhaps most importantly, disability culture is a social movement intended to unite a broad cross-section of people with disabilities (Gill, 1995). As part of the Disability Rights community, disability culture is not about a single disability-specific group, but rather a larger, universalistic approach to disability as a cultural identity.

Defining disability culture is difficult. Not even the Disability Rights community has agreed on a common language or description of acculturation (Peters, 2000). Embodied in art, music, literature, and other expressions, disability culture celebrates the ways in which people with disabilities view themselves (S. E. Brown, 2001). For instance, Golfus, a filmmaker, made the documentary *When Billy Broke His Head* (Golfus & Simpson, 1995) and chronicled his experiences after a traumatic brain injury. Sometimes shown in master's-level rehabilitation counseling courses, the most striking part of the documentary is the way in which Golfus situates rehabilitation in the larger experience of his disability and the perspectives of the Disability Rights community. Rehabilitation professionals who watch the film often express frustration with how Golfus portrays the rehabilitation system as ineffectual and removed from the lived experience of disability. Another well-known story is that of Christy Brown, an Irish author, painter, and poet who had severe cerebral palsy. Brown's autobiography *My Left Foot* (1954) is a complex portrayal of a very talented individual with multiple identities intersecting with class, religion, gender, and sexuality in the mid-20th century. In a review of the film, Longmore (2003) noted that Christy Brown's story is important because it is not an *essentialized* depiction of an individual with a disability as tragic or heroic, but captures the larger theme of people with disabilities who "fight bias and battle for control of their lives and insist that they will make their mark on the world" (p. 130). Many famous authors, including John Milton, James Joyce, and John Keats, have experienced disability (Davis, 2013). Today, artists use disability as a lens through which to express themselves in art, music, and theater in ways beyond essentialized portrayals as victims or villains (V. A. Lewis, 2006).

The rise of Web 2.0 applications (also known as "social media") now offers an endless supply of disability narratives that are promoting disability as a cultural identity (Hartley, Mapes, Taylor, & Bourgeois, 2016). Within the Disability Rights community, social media has become a preferred interface to "organize disability-rights actions, let others know about disability related news, promote events, or just find like-minded disability rights advocates" (Haller, 2010, p. 5). The emergence of popular social media tools, such as Twitter, Facebook, YouTube, blogs, and wikis, has led to a surplus of individuals using digital technologies and social media as platforms for media authorship (Brandt, 2009). For example, Baggs counters misconceptions that individuals with autism lack personhood in the YouTube video *In My Own Language* (www.youtube.com/watch?v=Jnyl M1hI2jc). As another example, Withers describes what it is like to experience symptoms such as depersonalization and hallucinations, including strategies for coping that include her dog: "if the animal doesn't react to the hallucination, then it's probably not real, she says" (Chen, 2016, p. 1) in the YouTube channel *Rachel Star Schizophrenic* (www .youtube.com/playlist?list=PL1wbyEW2jgnYSEOd5Vz7VO76MB2sif15QD). Finally, humor may be a particularly powerful avenue to promote social change, as is the case of Young in the YouTube video *I'm not Your Inspiration* (www.youtube.com/watch?v=8K9Ggl64Bsw); Moon in the YouTube video *I Got 99 Problems . . .* (www.youtube.com/watch?v=buRLc2e WGPQ); and Sherer in the YouTube series *My Gimpy Life* (www.youtube.com/user/ MyGimpyLife). In each case, first-person, authentic perspectives on disability are contributing to the notion of disability as a social and cultural identity.

It is particularly important for RCs to be exposed to disability culture (Barnes & Mercer, 2001; Conyers, 2003; Ingstad & Whyte, 1995; Snyder & Mitchell, 2006). Compared to the disability studies emphasis on intellectual arguments, disability culture is premised on the notion that the way to change society is by expression of the lived experience of disability through art, music, and literature (S. E. Brown, 2001). Disability culture responds to these negative societal messages by examining the complex identities of disability that intersect with gender, race, and sexuality, and by promoting the idea that an individual with a severe disability can live a fulfilling life. Complex narratives of disability may be used in the way that bibliotherapy has been incorporated into counseling practice for decades: to understand and promote the therapeutic needs of clients (Marrs, 1995). In the age of digital literacy (Carr & Porfilo, 2009), it is possible that media literacy and positive images of disability may assist individuals with disabilities to respond in successful and creative ways to disability concerns (Hartley et al., 2015, 2016). By offering positive representations of disability, social media has the potential to counter the negative images often found in the dominant cultural discourse. In fact, to promote self-advocacy of individuals with disabilities, the future of rehabilitation counseling practice may involve helping clients identify healthy and supportive Twitter feeds as well as therapeutic blogs that can assist individuals to respond creatively and successfully to disability concerns. The larger point is that an understanding of disability culture will lead to an approach to disability that questions the misrepresentation of disability in the dominant culture and encourages individuals to recognize the social and emotional experience of disability. Without an understanding of the social model, as embraced by the disability culture movement, counselors may inadvertently contribute to the perceptions of people with disabilities as diseased, broken, and in need of fixing (Baker, 2009; Bricher, 2000; Conyers, 2003; Donoghue, 2003; Illich et al., 2005). Thus, it is particularly important for RCs to be exposed to disability culture.

ONGOING CONSIDERATIONS

As in other specialized health fields, the medical model of disability has traditionally been the central focus of rehabilitation counseling research and policy decisions. As a consequence, many in the Disability Rights community have viewed this knowledge base as "oppressive" (Bricher, 2000, p. 781). Today, the rehabilitation counseling literature is increasingly influenced by the social model of disability (Armstrong & Fitzgerald, 1996; Carluccio & Patterson, 2001; Conyers, 2003; Kosciulek, 1999, 2000; McCarthy, 2003; McMahon & Shaw, 1999; Middleton, Rollins, & Harley, 1999; Szymanski, Parker, & Patterson, 2005), and the growing body of literature that moves away from the traditional medical model and toward the social model is a positive response to the Disability Rights community. However, if rehabilitation professionals are to incorporate the social model, a further dialogue is needed between RCs and the Disability Rights community. In developing such a dialogue, several ongoing issues must be addressed.

First, to collaborate with the Disability Rights community, rehabilitation professionals need to understand that the choice of language is never value-neutral, but rather represents an approach to understanding disability. In order to establish therapeutic relationships with individuals with disabilities, rehabilitation professionals need to move beyond simply adopting person-first language and consider underlying messages conveyed through language and the consequences to which each leads. Although the Disability Rights community is suspicious of overly medicalized or *essentialized* language depicting disability, it important to note that some individuals with disabilities may prefer identity-first language. As an example, self-advocates and their allies involved in the Autistic Self-Advocacy Network prefer "Autistic," "Autistic person," or "Autistic individual" to denote autism as a positive cultural identity status (retrieved from www.autisticadvocacy .org/home/about-asan/identity-first-language). The larger point is that the use of language is complex both in terms of intent and interpretation. It is therefore important that RCs be comfortable discussing language as well as understanding the underlying messages conveyed through language.

Second, as frontline service providers, RCs work directly with people with disabilities, and these interactions can have a major impact on how agency policies and practices are implemented. RCs need to consider the policies and practices that unintentionally limit the lives of people with disabilities (Gill, 1995; Pledger, 2003). For instance, rehabilitation services that are not flexible enough to address the holistic needs of individuals are not likely to make positive differences in their lives and may cause harm to families by using up already scarce resources. Without considering the social realities associated with disability, RCs may fail to address the social discrimination in the form of limited access to housing and transportation. As Deegan (1994) noted, it is particularly critical that rehabilitation services do not focus on "rehabilitating" individuals, but rather, place that focus on empowering individuals with disabilities with the skills to pursue their own individualized life goals (Brophy, Chan, & Mar, 1974; Stuntzner & Hartley, 2015; Vash, 1991). As an extension of this approach, RCs can serve as an important link between not-for-profit organizations and the Disability Rights community, bridging the gap between the medical and social model perspectives. Although many disability-specific groups, such as United Cerebral Palsy (2010) and National Alliance on Mental Illness (NAMI, 2010) originated from a medical model of disability perspective that looked to eradicate disability by finding a cure, these organizations are shifting toward the social model of disability perspective when people with disabilities assume leadership roles (Varela, 2001).

Third, the epistemological knowledge base of rehabilitation practice, including rehabilitation research and policy development, is an area where critical analysis should occur. Although practitioners typically do not conduct research, there is a need to understand fundamental concerns regarding the construction of rehabilitation knowledge. Specifically, there is concern that traditional rehabilitation knowledge was constructed from a medical model approach to disability (Bricher, 2000). From a Disability Rights perspective, most of this research has been conducted *on* rather than *with* people with disabilities (Barnes, 1996; Oliver, 1992; Shakespeare, 1996). Research influences health care policies and practices, and the Disability Rights community is rightfully wary of research on disability conducted without input from people with disabilities (Barnes, 1996; Oliver, 1992; Shakespeare, 1996). Noted by Charlton (1998), without input from individuals with disabilities, research on disability violates the notion of "Nothing About Us, Without Us" (p. 3). Rehabilitation researchers have responded to this concern, and participatory action research is growing in importance (Bruyère, 1993; Walker, 1993; White, 2002).

The goal of participatory action research is to enhance the relevance of research to the lives of people with disabilities by including people with disabilities in all aspects of the research process, beginning with the generation of research questions (Bruyère, 1993; Walker, 1993; White, 2002). Participatory action research is likely to lead to more collaboration; however, there will always be conflict between proponents of the medical model and the social model. As a result, rehabilitation counseling professionals without disabilities may find it "difficult to find a rightful place in relation to research with disabled people and the social model" and struggle to find a comfortable role in discussing traditional rehabilitation knowledge and research with individuals with disabilities (Bricher, 2000, p. 782). Perhaps it is most important for RCs to recognize disabilities as a social and emotional experience, not a medical issue that has to be solved or prevented, if they are to engage in a dialogue with the Disability Rights community (Baker, 2009; Barnes, 1996; Conyers, 2003; Donoghue, 2003). Critically examining how knowledge is constructed is an important part of developing a climate of respect and reciprocity with the Disability Rights community. Disability studies and disability culture both provide a critique of cultural misconceptions of disability.

Finally, rehabilitation counseling must continue its traditional focus on the employment of individuals with disabilities. Unfortunately, the relationship between disability and poverty is well established (Lustig & Strauser, 2007). For example, individuals with severe psychiatric disabilities have unemployment rates as high as 80% to 90% (Crowther, Marshall, Bond, & Huxley, 2001; Goldberg et al., 2001; Nobel, Honberg, Hall, & Flynn, 2001). Without an understanding of the social model, counselors may mistakenly conclude that the main reason is their psychiatric symptoms. However, research has shown that a major reason for the high unemployment rate is the stigma of mental illness:

Terms such as "unstable" and "volatile" have perpetuated the myth that employing workers with psychiatric disabilities is dangerous (Diksa & Rogers, 1996; Hazer & Bedell, 2000; Weber, Davis, & Sebastian, 2002). Surveys indicate that 50% of U.S. employers are reluctant to hire someone currently undergoing psychiatric treatment, and 70% are reluctant to hire someone currently taking antipsychotic medication (Scheid, 1999). Even after gaining employment, disclosure of a psychiatric disability can seriously limit a person's career advancement (Stuart, 2006). Workers who return to their jobs after a psychiatric leave of absence report receiving negative comments from colleagues who had previously been supportive and friendly (Wahl, 1999). Individuals with physical disabilities also are discriminated against, and employer fears of expensive accommodations and insurance claims contribute to unemployment rates of 60% to 70% (Stapleton, O'Day, & Livermore, 2005; Wilson-Kovacs, Ryan, Haslam, & Rabinovich, 2008). Besides unemployment, even career advancement can be difficult (Wilson-Kovacs et al., 2008). For instance, in a qualitative study one individual who had his eyesight and hearing affected by a genetic illness noted that senior management viewed him as having "half the capacity" and not up to challenging assignments associated with promotion (cited in Wilson-Kovacs et al., 2008, p. 709). In addition to offsetting the social and economic disadvantage associated with disability, rehabilitation counseling has to partner with the Disability Rights community to promote larger social change.

CONCLUSION

There is a clear need for interdisciplinary dialogue between disability studies and specialized professional fields such as rehabilitation counseling. With that said, collaboration is likely to be difficult because the two fields are so divergent in their missions and approaches to disability. The three models of disability (biomedical model, functional limitations model, and social model) are the best places for dialogue. With advances in gene therapy, biotechnology, neuroscience research, and assisted suicide (Braddock & Parish, 2001), none of the three models alone is complex enough to arrive at workable solutions to all issues experienced in rehabilitation counseling. Therefore, instead of viewing the three models as isolated constructs, our fields might recognize the relationships among the models as they inform rehabilitation practice. Finally, rather than forming opinions in a vacuum, RCs need to learn to listen to the Disability Rights community. For instance, how might the Disability Rights perspective influence the education of rehabilitation practitioners? How might the Disability Rights perspective view current rehabilitation policies and practices? How might collaborations between our fields lead to workable solutions to issues of health care and disability?

CONTENT REVIEW QUESTIONS

- With respect to the disability rights movement, what is meant by the phrase coined by Charlton (1998): "Nothing About Us, Without Us?"
- What are the principles of the independent living movement?
- What are three important domains for the critique of the dominant perspectives of disability?
- What is the significance of disability culture?

- What are the benefits of understanding the Disability Rights community prior to working as a RC?
- What are important considerations for respectful communication between rehabilitation counseling professionals and Disability Rights community members?

REFERENCES

Albrecht, G. L., Seelman, K. D., & Bury, M. (2001). Introduction: The formation of disability studies. In G. L. Albrecht, K. D. Seelman, & M. Bury (Eds.), *Handbook of disability studies* (pp. 1–10). Thousand Oaks, CA: Sage.

Amenábar, A. (Director). (2004). *The sea inside* [Motion picture]. Pozuelo de Alarcón, Spain: Sogepaqes.

American Psychiatric Association. (2013). *Diagnostic and statistical manual of mental disorders.* (5th ed.). Arlington, VA: American Psychiatric Publishing.

Americans with Disabilities Act. (1990). 42 U.S.C. § 12101 *et seq.* (July 26, 1990).

Armstrong, M. J., & Fitzgerald, M. H. (1996). Culture and disability studies: An anthropological perspective. *Rehabilitation Education, 10,* 247–304.

Association of Programs for Rural Independent Living. (2010). The united voice of independent living in rural America. Retrieved from http://www.april-rural.org

Badham, J. (Director). (1981). *Whose life is it anyway?* [Motion picture]. Beverly Hills, CA: Metro-Goldwyn-Mayer.

Baker, D. (2009). Bridging the deficiency divide: Expressions of non-deficiency models of disability in health care. *Disability Studies Quarterly, 29,* 6–12.

Barnartt, S. (1996). Disability culture or disability consciousness? *Journal of Disability Policy Studies, 7,* 1–19.

Barnartt, S., & Scotch, R. (2001). *Disability protests: Contentious politics 1970–1999.* Washington, DC: Gallaudet Press.

Barnes, C. (1996). Disability and the myth of the independent researcher. *Disability and Society, 7,* 115–124.

Barnes, C., & Mercer, G. (2001). Disability culture. In G. L. Albrecht, K. D. Seelman, & M. Bury (Eds.), *Handbook of disability studies* (pp. 515–534). Thousand Oaks, CA: Sage.

Barnes, C., Oliver, M., & Barton, L. (2002). *Disability studies today.* Malden, MA: Blackwell.

Baynton, D. (1996). *Forbidden signs.* Chicago, IL: University of Chicago Press.

Baynton, D. (2001). Disability and the justification of inequality in American history. In P. Longmore & L. Umansky (Eds.), *The new disability history: American perspectives* (pp. 33–57). New York: The New York University Press.

Baynton, D. (2013). Disability and the justification of inequality in American history. In L. J. Davis (Ed.), *The disability studies reader* (4th ed., pp. 17–33). New York, NY: Routledge.

Beers, C. W. (1908). *A mind that found itself.* New York, NY: Doubleday.

Bernstein, R. (2001). *Disintegrating systems: The state of state's public mental health system.* Washington, DC: Bazelon Center for Mental Health Law.

Block, P., Balcazar, F., & Keys, C. (2001). From pathology to power: Rethinking race, poverty, and disability. *Journal of Disability Policy Studies, 12,* 18–39.

Bolton, B., & Brookings, J. (1998). Development of a multifaceted definition of empowerment. *Rehabilitation Counseling Bulletin, 19,* 12–18.

Braddock, D. L., & Parish, S. L. (2001). An institutional history of disability. In G. L. Albrecht, K. D. Seelman, & M. Bury (Eds.), *Handbook of disability studies* (pp. 1–10). Thousand Oaks, CA: Sage.

Brandt, D. (2009). Writing over reading: New directions in mass literacy. In M. Baynham & M. Prinsloo (Eds.), *The future of literacy studies* (pp. 54–74). London, UK: Palgrave Macmillan.

Brophy, M. C., Chan, A., & Mar, B. M. (1974). The advocate counseling model. In T. Samore (Ed.), *Progress in urban librarianship* (pp. 40–48). Milwaukee, WI: Schools of Library.

Brannon, R. (1995). The use of the concept of disability culture: A historian's view. *Disability Studies Quarterly, 15,* 3–15.

Bricher, G. (2000). Disabled people, health professionals and the social model of disability: Can there be such a relationship? *Disability and Society, 15,* 781–793. doi:10.1080/713662004

Brockley, J. A. (2001). Martyred mothers and merciful fathers: Exploring disability and motherhood in the lives of Jerome Greenfield and Raymond Repouille. In P. Longmore & L. Umansky (Eds.), *The new disability history: American perspectives* (pp. 268–292). New York: New York University Press.

Brown, C. (1954). *My left foot*. London, UK: Secker & Warburg.

Brown, S. E. (2001). Editorial: What is disability culture? *Independent Living Institute Newsletter 2001–12*. Retrieved June 25, 2010, from http:www.independentliving.org/newsletter/12–01.html

Bruyère, S. M. (1993). Participatory action research: Overview and implications for family members of persons with disabilities. *Journal of Vocational Rehabilitation, 3*, 62–68.

Bruyère, S. M. (2000). Civil rights and employment issues of disability policy. *Journal of Disability Policy Studies, 11,* 18–28. doi:10.1177/104420730001100108

Byrom, B. (2001). A pupil and a patient. In P. Longmore & L. Umansky (Eds.), *The new disability history: American perspectives* (pp. 133–156). New York: New York University Press.

Campbell, J., & Oliver, M. (1996). *Disability politics*. London, UK: Routledge.

Carluccio, L. W., & Patterson, J. (2001). Promoting independent living in the rehabilitation curriculum. *Rehabilitation Education, 15,* 409–419.

Carr, P. R., & Porfilo, B. J. (2009). Computers, the media and multicultural education: Seeking engagement and political literacy. *Intercultural Education, 20*(2), 91–107. doi:10.1080/14675980902922200

Chamberlin, J. (1977). *On our own: Patient-controlled alternatives to the mental health system*. Lawrence, MA: National Empowerment Center.

Charlton, J. (1998). *Nothing about us without us*. Berkeley: University of California Press.

Chen, A. (2016, June 13). How YouTube videos help people cope with mental illness. *Morning Edition*. National Public Radio.

Chubon, R. A. (1992). Defining rehabilitation from a systems perspective: Critical implications. *Journal of Applied Rehabilitation Counseling, 23*, 27–32.

Cole, J. A. (2001). Developing new self-images and interdependence. In N. M. Crewe & I. K. Zola (Eds.), *Independent living for physically disabled people* (pp. 187–204). San Jose, CA: People with Disabilities Press.

Commission on Rehabilitation Counselor Certification. (2016). Rehabilitation counseling. Retrieved from http://www.crccertification.com/pages/rehabilitation_counseling/30.php

Conyers, L. M. (2003). Disability culture. *Rehabilitation Education, 3*, 139–154.

Corrigan, P. W. (2016). *Principles and practice of psychiatric rehabilitation: An empirical approach* (2nd ed.). New York, NY: Guilford Press.

Crewe, N. M., & Zola, I. K. (Eds.). (2001). *Independent living for physically disabled people*. San Jose, CA: People with Disabilities Press.

Crowther, R. E., Marshall, M., Bond, G. R., & Huxley, P. (2001). Helping people with severe mental illness to obtain work: Systematic review. *British Medical Journal, 322*, 204–208.

Cushing, P., & Smith, T. (2009). A multinational review of English-language disability studies degrees and courses. *Disability Studies Quarterly, 29*, 11–22.

Davidson, L., Tondora, J., Staeheli Lawless, M., O'Connell, M. J., & Rowe, M. (2009). *A practical guide to recovery-oriented practice*. New York, NY: Oxford University Press.

Davis, L. J. (Ed.). (2006). *The disability studies reader* (2nd ed.). New York, NY: Routledge.

Davis, L. J. (Ed.). (2013). *The disability studies reader* (4th ed.). New York, NY: Routledge.

Deegan, P. E. (1994). Recovery: The lived experience of rehabilitation. In L. Spaniol & M. Koehler (Eds.), *The experience of recovery* (pp. 54–59). Boston, MA: Center for Psychiatric Rehabilitation.

DeJong, G. (1979). Independent living: From social movement to analytic paradigm. *Archives of Physical Medicine and Rehabilitation, 60*, 435–446.

Diksa, E., & Rogers, E. S. (1996). Employer concerns about hiring persons with psychiatric disability. *Rehabilitation Counseling Bulletin, 40*, 31–44.

Donoghue, C. (2003). Challenging the authority of the medical definition of disability: An analysis of the resistance to the social constructionist paradigm. *Disability and Society, 18*, 199. doi:10.1080/09687590 32000052833

Eastwood, C. (Director). (2004). *Million dollar baby* [Motion picture]. Burbank, CA: Warner Bros. Pictures.

Farber, S. (1993). From victim to revolutionary: An interview with Lennard Frank. In *Madness, heresy, and the rumor of angels: The revolt against the mental health system*. Chicago, IL: Open Court.

Frain, M., Tschopp, M. K., & Bishop, M. (2009). Empowerment variables as predictors of outcomes in rehabilitation. *Journal of Rehabilitation, 75*(1), 27–35.

Frazer, E. (1999). *The problem of communitarian politics: Unity and conflict*. Oxford, UK: Oxford University Press.

Frieden, L. (2001). Understanding alternative program models. In N. M. Crewe & I. K. Zola (Eds.), *Independent living for physically disabled people* (pp. 62–72). San Jose, CA: People with Disabilities Press.

Gill, C. J. (1995). A psychological view of disability culture. *Disability Studies Quarterly, 15*, 16–19.

Goffman, E. (1961). *Asylums: Essays on the social situation of mental patients and other inmates*. New York, NY: Doubleday.

Goldberg, R. W., Lucksted, A., McNary, S., Gold, J. M., Dixon, L., & Lehman, A. (2001). Correlates of long-term unemployment among inner-city adults with serious and persistent mental illness. *Psychiatric Services, 52*, 101–103.

Golfus, B., & Simpson, D. (1995). *When Billy broke his head and other tales of wonder.* St. Paul, MN: Independent Television Series.

Grob, G. (1994). *The mad among us: A history of the care of America's mentally ill.* Cambridge, MA: Harvard University Press.

Hahn, H. (1988). The politics of physical differences: Disability and discrimination. *Journal of Social Issues, 44*(11), 39–47.

Hahn, H. (1991). Theories and values: Ethics and contrasting perspectives on disability. In R. P. Marinelli & A. E. Dell Orto (Eds.), *The psychological and social impact of disability* (pp. 18–22). New York, NY: Springer Publishing.

Haller, B. (2010). *Representing disability in an ableist world.* Louisville, KY: Avocado Press.

Hartley, M. T., Johnson, S. P., & Tarvydas, V. M. (2015). The ethics and practice of social media advocacy in rehabilitation counseling. *Journal of Rehabilitation, 81*(1), 43–52.

Hartley, M. T., Mapes, A. C., Taylor, A., & Bourgeois, P. (2016). Digital media technology and advocacy: Addressing attitudes toward disability on college campuses. *Journal of Postsecondary Education and Disability, 29*(3), 239–247.

Hazer, J. T., & Bedell, K. V. (2000). Effects of seeking accommodation and disability on preemployment evaluations. *Journal of Applied Social Psychology, 30*, 1201–1223. doi:10.1111/j.1559-1816.2000.tb02517.x

Hershenson, D. B. (1998). Systematic, ecological model for rehabilitation counseling. *Rehabilitation Counseling Bulletin, 42*, 40–50.

Hirsch, K. (1995). Culture and disability: The role of oral history. *Oral History Review, 22*, 1–27.

Hoggett, P. (1997). *Contested communities: Experiences, struggles, policies.* Bristol, UK: Policy Press.

Illich, I., Zola, I. K., McKnight, J., Caplan, J., & Shaiken, H. (2005). *Disabling professions.* London, UK: Marion Boyers.

Ingstad, B., & Whyte, S. R. (Eds.). (1995). *Disability and culture.* Los Angeles: University of California Press.

Jenkins, W., Patterson, J. B., & Szymanski, E. M. (1992). Philosophical, historic, and legislative aspects of the rehabilitation counseling profession. In R. M. Parker & E. M. Szymanski (Eds.), *Rehabilitation counseling: Basics and beyond* (2nd ed., pp. 1–41). Austin, TX: Pro-Ed.

Johnson, M. (1987). Emotion and pride: The search for a disability culture. *Disability Rag (January/February)*, 1–27.

Johnson, M. (2003). *Make them go away.* Louisville, KY: The Avocado Press.

Kilbury, R. F., Benshoff, J. J., & Rubin, S. E. (1992). The interaction of legislation, public attitudes, and access to opportunities for persons with disabilities. *Journal of Rehabilitation, 58*(4), 6–9.

Koestler, F. A. (1975). *The unseen minority.* New York, NY: American Foundation of the Blind.

Kosciulek, J. F. (1993). Advances in trait-and-factor theory: A person x environment fit approach to rehabilitation counseling. *Journal of Applied Rehabilitation Counseling, 24*, 11–14.

Kosciulek, J. F. (1999). The consumer directed theory of empowerment. *Rehabilitation Counseling Bulletin, 42*, 196–213.

Kosciulek, J. F. (2000). Implications of consumer direction for disability policy development and rehabilitation service delivery. *Journal of Disability Policy Studies, 11*, 82–89.

Kosciulek, J. F. (2005). Structural equation model of the consumer-directed theory of empowerment in vocational rehabilitation. *Rehabilitation Counseling Bulletin, 49*, 40–49.

Lane, H. (1984). *When the mind hears.* New York, NY: Random House.

Leahy, M. J., Chan, F., & Saunders, J. L. (2003). Job functions and knowledge requirements of certified rehabilitation counselors in the 21st century. *Rehabilitation Counseling Bulletin, 46*, 66–81. doi: 10.1177/0034355203046002010 1

Leahy, M. J., Muenzen, P., Saunders, J. L., & Strauser, D. (2009). Essential knowledge domains underlying effective rehabilitation counseling practice. *Rehabilitation Counseling Bulletin, 52*(2), 95–106. doi:10.1177/0034355208323646

Leahy, M. J., & Szymanski, E. M. (1995). Rehabilitation counseling: Evolution and current status. *Journal of Counseling and Development, 74*, 163–166.

Lewis, B. (2013). A mad fight: Psychiatry and disability activism. In L. J. Davis (Ed.), *The disability studies reader* (4th ed., pp. 100–114). New York, NY: Routledge.

Lewis, V. A. (2006). *Beyond victims and villains: Contemporary plays by disabled playwrights.* New York, NY: Theatre Communication Group.

Linton, S. (1998). *Claiming disability, knowledge and identity*. New York: New York University Press.

Lofquist, L. H., & Dawis, R. V. (1969). *Adjustment to work: A psychological view of man's problems in a work-orientated society*. New York, NY: Appleton-Century-Crofts.

Longmore, P. K. (1995). The second phase: From disability rights to disability culture. *Disability Rag* (September/October), 4–11.

Longmore, P. K. (2003). *Why I burned my book and other essays on disability*. Philadelphia, PA: Temple University Press.

Longmore, P. K., & Goldberger, E. (2003). The league of physically handicapped and the great depression. In P. Longmore (Ed.), *Why I burned my book and other essays on disability* (pp. 53–101). Philadelphia, PA: Temple University Press.

Longmore, P. K., & Umansky, L. (Eds.). (2001). *The new disability history*. New York: New York University Press.

Lustig, D. C., & Strauser, D. (2007). Causal relationships between poverty and disability. *Rehabilitation Counseling Bulletin, 50,* 194–202.

Lustig, D. C., Strauser, D. R., Rice, N. D., & Rucker, T. F. (2002). The relationship between working alliance and rehabilitation outcomes. *Rehabilitation Counseling Bulletin, 46,* 25–33.

Maki, D. R., McCracken, N., Pape, D., & Scofield, M. E. (1979). A systems approach to vocational assessment. *Journal of Rehabilitation, 45,* 48–51.

Maki, D. R., & Tarvydas, V. M. (2012). *The professional practice of rehabilitation counseling*. New York, NY: Springer Publishing.

Marrs, R. W. (1995). A meta-analysis of bibliotherapy studies. *American Journal of Community Psychology, 23*(6), 843–870. doi:10.1007/BF02507018

Matson, F. (1990). *Walking alone and marching together*. Baltimore, MD: National Federation of the Blind.

McCarthy, H. (2003). The disability rights movement: Experiences and perspectives of selected leaders in the disability community. *Rehabilitation Counseling Bulletin, 46,* 209–223.

McMahon, B. T., & Shaw, L. (Eds.). (1999). *Enabling lives: Biographies of six prominent Americans with disabilities*. New York, NY: CRC Press.

McRuer, R. (2006). *Crip theory: Cultural signs of queerness and disability*. New York: New York University Press.

Middleton, R. A., Rollins, C. W., & Harley, D. A. (1999). The historical and political context of the civil rights of persons with disabilities: A multicultural perspective for counselors. *Journal of Multicultural Counseling and Development, 27,* 105–120.

National Alliance on Mental Illness. (2010). National Alliance on Mental Illness. Retrieved from http://www.nami.org

National Council on Independent Living. (2010). National Council on Independent Living. Retrieved from http://www.ncil.org

Nobel, J. H., Honberg, R. S., Hall, L. L., & Flynn, L. M. (2001). Legacy of failure: The inability of the federal–state vocational rehabilitation system to serve people with severe mental illness. Retrieved from http://othermove.nbazhibo8.net/legacy-of-failure-the-inability-of-the-federal-state-vocational-rehabilitation-system-to-serve-people-with-severe-mental-illnesses.pdf

Noll, S., & Trent, J. (Eds.). (2004). *Mental retardation in America: A historical reader*. New York, NY: New York University Press.

Nosek, M. A., Zhu, Y., & Howland, C. (1992). The evolution of independent living programs. *Rehabilitation Counseling Bulletin, 35,* 174–179.

Not Dead Yet. (n.d.). Retrieved July 2010 from http://notdeadyetnewscommentary.blogspot.com

Oakes, D. (2002). *From patients to passion: A call for nonviolent revolution in the mental health system* (Plenary address alternatives 2002 Convention). Retrieved from http://www.mindfreedom.org

Oliver, M. (1990). *The politics of disablement*. London, UK: Macmillan Press.

Oliver, M. (1992). Changing the social relations of research production. *Disability, Handicap, and Society, 7,* 101–114.

Olmstead v. L. C. 527 U.S. 581 (1999).

Packard, E. (1868). *The prisoner's hidden life, or insane asylums unveiled: As demonstrated by the report of the investigating committee of the legislature of Illinois*. Chicago, IL: Author.

Parker, R., & Patterson, J. (Eds.). (2011). *Rehabilitation counseling: Basics and beyond* (5th ed.). Austin, TX: Pro-Ed.

Peters, S. (2000). Is there a disability culture? A syncretisation of three possible worldviews. *Disability and Society, 15,* 583–601. doi:10.1080/09687590050058170

Pledger, C. (2003). Discourse on disability and rehabilitation issues. *American Psychologist, 58,* 279–284. doi:10.1037/0003-066X.58.4.279

Porter, R. (1989). *A social history of madness.* New York, NY: Dutton.

Pratt, M. L. (1991). Arts of the contact zone. *Profession 91, 33*–40. Retrieved from http://www.jstor.org/stable/25595469

Price, M. (2013). Defining mental illness. In L. J. Davis (Ed.), *The disability studies reader* (4th ed., pp. 298–307). New York, NY: Routledge.

Richards, L., & Smith, Q. (n.d.). An orientation to independent living centers. *ILRU field work: A national technical assistance project for independent living* (pp. 1–6). Developed as part of the National Technical Assistance Project for Independent Living. Houston, TX: ILRU Research & Training Center on Independent Living at TIRR. Retrieved from http://www.ilru.org

Rubin, S., & Roessler, R. (2008). *Foundations of the vocational rehabilitation process.* Austin, TX: Pro-Ed.

Sales, A. (2007). *Rehabilitation counseling: An empowerment perspective.* Austin, TX: Pro-Ed.

Satel, S. (2000). *Review of P.C., M.D.: How political correctness is corrupting medicine.* New York, NY: Basic Books.

Saxton, M. (2001). Peer counseling. In N. M. Crewe & I. K. Zola (Eds.), *Independent living for physically disabled people* (pp. 171–186). San Jose, CA: People with Disabilities Press.

Scheid, T. L. (1999). Employment of individuals with mental disabilities: Business response to the ADA challenge. *Behavior Science and the Law, 17,* 73–91.

Schwab, L. (2001). Developing programs in rural areas. In N. M. Crewe & I. K. Zola (Eds.), *Independent living for physically disabled people* (pp. 73–87). San Jose, CA: People with Disabilities Press.

Schweik, S. M. (2008). *The ugly laws.* New York: New York University Press.

Scotch, R. K. (1988). Disability as the basis of a social movement: Advocacy and the politics of definition. *Journal of Social Issues, 44,* 159–172.

Shakespeare, T. (1996). Rules of engagement: Doing disability research. *Disability and Society, 11,* 115–119.

Shakespeare, T. (2013). The social model of disability. In L. J. Davis (Ed.), *The disability studies reader* (4th ed., pp. 214–221). New York, NY: Routledge.

Shakespeare, T., & Watson, N. (1997). Defending the social model. *Disability and Society, 12,* 293–300.

Shapiro, J. P. (1993). *No pity.* New York, NY: Three Rivers Press.

Sharrock, T. (Director). (2016). *You before me* [Motion picture]. Beverly Hills, CA: Metro-Goldwyn-Mayer.

Shreve, M. (1991). *Peer counseling in independent living centers* (pp. 1–29). Houston, TX: ILRU Program. Retrieved from www.ilru.org

Siebers, T. (2008). *Disability theory.* Ann Arbor: University of Michigan Press.

Smart, J. (2004). Models of disability. In T. Riggar & D. Maki (Eds.), *Handbook of rehabilitation counseling* (pp. 25–49). New York, NY: Springer Publishing.

Smart, J. (2015). *Disability, society, and the individual* (3rd ed.). Gaithersburg, MD: Aspen Press.

Snyder, S. L., & Mitchell, D. T. (2006). *Cultural locations of disability.* Chicago, IL: The University of Chicago Press.

Stapleton, D. C., O'Day, B., & Livermore, G. A. (2005, July). *Dismantling the poverty trap: Disability policy for the 21st Century.* Washington, DC: Cornell Institute for Policy Research, Rehabilitation Research and Training Center. Retrieved from http://digitalcommons.ilr.cornell.edu/edicollect/124

Stuart, H. (2006). Mental illness and employment discrimination. *Current Opinion in Psychiatry, 19,* 522–526. doi:10.1097/01.yco.0000238482.27270.5d

Stuntzner, S., & Hartley, M. T. (2014). Disability and the counseling relationship: What counselors need to know. In *Ideas and research you can use: VISTAS 2014.* Retrieved from www.counseling.org

Stuntzner, S., & Hartley, M. T. (2015). Balancing self-compassion with self-advocacy: A new approach for persons with disabilities learning to self-advocate. *Annals of Psychotherapy and Integrative Health.* Retrieved from http://www.annalsofpsychotherapy.com

Switzer, J. V. (2003). *Disability rights.* Washington, DC: Georgetown University Press.

Szymanski, E., Parker, R., & Patterson, J. (2005). Beyond the basics: Sociopolitical context of rehabilitation counseling practice. In R. Parker, E. Szymanski, & J. Patterson (Eds.), *Rehabilitation counseling: Basics and beyond* (4th ed., pp. 395–412). Austin, TX: Pro-Ed.

Tarvydas, V. M., Hartley, M. T., Jang, Y. J., Johnston, S., Moore, N., Walker, Q., . . . Whalen, J. (2012). Collaborating with the disability rights community: Co-writing a code of ethics as a vehicle for ethics education. *Rehabilitation Education, 26,* 243–256.

Tremain, S. (Ed.). (2006). *Foucault and the government of disability.* Ann Arbor: University of Michigan Press.

Trent, J. W. (1994). *Inventing the feeble mind.* Berkeley: University of California Press.

United Cerebral Palsy. (2010). United Cerebral Palsy. Retrieved from http://www.ucp.org

Varela, R. A. (2001). Changing social attitudes and legislation regarding disability. In N. M. Crewe & I. K. Zola (Eds.), *Independent living for physically disabled people* (pp. 28–48). San Jose, CA: People with Disabilities Press.

Vash, C. (1991). More thoughts on empowerment. *Journal of Rehabilitation, 57*(4), 13–16.

Wahl, O. F. (1999). *Telling is risky business.* Piscataway, NJ: Rutgers University Press.

Walker, M. L. (1993). Participatory action research. *Rehabilitation Counseling Bulletin, 37,* 2–5.

Weber, P. S., Davis, E., & Sebastian, R. J. (2002). Mental health and the ADA. *Employee Responsibilities and Rights Journal, 14,* 45–55.

White, G. W. (2002). Consumer participation in disability research: The golden rule as a guide for ethical practice. *Rehabilitation Psychology, 47,* 438–446. doi:10.1037/0090-5550.47.4.438

Wilson-Kovacs, D., Ryan, M. K., Haslam, S. A., & Rabinovich, A. (2008). Just because you can get a wheelchair in the building doesn't necessarily mean that you can still participate. *Disability and Society, 23,* 705–717. doi:10.1080/09687590802469198

Zola, I. K. (2001). Developing new self-images and interdependence. In N. M. Crewe & I. K. Zola (Eds.), *Independent living for physically disabled people* (pp. 49–59). San Jose, CA: People with Disabilities Press.

TEN

Disability Issues in a Global Context

LISA LOPEZ LEVERS

LEARNING OBJECTIVES

After reading this chapter, you should be able to:

- Define disability in an international context.
- Compare and contrast global disability issues in high-resource and low-resource countries.
- Understand the scope of rehabilitation counseling in an international context.
- Learn about the work of relevant disability-related international organizations.
- Identify some of the global epidemiological implications of disability.
- Identify some of the concerns regarding the lack of data related to global disability issues.
- Enhance awareness of current global contextual factors and other issues affecting disability, such as culture, poverty, trauma, crisis, large-scale disaster, HIV and AIDS, and psychosocial issues across the life span.
- Learn about some of the useful practices employed internationally to assist people with disabilities.
- Identify additional resources for promoting better understanding of disability and rehabilitation in an international context.

The world is changing rapidly and so are the multiple environments in which we all live. Social influencers such as globalization, migration, urbanization, and climate change affect us all. This is the current context in which disability issues and the role of rehabilitation counselors (RCs) are explored here. Yet even in the 21st century, accordance about what constitutes disability is not a settled matter (e.g., Officer & Groce, 2009; World Health Organization [WHO], 2011a). The most recent World Health Organization's *World Report on Disabilities* (WHO, 2011a) noted, "There is no agreement on definitions and little internationally comparable information on the incidence, distribution and trends of disability" (p. xxi). One common matter that emerges as salient is that people living with disabilities, internationally, often lack accessibility to and equality of opportunity in many areas, including employment, education, community living, built environments, and health care services (WHO, 2011a).

The purpose of this chapter is to parse out contemporary issues related to disability and to discuss and illuminate the expanding role of RCs within an international context, to the extent that the current knowledge base allows. In order to do this, it is imperative to understand relevant worldwide issues concerning disability, disability policy, and disability classification systems, especially as the needs in developing contexts compare and contrast with disability-related needs in North America and other developed countries. In this chapter, the reader is introduced to relevant disability demographics, constructs, and resources that relate to global perspectives of disability issues and the expanding role of RCs.

According to Human Rights Watch (2014), globally more than 1 billion people are living with some form of disability; this figure accounts for approximately 15% of the population. The World Bank (2016, para 1) reported that "one-fifth of the estimated global total, or between 110 million and 190 million people, experience significant disabilities." The WHO further indicated that "rates of disability are increasing due to population ageing [sic] and increases in chronic health conditions, among other causes" (WHO, 2015, para. 1).

Data indicated that about 80% of all people with disabilities reside in low-resource countries (WHO, 2011a). According to the WHO (2011a, p. 8), "disability disproportionately affects vulnerable populations. . . . People who have a low income, are out of work, or have low educational qualifications are at an increased risk of disability." The relationship between disability and poverty has become clear, and disability is considered both a cause and a consequence of poverty (Mitra, Posarac, & Vick, 2011; WHO, 2011a). Therefore, it is important to check assumptions regarding North American-based and other industrial-economies–based disability services and RC roles against the low-resource reality in which the majority of people with disabilities live. According to a *Lancet* editorial (2009), this majority of the world's people with disabilities who live in low-income countries have "little or no access to basic health services, including rehabilitation facilities" (p. 1793). It becomes essential to focus discussion on non-Western or developing, as well as Western or developed, systems of rehabilitation when addressing international disability concerns (DePoy & Gilson, 2011; United Nations Development Program [UNDP], 2016; WHO, 2015).

Well-established social safety mechanisms for people with disabilities exist in many high-resource countries; for example, Sweden, England, and Canada arguably have some of the strongest disability-related systems in the world (Levers, Magweva, & Mufema, 2010). Although popular thought would suggest that the United States has a comparable disability-related system, recent evidence of the quality versus cost of medical care in the United States (e.g., Agency for Healthcare Research and Quality [AHRQ], 2009b; Burke & Ryan, 2014; Commonwealth Fund, 2015; Kaiser Family Foundation, 2010; Shepard et al., 2009; U.S. Bureau of Labor Education, 2001), health inequity (e.g., AHRQ, 2009a), and still-prevalent negative perceptions about people with disabilities (e.g., Aiden & McCarthy, 2014; Martz, Strohmer, Fitzgerald, Daniel, & Arm, 2006) perhaps call this perception into question. Although the United States may not be at the forefront of health and quality of life (QOL) when compared to other developed countries, the major point is that higher-resource countries tend to have already-embedded social safety nets (SSNs) for people with disabilities, and rehabilitation services typically are delivered by relatively well-trained personnel. Although this situation is not necessarily the case in middle- and low-resource countries, disability-related needs for services continue to grow internationally.

Throughout the world, people with disabilities who live in poverty struggle with daily life activities, without the advantage of any state-sponsored assistance. In most low-resource areas, service provision by a master's-level RC simply is not financially feasible. This is not to say that services are completely unavailable, or that no one assumes the functions of rehabilitation counseling; however, the greater picture looks very different outside the protective structures of the SSNs that have been established in higher-resource societies. This chapter focuses on the relevant discrepancies between high- and low-resource conditions, as these relate to disability issues and rehabilitation counseling in a global context. This survey proceeds by discussing and illuminating the following areas: (a) definitions and scope, (b) trends in the relevant international literatures, and (c) useful practices. These discussions are followed by a conclusion that summarizes the key points of the chapter and offers recommendations for consideration of future actions by RCs in reference to international disability issues.

DEFINING DISABILITY AND THE SCOPE OF REHABILITATION COUNSELING IN AN INTERNATIONAL CONTEXT

The Rehabilitation Act of 1973, the Rehabilitation Act Amendments of 1998, and the Americans with Disabilities Act (ADA) of 1990 represent hallmark legislative efforts in the United States and offer benchmark definitions of relevant health-related and disability issues. A number of documents, somewhat parallel in terms of their international cachet, include the following globally relevant rights-based frameworks: the UN Convention on the Rights of Persons with Disabilities (CRPD; UN, 2006); the WHO's *International Statistical Classification of Diseases and Related Health Problems, 10th Revision* (*ICD-10*; World Health Organization, 2007b); the WHO's *International Classification of Functioning, Disability and Health* (*ICF*; World Health Organization, 2001); and the WHO's *Children and Youth Version of the International Classification of Functioning, Disability and Health* (2007a). It is important to note here that the United Nations Millennium Declaration, commonly referred to as the Millennium Development Goals (MDGs; United Nations [UN], 2000), is an important document related to international health goals. However, it has been widely criticized for originally ignoring the health needs of people with disabilities (e.g., *Lancet* Editorial, 2009; Levers et al., 2010; UN, 2011). Subsequently, in the UN's (2015) MDG Report, not only was extensive antipoverty progress reported, but issues concerning disability also were included in the text. The governments of many countries have demonstrated the political will to improve the lives of people with disabilities by taking action and signing important conventions such as the CRPD; however, the fiduciary power to follow through is not always available. This gap in power includes the attainability of human as well as material resources. In addition, the struggle for human rights has been trying at times for people with disabilities, when the security nets for which they have advocated do not materialize to meet concrete needs. For example, in an evaluation of the effects of poverty on people with disabilities in a Southern African country (Levers et al., 2010, p. 119), consumers of services indicated that "rights do not provide the immediate solution to problems of poverty such as lack of food . . . [arguing] that 'we do not eat rights.'" Yet in spite of obvious challenges, the important documents mentioned here have offered aspirations for strategic planning and have provided frameworks for setting goals that it is hoped will contribute to legislative and policy change that eventually can have a real impact on the quality of living for people with disabilities worldwide.

According to the UN (2006, Overview section, para. 12), comparative examinations of disability-related legislation indicated that "only 45 countries have anti-discrimination and other disability-specific laws," thereby highlighting the urgent need to advocate for disability-friendly policies worldwide. These important issues relate directly to (a) theoretical perspectives on disability, (b) definitions of disability, and (c) the role of RCs, all of which are discussed more fully in the following subsections.

Theoretical Perspectives on Disability

As mirrored by developments in North America, the international theoretical perspective on disability has shifted from a purely medical model to one with a greater social systems emphasis; that is, to a biopsychosocial or ecological model. This shift is so widely accepted that a special issue of the British-based *Lancet*, one of the world's leading medical journals, was dedicated to the topic of disability, and the title of the special issue was "Disability: Beyond the medical model" (*Lancet* Editorial, 2009, p. 1793).

A second shift in theoretical perspective relates to the issue of disability and cultural meaning. Many international organizations have begun to address this area by reevaluating baseline definitions of *disability*. One example rests with the WHO's nosologies of disability. In its earlier text, the *International Classification of Impairments, Disabilities and Handicaps* (*ICIDH*; WHO, 1980), the WHO classified disabilities from a more or less restrictive biomedical or disease-model perspective. However, the need eventually emerged for a more contextual consideration of disability and the community-based inclusion of people with disabilities, thus leading to the development of related guidelines. In its more recent text, the *ICF*, the WHO (2001) has engaged in a process of refining definitions of disability to reflect a biopsychosocial or ecological model, thereby having greater personal and international utility and applicability. In a review of the literature that was conducted three years after the publication of the *ICF*, Bruyère, VanLooy, and Peterson (2005) summarized discussions that reflect both support for and reservations about the *ICF*'s most recent conceptualization of disability. However, the *ICF* is considered by most as offering a contextual and holistic approach to disability, one that is applicable to a diversity of disability issues and a focus on QOL (e.g., Badley, 2008; Berg et al., 2009; Fleming & Leahy, 2014; Oltman, Neises, Scheible, Mehrtens, & Grüneberg, 2008; Pollard, Dixon, Dieppe, & Johnston, 2009; Steiner et al., 2002; Weigl, Cieza, Kostanjsek, Kirschneck, & Stucki, 2006).

Although national legal frameworks for disability policies remain relatively undeveloped around the world (Durocher, Lord, & Defranco, 2012), how disability is defined in governmental policies becomes extremely important because officially sanctioned definitions, in turn, determine eligibility of people with disabilities for social protection programs or SSNs. For example, impairment-oriented definitions, largely used in developing countries, tend to underreport the prevalence of disability and inadvertently exclude people with disabilities from eligibility for social protection services (Levers, Magweva, Maundeni, & Mpofu, 2008). Conversely, definitions of disability are more inclusive when based on activity and participation limitations, thus resulting in a higher census of people eligible for specific SSNs that are a part of the social protection model (Mitra, Posarac, & Vick, 2011). Additionally, most contemporary models of rehabilitation service delivery already tend to be humanitarian in nature. In contrast, by definition ecologically oriented models have allowed for greater incorporation of mechanisms that encourage empowerment and self-efficacy. The link between ecological and self-determination models is of particular importance to all counselors, including RCs (Lynch & Levers, 2007; O'Sullivan & Strauser, 2009). The issues of empowerment and self-efficacy have been instrumental in promoting and advancing the rights of people with disabilities throughout the world as well as advocacy for universal health care (Dye et al., 2013).

Defining Disability

The CRPD (UN, 2006, Article 1—Purpose, para. 2) defined disability as including people "who have long-term physical, mental, intellectual or sensory impairments which in interaction with various barriers may hinder their full and effective participation in society on an equal basis with others." The *ICF* also provides an ecological definition of disability, offering a common language and framework for considering health and health-related issues (WHO, 2002). Therefore, this ecological definition is essential as a disability-related tool in an international context. The *ICF* defines **disability** as "an umbrella term for impairments, activity limitations and participation restrictions," further stating that "[f]unctional limitations occur as a result of the interaction between an individual (with a health condition) and that individual's contextual factors (environmental and personal factors)" (WHO, 2001, p. 10). The *ICF* does not focus on the etiology of dysfunction or underlying pathology; rather, these are focal points of its companion classification, the *ICD-10* (WHO, 2007b).

The presence of impairments does not necessarily imply the presence of disorder or disease; rather, according to the WHO (2001, p. 12), they "represent a deviation from certain generally accepted population standards" of functioning. Determinations of impairment are made by "those qualified to judge physical and mental functioning according to these standards" (WHO, 2001, p. 12). **Disability**, then, refers to "the outcome or result of a complex relationship between an individual's health condition and personal factors, and of the external factors that represent the circumstances in which the individual lives" (WHO, 2001, p. 17). In this international and ecological context, the meaning of disability is intended to imply a focus on the comprehensive individual, societal, and body-related aspects of impairments, along with activity limitations and other participation restrictions in the environment. Its determination, also in this international and ecological context, may be made by various professionals or paraprofessionals. These individuals may or may not look a lot or a little like what are viewed as RCs in a Euro-American context.

In September 2007, the WHO published the *ICF-CY*. Although a number of ambitious objectives have been associated with the *ICF-CY*, much like the *ICF*, the *ICF-CY* has aimed to shift views regarding disability issues from a more medically oriented model to one that accounts for contextual and environmental factors (Simkiss, 2008). As an extension of a more contemporary focus on child and youth issues in the disability arena, recent literature has emphasized the importance of assessing and involving families (e.g., Mpofu, Levers, Mpofu, Tanui, & Hossain, 2015).

The **ecological model of functioning**, as operationally advanced in both the *ICF* and the *ICF-CY*, suggests dynamic and reciprocal relationships among various health-related conditions; these relationships occur within the context of multiple personal and environmental influences. Functional level and disability are then conceptualized within dynamic interactions between health conditions and contextual factors, including cultural considerations. The components and interactions that can be used to describe the relationship between disability and functioning are illustrated in Figure 10.1 (borrowed from Pollard et al., 2009, which was drawn from WHO, 2001, p. 18).

Disability, according to the *ICF* model, is defined by activity and participation limitations due to health conditions, particularly as these are linked to environments in which people live with disabilities. In concert with the underlying theory of the bioecological model of human development, social protection policies primarily are intended to mitigate or prevent activity restrictions and participation limitations. For example, poverty is a determinant that can affect environmental context, and disability is associated with poverty in most countries. Although this association suggests a complex situation that is not necessarily determined by a clear cause-and-effect relationship, it ultimately may lead to the socioeconomic exclusion of people with disabilities, which then influences

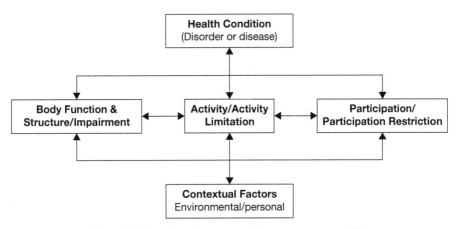

Figure 10.1   Interactions among the components of *ICF*.
From Pollard et al. (2009). This figure is from an Open Access article, permitting unrestricted use with proper citation; Pollard et al. drew from the *ICF* (WHO, 2001, p. 18).

other dimensions of living. Some performance-based benchmarks even indicate that the extent to which a country provides social protection programs may have a connection with international expenditure norms, thus emphasizing complex interactions between disability and economics (Besley, Burgess, & Rasul, 2003; Filmer, 2008; WHO, 2011a).

Regardless of socioeconomic status, activity restrictions, participation limitations, or environmental barriers, the *ICF* model recognizes that people can have disabilities and still be healthy (Lachapelle et al., 2005; Stein, Stein, Weiss, & Lang, 2009; WHO, 2001). Health or well-being is mediated by cognitive and bodily functions and structures that enable activity and participation (Murray et al., 2012, 2015). **Activity** is based on what a person is capable of doing to meet daily living needs, and **participation** arises from the roles that a person is able to fulfill. Both the environment and personal factors influence the conditions and pathways for activity and participation by people with disabilities. For example, people in chronic poverty may have significant health challenges and risk factors (Forouzanfar et al., 2015) that could be relieved by social protection programs. Due to living in such poverty, the bodily functions and structures of people with disabilities may perform less optimally in enabling a full range of activities and roles that are necessary for successful daily living. Personal factors such as self-attitudes can differentiate social outcomes for people who may have the same health conditions: while some may perceive a need to adapt and take control of their situations, others may not. Given the same objective environment and similar health conditions, people with disabilities may differ in their motivation to acquire the social protection services for which they are eligible. Based on all of these assumptions and derived from an ecological perspective of disability, a useful operational definition of **disability**, suggested by Levers et al. (2008, p. 22) in their evaluation of one African nation's disability system, is "[a]ny physical, sensory, cognitive, or psychiatric impairment that, when combined with environmental and societal barriers, limits the person's functional ability to perform major life activities."

Role of Rehabilitation Counselors

The Commission on Rehabilitation Counselor Certification (CRCC) website states that "The CRCC is the world's largest rehabilitation counseling organization," further indicating that "[w]hile the vast majority of Certified Rehabilitation Counselors (CRCs) practice in the United States, Certified Rehabilitation Counselors also practice in numerous other countries worldwide and in Canada as Canadian Certified Rehabilitation Counselors (CCRCs)" (CRCC, 2010, para. 2). According to the U.S. Bureau of Labor Statistics (BLS, 2015, What rehabilitation counselors do, para. 1), the scope of practice for RCs is defined in the following way: RCs help people with physical, mental, developmental, and emotional disabilities live independently. They work with clients to overcome or manage the personal, social, or psychological effects of disabilities on employment or independent living.

It may be arguable as to whether such comprehensive rehabilitation services are available in adequate proportions, even within the industrial societies where the need for such services emerged around industrialization and accelerated after World War II. For example, the large numbers of military personnel who have returned from international war zones with physical and psychological injuries may call into question the capacity of U.S. rehabilitation professionals to meet the need (Buck, 2012; Frain, Bishop, & Bethel, 2010). Furthermore, it is apparent that the onus of activity has tended to be on the RC to perform *for* rather than *with* the client, using a model that is relatively more agentic than collaborative. Conversely, in most low-resource countries, such a comprehensive set of costly rehabilitation services is not accessible to ordinary citizens. For example, rehabilitation services tend to be located in more centralized urban areas, and many people with disabilities live in rural regions; because they are unable to travel the required distances to obtain services, the cost of travel interferes with treatment (WHO, 2011a). Additionally, a scope of practice that favors individualism, which is a core component of the Western RC and other allied health care training models, would not be as productive in social structures that are more collectivist in nature and that exist in much of the non-Western low-resource areas of the world. In many non-Western societies, awareness of disability issues is not necessarily extended to associated rehabilitation practices.

Although professionals who work as RCs in the United States typically possess a master's degree or higher, this situation is not necessarily the case in other parts of the world. First, the field of counseling, regardless of specialty area, is not always viewed as a distinct profession in other countries. Psychology and social work are more universally recognized as organized fields of endeavor. Until very recently, preparing graduate students for careers specifically in professional counseling largely has been an American endeavor. However, there are indications that this approach has been changing, for example with students being trained in the West and returning to their non-Western homes to provide counseling (e.g., Cook, Lei, & Chiang, 2010) and rehabilitation counseling services (Alsaman, 2014). Additionally, there has been an international growth of counselor education (e.g., Astramovich & Pehrsson, 2009), promotion of a global counseling identity (e.g., Hoskins & Thompson, 2009), and greater focus on integrating modern counseling techniques with indigenous counseling (e.g., Bhusmane, 2007; Levers, 2006b, 2006c; Msimanga-Ramatebele, 2008). Second, in low-resource countries, a large treatment gap exists in relationship to services for psychiatric disabilities (Drake, Bond, Thornicroft, Knapp, & Goldman, 2012; Eaton et al., 2011). For people with these disabilities, human services are not always available; and when they are, it is not probable that they will be provided by a master's-level practitioner. Putting all of this together, it is likely that although the scope of practice for those fulfilling the role of RC is similar throughout the world, it is not as likely that the practitioner will have had the advantage of the same level of training or access to the same level of resources. With this understanding in mind, it is important to identify some of the relevant issues of concern that have global implications for those working in the disability and rehabilitation arena. This summary focuses on international trends that have been identified in the relevant professional literatures, and they are discussed in the next section.

INTERNATIONAL DISABILITY AND REHABILITATION LITERATURES

The presentation of a thorough and complete examination of global disability and rehabilitation issues is beyond the scope of this chapter. However, several salient trends emerge from the literature and serve to inform the discourse on disability issues and rehabilitation counseling in a global context. Although there is a plethora of transnational literature that relates to disability and rehabilitation issues—for example, comparisons of disability statistics between two or among several specific countries—there is little literature that integrates and synthesizes relevant international information in a meaningful way. Beyond the documents of global relevance that were identified earlier in this chapter, a review of the international literature has revealed two major currents of thought: first, a huge gap still exists in terms of any thorough examination of global disability issues (e.g., Freedman, 2014); and second, there are a number of identifiable trends or concerns that have emerged and that may have an impact on the delivery of rehabilitation services. These two currents of thought are discussed next.

Lacunae in the Disability and Rehabilitation Literatures

Lacunae (gaps) exist in the international literatures concerning comprehensive understandings of the epidemiological and evidentiary implications of, and the contextual factors associated with, disability and rehabilitation. Since the last version of this chapter (Levers, 2012a), more cross-national comparisons can be found in the relevant literature than previously (Forouzanfar et al., 2015; Kostanjsek et al., 2013; Murray et al., 2012, 2015; Salomon et al., 2012; Soerjomataram et al., 2012). Some of these more recent studies have compared risks and disease burden across as many as 188 countries (e.g., Murray et al., 2015) and as many as 12 regions of the world (e.g., Soerjomataram et al., 2012). The emerging literature begins to shed some light on understanding global disability and rehabilitation from a more comprehensive medical perspective, but the illumination of interdisciplinary and contextually relevant issues continues to be limited. This pattern of such modestly growing literatures amplifies the realization that disability is an even more complex and multifaceted issue in the global context.

Epidemiological Implications

Valid health-related statistics are vital across all levels of the health care system, and the ability to ascertain disease and injury levels and patterns related to most countries in the world has begun to emerge. Although various compilations of data regarding mortality, morbidity, and epidemiological trends exist at national and regional levels, one earlier publication has offered "comparable regional and global estimates and projections of disease and injury burden based on a common set of methods and denominated in a common metric" (Murray & Lopez, 1996, p. xxvii). *The Global Burden of Disease: A Comprehensive Assessment of Mortality and Disability from Diseases, Injuries, and Risk Factors in 1990 and Projected to 2020* (Murray & Lopez) is considered a landmark publication for its singularity in this arena. It has offered a mechanism for beginning to gather and analyze international disease- and disability-related data in a comprehensive and aligned fashion, as well as for using historical trends to project the mortality and disease burden forward to 2020.

The Murray and Lopez (1996) study has provided consistent estimates of disease and injury rates. More importantly, for the purposes of this chapter, it has "attempted to provide a comparative index of the burden of each disease or injury, namely the number of Disability-Adjusted Life Years (DALYs) lost as a result of either premature death or years lived with disability" (Henderson, 1996, p. xiii). The design of this common metric is even more unique in its inclusion of both physical and mental illnesses (Cole et al., 2000; Lopez, 2005), as psychiatric disability often has been viewed as a low priority in the international disability discourse (Drake et al., 2012; WHO, 2010a). This landmark study has offered a foundation for comparative and aggregate transnational research efforts.

Following Murray and Lopez (1996), the emerging literature presents a fuller and more comprehensive picture of globally significant epidemiological disability and rehabilitation issues. These more recent investigations and analyses focus on assessment of disease and injury risks (Forouzanfar et al., 2015; Kostanjsek et al., 2013; Murray et al., 2012, 2015; Salomon et al., 2012; Soerjomataram et al., 2012) as well as behavioral, environmental, occupational, and metabolic risks (Rehm et al., 2009, 2013).

One international investigation has indicated a relationship between QOL and self-determination (Lachapelle et al., 2005). Murray et al. (2015) have quantified what they term an epidemiological transition, from 1990 through 2013; they analyzed data for global, regional, and national disability-adjusted life years (DALYs) for 306 diseases and injuries, identifying healthy life expectancy (HALE) for 188 countries. Prüss-Ustün, Wolf, Corvalán, Bos, and Neira's (2016) assessment of global disease illuminated ways for improving the environment, and thus for promoting health and well-being.

Evidentiary Concerns

The WHO and World Bank have published a pioneering text, the *World Report on Disability and Rehabilitation* (2011a). The effort largely has responded to the reality that there was "no global document that compiles and analyses [sic] the way countries have developed policies and the responses to address the needs of people with disabilities" (WHO, n.d., I. Background and justification magnitude, para. 3).

The conception for the project was the outcome of the World Health Assembly's Resolution 58.23, of May 2005, regarding the provision *Disability, including prevention, management and rehabilitation*; the result was a request that the WHO "produce a World report on disability based on the best available scientific evidence" (WHO, n.d., I. Background and justification magnitude, para. 3). For the first time, a report has become available to the public that comprehensively outlines the evidence-based information regarding disability issues from an international perspective.

The WHO report (2011a) has been organized to convey the following key messages: (1) full and effective participation and inclusion of persons with disabilities in society is essential and within reach; (2) disability is a human rights issue; (3) poverty is a cause and effect of disability; (4) disability affects entire families; (5) disability is an economic development issue (particularly in low-resource countries); (6) disability is likely to affect most people at some time in their lives; (7) disability is a continuum of experience which varies across the life span; (8) disability is difficult to define, as it is varied, multidimensional, cross-cutting, and complex; (9) primary prevention must be balanced with respect for the integrity of people with disabilities; (10) (re)habilitation is important;

and, (11) evidence on what works is presented, it must be used, and much remains to be done (WHO, 2007c, Box 1: Key messages). The report was made available to the public at an official launch on June 9, 2011 (WHO, 2011b).

Contextual Factors

Gross inequalities in health care exist among the nations of the world (Marmot, 2005). The reality of so many people with disabilities throughout the world living in poverty underscores the numerous avoidable health inequities that punctuate the experience of so many people with disabilities. The notion of *social determinants of health* is an internationally accepted public health concept (Labonté, 2008; Marmot, Allen, Bell, Bloomer, & Goldblatt, 2012). The WHO's Commission on Social Determinants of Health (CSDH) has identified many contextual factors as social determinants of health. The CSDH has advanced the following three overarching recommendations and aligned principles of action:

1. Improve the conditions of daily life—the circumstances in which people are born, grow, live, work, and age.
2. Tackle the inequitable distribution of power, money, and resources—the structural drivers of those conditions of daily life—globally, nationally, and locally.
3. Measure the problem, evaluate action, expand the knowledge base, develop a workforce that is trained in the social determinants of health, and raise public awareness about the social determinants of health. (CSDH, 2008, p. 2)

The work of the CSDH has informed the discourse on social determinants of health and health inequities, advocating for less focus on individual behavioral change and greater emphasis on nurturing the conditions for health and well-being (Baum, 2008; Baum & Fisher, 2010; Levers, Magweva, & Mpofu, 2007; Springett, Whitelaw, & Dooris, 2010).

Culture

Nurturing the social conditions that promote health and well-being has everything to do with culture. As noted by Mpofu and Harley (2002), "[c]onceptions of disability vary widely across societies, and are influenced by the unique sociopolitical and cultural histories of those societies" (p, 26). Yet the biomedical model of disability and rehabilitation historically has ignored the relevance of local culture in general, and on an international scale, the importance of indigenous knowledge in particular. In terms of cultural understanding, rehabilitation counselor education (RCE) programs have begun to address this by a greater emphasis on including multicultural and diversity issues in the curriculum. In terms of the importance of acknowledging indigenous knowledge, researchers and scholars have begun to examine disability issues within their relevant cultural frameworks (e.g., Berman, 2009; Dalal, n.d.; Durie, 2004; Kakati, Ao, & Doulo, 2006; Levers, 2006a, 2006b, 2006c; Levers & Maki, 1994, 1995; Mpofu & Harley, 2002; Subrick, 2006).

Indigenous knowledge and ethnorehabilitation

In their inquiry into African traditional healing and indigenous knowledge, Levers and Maki (1994) proposed consideration for advancing the concept of **ethnorehabilitation** and advocated for its further examination by defining it as an:

> eco-systemic, praxeological construct which acknowledges the comprehensive nature of persons with disabilities through functional relationship to their respective

cultures . . . [in] interaction with their environments. . . . This view simultaneously permits a holistic and ecologic perspective which is vertically attentive to the spiritual dimensions of the person and horizontally reflective of the environmental dialectic. (Levers & Maki, 1994, p. 86)

Levers and Maki also indicated that it is only when ethical respect is paid to the person that this perspective can be measured, and the result is a philosophy of empowerment. Most people with disabilities live in low-resource areas of the world, thereby necessitating reliance on indigenous knowledge systems and traditional healing practices, an issue largely ignored by the Western, biomedically oriented community (Levers, 2006c; Levers, Radomsky, & Shefer, 2009).

Emerging Trends in the International Literature

A number of global trends have emerged in the disability and rehabilitation literature. The most salient are highlighted and discussed in the following subsections: (a) poverty; (b) trauma, crisis, and disaster; (c) HIV and AIDS; (d) psychosocial issues across the life span; and (e) international economic development.

Poverty

Social protection systems differ greatly in high-resource (developed) versus low-resource (developing) countries. As indicated earlier, this has led to numerous avoidable health and other life inequities. The association between poverty and disability is complex (Filmer, 2008; Handicap International, 2014; Levers et al., 2007, 2008, 2010; Palmer, 2011; Trani & Loeb, 2012; WHO, 2011a), as are the data that are linked to this intricate situation (Braithwaite & Mont, 2009).

Approximately 15% of the world's population has some form of disability, and the vast majority of all people with disabilities live in low- or middle-income countries (UN, 2011; WHO, 2011a, 2016). At least 20% (1 in 5) of the very poorest people, who are living in developing countries, have a disability (WHO, 2011a). According to World Bank estimates (as cited in Laurin-Bowie, 2005), about 43% of the people globally, who are living on less than $1.00 per day, have a disability. The UN review of disability and MDGs emphasized that:

> the most pressing issue faced globally by persons with disabilities is not their specific disability, but rather their lack of equitable access to resources such as education, employment, health care and the social and legal support systems, resulting in persons with disabilities having disproportionately high rates of poverty. (UN, 2011, p. vii)

Social systems often overlook people with disabilities, and yet current thinking suggests that it is preferable, more efficient, more cost-effective, and less stigmatizing to include people with disabilities in mainstream programs from the onset (Braithwaite & Mont, 2009; Groce & Trani, 2009; UN, 2011). In addition, social and economic exclusion typically does not affect the individual alone; rather, it results in high economic dependency on family members and relatives. People living with disabilities face enormous barriers to obtaining equitable services and opportunities. This phenomenon is due primarily to a combination of stigma, ignorance, discrimination, exclusion, and inaccessible environments. The ways in which poverty and disability interface with and reinforce one another not only negate the rights of people with disabilities, but they also perpetuate vulnerability and advance the vicious cycle of poverty (Handicap International, 2014).

Trauma, Crisis, and Disaster

Although global and regional statistics regarding injury-specific causes of disability are not available, by extrapolating data from various countries, the WHO (2016) suggested that up to 25% of disabilities are the result of injuries and violence. A United Nations International Children's Education Fund (UNICEF) fact sheet states that "persons with disabilities are more likely to be victims of violence or rape, according to a 2004 British study, and less likely to obtain police intervention, legal protection or preventive care" (UNICEF, n.d., Violence, para. 3). Traumatic experiences can affect individuals and communities, in profound ways, across the life span (Levers, 2012b), including people with disabilities (Johnson et al., 2012; Tarvydas & Ng, 2012). A few ways that such trauma may manifest, and constituting emerging issues associated with the disability literature, are war, climate change, and migration.

War

In warfare, three children are injured and permanently disabled for every one child killed (UNICEF, n.d.). Research further indicates that the annual rate of violence against children with disabilities is at least 1.7 times greater than for their peers who are not disabled (UNICEF, n.d.). Johnson et al. (2012) and Kett and van Ommeren (2009) emphasized the lack of inclusion concerning people with disabilities and disability issues in trauma-response efforts, particularly situations of armed conflict, disasters, and other emergencies. They also pointed to the fact that local disabled people's organizations (DPOs) are seldom included in the planning and coordination of crisis or disaster responses. This is echoed by Rathore et al. (2012) and Tarvydas, Levers, and Teahen (in press, a; in press, b). Tarvydas et al. further have suggested best ethical practices related to people with disabilities in trauma, crisis, and disaster situations.

Climate change

The change in climate is having an impact on the entire planet, causing both manmade and natural disasters. In this sense, people with disabilities may be particularly vulnerable (Abbott & Porter, 2013), both to physiological risks (e.g., Forouzanfar et al., 2015; Prüss-Ustün et al., 2016) and psychosocial challenges (e.g., Boikanyo & Levers, 2017) associated with climate change. Teahan, Levers, and Tarvydas (2017) have identified disability-related disaster and climate-change issues with regard to public health demands and the need for building social-ecological resilience.

Migration

Both war and climate change contextually have effected an increase in global migration. Refugees are arriving at new locations daily, many sustaining injury during dangerous treks in an attempt to leave war, poverty, famine, and drought behind. Levers, Biggs, and Strickler (2015) discuss the urgency of addressing immigrant and refugee health issues. The children of undocumented immigrant parents also constitute a vulnerable population, with the potential for experiencing both traumatizing and disabling conditions (Levers & Mancilla, 2013).

HIV and AIDS

A United Nations Programme on HIV/AIDS (UNAIDS, 2016) website reported that approximately 36.7 million people worldwide were living with HIV and AIDS in 2015. The pandemic has strained fragile health care systems throughout the world. Although there are resources available to respond to the AIDS pandemic, they have been woefully inadequate to meet public health needs. Data from the UNDP (2010) indicated that health care delivery has improved in many nations; in fact, UNAIDS (2016, AIDS-related deaths, para. 5) reported that "AIDS-related deaths have fallen by 45% since the peak in 2005." Various sources have detailed the disabling effects of HIV and AIDS on the lives of people who contract the virus (e.g., Hanass-Hancock, 2009; Levers, 2006a, 2006b; McReynolds & Garske, 2001). Researchers at Yale University and the World Bank (Groce, 2004) conducted a Global Disability Survey to further assess the impact. The most salient issue to report here regards the risk of HIV infection for people with disabilities and the reality that they largely have been ignored by prevention and care services (Levers et al., 2010).

The prevalence of HIV/AIDS among people with disabilities is equal to or higher than that among the rest of the population, yet they are largely excluded from HIV and AIDS services (WHO, 2011a). Groce (2003) has captured the essence of the problem by noting that while research has identified disabling aspects of HIV and AIDS, little has been gleaned regarding the risk of HIV and AIDS for people with disabilities. It appears that people with disabilities generally have not been included in outreach efforts due to the stereotype that they are not sexually active, and therefore not at risk (De Beaudrap, Mac-Seing, & Pasquier, 2014; Groce, 2003; World Bank, 2004). This fact has obvious and dire implications, and Handicap International (2014) has strongly advocated the inclusion of disability in HIV policy and programming on the international stage. Finally, children and youth with disabilities, who also are affected by HIV and AIDS, may face additional challenges (Maundeni & Levers, 2017; Rohleder, Swartz, Schneider, & Eide, 2011).

Psychosocial Issues Across the Life Span

Psychosocial issues, both related and not related to disability, have an impact on people with disabilities across the life span. These are discussed briefly, in global perspective, in the following subsections.

Gender

In many developing countries, females report higher incidences of disability than males (UNICEF, n.d.). In addition, females with disabilities typically experience stigmatization on multiple levels; that is, exclusion due to both gender and disability. Women and girls are particularly vulnerable to maltreatment and abuse. According to the UNICEF fact sheet, a small 2004 survey in India "found that virtually all of the women and girls with disabilities were beaten at home, 25% of women with intellectual disabilities had been raped and 6% of disabled women had been forcibly sterilized" (UNICEF, n.d., Overview, para. 9). These findings are consistent with assessments carried out in other developing countries (e.g., Levers, 2006a; Levers et al., 2008, 2010; Levers, Kamanzi, Mukamana, Pells, & Bhusumane, 2006; Levers & Magweva, 2005). A U.S.-based publication (Office on Women's Health, 2015) cited research suggesting that "that women with disabilities are more likely to suffer domestic violence and sexual assault than women without disabilities. And women with disabilities report abuse that lasts longer and is more intense than women without disabilities" (para. 1). Gender-related rites of passage across the life span, such as dating, courtship, marriage, and childbirth, may pose additional challenges for both male and female people with disabilities. Additionally, people with disabilities coming out as gay or wishing to transition genders may face added layers of gender bias.

Children and youth

Although comparative studies of childhood disabilities exist (e.g., Gottlieb, Maenner, Cappa, & Durkin, 2009; Mpofu, 2003; WHO, U.S. Centers for Disease Control and Prevention [CDC], & International Clearinghouse for Birth Defects Surveillance and Research [ICBDSR], 2014), they tend to focus on a cluster of countries or a region, offering little comprehensive information regarding childhood disability issues. Trani (2009) asserted the importance of early screening of children for disabilities. Congenital anomalies, or birth defects, have a wide range of causes globally. The WHO, CDC, and ICBDSR (2014) have called for prevention approaches related to sexually transmitted infections, vaccinations, legislation management involving toxic chemicals, and fortification of staple foods.

According to the United Kingdom's Department for International Development, "[m]ortality for children with disabilities may be as high as 80% in countries where under-five mortality as a whole has decreased below 20% . . . [and] in some cases it seems as if children are being 'weeded out'" (cited in UNICEF, n.d., Overview, para. 11). Such apprehension begs the question of disability-related infanticide. Although a full discussion of this complex issue is beyond the scope of this chapter, in a UNICEF-sponsored report on violence against children with disabilities, Groce and Paeglow (2005) have asserted that infanticide (done immediately or soon after birth) and "mercy killings" (done at a later time after birth, sometimes years later) continue to be global manifestations of violence against children with disabilities. As with information regarding other childhood disability issues, there is little comprehensive data concerning infanticide on an international level. UNICEF has taken on a key role in promoting the rights of children with disabilities on an international scale.

Education

According to UNESCO, about 98% of children living with disabilities in developing countries do not attend school (cited in ILO, 2009), and approximately 30% of street youths are disabled (UNICEF, n.d.). The UNICEF fact sheet reports that in some developing countries, disability rates are significantly higher among groups with lower educational levels, and that, "[o]n average, 19% of less educated people have disabilities, compared to 11% among the better educated" (UNICEF, n.d., Overview, para. 5). Based on a 1998 UNDP study (cited in UNICEF, n.d., Education, para. 2), UNICEF reported that "the global literacy rate for adults with disabilities is as low as 3%, and 1% for women with disabilities." Assessment (Gottlieb et al., 2009), early intervention (Gottlieb et al., 2009), and access to assistive technology (Borg, Lindström, & Larsson, 2009) are linked with the issue of education and disability. Studies continue to emerge regarding the inclusion of children with intellectual disabilities (e.g., Aderemi, 2013; Peters, 2007; Sideridis, 2007; Schalock, Verdugo, & Gomez, 2011), with an emphasis on their educational processes. Finally, a recent U.S.-based study showed that accommodations as simple as course and test adjustments, like extension of time and modification of materials, had a significant positive influence on college students with disabilities (Kim & Lee, 2016).

Work

The International Labour Organization ([ILO] 2007, 2009) reported that people with disabilities face higher unemployment rates and lower earnings than people without disabilities; they often are excluded and marginalized, being particularly vulnerable during times of economic crisis. Automation is a swiftly emergent phenomenon. However, in a review of academic literature and popular print media, Wolbring (2016, p. 1) could not identify a single article that "thematized the potential negative impact of robots on the employability situation of disabled people or the relationship of disabled people and robots as co-workers." Unemployment rates vary among the types of disabilities; the highest rates tend to exist among those people having psychiatric disabilities (ILO, 2007). Men with disabilities are nearly twice as likely as women with disabilities to have gainful employment (ILO, 2007).

If work conditions are conducive, supportive, and adaptive, people with disabilities have proven that they can contribute and produce at all levels (ILO, 2007, 2009; Shrey & Hursh, 1999). Yet a prevalent bias is that workers with disabilities cost employers extra money, when in reality their exclusion from the workplace "deprives societies of an estimated $1.37 to 1.94 trillion in annual loss in GDP" (ILO, 2007, para. 1). Assistive technology clearly has implications in this arena (Borg et al., 2009), and greater access is needed. Some of the international donor and nongovernmental organizations (NGOs) have begun to implement income-generation projects among people with disabilities, but real employment opportunities in the governmental and private sectors have been slow to emerge.

Aging

A number of contemporary issues face aging populations around the world, and this has implications for RCs (Dixon, Richard, & Rollins, 2003). According to the WHO (2011a), in higher-resource countries where life expectancies are over age 70, people spend an average of about 8 years, or 11.5% of the life span, living with disabilities. Regardless of the geopolitical advantages of living in a high- versus low-resource country, most people surviving to an older age are likely to experience increasing disability in their elder years (Robine & Michel, 2004). Sabat (2009) reported, for example, that dementia is on the rise in developing countries, and Sousa et al. (2009) noted the increase of dementia and the contribution of other chronic diseases to disability in elderly people in both low- and middle-income countries. Studies also suggested an association between the impact of metabolic syndrome on aging adults and an increase in disability (Forouzanfar et al., 2015; Liaw et al., 2016).

Economic Development

According to the WHO (2011a, p. 10), "disability is a development issue, because of its bidirectional link to poverty: disability may increase the risk of poverty, and poverty may increase the risk of disability." Officer and Groce (2009, p. 1795) assert that "[d]isability is a neglected development issue," and that people with disabilities, for the most part, have not benefited from international economic development efforts (Kuipers, 2009). As indicated earlier in this chapter, people with disabilities are underrepresented disproportionately in the development arena universally, and this fact has a direct relationship to their poverty levels; they also tend to be poorer than people without disabilities (Metts, 2004). MacLachlan and Swartz (2009) advocated for greater inclusion of people with disabilities in international development efforts.

USEFUL PRACTICES

Trends in the international disability and rehabilitation literatures have raised many important issues, concerns, and challenges. As noted, these data are not sufficient, and the need for more research related to disability and rehabilitation interventions in international context is great; therefore, it is difficult to identify *best practices* in the sense that usually is intended in the behavioral and social sciences. However, in terms of the salient issues that have emerged from the relevant international literatures, it is possible to identify several *useful practices* that have real implications for RCs and that hold promise for further examination. These useful practices are discussed briefly as follows: (a) rights-based approach, (b) community-based rehabilitation (CBR), (c) professional training, (d) Web-resource access, and (e) research.

Rights-Based Approach

The rights-based approach fortunately has replaced the charity model. The CSDH has emphasized the relevance of Article 25(a) of the UN *Universal Declaration on Human Rights* (UN, 1948, cited in CSDH, 2008, p. 84):

> Everyone has the right to a standard of living adequate for the health and well-being of himself and of his family, including food, clothing, housing and medical care and necessary social services, and the right to security in the event of unemployment, sickness, disability, widowhood, old age or other lack of livelihood in circumstances beyond his control.

The core principles of the UN's CRPD include respect for all aspects of human dignity and participation; rights related to equal access to health care are found in separate disability- and rehabilitation-related articles. Additional articles of the CRPD deal with the special needs of women and of children with disabilities, as well as with issues of accessibility, mobility, and the responsibilities of the professionals providing care to people with disabilities, among others. To date, some 167 nation-states have signed on to the CRPD (UN, 2016).

Clearly, in the international arena, disability is viewed as an issue of human rights and social justice. Although this obviously is significant, rights alone do not provide the immediate solution to problems of poverty such as lack of food, shelter, and employment. A tension exists between *human rights* in idealist abstraction, and *human rights* in terms of the pragmatic and concrete reality of everyday needs. This tension is articulated by people with disabilities the world over. Social justice must inform the discourse, and social justice *action* must mediate the results related to fully realizing the rights-based approach. For example, although social justice advocacy for equity is essential, people with disabilities and DPOs assert that it must be followed by action that leads to ensuring that concrete needs are met, like food and shelter. As noted earlier in this chapter, some African consumers of rehabilitation services have clearly echoed this sentiment: "We do not eat rights" (Levers et al., 2010, p. 119).

Community-Based Rehabilitation

First introduced by the WHO in the late 1970s, **community-based rehabilitation** (CBR) has been influenced and strengthened by people with disabilities and DPOs as it has developed over the last several decades (Musoke & Geiser, 2013). According to the WHO (2010a, para. 1), CBR "has evolved to become a multi-sectoral strategy that empowers persons with disabilities to access and benefit from education, employment, health and social services." Its scope has broadened significantly over the past 30 years, with an increased readiness of community-based rehabilitation organizations (CBROs) to implement CBR (Pfaller et al., 2016; WHO, 2010b).

Much more than an intervention, CBR is a system of care and service delivery that has involved all relevant stakeholders in the community, including people with disabilities and their families. Regarded as a general strategy for community development of rehabilitation, CBR has positively affected social inclusion of people with disabilities as well as equalizing opportunities (Mpofu, 2015). Research has shown that participation in CBR programs can have a positive impact on people with disability (Biggeri et al., 2014). Major aims of CBR have included enhancing the QOL for people with disabilities and their families and ensuring that basic needs are met in least restrictive environments (Mpofu et al., 2015). As noted by Hartley, Finkenflugel, Kuipers, and Thomas (2009), CBR's goals are to "support access to regular services and opportunities and assist people with disabilities to actively contribute to their own communities as well as encouraging communities to promote and respect their human rights" (p. 1803).

The WHO (2010b) has published guidelines for CBR, including a matrix that covers the five components of health, education, livelihood, social dimension, and empowerment. The information is presented in seven separate booklets, all of which are available online. The seven booklets include an introduction, examinations of the five components, and a supplementary booklet that focuses on specific issues that have been overlooked, to date, in most CBR programs (i.e., mental health, HIV and AIDS, leprosy, and humanitarian crises). Hartley et al. (2009) reported that the WHO guidelines and matrix also reflect critiques of CBR and are aimed at improving the implementation and efficacy of CBR. Although more rigorous research needs to be conducted in this area, CBR shows great promise, especially as it relates to efficacy, and is associated with positive social outcomes.

Professional Training

The preservice training of RCs and other rehabilitation personnel is critical to an enhanced understanding of disability and rehabilitation issues in a global context (Shakespeare, Iezzoni, & Groce, 2009), and a number of examples can be found in the literature. Alsaman (2014) has examined the efficacy of educating international RCs and ways that university-based programs can contribute to and enhance the advocacy of disability-related training globally. Astramovich and Pehrsson (2009) have promoted the advancement of counselor education, in general, as a means for fostering international perspectives. Stein et al. (2009) have suggested that disability be included with other diversity issues in training programs. Wilson, Henry, Sayles, Senices, and Smith (2003) have suggested that multicultural counseling competencies are imperative in training vocational counselors to meet the demands of globalized understandings of disability.

Some academics have espoused the utility of international exchanges of rehabilitation scholars (e.g., Fabian & Madsen, 2007) and cross-cultural field exchanges for rehabilitation students (e.g., Luecking, Cuozzo, McInerney, Cury, & Lorca, 2007) as mechanisms for training RCs about the importance of global context. A special issue of *Rehabilitation Education* (Nemec, Spaniol, & Dell Orto, 2001) was devoted to the necessity of training counselors in psychiatric rehabilitation. Finally, Tingey, Millington, and Graham (2007) have recommended a **communities-of-practice** approach to training RCs; *communities of practice* is a term that has been borrowed from social learning theory which, as used here, refers to building an evidence-based theory of shared knowledge and practice among RCs. Advancing quality preservice and in-service training for rehabilitation personnel is an essential practice and is important in enhancing service delivery for and with people with disabilities throughout the world.

Web-Resource Access

A UNICEF publication (n.d., Overview, para. 13) noted that in the United Kingdom, "75% of the companies of the FTSE 100 Index on the London Stock Exchange do not meet basic levels of web accessibility, thus missing out on more than $147 million in revenue." Web accessibility for people with disabilities is a growing concern (Thompson, Burgstahler, Moore, Gunderson, & Hoyt, 2007). The W3C Web Accessibility Initiative ([W3C WAI], 2010) offered strategies, guidelines, and resources to make the web accessible to people with disabilities. Tim Berners-Lee, W3C Director and inventor of the World Wide Web, has stated that "the power of the Web is in its universality. Access by everyone regardless of disability is an essential aspect" (W3C WAI, 2010, column 1, text block 3).

Research

The unmet health and rehabilitation needs of people with disabilities worldwide are open for inquiry. For example, Stein et al. (2009, p. 1797) suggested that more "research is required on how disability affects relative access to health care and medical outcomes." Salvador-Carulla and Saxena (2009) have identified a research gap between intellectual disability and other neuropsychiatric disorders. Although publications such as the *ICF* (WHO, 2001), *The Global Burden of Disease* (Murray & Lopez, 1996), and the *World Report on Disability* (WHO, 2011a) make the need for robust epidemiological and statistical analyses obvious, Hanley-Maxwell, Al Hano, and Skivington (2007) and Levers (2001) suggested that qualitative and ethnographic understandings of the lived experiences of people with disabilities and in-depth examinations of disability-related phenomena also are essential in the global context of rehabilitation. Community-based research with indigenous populations with disabilities such as Native American Indians (Marshall et al., 2002), or with indigenous practitioners such as African traditional healers (Levers, 2006c), can yield important information that informs the cross-cultural discourse. Tomlinson et al. (2009) have suggested that, because accurate information about the health patterns of people with disabilities is inadequate, and in light of the scarcity of resources, disability-related research should be systematically prioritized and involve relevant stakeholders. The National Disability Authority (2009) offers ethical guidance for research with people with disabilities, in accordance with the ethical principles involving any research with human subjects.

CONCLUSION

This chapter introduced germane disability and rehabilitation issues in a global context. Those topics that have been emphasized are definitions of disability, the scope of rehabilitation counseling in an international context, theoretical perspectives on disability, the role of RCs, the international disability and rehabilitation literatures, and useful practices. A number of available, recently published, and soon-to-be-published resources have been identified concerning disability and rehabilitation in an international context. Additional useful resources are listed in Box 10.1.

BOX 10.1   Internet Resources

International Association of Rehabilitation Professionals (IARP; www.rehabpro.org)
Disabled World (www.disabled-world.com)
International Disability Alliance (www.internationaldisabilityalliance.org)
World Institute on Disability (www.wid.org)
WHO, Global Health Observatory (GHO) data (www.who.int/gho/en)
ICF Browser (http://apps.who.int/classifications/icfbrowser)
Handbook for Parliamentarians on the Convention on the Rights of Persons with Disabilities (www.un.org/disabilities/default.asp?id=212)
Linking CBR, disability, and rehabilitation (www.iddcconsortium.net/sites/default/files/resources-tools/files/cbr_africa_final_2013_en.pdf)
A Practical Guide for Creating Trauma-informed Disability, Domestic Violence and Sexual Assault Organizations (www.disabilityrightswi.org/wp-content/uploads/2012/05/Trauma-Informed-Guide.pdf)
International Encyclopedia of Rehabilitation (http://cirrie.buffalo.edu/encyclopedia/en)
W3C: Accessibility (www.w3.org/standards/webdesign/accessibility)

A dearth of evidence concerning global disability and rehabilitation issues exists and only begins to intersect with the lived experiences and paramount needs of people with disabilities. There is a great deal of work yet to be done at the international level, which calls for our attention. Several pertinent recommendations can be derived from this discussion; it is hoped that RCs, educators, and researchers might take these topics under consideration for future action in reference to international disability issues.

First, the issue of advocacy merits further consideration. RCs can advocate for improvements for people with disabilities in terms of infrastructural access, access to services, and, especially in the 21st century, access to web resources. RCs can advocate for continual reinforcement of the rights-based approach, for poverty mitigation efforts, and for expanded global ways of applying the ecological model. RCs are positioned to advocate for greater professionalization opportunities within the field, especially related to preservice and in-service training, while at the same time understanding that indigenous knowledge systems may offer culturally relevant sources of information as well.

Second, the number of people with disabilities is growing worldwide, in both low- and high-resource countries. Issues such as poverty, diseases such as HIV and AIDS, illnesses such as psychiatric disabilities, and life-span conditions such as aging, along with circumstances involving trauma, crises, and disasters, have a global impact on programming aimed at improving the lives of people with disabilities, and at mitigating the negative impact of barriers. RCs have the expertise to construct new ways of building capacity so that relevant rehabilitation services are available to all who need them.

Third, the importance of disability- and rehabilitation-related training beyond the industrialized West cannot be emphasized enough. A number of evaluations have reported the lack of basic training in developing countries, along with a hunger for more education among the people working in such rehabilitation settings (e.g., Levers et al., 2006, 2008, 2010; Levers & Magweva, 2005; Levers & Maki, 1994, 1995). RCs in high-resource countries need to find ways to share instructional resources with and construct training opportunities for colleagues in low-resource countries (Alsaman, 2014). RCs can support related endeavors through service learning, advocacy projects, volunteerism, and grant writing activities.

Finally, the paucity of research related to international disability and rehabilitation issues illuminates the need for inquiry that is pertinent to the lives of people with disabilities and the systems that serve them. RCs have a wide-open field for identifying important issues and pursuing research agendas that can contribute to the expansion of thinking and the increased understandings of related global issues.

In summary, little has been written about international disability issues from a comprehensive and synthesis-oriented perspective. However, we know that a number of avoidable inequities continue to have deleterious effects on the lives of children and adults living with disabilities. RCs, in all of our international and cultural permutations, have the opportunity and the responsibility to assist people with disabilities to empower themselves. We also have the opportunity and the responsibility to contribute to the international knowledge base in ways that continue to close the disability-related gaps—gaps in knowledge, practice, service delivery, social justice, and equity—in the global context.

CONTENT REVIEW QUESTIONS

- How does culture play a role in understanding disability issues on an international scale?
- How does the *ICF* model of rehabilitation differ from the more traditional medical model? Why is this significant?
- In what ways does the role of the RC enhance opportunities for people with disabilities globally, and in what ways can RCs serve in an advocacy capacity for global disability concerns? Why does this matter?
- What roles do international organizations such as the WHO and the UN play in advancing disability issues throughout the world? Why is this important?
- In what ways does a more ecologically oriented model of rehabilitation universally support the rights-based approach and the CBR approach? How does this relate to equity and social justice?
- What kinds of training experiences can help to prepare RCs for international work?

REFERENCES

Abbott, D., & Porter, S. (2013). Environmental hazard and disabled people: From vulnerable to expert to interconnected. *Disability and Society, 28*, 839–852.

Aderemi, T. J. (2013). Teachers' perspectives on sexuality and sexuality education of learners with intellectual disabilities in Nigeria. *Sexual Disability Journal*, July. doi:10.1007/s11195-013-9307-7.

Agency for Healthcare Research and Quality. (2009a). *2009 national healthcare disparities report* (AHRQ Publication No. 10-0,004). Rockville, MD: U.S. Department of Health and Human Services. Retrieved from http://www.ahrq.gov/qual/nhdr09/nhdr09.pdf

Agency for Healthcare Research and Quality. (2009b). *2009 national healthcare quality report* (AHRQ Publication No. 10-0003). Rockville, MD: U.S. Department of Health and Human Services. Retrieved from http://www.ahrq.gov/qual/nhqr09/nhqr09.pdf

Aiden, H., & McCarthy, A. (2014, May). Current attitudes towards disabled people. Scope. Retrieved from http://www.scope.org.uk/Scope/media/Images/Publication%20Directory/Current-attitudes-towards-disabled-people.pdf

Alsaman, M., (2014). Rehabilitation research, policy, and education. *Rehabilitation Research, Policy, and Education, 28*(2), 66–79.

Astramovich, R. L., & Pehrsson, D-E. (2009). Advancing counselor education: Fostering international perspectives and open access scholarship. *Journal for International Counselor Education, 1,* 1–6. Retrieved from http://digitalcommons.library.unlv.edu/jice

Badley, E. M. (2008). Enhancing the conceptual clarity of the activity and participation components of the International Classification of Functioning, Disability, and Health. *Social Science and Medicine, 66,* 2335–2345. Retrieved from http://citeseerx.ist.psu.edu/viewdoc/download?doi=10.1.1.469.2252&rep=rep1&type=pdf

Baum, F. (2008). The Commission on the Social Determinants of Health: Reinventing health promotion for the twenty-first century? *Critical Public Health, 18,* 457–466. doi:10.1080/09581590802443612

Baum, F., & Fisher, M. (2010). Health equity and sustainability: Extending the work of the Commission on the Social Determinants of Health. *Critical Public Health, 20,* 311–322. doi:10.1080/09581596.2010.503266

Berg, K., Finne-Soveri, H., Gray, L., Henrard, J. C., Hirdes, J., Ikegami, N., . . . Teare, G. (2009). Relationship between interRAI HC and the ICF: Opportunity for operationalizing the ICF. *BMC Health Services Research, 9.* doi:10.1186/1472-6963-9-47

Berman, N. (2009). Negotiating local knowledge: Networking disability on the community level. *Disability Studies Quarterly, 29*(4). Retrieved from http://www.dsq-sds.org/article/view/967/1176

Besley, T., Burgess, R., & Rasul, I. (2003). *Benchmarking government provision of social safety nets* (Social Protection Discussion Paper Series, No. 0315). Washington, DC: The World Bank.

Bhusmane, D-B. (2007). *Mechanisms of indigenous counseling in Botswana* (Unpublished doctoral dissertation). Pittsburgh, PA: Duquesne University.

Biggeri, M., Deepak, S., Mauro, V., Trani, J-F., Kumar, J., & Ramasamy, P. (2014). Do community-based rehabilitation programmes promote the participation of persons with disabilities? A case control study from Mandya District, in India. *Disability and Rehabilitation, 36,* 1508–1517.

Boikanyo, M. N., & Levers, L. L. (2017). The effects of climate change on water insecurity in Botswana: Links to the criminal justice system. In G. Magill & K. Aramesh (Eds.), *The urgency of climate change: Pivotal perspectives* (pp. 434–449). Newcastle Upon Tyne, England: Cambridge Scholars Publishing.

Borg, J., Lindström, A., & Larsson, S. (2009). Assistive technology in developing countries: National and international responsibilities to implement the Convention on the Rights of Persons with Disabilities. *Lancet, 374,* 1863–1865.

Braithwaite, J., & Mont, D. (2009). Disability and poverty: A survey of World Bank poverty assessments and implications. *ALTER, European Journal of Disability Research, 3,* 219–232.

Bruyère, S., VanLooy, S., & Peterson, D. (2005). The International Classification of Functioning, Disability and Health (ICF): Contemporary literature overview. *Rehabilitation Psychology, 50*(2), 113–121.

Buck, R. P. (2012). The impact of war on military veterans. In L. L. Levers (Ed.), *Trauma counseling: Theories and interventions* (pp. 434–453). New York, NY: Springer Publishing.

Burke, L. A., & Ryan, A. M. (2014, February). The complex relationship between cost and quality in US health care. *Virtual Mentor: American Medical Association Journal of Ethics, 16*(2), 124–130.

Cole, B., Kane, C., Killeen, M., Mohr, W., Nield-Anderson, L., & Kurlowicz, L. (2000, April). *Responding to the global burden of disease* (International Society of Psychiatric-Mental Health Nurses White Paper). Retrieved from http://www.ispn-psych.org/docs/4-00Global-Burden.pdf

Commission on Rehabilitation Counselor Certification. (2010). About CRC certification. Retrieved from http://www.crccertification.com/pages/aboutcertification/46.php

Commission on Social Determinants of Health. (2008). *Closing the gap in a generation: Health equity through action on the social determinants of health* (Final Report of the Commission on Social Determinants of Health). Geneva, Switzerland: World Health Organization.

Commonwealth Fund. (2015). U.S. health care from a global perspective. Retrieved from http://www.commonwealthfund.org/publications/issue-briefs/2015/oct/us-health-care-from-a-global-perspective

Cook, A. L., Lei, A., & Chiang, D. (2010). Counseling in China: Implications for counselor education preparation and distance learning instruction. *Journal for International Counselor Education, 2,* 60–73. Retrieved from http://digitalcommons.library.unlv.edu/jice

Dalal, A. K. (n.d.). Disability rehabilitation in a traditional Indian society. Retrieved from http://webcache
.googleusercontent.com/search?q=cache:TAHGKD7nkhMJ:english.aifo.it/disability/apdrj/selread102/
dalal.doc+&cd=1&hl=en&ct=clnk&gl=us

De Beaudrap, P., Mac-Seing, M., & Pasquier, E. (2014). Disability and HIV: A systematic review and a meta-
analysis of the risk of HIV infection among adults with disabilities in sub-Saharan Africa. *AIDS Care, 26,*
1467–1476. doi:10.1080/09540121.2014.936820

DePoy, E. G., & Gilson, S. F. (2011). *Studying disability: Multiple theories and responses.* Thousand Oaks, CA: Sage.

Dixon, C. G., Richard, M., & Rollins, C. W. (2003). Contemporary issues facing aging Americans: Implications for rehabilitation and mental health counseling. *Journal of Rehabilitation, 69*(2), 5–12.

Drake, R. E., Bond, G. R., Thornicroft, G., Knapp, M., & Goldman, H. H. (2012). Mental health disability:
An international perspective. *Journal of Disability Policy Studies, 23*(2), 110–120. doi:10.1177/10442
07311427403

Durie, M. (2004). Understanding health and illness: Research at the interface between science and indigenous knowledge. *International Journal of Epidemiology, 33,* 1138–1143. doi:10.1093/ije/dyh250

Durocher, J., Lord, J., & Defranco, A. (2012). Disability and global development. *Disability and Health Journal,*
5, 132–135.

Dye, C., Boerma, T., Evans, D., Harries, A., Lienhardt, C., McManus, J., . . . Zachariah, R. (2013). *World*
health report 2013: Research for universal health coverage. Geneva, Switzerland: World Health Organization. Retrieved from http://apps.who.int/iris/bitstream/10665/85761/2/9789240690837_eng.pdf?ua=1

Eaton, J., McCay, L., Semrau, M., Chatterjee, S., Baingana, F., Araya, R., . . . Saxena, S. (2011). Global mental
health 4: Scale up of services for mental health in low-income and middle-income countries. *Lancet, 378,*
1592–1603.

Fabian, E. S., & Madsen, M. K. (2007). International exchange in disability and social inclusion: American
educators' perspectives. *Journal of Rehabilitation Counseling, 38*(3), 12–17.

Filmer, D. (2008). Disability, poverty, and schooling in developing countries: Results from 14 household
surveys. *World Bank Economic Review, 22*(1), 141–163.

Fleming, A. R., & Leahy, M. J. (2014). Using the International Classification of Functioning to conceptualize quality of life among rehabilitation services recipients. *Rehabilitation Research, Policy, and Education,*
28(1), 2–23.

Forouzanfar, M. H., Alexander, L., Anderson, H. R., Bachman, V. F., Biryukov, S., . . . Murray, C. J. L. (2015).
Global, regional, and national comparative risk assessment of 79 behavioural, environmental and
occupational, and metabolic risks or clusters of risks in 188 countries, 1990–2013: A systematic analysis for the Global Burden of Disease Study 2013. *Lancet, 386,* 2287–2323. Retrieved from http://www
.thelancet.com/pdfs/journals/lancet/PIIS0140-6736(15)00128-2.pdf

Frain, M. P., Bishop, M., & Bethel, M. (2010). A roadmap for rehabilitation counseling to serve military veterans with disabilities. *Journal of Rehabilitation, 76*(1), 13–21.

Freedman, V. A. (2014). Research gaps in the demography of aging with disability. *Disability and Health Jour-*
nal, 7(1), S60–S63.

Gottlieb, C. A., Maenner, M. J., Cappa, C., & Durkin, M. S. (2009). Child disability screening, nutrition,
and early learning in 18 countries with low and middle incomes: Data from the third round of UNICEF's
Multiple Indicator Cluster Survey (2005–06). *Lancet, 374,* 1821–1830.

Groce, N. E. (2003). HIV/AIDS and people with disability. *Lancet, 26,* 1401–1402.

Groce, N. E. (2004). *HIV/AIDS and disability: Capturing hidden voices.* The World Bank/Yale University.
Retrieved from http://siteresources.worldbank.org/DISABILITY/Resources/Health-and-Wellness/HIV
AIDS.pdf

Groce, N. E., & Paeglow, C. (2005, July). *Summary report: Violence against disabled children* (UN Secretary
General's Report on Violence against Children). Thematic Group on Violence against Disabled Children,
Findings and Recommendations, Convened by UNICEF at the United Nations, New York, NY. Retrieved
from http://www.unicef.org/videoaudio/PDFs/UNICEF_Violence_Against_Disabled_Children_Report_
Distributed_Version.pdf

Groce, N. E., & Trani, J-F. (2009). Millennium Development Goals and people with disabilities. *Lancet, 374,*
1800–1801.

Hanass-Hancock, J. (2009). Disability and HIV/AIDS—a systematic review of literature on Africa. *Journal of*
the International AIDS Society, 12(34). doi:10.1186/1758-2652-12-34

Handicap International. (2014, December). *Including disability in HIV policy and programming: Good prac-*
tices drawn from country-based evidence (LL N° 07 Brief). Retrieved from http://www.hiproweb.org/uploads/
tx_hidrtdocs/LL07Brief.pdf

Hanley-Maxwell, C., Al Hano, I., & Skivington, M. (2007). Qualitative research in rehabilitation counseling. *Rehabilitation Counseling Bulletin, 50*(2), 99–110.

Hartley, S., Finkenflugel, H., Kuipers, P., & Thomas, M. (2009). Community-based rehabilitation: Opportunity and challenge. *Lancet, 374,* 1803–1804.

Henderson, R. H. (1996). Foreword. In C. J. L Murray & A. D. Lopez (Eds.), *The global burden of disease: A comprehensive assessment of mortality and disability from diseases, injuries, and risk factors in 1990 and projected to 2020* (pp. xiii–xiv). Cambridge, MA: The Harvard School of Public Health on behalf of the World Health Organization and the World Bank, distributed by Harvard University Press.

Hoskins, W. J., & Thompson, H. C. (2009). Promoting international counseling identity: The role of collaboration, research, and training. Retrieved from http://counselingoutfitters.com/vistas/vistas_2009_Title.htm

Human Rights Watch. (2014). One billion forgotten: Protecting the human rights of persons with disabilities. Retrieved from https://www.hrw.org/sites/default/files/related_material/2014%20disabilities_program_low.pdf

International Labour Organization. (2007, November). Facts on disability in the world of work. Retrieved from http://www.ilo.org/wcmsp5/groups/public/@dgreports/@dcomm/documents/publication/wcms_087707.pdf

International Labour Organization. (2009, November). Facts on disability and decent work. Retrieved from http://www.ilo.org/wcmsp5/groups/public/---ed_emp/---ifp_skills/documents/publication/wcms_117143.pdf

Johnson, E. T., Brooks, J. M., Mpofu, E., Anwer, J., Brock, K., Ngazimbi, E., & Magweva, F. I. (2012). Trauma survivorship and disability. In L. L. Levers (Ed.), *Trauma counseling: Theories and interventions* (pp. 98–131). New York, NY: Springer Publishing.

Kaiser Family Foundation. (2010). U.S. health care costs. Retrieved from http://www.kaiseredu.org/Issue-Modules/US-Health-Care-Costs/Background-Brief.aspx

Kakati, L. N., Ao, B., & Doulo, V. (2006). Indigenous knowledge of zootherapeutic use of vertebrate origin by the Ao tribe of Nagaland. *Journal of Human Ecology, 19*(3), 163–167.

Kett, M., & van Ommeren, M. (2009). Disability, conflict, and emergencies. *Lancet, 374,* 1801–1803.

Kim, W. H., & Lee, J. (2016). The effect of accommodation on academic performance of college students with disabilities. *Rehabilitation Counseling Bulletin, 60*(1), 40–50.

Kostanjsek, N., Good, A., Madden, R. H., Üstün, T. B., Chatterji, S., Mathers, C. D., & Officer, A. (2013). Counting disability: Global and national estimation. *Disability and Rehabilitation, 35,* 1065–1069.

Kuipers, P. (2009). Review of the book *Disability and international development: Towards inclusive global health. Lancet, 374,* 1813.

Labonté, R. (2008). Global health in public policy: Finding the right frame? *Critical Public Health, 18,* 467–482.

Lachapelle, Y., Wehmeyer, M. L., Hailewyck, M. C., Courbois, Y., Keith, K. D., Schalock, R., . . . Walsh, P. N. (2005). The relationship between quality of life and self-determination: An international study. *Journal of Intellectual Disability Research, 49,* 740–744. doi:10.1111/j.1365-2788.2005.00743.x

Lancet Editorial. (2009). Disability: Beyond the medical model [Editorial]. *Lancet, 374,* 1793.

Laurin-Bowie, C. (2005). Poverty, disability and social exclusion: New strategies for achieving inclusive development. *Journal for Disability and International Development, 2,* 51–56.

Levers, L. L. (2001). Representations of psychiatric disability in fifty years of Hollywood film: An ethnographic content analysis. *Theory and Science, 2*(2). Retrieved from http://theoryandscience.icaap.org/content/vol002.002/lopezlevers.html

Levers, L. L. (2006a, April). *Report on the need for trauma counseling in post-genocide Rwanda.* An unpublished report prepared for the Kigali Health Institute (KHI), Kigali, Republic of Rwanda.

Levers, L. L. (2006b). Samples of indigenous healing: The path of good medicine. *International Journal of Disability, Development and Education, 54,* 479–488.

Levers, L. L. (2006c). Traditional healing as indigenous knowledge: Its relevance to HIV/AIDS in Southern Africa and the implications for counselors. *Journal of Psychology in Africa, 16,* 87–100.

Levers, L. L. (2012a). Disability issues and the role of rehabilitation counselors in a global context. In D. R. Maki & V. Tarvydas (Eds.), *The professional practice of rehabilitation counseling: Formative perspective and features* (pp. 163–188). New York, NY: Springer Publishing.

Levers, L. L. (2012b). Introduction to understanding trauma. In L. L. Levers (Ed.), *Trauma counseling: Theories and interventions* (pp. 521–539). New York, NY: Springer Publishing.

Levers, L. L., Biggs, B-A., & Strickler, A. (2015). International implications for addressing immigrant and refugee health issues. In E. Mpofu (Ed.), *Community-oriented health services: Practices across disciplines* (pp. 271–292). New York, NY: Springer Publishing.

Levers, L. L., Kamanzi, D., Mukamana, D., Pells, K., & Bhusumane, D-B. (2006). Addressing urgent community mental health needs in Rwanda: Culturally sensitive training interventions. *Journal of Psychology in Africa, 16,* 261–272.

Levers, L. L., & Magweva, F. I. (2005, March). *Report on a national rehabilitation plan and training programme.* Windhoek, Namibia: Ministry of Lands, Resettlement, and Rehabilitation (Government of the Republic of Namibia).

Levers, L. L., Magweva, F. I., Maundeni, T., & Mpofu, E. (2008). *A report on a comprehensive study of social safety nets for people with disabilities in Botswana* (A study sponsored by the Botswana Ministry of Health, at the request of the Botswana Office of the President). Gaborone, Botswana: Ministry of Health.

Levers, L. L., Magweva, F. I., & Mpofu, E. (2007). *A review of district health systems in east and southern Africa: Facilitators and barriers to participation in health* (EQUINET Discussion Paper No. 40). Regional Network for Equity in Health in East and Southern Africa (EQUINET). Retrieved from http://www.equinetafrica.org/bibl/docs/DIS40ehsLOPEZ.pdf

Levers, L. L., Magweva, F. I., & Mufema, E. (2010, March). *Poverty levels among people with disabilities: An evaluation of the need for developing a disability social protection scheme in Zimbabwe* (Final Report to the Terms of Reference Committee Regarding the Consultancy for the National Association of Societies for the Care of the Handicapped [NASCOH], the National Association of Non-Governmental Organizations [NANGO], and the Republic of Zimbabwe Ministry of Labour and Social Services [MoLSS]). Harare, Zimbabwe: National Association of Societies for the Care of the Handicapped.

Levers, L. L., & Maki, D. R. (1994). *An ethnographic analysis of traditional healing and rehabilitation services in southern Africa: Cross-cultural implications* (An International Exchange of Experts and Information in Rehabilitation [IEEIR] Research Fellowship Monograph prepared for the World Rehabilitation Fund, National Institute on Disability and Rehabilitation Research, U.S. Dept. of Education. Oklahoma State University). Stillwater, OK: National Clearing House of Rehabilitation Training Materials.

Levers, L. L., & Maki, D. R. (1995). African indigenous healing, cosmology, and existential implications: Toward a philosophy of ethnorehabilitation. *Rehabilitation Education, 9,* 127–145.

Levers, L. L., & Mancilla, R. (2013). Educating the children of undocumented immigrant parents: The impact of trauma on citizen children's development. In F. E. McCarthy, M. H. Vickers, & E. Brown (Eds.), *International advances in education: Global initiatives for equity and social justice* (Vol. 6: *Migrants and refugees: equitable education for displaced populations,* pp. 51–72). Charlotte, NC: Information Age.

Levers, L. L., Radomsky, L., & Shefer, T. (2009). Voices of African traditional healers: Cultural context and implications for the practice of counselling in sub-Saharan Africa. *Journal of Psychology in Africa, 19,* 501–506.

Liaw, F-Y., Kao, T-W., Wu, L-W., Wang, C-C., Yang, H-F., Peng, T-C., . . . Chen, W-L. (2016). Components of metabolic syndrome and the risk of disability among the elderly population. *Scientific Reports, 6,* 1–9. Retrieved from http://www.ncbi.nlm.nih.gov/pmc/articles/PMC4780009/pdf/srep22750.pdf

Lopez, A. D. (2005). The evolution of the Global Burden of Disease framework for disease, injury and risk factor quantification: Developing the evidence base for national, regional and global public health action. *Globalization and Health* 2005, *1*(5). doi:10.1186/1744-8603-1-5

Luecking, R. G., Cuozzo, L., McInerney, C., Cury, S. H. M., & Lorca, M. C. B. C. (2007). Cross-cultural field exchange as a rehabilitation professional development experience. *Journal of Rehabilitation Counseling, 38*(3), 18–24.

Lynch, M. F., & Levers, L. L. (2007). Ecological-transactional and motivational perspectives in counseling. In J. Gregoire & C. Jungers (Eds.), *Counselor's companion: Handbook for professional helpers* (pp. 586–605). Mahwah, NJ: Lawrence Erlbaum.

MacLachlan, M., & Swartz, L. (Eds.). (2009). *Disability and international development: Towards inclusive global health.* New York, NY: Springer.

Marmot, M. (2005). Social determinants of health inequalities. *Public Health, 365,* 1099–1104.

Marmot, M., Allen, J., Bell, R., Bloomer, E., & Goldblatt, P. (2012). WHO European review of social determinants of health and the health divide [on behalf of the Consortium for the European Review of Social Determinants of Health and the Health Divide]. *Lancet, 380,* 1011–1029.

Marshall, C. A., Johnson, S. R., Kendall, E., Busby, H., Schacht, R., & Hill, C. (2002, April). Community-based research and American Indians with disabilities: Learning together methods that work. In Work Group on American Indian Research and Program Evaluation Methodology (AIRPEM), *Symposium on Research and Evaluation Methodology: Lifespan Issues Related to American Indians/Alaska Natives with Disabilities.* Symposium conducted at the meeting of AIRPEM, Washington, DC. Retrieved from http://www.fnbha.org/pdf/AIRPEMMonograph.pdf

Martz, E., Strohmer, D., Fitzgerald, D., Daniel, S., & Arm, J. (2006). Disability prototypes in the United States and the Russian Federation: An international comparison. *Rehabilitation Counseling Bulletin, 53*(1), 16–26.

Maundeni, T., Jankey, O., & Levers, L. L. (2017). Social welfare issues in childhood: The Botswana Experience. In I. Tshabangu (Ed.), *Global ideologies surrounding children's rights and social justice* (pp. 57–73). Hershey, PA: IGI Global.

McReynolds, C. J., & Garske, G. G. (2001). Current issues in HIV disease and AIDS: Implications for health and rehabilitation professionals. *Work: A Journal of Prevention, Assessment and Rehabilitation, 17*(2), 117–124.

Metts, R. (2004, November 16). *Disability and development: Background paper prepared for the disability and development research agenda meeting.* Washington, DC: World Bank Headquarters. Retrieved from http://siteresources.worldbank.org/DISABILITY/Resources/280658-1172606907476/mettsBGpaper.pdf

Mitra, S., Posarac, A., & Vick, B. (2011). Disability and poverty in developing countries: A snapshot from the world health survey. *SP Discussion Paper No. 1109*, the World Bank, Social Protection and Labor Unit, Human Development Network (HDNSP). Retrieved from http://siteresources.worldbank.org/SOCIAL PROTECTION/Resources/SP-Discussion-papers/Disability-DP/1109.pdf

Mpofu, E. (Ed.). (2015). *Community-oriented health services: Practices across disciplines.* New York, NY: Springer Publishing.

Mpofu, E., & Harley, D. (2002). Rehabilitation in Zimbabwe: Lessons and implications for rehabilitation practice in the United States. *Journal of Rehabilitation, 68*(4), 26–33.

Mpofu, E., Levers, L. L., Mpofu, K., Tanui, P., & Hossain, Z. S. (2015). Family assessments in rehabilitation service provision. In M. Millington & I. Marini (Eds.), *Families in rehabilitation counseling: A community-based rehabilitation approach* (pp. 251–266). New York, NY: Springer Publishing.

Msimanga-Ramatebele, S. H. (2008). *Lived experiences of widows in Botswana: An ethnographic examination of cultural rituals of death, loss, grief, and bereavement—implications for professional counseling* (Unpublished doctoral dissertation). Duquesne University, Pittsburgh, PA.

Murray, C. J. L., Barber, R. M., Foreman, K. J., Ozgoren, A. A., Abd-Allah, F., Abera, S. F., . . . Vos, T. (2015). Global, regional, and national disability-adjusted life years (DALYs) for 306 diseases and injuries and healthy life expectancy (HALE) for 188 countries, 1990-2013: Quantifying the epidemiological transition. *Lancet, 386*, 2145–2191.

Murray, C. J. L., & Lopez, A. D. (Eds.). (1996). *The global burden of disease: A comprehensive assessment of mortality and disability from diseases, injuries, and risk factors in 1990 and projected to 2020.* Cambridge, MA: Harvard University Press.

Murray, C. J. L., Vos, T., Lozano, R., Naghavi, M., Flaxman, A. D., Michaud, C., . . . Lopez, A. (2012). Disability-adjusted life years (DALYs) for 291 diseases and injuries in 21 regions, 1990-2010: A systematic analysis for the Global Burden of Disease Study 2010. *Lancet, 380*, 2197–2223.

Musoke, G., & Geiser, P. (Eds.). (2013). *Linking CBR, disability and rehabilitation.* Kyambogo: CBR Africa Network, Handicap International. Retrieved from http://www.iddcconsortium.net/sites/default/files/resources-tools/files/cbr_africa_final_2013_en.pdf

National Disability Authority. (2009). Ethical guidance for research with people with disabilities. *Disability Series, 13.* Retrieved from http://nda.ie/nda-files/Ethical-Guidance-for-Research-with-People-with-Disabilities.pdf

Nemec, P. B., Spaniol, L., & Dell Orto, A. E. (2001). Psychiatric rehabilitation education. *Rehabilitation Education, 15*(2), 115–118.

Office on Women's Health. (2015, September 4). Violence against women with disabilities. Retrieved from http://www.womenshealth.gov/violence-against-women/types-of-violence/violence-against-women-with-disabilities.html

Officer, A., & Groce, N. E. (2009). Key concepts in disability. *Lancet, 374*, 1795–1796.

Oltman, R., Neises, G., Scheible, D., Mehrtens, G., & Grüneberg, C. (2008). ICF components of corresponding outcome measures in flexor tendon rehabilitation: A systematic review. *BMC Musculoskeletal Disorders, 9.* doi:10.1186/1471-2474-9-139

O'Sullivan, D., & Strauser, D. R. (2009). Operationalizing self-efficacy, related social cognitive variables, and moderating effects: Implications for rehabilitation research and practice. *Rehabilitation Counseling Bulletin, 52*, 251–258. doi:10.1177/0034355208329356

Palmer, M. (2011). Disability and poverty: A conceptual review. *Journal of Disability Policy, 21*(4), 210–218.

Peters, S. J. (2007). "Education for All?" A historical analysis of international inclusive education policy and individuals with disabilities. *Journal of Disability Policy Studies, 18*(2), 98–108. doi:10.1177/10442073070180020601

Pfaller, J. S., Wei-Mo, T., Morrison, B., Chan, F., Owens, L., Anderson, C. A., . . . Menz, F. E. (2016). Social-cognitive predictors of readiness to use evidence-based practice: A survey of community-based rehabilitation practitioners. *Rehabilitation Counseling Bulletin, 60*(1), 7–15.

Pollard, B., Dixon, D., Dieppe, P., & Johnston, M. (2009). Measuring the ICF components of impairment, activity limitation and participation restriction: An item analysis using classical test theory and item response theory. *Health and Quality of Life Outcomes, 7.* doi:10.1186/1477-7525-7-41

Prüss-Ustün, A., Wolf, J., Corvalán, C., Bos, R., & Neira, M. (2016). *Preventing disease through healthy environments: A global assessment of the burden of disease from environmental risks.* Geneva, Switzerland: World

Health Organization. Retrieved from http://apps.who.int/iris/bitstream/10665/204585/1/9789241565196_eng.pdf?ua=1

Rathore, F. A., Gosney, J. E., Reinhardt, J. D., Haig, A. J., Li, J., & DeLisa, J. A. (2012). Medical rehabilitation after natural disasters: Why, when, and how? *Archives of Physical Medicine and Rehabilitation*, 93, 1875–1881. Retrieved from http://www.archives-pmr.org/article/S0003-9993(12)00393-0/pdf

Rehm, J., Borges, G., Gmel, G., Graham, K., Grant, B., Parry, C., . . . & Room, R. (2013). The comparative risk assessment for alcohol as part of the Global Burden of Disease 2010 Study: What changed from the last study? *International Journal of Alcohol Drug Research*, 2(1), 1–5.

Rehm, J., Mathers, C., Popova, S., Thavorncharoensap, M., Teerawattananon, Y., & Patra, J. (2009). Global burden of disease and injury and economic cost attributable to alcohol use and alcohol-use disorders. *Lancet*, 373, 2223–2233.

Rohleder, P., Swartz, L., Schneider, M., & Eide, A. H. (2011). Challenges to providing HIV prevention education to youth with disabilities in South Africa. *Disability and Rehabilitation*, 34, 619–624.

Robine, J. M., & Michel, J. P. (2004). Looking forward to a general theory on population aging. *Journal of Gerontology: Medical Sciences*, 59(6), M590–M597.

Sabat, S. R. (2009). Dementia in developing countries: A tidal wave on the horizon. *Lancet*, 374, 1805–1806.

Salomon, J. A., Vos, T., Hogan, D. R., Gagnon, M., Naghavi, M., Mokdad, A., . . . Jonas, J. B. (2012). Comman values in assessing health outcomes from disease and injury: Disability weights measurement study for the Global Burden of Disease Study 2010. *Lancet*, 380, 2129–2143.

Salvador-Carulla, L., & Saxena, S. (2009). Intellectual disability: Between disability and clinical nosology. *Lancet*, 374, 1798–1799.

Schalock, R. L., Verdugo, M. A., & Gomez, L. E. (2011). Evidence-based practices in the field of intellectual and developmental disabilities: An international consensus approach. *Evaluation and Program Planning*, 34, 273–282. Retrieved from https://www.researchgate.net/profile/Laura_Gomez10/publication/237004341_The_development_and_use_of_Provider_Profiles_at_the_organizational_and_systems_level/links/54a3e9260cf256bf8bb2a576.pdf

Shakespeare, T., Iezzoni, L., & Groce, N. E. (2009). The art of medicine: Disability and the training of health professionals. *Lancet*, 374, 1815–1816.

Shepard, M., Kocot, S. L., Brennan, N., Morrison, M., Nguyen, N., Williams, R. D., . . . & McKethan, A. (2009, August 21). *Improving quality and value in the U.S. health care system*. Washington, DC: Bipartisan Policy Center. Retrieved from https://www.brookings.edu/wp-content/uploads/2016/06/0821_bpc_qualityreport.pdf

Shrey, D. E., & Hursh, N. C. (1999). Workplace disability management: International trends and perspectives. *Journal of Occupational Rehabilitation*, 9(1), 45–59.

Sideridis, G. D. (2007). International approaches to learning disabilities: More alike or more different? *Learning Disabilities: Research and Practice*, 22(3), 210–215. doi:10.1111/j.1540-5826.2007.00249.x

Simkiss, D. (2008). The International Classification of Functioning, Disability and Health. *Journal of Tropical Pediatrics*, 54(3), 149–150. doi:10.1093/tropej/fmn047

Soerjomataram, I., Lortet-Tieulent, J., Parkin, D. M., Ferlay, J., Mathers, C., Forman, D., & Bray, F. (2012). Global burden of cancer in 2008: A systematic analysis of disability-adjusted life-years in 12 world regions. *Lancet*, 380, 1840–1850.

Sousa, R. M., Ferri, C. P., Acosta, D., Albanese, E., Guerra, M., Huang, Y., . . . Prince, M. (2009). Contribution of chronic diseases to disability in elderly people in countries with low and middle incomes: A 10/66 Dementia Research Group population-based survey. *Lancet*, 374, 1821–1830.

Springett, J., Whitelaw, S., & Dooris, M. (2010). Sustainable development, equity and health—time to get radical. *Critical Public Health*, 20, 275–280. doi:10.1080/09581596.2010.502932

Stein, M. A., Stein, P. J. S., Weiss, D., & Lang, R. (2009). Health care and the UN Disability Rights Convention. *Lancet*, 374, 1796–1798.

Steiner, W. A., Ryser, L., Huber, E., Uebelhart, D., Aeschlimann, A., & Stucki, G. (2002). Use of the ICF model as a clinical problem-solving tool in physical therapy and rehabilitation medicine. *Physical Therapy*, 82, 1098–1107.

Subrick, R. (2006). *AIDS and traditional belief: How an inappropriate AIDS prevention strategy undermined Botswana's health* (International Policy Network Paper). Retrieved from http://www.policynetwork.net/health/publication/aids-and-traditional-belief

Tarvydas, V., Levers, L. L., & Teahen, P. (in press, a). Ethics narratives from lived experiences of disaster and trauma counselors. In J. Webber & J. B. Mascari (Eds.), *Disaster mental health counseling: A guide to preparing and responding* (4th ed.). Alexandria, VA: American Counseling Association.

Tarvydas, V., Levers, L. L., & Teahen, P. R. (in press, b). Learning from lived experiences: Ethical responses to trauma, crisis, and disaster. *Journal of Counseling and Development*.

Tarvydas, V., & Ng, H. K. Y. (2012). Ethical perspectives on trauma work. In L. L. Levers (Ed.), *Trauma counseling: Theories and interventions* (pp. 521–539). New York, NY: Springer Publishing.

Teahan, P., Levers, L. L., & Tarvydas, V. (2017). Disaster, climate change, and public health: Building social-ecological resilience. In G. Magill & K. Aramesh (Eds.), *The urgency of climate change: Pivotal perspectives* (pp. 133–160). Newcastle Upon Tyne, England: Cambridge Scholars Publishing.

Thompson, T., Burgstahler, S., Moore, E., Gunderson, J., & Hoyt, N. (2007). International research on web accessibility for persons with disabilities. Retrieved from https://staff.washington.edu/tft/research/international

Tingey, K. B., Millington, M. J., & Graham, M. (2007, October). *A communities of practice approach to training and education: Building sociocognitive networks in rehabilitation counseling* (White Paper). Logan, UT: National Clearinghouse of Rehabilitation Training Materials.

Tomlinson, M., Swartz, L., Officer, A., Chan, K. Y., Rudan, I., & Saxena, S. (2009). Research priorities for health of people with disabilities: An expert opinion exercise. *Lancet, 374*, 1857–1862.

Trani, J-F. (2009). Screening children for disability. *Lancet, 374*, 1806–1807.

Trani, J-F., & Loeb, M. (2012). Poverty and disability: A vicious circle? Evidence from Afghanistan and Zambia. *Journal of International Development*. Retrieved from http://openscholarship.wustl.edu/cgi/viewcontent.cgi?article=1032&context=brown_facpubs

United Nations. (2000, 18 September). United Nations Millennium Declaration. Retrieved from http://www.un.org/millenniumgoals/bkgd.shtml

United Nations. (2006). United Nations Convention on the Rights of Persons with Disabilities. Retrieved from http://www.un.org/disabilities/convention/conventionfull.shtml

United Nations. (2011). Disability and the Millennium Development Goals: A review of the MDG process and strategies for inclusion of disability issues in Millennium Development Goal efforts. Retrieved from http://www.un.org/disabilities/documents/review_of_disability_and_the_mdgs.pdf

United Nations. (2016, September 23). Iceland ratifies CRPD (total: 167). *Division for Social Policy and Development Disability*. Retrieved from https://www.un.org/development/desa/disabilities/news/dspd/iceland-ratifies-crpd-total-167.html

United Nations Development Program. (2010, November). *Human development report 2010, The real wealth of nations: Pathways to human development* (20th anniversary edition). Retrieved from http://hdr.undp.org/en/media/HDR_2010_EN_Complete.pdf

United Nations Development Program. (2016). Disability rights. Retrieved from http://www.undp.org/content/undp/en/home/ourwork/povertyreduction/focus_areas/focusinclusive_development/disability-rights.html

United Nations International Children's Education Fund. (n.d.). Voices of youth: Be in the know: Fact sheet. Retrieved from http://www.unicef.org/explore_3893.html

United Nations Programme on HIV/AIDS. (2016). Fact sheet 2016. Retrieved from http://www.unaids.org/sites/default/files/media_asset/UNAIDS_FactSheet_en.pdf

U.S. Bureau of Labor Education. (2001, Summer). *The U.S. health care system: Best in the world, or just the most expensive?* Orono: The University of Maine. Retrieved from https://umaine.edu/ble/wp-content/uploads/sites/181/2011/01/US-healthcare-system.pdf.

W3C Web Accessibility Initiative. (2010). W3C: Web accessibility initiative. Retrieved from http://www.w3.org/WAI

Weigl, M., Cieza, A., Kostanjsek, N., Kirschneck, M., & Stucki, G. (2006). The ICF comprehensively covers the spectrum of health problems encountered by health professionals in patients with musculoskeletal conditions. *Rheumatology, 45*, 1247–1254.

Wilson, K. B., Henry, M. L., Sayles, C. D., Senices, J., & Smith, D. R. (2003). Multicultural counseling competencies in the 21st century: Are vocational rehabilitation counselors primed for the next millennium? *Journal of the Pennsylvania Counseling Association, 5*(1), 5–18.

Wolbring, G. (2016). Employment, disabled people and robots: What is the narrative in the academic literature and Canadian newspapers? *Societies, 6*(15), 1–16.

World Health Organization. (n.d.). Concept note: World report on disability and rehabilitation. Retrieved from http://www.who.int/disabilities/publications/dar_world_report_concept_note.pdf

World Health Organization. (1980). *International classification of impairments, disabilities and handicaps.* Geneva, Switzerland: Author. Retrieved from http://apps.who.int/iris/bitstream/10665/41003/1/9241541261_eng.pdf

World Health Organization. (2001). *International classification of functioning, disability and health [ICF].* Geneva, Switzerland: Author.

World Health Organization. (2002). *Towards a common language for functioning, disability and health: ICF.* Geneva, Switzerland: Author. Retrieved from http://www.who.int/classifications/icf/training/icfbeginnersguide.pdf

World Health Organization. (2007a). *Children and youth version of the international classification of functioning, disability and health (ICF-CY)*. Geneva, Switzerland: Author.

World Health Organization. (2007b). *International statistical classification of diseases and related health problems, 10th revision [ICD-10]*. Geneva, Switzerland: Author.

World Health Organization. (2007c, April). WHO world report on disability and rehabilitation update no. 1. Retrieved from http://siteresources.worldbank.org/DISABILITY/Resources/News---Events/BBLs/20070411 WHOissue1.pdf

World Health Organization. (2010a). Community-based rehabilitation (CBR). Retrieved from http://www.who.int/disabilities/cbr/en/index.html

World Health Organization. (2010b, October). Community-based rehabilitation (CBR) guidelines. Retrieved from http://www.who.int/disabilities/cbr/guidelines/en/index.html

World Health Organization. (2011a). A world report on disability. Retrieved from http://www.who.int/disabilities/world_report/2011/report.pdf

World Health Organization. (2011b, February). *The WHO Newsletter on Disability and Rehabilitation, 12*. Retrieved from http://www.who.int/disabilities/publications/newsletter/dar_issue12.pdf?ua=1

World Health Organization. (2015, December). Disability and health (Fact Sheet No. 352). Retrieved from http://www.who.int/mediacentre/factsheets/fs352/en/#

World Health Organization. (2016). Injury-related disability and rehabilitation. *Violence and Injury Prevention*. Retrieved from http://www.who.int/violence_injury_prevention/disability/en

World Health Organization, National Center on Birth Defects and Developmental Disabilities from the United States Centers for Disease Control and Prevention, & International Clearinghouse for Birth Defects Surveillance and Research. (2014). Birth defects surveillance: A manual for programme managers. Retrieved from https://www.cdc.gov/ncbddd/birthdefectscount/documents/bd-surveillance-manual.pdf

ELEVEN

Assessment

ELIAS MPOFU AND NGONIDZASHE MPOFU

LEARNING OBJECTIVES

After reading this chapter, you should be able to:

- Define the construct of person-centric assessments as it applies to rehabilitation counseling practice settings.
- Differentiate person-centric assessments from those focused on impairment and disability.
- Describe the structure of the World Health Organization (WHO) *International Classification of Functioning, Disability and Health (ICF)*.
- Discuss applications of the *ICF* as a framework for the design, selection, and implementation of person-centric assessments.
- Propose prospective use of the *ICF* together with the *Diagnostic and Statistical Manual of Mental Disorders* (5th ed.; *DSM-5*) and *International Statistical Classification of Diseases and Related Health Problems, Tenth Revision (ICD-10)* and *ICD-11* (in preparation) for person-centric rehabilitation support assessments.
- Evaluate the incremental value of person-centric data for rehabilitation support interventions.

This chapter discusses the nature and significance of person-centric assessments to rehabilitation support interventions for people with disabilities. It defines person-centric assessments and positions them within the framework of the WHO's (2001) *International Classification of Functioning, Disability and Health (ICF)*. The *ICF* provides a universally accepted biosocial conceptual framework for understanding health and disability. Its full implementation in rehabilitation service provisioning requires acquiring and integrating information on three health conditions (body structure and functions, activities, and participation) and two contextual conditions (environmental and personal factors) to optimize personal functioning. This chapter discusses the ways in which the *ICF* can be used in conjunction with the *Diagnostic and Statistical Manual of Mental Disorders* (5th ed.; *DSM-5*; American Psychiatric Association [APA], 2013) and other WHO classification systems to provide person-centric data for rehabilitation support interventions with people with disabilities. Finally, the chapter proposes a conceptual model for applying *ICF* framework concepts to the design, selection, and use of person-centric rehabilitation assessments for life design with disability.

A priority goal of rehabilitation counseling is to ensure that people with disabilities have access to regular community services and the same opportunities to engage in full community citizenship roles as their peers without disabilities (United Nations, 2009,

2012). In the context of the day-to-day reality of people with disabilities and their support systems (family, significant others, rehabilitation and health service providers), priorities include the successful orchestration of basic resources, services, and supports for enhancing their capacity to attain a satisfactory life with full community inclusion (Mpofu et al., 2012; Thompson & DeSpain, 2016). A satisfactory life is defined by two complementary statuses: hedonic and eudaimonic well-being (Diener, 1984; Kahneman, Diener, & Schwarz, 1999; Ryff & Singer, 2008; Waterman, 1993). **Hedonic well-being** is associated with experiencing a sense of enjoyment, contentment, and happiness (Diener, 1984; Waterman, 1993) with pleasurable positive affect (Diener, 1984; Kahneman et al., 1999; Ryff & Singer, 2008), and the absence of emotional pain (Ryan et al., 2008). **Eudaimonic well-being** is associated with opportunities for self-realization, personal expressiveness (Waterman, 1993), being fully functional and successful in attaining a meaningful life (Ryff & Singer, 2008), living well with disability (Mpofu, 2013), or successful participation (Thompson et al., 2015). Many people with disabilities are able to participate meaningfully in their communities with appropriate long-term rehabilitation counseling supports (Putman & Frieden, 2014), and rehabilitation counselors can play a critical role in identifying and providing the rehabilitation supports necessary for a person with a disability to "participate in activities linked to normative human functioning" (Schalock et al., 2010, p. 105).

Working around the realities of accessing supports for a satisfying life requires interlinked and person-centric information on what is needed, how, when, by whom, and for what personal function purposes (Madden, Fortune, Cheeseman, Mpofu, & Bundy, 2013; Stancliffe, Arnold, & Riches, 2016). In most cases, people with disabilities are the most valuable informants on their individual needs for support—yet often they are neither listened to nor asked about their priorities (Bond, Mpofu, & Millington, 2015; Mpofu, 2013). Person-centric assessment places the life choices of people with disabilities at the center of the rehabilitation counseling process, tapping into the lived experience with disability to construct solutions for meaningful community involvement (Mpofu, 2013).

Person-centric assessment involves the active participation of people with disabilities in generating the evidence on which interventions are based (Peterson & Elliott, 2008; Stancliffe et al., 2016). Assessment is critical because it involves managing complexity in types of data and data sources to inform interventions. The specific instruments for person-centric data gathering may include use of self-report measures, information from support providers, unstructured and structured interviews, and personal portfolios, as well as standard assessments (see Mpofu & Oakland, 2010a, 2010b for a comprehensive discussion of related procedures and instruments). With the right types of data, it is possible to construct optimal solutions for maximizing personal and community living with disability (Kellet, Mpofu, & Madden, 2013). Rehabilitation support interventions are a disability right (United Nations, 2012), and what constitutes the data on which such supports are premised is an important consideration (Umeasiegbu, Bishop, & Mpofu, 2013). The person-centric approach to rehabilitation counseling interventions (Schalock et al., 2010; Thompson et al., 2009) is in recognition of the fact that with appropriate personal and environmental enablers, the impact of disability on human functioning can be minimized if not eliminated (Harley, Mpofu, Scanlan, Umeasiegbu, & Mpofu, 2015).

Person-centric assessment aligns well with the rehabilitation counseling emphasis on the whole person, rather than a purely medical focus on disease and disorders (Madden et al., 2013; Mpofu et al., 2016), to inform rehabilitation counseling supports and interventions (Dune & Mpofu, 2015; Mpofu et al., 2012). Person-centered care has been studied more in primary care practice settings (de Silva, 2014) than in rehabilitation counseling practice settings (Mpofu et al., 2012, 2016). With this in mind, there is an urgent need for consideration of the types and nature of person-centric assessments with people with disabilities to inform the design and implementation of rehabilitation counseling supports and interventions.

PERSON-CENTRIC ASSESSMENTS

Person-centric assessments are designed to yield or provide data on supports needed by a person with a disability to attain his or her optimal "functioning vector" within "his or her reach" (Sen, 1985, p. 201). Data from person-centric assessments are useful in activity and participation decisions with chronic illness and disability across a number of life domains or for life design (Mpofu et al., 2016). **Life design** is a whole-person concept that is consistent with a disability rights approach to creating linkages and synergies among personal and environmental assets for successful living. From a disability rights perspective, people with disabilities are competent to lead and advise on their own health and well-being (Sepucha, Uzogarra, & O'Connor, 2008) as well as their inclusion in the community (Mpofu, 2013). From their experience living with disability, these individuals are the most knowledgable about the supports necessary for successful living with disability. People with disabilities are continually engaged in exploring and enacting choices to optimize successful living with disability in particular environments (Mpofu & Bishop, 2006), and person-centric assessment data are essential to best configure personal and environmental qualities that optimize life design choices for living well with a disability (Mpofu et al., 2012).

Person-centric assessments can be distinguished from other types of assessments because of their focus on individualized interventions to support the self-determination of people with disabilities. In contrast, other assessment procedures focused primarily on impairment rather than life design may inadvertently contribute to the disablement process because of their exclusive focus on the impact of health conditions on the "functioning in specific body systems, generic physical and mental actions and activities of daily living," considering personal and environmental factors only to the extent they "speed or slow disablement" (Verbrugge & Jette, 1994, p. 1). Often, assessments preselected by service providers to collect data on specific aspects of disability may not address the individualized concerns of people with disabilities (Iglehart, 2011; Üstün & Kennedy, 2009). Although some assessment procedures may be preordained or dictated by funding-stream policies about which aspects of disability they will record, how they will gather the information, and how they will interpret and summarize it and for what purposes (Iglehart, 2011; Kaiser Family Foundation, 2011), rehabilitation counselors may also collect person-centric data. Rather than being preoccupied with impairment, person-centric assessment focuses on how impairment restricts functioning in ways that are unique to the individual, which may have important implications for disability eligibility assessments that are mandated by policy (Madden, Glozier, Mpofu, & Llewellyn, 2011) or to support the provision of integrated care service as medically necessary (Cloninger, 2011).

With person-centric assessments, people with disabilities and rehabilitation counselors are equal partners as to the types and sources of data that are needed to maximize living well with a disability. Person-centric data prioritize the preferences or expressed needs of people with disabilities for rehabilitation supports helpful to their activity and participation (Dijkstra, Niessen, Braspenning, Adang, & Grol, 2006) and community living (Mpofu, 2013; Mpofu et al., 2012). A benefit of person-centric assessment is that people with disabilities are more likely to follow through with treatment decisions that have prioritized their individual needs rather than decisions based on what are perceived to be routine, provider-oriented assessment procedures (de Silva, 2014; Olsson, Jakobsson Ung, Swedberg, & Ekman, 2013). Consistent with the rehabilitation counseling emphasis on the person–environment fit, the WHO's (2001) *ICF* provides a framework for a whole-person approach to the use of person-centric assessment for rehabilitation support interventions.

THE INTERNATIONAL CLASSIFICATION OF FUNCTIONING, DISABILITY AND HEALTH FRAMEWORK FOR PERSON-CENTRIC ASSESSMENTS

The *ICF* is not an assessment tool; rather, it is a framework for describing human functioning on the basis of which person-centric assessments may be selected or designed and implemented with people with disabilities. The *ICF* has been described as an information system with the goals to "represent and process information . . . to create new knowledge" (Hollenweger, 2013, p. 1091), as would be the case with person-centric assessments for life design with disability. A brief overview of the *ICF* follows to provide context for the discussion of the person-centric assessment applications.

Structure of the *ICF*

The *ICF* considers health and disability to be defined by the interaction between body structure and function of people, and impairments they may experience; activities of people and the limitations they may experience on their ability or performance; participation or involvement in all areas of life and restrictions people may experience; and environmental and personal factors that affect physical functioning as well as the activities people can or will do and their participation in life roles (see Figure 11.1).

According to the *ICF*, disability involves dysfunction at one or more of these levels: biological impairments, activity limitations, and participation restrictions. *Biological impairment* refers to differences in anatomical structure or function, such as the ability to move one's arms or legs. In contrast, *disability* refers to the restriction or lack of

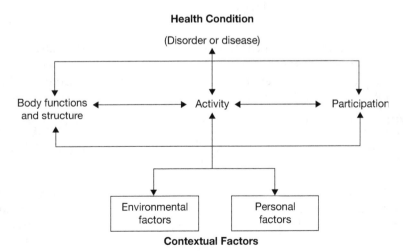

Figure 11.1 *International Classification of Functioning, Disability and Health* structure for understanding health and disability.
Source: WHO (2001, p. 18).

ability that arises from the interaction between features of the person and features of the overall context in which the person lives. This is not to deny the fact that some aspects of disability are almost entirely internal to the person (from impairment), whereas other aspects are almost entirely external (from environmental restrictions). In other words, data on both the medical aspects (impairment-oriented) and social aspects (environment-oriented) of disability are important for successful living with disability.

The *ICF* is a biosocial model of disability in that it synthesizes what is true from the medical and social models of disability without overly privileging one of the aspects or reducing the whole, complex notion of disability to one of its aspects. The *ICF* model, with its emphasis on functioning, proposes a view of "health" and

---

BOX 11.1 *ICF* Definition of Terms

Body functions—the physiological functions of body systems (including psychological functions).

Body structures—anatomical parts of the body such as organs, limbs, and their components.

Impairments—problems in body function or structure such as a significant deviation or loss.

Activity—the execution of a task or action by an individual.

Participation—involvement in a life situation.

Activity limitations—difficulties an individual may experience in involvement in life situations.

Participation restrictions—problems an individual may experience in involvement in life situations.

Environmental factors—make up the physical, social, and attitudinal environment in which people live and conduct their lives. These are either barriers to or facilitators of the person's functioning.

Functioning—an umbrella term encompassing all body functions, activities, and participation. It denotes the positive or neutral aspects of the interaction between a person's health condition(s) and that individual's contextual factors (environmental and personal factors).

Source: WHO (2001, pp. 3, 8, 10).

"disability" in which every human being can experience a decrement in health and thereby experience some level of disability. From this perspective, good health and living well with disability are both possible with the right supports or resources (Schalock et al., 2010; Thompson et al., 2015). Box 11.1 presents the definitions of components of the *ICF* framework.

Boxes 11.2 and 11.3 present case conceptualizations utilizing the *ICF*. The *ICF* components are indications for the clinical and personal function presentations of a person

---

BOX 11.2 Case Conceptualization Utilizing the *ICF*: A Person With a Spinal Cord Injury

Mr. Sig is a 26-year-old man with a T9 complete spinal cord injury from a motor vehicle accident. He has received care from a multidisciplinary spinal rehabilitation unit following initial care in an acute surgical ward. Mr. Sig's complete paraplegia translates into problems of lower muscle power and sensations (*body structure/function*). This impairment results in difficulty walking and moving (*activity limitation*). Mr. Sig is slowly improving with wheelchair mobility and requires ongoing assistance with bathroom transfers. He would have complete difficulty in a nonmodified home environment without use of equipment or aids and assistance of others. He would have difficulty returning to his usual work as a bricklayer (*participation restriction*). Mr. Sig is supported by both his long-term girlfriend and his parents (*environmental factors*). He prefers outdoor living and wilderness adventure with boyhood friends (*personal factors*).

BOX 11.3 Case Conceptualization: A Person With Guillain-Barré Syndrome

Ms. Blandish is a 37-year-old woman with Guillain-Barré syndrome. She presented with weakness in all four limbs, paraesthesia, and decreased balance (*body function and structure*). She was initially bedbound, dysphagic, and dysphonic. On admission to a rehabilitation unit, she was independent with bed mobility, mobilized with four-wheeled walker and standby assistance. Ms. Blandish needs assistance with feeding and some aspects of self-care due to upper limb weakness and reduced dexterity. She experiences fatigue during the day with resultant impaired concentration (*activity limitations*). Ms. Blandish is a self-employed chef in the family catering business. She worked a busy schedule of 50–60 hours per week and has had to cut down on work hours significantly because of the illness (*participation restriction*). Ms. Blandish was previously well and healthy, with no medical history (*personal factors*). She was an avid long-distance runner, nonsmoker, drank alcohol occasionally, and drove a sports car (personal factors). She lives with her father in a single-story house with two steps and no rail at the front (*environmental factor*).

---

with a complete spinal cord injury (Box 11.2) and with Guillain-Barré syndrome, an autoimmune disorder in which the body's immune system attacks part of the peripheral nervous system (Box 11.3).

As should be apparent from these two case conceptualizations, applying the ICF framework has the unique advantage of establishing a transparent language for describing health- and disability-related personal function statuses in nontechnical terms accessible to a variety of users and audiences (WHO, 2002). The next sections describe in more detail each of the components of the ICF. In each case, consideration is given to person-centric assessment applications associated with each of the ICF components (see Figure 11.2 for a summary).

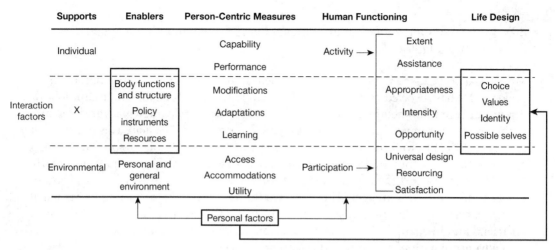

Supports		Enablers	Person-Centric Measures	Human Functioning		Life Design
Individual			Capability	Activity →	Extent	
			Performance		Assistance	
Interaction factors	X	Body functions and structure	Modifications		Appropriateness	Choice
						Values
		Policy instruments	Adaptations		Intensity	Identity
		Resources	Learning		Opportunity	Possible selves
Environmental		Personal and general environment	Access	Participation →	Universal design	
			Accommodations		Resourcing	
			Utility		Satisfaction	

Personal factors

Figure 11.2 The central role of person-centric measures in rehabilitation support interventions for life design.

TABLE 11.1 *International Classification of Functioning, Disability and Health* **Components and Chapters**

Body Functions
- Mental functions
- Sensory functions and pain
- Voice and speech functions
- Functions of the cardiovascular, hematological, immunological, and respiratory systems
- Functions of the digestive, metabolic, and endocrine systems
- Genitourinary and reproductive functions
- Neuromusculoskeletal and movement-related functions
- Functions of the skin and related structures

Body Structures
- Structure of the nervous system
- The eye, ear, and related structures
- Structures involved in voice and speech
- Structure of the cardiovascular, immunological, and respiratory systems
- Structures related to the digestive, metabolic, and endocrine systems
- Structure related to genitourinary and reproductive systems
- Structures related to movement
- Skin and related structures

Activities and Participation
- Learning and applying knowledge
- General tasks and demands
- Communication
- Mobility
- Self-care
- Domestic life
- Interpersonal interactions and relationships
- Major life areas
- Community, social, and civil life

Environmental Factors
- Products and technology
- Natural environment and human-made changes to environment
- Support and relationships
- Attitudes
- Services, systems, and policies

Source: WHO (2001, pp. 29–30).

ICF Components and Chapters

In the *ICF* manual, the core components are presented as chapters, as outlined in Table 11.1.

Body Structures and Function

As listed in Table 11.1, the *ICF* defines disability in body functions and structures as a deviation from population norms. According to the *ICF*, "structures" are anatomically based, as in the physical components of the cardiovascular and respiratory systems. "Functions" are defined as physiological correlates of such structures in regard to how they support bodily activities. Different health conditions often imply a need for disability-specific assessments. In the last decade, *ICF*-based core sets have been proposed that list common impairments for prevalent health conditions such as stroke (Geyh et al., 2004). Similarly, modular forms of assessments have been proposed with common core indicators and different branches of indicators from differential diagnosis of disease subtypes (Leone, Beghi, Righini, Apolone, & Mosconi, 2005). For example, with stroke the body functions likely impacted are consciousness, orientation, memory, and muscle tone and power. The impact of the stroke experience on these body structures and functions would depend on site and severity of lesion (Andelman, Zuckerman-Feldhay, Hoffien, Fried, & Neufeld, 2004; Keenan & Gorman, 2007), the specification of which would make for better targeted rehabilitation intervention (Jacoby, Baker, Crossley, & Schachter, 2013). For another example, people with epilepsy, with right-hemisphere lesions, might lack in self-awareness and report less reliably regarding existing difficulties (Keenan & Gorman, 2007). Person-centric assessments with people with right-hemisphere lesion would prioritize support tools for self-monitoring for seizure control medications and physical safety with seizure occurence.

Nonetheless, even with the benefit of core set listings, assessment for rehabilitation supports must still be individualized, as a person's premorbid functioning and life circumstances may influence recovery and personal functioning in significant life domains.

Activity

The *ICF* defines activity as the execution of a task or action by an individual (WHO, 2002). A person can have activity limitations due to an impairment in bodily structure or function that might constrain participation in a preferred or normative role. Alternatively, it is possible for a person to have the ability to engage in an activity, yet not be able to carry out the activity due to a lack of opportunity or support (Stancliffe et al., 2016). Nonetheless, a certain level of activity capability or potential is necessary for meaningful participation in key life areas. For instance, if a person is independent in performance of certain core activities such as mobility, body transfers, and personal activities of daily living, he or she would also likely have an enhanced capacity to participate in life domains that presume such competencies.

There is a certain degree of overlap between "activity" and "participation" in Table 11.1. For practical purposes, the first five aspects listed under "Activities and Participation" (learning and applying knowledge, general tasks and demands, communication, mobility, and self-care) fall under activities, whereas the last four aspects (domestic life, interpersonal interactions and relationships, major life areas, and community, social, and civil life) fall under participation.

ICF qualifiers are utilized to frame and collect person-centric data for rehabilitation support interventions for identified activities and participation roles. When using *ICF* qualifiers, a numerical code is used to record the impact of a problem on the individual across the domains of impairment, activity limitation, participation restrictions, and environmental factors. The numeric qualifiers are on a scale from 0 (no problem) to 4 (complete problem). (There are two additional qualifiers: 8, not specified; and 9, not applicable.) For example, Australian health and community services data standards for functioning and disability are based on the *ICF* and are person-centric in their emphasis on person-reported difficulties with activities (applying the *ICF* generic qualifier, noted previously) and perceived need for assistance (0 = no assistance; 4 = high assistance; Madden, 2010).

Participation

The *ICF* framework considers participation to be "involvement in life situations" (WHO, 2001, p. 10). For instance, participation in work, family, recreation and leisure, and education is primary to a satisfying life. Successful participation is defined by "engagement in all aspects of an activity as judged against contemporary . . . community standards and resulting in maximal involvement of the person in the activity" (Thompson et al., 2015, p. 13). Person-centric data on participation are those related to the individual autonomy and independence of people with disabilities, including their freedom to make their own choices regarding priority life areas to invest in, and opportunity to be actively involved in decision-making processes about policies and programs concerning them. The selection or use of person-centric assessments for participation should prioritize those that yield data usable for the design and implementation of rehabilitation supports for meaningful involvement in life situations. Sample person-centric participation-oriented questions might include: *What would you like for yourself?* and *How would you like to get that?*; for the participation in life domains, the generic *ICF* extent of participation qualifier would be used (0 = full participation; 4 = complete restriction).

Generic qualifiers to record the extent of functioning or disability in a life domain or category are interpreted so that "0" means *no problem,* "2" means mild problem, "3" means *severe problem,* and "4" is indicative of *complete problem.* For example, a record of *mild problem* means participation restrictions in a life domain that are present less than 25% of the time and with an intensity a person can tolerate, with relatively rare problem instances over the last 30 days. A record of *complete problem* means participation restrictions are pervasive and present more than 95% of the time, with an intensity that totally disrupts the person's day-to-day life and with problems experienced every day over the last 30 days.

Standards for person-centric measures of pariciption are evolving (Madden, 2010), and thus far only Australian standards apply the degree of satisfaction with participation (0 = high satisfaction; 5 = complete restriction and dissatisfaction; Madden, 2010). Regardless of practice jurisdiction, person-centric measures of participation should be collected on at least three areas of life that the person with a disability identifies as important to start with, and with a focus on (a) *where they are very pleased with their participation/involvement,* and (b) *where they want to see change.* Ancillary questions should ask about things and people around the person in the everyday environment that help his or her participation in priority life domains. This should include questions about equipment used (or needed), building design, people, attitudes, and services.

Environment

The *ICF* defines environmental factors as those that constitute the physical, social, and attitudinal environment in which individuals live and conduct their lives. In rehabilitation service provisioning, a key consideration is to surmount and not circumvent the participation restrictions on the individual (Thompson et al., 2015). The physical, social, and attitudinal environments in which people live or conduct their lives are important for the supports they would require for a satisfying life. These include their use of products and technology as well as social networks for health and well-being.

With physical disability or cognitive impairment, assessment for accessibility of environments and attention to modifiable falls risk factors are important to participation support considerations. This would be the case in, for example, home environment assessments to provide supports needed for safety from injuries (Lockwood, Taylor, & Harding, 2015). However, the definition of physical environment is much broader than just the home setting, and includes the built environment for which health impact assessments may be needed as a part of comprehensive rehabilitation (Dannenberg et al., 2008). Social and attitudinal barriers consist of elements that often are outside the individual's control, although also modifiable through supportive prodisability policy implementation. Within the disability and health policy frameworks, practices cognizant of *ICF* environmental social–attitudinal barriers to living with a disability include eligibility criteria to access disability support funding and enforcing accessibility requirements for transport or for public spaces.

The environmental factors domain attributes are scored on two qualifiers. The first qualifier addresses access/barriers issues with reverse scoring, so that a higher value denotes less access or more barriers: 0 (no barrier); 4 (complete barrier). The second qualifier addresses the activity or participation facilitation that would be needed, with a higher value denoting greater need for support: 0 (no facilitator); 4 (complete facilitator).

Person-centric assessments consider possible environmental influences on goal attainment and value realization. They seek to address solution-focused questions about the environment of participation, such as (a) How might the environmental context (actual or perceived) affect the scope and nature of personal goals in rehabilitation? (b) What aspects of the environment can be changed? (c) What perceptions of the environment can be changed?

Personal Factors

Personal factors refer to "the particular background of an individual's life and living, including features of the individual that are not part of a health condition or health states, and which can impact functioning positively or negatively" (Grotkamp, Cibis, Nuchtem, von Mittelstaedt, & Seger, 2012). They include individual differences such as gender, age, ethnicity, learning orientation, educational level, personality traits, "coping styles, social background, education, profession, past and current experience, overall behaviour pattern, character and other factors that influence how disability is experienced by the individual. Their assessment is left to the user, if needed" (WHO, 2001, p. 19).

Some personal factors, such as age, gender, and ethnicity, are not modifiable even though they may carry risk factors for disability. For example, the risk factor for colorectal cancer increases with age (Danaei et al., 2005) and the risk of Tay–Sachs disease is higher with Ashkenazi Jewish ancestry (Bach, Tomczak, Risch, & Ekstein, 2001). Other factors are changeable or modifiable, and important for rehabilitation goal setting, intervention design, implementation, and evaluation (Mpofu & Oakland, 2010a). These include personal psychological assets such as learning or applying knowledge, coping and resilient living, and so forth. Grotkamp et al. (2012) classified personal factors into 72 categories, arranged in chapters as follows: general factors normally unchangeable; a person's inherent physical and mental constitution; more modifiable factors such as attitudes, basic skills, and behaviour patterns; life situation and socioeconomic/

sociocultural factors; and other health factors (premorbid functioning, preexisting health conditions, prior interventions).

Person-centric assessments for personal factors tap into the priority value preferences of the person with a disability for types of activities and participation across life domains (Mpofu, Bishop, & Hirschi, 2010). For each area of life, person-centric assessments should address (a) how *important* this area of life is to the person; (b) whether he or she has good *opportunities* to participate and the *choice* about participating; (c) whether he or she feels able to *control* his or her involvement in this area of life; (d) whether he or she spends enough *time* on activities in this area (and frequently enough); and (e) whether he or she feels fully *involved* and pleased with the way he or she is able to participate. Person-centric assessment of personal factors presumes adherence to ethical aspects of nonmaleficence as characterized by respect for privacy issues, personal autonomy and choices, and use of the data in nonstigmatizing ways (Grotkamp et al., 2012; Peterson & Threats, 2005).

THE *ICF* AND OTHER NOSOLOGIES OF DISABILITY, FUNCTIONING, AND HEALTH

The *ICF* classifies functioning and disability associated with health conditions. It can be used to complement other medical-oriented systems, such as the *DSM-5* (APA, 2013), *WHO Disability Assessment Schedule 2.0* (*WHODAS 2.0*; WHO, 2012), and the *International Statistical Classification of Diseases and Related Health Problems, Tenth Revision* (*ICD-10*; WHO, 2011, 2014). The *DSM-5* is a diagnostic tool for mental disorders, whereas the *ICD-10* gives users an etiological framework for classification by diagnosis of diseases, disorders, and other health conditions. The *WHODAS 2.0* is a measure of general functioning with mental disorder and is used together with the *DSM-5*. The *ICD-10* belongs to the WHO family of international classifications, including the *ICF* and the *WHODAS 2.0* (WHO, 2012).

The *DSM-5* and *ICD-10* enable comprehensive assessment of the anatomical or physiological, structural, and mental health aspects of disability to inform interventions framed on the *ICF*, including the impact that the specific health condition may have on activity restrictions and participation limitations for which rehabilitation support interventions would be needed (Mpofu et al., 2016; Peterson, 2011; WHO, 2013). Moreover, data on disease or disorders (from the *DSM-5*, *ICD-10*) may have implications for policies on health and functioning at the population level, as in disability support funding-stream eligibility. For person-centric assessments, information on incidence and prevalence of disease, disorders, and health conditions (provided by *DSM-5*, *ICD-10*), and information about health and health-related functioning (provided by *ICF*, *WHODAS 2.0*) can be combined to inform person-oriented health and well-being support systems. Use of these health and disability systems together in a person-centric way would enable the appropriate targeting of supports for living well with disability.

Physical and psychological functioning (as framed in the *ICF*) does not necessarily overlap with severity or clinical significance of a diagnosis (as diagnosed per the *DSM-5*). This is because personal functioning is realized in interaction with one's environment, which includes the available supports for enacting specific life roles. Thus, a person with a severe psychiatric disorder and with supports for work participation (flexible hours; digital task prompting; coworker/supervisor task sharing) may be successful in a competitive work environment, the vocational outcome of which would be

---

BOX 11.4 Case Conceptualization Utilizing the *ICF* and *DSM-5:* A Person With a Somatic Symptom Disorder

Ms. Chandler had lower-right below-the-knee amputation following a car accident. She has successfully recovered from the physical treatment with a healthy amputation stump and uses a prosthesis. She reports that she experiences ongoing pain from "the leg" (i.e., the prosthesis). Her physician treatment team cannot find probable cause for the pain. Ms. Chandler has been taking pain medications for suspected stump neuromas (sensitive nerve endings that may form under an amputation stump). The pain did not improve on opioids, and she experienced side effects, including severe constipation. Ongoing monitoring of analgesia and side effects of pain relief medication has been a critical part of the medical treatment plan, as pain was a central problem for Ms. Chandler. Nonetheless, she reports significant distress and anxiety from the pain around the amputation stump, despite a seemingly well-fitting prosthetic device. She states that she experiences significant restrictions to her mobility in her house, with pain that escalates when climbing stairs or transferring onto the driver's seat of her high-ride-height sport utility vehicle. Ms. Chandler uses adaptive seating in her workplace, including a flexi-desk that allows her to work while standing, which improves her back and leg muscle tone. However, she reports restrictions to her leisure activities, such as shopping. Rehabilitation support interventions for Ms. Chandler to enhance her mobility included gait retraining, balance training, strengthening exercises, and fall prevention education. Other rehabilitation supports included weight control with dietician support, assessment of activities of daily living, and home modifications with an occupational therapist.

---

contraindicated by a reliance on *DSM-5* (or *ICD-10*) diagnosis alone. This clinical reality calls for psychiatric diagnosis (per *DSM-5*) to be considered separate and apart from personal functioning with psychiatric disability (per the *ICF* framework; see also WHO, 2001).

Successful living with a health condition often requires attention to influences on personal functioning beyond those predicated on the clinical diagnosis per se. Moreover, physical health conditions may influence mental health functioning, necessitating treatment for the mental health condition as part of a comprehensive health management plan. Consider the case described in Box 11.4 of a woman who sustained a below-the-knee amputation from a motor vehicle accident, and the extent to which the *ICF* framework can be used together with *DSM-5* for a comprehensive treatment plan. Ms. Chandler would be diagnosed, using the *DSM-5*, with somatic symptom disorder. However, as should be apparent from the case description, comprehensive treatment would have to consider both her *DSM-5* diagnosis and her personal functioning have framed per the *ICF*.

ICF FRAMEWORK APPLICATIONS TO LIFE DESIGN WITH DISABILITY

The *ICF* is a highly adaptable framework for the provision of rehabilitation counseling services (Hollenweger, 2013). Thus far, these applications have tended to address rehabilitation support needs in the context of physical medicine and rehabilitation with priority goals to restore, maintain, and augment functioning with disability. This will remain an important goal of rehabilitation services. However, life design with disability goes beyond the interventions aimed at restoring, maintaining, and augmenting functioning to reach toward enhancing participation in life domains of significance to the person with a disability in the context of his or her environment. The *ICF* framework concepts are adaptable for the design, selection, and use of person-centric assessments in the context of a rehabilitation counseling approach to support the maximum self-determination and inclusion of individuals with disabilities.

Figure 11.2 presents an assessment model in which person-centric assessments are at the core of support interventions for life design with disability. According to Figure 11.2, rehabilitation supports are required at the individual and environmental levels with requisite enablers. Data from person-centric assessments are needed to inform the supports for human functioning in regard to activities and participation to enable life design with disability. Personal factors or the attributes of the individual (as stated earlier) underlie individualized rehabilitation support interventions for life design with disability. Ongoing life design choices and outcomes influence the types of evidence needed for their sustenance through the agency of personal factors, making for a cyclic or mutually reinforcing system for human functioning with disability. The components of the rehabilitation supports model based on person-centric assessments are explained next.

Individual and Environmental Supports

Individual supports have been defined as the "resources and strategies that aim to promote the development, education, interests and personal well-being of a person and enhance individual functioning" (Schalock et al., 2010, p. 224). Examples of individual supports include information and education on living well with disability, technology to enable the person to function optimally, and other supports for successful transactions with the environment. The individual and environmental support needs are interactive, in that supports to enhance a person's capabilities also enable his or her participation in the environment as much as environmental support enhances the person's functioning.

Environmental supports are those aimed at bridging the gap between a person's capabilities and the demands for successful living with disability. The specific nature and function of environmental supports will depend on the level of environment for personal functioning. Two levels of environment are relevant to human functioning: personal and typical or general. The typical or general environment is one in which everyone participates. Examples include community venues and amenities such as shopping, recreation, work setting, health, and public transportation systems. This typical or normative environment is what the *ICF* framework describes in regard to participation needs when a person has a health condition for which support may be indicated. It is objective and verifiable as to its characteristics and often policy instruments for its regulation exist.

By contrast, the personal environment is defined by the individual's lived experiences. The personal environment is mostly subjective. For example, workplace social climate may be different for a person with a disability, in how he or she perceives being treated by peers and supervisors. If a workplace social climate is discriminatory, an inequitable work participation situation exists for people with disabilities, suggesting needs for evidence on the employing organization's implementation of disability-inclusive work practices. The extent to which the personal environment overlaps the typical environment as interpreted by the individual largely determines the levels of environmental supports needed. The larger the overlap between the personal and normative environments, the lower the need for individualized environmental supports. General environments with universal design features (those with wide scope to accommodate diversity in human performance attributes) have person-centric qualities (Mpofu & Oakland, 2010a, 2010b). Person-centric rehabilitation support interventions may be aimed at bridging the gap between the personal and typical environments.

Enablers

Enablers are the supports needed for engagement in activities and environments of choice. In the *ICF* framework, body structure and function are enablers in that type and severity of disability from impairment affect personal functioning. In other words, some level of physical functioning would enable participation (with personal and environmental supports). Disability support policy instruments and their implementation mechanisms are enablers to living with disability if appropriately targeted to the needs of the person with a disability (Putman & Frieden, 2014). However, some policy-determined disability supports may not address the needs for meaningful community living with disability, and evidence is needed as to which aspects of policy-determined tools are enablers or barriers to successful community living with disability (Wallace, 2011). Finally, the resources available to the individual (material, financial, social) are significant enablers of rehabilitation supports for life design with disability. For instance, health needs that may arise from living with disability may be materially and financially costly (Iglehart, 2011; Kaiser Family Foundation, 2011; National Council on Disability, 2009), requiring innovative management solutions for successful living with disability. Assessments that provide data on disability supports enablers are critical to provision of person-centric rehabilitation care service.

Person-Centric Assessments

As previously discussed, person-centric assessments for individual supports are those that yield data on the person's capabilities (what a person can do) and performance (what a person does). Assessments for environmental supports will provide data on environmental access for and accommodations of disability. In addition, person-centric assessments would also provide data on the utility of specific environmental supports for disability, including on environmental modifications and adaptations to bridge the gap between the person's abilities (capacities and performance) and the personal learning required for successful living with disability.

Human Functioning

Human functioning is defined primarily as engagement or participation in the major life areas (WHO, 2001). Types of person-centric assessment indicators for activity (i.e., need for assistance) and participation (i.e., satisfaction with participation) with disability were previously considered in some detail following the *ICF* framework guidelines. As previously noted, activity and participation overlap only partially, in that a person capable of specific activities may not necessarily participate in life domains in which those activity abilities would be required. The gap between activity and participation involvement may be explained variously, including perceived (in)appropriateness (Mpofu & Oakland, 2006), intensity of support demands (Stancliffe et al., 2016; Thompson et al., 2015), or lack of opportunity (Mpofu & Wilson, 2004; Stancliffe et al., 2016). Person-centric assessments for rehabilitation supports provide data on the appropriateness, intensity demands, and opportunity affordances for a satisfying life with disability.

Life Design

Previous sections considered the significance of a life design approach to rehabilitation supports with disability. Appropriate person-centric outcome measures for life design would include those regarding prioritized choices (autonomy), personal values and salient identities (relational worth, possible selves; Mpofu & Conyers, 2004), and aspirations for present and future living (competencies; Dune & Mpofu, 2015; Mpofu, 2013) and satisfaction with life (e.g., Diener, Emmons, Larsen, & Griffen, 1985; Waterman et al., 2010).

Autonomy refers to the need to feel that one is free to regulate one's own behavior, rather than being controlled by external sources (Deci & Ryan, 2000); it indicates a sense of personal choice, free will, and ownership of one's behavior (Haivas, Hofmans, & Pepermans, 2014). *Competence* refers to the need to interact effectively with one's environment to take opportunities to engage in activities within one's ability (Deci & Ryan, 2000; Haivas et al., 2014). *Relatedness* refers to being connected to others, in meaningful reciprocal relationships in which the individual is supported by and also cared for by others (Deci & Ryan, 2000; Haivas et al., 2014; Mpofu, 2013). As people with disabilities are supported in achieving their choices in the context of meaningful relationships with their allies and the community in general, they realize the wide array of possible selves they can aspire to be in their life settings.

CONCLUSION

Person-centric assessments have the unique strength of adopting a whole-person perspective premised on capabilities and potential, rather than being overly focused on disability and participation restrictions. Assessments for treating impairment alone, though important, may lack person-centric qualities and undervalue the individualized needs of people with disabilities from a life design perspective. Person-centric assessment is premised on personal choices, values, and attainment of a satisfying life with disability, and uses appropriate data for understanding how people with disabilities construct meaning in activities and participation. Person-centric interventions are aligned with disability rights-based approaches in rehabilitation counseling that value the views of people with disabilities regarding their self-determination and full community inclusion. The WHO *ICF* provides a framework for a whole-person approach to assessment in which biological impairments are considered in the context of personal functioning, while also taking into account the environmental factors. Use of *ICF* qualifiers personalizes assessment data to be responsive to specific competences, offering the potential for assessments to be supported with customized rehabilitation counseling interventions. The *ICF* can be used to complement the *DSM-5*, *WHODAS 2.0*, and *ICD-10/ICD-11* approaches to gather data usable in person-centric ways to optimize the effectiveness of rehabilitation counseling interventions.

CONTENT REVIEW QUESTIONS

- How does prioritizing person-centric data in rehabilitation assessments enable the identification of competencies and resources for effective life design with disability?
- How does the construct of person-centric assessment apply to rehabilitation counseling practice settings?
- What differentiates person-centric assessments from those focused on impairment and disability?
- How does the *ICF* framework apply to the design, selection, and implementation of person-centric assessments?
- Describe the structure of the WHO *ICF*.
- How does using the *ICF* together with the *DSM-5* and *ICD-10/ICD-11* give incremental value to person-centric data for rehabilitation support interventions?

REFERENCES

American Psychiatric Association. (2013). *Diagnostic and statistical manual of mental disorders* (5th ed.). Arlington, VA: American Psychiatric Publishing.

Andelman, F., Zuckerman-Feldhay, E., Hoffien, D., Fried, I., & Neufeld, M. Y. (2004). Laterization of deficit in self-awareness of memory in patients with intractable epilepsy. *Epilepsia, 45*(7), 826–833. doi:1111/j .0013-9580.2004.51703x

Bach, G., Tomczak, J., Risch, N., & Ekstein, J. (2001). Tay-Sachs screening in the Jewish Ashkenazi population: DNA testing is the preferred procedure. *American Journal of Medical Genetics, 99*(1), 70–75.

Bond, K. S., Mpofu, E., & Millington, M. (2015). Treating women with genito-pelvic pain/penetration disorder: Influences of patient agendas on help-seeking. *Journal of Family Medicine, 2*(4), 1033–1041.

Cloninger, C. R. (2011). Person-centred integrative care. *Journal of Evaluation in Clinical Practice, 17*(2), 371–372.

Danaei, G., vander Hoorn, S., Lopez, A. D., Murray, C. J., Ezzati, M., & Comparative Risk Assessment Collaborating Group. (2005). Causes of cancer in the world: Comparative risk assessment of nine behavioural and environmental risk factors. *Lancet, 366*(9499), 1784–1793.

Dannenberg, Al. L., Bhatia, R., Cole, B. L., Heaton, S. K., Feldman, J. D., & Rutt, C. D. (2008). Use of health impact assessment in the US: 27 case studies, 1999–2007. *American Journal of Preventive Medicine, 34*(3), 241–256.

de Silva, D. (2014). *Helping measure person-centred care*. London, UK: The Health Foundation.

Deci, E., & Ryan, R. M. (2000). The "what" and "why" of goal pursuits: Human needs and the self-determination of behaviour. *Psychological Inquiry, 11*(4), 227–268.

Diener, E. (1984). Subjective well-being. *Psychological Bulletin, 95*(3), 542–575.

Diener, E., Emmons, R. A., Larsen, R. J., & Griffin, S. (1985). The Satisfaction with Life Scale. *Journal of Personality Assessment, 49*(1), 71–75.

Dijkstra, R. F., Niessen, L. W., Braspenning, J. C., Adang, E., & Grol, R. T. (2006). Patient-centred and professional-directed implementation strategies for diabetes guidelines: a cluster-randomized trial-based cost-effectiveness analysis. *Diabetes Medicine, 23*(2), 64–170.

Dune, T., & Mpofu, E. (2015). Evaluating person-centered measures to understand sexuality with cerebral palsy: Procedures and applications. *International Journal of Social Sciences, 3*(4), 144–155.

Geyh, S., Cieza, A., Schouten, J., Dickson, H. Frommelt, P., Omar, Z., & Stucki, G. (2004). ICF core sets for stroke. *Journal of Rehabilitation Medicine, 36*, 135–141.

Grotkamp, S. L., Cibis, W. M., Nuchtem, N., von Mittelstaedt, G., & Seger, W. F. K. (2012). Personal factors in the International Classification of Functioning, Disability and Health: Prospective evidence. *Australian Journal of Rehabilitation Counselling, 18*(1), 1–24.

Haivas, S., Hofmans, J., & Pepermans, R. (2014). "What motivates you doesn't motivate me": Individual differences in the needs satisfaction-motivation relationship of Romanian volunteers. *Applied Psychology: An International Review, 63*(2), 326–343. doi:10.1111/j.1464-0597.2012.00525.x

Harley, D., Mpofu, E., Scanlan, J., Umeasiegbu, V., & Mpofu, N. (2015). Disability social inclusion and community health. In E. Mpofu (Ed.), *Community-oriented health services: Practices across disciplines* (pp. 207–222). New York, NY: Springer Publishing.

Hollenweger, J. (2013). Developing applications of the ICF in education systems: Addressing issues of knowledge creation, management and transfer. *Disability and Rehabilitation, 35*(13), 1087–1091. doi:10.3109/09638288.2012.740135

Iglehart, J. K. (2011). Desperately seeking savings: States shift more Medicaid enrollees to managed care. *Health Affairs, 30*(9), 1627.

Jacoby, A., Baker, G. A., Crossley, J., & Schachter, S. (2013). Tools for assessing quality of life in epilepsy patients. *Expert Review of Neurotherapeutics, 13*(12), 1355–1369. doi:10.1586/1473715.2013.850032

Kahneman, D., Diener, E., & Schwarz, N. (1999). *Well-being: The foundations of hedonic psychology*. New York, NY: Russell Sage.

Kaiser Family Foundation. (2011). Managing costs and improving care: Team-based care of the chronically ill. Retrieved from http://kff.org/health-costs/event/managing-costs-and-improving-care-team-based

Keenan, J. P., & Gorman, J. (2007). The causal role of the right hemisphere in self-awareness: It is the brain that is selective. *Cortex, 43*(8), 1074–1082.

Kellet, D., Mpofu, E., & Madden, R. (2013). Reflective action assessment with a prospective clinical problem solving tool in the context of rehabilitation medicine: An illustrative case study. *Disability and Rehabilitation, 35*, 1048–1054.

Leone, M. A., Beghi, E., Righini, C., Apolone, G., & Mosconi, P. (2005). Epilepsy and quality of life in adults: A review of the instruments. *Epilepsy Research, 66*(1), 23–44. doi:10.1016/j.eplespyres.2005.02.009

Lockwood, K. J., Taylor, N. F., & Harding, K. E. (2015). Pre-discharge home assessment visits in assisting patients' return to community living: A systematic review and meta-analysis. *Journal of Rehabilitation Medicine, 101*(4), 289–299.

Madden, R. H. (2010). Self-reporting on participation and environment: Can we make more use of Australia's national data standards. Australian ICF Disability and Rehabilitation Research Program. Bruce, Australia: Australian Institute of Health and Welfare.

Madden, R. H., Fortune, N., Cheeseman, D., Mpofu, E., & Bundy, A. (2013). Fundamental questions before recording or measuring functioning and disability. *Disability and Rehabilitation, 35*(13), 1092–1096.

Madden, R. H., Glozier, N., Mpofu, E., & Llewellyn, G. (2011). Eligibility, the ICF and the UN Convention: Australian perspective. *BMC Public Health, 11*(Suppl. 4), 56–67.

Mpofu, E. (2013). Qualities of life design measures with chronic illness or disability. *Disability and Rehabilitation, 35*, 1055–1058.

Mpofu, E., & Bishop, M. (2006). Value change and adjustment to disability: Implications for rehabilitation education and practice. *Rehabilitation Education, 20*, 141–161.

Mpofu, E., Bishop, M., & Hirschi, A. (2010). Assessment of values. In E. Mpofu & Oakland, T. (Eds.), *Rehabilitation and health assessment: Applying ICF guidelines* (pp. 381–407). New York, NY: Springer Publishing.

Mpofu, E., & Conyers, L. M. (2004). A representational theory perspective of minority status and people with disabilities: Implications for rehabilitation education and practice. *Rehabilitation Counseling Bulletin, 47*, 142–151.

Mpofu, E., Madden, R., Athanasou, J. A., Manga, R. Z., Gitchel, W. D., Peterson, D. B., & Chou, C. (2012). Person-centered assessment in rehabilitation and health. In P. J. Toriello, M. Bishop, & P. D. Rumrill (Eds.), *New directions in rehabilitation counseling: Creative responses to professional, clinical, and educational challenges* (pp. 209–235). Linn Creek, MO: Aspen Professional Services.

Mpofu, E., Madden, R., Madden, R., Kellett, D., Peterson, D. B., Gitchel, W. D., & Lee, E. J. (2016). Advances in rehabilitation and health assessments. In F. T. L. Leong, D. Bartram, F. M. Cheung, K. F. Geisinger, & D. Iliescu (Eds.), *The ITC International Handbook of Testing and Assessment* (pp. 244–255). New York, NY: Oxford University Press.

Mpofu, E., & Oakland, T. (2006). Assessment of value change in adults with acquired disabilities. In M. Hersen (Ed.), *Clinician's handbook of adult behavioral assessment* (pp. 601–630). New York, NY: Elsevier.

Mpofu, E., & Oakland, T. (Eds.). (2010a). *Rehabilitation and health assessment: Applying ICF guidelines*. New York, NY: Springer Publishing.

Mpofu, E., & Oakland, T. (Eds.). (2010b). *Assessment in rehabilitation and health*. Upper Saddle River, NJ: Merrill/Pearson.

Mpofu, E., & Wilson, K. B. (2004). Opportunity structure and transition practices with students with disabilities: The role of family, culture, and community. *Journal of Applied Rehabilitation Counseling, 35*(2), 9–16.

National Council on Disability. (2009). The current state of health care for people with disabilities. Retrieved from http://www.ncd.gov/rawmedia_repository/0d7c848f_3d97_43b3_bea5_36e1d97f973d.pdf

Olsson, L. E., Jakobsson Ung, E., Swedberg, K., & Ekman, I. (2013). Efficacy of person-centred care as an intervention in controlled trials: A systematic review. *Journal of Clinical Nursing*, 22(3–4), 456–465.

Peterson, D. B. (2011). *Psychological aspects of functioning, disability and health*. New York, NY: Springer Publishing.

Peterson, D. B., & Elliott, T. R. (2008). Advances in conceptualizing and studying disability. In S. Brown & R. Lent (Eds.), *Handbook of counseling psychology* (4th ed., pp. 212–230). Hoboken, NJ: Wiley.

Peterson, D. B., & Threats, T. T. (2005). Ethical and clinical implications of the International Classification of Functioning, Disability and Health (ICF) in rehabilitation education. *Rehabilitation Education*, 19, 129–138.

Putman, M., & Frieden, L. (2014). Sharpening the aim of long-term services and supports policy. *Public Policy and Aging Report*, 24(2), 60–64.

Ryff, C. D., & Singer, B. H. (2008). Know thyself and become what you are: A eudaimonic approach to psychological well-being. *Journal of Happiness Studies*, 9, 13–39. doi:10.1007/s10902-006-9019-0

Schalock, R., Borthwick-Duffy, S., Bradley, V., Buntinx, W., Coulter, D., Craig, E., . . . Yeager, M. H. (2010). *Intellectual disability: Definition, classification, and systems of support* (11th ed.). Washington, DC: American Association on Intellectual and Developmental Disabilities.

Sen, A. (1985). Well-being, agency and freedom: The Dewey lecturers. *Journal of Philosophy*, 82(4), 169–221.

Sepucha, K. R., Levin, C. A., Uzogara, E. E., Barry, M. J., O'Connor, A. M., & Mulley, A. G. (2008). Developing instruments to measure the quality of decisions: Early results for a set of symptom-driven decisions. *Patient Education and Counseling*, 73(3), 504–510.

Stancliffe, R. J., Arnold, S. R. C., & Riches, V. C. (2016). The supports paradigm. In R. L. Schalock & K. D. Keith (Ed.), *Cross-cultural quality of life: Enhancing the lives of persons with intellectual disability* (2nd ed., pp. 133–142). Washington, DC: American Association on Mental Retardation.

Thompson, J. R., Bradley, V., Buntinx, W. H. E., Schalock, R. L., Shogran, K. A., Snell, M. E., . . . Yeager, M. H. (2009). Conceptualizing supports and the support needs of people with intellectual disability. *Intellectual and Developmental Disabilities*, 47, 135–146. doi:10.1352/1934-9556-47.2.135

Thompson, J. R., Bryant, B., Schalock, R. L., Shogren, K. A., Tassé, M. J., Wehmeyer, M. L., . . . Rotholz, D. A. (2015). *Supports Intensity Scale—Adult Version: Users manual*. Washington, DC: American Association on Intellectual and Developmental Disabilities.

Thompson, J. R., & DeSpain, S. N. (2016). Community support needs. In N. N. Singh (Ed.), *Handbook of evidence-based practices in intellectual and developmental disabilities* (pp. 137–168). New York, NY: Springer.

Umeasiegbu, V. I., Bishop, M., & Mpofu, E. (2013). The conventional about disability conventions: A reflective analysis of United Nations Convention on the Rights of Persons with Disabilities. *Rehabilitation Education, Policy and Research*, 27(1), 58–72.

United Nations. (2009). Rights and dignity of persons with disabilities. Retrieved from http://www.un.org/disabilities

United Nations. (2012). Convention on the rights of persons with disabilities: Latest development. Retrieved from http://www.un.org/disabilities

Üstün, B., & Kennedy, C. (2009). What is "functional impairment"? Disentangling disability from clinical significance. *World Psychiatry*, 8, 82–85.

Verbrugge, L. M., & Jette, A. M. (1994). The disablement process. *Social Science and Medicine*, 38(1), 1–14. doi:10.1016/0277-9536(94)90294-1

Wallace, J. (2011). Assistive technology funding in the United States. *NeuroRehabilitation*, 28(3), 295–302.

Waterman, A. S. (1993). Two conceptions of happiness: Contrasts of personal expressiveness (eudaimonia) and hedonic enjoyment. *Journal of Personality and Social Psychology*, 64, 678–691.

Waterman, A. S., Schwartz, S. J., Zamboanga, B. L., Ravert, R. D., Williams, M. K., Agocha, V. B., . . . Donnellan, M. B. (2010). The Questionnaire for Eudaimonic Well-Being: Psychometric properties, demographic comparisons, and evidence of validity. *Journal of Positive Psychology*, 5(1), 41–61. doi:10.1080/17439760903435208

World Health Organization. (2001). *International classification of functioning, disability and health: ICF*. Geneva, Switzerland: Author.

World Health Organization. (2002). Towards a common language for functioning disability and health: ICF. Geneva, Switzerland: Author.

World Health Organization. (2011). *International statistical classification of diseases and related health problems, tenth revision.* Geneva, Switzerland: Author.

World Health Organization. (2012). *Measuring health and disability: Manual for WHO Disability Assessment Schedule (WHODAS 2.0).* Geneva, Switzerland: Author.

World Health Organization. (2013). *How to use the ICF: A practical manual for using the International Classification of Functioning, Disability and Health.* Geneva, Switzerland: Author. Retrieved from http://apps.who.int/classifications/network/en

World Health Organization. (2014). *ICD-11.* Retrieved from http://www.who.int/classifications/icd/revision/en

TWELVE

Counseling

MARK A. STEBNICKI

LEARNING OBJECTIVES

After reading this chapter, you should be able to:

- Understand the current scope of practice in rehabilitation counseling and the impact that counselor licensure legislation has on the field concerning eligibility for counselor licensure and becoming an independent rehabilitation practitioner.
- Define the foundational skills and scope of practice required for effective, competent, and ethical rehabilitation counseling practice.
- Explain a psychosocial model for rehabilitation counselors (RCs) who want to structure therapeutic interactions with clients who have chronic illnesses and disabilities.
- Explore a career path of professional rehabilitation counseling that brings meaning and purpose to a livelihood much better than average occupational outlook of most other counseling professions.

Defining the construct of counseling is a considerable task. It is often misunderstood by the general public and clients themselves because of the multiple specialty areas within the larger practice of professional counseling. State counselor licensure laws, credentialing boards, and national counselor certification organizations have even disagreed about the definition and scope of practice for professional counselors in the past. To unify the profession of counseling, the American Association of State Counseling Boards (AASCB), in partnership with and the American Counseling Association (ACA), the largest professional counseling association internationally, defined *counseling* during a March 2010 meeting at ACA's annual conference in Pittsburg, Pennsylvania (ACA, 2016). This joint oversight committee, charged with defining the vision and scope of practice within the counseling profession, represented more than 29 other professional counseling associations and organizations (including those representing rehabilitation counseling) with the intention of unifying the profession of counseling. The committee was charged with utilizing a systematic research approach involving work groups and focus or study groups for developing a clear, brief, concise definition for the field of counseling. This committee approved by consensus the following definition:

> *Counseling is a professional relationship that empowers diverse individuals, families, and groups to accomplish mental health, wellness, education, and career goals.*

ACA's and AASCB's oversight committee anticipated an expanded definition of counseling in the coming years as the evolving field of counseling continues to offer therapeutic services to a variety of individuals, families, and groups in a diversity of therapeutic settings (e.g., Internet, face-to-face, in-patient psychiatric and substance abuse rehabilitation facilities and health care settings).

To capture the diversity of specializations within the counseling profession, Schneider Corey and Corey (2016) highlight how each counseling specialty (e.g., addiction, career, school, mental health, and rehabilitation counseling) defines its specialty area of practice by both the population and the setting in which services are provided. Based on these specialty areas, individuals, groups, and families are offered therapeutic programs and services that are unique to a particular environment. For instance, school counselors work primarily in school settings; substance abuse counselors work primarily in residential, inpatient, and/or outpatient rehabilitation treatment programs; career counselors work in vocational and career counseling centers; and pastoral counselors work primarily in faith-based and hospital settings.

Counseling also varies by the individual needs that clients bring. Hackney and Cormier (2009) note that the various professional counseling specialties have emerged as a result of the individual's interpersonal and intrapersonal needs. In other words, the specialization of rehabilitation counseling may respond to the personal, vocational, and independent living needs of individuals with disabilities, whereas other specializations such as school counseling may respond to the developmental needs of youth. Thus, client needs relate to the individual's personality traits, behaviors, cognitive abilities, emotional and psychological wellness, unique cultural aspects, and developmental phase of life. Viewing a client through this counseling lens, each professional counseling specialization then selects specific therapeutic interventions based on their academic and clinical training. Therapeutic effectiveness is enhanced by knowing each client's coping resources, external supports, and resiliency traits.

Ivey, Bradford Ivey, and Zalaquett (2014) suggest that the terms *counseling, interviewing*, and *therapy* have considerable overlap within the counseling literature because of the diversity of counseling specializations. The terms and constructs are often used interchangeably and the counseling process is described both the same and differently depending upon the populations served and the counseling setting. The term *interviewing* typically refers to the basic process of gathering information, problem solving, and dealing with the psychosocial aspects of individuals by facilitating brief short-term counseling strategies. However, the process of counseling and psychotherapy is more long term and intensive by nature. This process has the intention to form a deeper personal therapeutic relationship with the individual. Counselors often use the terms *counseling* and *psychotherapy* interchangeably without a standard or agreed-upon definition. In several states, licensed professional counselors (LPCs) may legally refer to their occupation using either of the terms *counselor* or *psychotherapist*. For clarity purposes, the terms *counselor* and *counseling* are used throughout this chapter.

COUNSELING AS A DYNAMIC PROCESS

The process of becoming a skilled and competent professional counselor includes learning basic counseling theories and approaches, skills of interviewing, use of empathy in session, and other strategies that assist in building client rapport with the intention of achieving an optimal working alliance. It is beyond the scope of this chapter to provide a comprehensive overview of the process or helping skills used during therapeutic interactions. There are excellent counseling texts related to counseling theories and strategies that assist professionals in developing the foundational skills to use during therapeutic interactions. These texts basically prepare professional counselors in establishing client rapport (e.g., use of attending, listening, empathic responses, open-ended questioning, clarifying, paraphrasing, and summaries) and in gaining therapeutic alliance (e.g., use of challenging skills, goal setting, and cultivating optimal wellness strategies) so that professional counselors can achieve meaningful and working alliances with their clients.

At the core of counselor preparation is a keen awareness and mastery of interpersonal communication skills that help facilitate relationship values that are fundamental to the counseling process. At the foundation of the counseling relationship are the principles of respect, warmth, understanding, genuineness, congruency, authenticity, and positive regard. The success of this relationship comes when a therapeutic alliance can be created with the client. This alliance is developed based on trust and mutual agreement related to client concerns. Lustig, Strauser, Rice, and Rucker (2002) noted how the working alliance is strengthened through *goals* (i.e., target or outcome of the interventions), *tasks* (i.e., behaviors and cognitions engaged in during counseling), and *bonds* (i.e., interactions between the counselor and client). Based on these facilitative skills, the client and counselor engage in a therapeutic interaction with intention to develop increased awareness and meaning of the client's specific issues for therapy. The ultimate goal of counseling is to empower the client with an optimal level of overall mental, physical, and psychosocial functioning. This dynamic structural process assists the client to sequentially grow and develop from the "problem issue" to the desired change. This recurring interaction relies on skilled and competent counselors to use the strategies and techniques of counseling as a means for client self-reflection and personal growth, which ultimately assists clients in making meaning of their presenting problem issues.

Motivated clients naturally try to understand the meaning of events and experiences that have occurred in their past and present lives. The counselor uses the counseling relationship to help clients draw from their personal history, knowledge, awareness, coping abilities, resiliency skills, and overall life experiences to derive meaning. The resulting self-discovery and awareness generate energy that is focused toward an intentional way of being that ultimately leads to interpersonal effectiveness and action that generalizes to multiple life areas. In addition, the counselor and client, through a variety of counseling strategies and approaches, continually seek insight and self-reflection. Central to this process is the client's readiness and motivation to take action. Once the client is ready and motivated to change, then positive forward progress occurs at multiple cognitive, emotional, behavioral, and spiritual levels. Typically, this change results in an increased ability for clients to deal with significant concerns or the issues that brought them initially into the counseling process (Lopez Levers, 2012).

Ivey et al. (2014) assert that there are core skills that counselors and psychotherapists use in the helping process. These therapeutic engagements are required to build a therapeutic relationship and help clients work through their specific problem issues. These authors propose a hierarchy or pyramid of micro-counseling skills where the foundation is built upon intentional interviewing that integrates the counselor's ethical behavior, cultural competence, and facilitation of client wellness. The foundation for building and sustaining a working alliance is an ongoing task in the counseling process. The essential core skills that must be acquired by the professional counselor or psychotherapist include the following, which can be taught and practiced through education, awareness, modeling, and experience:

- Attending and listening
- Open and closed questions
- Client observation skills
- Encouraging, paraphrasing, and summarizing
- Reflection of feeling
- A multi-stage interview structure
- Confrontation
- Focusing
- Reflection of meaning and interpretation/reframing
- Influencing skills and counseling strategies
- Skill integration
- Determining personal style and theory

Overall, Ivey et al. (2014) suggest that as counselors or psychotherapists gain a sense of mastery, they will then learn that each client has unique needs that are communicated with an array of verbal and nonverbal responses. Thus, it is incumbent upon the professional to identify the client's unique style of expression and communication.

From Egan's (2014) perspective, the skilled helper engages in the counseling process within a three-stage Skilled Helper Model, as follows:

- *Stage I:* What is going on? (Counselors help clients clarify key issues for change.)
- *Stage II:* What solutions make sense? (Counselors help their clients determine outcome.)
- *Stage III:* What do I have to do to get what I need or want? (Counselors develop strategies for helping clients accomplishing their goals.)

This three-stage model involves two basic goals. The first is recognizing how clients manage specific problems in their day-to-day lives. This goal relates to the way in which professional counselors assist their clients by facilitating opportunities and resources so that clients can live more optimally. The second goal relates to the client's general ability to manage his or her problems, develop better coping skills, and recognize opportunities for everyday living. Accordingly, counseling is about increasing the client's levels of emotional and psychological functioning. Egan (2014) posits a flexible model of skilled helping. However, therapeutic interactions must be structured so that clients will not lose focus on their problem situations and lose or waste opportunities. Thus, counseling from Egan's perspective is about helping individuals achieve results, view the outcomes, and have a sense of accomplishment that is achieved by their difficult work in the counseling process.

Perhaps universal within the counseling process is an understanding of how to establish client rapport and achieve a meaningful working alliance within a multicultural context. Integrating the knowledge, awareness, and skills to work with the individual's cultural attributes, such as gender, race, ethnicity, sexual orientation, socioeconomic status, spiritual and religious beliefs, and disability, is of paramount importance. The RESPECT-FUL Model provides a comprehensive and functional approach to cultural competence within the counseling process (D'Andrea & Daniels, 2001). Accordingly, counseling theory and approach should not replace the professional counselor's ability to achieve meaningful rapport with clients in a multicultural context. Without client rapport, a meaningful working alliance will be difficult to achieve and clients will likely terminate services prematurely.

THE EVOLVING DEFINITION AND SCOPE OF REHABILITATION COUNSELING PRACTICE

The foundational skills of person-centered interactions within a humanistic model of counseling have always been at the foundation of the RC's scope of practice (Stebnicki, 2008a). Perhaps it is time to revisit our professional identity by reviewing the collective wisdom of early rehabilitation counselor educators, researchers, and practitioners (i.e., Patterson, 1957, 1966; Rubin Roessler, 1978; Whitehouse, 1975; Wright, 1980). The field of counseling evolved primarily as a group of specialty areas (e.g., vocational, school, mental health, and rehabilitation) that practiced with a common core of competencies and foundational skills (Leahy, Rak, & Zanskus, 2016). Today, there is a much expanded job market for RCs because of the diversity of job settings and titles into which recent graduates of Council on Rehabilitation Education (CORE)-accredited programs have been hired. In the past, Goodwin (2006) reported that 60% of all rehabilitation counselor education (RCE) programs offered a specialty concentration. The most frequently identified concentrations were substance abuse counseling, clinical mental health counseling, and deafness and hearing impairment counseling. Goodwin also identified 11 programs with a psychiatric rehabilitation specialization. Bernacchio, Burker, Falvo, Porter, and Carone (2008) identified four additional programs with a psychiatric rehabilitation concentration. The number of RCE programs with specializations in substance abuse, mental health counseling, and psychiatric rehabilitation was a contributing factor in the merger between CORE and the Council for Accreditation of Counseling and Related Educational Programs (CACREP; CORE, 2016; Tarvydas, Hartley, & Gerald, 2016). With the merger, it is anticipated that RCs will have expanded job opportunities in the larger counseling profession, as well as be eligible for the LPC credential across all 50 states and other counseling-related certifications in the near future.

There are multiple indicators that suggest a shift in the foundational principles and practices in rehabilitation counseling. Tarvydas et al. (2016) opine that one of the most critical components in counselor licensure legislation is the professional scope of practice statement. If RCs have limited clinical experiences and insufficient appropriate clinical counseling versus case management interactions, then rehabilitation counseling professionals may not be perceived by others in the larger counseling profession as being qualified practitioners. Generally, CORE- and CACREP-accredited programs have provided graduate trainees with the foundational knowledge, awareness, and clinical experiences to prepare them for career opportunities as independent practitioner counselors. However, it is important for professionals who want to become professionally licensed to contact their state counselor licensure board for an evaluation of any deficits that might exist in their academic program or supervised clinical experiences. Issues regarding licensing eligibility should become a career decision, and should be made at the beginning, not at the completion, of the counselor education program. The ACA's website has a listing of contact information for counselor licensure boards across all 50 states. The overall structure of professional credentialing in counseling is given extended consideration in Chapter 3. This chapter provides detail on how the specific professional function or service of counseling interacts with these aspects of credentialing.

Indeed, there are critical issues affecting RCs that relate to third-party reimbursement, mental health and disability legislation, the ability to diagnose and treat mental health and substance abuse conditions, and the expanding specialty areas in counseling that require certification and/or a license to practice (e.g., mental health and substance abuse counseling). In the past, the number of private insurance companies and state counselor licensure boards that accepted RCs as independent practitioners has varied from state to state. Moving forward, we must be vigilant about keeping a watch on our profession. One area in which professional RCs can increase their knowledge is an understanding of the concepts and language of managed health care as it relates to mental health services. This can be quite confusing for RCs who choose to be licensed as independent counseling practitioners. Graduate programs in rehabilitation counseling are designed to teach the necessary skills to become competent and ethical practitioners, rather than developing business skills to promote one's private practice.

There are comprehensive guides for private practitioners that describe the credentialing aspects of becoming a provider and getting on managed care plans, marketing, and the promotion of one's private counseling practice (Walsh, 2016; Walsh & Dasenbrook, 2009). These guides are an excellent resource for RCs who choose to become entrepreneurs and work with individuals, families, and groups within the system of managed care, as opposed to working only in state and federal vocational rehabilitation (VR) programs. Today, accredited RCE programs provide new graduates with the foundational knowledge, awareness, and clinical experiences to prepare for new and exciting career opportunities in rehabilitation counseling.

INTEGRATING BEST PRACTICES INTO THE REHABILITATION COUNSELING PROCESS

It is essential that we develop a clear understanding of how to integrate best practices into the rehabilitation counseling process. Facilitating therapeutic relationships lies at the foundation of the person-centered approaches of attending, listening, and empathic responding. Rehabilitation counseling professionals are accountable to those individuals, families, and groups whom we serve in terms of providing competent and ethical services. The counseling field itself has taken on a much more outcome-based, solution-focused approach, which has been driven by counselor accreditation standards, managed care, and private practice insurance panels (Stout & Hayes, 2005; Walsh, 2016; Walsh & Dasenbrook, 2009). The implied meaning suggests that "best practices" are "evidence-based," which must be evaluated in terms of client treatment and the continuum of services. The counseling process must be evaluated throughout various phases of the client's individual rehabilitation treatment plan; these evaluations include, but are not limited to, how the RC, agency, or organization performs the following:

- Establishes the first contact and makes connections with clients
- Establishes and builds a therapeutic rapport with clients
- Assesses, evaluates, and defines the clients' presenting problem issues in a culturally sensitive manner
- Identifies salient goals and objectives that include client participation in the rehabilitation treatment plan
- Chooses specific interventions and approaches that are culturally appropriate
- Engages clients in the continuum and termination of services with appropriate follow-up referral sources and natural support systems

It is important for RCs to be perceived by their clients as competent and ethical, as well as to maintain confidence among counselor licensure and certification organizations, private and public insurers, state legislators, and other stakeholders. To do this, the profession itself should strive for innovative practices that are evidence-based and are specific to working with people with chronic illnesses and disabilities. The evaluation of the outcome of services must take place on various levels. In other words, the evaluation of "client improvement" or "degree of satisfaction" must be measurable and consistent with rehabilitation counseling accreditation standards, client feedback, and other health and human service practice standards.

Integrating best practices within the rehabilitation counseling process can be communicated and advanced on multiple levels. This includes, but is not limited to, services provided by a sole practitioner (e.g., where the RCs act in an advocacy role), agency or organization (e.g., lobbying for a specific program or service for people with disabilities), university-based grant-funded programs (e.g., a demonstration project) where empirical data are published about the effectiveness of a specific program or approach, or a professional rehabilitation counseling association (e.g., a national voice that promotes services to people with disabilities by the most qualified practitioners: the rehabilitation professionals).

Advancing evidence-based practices in the rehabilitation counseling profession can be done at the national level through such means as presentations at professional rehabilitation conferences. The National Council on Rehabilitation Education (NCRE, 2016) is one example of a professional association concerned with education of competent and ethical rehabilitation practitioners for the primary purpose of improving rehabilitation services for people with disabilities. The Commission on Rehabilitation Counselor Certification (CRCC, 2016) is another example of an organization that promotes, both in the United States and other partnering countries, the rehabilitation counseling profession as a group dedicated to improving the lives of people with chronic illnesses and disabilities. The CRCC, which administers the certified rehabilitation counselor (CRC) credential, sets the standards for the quality delivery of services and competencies required for professional practice as a CRC. Overall, these organizations reflect a model of rehabilitation counseling teaching, research, service, and practice that portrays the ideal standards for best practices. Ultimately, opportunities such as these enrich personal and professional growth that brings meaning and purpose to one's practice.

Personal and Professional Growth as a Standard of Best Practices

Corey (2010) suggests that "counseling professionals tend to be compassionate people who are good at taking care of others, but often we do not treat ourselves with the same level of care" (p. 185). This statement suggests that integrating best practices may begin with the professional who can maintain his or her own self-care throughout different career experiences that include the ebb and flow of personal and professional growth. Accordingly, some of the most effective RCs are those who are seen by self and others as empathetic, competent, and ethical practitioners. The portrait of the ideal RC is an empathetic professional who has the awareness, knowledge, and skills to work effectively with the interpersonal challenges posed by clients. Some of these challenges include working with those who have experienced significant loss, grief, trauma, addictions, chronic illness, and disability.

If the professional counselor has a decreased capacity for empathy, he or she may be at risk for empathy fatigue or other counselor impairments (Stebnicki, 2008b, 2016).

Empathy fatigue, a word and construct coined by Stebnicki in 1998, results from "a state of mental, emotional, social, physical, spiritual, and occupational exhaustion that occurs as the counselor's own wounds are continually revisited by his or her clients' life stories of chronic illness, disability, trauma grief, loss, and extraordinary stressful events" (p. 16). A functional self-assessment of empathy fatigue indicates that there are multiple variables that coexist on a continuum of low, moderate, to high that measures the professional's qualitative experience (Stebnicki, 2016). These variables include counselors' (a) cognitions and perceptions about therapeutic interactions with their clients; (b) behaviors in session that might detract from exhibiting warmth, genuineness, and empathy; (c) spiritual beliefs that may be imposed on self or others about the clients' mental or physical condition; (d) counseling approach and style that may be culturally insensitive; (e) emotional involvement within a session where there may be diminished mood or negativity toward self and others in session; (f) physical capacity to maintain attention in difficult sessions; and (g) occupational characteristics of the professional that may include poor job match between professionals and their work environment or the population they serve. The interested reader may want to consult the reference list for further details on assessing the empathy fatigue experience.

Ideal helpers are also committed to an honest assessment of their own strengths and limitations, have a basic curiosity and openness to learning new approaches, genuinely care about people, are willing to draw upon multiple resources for maintaining self-care practices, have the ability to respect others who are culturally different, have the capacity to establish meaningful relationships, and have a healthy sense of self (Schneider, Corey & Corey, 2016). Other characteristics of effective counselors are increased self-awareness and understanding, good psychological health, sensitivity to cultural differences, open-mindedness, objectivity, trustworthiness, and having interpersonal skills that are genuine and empathetic (Hackney & Cormier, 2009, p. 13).

Students choose to become RCs for many reasons. They may be drawn to the counseling profession because either they or a family member may have experienced a significant life event related to addiction, mental health, chronic medical condition, or acquired mental or physical disability. Whatever the motivation and inspiration used to make the career choice, it is essential that professionals examine personal motives for choosing rehabilitation counseling by exploring (a) their personal stress levels and how it relates to working with people who, at times, may have intense psychological, emotional, physical, medical, or occupational needs; (b) their attitudes, values, and beliefs about working with different populations of people (i.e., physical versus psychiatric disability) or in different occupational settings; (c) their career goals related to personal and professional growth in a humanistic-oriented work environment; and (d) other areas where the professional has recognized certain reactions that may trigger a sympathy, fatigue, or burnout response.

Competent and Ethical Treatment Strategies as Best Practices

There has been a trend in recent years toward greater emphasis on client or patient rights, as evidenced by specific counseling-related state and federal client protection legislation. With the passage of the 1996 Health Insurance Portability and Accountability Act (HIPAA, 2010), there are multiple areas of which RCs should be mindful when providing services. It is beyond the scope of this chapter to fully discuss specific laws relating to health care, mental health, and rehabilitation. The interested reader should consult Robles (2016) for an expanded discussion concerning HIPAA and the Affordable Care Act. However, best practices of RCs include an understanding of client protection laws relating to client confidentiality, the provision of treatment, documentation of psychocounseling services, and standards governing how information must be kept in electronic files, as well as many other areas.

One particular area of client protection salient for RCs is the way in which clients are to be provided with accurate information about the nature and intent of the counseling relationship. Professional disclosure statements are one tool used by professional counselors; these documents indicate that clients have been fully informed about the nature and intent of services being offered (Goodwin, 2016). Disclosure statements become a legal contract between the client and the counselor and should include issues that relate to the professional's statement regarding the following:

- Credentials (i.e., certifications and licenses)
- Counseling approaches, strategies, and theoretical orientation
- Populations served, both past and current
- Potential benefits and risks of counseling
- Client confidentiality
- Dual relationships, if any
- Length and frequency of sessions or services
- Expectations regarding treatment outcome
- Fees and method of payment
- Billing and insurance reimbursement policies
- Clients' rights to view their files
- Termination of services
- Emergency contact information
- Vacation, retirement, death, or impairment
- Alternatives to counseling
- Complaint procedures

Research supports the notion that many ethical dilemmas can be avoided if the client is provided with the appropriate amount of information that clarifies the nature and intent of treatment and services to be provided (Cottone & Tarvydas, 2007; Remley & Herlihy, 2005; Corey, Schneider Corey, Corey, & Callahan, 2015). Although the professional disclosure statement is essential for obtaining consent and informing clients of the nature and intent of the counseling relationship, the client's individualized treatment plan is the primary tool used to communicate and define the counseling process for identifying outcomes for client change (Hackney & Cormier, 2009). As part of a best practices approach, RCs need to work with clients and their family members in an active, solution-focused manner when it comes to the rehabilitation treatment process. Cormier and Nurius (2003, p. 331) provide the following guidelines for assessing client progress throughout the treatment process:

- A description of all relevant and potentially useful treatment approaches
- A rationale for each procedure that will be used
- A description of the counselor's role in each intervention
- A description of the client's role in each intervention
- Possible discomforts or risks that may occur as a result of the intervention
- Expected benefits that will occur as a result of the intervention
- The estimated time and cost of each intervention

The assumption stated in these guidelines implies that flexibility is required in any rehabilitation treatment plan; there is not just one "best practice" plan. Rather, there are multiple paths to get to the desired outcome because there are many therapeutic approaches and client variables involved. For instance, the counselor, agency, or organization may use affective, cognitive, behavioral, interactional (systemic), or any combination of these interventions. Because client problem issues are multidimensional, each goal may require different needs and resources at different times throughout the counseling process.

Johnston, Tarvydas, and Butler (2016) note that it is critical for counselors to stay current with the various codes for ethical practice, maintaining a good awareness, knowledge, and interpretation of the language within the codes so as to minimize the chances of being involved in an ethical or legal complaint. Possessing a good working knowledge of an ethical decision-making model can also assist counselors in providing competent and ethical services to their clients (Cottone & Tarvydas, 2007) and can enhance best practice standards for client protection.

COUNSELING PEOPLE WITH DISABILITIES

Most counseling texts offer strategies and techniques to work with the general mental health needs of individuals requiring counseling services. However, there are unique issues that relate to counseling people with disabilities. Besides considering the reduction in a client's physical capacity, there are psychological, mental, and emotional health concerns to consider. In addition, there are other contextual issues related to the psychosocial reaction to chronic illness or disability that can hinder full participation and achieving optimal wellness across multiple life areas.

There are both universal and specific counseling techniques to use in therapeutic interactions for people with disabilities. However, little is known about best practices in working with individuals who have coexisting mental health issues and physical disability. Most of the research related to the psychosocial reactions of people with disabilities is qualitative in nature. For example, actor Christopher Reeve, now deceased, acquired a C-1 level spinal cord injury and became quadriplegic and ventilator dependent after an equestrian competition in Virginia in May of 1995. As Frey and Hutchins Pirnot (2008, p. 160) account, Reeve's life, he always believed that he would someday walk again. After years of intensive physical and occupational therapy, Reeve was able to move his index finger and later gain some sensation in his left leg and arm. As an outside observer, it is unclear whether this rigorous physical regimen or his ability to pay for multiple specialists contributed to the return of sensation and physical capacity or whether the sensation would have returned on its own.

The point being made is that there are multiple physical disabilities and chronic health conditions to consider (e.g., spinal cord injury, diabetes, HIV/AIDS, cancer, chronic pain, and muscular skeletal disorders) when providing psychosocial support and services. This results in a complex interplay between a client's physical, psychological, emotional, social, and independent functioning. Thus, counseling strategies and techniques facilitated by rehabilitation professionals must be culturally centered as it relates to understanding how clients identify themselves in terms of their functioning and health. To assist in understanding these concepts, this section offers essential guidelines to facilitate therapeutic interactions for counseling people who have a variety of chronic illnesses and disabilities.

Counseling people with disabilities have primarily focused on the psychosocial aspects of the individual. Historically, the terms used to describe counseling issues have been directed toward psychosocial *adjustment, adaptation,* or *acceptance* of the individual with a disability. Traditionally, these terms have been used to describe individual's coping skills and how successfully they integrate their mental and physical functioning, and overall health into their disability identity. Disability scholars have delineated how psychosocial adjustment and adaptation is expressed through a series of phases or stages that individuals work their way through, finally ending in the theoretical stage of *acceptance* of their disability.

Smart (2001, p. 229) suggests that the more appropriate term *individual's response to disability* communicates more fully that (a) the disability itself does not define the individual; rather it is the meaning ascribed by the disability and how the individual views his or her residual functional capacity; (b) *adjustment* does not represent a total life experience or final endpoint of the individual; rather it reflects a range of experiences that include, but are not limited to, physical, psychological, emotional, cognitive, social, occupational, and spiritual response to a disability; and (c) *adjustment, adaptation,* and *acceptance* tend to pathologize the experience of disability and make the assumption that only those individuals who have a disability go through a phase or stage of *adjustment,* but in reality, all individuals have critical life issues to deal with that cannot be described as having a beginning and end point.

Indeed, all individuals have many critical life events (e.g., divorce, death of a parent, child, or spouse, loss of job and financial security, physical loss of a body part, and acquired disease or chronic illness) that do not fit neatly into a model of *adjustment, adaptation,* or *acceptance* (Stebnicki, 2017). Besides, what is considered by society to be *acceptance* of a disability does not typically occur as a one-time event. Accordingly, there are unique cultural differences that define the identity of the individual. This accentuates the point that one of the primary differences between the specialty areas of rehabilitation counseling and other counseling disciplines (e.g., school counseling, counseling psychology, clinical social work) is that the society's attitude toward people with disabilities may actually be more disabling than the disability itself. This philosophy is espoused by many authors in the field (Arokiasamy, 1993; Smart, 2016; Smart & Smart, 2006; Vanier, 2007; Vash, 1994; Vash & Crewe, 2004), who further advocate that people with mental and physical disabilities desire the same genuineness, respect, empathy, support, and opportunities as all other clients. Accordingly, the person's psychosocial reaction to disability is a complex interplay of variables that include, but are not limited to, the following issues:

1. *Time of onset.* There are a range of congenital and acquired disabilities that vary across the life span from birth to near death each having have their own unique psychosocial issues. The onset affects the individual emotionally, psychologically, physically, socially, spiritually, cognitively, academically, vocationally, and affects the level of independent functioning throughout the life span.
2. *Type of disability.* Counselors must consider the range of mental, physical, psychological, cognitive, developmental, acquired health, chronic health, life-threatening, and other conditions affecting various functional capacities, body systems, and life areas. It is also important to have a good working knowledge of the course, pattern, prognosis, exacerbation, and remission of the individual's specific type of disability.
3. *Individuals' perceptions of their disabilities.* Counselors must consider the individual's perception of his or her particular disabling condition and view this in terms of the types of losses the individual may be reporting. Depending upon the individual's

disability, losses occur in many contexts that include a combination of economic loss, loss of independence, loss of cognitive abilities, loss of physical capacity, loss of immune functioning, loss of emotional or psychological functioning, loss of vocational, educational, occupational, or career opportunities, loss of faith in God or a higher power, loss of belief in fairness or justice, and the loss of existential meaning of life itself. There is a complex interplay with what the individual experiences with varying degrees of intensity and duration.

4. *Cultural attributes and context of the disability.* Counselors must understand the individual and family within the context of their particular unique cultural attributes, level of acculturation, within-group differences, and overall cultural identity. Culturally competent counselors also try to gain an understanding of the individual's experience with outside influences that may spark negative attitudes, discrimination, stereotyping, or being marginalized by other individuals or groups in society. These outside influences may affect a range of issues related to the individual's self-esteem, confidence, mood, self-depreciation, and other issues related to psychological and emotional well-being.

5. *Continuum of disability.* Counselors must be mindful that disability occurs on a continuum of abilities. There are few, if any, individuals who have absolutely no abilities, and few, if any, who have superior mental, physical, cognitive, or intellectual attributes. Thus, we all exist on a continuum of abilities rather than disabilities.

6. *Psychosocial reaction or response of disability.* Psychosocial reaction or response is a highly individualized experience that is a complex interplay between the person's developmental phase of life, which has varying degrees of intensity, adjustment, and adaptation to the disability. There are physical, psychological, emotional, social, cognitive, vocational, and spiritual reactions to disability that cannot be represented by a theoretical model that has a beginning and end point. It is of paramount importance to also understand that psychosocial reaction or response to disability is a parallel process that affects family, friends, and significant others.

7. *Counseling from a coping skills and resiliency focus.* Competent counselors understand how to work with the individual and family members from a coping skills perspective and know how to assess the individual's resiliency traits. Cultivating resiliency skills are essential so that the individual can generalize past positive coping and resiliency resources to handle future critical life tasks and goals.

8. *Understanding the disability experience.* It is critical for counselors to understand that disability is a unique experience of a particular individual. Professionals and nonprofessionals alike, even if suffering from the same chronic illness or disability (i.e., cancer, diabetes, alcoholism, and spinal cord injury), should not assume that they know what the other person is experiencing. Competent counselors also understand that they should not enable, protect, or sympathize with their clients. Some individuals with disabilities may be difficult to work with, behaviorally and emotionally, because they may have multiple intense issues. Thus, professional counselors must empower their clients with numerous resources, remain objective, facilitate high levels of empathy (not sympathy), and facilitate optimal levels of functioning to increase the individual's quality of life (QOL). If the rehabilitation professional feels that he or she cannot serve the individual client because of his or her own personal issues (i.e., countertransference), has difficulty with being objective, and/or a lack of the appropriate skills or competence to work with a particular individual, then, ethically, the professional needs to consult the CRC Code of Ethics, consult with a supervisor, and perhaps refer this particular client to a different qualified professional.

9. *Recognize the individual as a survivor.* Viewing people with disabilities as victims of a traumatic event (e.g., traumatic brain injury and spinal cord injury) or those who have acquired a life-threatening disability (e.g., amyotrophic laterals sclerosis [ALS], cancer, and HIV/AIDS) diminishes the individual's survival, coping, and resiliency skills. The use of victim language negatively reinforces the stereotypes of the individual as being helpless and dependent and that his or her total identity is related to the multiple limitations confronting the individual's functionality and overall well-being. Viewing a person with disabilities as a survivor places the emphasis on the individual's ability to transcend some of life's most difficult challenges. When the individual is empowered with resources that cultivate increased resiliency, independence, and functional capacity, then the individual is a survivor, which is a starting point to live life optimally.

In summary, it is of paramount importance for counselors to recognize and understand that people with disabilities are not a member of one cultural group. Rather, these individuals comprise multiple roles, identities, attributes, and capabilities. There are many other guidelines that could be offered that relate to the individual's reaction to a disability as the individual changes and evolves throughout the life span. However, the aforementioned foundational guidelines are, in part, the basis for providing competent and ethical services to people with disabilities. If counselors cannot establish a rapport with their clients, they may have difficulty in forming a therapeutic alliance. Despite the paucity of quantitative data related to best practices, counselors who exhibit honest, direct, and empathic therapeutic relationships in a cultural-centered manner can offer clients a very good beginning point for counseling. Common issues related to specific disabilities are discussed using case study scenarios and discussion questions (see the Content Review Questions at the end of this chapter).

ONGOING CONSIDERATIONS

The Culture of Disability

There tends to be the myth that people with disabilities comprise one single group of individuals. However, there are a growing number of chronic illnesses and disabling conditions (i.e., HIV/AIDS, autism spectrum disorder, type 1 diabetes, and obesity) that affect the individual's mental, physical, cognitive, social, and vocational functioning and each condition has its own unique physiological, psychological, and cultural attributes. Fujiura and Yamaki (2000) suggest that as cultural diversity increases in the United States, the number of individuals with disabilities who come from diverse cultural backgrounds also increases. Counselors across a variety of work settings and theoretical orientations must be proficient, competent, and ethical in working with a range of people with disabilities who may be culturally different.

In a content analysis of multicultural counseling syllabi from CORE-accredited programs, Stebnicki and Cubero (2008) found that multicultural awareness and knowledge areas were addressed in course syllabi in terms of the course content and objectives. However, little attention was given to assisting professional RCs in developing the necessary and sufficient skills to work with people from diverse backgrounds in terms of counseling strategies and techniques. Indeed, there are universal and specific ways to engage in therapeutic interactions with people from a variety of cultural backgrounds. Yet, there is a unique overlay in terms of the level of awareness, knowledge, and skills required to work effectively with individuals who identify themselves as having a chronic illness or disability.

In a comprehensive work relating to the impact that race and culture has on people with disabilities, Balcazar, Suarez-Balcazar, Taylor-Ritzler, and Keys (2010) suggest that guidelines for best practices are rarely discussed in research and practice. As a consequence, the cultural implications of disability and the best counseling practices to facilitate work with this group are not clear. This situation is because there is little empirical evidence to guide RCs in facilitating specific therapeutic strategies, techniques, and services that would potentially work with the diversity of disabilities that exist. In research and practice, the language and constructs related to counseling people with disabilities tends to be described within the context of multicultural counseling skills. Although such models of multicultural counseling can be very applicable in practice, there are unique cultural attributes, differences, and similarities that relate to individuals who have a variety of medical, physical, cognitive, and mental health conditions that should be addressed by counselors.

Particular attention must be given to the counselor's perception of viewing the individual from purely a biological, medical, or psychopathology model of treatment. This perspective is one of the primary differences between rehabilitation counseling and other specialty practice areas (e.g., mental health counseling, community counseling, marriage and family counseling). Because rehabilitation counseling is a specialty that works with the medical, psychosocial, and vocational impact of people with disabilities, there is a complex overlay of the disability itself and its own unique cultural attributes that affect the individual's life functioning.

RCs not only are obligated to work with the mental health aspects of the individual, but also consider the complex psychosocial reactions that one might have with an acquired disability. Thus, it is imperative that professional counselors do not treat people with disabilities from purely a mental health or diagnostic category using traditional treatment protocols and counseling theories that are not culturally sensitive. For some individuals, the disability and the accompanying functional limitations may or may not pose a hindrance, obstacle, or challenge. Rather, it may be societal attitudes or architectural barriers that are the most difficult hurdle for the individual.

As Smart (2016) notes, there is not one single type of individual that comprises the total population we refer to as "people with disabilities" because there are multiple identities, roles, functional capacities, environments, and assets that encompass this group of individuals. In fact, people with disabilities consist of many other groups including, but not limited to, people who are older adults, gays or lesbians, African Americans, and Hispanics, as well as people representing a variety of professions (i.e., plumbers, politicians, teachers, lawyers, and physicians). Crabtree, Royeen, and Benton (2006, p. 4) note that being culturally proficient in rehabilitation practice is to truly understand the personal wishes, beliefs, preferences, choices, expectations, and values of people with disabilities. Likewise, Riggar and Maki (2004, p. 4) suggest that individuals with disabilities should be conceptualized as interacting within multiple contexts of life by viewing the person in a holistic and ecological perspective with the counselor facilitating strategies that focus on achieving a meaningful QOL.

In an ideal world, all counselor education programs would have course work relating to working with the cultural aspects of counseling people with disabilities. This course work would include the foundational concepts in rehabilitation and content areas related to the medical, psychosocial, and vocational aspects of various chronic illnesses and disabilities. Integral to providing services to people with disabilities in a competent and ethical manner is having the ability to generalize this awareness and knowledge into actual counseling strategies and techniques. Competencies in the rehabilitation counseling scope of practice begin by understanding that there is a continuum of abilities everyone possesses. Any differences that depart from "normal" biological, psychological, physical, cognitive, and developmental functioning should not be viewed as psychopathological or abnormal functioning. Rather, it is an expression of the unique cultural attributes that may have been acquired by birth or somewhere along the continuum of abilities within the personal growth and development of the individual.

Paradigm Shift

There has been a paradigm shift in the last 25 years from working with the individual who has a disability as the *patient* to the *client* (Smart & Smart, 2006; Vash, 1994). Working from the biomedical or *patient* model of disability does little to empower the individual with achieving optimal levels of wellness and independence. Hence, the biomedical model suggests that the "problem of disability" resides within the individual regardless of one's personal assets, attributes, and other abilities. As a consequence of this perceptual pattern, people with physiological deficits and psychopathology are viewed as deviating from the norm.

The use of various classification and diagnostic systems such as the *Diagnostic and Statistical Manual of Mental Disorders* (5th ed.; *DSM-5*; American Psychiatric Association [APA], 2013) further depreciates the individual's worth. As a consequence, the diagnostic category attributed to the person (e.g., borderline personality disorder, depression, and polysubstance abuse disorder) reinforces society's negative attitudes about the individual. This diagnosis can result in the perception that any mental, physical, or biological difference that deviates from the norm should be considered aberrant, flawed, or abnormal. As a consequence of not being perceived as "normal" in society, it is often concluded that the "problem" of the person's mental or physical condition resides within the individual. When people with disabilities are not provided opportunities or are intentionally marginalized in the workplace, recreational areas, social institutions, educational settings, and other public places, then this negative designation creates a majority–minority conflict. The emotional and psychological cost to the individual with the disability can be significant if they integrate such stereotypes and intentional acts of discrimination into their psychological and emotional well-being. As a consequence, Taylor and Epstein (1999) suggest that individuals with disabilities, particularly those with hidden disabilities, have significant mental health challenges of transforming feelings such as anger, depression, doubt, and shame into more healthy coping and resiliency functioning.

It is essential that counseling professionals recognize the paradigm when it comes to diagnosing and treating people with psychological conditions as delineated in the *DSM-5* (APA, 2013). Because there is a wide range of professionals involved with programs and services for people with psychological problems, it is critical that these professionals understand the fundamental concepts in dealing with people with disabilities during therapeutic interactions. People with occupational titles such as psychiatrists, psychologists, licensed clinical social workers, LPCs, RCs, mental health counselors, psychiatric nurses, psychiatric technicians, and mental health workers all have the responsibility and ethical obligation to work in a culturally sensitive manner with this unique population of individuals. Accordingly, any system that classifies the individual in relation to a "disorder" must be taken within context of the person's mental and physical capacity, holistic health functioning, and other contextual factors that may hinder full environmental participation and expression of the person's own unique cultural attributes.

The *International Classification of Functioning, Disability, and Health*; Beta-2 draft (*ICFDH-2*; World Health Organization [WHO], 2001)—referred to as the *ICF*—is an example of a classification system that is not based on a "disorder" of abnormal functioning. Peterson's (2011, 2016) research contributions with the revised *ICF* challenge professionals who serve individuals with psychological or psychiatric disabilities to view the person from a biopsychosocial model of diagnosis and treatment. Peterson's work delineates how psychopathology can be integrated into the *ICF* to assist mental health professionals in viewing their client's mental health functioning from (a) a body function and structure perspective, (b) the types of activities from which individuals are limited and restricted from participating, and (c) contextual factors such as environmental conditions and other sociocultural and personal factors.

Diagnosis and treatment of mental and physical disabilities require professionals to understand functioning from a holistic or biopsychosocial perspective. This necessity is because disabling conditions can affect multiple life areas such as the individual's mental, physical, cognitive, behavioral, social, vocational, and spiritual health and functioning. Because the *DSM-5* (APA, 2013) differs from the *ICF* classification system, Peterson (2011, 2016) suggests that the stakeholders of the *DSM-5* (APA, 2013) do not endorse the duality of the mind and body, which separates the physical from mental health aspects of "disorders" and health." Accordingly, rehabilitation professionals must provide services with concern for the individual's level of functioning, type of disability, and holistic health.

CONCLUSION

Building a rapport with a client in a person-centered and culturally sensitive manner requires that the counselor's own attitude toward people with disabilities be open, flexible, and genuine. Schneider Corey & Corey, (2016) suggest that person-centered approaches emphasize that counselors' attitudes toward their clients will affect the quality of the client–counselor relationship. This counselor reaction is communicated both verbally and nonverbally by genuineness, warmth, accurate empathy, unconditional acceptance, respect, and interpersonal communication skills that model culturally competent strategies and approaches.

Professionals who provide counseling services to people with disabilities must be competent not only in the foundational process skills of counseling, but also must pay particular attention to the cultural differences of disability and how their counseling approaches are communicated both verbally and nonverbally to their clients. Building client rapport and maintaining a strong working alliance can be a prime determinant of a positive outcome during therapeutic interactions.

CONTENT REVIEW QUESTIONS

- RCs possess a unique knowledge, awareness, and skill-set to work with the challenges people with disabilities face on a day-to-day basis across multiple life areas. Discuss

how does the rehabilitation counseling profession differ from other counseling specialty areas?
- Defining the construct of counseling is a considerable task. It is often misunderstood by the general public and clients themselves because of the multiple specialty areas within the larger practice of professional counseling. Compare and contrast the scope of practice and specific job functions/job settings in the rehabilitation counseling profession and other counseling-related professions. How are they similar? How do they differ?
- There are core skills that counselors use in the helping process. These therapeutic engagements are required to build a therapeutic relationship and help clients work through their specific problem issues. Name some specific core skills (e.g., attending, listening, empathy, challenging) and describe the intention of their use during the therapeutic process. Provide specific examples of these core skills and how they could be facilitated during client–counselor interactions.
- The most effective RCs are those described by self and others as empathetic, competent, and ethical practitioners. What are some elements or evaluative measures that lead to this perception of "the most effective RCs"?
- There are both universal and specific counseling approaches, programs, and services used during therapeutic interactions for people with disabilities. Provide some examples of specific therapeutic approaches, programs, and services typically facilitated for people with disabilities.

REFERENCES

American Counseling Association. (2016). 20/20: A vision for the future of counseling. Retrieved from http://www.counseling.org/knowledge-center/20-20-a-vision-for-the-future-of-counseling/consensus-definition-of-counseling

American Psychiatric Association. (2013). *Diagnostic and statistical manual of mental disorders* (5th ed.). Arlington, VA: American Psychiatric Publishing.

Arokiasamy, C. V. (1993). A theory for rehabilitation? *Rehabilitation Education, 7,* 77–98.

Balcazar, F. E., Suarez-Balcazar, Y., Taylor-Ritzler, T., & Keys, C. B. (2010). *Race, culture, and disability: Rehabilitation science and practice.* Sudbury, MA: Jones & Bartlett.

Bernacchio, C., Burker, E. J., Falvo, D., Porter, P., & Carone, S. (2008). Specializations in rehabilitation counseling: One Program's vision. *Rehabilitation Education, 22*(3/4), 185–192.

Cormier, S., & Nurius, P. S. (2003). *Interviewing and change strategies for helpers* (5th ed.). Pacific Grove, CA: Brooks/Cole.

Commission on Rehabilitation Counselor Certification. (2016). CRC/CRCC scope of practice. Retrieved June 28, 2016, from https://www.crccertification.com/crc-crcc-scope-of-practice

Corey, G., Schneider Corey, M. S., Corey, C., & Callahan, P. (2015). *Issues and ethics in the helping professions* (9th ed.). Belmont, CA: Brooks/Cole, Cengage.

Corey, M. S. (2010). *Creating your professional path: Lesson from my journey.* Alexandria, VA: American Counseling Association.

Cottone, R. R., & Tarvydas, V. M. (2007). *Counseling ethics and decision making* (3rd ed.). Upper Saddle River, NJ: Merrill/Prentice Hall.

Council on Rehabilitation Education. (2016). Clinical rehabilitation counseling. Retrieved from http://www.core-rehab.org/Files/Doc/PDF/Clinical%20Rehabilitation%20Counseling%20Standards.%20FINAL.pdf

Crabtree, J. L., Royeen, M., & Benton, J. (2006). Cultural proficiency in rehabilitation: An introduction. In M. Royeen & J. L. Crabtree (Eds.), *Culture in rehabilitation: From competency to proficiency* (pp. 1–16). Upper Saddle River, NJ: Pearson Prentice Hall.

D'Andrea, M., & Daniels, J. (2001). Respectful counseling: An integrative model for counselors. In D. Pope-Davis & H. Coleman (Eds.), *The interface of class, culture, and gender in counseling* (pp. 417–466). Thousand Oaks, CA: Sage.

Egan, G. (2014). *The skilled helper: A problem-management and opportunity-development approach to helping* (10th ed.) Belmont, CA: Brooks/Cole.

Frey, G. L., & Hutchins Pirnot, K. (2008). *As I am: A true story of adaptation to physical disability*. Sarasota, FL: The Peppertree Press.

Fujiura, G. T., & Yamaki, K. (2000). Trends in demography of childhood poverty and disability. *Exceptional Children, 66*(2), 187–199.

Goodwin, L. R. (2006). Rehabilitation counselor specialty areas offered by rehabilitation counselor education programs. *Rehabilitation Education, 20*(2), 133–134.

Goodwin, L. R. (2016). Professional disclosure in counseling. In I. Marini & M. A. Stebnicki (Eds.), *The professional counselor's desk reference* (2nd ed., pp. 69–79). New York, NY: Springer Publishing.

Hackney, H. L., & Cormier, S. (2009). *The professional counselor: A process guide to helping*. Upper Saddle River, NJ: Pearson.

Health Insurance Portability and Accountability Act. (2010). Understanding HIPPA privacy. Retrieved from http://www.hhs.gov/ocr/privacy/hipaa/understanding/index.html

Ivey, A. E., Bradford Ivey, M., & Zalaquett, C. P. (2014). *Intentional interviewing & counseling: Facilitating client development in a multicultural society* (8th ed.). Belmont, CA: Brooks/Cole, Cengage.

Johnston, S. P., Tarvydas, V. M., & Bulter, M. (2016). Managing risk in ethical and legal situations. In I. Marini & M. A. Stebnicki (Eds.), *The professional counselor's desk reference* (2nd ed., pp. 61–68). New York, NY: Springer Publishing.

Leahy, M. J., Rak, E., & Zanskus, S. A. (2016). A brief history of counseling and specialty areas of practice. In I. Marini & M. A. Stebnicki (Eds.), *The professional counselor's desk reference* (2nd ed., pp. 3–8). New York, NY: Springer Publishing.

Lopez Levers, L. (2012). Disability issues in a global context. In D. R. Maki & V. M. Tarvydas (Eds.), *The professional practice of rehabilitation counseling* (pp. 165–190). New York, NY: Springer Publishing.

Lustig, D. C, Strauser, D. R., Rice, N. D, & Rucker, T. F. (2002). The relationship between working alliance and rehabilitation outcomes. *Rehabilitation Counseling Bulletin, 46,* 25–33.

National Council on Rehabilitation Education. (2016). Website. Retrieved from https://ncre.org

Patterson, C. H. (1957). Counselor or coordinator. *Journal of Rehabilitation, 23*(3), 13–15.

Patterson, C. H. (1966). The rehabilitation counselor: A projection. *Journal of Rehabilitation, 32*(1), 31, 49.

Peterson, D. B. (2011). *Psychological aspects of functioning, disability, and health*. New York, NY: Springer Publishing.

Peterson, D. B. (2016). The International Classification of Functioning, Disability, and Health: Applications for professional counseling. In I. Marini & M. A. Stebnicki (Eds.), *The professional counselor's desk reference* (2nd ed., pp. 329–341). New York, NY: Springer Publishing.

Remley, T. P., & Herlihy, B. (2005). *Ethical, legal, and professional issues in counseling* (2nd ed.). Upper Saddle River, NJ: Prentice Hall.

Riggar, T. F., & Maki, D. R. (2004). *Handbook of rehabilitation counseling*. New York, NY: Springer Publishing.

Robles, B. (2016). A synopsis of the Health Insurance and Portability and Accountability Act and the Affordable Care Act. In I. Marini & M. A. Stebnicki (Eds.), *The professional counselor's desk reference* (2nd ed., pp. 43–48). New York, NY: Springer Publishing.

Rubin, S. E., & Roessler, R. T. (1978). *Foundations of the vocational rehabilitation process*. Baltimore, MD: University Park Press.

Schneider Corey, M., & Corey, G. (2016). *Becoming a helper* (7th ed.). Belmont, CA: Brooks/Cole, Cengage.

Smart, J. F. (2001). *Disability, society, and the individual*. Gaithersburg, MD: Aspen.

Smart, J. F. (2016). Counseling individuals with disabilities. In I. Marini & M. A. Stebnicki (Eds.), *The professional counselor's desk reference* (2nd ed., pp. 417–421). New York, NY: Springer Publishing.

Smart, J. F., & Smart, D. W. (2006). Models of disability: Implications for the counseling profession. *Journal of Counseling and Development, 84,* 29–40.

Stebnicki, M. A. (2008a). A call for integral approaches in the professional identity of rehabilitation counseling: Three specialty areas, one profession. A joint special issue in *Rehabilitation Counseling Bulletin and Journal of Applied Rehabilitation Counseling. Journal of Applied Rehabilitation Counseling, 39*(4), 64–68.

Stebnicki, M. A. (2008b). *Empathy fatigue: Healing the mind, body, and spirit of professional counselors*. New York, NY: Springer Publishing.

Stebnicki, M. A. (2016). From empathy fatigue to empathy resiliency. In I. Marini & M. A. Stebnicki (Eds.), *The professional counselor's desk reference* (2nd ed., pp. 533–545). New York, NY: Springer Publishing.

Stebnicki, M. A. (2017). *Disaster mental health counseling: Responding to trauma in a multicultural context*. New York, NY: Springer Publishing.

Stebnicki, M. A., & Cubero, C. (2008). A content analysis of multicultural counseling syllabi from rehabilitation counseling programs. *Rehabilitation Education, 22*(2), 89–100.

Stout, C. E., & Hayes, R. A. (2005). *Evidence-based practice: Methods, models, and tools for mental health professionals.* Hoboken, NJ: Wiley.

Tarvydas, V. M., Hartley, M. T., & Gerald, M. (2016). What practitioners need to know about professional credentialing? In I. Marini & M. A. Stebnicki (Eds.), *The Professional counselor's desk reference* (2nd ed., pp. 17–22). New York, NY: Springer Publishing.

Taylor, S., & Epstein, R. (1999). *Living well with a hidden disability: Transcending doubt and shame and reclaiming your life.* Oakland, CA: New Harbinger.

Vanier, J. (2007). The contributions of the physically and mentally handicapped to development. In A. E. Dell Orto & P. W. Power (Eds.), *The psychological and social impact of illness and disability* (5th ed., pp. 101–107). New York, NY: Springer Publishing.

Vash, C. L. (1994). *Personality and adversity: Psychospiritual aspects of rehabilitation.* New York, NY: Springer Publishing.

Vash, C. L., & Crewe, N. M. (2004). *Psychology of disability* (2nd ed.). New York, NY: Springer Publishing.

Walsh, R. J. (2016). Contracting strategies with managed care and other agencies. In I. Marini & M. A. Stebnicki (Eds.), *The professional counselor's desk reference* (2nd ed., pp. 49–54). New York, NY: Springer Publishing.

Walsh, R. J., & Dasenbrook, N. C. (2009). Contracting strategies with managed care and other agencies. In I. Marini & M. A. Stebnicki (Eds.), *The professional counselor's desk reference* (pp. 79–87). New York, NY: Springer Publishing.

Whitehouse, F. A. (1975). Rehabilitation clinician. *Journal of Rehabilitation, 41*(3), 24–26.

World Health Organization. (2001). *International classification of functioning, disability and health: ICF.* Geneva, Switzerland: Author.

Wright, G. N. (1980). *Total rehabilitation.* Boston, MA: Little, Brown.

THIRTEEN

Case Management

MARTHA H. CHAPIN, MAGGIE K. BUTLER, AND VANESSA M. PERRY

LEARNING OBJECTIVES

After reading this chapter, you should be able to:

- Define case management and caseload management.
- Describe the role of a case manager in the rehabilitation process.
- Understand the purpose of medical, psychological, and vocational case management.
- Explain how your client would benefit from medical, psychological, and vocational case management.
- Explain how Lewy body dementia (LBD) can affect a client's rehabilitation.

As rehabilitation counselors (RCs), we are trained to research and problem-solve the services our clients need to help them "achieve their personal, social, psychological, and vocational goals" (Rehabilitation Counseling Consortium [RCC], as cited in Maki & Tarvydas, 2012, p. 4). We have an arsenal of tools at our disposal, including knowledge of medical, psychological, and vocational resources, as well as the administrative expertise to communicate our needs, wants, and desires to other professionals in the field. All of these services have the end goal of helping our clients reach their desired goals.

In this chapter, we describe the value of case management for RCs. We then present a case and walk the reader through the case management process required of the RC assisting this client, discussing her medical, psychological, and vocational case management needs from initial referral to case closure. Because a client's needs may change as the client ages, we review this same case each decade of the client's life to see how her needs change throughout her life span.

VALUE OF CASE MANAGEMENT

RCs use case management skills in both their professional and their personal lives. **Case management** is "a collaborative process of assessment, planning, facilitation, care coordination, evaluation and advocacy for options and services to meet an individual's and family's comprehensive health needs through communication and [the use of] available resources to promote patient safety, quality of care, and cost-effective outcomes" (Case Management Society of America [CMSA], 2016, p. 11). This definition includes family, based on "legislative and regulatory changes affecting professional case management practice" (CMSA, 2016, p. 10), because family members or family caregivers are part of the client's support system and play an integral role in caring for the client. As RCs, our job is to be aware of family dynamics. Depending on the RC's role and the client's request, the RC may assess the needs of the client and the family and, through collaboration with the client and family, create a case management plan that will effectively serve the client. This plan includes educating the client and family about available resources, linking them to these resources, discussing financial responsibility, and facilitating the client's access to these resources (CMSA, 2016).

RCs use case management skills in a variety of work settings, including public rehabilitation, private for-profit rehabilitation, behavioral health treatment programs, community-based rehabilitation, private not-for-profit rehabilitation programs, and managed care (CMSA, 2016; Shaw, Leahy, & Chan, 2005). Case management is also used in hospitals and integrated care delivery systems; ambulatory care clinics and community-based organizations; corporations; schools; public health insurance and benefit programs; private health insurance programs; government-sponsored programs; geriatric services; long-term care; end-of-life, hospice, palliative, and respite care programs; physician and medical groups; life care planning (LCP); as well as health, wellness, prevention, and disease management programs (CMSA, 2016, p. 14). The number of work sites using case management demonstrates how RCs might use these same skills throughout their own life span to help themselves and their families traverse life's challenges.

Knowledge of case management can be demonstrated through credentialing in this specialized area of expertise. There are three primary certifications for RCs who provide case management services. These certifications include becoming a certified rehabilitation counselor (Commission on Rehabilitation Counselor Certification [CRCC], 2016), a certified disability management specialist (Certification of Disability Management Specialist [CDMS], 2014a), or a certified case manager (Commission for Case Management Certification [CCMC], n.d.; Shaw et al., 2005). Certification as an RC is the credential specifically designated for RCs (CRCC, 2016) and is recommended for graduates of rehabilitation counseling programs. RCs obtain certification as disability management specialists when they practice in insurance-based rehabilitation (CDMS, 2014b) and as case managers when their primary job duty is case management (CCMC, n.d.; see Chapter 3).

Caseload management has been defined as "how to work with more than one case at a time, how to select which case to work with, how to move from one case to another, how to establish a system to insure movement of all cases, and how to meet objectives one has established" (Henke, Connolly, & Cox, 1975, as cited in Greenwood & Roessler, 2006). This definition focuses on the management of all cases on the RC's caseload. For public RCs, caseload sizes range from 85 to 205 cases, with an average caseload size of 143 cases (Dew, Alan, & Tomlinson, 2008), whereas disability management specialists have caseload sizes ranging from 26 to 50 cases (Rosenthal, Hursh, Lui, Isom, & Sasson, 2007). The clients on the RC's caseload have to be in different phases of the rehabilitation process for the RC to meet quotas for successful case closure. Therefore, caseload management requires that RCs effectively plan, manage, and evaluate each client's case to help clients accomplish their goals in a timely manner. The RC also needs to manage his or her own time effectively and prioritize which cases to service first (Greenwood & Roessler, 2006). This includes allowing time for unexpected caseload needs to arise during the course of the day and anticipating that caseload management tasks will take longer than projected. One way to effectively manage a caseload is for the RC to "touch" each case on his or her caseload monthly. This would require the RC to divide all of the cases by the number of days available in the month and each day check the status of the clients on that day's schedule and provide these clients with the needed services. Through the course of the month, the RC would have "touched" each case (Emmerton, 2016).

One key aspect of caseload management is case documentation. **Case documentation** may include case notes documenting the RC's interactions with the client and other service providers (CRCC, 2017). Typically, the RC schedules an initial interview with the client to gather medical, psychological, vocational, and financial information. Following this meeting, the RC writes an initial assessment report and establishes recommendations or treatment goals. These recommendations may include contacting the client's medical and psychological providers to gather information to document the existence of a disability, which may be required for the client to be eligible for services. Letters to request information and to refer the client for services may also be needed. Progress reports or case notes are written to document the activities completed based on the recommendations. Additional recommendations will be made to move the client toward medical or psychological stability, return to work, and a more independent lifestyle. The frequency of these reports depends upon agency guidelines, but likely occurs every 30, 60, or 90 days. If the RC is working for a fee-for- service agency, a bill documenting the time spent by the RC providing these case services will be included with the initial assessment or progress reports. Today electronic health records are used more often than paper case files.

CASE MANAGEMENT PROCESS

The case management process is cyclical rather than linear, and recurrent rather than unidirectional (CMSA, 2016). There are six primary steps in this process: (1) "client identification, selection and engagement in professional case management; . . . (2) assessment and opportunity identification; . . . (3) development of the case management plan of care; . . . (4) implementation and coordination of the case management plan of care; . . . (5) monitoring and evaluation of the case management plan of care; . . . and (6) closure of the professional case management services" (CMSA, 2016, pp. 18–19).

To implement these steps, the RC usually receives a referral either directly from the client or from another agency. Once the referral is received, the RC reviews the client's case file, meets with the client to complete an initial assessment, and then explores the client's medical, psychological, and vocational case management needs (Chapin, 2005a, 2005b; Roessler & Rubin, 2006; Rubin & Roessler, 2008). If the client is eligible for services, the RC develops a treatment plan and decides which steps are needed to help the client achieve his or her goals. Throughout the case management process, the RC monitors and evaluates the services the client is receiving and modifies the treatment plan as needed. Additional details on each stage of the case management process will follow.

File Receipt and Review

When receiving referrals for new clients, RCs will likely receive some basic background information about them, such as their name, age, gender, type of disability, and reason for referral. In order to comprehend clients' stories, RCs should review each of the documents found in clients' files. RCs can expect to review educational records, medical records, psychological evaluations, vocational evaluations, and so forth. In reviewing what documents are present in case files, RCs will also be able to observe what information is notably absent (Roessler & Rubin, 2006; Rubin & Roessler, 2008).

Conferring with previous service providers may help RCs gain insight into the history of clients' presenting condition(s), supports clients have utilized in the past, and clients' prognoses. In order for RCs to request records from other service providers, clients must complete a written release of information. Releases of information should be prepared by RCs and should include the client's name and the nature of documents requested (e.g., vocational evaluation report, counseling diagnosis and clinical impressions, medical history). RCs should take care to interpret documents within their scope of practice and consult with experts when interpreting documents beyond their scope. This is true for the medical, psychological, and vocational case management areas described next.

Medical Case Management

Each step in the rehabilitation process has multiple facets. For example, medical case management can encompass discharge planning and assist a client in the client's transfer to long-term care, a skilled nursing facility, or home. Skilled nursing facilities include nursing homes, intermediate care facilities, and extended care facilities. Hospice care may also be needed by a client (Powell & Tahan, 2010), but most RCs will not coordinate transfer to hospice care. A client who transfers home may need the RC's assistance in finding and compensating home health aides, coordinating environmental modifications, hiring a personal care attendant, and ensuring that home health care services are provided. Home health care services and outpatient treatment may require coordination with nurses, occupational and physical therapists, speech and language pathologists, audiologists, prosthetists, and orthotists, to name just a few areas of medical case management. Follow-up with a client's treating physician or referral to a new physician may also be necessary (Chapin, 2005a, 2005b; Roessler & Rubin, 2006). In conjunction with medical case management, psychological issues may also have to be addressed. Box 13.1 summarizes information to be included in a referral letter or a letter requesting information about a client.

Psychological Case Management

Psychological case management may require assisting the client in referral to a mental health professional. The mental health professional may treat the client's mental health or addiction concerns, assist in adjustment to disability, address issues of domestic violence, or help the client cope with surviving a crisis or disaster, as well as deal with issues of sexuality that occur as a result of the client's disabling condition. Pain management treatment may also be required (Chapin, 2005b). For clients with substance abuse or mental health concerns, referral to a day treatment program or halfway house may be required. A psychological or neuropsychological evaluation may be completed if additional information regarding the client's cognitive and emotional functioning is required (Roessler & Rubin, 2006). Although medical and psychological case management is being pursued, discussions regarding return to work may also occur.

Vocational Case Management

Vocational case management requires that RCs have knowledge of their clients' educational background and prior work and volunteer experiences. This information, in conjunction with medical and psychological knowledge, facilitates decisions regarding

---

BOX 13.1   Information to Include in a Referral Letter and Letter Requesting Information

Referral letter

- Return address
- Date
- Mailing address
- Regarding line
- Introduction of you and your relationship to the client—why are you helping this client?
- Purpose of the letter—reason for referral, current issue(s) to be resolved
- Appointment date if already scheduled
- Biopsychosocial history relevant to the diagnosis (Ask yourself, does the person to whom I am making the referral need to know this information about my client to facilitate effective treatment?)
- Desired outcome—diagnosis, prognosis, current treatment plans, specific questions you need answered
- If you are making a referral for physical therapy, occupational therapy, or work hardening, include the prescription from the physician for treatment
- Statement related to the release of information, if attached
- Signature line
- Enclosures, if applicable—list information enclosed

Letters requesting information

- Return address
- Date
- Mailing address
- Regarding line
- Introduction of you and your relationship to the client—why are you helping this client?
- Purpose of the letter—reason for referral, current issue to be resolved
- Desired outcome—diagnosis, prognosis, current treatment plans, specific questions you need answered
- Statement related to the release of information, if attached
- Signature line
- Enclosures, if applicable—list information enclosed

Remember to write the letters clearly and succinctly.

---

the client's ability to return to work. The return-to-work process includes exploring return to work with the same or a different employer in the same job or in a new job with or without job modifications. If employment is not possible, then coordinating short-term retraining to facilitate return to work with the same or a new employer, or self-employment, may be pursued (Matkin, 1981; Welch, 1979). To facilitate return to work, the RC will contact the employer, if one exists at the time of injury or illness, and discuss the client's ability to return to work. If returning to work with the former employer is possible, the RC may obtain a functional capacity evaluation from the treating physician or another health care professional and may complete a job analysis that is reviewed with the treating physician to ensure placement into a physically appropriate job (Chapin, 2005a, 2005b; Roessler & Rubin, 2006).

If returning to work with the same employer in the same or a similar job is not possible, the RC may need to look at developing a new job goal and alternate job placement. Techniques the RC may use to help determine a new job goal within the client's physical capabilities include a transferable skills analysis and labor market survey. The RC may also use an on-the-job evaluation to determine if a new job or short-term retraining is appropriate or if on-the-job training is needed to transition a client into a new job. If a new job is pursued, the client may also need assistance with developing a résumé and cover letter and learning job-seeking skills. A functional capacity evaluation may be needed and a job analysis may be completed and reviewed with the treating physician in order for the RC to obtain a release to return to work (Chapin, 2005a, 2005b).

If the aforementioned techniques are not beneficial in helping the client return to work, the client may benefit from the RC providing interest and aptitude testing to help the client develop a job goal. If more in-depth testing is required to help a client develop a job goal, the RC may refer the client for a vocational evaluation. Some of these techniques are discussed in the case study of Carla. The reader should note how medical, psychological, and vocational aspects of the case management process overlap in the following case study.

CASE STUDY

CASE NARRATIVE

Carla is a 45-year-old woman with major depressive disorder who was recently diagnosed with early onset LBD with hallucinations. Carla has scheduled an appointment with an RC at her public vocational rehabilitation (VR) services office. The RC reviews the initial assessment and researches LBD in preparation for Carla's visit.

LBD is a brain disorder that affects more than 1 million Americans. Often compared to Alzheimer's disease and Parkinson's disease, LBD is characterized by abnormal protein deposits in the brain. Consequently, thought, movement, behavior, and mood are negatively affected. Because LBD affects many parts of the brain, clients may have both physical and psychological manifestations. Physical manifestations may include problems with motor functioning, including difficulty walking or rigidity (parkinsonism), rapid eye movement (REM) sleep behavior disorders, and difficulty recognizing smells (National Institutes of Health [NIH], National Institute of Aging, National Institute of Neurological Disorders and Stroke, 2015). From a physical perspective, clients may also experience syncope (fainting) and frequent falls (Galvin et al., 2008).

People affected by LBD may have difficulty performing activities of daily living or managing personal finances, and may experience hallucinations. LBD is progressive in

(continued)

CASE STUDY *(continued)*

nature and most commonly diagnosed at age 50 or later. Individuals with LBD often live with the disease for 5 to 7 years (from diagnosis to death), but the disease may also span 2 to 20 years. At onset, individuals with LBD may express symptoms of dementia, unpredictable changes in ability to concentrate, and depressed mood. Up to 8% of people with LBD experience hallucinations. As LBD becomes terminal, people with LBD may rely almost entirely on others for care. The etiology of LBD remains unknown (NIH et al., 2015).

Initial Assessment

When the initial referral was received, the RC would likely have received records such as a neurological assessment and medical report. Carla's RC should consult with a medical expert when interpreting her neurological assessment. Medical records would provide information about Carla's diagnosis of having LBD. The RC has gathered the following information about Carla.

Carla, in her mid-40s, has been experiencing difficulty at work and will be terminated from her position as a nursing assistant at the end of the month due to her lack of interpersonal skills and causing dissension among coworkers. Carla has worked with an RC in the past and believes she will need assistance in finding new employment, as she now has the responsibility of maintaining medical insurance for herself and her husband (who is not working due to illness). Carla is extremely anxious because her husband physically abuses her and she knows that a loss of employment and a new diagnosis will trigger his abuse.

Carla explained that she feels as if she gets along with her coworkers; however, she believes that they plotted against her and that is the reason she was terminated. She states that her employer never gave her a warning and just informed her that she would lose her job. Carla reports that she uncovered that her employer was a prostitute and that is why she was fired by her employer.

Carla explains to the RC that there is no cure for her LBD and the doctors have given her clozapine for her hallucinations. Carla does not believe she has hallucinations and does not want to take the medication, but has agreed to take it to see how it makes her feel. Carla states that she has to make regular appointments with her physician to have her blood drawn, so she does not acquire a rare blood disease due to the clozapine. Blood tests are needed because "clozapine can decrease the number of neutrophils, a type of white blood cell, that function in the body to fight off infections" (U.S. Food and Drug Administration, 2015, para. 2). Carla believes this blood work may impede her work schedule.

Medical Case Management

One of the recommendations from the initial assessment is to obtain medical documentation of Carla's LBD. Physicians who treat LBD include neurologists, geriatric psychiatrists, and neuropsychologists (Lewy Body Dementia Association [LBDA], 2016a). Since a neurologist is treating Carla, medical records will be requested from the neurologist to

(continued)

CASE STUDY (*continued*)

gain a better understanding of Carla's diagnosis and how LBD is affecting Carla. Medical testing that might be received from the neurologist includes results from a magnetic resonance imaging, electroencephalography reports, and a cerebrospinal fluid analysis (Moellenhauer et al., 2010). Because Carla will soon be terminated from her job as a nursing assistant, the RC will ask the physician about Carla's functional capabilities for work. Contact with Carla's neurologist reveals that she is experiencing cognitive rather than physical limitations from her LBD.

Psychological Case Management

Overall, Carla could benefit from counseling support to help her navigate the many obstacles she is facing in her life, such as loss of employment, adjustment to disability, domestic violence, poor interpersonal communication, and symptoms of depression. If Carla's RC works at an agency that does not allow RCs to provide mental health counseling and Carla is not currently receiving counseling services, the RC should refer Carla to a clinical mental health counselor so that she may receive additional support as she navigates life with LBD.

Counseling could also help Carla explore and improve her interpersonal skills, given that they are the reason for dismissal from her previous employer. In counseling, Carla may also have the opportunity to explore what losing her job has meant to her and what effect it might have had on her self-concept. As LBD progresses, counseling may also help Carla process what having a disability is like and teach her positive coping strategies. Counseling could also provide an opportunity for Carla to discuss her marriage, the cycle of abuse, and supports available to her as a woman in a domestic violence situation.

Carla reports a diagnosis of major depressive disorder. This diagnosis indicates that Carla's mental health has been treated in the past. Requesting her mental health records will help the RC understand her diagnosis and how it affects Carla. Since Carla has already been diagnosed with LBD, the RC should request a neuropsychological assessment, which will provide medical documentation so Carla will be eligible for services from state VR.

Vocational Case Management

After the RC has acknowledged and discussed the impact of Carla's medical, psychological, and familial issues with Carla, vocational exploration can begin. Reviewing the functional capacity evaluation prior to creating Carla's vocational plan will prove advantageous due to Carla's comorbidity (depression and LBD). Depending on the results of that evaluation, maintaining employment as a nursing assistant may or may not be a viable vocational option for Carla. If working as a nursing assistant is determined to be an option, identification of workplace accommodations should be explored for medication management and interpersonal issues (e.g., use of a mentor or supervisor when behavior become unprofessional; Job Accommodation Network, 2016).

In the event Carla is unable to pursue employment as a nursing assistant, vocational exploration will be necessary. Vocational exploration may include activities such as vocational evaluations/assessments, which assess work preferences, skills, and capacity

(*continued*)

CASE STUDY (*continued*)

to work in a variety of roles (Roessler & Rubin, 2006). Equally important is an assessment of prospective work environments Carla is interested in pursuing. Conducting a job analysis will help Carla and the RC identify the physical and mental demands of jobs, environmental stressors, hazards, and characteristics of the work environment (Roessler & Rubin, 2006).

RCs have an ethical obligation to maintain case files in an appropriate manner (American Counseling Association [ACA, 2014] *Code of Ethics*; CRCC *Code of Professional Ethics for Rehabilitation Counselors* (2017); National Board for Certified Counselors *Code of Ethics* [NBCC, 2012]). In the case of Carla, case file management is imperative. Carla's history of ruptured relationships may recur in the counselor–client dynamic. Maintaining appropriate and consistent case files will assist in documenting conflicts and monitoring Carla's progress in her vocational endeavors.

CASE MANAGEMENT THROUGH THE LIFE SPAN

Viewing Carla's case management needs throughout her life span demonstrates the cyclical and recurrent nature of case management (CMSA, 2016).

Carla in Her Mid-50s

Carla has found herself back at Vocational Rehabilitation Services because she was just released from a mental health facility. Carla reports that her relationship with her only son is strained because he had Carla committed. Carla believes the reason for her committal was that she uncovered that her daughter-in-law was laundering money from her place of employment. Since the last time working with the RC, Carla reports her LBD has been the same and that she does not need to continue the use of medication.

Carla's husband has since passed away and she is living in their house, which is about 45 minutes away from her son. Carla would like to pursue a nursing assistant position, as that is the only work she enjoys; however, Carla is trying to pass the Certified Nursing Assistant examination (American Red Cross, 2016) without much success.

Medical Case Management

Although there are no physical issues for the RC to address at this time, the RC should request updated medical information from Carla's neurologist to stay abreast of Carla's medical status.

Psychological Case Management

Upon release from mental health inpatient care, clients usually have follow-up mental health services coordinated by a discharge planner. The RC should seek permission from Carla to follow up with aftercare providers to ensure streamlined services for Carla. Her son's involvement in her involuntary commitment would have likely damaged their relationship and put strain on their family as a whole. The RC should ask Carla about family

(*continued*)

CASE STUDY (*continued*)

members' relationships with one another and see if additional support is needed. A referral to a marriage and family therapist could help Carla's family address conflict and concerns about Carla. The RC may want to address possible unresolved grief and bereavement from the passing of Carla's husband and how the family as a whole is handling his loss. Additionally, Carla should continue to receive medication management.

Vocational Case Management

Collaborating with providers is an essential function of case management for RCs (Leahy & Kline, 2014). Carla's RC should gather as much information as possible concerning the committal from Carla and the appropriate medical professionals. Obtaining current medical information can assist in identifying whether Carla has a release to return to work from her treating provider and factors that may impact her vocational plan (i.e., noncompliance with medication). In addition, updating the functional capacity evaluation is necessary to develop appropriate vocational goals.

Carla's difficulty in passing the Certified Nursing Assistant examination (American Red Cross, 2016) may cause frustration and conflict within the counselor–client alliance. Carla may express resistance to pursuing employment that is out of her comfort zone. Revisiting vocational assessments and evaluations will aid Carla in identifying additional employment opportunities she enjoys and has the skills to pursue. RCs can further support clients in new positions by providing on-the-job training. On-the-job-training allows clients to have one-on-one training, which should acclimate them to their work responsibilities and the work environment.

Carla in Her Mid-60s

Carla is about to lose a job she obtained through a neighbor. She reports that she recently was diagnosed with breast cancer, but doesn't believe the diagnosis and has refused treatment. Carla states that she feels just fine and really needs to work. She has changed treating physicians and is no longer taking her medication for LBD. Carla does not want to receive financial help from her son and is resistant to applying for supplemental security income (SSI) due to the lengthy application process and the fact that none of the people she knows was ever able to receive the benefit.

Carla is now living in a low-income independent living community because maintaining her home was too much for her. She enjoys the people in the community, but needs work to maintain her living expenses. Carla is determined to be as independent as possible and plans to work hard until the end of her life.

Medical Case Management

The RC would request medical information regarding the breast cancer diagnosis from Carla's treating physician. If further medical treatment is recommended, the RC will discuss treatment options with Carla. However, if Carla refuses treatment, the RC must honor Carla's decision and would document in Carla's case file concerning her decision to refuse treatment.

(continued)

CASE STUDY (*continued*)

Psychological Case Management

Carla has recently received a serious diagnosis: breast cancer. Denying the veracity of her diagnosis is a significant barrier to Carla's treatment. The RC should review medical documentation of the diagnosis with Carla and explore her denial of the diagnosis and general feelings about cancer. Particularly, what previous experience with cancer does Carla have? What are her thoughts about loved ones' cancer treatments? Carla has had difficulty maintaining employment throughout the years. The RC should explore how Carla's self-concept related to employment has evolved throughout the years and offer support as she faces dismissal from a job. Carla's perspective about the role employment may take in her life will evolve as she ages and considers whether or not she would like to be a member of the workforce. Carla's psychiatrist should continue to monitor hallucinations and provide medication management.

Vocational Case Management

Assessing Carla's functional capacity to work is central to moving forward with a vocational plan. Understanding how Carla's new diagnosis of breast cancer will impact her overall health, medications, treatments, and psychological health is imperative to identifying her capacity to carry out job functions. Case management is grounded in the premises of client choice and minimizing value imposition at all costs (Leahy & Kline, 2014). Some RCs may struggle with Carla's choice to continue to work given her previous work history and her medical conditions. As long as Carla is medically cleared to work with supports, she should be afforded the opportunity to seek vocational opportunities.

As Carla's medical issues have increased, she may require a comprehensive employment accommodation evaluation. Consequently, reviewing a job analysis with her medical provider would be helpful to identify the most appropriate vocational environment. As Carla's interpersonal issues continue to persist, a behavioral plan may have to be developed to monitor relationships with employees and employers. Carla can be successful with attention to medical, physical, psychological, and vocational needs.

Carla at Her Mid-70s

Carla did not show up for work, and the employer contacted the RC on file. Because the RC had a release of information on file to talk with Carla's personal care attendant, the RC called the attendant and asked the personal care attendant to check on Carla. The attendant found Carla passed out at her home. Carla was taken to a local hospital where doctors informed Carla and her family that she had 6 months to 1 year to live. The doctor recommended locating hospice care for Carla.

Medical Case Management

Because Carla was hospitalized, the RC would gather current medical information regarding the recent hospitalization and the recommendation for hospice care. If the RC works at an agency whose purpose is to assist Carla with employment, then the RC will be

(*continued*)

CASE STUDY (*continued*)

required to refer Carla to another agency to coordinate her hospice care. The RC or new case manager may attend the treatment team meeting and work directly with the discharge planner at the hospital to coordinate hospice care. Carla and her son, in conjunction with Carla's physician, will decide whether Carla will receive home hospice care or inpatient care. Because a personal care attendant has assisted Carla in her home, Carla's home may already be equipped with a temporary ramp to allow easy entrance and exit. Carla might also benefit from home health care services, including a nurse to draw her blood because she is still on clozapine.

As Carla's condition deteriorates, she may benefit from physical therapy to decrease the rapid decline of physical functioning and mobility and from occupational therapy to assist her in activities of daily living, particularly self-care needs (Galvin et al., 2008). Grab bars, a raised toilet seat, and a tub transfer chair for the bathroom may be required to assist Carla in her activities of daily living. If Carla has difficulty ambulating, a walker, and then a wheelchair, would assist her with mobility. Carla has previously been using the services of a personal care attendant, and the need for the attendant will increase as her health declines. Furthermore, Carla's dementia will affect her thinking, remembering, and reasoning skills. At some point, the cost of inpatient care, possibly in an Alzheimer's unit, at a nursing home or assisted living facility may be less than the cost of a personal care attendant. Also, as Carla's health declines, she may need inpatient hospice care (U.S. Department of Health and Human Services, NIH, National Institute of Aging, 2016). Since Carla is in her 70s, she would be eligible for Medicare. Medicare should cover Carla's hospice care expenses, but Carla would still be required to pay her monthly premiums, deductibles, and coinsurance for treatment unrelated to her terminal illness (Medicare .gov, n.d.). Support for the family will be essential during Carla's life transitions.

Psychological Case Management

Carla has faced serious deterioration of her physical health. Because LBD has negatively impacted her cognitive skills, the RC should follow up with Carla's neurologist for more detailed information on her cognitive functioning. Carla's ability to live independently has decreased and will continue to decrease over time. She would need to discuss what relying on others means to her and ways she might age with dignity. Watching Carla's slow decline may also have a negative impact on Carla's family, who would likely benefit from caregiver and family supports. Support groups and group counseling are two of many resources available to loved ones of people with dementia that the RC could coordinate for Carla's family.

Vocational Case Management

There would be no further need for vocational case management, as Carla will not be returning to work.

Life Care Planning

The National LBDA recommends life care planning (LCP) for individuals with this diagnosis (LBDA, 2016b). In the case of Carla, LCP may be a viable consideration. According

(*continued*)

CASE STUDY (*continued*)

to Reid, Deutsch, and Kitchen (2005), LCP is a "systematic methodology for identifying and quantifying the multidimensional, disability-related needs of an individual" (p. 229). Some RCs are qualified to become certified LCP practitioners, whereas others may refer clients to LCP providers. In either situation, case management skills are essential to LCP. RCs working with LCPs may need to forward vocational assessments/evaluations, particularly for a client who "has no clear vocational goal, has no work history or a series of short, sporadic jobs, [and] who has not been determined ineligible for vocational opportunities" (Berens & Weed, 2009, p. 44). While practicing, LCPs may need to negotiate cost services over a life span for a client. RCs can view LCP as a "problem-solving approach that promotes continuity and consistency of care" (Reid et al., 2005, p. 228).

CONCLUSION

In this chapter, we have provided a brief overview of case management, defined case and caseload management, discussed the value of case management, and reviewed the steps in the case management process. The case study of Carla was examined to show the application of case management skills.

This chapter provides an introduction to case management. For additional information on case management and the case management process, the reader is directed to *Case Management and Rehabilitation Counseling* (Roessler, Rubin, & Rumrill, in press) and *The Case Manager's Handbook* (Mullahy, 2014).

CONTENT REVIEW QUESTIONS

- How might case management in VR differ from other professions?
- What are some ways that RCs can invite clients' family members to be partners in the case management process?
- What are some settings in which RCs use case management?
- Examine the pros and cons of an injured or ill client returning to a previous job or finding a new job.
- How can RCs avoid impeding a client's autonomy while providing case management?

REFERENCES

American Counseling Association. (2014). *Code of ethics.* Alexandria, VA: Author. Retrieved from https://www.counseling.org/resources/aca-code-of-ethics.pdf

American Red Cross. (2016). Prepare for your CNA test. Retrieved from http://www.redcross.org/take-a-class/cna/cna-preparaton/cna-practice-test

Berens, D. E., & Weed, R. O. (2009). The role of the vocational rehabilitation counselor in life care planning. In R. O. Weed & D. E. Berens (Eds.), *Life care planning and case management handbook* (3rd ed., pp. 41–61). Boca Raton, FL: Taylor & Francis.

Case Management Society of America. (2016). *Standards of practice for case management.* Little Rock, AR: Author. Retrieved from http://solutions.cmsa.org/acton/media/10442/standards-of-practice-for-case-management

Certification of Disability Management Specialist. (2014a). About. Retrieved from http://www.cdms.org/index.php/About/Content/about-cdms.html

Certification of Disability Management Specialist. (2014b). Scope of practice. Retrieved from http://www.cdms.org/index.php/About/Content/scope-of-practice.html

Chapin, M. H. (2005a). Case management in private sector rehabilitation. In F. Chan, M. J. Leahy, & J. L. Saunders (Eds.), *Case management for rehabilitation health professionals* (2nd ed., Vol. 1, pp. 304–329). Osage Beach, MO: Aspen Professional Services.

Chapin, M. H. (2005b). Community resources. In F. Chan, M. J. Leahy, & J. L. Saunders (Eds.), *Case management for rehabilitation health professionals* (2nd ed., Vol. 1, pp. 176–196). Osage Beach, MO: Aspen Professional Services.

Commission for Case Management Certification. (n.d.). Home. Retrieved from https://ccmcertification.org

Commission on Rehabilitation Counselor Certification. (2016). About CRCC certification. Retrieved from https://www.crccertification.com/about-crc-certification

Commission on Rehabilitation Counselor Certification. (2017). *Code of professional ethics for rehabilitation counselors*. Schaumburg, IL: Author. Retrieved from https://www.crccertification.com/filebin/pdf/Final_CRCC_Code_Eff_20170101.pdf

Dew, D. W., Alan, G. M., & Tomlinson, P. (Eds.). (2008). *Recruitment and retention of vocational rehabilitation counselors* (Institute on Rehabilitation Issues Monograph No. 33). Washington, DC: The George Washington University, Center for Rehabilitation Counseling Research and Education.

Emmerton, B. (2016, October 26). *Re: Case Management* [Online forum comment]. Retrieved from http://engage.crccertification.com/communities/community-home/digestviewer/viewthread?MID=2246&GroupId=19&tab=digestviewer&UserKey=48b27495-dc4a-4d5b-9153-12ad42667a21&sKey=ab002621bc4e45cf942f#bm2

Galvin, J. E., Boeve, B. F., Duda, J. E., Galasko, D. R., Kaufer, D., Leverenz, J. B., . . . Lopez, O. L. (2008). Current issues in LBD diagnosis, treatment and research. Retrieved from https://www.lbda.org/sites/default/files/current_issues_in_lbd_-_for_2012_template.pdf

Greenwood, R., & Roessler, R. T. (2006). Systematic caseload management. In R. T. Roessler & S. E. Rubin (Eds.), *Case management and rehabilitation counseling* (4th ed., pp. 233–246). Austin, TX: Pro-Ed.

Job Accommodation Network. (2016). Accommodation and compliance series: Employees with mental health impairments. Retrieved from http://askjan.org/media/Psychiatric.html

Leahy, M. J., & Kline, K. M. (2014). Case management practices in rehabilitation and human services. In J. D. Andrew & C. W. Faubion (Eds.), *Rehabilitation services: An introduction for the human services professional* (3rd ed., pp. 326–341). Linn Creek, MO: Aspen Professional Services.

Lewy Body Dementia Association. (2016a). Finding a doctor to diagnose and treat LBD. Retrieved from https://www.lbda.org/node/1320

Lewy Body Dementia Association. (2016b). Treatment. Retrieved from https://www.lbda.org/content/treatment-options

Maki, D. R., & Tarvydas, V. M. (2012). Rehabilitation counseling: A specialty practice of the counseling profession. In D. R. Maki & V. M. Tarvydas (Eds.), *The professional practice of rehabilitation counseling* (2nd ed., pp. 3–13). New York, NY: Springer Publishing.

Matkin, R. E. (1981). Program evaluation: Searching for accountability in private rehabilitation. *Journal of Rehabilitation*, 47(1), 65–68.

Medicare.gov. (n.d.). How hospice works. Retrieved from https://www.medicare.gov/what-medicare-covers/part-a/how-hospice-works.html

Moellenhauer, B., Förstl, H., Deuschl, G., Storch, A., Oertel, W., & Trenkwalder, C. (2010). Lewy body and parkinsonian dementia: Common, but often misdiagnosed conditions. *Dtsch Arztebel International*, 107(39), 684–691. doi:10.3238/arztebl.2010.0684

Mullahy, C. M. (2014). *The case manager's handbook* (5th ed.). Burlington, MA: Jones & Bartlett.

National Board for Certified Counselors. (2012). *National Board for Certified Counselors code of ethics*. Greensboro, NC: Author. Retrieved from http://www.nbcc.org/Assets/Ethics/NBCCCodeofEthics.pdf

National Institutes of Health, National Institute of Aging, National Institute of Neurological Disorders and Stroke. (2015). *Lewy body dementia: Information for patients, families, and professionals* (NIH Publication No. 15-7907). Retrieved from https://www.nia.nih.gov/alzheimers/publication/lewy-body-dementia/introduction

Powell, S. K., & Tahan, H. A. (2010). *Case management: A practical guide for education and practice* (3rd ed.). Philadelphia, PA: Wolters Kluwer/Lippincott Williams & Wilkins.

Reid, C., Deutsch, P., & Kitchen, J. (2005). Life care planning. In F. Chan, M. Leahy, & J. Saunders (Eds.), *Case management for rehabilitation health professionals* (2nd ed., Vol. 1, pp. 228–263). Osage Beach, MO: Aspen Professional Services.

Roessler, R. T., & Rubin, S. E. (2006). *Case management and rehabilitation counseling* (4th ed.). Austin, TX: Pro-Ed.

Roessler, R. T., Rubin, S. E., & Rumrill, P. D. (in press). *Case management and rehabilitation counseling* (5th ed.). Austin, TX: Pro-Ed.

Rosenthal, D. A., Hursh, N., Lui, J., Isom, R., & Sasson, J. (2007). A survey of current disability management practice: Emerging trends and implications for certification. *Rehabilitation Counseling Bulletin, 50,* 76–86. doi:10.1177/00343552070500020601

Rubin, S. E., & Roessler, R. T. (2008). Utilizing rehabilitation facilities and support services. In S. E. Rubin & R. T. Roessler (Eds.), *Foundations of the vocational rehabilitation process* (6th ed., pp. 365–397). Austin, TX: Pro-Ed.

Shaw, L. R., Leahy, M. J., & Chan, F. (2005). Case management: Historical foundations and current trends. In F. Chan, M. J. Leahy, & J. L. Saunders (Eds.), *Case management for rehabilitation health professionals* (2nd ed., Vol. 1, pp. 3–27). Osage Beach, MO: Aspen Professional Services.

U.S. Department of Health and Human Services, National Institutes of Health, National Institute of Aging. (2016). *End of life: Helping with comfort care* (NIH Publication No. 16-6036). Retrieved from https://www .nia.nih.gov/health/publication/end-life-helping-comfort-and-care/introduction

U.S. Food and Drug Administration. (2015). Information on clozapine. Retrieved from http://www.fda.gov/ Drugs/DrugSafety/PostmarketDrugSafetyInformationforPatientsandProviders/ucm497790.htm?source= govdelivery&utm_medium=email&utm_source=govdelivery

Welch, G. T. (1979). The relationship of rehabilitation in industry. *Journal of Rehabilitation, 45*(3), 24–25.

FOURTEEN

Advocacy

WILLIAM MING LIU AND REBECCA L. TOPOREK

LEARNING OBJECTIVES

After reading this chapter, you should be able to:

- Understand the relationship between advocacy, empowerment, and social justice.
- Understand advocacy in connection to multicultural competencies and rehabilitation.
- Understand the advocacy competencies.

Advocacy in rehabilitation counseling is not new. In fact, "[a]dvocacy is embedded in the very nature of the rehabilitation counseling field" (Middleton, Robinson, & Mu'min, 2010, p. 175). Rehabilitation counselors, in many professional practices, often find themselves at the forefront of helping clients in multiple ways to create optimal environments for growth and development (Maki & Riggar, 1997; Toporek, Blando, et al., 2009). Yet, there have been some challenges to advancing the practice of advocacy within rehabilitation counseling. We propose that a multicultural counseling framework may serve as a valuable resource to meet this challenge. Two issues are illuminated when considered through the lens of multiculturalism. First, the intersections of identity and oppression operate across all specializations in counseling, including rehabilitation counseling. For example, Middleton et al. (2010) asserted that advocacy in rehabilitation counseling has tended to focus on facilitating access to services and has been somewhat slower to address advocacy with individuals who are marginalized within the rehabilitation system based on other aspects of identity such as race and ethnicity. As with other areas of human services, there also has been research pointing to differential access and referral to rehabilitation services related to racial identity of the client (e.g., Reed, Holloway, Leung, & Menz, 2005; Wilson, 2002). Second, a deficit approach, present when the medical model of disability is used, parallels historic conceptualizations and treatment used by counseling and psychology regarding individuals from other identity communities that have faced oppression (e.g., race or ethnicity, sexual orientation). Advocacy has been one way for counseling professionals to begin to address problematic circumstances within the profession, whether it be neglect, bias, or mistreatment based on racism, sexism, and other forms of oppression. Furthermore, a broad approach to advocacy, including individual, organizational, and societal levels, as described in the ACA Advocacy Competencies (J. A. Lewis, Arnold, House, & Toporek, 2002) can be useful.

Multicultural counseling literature has critiqued traditional counseling practices, research, and education for cultural bias toward individualism, middle-classness, and certainly ability (Olkin, 1999, 2002; Prilleltensky, 1997). The combination of an individualism bias and the social class or ability bias can create a situation in which anyone outside those norms is viewed as having a deficit. This focus centers attention on the individual and results in a neglect of the role of systemic barriers. Treatment focuses on "fixing" the individual or community experiencing difficulties rather than addressing the system. Parallel issues can arise in rehabilitation services when the medical model implicitly, or explicitly, shapes the way an individual's presenting issues are viewed. Within the framework of the medical model, the problem and pathology are located within the individual (Jun, 2010). When rehabilitation practice operates through a medical model, it focuses on the disability and the characteristics of the individual with the intent of minimizing pathology and treating symptoms rather than addressing problems in the environment (Middleton et al., 2010). Alternatively, the disability rights movement consistently has advocated for a social model that identifies the environment as problematic, rather than the individual with the disability. In this model, dominant power systems shape the environment in ways that cater to the majority population and those with privilege, rather than to all individuals, hence creating barriers for those with disability. In reality, there are a range of practice settings, each with constraints, policies, and practices shaped by sources of funding. When eligibility for services is dependent on a diagnosis, the medical model may be the entree to services—yet it is to be hoped that the actual services themselves will shift to focusing on the environment to reduce barriers rather than working to "fix" the individual. This blend may be considered closer to a biopsychosocial model. At its best, rehabilitation counseling integrates, or even prioritizes, advocacy with the individual or community to effect change in the system.

Within the counseling profession broadly, an individual focus is often perpetuated when traditional counseling theories are the basis of practice. The denial of power systems that perpetuate marginalization of "minority" peoples has been identified as a problematic theme reflected in many theoretical orientations (Caldwell & Vera, 2010; Liu & Hernandez, 2010; Pieterse, Evans, Risner-Butner, Collins, & Mason, 2009; Singh et al., 2010; Toporek & Liu, 2001; Toporek & Vaughn, 2010). When these models shape practice, a client's "failure" to be "self-actualized" and be "productive" is often considered to be the fault of the client rather than context, history, or access to resources. This type of bias has also been found within rehabilitation counseling, when bias based on identity dimensions such as ethnic minority race and ethnicity is present along with disability. To correct these issues and more fully integrate context into professional practice, many in the counseling profession have taken upon themselves the responsibility to work beyond the confines of the counseling space and to engage directly in social action and advocacy. Within rehabilitation counseling, advocacy with and for individuals with disabilities continues in its strong tradition.

The focus of this chapter is to describe advocacy in rehabilitation counseling by attending to the contribution of multicultural counseling perspectives. To meet this goal, we first discuss the relevance of incorporating multicultural competency and advocacy in rehabilitation counseling. Second, we discuss the role of advocacy in professional practice and describe various models and definitions of advocacy. Finally, we discuss education and practice implications, with particular attention to the professional responsibilities of RCs and the challenges they face as they attempt to advocate for their clientele.

MULTICULTURAL COUNSELING COMPETENCIES

By now, most counselors understand the necessity of multicultural competencies. The best-known framework for **multicultural competencies**—as articulated by D. W. Sue, Arredondo, and McDavis (1992)—stated that counselors need to have knowledge, awareness, and skills in three areas of understanding: their biases, their client's worldviews, and culturally congruent interventions. Newer scholarship complements the competency framework by focusing on multiculturally oriented counselors (Owen, 2013). **Multicultural orientation** is focused on the counselor's humility or "other-oriented stance which is marked by openness, curiosity, lack of arrogance, and genuine desire to understand clients' cultural identities" (Owen et al., 2016, p. 31). Although advanced cultural competence may be aspirational (to be worked on and improved continually), a basic multicultural orientation suggests a form of cultural humility as a critical counselor characteristic. Furthermore, a recently proposed model of cultural competencies (Ratts, Singh, Nassar-McMillan, Butler, & McCullough, 2016) attempted to integrate the original multicultural competencies (D. W. Sue et al., 1992) with the advocacy competencies (J. A. Lewis et al., 2002). In addition, they sought to expand on previous models to centralize the role of the counselor and client experiences of oppression and privilege and assert that those are brought into the counseling relationship.

The argument for the integration of multiculturalism (both competency and orientation) into counseling has rested on the changing racial and ethnic demographics of the United States (Ridley & Kleiner, 2003; Smith & Trimble, 2016). Problematically, however, this argument often overlooks other existing aspects of diversity (e.g., sexual orientation, gender, and ability) and situates multiculturalism with race and ethnicity. On the contrary, it is important that multiculturalism be defined in general and overarching cultural dimensions—to be expansive and inclusive (Stone, 1997). There are several works that support this broader definition and thus can effectively contribute to the relevance of multicultural competencies to rehabilitation counseling. First, Arredondo et al. (1996) discussed an inclusive perspective of multiculturalism and elaborated the competencies within the framework of personal dimensions of identity. They suggested that counselors must consider the multiple ways that individuals define themselves as well as the multiple communities of importance to clients. Arredondo et al. asserted that counselors must strive for competence in these different realms.

In keeping with the expansive definition of multiculturalism, it is easy to understand how advocacy, multiculturalism, and rehabilitation counseling may form a strong partnership. A number of authors have supported the need to attend to intersection of identity when working with ethnic minority clients with disabilities (e.g., Hennessey, Rumrill, Fitzgerald, & Roessler, 2008; Wilson, 2002). There has been some consideration of multicultural counseling competence when working with clients with disabilities (e.g., Artman & Daniels, 2010; Olkin, 2002, 2007), yet attention to intersections of identity beyond disability has been inconsistent. Middleton et al. (2000) recognized these limitations and advocated for the adoption of multicultural rehabilitation competencies. These competencies articulate the importance of cultural competence including awareness, knowledge, and skills. Middleton and her colleagues endorsed and provided practical guidance regarding the implementation of these competencies. This move reinforces the connection between rehabilitation counseling and multicultural competence. Later, Middleton et al. (2010) noted that, although the multicultural rehabilitation competencies had been developed, the field was still slow to advocate for underrepresented groups.

It is important to note that within the past 5 years or so, there has been significant growth in literature attending to the need for integration of multiplicity of identities in working with individuals with disabilities (e.g., Chronister & Johnson, 2009; Cordes, Cameron, Mona, Syme, & Coble-Temple, 2016; Middleton et al., 2010; Mpofu & Harley, 2015). One example is advocacy around the inclusion of specific attention to ethical practice in rehabilitation counseling when working with culturally diverse individuals (Cartwright & Fleming, 2010). Cartwright, Harley, and Burris (2012) built on this work and provided a discussion and application of models for RCs to use for working with multiple dimensions of identity that might be presented by clients.

It is heartening that there has been increased recognition of historical bias within rehabilitation services, as with other areas of mental health and counseling, and movement toward better service. The history of advocacy generally within rehabilitation counseling and the recent increased attention to multicultural perspectives points to potential for integrating multicultural competence and advocacy. To facilitate further development of this integration, reflecting on how the broader multicultural movement has expanded to integrate these two frameworks can be helpful. Toporek and Reza (2000) used the base of multicultural counseling competencies provided by D. W. Sue et al. (1992) to assert that multicultural competencies should include attention to institutional dimensions as well as professional and personal realms. They described institutional cultural competence as actions that counselors may need to take in addressing institutional issues that impact the well-being of clients. Counselors may do this work through administrative roles, coordinator roles, as members of an organization, or in a variety of other functions. This attention to institutional competence directly suggests that advocacy may be critical in working in culturally competent ways—beyond one-on-one work with clients.

Focusing on rehabilitation counseling specifically, Middleton et al. (2010) asserted that advocacy is inherent in the multicultural counseling competencies (D. W. Sue et al., 1992) and the multicultural rehabilitation counseling competencies. Acknowledging the importance of self-advocacy within rehabilitation, Middleton and her colleagues also noted that access to institutional power varies based on a number of identity variables, such as race, gender, sexual orientation, and disability status. Consequently, advocacy may be needed from others who have greater access to institutional power: namely, counselors. Middleton and her colleagues charged that there are two major gaps in the rehabilitation counseling profession: the lack of endorsement of multicultural competencies and the absence of common language, definitions, and competencies for advocacy.

In general, multiculturalism encourages institutions and individuals to seek out transformation of systems rather than to settle for additive changes or superficial reorganizing (Liu & Pope-Davis, 2003). As such, advocacy becomes an implicit activity of those who identify themselves as multiculturally competent and oriented counselors. In a similar manner, RCs may find themselves in situations where they must facilitate client self-advocacy or advocate for client welfare—with or on behalf of the client—to make environmental accommodations and facilitate change with and for the client. This advocacy activity is congruent with the aims of multiculturalism because environments that are not adaptive or accommodating may be construed as marginalizing and oppressive milieus for clients. As a function of their role, RCs acting as advocates in promoting changes in a client's environment are engaging in multiculturally competent work for the betterment of their clients.

Although it may appear that there is a dichotomy between counseling and advocacy, Lerner (1972) believed that this perception results in a false dichotomy between social action and counseling. For some counselors, the idea of advocacy is perceived as a confluence between the personal and the private world of counseling versus the public and the political world of social action (Pope-Davis, Liu, Toporek, & Brittan, 2001). Consequently, reluctance toward advocacy may be construed as a fear of politicizing counseling (Pope-Davis et al., 2001). This fear, of course, assumes that counseling is a nonpolitical activity (Liu & Pope-Davis, 2003). But if counselors understood "political and politics" as a venue or situation in which a person's values, beliefs, and worldviews are used to facilitate another person's movement toward some intrapersonal and interpersonal change, then counselors would see that politics is inflected in every personal and professional activity.

Advocacy in counseling, especially rehabilitation counseling, challenges many of the values inherent in traditional counseling and psychotherapy (Toporek & Liu, 2001). Among these conflicts are the value of individualism, insight as a cure, and ableism (Olkin, 2002). It also challenges the notion of time-limited or brief therapy, psychological distance between the client and the counselor, and dual relationships. Advocacy and being an advocate confront the notion that clients are, by themselves, responsible for their situations (i.e., it is their distorted perceptions that are creating the problem) and that only they can change their environment. Often, many of these values are implicit in the way clients are treated (i.e., diagnosed) in counseling (Follette & Houts, 1996). Moving away from this dualistic worldview, rehabilitation counseling recognizes that the environment significantly impacts their clients. However, the controversy in rehabilitation counseling is often the extent to which counselors use their own power and privilege for the benefit of their client (Liu, Pickett, & Ivey, 2007). Consequently, advocacy actions risk and threaten the status quo on which the counselor may depend. That is, RCs may be at risk of losing their jobs if their advocacy actions challenge the system in which they exist. Kivel (2009) presented a particularly provoking argument along this vein. He charged that helping professionals and the systems within which they work intentionally and actively, albeit unconsciously, function to maintain oppressive power structures. Teaching and empowering clients to advocate for themselves is a critical role for rehabilitation counselors (Vash, 1991). Self-advocacy, as history shows, is the basis for civil rights movements such as the disability rights movement that emerged when individuals exerted their civil rights within the context of their own lives (McCarthy, 2003). Although self-advocacy is certainly an important rehabilitation counseling goal, we also believe that the RC may need to consider situations in which it is appropriate to intervene directly in organizations or systems, even those in which they work.

One of the principles in multicultural counseling is the idea of collaboration with clients. For example, according to the Commission on Rehabilitation Counselor Certification (CRCC, 2017) *Code of Ethics*, "Rehabilitation counselors work to help clients, parents, or legal guardians understand their rights and responsibilities, speak for themselves, and make informed decisions. When appropriate and with the consent of a client, parent, or legal guardian, rehabilitation counselors act as advocates on behalf of that client at the local, regional, and/or national levels" (Standard C.1.b., p. 12). Rather than wallow in the ambiguity between what we do "with" or "for" a client (Lerner, 1972), the focus should always be on what we can do "along" with clients in order to better their environment, situation, or condition (e.g., Freire, 1989). In traditional psychotherapy, clients tend to be disempowered and may feel a lack of agency due to the assumptions many counselors may hold about clients. These assumptions may be that the counselor knows what is best for the client, does not include clients in decisions, and stigmatizes individuals through deficit-oriented labels (e.g., disabled client versus a client with a disability; Prilleltensky, 1997). Based on the disability rights mantra "nothing about us without us" (Charlton, 1998, p. 3), the necessity of collaborating with clients is central in client advocacy as defined by J. A. Lewis et al. (2002). It is particularly important in rehabilitation counseling to work collaboratively with clients to identify the part of the problem that is internal (intrapsychic) and the part that is external (systemic), as well as actions that the client may take to change the systemic issues.

An example of multicultural collaboration with a client may be reflected in understanding how the client's culture constructs a person's illness via **culturally adapted psychotherapy (CAP;** Benish, Quintana, & Wampold, 2011; Griner & Smith, 2006). In CAP, the focus is on exploring the ways in which illness is explained in the client's particular culture (illness myth). Understanding how the client conceptualized illness also allows the counselor to adapt current psychotherapy interventions to help with the client. Mental illness and interventions for recovery are both culturally constructed. That is, the manifestations may be similar (e.g., depressive symptoms), but often the explanations may vary as well as what may be considered to be healing interventions. As a part of a culturally adapted therapy, the counselor works with the client to explore what the client believes is causing the illness. This practice involves "asking explicit questions about what the client believed caused the problems, symptoms experienced, consequences of the illness, and treatments that were acceptable to the client" (Benish et al., 2011, p. 287).

In addition, there are times when it is appropriate for counselors to recognize their responsibility in addressing systemic issues. The CRCC (2017) *Code of Ethics* requires, for instance, that "rehabilitation counselors remain aware of actions taken by their own and cooperating organizations on behalf of clients. When possible, to ensure effective service delivery, rehabilitation counselors act as advocates for clients who cannot advocate for themselves" (Standard C.1.c., p. 12). Thus, when the help-giving organization is one that is perpetuating barriers, not only is it important for clients to voice their concerns, but it is also a responsibility of the counselor—as a member of the organization— to actively facilitate change within the organization (Hopps & Liu, 2006). If counselors do not take such action, they are in danger of colluding with the problematic system. The client may sense the counselor's implicit collusion and may interpret counselor– client discourse in counseling as a double-bind message of "I'll help you only if I don't risk anything on my part." Consequently, the counselor's trustworthiness, credibility, and ability to conduct counseling may be jeopardized (S. Sue & Zane, 1987). In fact, the American Counseling Association (ACA) *Code of Ethics* stipulates that if policies or practices of the organization are "potentially disruptive or damaging to clients or may limit the effectiveness of services provided and change cannot be affected, counselors take appropriate further action" (ACA, 2014, p. 10).

It is important to see counseling as an interactional process in which the client and counselor are conceived as collaborators. The counselor is open to change as much as the client, and they both must envision potential changes within their environment. Because it is important to construe the "client" or "consumer" as a participant in his or her own change, we would like to posit that the consumer language often used in rehabilitation counseling be challenged for not fully incorporating the notion of client agency in the environment. The consumer label for clientele is popular because it puts the potential "power" within the consumer and not necessarily with the service provider. However, the marketplace metaphor still resonates with an adversarial theme. If the consumer is unhappy with a particular service, then the service provider is to change and meet the new demands. Yet implicit in this notion of the consumer and the market is also a "bottom line." Based on cost-benefit calculations, some agencies may not change at all, and eventually clients may find themselves without adequate services altogether. The notion of collaboration or equality is not inherent in an economic model of service provision (e.g., Eriksen, 1997, 1999). Consequently, we will use the language of collaboration to denote the role of the client and counselor rather than using the common language of the consumer in this chapter.

Before continuing, it is necessary to understand the role advocacy has in counseling and in the counseling profession. In addition, we discuss the various models from which advocacy can be operationalized. The following section is a brief overview of these two facets of advocacy in counseling.

ADVOCACY IN COUNSELING

Historical Perspective

The issue of advocacy is partly a professional identity issue and not solely a practical concern. Actions that benefit clients by eliminating or diminishing institutional and cultural barriers may have a secondary effect of empowering clients and encouraging future social action by clients and counselors. Many sentiments toward institutional and cultural change were elements of advocacy and community organizing in the 1970s when changing structural inequities was considered an appropriate professional role (J. A. Lewis & Lewis, 1983). Yet, through the 1980s and 1990s, the advocacy perspective seemingly lost its prominence (McClure & Russo, 1996; Toporek & Liu, 2001). McClure and Russo (1996) speculated that a focus by the counseling profession toward credibility and individualism has contributed to the decreasing emphasis on advocacy as a legitimate professional role.

With the increasing emphasis on multiculturalism and multicultural competencies, it appears that the pendulum may be swinging back toward advocacy and social justice. With the advent of multiculturalism and feminist orientations, traditional notions of psychotherapy and counseling are being challenged to become relevant for historically marginalized groups (Toporek & Liu, 2001). Because multiculturalism is concerned with social justice, especially for disenfranchised and marginalized groups, and because advocacy also is typically aligned with combating marginalization (Chesler, Bryant, & Crowfoot, 1976), advocacy has become an important professional concern. Recognizing that counseling has been effective differentially and sometimes biased against minority individuals, there have been increasing challenges to the profession to explore the individual, cultural, and institutional barriers that perpetuate oppression (Hopps & Liu, 2006; Middleton et al., 2010; Ridley, 1995; Sutton & Kessler, 1986). Although some oppression can be acted upon in dyadic interactions, some can only be targeted through advocacy (Atkinson, Thompson, & Grant, 1993; Middleton et al., 2010). For instance, a negative sense of self related to internalizing negative stereotypes of his or her racial group (i.e., internalized racialism; Cokley, 2002) can be a pertinent dyadic issue in individual counseling. But if a client reports that he or she cannot gain access to a building due to wheelchair restrictions to doorways and steps, the "in-session" (individual-focused) counseling is likely to be unsuccessful in ameliorating client distress, anger, and frustration. Only through appropriate advocacy and "out-of-session" actions will clients start to build a sense of efficacy and empowerment (McWhirter, 1994). Gruber and Trickett (1987) posit that advocacy operationalizes the privileges and power of the advocate, which are the intimate knowledge of rules, norms, and systems and are the resources that counselors can use to work with clients in a concerted and effective way for change. In the latter case, the counselor is the most effective agent to start the change process to make the agency more accessible. Within rehabilitation counseling, the role of counselor as advocate has been relatively widely accepted in regard to issues related to disabilities. This has not necessarily carried over to issues related to other ways in which clients or communities may experience marginalization or oppression.

Definitions and Models

Although we focus specifically on advocacy in this chapter, one of the confusions that can occur is between definitions of advocacy, empowerment, and social action. Sometimes, all three labels can be used synonymously to describe a particular activity, and we would draw some distinctions that may not be apparent. For us, **advocacy** is "the action a mental health professional, counselor, or psychologist takes in assisting clients and client groups to achieve therapy goals through participating in clients' environments" (Toporek & Liu, 2001, p. 387).

Historically, authors have sought to refine the overall idea of advocacy to include a variety of activities. J. A. Lewis and Lewis (1983) differentiated between case advocacy, which is advocacy on behalf of a client, and class advocacy, which is advocacy on a systemic level. They also describe three types of advocacy as "here and now" advocacy or responding to a situation, "preventive" advocacy or actions to create a just environment, and "citizen" advocacy or action encouraging others to challenge social issues. Chan, Brophy, and Fisher (1981) elaborated further on the concept of advocacy and suggested three types of advocacy that may be used. First, **representative advocacy** is when a counselor takes on the issues of his or her client because the client is unable to express or act upon his or her needs. This is similar to the counselor–advocate model of Atkinson, Morten, and Sue (1993), in which the counselor "speaks on behalf of the client, often confronting the institutional sources of oppression that are contributing to the client's problem" (p. 301). Second, **group advocacy** is when a "group seeks to intervene in a problem situation in order to achieve a goal consistent with the interest of the members of the group or others" (Chan et al., 1981, p. 195). Finally, there is **self-advocacy** when the individual is taught agentic knowledge, actions, and behaviors. In this last case, Chan et al. (1981) illustrated their "self-advocacy" by presenting cases wherein clients are faced with a problematic situation. Counselors, working in this model, help clients define the problem and develop a list of possible actions from which the client chooses alternatives. Importantly, while self-advocacy means that the RC will not act on behalf of the client, a collaborative interaction between the counselor and the client is critical to ensure that the client is ready to take on the responsibilities necessary to learn to assert control over the social justice problem (Chan et al., 1981).

In considering advocacy in counseling, we have found it useful to describe advocacy as a continuum of activity on which empowerment and social action reside (Toporek & Liu, 2001). For us, empowerment is considered to be on one end of the agentic continuum. In this model, **empowerment** implies that the counselor and client work to develop efficacy within the client's and counselor's sociopolitical world (McWhirter, 1994, 1997; Toporek & Liu, 2001). Thus, empowerment encompasses a specific action and behavior with a specific client. As a result of empowerment, clients are able to cope with specific situational problems and concerns, and have a sense of self-efficacy to contend with similar problems in the future. **Social action**, in contrast, means that the counselor is working constantly on removing institutional and cultural barriers for a community or population. Social action implies advocacy on a societal level on issues such as legislation or public policy that affect all clients. Thus, social action implies broad-based action and not specific activities focused on the issues of just one individual. Social action also means that counselors are working toward a socially just world: one in which benefits, rights, privileges, and resources are equally distributed as well as social costs and vulnerabilities (i.e., everyone shares equally in the good and bad in society; B. L. Lewis, 2010). Within this model, there are a range of behaviors in which counselors may engage to remove barriers and address injustice. We assert that all these activities may be considered under the umbrella of advocacy and that each of these behaviors may be appropriate at various times in work with clients.

In recognition of the fact that many counselors across specializations may need to utilize advocacy in their work, but may not have training to do so effectively, the ACA adopted a set of **advocacy competencies** (J. A. Lewis et al., 2002). These advocacy competencies were designed to facilitate the ethical implementation of advocacy and assist counselors in identifying advocacy actions that would be appropriate at individual, community or school, and public or societal levels (Toporek, Lewis, & Crethar, 2009). Furthermore, the advocacy competencies acknowledged that some types of advocacy may be collaborative actions in which the client and the counselor work together and other types where the counselor may take action on behalf of the client. This framework resulted in six domains, including empowerment and client advocacy (individual level), community collaboration and systems advocacy (community or school level), and public information or social/political action (societal). Middleton et al. (2010) examined the advocacy competencies and integrated the Multicultural Rehabilitation Counseling Competencies providing guidelines for appropriate advocacy within rehabilitation counseling. Furthermore, they illustrate concrete examples of advocacy for a number of common situations that RCs may encounter.

A common thread through advocacy, empowerment, and social action is that any action along all these dimensions may be positive for clients and counselors alike. In all of these cases, changing environments for the optimal growth and development of the client is the goal. Although these actions are necessary and important in the professional lives of RCs, the challenge is to ensure that counselors learn and train to be effective advocates for their clients.

PRACTICE

Advocacy in practice may take many forms, as suggested by the continuum model we described earlier. Hershenson's (1990) "C-C-C" **model of rehabilitation counseling** may be used as a framework for considering how advocacy may be an integral part of the role. In this model, the RC's role includes three primary functions: coordinating, counseling, and consulting. Within each aspect of this role, the counselor may find that some form of advocacy is an appropriate intervention. Because the practice of rehabilitation counseling also takes many forms, we will address examples and possible advocacy roles throughout counseling, coordination, and consultation.

The counseling function of rehabilitation counseling lends itself to advocacy in relation to individual issues. Chan et al. (1981) provided some excellent examples of self-advocacy and a model for working with individual clients to facilitate their knowledge and agency in addressing barriers. In addition to self-advocacy, there are other examples of advocacy behaviors in counseling. For example, advocating for clients in their presence can serve as a model of agentic behavior for clients as well as serving an advocate function. With this type of behavior, it is critical that the counselor and client collaboratively decide on what action the counselor might take, including goals and strategy for the action. This type of behavior may be appropriate in a situation in which the power and privilege of the counselor's role lends something that is not attainable by the client. The modeling involved in this action can provide a visible demonstration for situations in which self-advocacy is more important.

The coordinating function of rehabilitation counseling also lends itself to advocacy. Advocacy at this level may address individual or group concerns. Within the coordination function, counselors may be participants in decision- and policy-making bodies such as clinical and administrative management teams, and as such have access at a level different from that available to the client or client groups. Advocacy at the coordination level may also include actions such as identifying client needs that are not being met by the institution and then working to establish funding and institutional support for programs that may meet the needs of a specific population.

The consultation role provides a noteworthy avenue for advocacy. As with coordination, advocacy in this role may serve individuals or groups. One example of advocacy at this level would be to engage legislators as consultees around issues that represent barriers to clients from marginalized groups. Other examples might include consulting with social service agency staff to provide training around multicultural competence, prejudice and discrimination, or consulting with faculty to ensure that new curriculum includes issues-related disabilities and other issues. The expertise of people with disabilities could be honored by ensuring that there is representation either by client groups or community groups in these efforts. The Community Collaboration or Public Information domain of advocacy from the advocacy competencies (J. A. Lewis et al., 2002) provides guidance for partnering in advocacy with communities and clients. A final example of this would be lobbying the institution to include a permanent advocate on planning committees for access issues in remodeling or construction.

The advocacy choices that RCs and clients make are complex. It is imperative that RCs have the knowledge, competency, and orientation necessary to be ethical and effective advocates. With this in mind, the recently revised CRCC (2017) *Code of Ethics* provides ethical guidance for implementing advocacy within rehabilitation counseling practice. With regard to informed consent, the Code requires that "rehabilitation counselors obtain client consent prior to engaging in advocacy efforts on behalf of an identifiable client to improve the provision of services and to work toward removal of systemic barriers or obstacles that inhibit client access, growth, and development" (Standard C.1.d., p. 12). Thus, while RCs have an ethical obligation to advocate at times, they also negotiate the tensions related to the principles of social justice and the needs and desires of the individual client. As an example, RCs need to obtain and document a client's consent about disclosing client confidential information "when in engaging in advocacy on behalf of clients" (Standard C.1.d., p. 12). Considering the multifaceted role required in the practice of rehabilitation counseling, effective training for advocacy is a necessary, yet complex, endeavor.

Training

Advocacy training may be one of the most challenging issues in counselor education. Along with coursework, counselor education centralizes the need for face-to-face work with clients as well as competent supervision. But how does one go about receiving competent supervision for advocacy work? One possible answer may come from the advocacy literature as well as training strategies described within multicultural competencies.

First, a distinction must be made between advocacy self-efficacy and specific competent behaviors (B. L. Lewis, 2010). For example, multicultural competency can be perceived as the sense of self-efficacy that counselors may have about working with diverse peoples and groups, and multicultural competencies may be the specific proficiencies counselors have in working with diverse peoples (Pieterse et al., 2009). Although counselors sometimes have a high sense of self-efficacy (competency), they may not have the exact proficiencies that allow them to work effectively with diverse peoples and groups (Ridley & Kleiner, 2003). For instance, it is possible that counselors who perceive themselves as highly multiculturally competent may not be experienced as such by their clients (Pope-Davis et al., 2002). This issue is pertinent to advocacy in rehabilitation counseling because counselors may have a sense of competency in being an advocate for their clients, but may find themselves at a loss when it comes to the real behavior and action of advocacy. Thus, training and supervision become integral aspects of rehabilitation counseling advocacy.

Another training issue for RCs is that the very environment that they are challenging for their client may be the one that employs them. Hence, as RCs seek to engage and transform environments for their clients, they may become acutely aware that their jobs may be threatened. Power differentials in supervision and in the field are considerable forces for trainees (Toporek & Vaughn, 2010). For many trainees, there is a delicate balance between maintaining openness to a new system while also recognizing systemic barriers that may require advocacy. This balance is difficult and trainees often need guidance regarding the timing and appropriateness of challenging the systems in which they are often some of the least powerful players. At the same time, trainees may have a tendency to observe injustice and feel angry with the system without a full understanding of the larger context. Training regarding ways of identifying and resolving these dilemmas would be useful.

One model that may provide a good guide is that of a portfolio approach to advocacy training. Coleman and Hau (2003) provide a model of using portfolio assessment to evaluate and support students' development around multicultural issues. A similar model may be applied for advocacy in rehabilitation counselor education (RCE). Using this type of model, students would develop a portfolio of training and practice activities related to advocacy work they have completed throughout the program. The portfolio may include examples of specific cases within practicum, papers they have written, workshops they have attended, and so forth. This process would provide the student with the opportunity to do a comprehensive self-review and the program faculty with more data on which to evaluate the students' progress.

Currently, a major challenge in rehabilitation counseling is that training on the issue of being an advocate for clients may not be well integrated into curriculum or internship (Collison et al., 1998; Ebener, 2007; Eriksen, 1997, 1999). Effective training could be enhanced with exercises such as developing skills in identifying problem situations and determining which type of advocacy might be appropriate. The ACA advocacy competencies (J. A. Lewis et al., 2002) may be helpful with that. In addition, it would be important for counselors to be able to identify the consequences of advocacy actions for both clients and themselves; for example, living with a changed system, or less optimistically, the ramifications of challenging a hostile system. Although advocacy issues are not new for rehabilitation counseling, there is a need for more attention to course-work, curriculum, and supervision necessary to be an effective rehabilitation counseling advocate.

OPPORTUNITIES AND CHALLENGES IN IMPLEMENTING ADVOCACY IN REHABILITATION COUNSELING

The movement toward advocacy within the counseling professions is not without its detractors. Some argued that counselors cannot be involved in clients' environments and that advocacy is an unrealistic expectation (Weinrach & Thomas, 1998), or that it is a dangerous ideology (Ramm, 1998). This attitude, of course, assumes that the counseling profession is value-neutral and that we are not constantly practicing our politics in session (Pope-Davis et al., 2001). In fact, counselors are constantly negotiating their values in session and practicing their worldviews out of session.

Others have noted the need for intentionality and awareness in advocacy so as not to create unrealistic dependencies (Pinderhughes, 1983) or disempower clients (McWhirter, 1994). It is important to emphasize that dependency building does not represent the type of advocacy about which we are speaking. Rather, actions that promote dependency building are problematic and represent values and worldviews imposed by the counselor on the client in a noncollaborative relationship, wherein the counselor retains his or her position as "healer" and the client's position as that of the "sick person." Both are examples of nonadvocacy relationships and are more likely traditional counseling relationships masquerading as advocacy.

There are some promising developments in rehabilitation counseling practice and training. For example, models for community-based rehabilitation have placed collaboration with clients and consumers as guiding practice (Millington, 2016). In this approach, the counselor collaborates with the client's family and community, their social network, to facilitate empowerment, inclusion, and ensure a safety net of care. The goals of this approach, according to Millington, go further than individual care, and he stated that "its communitarian aims include: reducing poverty, promoting local ownership of programs and the health issues they address; building capacity in support networks; engaging disability **advocacy** groups in CBR programming; and pursuing evidence-based practice" (p. 111). Models such as this provide ways of reconceptualizing the role of counselor as partner in advocacy and social change.

CONCLUSION

Rehabilitation counseling provides a natural forum for integrating advocacy into practice and education, and there is an increasing body of literature and models to facilitate with implementation. In order for the field to advance, there are some philosophical and ethical issues as well as skills training that must be included in order for counselors and education programs to effectively use this approach with clients. Some of these issues include concerns about creating dependency, balancing client agency with counselors' responsibilities to address systemic barriers, dilemmas regarding conflict of interest between counselors and their home institution, and many others. In addition, research is needed regarding the nuances of process and client outcomes using advocacy in rehabilitation practice. Training will be critical in providing RCs an avenue for developing appropriate skills in resolving these issues and identifying appropriate times and strategies for advocacy. Multicultural counseling competencies can provide useful guidance in terms of training models and the establishment of competency standards that recognize issues faced by clients who are marginalized and impeded by systemic barriers. It is hoped that this chapter provided a useful framework as well as tools that may help RCs and educators to integrate advocacy thoughtfully and effectively.

CONTENT REVIEW QUESTIONS

- How are the definitions of advocacy and empowerment similar and divergent?
- What is the C-C-C model?
- What are the professional and ethical issues related to advocacy?
- What is a double-bind message in advocacy?
- What is the definition of social justice and social action?
- What is the relationship between the multicultural counseling competencies and the Multicultural Rehabilitation Counseling Competencies?
- What are some of the recent advances in the field of rehabilitation counseling that address issues of intersectionality and multicultural identities beyond disability?

REFERENCES

American Counseling Association. (2014). *Code of ethics.* Alexandria, VA: Author.

Arredondo, P., Toporek, R., Brown, S., Jones, J., Locke, D., Sanchez, J., . . . Stadler, H. (1996). Operationalization of multicultural counseling competencies. *Journal of Multicultural Counseling and Development, 24*(1), 42–78.

Artman, L. K., & Daniels, J. A. (2010). Disability and psychotherapy practice: Cultural competence and practical tips. *Professional Psychology: Research and Practice, 41*(5), 442–448. doi:10.1037/a0020864

Atkinson, D. R., Morten, G., & Sue, D. W. (1993). *Counseling American minorities: A cross-cultural perspective* (4th ed.). Dubuque, IA: William C. Brown.

Atkinson, D. R., Thompson, C. E., & Grant, S. K. (1993). A three-dimensional model for counseling racial/ethnic minorities. *The Counseling Psychologist, 21,* 257–277.

Benish, S. B., Quintana, S., & Wampold, B. E. (2011). Culturally adapted psychotherapy and the legitimacy myth: A direct-comparison meta-analysis. *Journal of Counseling Psychology, 58,* 279–289. doi:10.1037/a0023626

Caldwell, J. C., & Vera, E. M. (2010). Critical incidents in counseling psychology professionals' and trainees' social justice orientation development. *Training and Education in Professional Psychology, 4,* 163–176.

Cartwright, B. Y., & Fleming, C. L. (2010). Multicultural and diversity consideration in the new Code of Professional Ethics for Rehabilitation Counselors. *Journal of Applied Rehabilitation Counseling, 41*(2), 20–24.

Cartwright, B. Y., Harley, D. A., & Burris, J. L. (2012). Cultural competence. In D. R. Maki & V. M. Tarvydas (Eds.), *The professional practice of rehabilitation counseling* (pp. 371–389). New York, NY: Springer Publishing.

Chan, A., Brophy, M. C., & Fisher, J. C. (1981). Advocate counseling and institutional racism. In *National Institutes of Mental Health, institutional racism and community competence (ADM 81-907)* (pp. 194–205). Washington, DC: U.S. Department of Health and Human Services.

Charlton, J. I. (1998). *Nothing about us without us: Disability oppression and empowerment.* Los Angeles: University of California Press.

Chesler, M. A., Bryant, B. I., & Crowfoot, J. E. (1976). Consultation in schools: Inevitable conflict, partisanship, and advocacy. *Professional Psychology, 7*(4), 637–645.

Chronister, J., & Johnson, E. (2009). Multiculturalism and adjustment to disability. In F. Chan, E. Da Silva Cardoso, & J. A. Chronister (Eds.), *Understanding psychosocial adjustment to chronic illness and disability: A handbook for evidence-based practitioners in rehabilitation* (pp. 479–518). New York, NY: Springer Publishing.

Cokley, K. O. (2002). Testing Cross's revised racial identity model: An examination of the relationship between racial identity and internalized racialism. *Journal of Counseling Psychology, 49,* 476–483.

Coleman, H. L. K., & Hau, J. M. (2003). Multicultural counseling competency and portfolios. In D. B. Pope-Davis, H. L. K. Coleman, W. M. Liu, & R. L. Toporek (Eds.), *Handbook of multicultural counseling competencies in counseling and psychology* (pp. 168–182). Thousand Oaks, CA: Sage.

Collison, B. B., Osborne, J. L., Gray, L. A., House, R. M., Firth, J., & Lou, M. (1998). Preparing counselors for social action. In C. C. Lee & G. R. Walz (Eds.), *Social action: A mandate for counselors* (pp. 263–278). Alexandria, VA: American Counseling Association.

Commission on Rehabilitation Counselor Certification. (2017). *Code of professional ethics for rehabilitation counselors.* Schaumburg, IL: Author.

Cordes, C. C., Cameron, R. P., Mona, L. R., Syme, M. L., & Coble-Temple, A. (2016). Perspectives on disability within integrated health care. In J. M. Casas, L. A. Suzuki, C. M. Alexander, & M. A. Jackson (Eds.), *Handbook of multicultural counseling* (4th ed., pp. 401–410). Thousand Oaks, CA: Sage.

Ebener, D. J. (2007). Skill emphases in rehabilitation counselor education curricula. *Rehabilitation Education, 21*(3), 195–204. doi:10.1891/088970107805059652

Eriksen, K. (1997). *Making an impact: A handbook on counseling advocacy.* Washington, DC: Taylor & Francis/Accelerated Development.

Eriksen, K. (1999). Counseling advocacy: A qualitative analysis of leaders' perceptions, organizational activities, and advocacy documents. *Journal of Mental Health Counseling, 21*(1), 33–49.

Follette, W. C., & Houts, A. C. (1996). Models of scientific progress and the role of theory in taxonomy development: A case study of the *DSM. Journal of Consulting and Clinical Psychology, 64,* 1120–1132.

Freire, P. (1989). *Pedagogy of the oppressed.* New York, NY: Continuum.

Griner, D., & Smith, T. B. (2006). Culturally adapted mental health interventions: A meta-analytic review. *Psychotherapy: Theory, Research, Practice, and Training, 43,* 531–548.

Gruber, J., & Trickett, E. J. (1987). Can we empower others? The paradox of empowerment in the governing of alternative public schools. *American Journal of Community Psychology, 15*(3), 355–371.

Hennessey, M. L., Rumrill, P. D., Fitzgerald, S., & Roessler, R. (2008). Disadvantagement-related correlates of career optimism among college and university students with disabilities. *Work: Journal of Prevention, Assessment and Rehabilitation, 30*(4), 483–492.

Hershenson, D. (1990). A theoretical model for rehabilitation counseling. *Rehabilitation Counseling Bulletin, 33,* 268–278.

Hopps, J., & Liu, W. M. (2006). Working for social justice from within the health care system: The role of social class in psychology. In R. L. Toporek, L. H. Gerstein, N. A. Fouad, G. Roysircar, & T. Israel (Eds.), *Handbook for social justice in counseling psychology: Leadership, vision, and action* (pp. 318–337). Thousand Oaks, CA: Sage.

Jun, H. (2010). *Social justice, multicultural counseling and practice: Beyond a conventional approach.* Thousand Oaks, CA: Sage.

Kivel, P. (2009). Social service or social change? In INCITE: Women of Color Against Violence (Ed.), *The revolution will not be funded: Beyond the non-profit industrial complex* (pp. 129–149). Cambridge, MA: South End Press.

Lerner, B. (1972). *Therapy in the ghetto: Political impotence and personal disintegration.* Baltimore, MD: Johns Hopkins University.

Lewis, B. L. (2010). Social justice in practicum training: Competencies and developmental implications. *Training and Education in Professional Psychology, 4,* 145–152.

Lewis, J. A., Arnold, M. S., House, R., & Toporek, R. L. (2002). ACA advocacy competencies. Retrieved from http://www.counseling.org/Publications

Lewis, J. A., & Lewis, M. D. (1983). *Community counseling: A human services approach.* New York, NY: Wiley.

Liu, W. M., & Hernandez, N. (2010). Counseling those in poverty. In M. J. Ratts, J. A. Lewis, & R. L. Toporek (Eds.), *American Counseling Association Advocacy Competencies: An advocacy framework for counselors* (pp. 43–54). Alexandria, VA: American Counseling Association.

Liu, W. M., Pickett, T., Jr., & Ivey, A. E. (2007). White middle-class privilege: Social class bias and implications for training and practice. *Journal of Multicultural Counseling and Development, 35,* 194–206.

Liu, W. M., & Pope-Davis, D. B. (2003). Moving from diversity to multiculturalism: Exploring power and the implications for psychology. In D. B. Pope-Davis, H. L. K. Coleman, W. M. Liu, & R. L. Toporek (Eds.), *The handbook of multicultural competencies* (pp. 90–102). Thousand Oaks, CA: Sage.

Maki, D. R., & Riggar, T. F. (1997). Rehabilitation counseling: Concepts and paradigms. In D. R. Maki & T. F. Riggar (Eds.), *Rehabilitation counseling: Profession and practice* (pp. 3–31). New York, NY: Springer Publishing.

McCarthy, H. (2003). The disability rights movement: Experiences and perspectives of selected leaders in the disability community. *Rehabilitation Counseling Bulletin, 46*(4), 209–223.

McClure, B. A., & Russo, T. R. (1996). The politics of counseling: Looking back and forward. *Counseling and Values, 40*(3), 162–174.

McWhirter, E. H. (1994). *Counseling for empowerment.* Alexandria, VA: American Counseling Association.

McWhirter, E. H. (1997). Empowerment, social activism, and counseling. *Counseling and Human Development, 29*(8), 1–14.

Middleton, R. A., Robinson, M. C., & Mu'min, A. S. (2010). Rehabilitation counseling: A continued imperative for multiculturalism and advocacy competence. In M. J. Ratts, R. L. Toporek, & J. A. Lewis (Eds.), *ACA Advocacy Competencies: A social justice framework for counselors* (pp. 173–183). Alexandria, VA: American Counseling Association.

Middleton, R. A., Rollins, C., Sanderson, P., Leung, P., Harley, D., & Leal-Idrogo, A. (2000). Endorsement of professional multicultural rehabilitation competencies and standards: A call to action. *Rehabilitation Counseling Bulletin, 48,* 233–244.

Millington, M. J. (2016). Community-based rehabilitation: Context for counseling. In I. Marini, & M. A. Stebnicki (Eds.), *The professional counselor's desk reference* (2nd ed., pp. 111–116). New York, NY: Springer Publishing.

Mpofu, E., & Harley, D. A. (2015). Multicultural rehabilitation counseling: Optimizing success with diversity. In F. Chan, N. L. Berven, & K. R. Thomas (Eds.), *Counseling theories and techniques for rehabilitation and mental health professionals* (2nd ed., pp. 417–441). New York, NY: Springer Publishing.

Olkin, R. (1999). *What psychotherapists should know about disability.* New York, NY: Guilford Press.

Olkin, R. (2002). Could you hold the door for me? Including disability in diversity. *Cultural Diversity and Ethnic Minority Psychology, 8,* 130–137.

Olkin, R. (2007). Disability affirmative therapy and case formulation: A template for understanding disability in clinical context. *Counseling and Human Development, 39*(8), 1–20.

Owen, J. (2013). Early career perspectives on psychotherapy research and practice: Psychotherapist effects, multicultural orientation, and couple interventions. *Psychotherapy, 50,* 496–502. doi:10.1037/a0034617

Owen, J., Tao, K. W., Drinane, J. M., Hook, J., Davis, D. E., & Kune, N. F. (2016). Client perceptions of therapists' multicultural orientation: Cultural (missed) opportunities and cultural humility. *Professional Psychology: Research and Practice, 47,* 30–37. doi:10.1037/pro0000046

Pieterse, A. L., Evans, S. A., Risner-Butner, A., Collins, N. M., & Mason, L. B. (2009). Multicultural competence and social justice training in counseling psychology and counselor education: A review and analysis of sample multicultural course syllabi. *The Counseling Psychologist, 37,* 93–115.

Pinderhughes, E. B. (1983). Empowerment for our clients and ourselves. *Social Casework, 64*(6), 331–338.

Pope-Davis, D. B., Liu, W. M., Toporek, R., & Brittan, C. (2001). How do we identify cultural competence in counseling: Review, introspection, and recommendations for future research. *Cultural Diversity and Ethnic Minority Psychology, 7,* 121–138.

Pope-Davis, D. B., Toporek, R. L., Ortega-Villalobos, L., Ligiero, D. P., Brittan-Powell, C. S., Liu, W. M., . . . Liang, C. T. H. (2002). A qualitative study of clients' perspectives of multicultural counseling competence. *The Counseling Psychologist, 30,* 355–393.

Prilleltensky, I. (1997). Values, assumptions, and practices: Assessing the moral implications of psychological discourse and action. *American Psychologist, 52,* 517–535.

Ramm, D. R. (1998). Consider the scientific study of morality. *American Psychologist, 53,* 323–324.

Ratts, M. J., Singh, A. A., Nassar-McMillan, S., Butler, S. K., & McCullough, J. R. (2016). Multicultural and Social Justice Counseling Competencies: Guidelines for the counseling profession. *Journal of Multicultural Counseling and Development, 44,* 28–48. doi:10.1002/jmcd.12035

Reed, J. M., Holloway, L. L., Leung, P., & Menz, F. E. (2005). Barriers to the participation of Hispanic/Latino individuals in community rehabilitation programs. *Journal of Applied Rehabilitation Counseling, 36*(2), 33–41.

Ridley, C. R. (1995). *Overcoming unintentional racism in counseling and therapy.* Thousand Oaks, CA: Sage.

Ridley, C. R., & Kleiner, A. J. (2003). Multicultural counseling competence: History, themes, and issues. In D. B. Pope-Davis, H. L. K. Coleman, W. M. Liu, & R. L. Toporek (Eds.), *The handbook of multicultural competencies* (pp. 3–20). Thousand Oaks, CA: Sage.

Singh, A. A., Hofsess, C. D., Boyer, E. M., Kwong, A., Lau, A. S. M., McLain, M., . . . Haggins, K. L. (2010). Social justice and counseling psychology: Listening to the voices of doctoral trainees. *The Counseling Psychologist, 38,* 766–795.

Smith, T. B., & Trimble, J. E. (2016). *Foundations of multicultural psychology: Research to inform effective practice.* Washington, DC: American Psychological Association.

Stone, G. L. (1997). Multiculturalism as a context for supervision: Perspectives, limitations, and implications. In D. B. Pope-Davis & H. L. K. Coleman (Eds.), *Multicultural counseling competencies: Assessment, education and training, and supervision* (pp. 263–289). Thousand Oaks, CA: Sage.

Sue, D. W., Arredondo, P., & McDavis, R. J. (1992). Multicultural counseling competencies and standards: A call to the profession. *Journal of Counseling and Development, 70,* 477–486.

Sue, S., & Zane, N. (1987). The role of culture and cultural techniques in psychotherapy: A critique and reformulation. *American Psychologist, 42,* 37–45.

Sutton, R. G., & Kessler, M. (1986). National study of the effects of socioeconomic status on clinical psychologists' professional judgment. *Journal of Consulting and Clinical Psychology, 54,* 275–276.

Toporek, R. L., Blando, J. A., Chronister, J., Kwan, K.-L. K., Liao, H.-Y., & VanVelsor, P. (2009). Counselor to the core: Serving the whole client through creative blending of counselor roles. *Counseling and Human Development, 41*(5), 1–16.

Toporek, R. L., Lewis, J., & Crethar, H. C. (2009). Promoting systemic change through the advocacy competencies: Special section on ACA advocacy competencies. *Journal of Counseling and Development, 87,* 260–268.

Toporek, R. L., & Liu, W. M. (2001). Advocacy in counseling: Addressing race, class, and gender oppression. In D. B. Pope-Davis & H. L. K. Coleman (Eds.), *The intersection of race, class, and gender in multicultural counseling* (pp. 385–416). Thousand Oaks, CA: Sage.

Toporek, R. L., & Reza, J. V. (2000). Context as a critical dimension of multicultural counseling: Articulating personal, professional, and institutional competence. *Journal of Multicultural Counseling and Development, 29*(1), 13–30.

Toporek, R. L., & Vaughn, S. R. (2010). Social justice in the training of professional psychologists: Moving forward. *Training and Education in Professional Psychology, 4,* 177–182.

Vash, C. (1991). More thoughts on empowerment. *Journal of Rehabilitation, 57*(4), 13–16.

Weinrach, S. G., & Thomas, K. R. (1998). Diversity-sensitive counseling today: A postmodern clash of values. *Journal of Counseling and Development, 76,* 115–122.

Wilson, K. (2002). Exploration of VR acceptance and ethnicity: A national investigation. *Rehabilitation Counseling Bulletin, 45,* 168–176.

FIFTEEN

Career Development and Employment of People With Disabilities

DAVID R. STRAUSER, DEIRDRE O'SULLIVAN, AND ALEX W. K. WONG

LEARNING OBJECTIVES

After reading this chapter, you should be able to:

- Understand the relationship between work, human needs, and development.
- Know how to assess basic human needs related to survival and power, social connection, well-being, and self-determination.
- Understand the Illinois Work and Well-Being Model and how rehabilitation counselors (RCs) can implement this model when working with people with disabilities.
- Understand the basic tenets of five important career development theories, as well as the limitations of each when working with individuals with disabilities.
- Understand rehabilitation counseling interventions using theory in conjunction with the Work and Well-Being Model.

Historically, the field of rehabilitation counseling has been concerned with the career development, employment, and vocational behavior of individuals with disabilities (Patterson, Szymanski, & Parker, 2005; Wright, 1980). Underlying the vocational focus of rehabilitation counseling is the philosophy that work is a fundamental and central component of people's lives and is the primary means by which individuals define themselves in society (Blustein, 2008; Gottfredson, 2002; Super, 1969; Szymanski & Hershenson, 2005). RCs who provide career and vocational services to individuals with disabilities must understand the complex interaction among work, society, and the individual in order to facilitate and maximize individuals with disabilities in career development, employment, and overall work adjustment. This chapter provides an introduction to the constructs, theories, and strategies that are relevant for practicing RCs to assist individuals with disabilities to attain work, maximize productivity, and successfully adjust to the contemporary social, organizational, and personal dynamics in the work environment. Topics covered in this chapter that highlight the vocational focus of rehabilitation counseling are (a) centrality of work in people's lives, (b) how work relates to individuals' basic needs (Blustein, 2008) and how these needs can be used to develop multidimensional outcomes to measure the effectiveness of rehabilitation counseling, (c) the Illinois Work and Well-Being Model, (d) relevant theories of career development and work adjustment, and (e) basic career and employment development interventions.

In addition to the core value that work is central to people's lives, this chapter is based on several assumptions that the authors believe are not only relevant, but also fundamental to the field and practice of rehabilitation counseling. First, the practice of rehabilitation counseling is focused on bringing about positive behavior change. This change in behavior can be big or small, involve the development of new skills, or stress the enhancement of existing skills; nevertheless, there is focus on positive change. Even when the focus of rehabilitation counseling is on job maintenance, we believe that this is a focus on positive behavior change, because the individual would not need rehabilitation counseling services if the individual had the necessary skills to achieve this goal independently. Second, the focus of rehabilitation counseling is to maximize the individual's ability to function independently in the environment of his or her choice. We think that the key words are "independently" and "choice." Individuals with disabilities must have the independent desire to bring about change and be empowered to be change agents in their lives. Third, as discussed in other chapters of this book, we feel that counseling and the relationship between the RC and the individual with disability are the fundamental tools that RCs have to bring about effective and positive behavioral change.

CENTRALITY OF WORK

Work has been—and will undoubtedly continue to be—central to all human societies. Work provides opportunities to advance, for social support systems, and for self-expression and self-determination—all necessary components of psychological health (Blustein, 2008; Neff, 1985). In a sense, the activity of work itself is healthy and can be therapeutic for all people, but may be particularly beneficial for people with disabilities due to the common experiences of greater social isolation, stigma, and financial burdens compared to people without disabilities (Blustein, 2008; Strauser, O'Sullivan, & Wong, 2010). Besides the commonly experienced negative financial impact following a chronic illness or disability, people often become isolated and experience a decrease in self-esteem. The work environment can offset this experience by providing opportunities for income, social interaction, and support. According to Neff (1985), most work environments provide social environments that require a person to interact with others, perform rituals and customs that are meaningful, and provide opportunities for growth. These are the activities that sustain mental health (Blustein, 2006, 2008).

The evidence supporting the positive mental health impact of work is not meant to dismiss the potentially hazardous impact of certain working environments on individuals. Specifically, an incongruent person–environment fit can lead to higher levels of depression and stress (Neff, 1985; O'Sullivan & Strauser, 2010). An **incongruent fit** is one where the individual's personal work style and value system do not fit well with the work environment (Hershenson, 1981; Holland, 1985; Neff, 1985). Service sector positions (common employment sites for individuals with disabilities); work environments that are noisy, dirty, require long hours; and extreme weather conditions will also likely lead to increased stress levels (Szymanski & Parker, 2010). Other factors that contribute to reduction in mental health include job role ambiguity, lack of control or input, lack of support in high-responsibility jobs, and very low pay (Neff, 1985; Strauser et al., 2010). Work stress has been a topic of considerable concern for both psychology and business and has a significant negative impact on the overall work environment (Baron & Greenberg, 1990; Kahn & Byosiere, 1990; Quick, Quick, Nelsom, & Hurrell, 1997; Szymanski & Parker, 2010). For an individual with disabilities, the relationship between the individual's job and work stress is complex, with the presence of a disability or chronic health condition further complicating the individual's ability to manage stress in the workplace. Managing work stress for individuals with disabilities is an important factor for RCs to consider and much more research is needed in this particular area.

Because of the centrality of work across the life span and its impact on well-being, an understanding of how people must adapt to work after any life-changing event or congenital illness is worthy of exploration and an important and necessary goal of rehabilitation researchers, educators, and counselors. Competitive employment not only improves a person's financial standing, but has also been shown to improve self-esteem and mental health (Blustein, 2008). Competitive employment leads to improvements in physical and psychological health for many reasons. First, employment means income and a social role, both of which lead to improvements in social status (Wolfensberger, 2002). There can also be improved access to better housing, health care, nutrition, neighborhood, and school districts, as well as crime-free communities and better family relationships (Blustein, 2008; Bond et al., 2001; Larson et al., 2007). From a community perspective, a study of urban Chicago (Wilson, 1996) found that loss of employment empirically connected to a lower quality of life (QOL), including increased drug use, violence, and crime. According to Wilson (1996), employment status is more important than poverty for predicting family discord, violence in neighborhoods, and low-functioning school systems. Wilson (1996) explained that families who function in communities with high employment and who are poor experience fewer problems than families who function in communities with high unemployment and high poverty. From the individual perspective, loss of employment is linked to higher rates of depression, anxiety, and substance abuse (Blustein, 2008), as well as overall reduction in well-being and health status. These states were found not to rebound back to levels prior to loss of employment despite eventual reemployment (Blustein, 2008; Blustein, Kenna, Gill, & DeVoy, 2008). This finding points to the lasting negative physical and psychological impacts experienced by those who lose their employment status, even after regaining it.

Across disability categories, employment rates are much lower for people with disabilities compared to the national average. A U.S. Bureau of Labor Statistics (BLS) employment situation report for 2015 estimated the employment rate of individuals with disabilities to be 17.5% compared to 65.0% for people without disabilities (Bureau of Labor Statistics, 2016). For workers with disabilities, the unemployment rate of 10.7% was significantly higher than the 5.1% rate for workers without disabilities (Bureau of Labor Statistics, 2016). The recession that began in 2008 has had a disproportionate impact on workers with disabilities, with the number of employed workers with disabilities declining at a rate more than three times that of workers without disabilities and the unemployment rate rising dramatically to levels exceeding that of other workers (Fogg, Harrington, & McMahon, 2010). Disability employment statistics also indicate that a large percentage of people with disabilities are no longer looking for employment. In 2012, approximately 80% of adults with a disability were not in the labor force, compared with only 30% of people with no disability (Bureau of Labor Statistics, 2016). Between 1970 and 2009, the number of people receiving Social Security Disability Insurance (SSDI) benefits more than tripled, from 2.7 million to 9.7 million. Less than 1% of individuals on the rolls of the Disability Insurance (DI) and Supplemental Security Income (SSI) programs ever resume employment (Lui et al., 2010). As a result of the low employment and underemployment rates, individuals with disabilities are at increased risk for experiencing decreased levels of physical and psychological health—further complicating future career development and employment. Without a doubt, lack of employment opportunities excludes people with disabilities and chronic health conditions from full community participation, significantly affecting the quality of their lives.

WORK AND HUMAN NEEDS

Due to the centrality of work and its positive effect on individuals' physical and psychological health, work has been identified as a foundation for meeting human needs. According to Blustein (2006, 2008) and Blustein et al. (2008), work provides a means by which individuals can fulfill the following three basic human needs: (a) survival and power, (b) social connection, and (c) self-determination and well-being. In providing vocational and career services, it is important for RCs to understand from the perspective of the individual with disability how his or her educational experiences, conceptualization of work, work experience, familial and cultural background, and disability-related factors impact these three basic human needs. Understanding the impact of work on these three fundamental human needs also highlights the complex way in which working functions in the human experience and the need for multidimensional outcomes in measuring the effectiveness of rehabilitation counseling interventions. Specifically, the traditional dichotomous outcome of *employed* versus *unemployed* does not cover the multidimensional impact of work in the lives of individuals with disabilities. Being employed only tells us that the person is working and nothing about the quality of employment, how integrated the individual is in the social environment, and the autonomy with which the individual is functioning as a result of working or not working. Therefore, to gain a true understanding of the effectiveness of rehabilitation counseling, it is critical to employ a multidimensional outcome analysis model. In the remainder of this section, we provide a brief overview of the three sets of human needs that can be fulfilled by working (Blustein, 2008). We then discuss domains that can be used to guide the evaluation of the impact of rehabilitation services on enhancing the career development and employment of individuals with disabilities.

Basic Need of Survival and Power

Work provides a means for individuals with disabilities to survive and derive power (Blustein, 2006; Blustein et al., 2008). In contemporary labor market terms, survival can be equated with the individual being able to meet his or her basic needs. Ideally, through competitive employment, individuals with disabilities should be able to generate enough income and benefits to meet their most basic needs. However, research continuously has found that individuals with disabilities are employed at a much lower rate than their counterparts without disabilities, likely are employed in positions with no real career path and no benefits, are underemployed, and when employed, occupy low-paying positions (Lustig & Strauser, 2007). A reciprocal relationship between disability and poverty has been established and is exacerbated by high rates of unemployment and underemployment for individuals with disabilities (Edgell, 2006; Lustig & Strauser, 2007). Globalization and the changing labor market have made it more difficult for individuals with disabilities to escape poverty (Szymanski & Parker, 2010). As a result, many individuals with disabilities are unable to meet their most basic human needs independently, thus often creating a state of dependence with no real promise for achieving higher states of vocational or career functioning.

The human need for the acquisition of psychological, economic, and social power is tied closely to meeting basic needs (Blustein, 2006). What this association means for individuals with disabilities is that working should provide material and social resources that increase an individual's agency within society. In essence, work should give an individual purpose and relevance within the broader environment. Individuals who are working assume an increased social role that ultimately increases their ability to derive psychological, social, and economic power (Wolfensberger, 2002). However, there are many structural and cultural barriers that negatively impact individuals' (with disabilities) access to high-status employment, ultimately relegating them to disempowered and low-status occupational and social roles (Szymanski & Parker, 2010). Occupying these disempowered and low-status roles perpetuates dependence on others (individuals, institutions, and programs) and does not fulfill the individual's personal needs.

RCs need to be aware that individuals with whom they work have an inherent need for survival and power, and that work is critical to meeting these individual needs. Vocational and career services should be directed at increasing career and employment opportunities to maximize individuals' abilities to sustain themselves and increase their power by obtaining positions that have increased social value. Table 15.1 provides a list of potential outcomes that could be used to measure individuals' ability to meet their needs for survival and power.

TABLE 15.1   Need, Outcome Construct, and Specific Outcome Domains Related to Rehabilitation Counseling Outcomes

Need	Outcome Constructs	Specific Outcome Domains
Survival and power	Compensation	Salary
		Benefits
		Pay incentives
		Indirect compensation
	Employee development	Internal development
		External development
	Perceived occupational status	Low-status positions
		High-status positions
Social connection	General integration	Conformity
		Acceptance
		Orientation
	Social support	Close interpersonal relationships
		Diffuse relationships
	Leisure	Leisure activities
		Recreational activities
	Independent living	Individual's living situation
Self-determination and well-being	Well-being	Quality of life
		Satisfaction with life
		Physical health status
		Psychological health status
	Self-determination	Autonomy
		Relatedness
		Capacity
		Values and goals

Basic Need for Social Connection

Individuals are social beings who have strong needs to be connected with broader society and develop strong interpersonal relationships (Blustein, 2006; Bowlby, 1982). Participation in work-related activities provides an opportunity for individuals with disabilities to connect with other individuals and their broader social and cultural environments (Blustein, 2008). Ideally, through work, individuals develop positive relationships that supply the support needed to manage work-related stress and foster identity development (Blustein, 1994; Schein, 1990). In contrast, if individuals experience a negative work environment, where the individual feels isolated, disconnected, and under stress, the individual's job performance and work adjustment will most likely be negatively affected. Finally, working provides a mechanism for individuals with disabilities to develop a sense of connection with their broader social world through contributing to the larger economic structure of society (Blustein, 2006). Earning a paycheck and contributing to society's well-being by paying fair and reasonable taxes is a valued social role.

Rehabilitation counseling should not only be focused on finding employment, but also on how employment can increase individuals' levels of social integration. Many times in rehabilitation counseling, the focus of work and socialization are directed at enhancing the person's socialization on the job and with coworkers. However, Blustein (2008) highlighted that the social impact and benefits of work are not limited to the work environment, but also include the broader community. As a result, RCs need to ensure that their efforts regarding socialization not only include the work environment, but also how work can be leveraged to increase individuals' overall level of social integration in roles and communities that they wish to occupy and participate. Potential outcomes for measuring an individual's level of social connection are highlighted in Table 15.1.

Basic Need for Self-Determination and Well-Being

Individuals search for environments that promote self-determination, self-expression, and well-being. RCs have been instrumental in conceptualizing and facilitating work environments that promote physical and psychological well-being for people with disabilities. This work has included job placement in safe environments, promotion of accommodations such as flexibility, and facilitation of environments and tasks that do not exacerbate symptoms. Although all these met objectives are necessary for well-being, they are not sufficient. Ideally, individuals work in environments that provide them with opportunities to exercise self-determination and self-expression, and promote individual well-being by participating in work that is consistent with their skills and interests. However, very few individuals with disabilities have the opportunity to participate in work-related activities that correspond to their personal skills and interests, and they often pursue employment for extrinsic reasons such as income (Blustein, 2008). Research has suggested that promoting *autonomy*, *relatedness*, and *competence* in relation to work that is initially pursued for extrinsic reasons can increase the individual's level of self-determination and well-being related to work (Ryan & Deci, 2000). Blustein (2008) also suggested that when an individual's personal values and goals coincide with those of the work organization, and when the work environment provides individuals with resources and supports that foster successful work experiences, the individual's level of well-being increases.

It is important to note that we are not suggesting that the promotion of autonomy, relatedness, and competence can transform a job with low pay, high stress, and an overall poor work environment into a positive and rewarding work experience. What we are suggesting is that for individuals with disabilities who are not employed in jobs that are consistent with their interests and abilities, RCs can address these constructs of *autonomy*, *relatedness*, and *competence* to promote a better work experience for individuals with disabilities. Specifically, addressing these issues through counseling and careful analysis of how individuals with disabilities derive meaning from their work is important. It can help provide RCs the knowledge to enhance the employment conditions that frame the experience of most people with disabilities, who must accept employment options that have low pay, no benefits, and limited opportunities for advancement, so that they can support themselves and their family (Blustein, 2008). Potential outcomes for measuring self-determination and well-being are highlighted in Table 15.1.

WORK AND WELL-BEING MODEL

As rehabilitation practitioners, researchers, and administrators work to maximize the career development and employment of people with disabilities, they will find it important to have a conceptual model to guide services, assist with the allocation of limited resources, and guide the measurement of effective vocational rehabilitation (VR) outcomes. We introduce the **Illinois Work and Well-Being Model** (Figure 15.1) that can be used by rehabilitation professionals, service providers, and policy makers as a foundation for addressing the important domains and factors related to the career development of individuals with disabilities. The model presented is designed to be parsimonious in nature, to facilitate broad application, yet refined enough to promote in-depth research related to each of the domains and factors making up the model. The primary objective of this model is to inform service, research, and policy related to the career and employment development of individuals with disabilities with the goal of increasing employment, well-being, and overall participation in broader society of people with disabilities.

The overall objective of the Illinois Work and Well-Being Model (Figure 15.1) is to provide a framework for conceptualizing the career and employment development of individuals with disabilities, with the goal of improving individual participation in

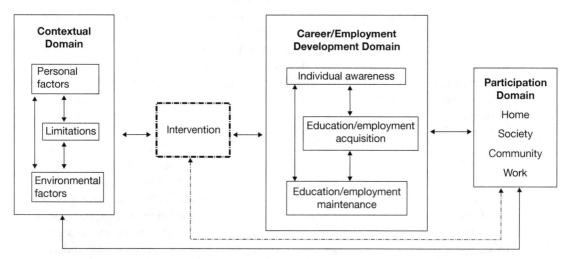

Figure 15.1   Illinois Work and Well-Being Model.

work-related activities and broader society. Specifically, the model identifies the interaction of contextual, career/employment development, and participation domains as key in explaining how personal, environmental, treatment, educational, career/employment development, and potential interventions serve as facilitators or barriers related to overall societal participation. The proposed conceptual model is grounded in the major tenets of the *International Classification of Functioning, Disability and Health* (ICF) model and theory-driven research related to the career development and employment of individuals with chronic health conditions to operationalize the three major model domains. The intervention component facilitates the interaction between the contextual and career development domains and conceptually has a direct and indirect effect on the participation domain. The type and focus of interventions are not specified and no theoretical orientation is preferred. Conceptually, the three domains and the intervention component of the model provide a structure to operationalize how career/employment development is related to participation of individuals with disabilities. Specifically, the model is designed to serve as a guide for researchers, practitioners, and policy makers to identify specific areas of need, conceptualize how contextual and career/employment development domains and factors interact to impact participation, and develop and evaluate the efficacy of specific career-focused interventions.

The conceptual model is not designed to replace specific theories that attempt to explain or describe important career constructs such as decision making, motivation, interest, value, or personality development. Instead, in applying the proposed conceptual model, those constructs and theories are viewed as important process-oriented factors that are inherent to the model, and are embedded within the model. In addition, like the model's domains and factors, these process factors should be points of relevant and valuable career development and employment research. Prior research has provided substantial support suggesting that many of these process-oriented constructs and theories are extremely relevant and may be the operational mechanisms that provide the foundation for interventions that promote and enhance the interaction between the contextual and career/employment development domains, with the ultimate goal of increasing participation.

Conceptual Model Domains

The proposed conceptual model consists of *Contextual, Career/Employment Development,* and *Participation* domains that interact to provide a structure for understanding the career and employment development of people with disabilities (Figure 15.1). The *interventions* component is purposefully situated between the *Contextual* and *Career/Employment Development* domains. As a result, the model implies that interventions directly and indirectly influence both of these domains (*Contextual* and *Career/Employment Development*) and have an indirect effect on the *Participation* domain. Each domain is comprised of factors, which allows for analysis at both the individual domain level and the factor level. As a result, domains and factors can be conceptualized as both independent and interdependent in nature. All arrows between domains and factors are bidirectional, indicating a reciprocal effect between the model components. Relationships between domains, factors, and interventions can be positive, negative, or neutral, indicating that the value of the directional impact is determined by the situation-specific activities, expressions, and reactions to both specific and broad stimuli. In the following sections, each domain is described with an emphasis on structure and the reciprocal interaction between major domains.

Contextual Domain

The *Contextual* domain applies the *ICF* Model as a guide to operationalize how personal and environmental factors interact with medical and treatment-related limitations and restrictions. Because this domain applies the *ICF* Model, the specific domain factors of personal, environmental, and limitations should be conceptualized according the guidelines offered by the *ICF*. The bidirectional arrows between the domain factors indicate a reciprocal relationship, implying that growth or change in one factor can directly or indirectly impact growth or change in the other factors. The solid bidirectional arrow between the *Contextual* and *Career/Employment Development* domains indicates a direct reciprocal connection between these two major domains independent of any intervention, implying a mutually interdependent developmental process. The solid bidirectional arrow along the bottom of the model between the *Contextual* and *Participation* domains implies a reciprocal relationship independent of the *Career/Employment Development* domain and any career interventions. Specifically, it indicates that the factors that make up the *Contextual* domain collectively or individually impact the individual's participation in home, society, community, and work. Likewise, any of the *Participation* domain areas can impact the *Contextual* domain or specific factors individually or collectively. What this inherently implies is that independent of any career development activities or processes, the interaction of personal, environmental, or medical or treatment-related factors impacts participation. By default, the *Career/Employment Development* domain is a cognitive, affective, and behavioral process serving as a moderator that facilitates or creates barriers between the contextual factors and the individual's participation in life's major *Participation* domain factors.

Career/Employment Development Domain

The *Career/Employment Development* domain is based on career and employment research related to individuals with chronic health conditions and disabilities. The domain consists of the following three factors: *Individual Awareness, Educational and Employment Acquisition,* and *Educational and Employment Maintenance.* The *Individual Awareness* factor addresses an individual's levels of personal awareness regarding how his or her skills, abilities, interests, values, needs, personality, assets, limitations, and preferences relate to broader societal and work-related activities and participation. Specifically, awareness is developmentally mediated, with the individual becoming aware of how he or she relates to the world and what activities he or she may choose to participate in. Ideally, this developmental process should be based on self-exploration that facilitates the expression of personal choice. However, as previously noted in the career research, many times individuals are not afforded the opportunity to engage in self-awareness activities and exercise personal choice (Blustein, 2006). Therefore, in all likelihood the outcome of self-awareness is the individual gaining an understanding of personal identity and what education and work-related activities would be physically, cognitively, behaviorally, and emotionally advantageous to pursue. The *Individual Awareness* factor theoretically provides the foundation for the acquisition and maintenance factors although, as implied by the bidirectional arrows, all factors have a reciprocal impact influencing the continual development of each factor.

The *Education and Employment Acquisition* factor addresses the process in which individuals go about acquiring access to educational and employment-related activities. From an educational perspective, acquisition includes, but is not limited to, the process and activities associated with applying for appropriate education-related activities, including trade, 2-year, and 4-year training programs. Acquisition can include leveraging participation in the state-federal VR program and securing appropriate financial aid. Education-related acquisition can occur at multiple points of educational transition and may occur multiple times over one's life course. Employment-related acquisition primarily focuses on activities related to job development, placement, and job-seeking activities. Impression management and appropriate job-seeking techniques are significant parts that affect employment acquisition and are grounded in the preceding awareness factor. Like educational acquisition, employment-related acquisition in all likelihood will occur multiple times throughout the life course and, depending on the developmental stage, may have different requirements to meet the specified acquisition demands. The Employment and Educational Acquisition factor provides the foundation for the Maintenance-related activities and has a reciprocal impact on individual awareness.

The *Educational and Employment Maintenance* factor addresses the activities and behaviors associated with maintaining engagement and participation in education- and occupation-related activities. Being able to manage educational and work-related stresses, employing functional and appropriate social skills, and being able to make appropriate adjustments to personal and environmental demands are the important components of the maintenance factor. Individuals with chronic health conditions will also have to manage the functional limitations associated with their medical condition and related treatment. Although Maintenance occurs after Acquisition and is typically conceptualized as an outcome, it too has a reciprocal effect on the preceding factors. For example, unsuccessful educational or employment maintenance may have a negative impact on an individual's level of awareness by creating doubt regarding his or her skills and abilities, which, in turn, could affect the individual's motivation to pursue and participate in educational and employment acquisition related activities.

Participation Domain

The Participation domain utilizes the *ICF* Model as a guide to identify meaningful and broad-based participation in major life areas, which is conceptualized as contributing to one's overall level of well-being. In this conceptual model, the life areas of *home, society, community*, and *work* have been identified and can serve as outcomes of interest. Although the work area may seem an obvious focal area for those working to improve career development and employment outcomes for individuals with chronic health conditions, the model stresses the interconnectivity of all participation areas. What this means in practical terms is that participation in one area directly and indirectly impacts participation in the other three remaining areas. The concept of participation area interconnectivity is important because it reinforces the understanding that work has a broad impact on the individual, not only in terms of employment outcomes, but also in terms of how individuals are able to function in their homes, participate in broader societal activities, and engage in community activities that provide social, recreational, and leisure opportunities. Overall, a fundamental tenet embedded in the model is that increased positive participation in the areas identified in the Participation domain will lead to an overall increase an individual's well-being and overall QOL.

Interventions

According to the conceptual model, the *Intervention* component is situated between the *Contextual* and *Career/Employment Development* domains. This placement suggests that the primary goal of career, educational, and employment interventions is to facilitate and maximize the direct interaction between the *Contextual* and *Career/Employment* domains, which will in turn indirectly impact the *Participation* domain. Historically, career and employment interventions have been conceptualized as existing within the career/employment development domain, excluding or minimizing the impact of the contextual factors identified in this model. VR research has provided some exceptions to this formulation through the inclusion of contextual factors in interventions such as the Individualized Supportive Employment (ISE) model. However, most vocational and VR research has not focused on how the interaction of the contextual factors affects career development, and, ultimately, broader societal participation. By pulling the Intervention component outside of the *Career/Employment Development* domain and placing it between the *Contextual* and *Career/Employment Development* domains, the model implies that interventions should focus on the correspondence between the two respective domains. Effective interventions should focus on maximizing the personal, environmental, and medical-related limitations to impact the *Career/Employment Development* domain and specific career/employment development domain factors. For example, the model implies that for an intervention addressing a deficiency in job-seeking skills (Acquisition factor) to be effective, the intervention should take into account how an individual's age, education, gender (personal factors); labor market, culture, familial factors (environmental factors); and depreciated executive processing, fatigue, and limited mobility (disability-related limitations) affect the efficacy, adequacy, and acceptability of the intervention. Finally, the dashed bidirectional arrow between the *Intervention* component and the *Participation* domain implies that interventions can have an impact independent of the *Career/Employment Development* domain.

There are multiple ways in which to apply this model to improving the overall participation of individuals with disabilities in broader society. The model presented provides a basic guide for practitioners, policy makers, and researchers in examining the domains, factors, and participation outcomes related to career development and employment of individuals with disabilities. The model provides a means for practitioners to operationalize the factors and domains that may be contributing to decreased career and participation outcomes. Practitioners can use the model to gain an understanding of service delivery strengths and potential areas of need. The model presents researchers with both within- and across-domain analysis and examination at the factorial level. From a policy perspective, this conceptual model provides a way to analyze current resource allocation and the potential need to expand services to include career and vocational development as an important part of expanding broader societal participation.

THEORIES OF VOCATIONAL BEHAVIOR AND CAREER DEVELOPMENT

Theories provide language and explanation for a given phenomenon. Before a practitioner can implement a treatment plan effectively, the problem, as well as the possible range of solutions, must be understood. Science provides a process to test ideas about which solutions work for different populations. Over time, consistency in research findings from these tests generates theories that help explain what is observable. Practices that are guided by research findings are known as **evidence-based practices**. Counselors who do not understand and use research findings and theory are not practicing from an "evidence base." In this chapter, vocational behavior and career development are the phenomena of interest. The population of interest is people with disabilities. Here we outline the key principles of major theories so that rehabilitation professionals can use these theoretical principles when conceptualizing their clients. Models and conceptual models, like the model introduced in this chapter, help practitioners use theories in practical ways. As we outline each theory, we explain how the key points from each can be used to guide practice and interventions with clients. Keeping in mind that all theories have limits, and that a comprehensive discussion of each theory is beyond the scope of this chapter, we provide a summary of major theories applicable to those with disabilities in vocational and career contexts. The additional lens of the Work and Well-Being Model can help the practitioner fill in the gaps of any given theory and personalize practice to each client.

When reading the rest of the chapter, keep in mind key points derived from the culmination of career and vocational theories: (a) there are likely *multiple vocational options* for which a person is qualified and well suited; (b) success at work is most likely when the *person fits the environment*; and (c) people and environments change over time, so vocational and career decision making must be considered a *developmental process*.

Super's Life-Span and Life-Space Theory of Career Development

Super's theory is a multifaceted view of career development based on constructs from developmental, social, and personality psychology combined with learning and self-concept theory (Super, 1990, 1994). Super's theory is developmental in nature and examines the notion of trait and factor congruence (Szymanski, Enright, Hershenson, & Ettinger, 2010; Szymanski & Hershenson, 2005). Super (1990) posited that each occupation requires a characteristic pattern of ability and personality characteristics (i.e., needs, values, interests, traits, and self-concept). As a result of these characteristics, people are qualified for a number of occupations. The vocational preferences, competencies, and environments in which people live and work change with time and experience. A key component of Super's model is the **life career rainbow** that combines situational and personal determinants with life roles and life stages. **Life roles** proposed by Super include *child, student, leisurite, citizen, worker,* and *homemaker.* The following **life stages** and corresponding ages reflect the developmental nature of Super's theory: *growth (birth–14), exploration (15–24), establishment (26–44), maintenance (45–64),* and *decline (65+).* Although age ranges for stage transition are offered, actual transition ages are flexible and "each transition involves a recycling through one or more stages—a mini-cycle" (Super, 1990, p. 215). Super (1994) further suggested that success in coping with demands of the environment depends on the readiness of the individual to cope with these demands (i.e., **career maturity**). The nature of an individual's career pattern is determined by the individual's parental socioeconomic level, mental ability, education, skills, personalities, and career maturity, and by the opportunities to which he or she is exposed.

Super's (1990) conceptualization of career development has been applied frequently to the practice of career counseling. For example, his work on the life career rainbow, which combines situational and personal antecedents with life roles and stages and career maturity, has been applied in a number of ways, including underpinning instruments such as the *Career Development Inventory* (Thompson & Linderman, 1984) and the *Career Maturity Inventory* (Crites, 1978). Super's theory has been found to be useful in addressing the special career needs of individuals with disabilities, particularly those with congenital problems. The limitations in early experiences—including opportunities for play, work role fantasies, and career-related role playing—hinder people with congenital disabilities from full participation in career planning and decision making (Szymanski et al., 2010; Szymanski & Hershenson, 2005; Thomas & Parker, 1992; Turner & Szymanski, 1990).

Holland's Theory of Vocational Personalities and Work Environments

As its name implies, Holland's theory focuses on a person–environment fit that depends upon the congruence between individual personalities and environmental characteristics (Holland, 1997). According to Holland's theory, individuals exhibit aspects of the following six **work personalities**: realistic (R), investigational (I), artistic (A), social (S), enterprising (E), and conventional (C). "The more closely a person resembles a particular personality type, the more likely he or she is to exhibit the personal traits or behaviors associated with that type" (Holland, 1997, pp. 1–2). The **work environment** consists of the same six traits that can be applied to describe the characteristics of various educational and employment opportunities (Holland, 1997). The matching of the individual's work personality type and environment leads to the increased prediction of vocational and educational outcomes, including vocational choice and achievement, educational choice and achievement, competence, social behavior, and vulnerability to influence. The RIASEC hexagon is a structural model used to represent the interrelationships among the six types and work environments, and it has been central to Holland's theory and its application in applied settings (Tracey & Rounds, 1995). Over the past 20 to 30 years, comprehensive meta-analyses (Rounds & Tracey, 1996; Tracey & Rounds, 1993), combined with research using more representative samples (Day, Rounds, & Swaney, 1998; Fouad, Harmon, & Borgen, 1997), and increasingly sophisticated structural methods (Armstrong, Hubert, & Rounds, 2003; Deng, Armstrong, & Rounds, 2007) have provided some empirical support for Holland's structural model. Personal identity and environmental identity are important constructs related to Holland's theory. **Personal identity** is defined as "the possession of a clear and stable picture of one's goals, interests, and talents," and **environmental identity** is defined as being "present when an environment or organization has clear and integrated goals, tasks, and rewards that are stable over time intervals" (Holland, 1997, p. 5).

Due to its ease of use and strong research support, Holland's model has been applied widely in current counseling settings, although some criticisms have appeared that question the possibility of application to various disability populations (Conte, 1983; Hagner & Salomone, 1989). However, Szymanski et al. (2010) and Szymanski and Hershenson (2005) suggested that this model can be applied with important precautions. For example, the *My Vocational Situation* assessment (Holland, Daiger, & Power, 1980), which addresses vocational identity, is also useful for appraising the readiness of career planning for people with disabilities. The *Self-Directed Search* (SDS; Holland, 1985) is another instrument that operationalizes the RIASEC typology, and it has a version for people with low reading levels. It is useful for engaging people with disabilities in career planning. RCs should be aware of the potential impact of disability in limiting expressed interests: individuals with disabilities may respond negatively to SDS items because they may believe that they cannot perform the required tasks due to physical and cognitive limitations. Another caution for RCs is that limited early life and educational experiences may hinder the vocational development of people with congenital disabilities, resulting in a flat interest profile (Conte, 1983; Turner & Szymanski, 1990).

Minnesota Theory of Work Adjustment

The original development of the Minnesota theory of work adjustment was supported by a federally funded rehabilitation program to address how the individuals being evaluated in the VR program adjusted to work (Lofquist & Dawis, 1969). This theory is based on a series of person–environment constructs emphasizing the work personality–work environment correspondence leading to job satisfaction and satisfactoriness (Dawis, 2000, 2005). Theoretically, *work adjustment* is defined as the process by which the person achieves and maintains correspondence with the work environment (Lofquist & Dawis, 1969). According to this model, the constructs of *skills* and *needs* are used to describe the person's work personality, whereas the two complementary terms *reinforcers* and *skill requirements* are used to describe the work environment. The correspondence between the person's skills and the skill requirements of the work environment determines **satisfactoriness** (i.e., the extent to which the individual is capable of performing the job). The correspondence between the person's needs and the reinforcers of work environment determines the person's **satisfaction** with the job. Satisfactoriness and satisfaction result in **tenure** (i.e., the period of time the individual holds the job), which is the principal indicator of work adjustment (Lofquist & Dawis, 1969). **Work adjustment** is defined as "the continuous and dynamic process by which the individual seeks to achieve and maintain correspondence with the work environment" (Lofquist & Dawis, 1969, p. 46).

Lofquist and Dawis (1969) initially suggested that, due to the ease of administration of the instruments associated with the theory, RCs should be able to spend more time and resources on counseling individuals with disabilities. Assessment instruments and supporting materials used to operationalize, test, and apply the Minnesota theory of work adjustment have been developed widely. Readers are referred to the website (www.psych .umn.edu/psylabs/vpr/default.htm) from Vocational Psychology Research Program of the Department of Psychology, University of Minnesota, to get more information. Readers can also review two textbooks from Szymanski et al. (2010) and Szymanski and Hershenson (2005) for a detailed description of the theory and its application.

Social Cognitive Career Theory

The development of the social cognitive career theory was based on Bandura's general social cognitive theory (Bandura, 1986). This theory emphasizes the complex ways in which individuals' personal attributes, external environmental factors, and overt behaviors operate as interlocking mechanisms that mutually influence one another and the individuals' learning experiences (Lent, 2005; Lent, Brown, & Hackett, 1996, 2002). Following the basic tenets of social cognitive theory, social cognitive career theory highlights the interplay of three variables that enable the exercise of personal agency in career development: namely, **self-efficacy** (i.e., judgments of one's own capabilities to attain specific tasks), **outcome expectations** (i.e., beliefs about the anticipated results of performing particular behaviors), and **personal motivations** (i.e., intention to carry out a particular activity or to produce a particular outcome). The theory acknowledges that people are capable of directing their own vocational behavior (**human agency**) and even negotiating personal (e.g., predispositions, race, ethnicity, gender, disability, and health status) and contextual variables (e.g., sociostructural barriers, support, and culture) to prevail in career development. Social cognitive career theory intends to provide a potentially unifying model to explain how people develop vocational interests, make career choices, and achieve varying levels of career success and stability (Lent, 2005; Lent et al., 1996, 2002).

Social cognitive career theory shares certain goals and features with trait factor (or person–environment fit) and developmental career theories. It has been useful in guiding practice and research on career counseling and vocational intervention for people with disabilities (Strauser, Ketz, & Keim, 2002) and minorities (Lent et al., 2002). In particular, this theory offers a unifying model to guide RCs as they assist clients in examining and overcoming barriers engendered by personal limitations, environmental factors, and/ or learning experiences. In addition, this theory also provides a blueprint for guiding rehabilitation counseling research and practice of facilitating career choice making, promoting career aspirations, expanding vocational alternatives, improving self-efficacy, and promoting work satisfaction among people with disabilities.

Hershenson's Theory of Work Adjustment Development

Work adjustment is comprised of two essential elements: the person and the person's environment (Hershenson, 1996b). The person consists of the following three subsystems that develop sequentially: *work personality, work competencies,* and *work goals.* **Work personality** develops during the preschool years and is influenced mostly by the family. It consists of one's self-concept as a worker, work motivation, and work-related needs and values. Work competencies develop during the school years and are influenced by successes and failures in school settings. **Work competencies** consist of work habits, physical and mental skills, and work-related interpersonal skills (Strauser et al., 2002; Szymanski & Hershenson, 2005). Appropriate work goals develop prior to leaving school and are influenced by one's peer or reference groups (Hershenson, 1996a). **Work goals** should be clear, realistic, and consistent with the person's work personality and work competencies. Hershenson (1996b) mentioned three components in the person's environment, including *organizational culture and behavioral expectations, job demands and skill requirements,* and the *rewards and opportunities* available to the worker. Szymanski et al. (2010) and Szymanski and Hershenson (2005) suggested that the product of the interaction of the person's subsystems and work environment is work adjustment. Hershenson also discussed the following three domains of work adjustment: work role behavior, task performance, and work satisfaction. **Work role behavior** refers to displaying appropriate behaviors in the work setting, which is primarily related to work personality in the person and the behavioral expectations of the work setting. **Task performance** refers to the quality and quantity of one's work output, which is related primarily to work competencies in the person and the skill requirements of the work setting. **Work satisfaction** refers to one's degree of gratification resulting from work, which is related primarily to the work goals of the person, and the rewards and opportunities in the work setting.

Hershenson's theory was designed particularly to be applicable to people with disabilities. Theoretically, individuals must address two major environmental transitions in facilitating work adjustment: the transition from home to school and the transition from school to work. However, for individuals who experience an impediment in the course of their career track, there may be a third or fourth environmental transition (rehabilitation counseling or a shifting of careers). Success in the current transition will depend on the individual's experience during previous transitions (Szymanski et al., 2010; Szymanski & Hershenson, 2005). Research has found that individuals with disabilities who had higher levels of work personality have higher levels of job readiness, self-efficacy, and more internalized work locus of control (Strauser et al., 2002).

USING THE WORK AND WELL-BEING MODEL

The five career development and work adjustment theories discussed in the previous section have their strengths and utiliy, but also have limitations that preclude their exclusive application to the career and vocational counseling of individuals with disabilities

(Conte, 1983; Szymanski & Hershenson, 2005). Research regarding the career development and employment of individuals with disabilities has identified the following three factors that limit the application of existing career and vocational theories: (a) limitations in career exploratory experiences, (b) limited opportunities to develop decision-making abilities, and (c) a negative self-concept resulting from negative societal attitudes toward individuals with disabilities (Curnow, 1989). Because of the various limitations, the five theories discussed herein are of questionable use in describing, predicting, planning, and implementing career development and employment interventions designed to facilitate better career and employment outcomes of individuals with disabilities.

Over the past 15 years, several attempts have been made to address the limitations noted and develop a comprehensive model that would address these issues (Hershenson & Szymanski, 1992; Szymanski & Hershenson, 1998; Szymanski, Hershenson, Enright, & Ettinger, 1996). Despite the efforts to develop a comprehensive theory, some have questioned this need given the diversity and heterogeneity of individuals with disabilities (Thomas & Berven, 1990). One alternative to developing a comprehensive theory is employing a model to guide RCs in their provision of VR services to individuals with disabilities. **The Work and Well-Being** model is based on the World Health Organization's *ICF* model, and thus can be applied to all clients regardless of specific disability, life factors, or career goals. The two domains contained within this model are *career* and *context*, or *work* and *well-being*. Figure 15.1 depicting the model reminds us how closely linked life factors are, and how interventions, when appropriately prioritized and designed with an appreciation of this relationship in mind, can positively impact both work and well-being. The model facilitates comprehensive conceptualization of diverse clients, with the ultimate goal being selection of appropriate interventions using

TABLE 15.2   Summary of Major Vocational and Career Theories

Theory	Key Concepts	Possible Limitations for PWD
Super's Life-Span, Life-Space Theory	Career rainbow Life roles Life stages Career maturity	PWD have reduced opportunities across the life span that can impact career maturity, roles, and stages.
Minnesota Theory of Work Adjustment	Satisfaction Satisfactoriness Reinforcers Skill requirements	Emphasizes current person–environment congruence at the expense of considering earlier life experiences known to impact career/vocational behavior.
Bandura's Social Cognitive Career Theory	Self-efficacy Outcome expectations Motivations	Applicable in Western societies that promote and value personal agency; may have limited utility with people with other worldviews.
Hershenson's Theory of Work Adjustment	Work personality Work competencies Work goals/values	Can be difficult for the rehabilitation counselor to determine which subsystem is most likely the source of work-related failure when factors overlap all three subsystems
Holland's Theory of Person–Environment Fit	RIASEC hexagon Congruence Personal identity Environmental identity	Disability can limit one's expressed interests. People can have high interest and low capacity to obtain necessary skills and education.

PWD, people with disability.

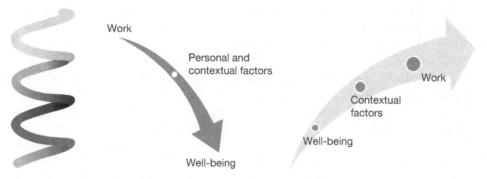

Figure 15.2   Linkage of work and well-being.

tenets of career and vocational theory in combination with prioritization of health and contextual factors that are impacting work. Preventing a downward spiral is critical. Facilitation of an upward spiral is possible and likely when appropriate interventions are employed.

As outlined earlier in this chapter, work and well-being are intricately linked. As one's health deteriorates, work capacity will inevitably be negatively affected (see Table 15.2). Imagine a spiral where factors move up or down together. Having upward momentum in one domain, such as work, can propel one's health to move in the same direction. One primary goal of rehabilitation counseling is to facilitate stable health, so that a downward spiral is avoided. The spiral relationship between work and well-being is mediated by personal and environmental factors. When they are positive and protective, they serve to buffer a potentially downward spiral when health is deteriorating; these factors, when negative, serve as risk factors for worsening health and career status. Effective RCs can use theory and the Work and Well-Being Model to ensure that protective personal and environmental factors are in place to promote an upward momentum. As you read the next section on rehabilitation counseling interventions, keep the Work and Well-Being Model, and the image of the spiral depicted in Figure 15.2, in mind.

REHABILITATION COUNSELING INTERVENTIONS

Individual and Group Career Counseling

Individual career counseling is a largely verbal process in which the counselor and client engage in a dynamic interaction where the counselor employs a repertoire of diverse behaviors. These behaviors are used to help bring about self-understanding and action in the form of "good" decision making on the part of the individual who has responsibility for his or her own actions (Herr & Cramer, 1996). Recent research regarding the vocational behavior of individuals receiving VR services has indicated that the core elements of the working alliance are especially powerful facilitators of change when providing individual career counseling services (Strauser, Lustig, & Donnell, 2004). The **working alliance** is a transtheoretical process that consists of the following three elements: (1) bonds, (2) goals, and (3) tasks (Strauser et al., 2004). Individuals who reported higher levels of working alliance with their VR counselor reported more satisfaction with their rehabilitation services and increased vocational outcomes (Lustig, Strauser, Weems, Donnell, & Smith, 2003). Research also has suggested that individuals receiving vocational services reported that they would have liked to receive more vocational counseling and desired a strong working relationship with their RC (Lustig et al., 2003). Group counseling is beneficial when counseling for career exploration, using visual imagery, developing locally relevant occupational information, teaching career decision making, and teaching job interviewing skills (Pope, 1999).

Vocational Evaluation

Vocational evaluation is a comprehensive and systematic process in which RCs and clients work together to assess and identify the client's vocational interests, abilities, aptitudes, work values, functional limitations, and barriers to employment. The main function of vocational evaluation services provided by RCs is to identify the client's strengths and weaknesses relative to the rehabilitation goal and employment outcome. According to the INCOME Model, the client in the iNforming status may benefit from a vocational evaluation, in which the client acquires information about himself or herself, the world of work, and potential supports and barriers.

Situational Assessment

Situational assessment is a valuable tool for RCs when assisting clients to make choices about the types of jobs and work environments that would be of interest. A **situational assessment** is an assessment that commonly involves actual employment and community settings, but can also be developed within the private sector for people with disabilities to explore their interests, assess current skill level, and provide training (Fraser & Johnson, 2010). Situational assessment allows information to be generated quickly concerning employment options that are worth pursuing further, and avoids wasting time on inappropriate job searches. In addition, many situational assessments can provide a transition to actual paid employment. Situational assessments can assist RCs and individuals with disabilities in determining potential accommodations that will be necessary for successful competitive employment. The client in the Choosing and Obtaining statuses may benefit from situational assessments. RCs can assist clients in the Choosing status to make career choices by understanding the fit between the individual and the work environment. RCs working together with the client in the Obtaining status can identify barriers to obtaining employment.

Job Site Accommodation

The Americans with Disabilities Act (ADA) of 1990 instituted the policy that employers must make a reasonable accommodation to the known physical and mental limitations of a qualified applicant or employee with a disability. RCs involved in the accommodation process can work with other rehabilitation professionals to determine what type of workplace accommodation may be needed or beneficial to facilitate competitive employment. According to the INCOME Model, a client in the Maintaining status may benefit from a job site accommodation, so that the client can adjust to the work demands and the work environment in order to maintain the job.

Job Development and Placement

Job development and placement interventions help clients with disabilities connect with the jobs that match their knowledge, skills, and abilities. RCs can assist with revising a resume, preparing the individual for a job interview, finding job leads, assisting with the submission of a job application, and setting up and attending interviews. They can also provide the assistance and support needed to help the individual attain the desired employment outcome. In accordance with the INCOME Model, the client in the Choosing and Obtaining statuses may benefit from job development and placement services.

Supported Employment

According to the Rehabilitation Act Amendments of 1998, **supported employment** is a program to assist people with the most significant disabilities to become and remain successfully and competitively employed in integrated workplace settings. It is targeted at individuals with the most significant disabilities for whom competitive employment has not occurred traditionally, or for whom competitive employment has been interrupted or has been intermittent because of a disability. Supported employment usually provides assistance such as job coaches, transportation, assistive technology, specialized job training, and individually tailored supervision. Typically, supported employment is a way to move people from dependency on a traditional service delivery system to independence via competitive employment (Wehman, 1996). There are several features of supported employment programs that differ from traditional job placement service approaches. First, supported employment programs seek to identify jobs that provide wages above the minimum wage, fringe benefits, and positions with career trajectories. Second, supported employment programs focus on providing the ongoing support required to get and keep a job rather than on getting a person ready for future employment. Third, supported employment programs emphasize creating opportunities to work rather than simply providing services to develop job skills for people with disabilities. Fourth, supported employment programs encourage full participation. Thus, all people— regardless of the degree of their disability—have the capacity to undertake supported employment if appropriate support services can be provided. Fifth, supported employment programs promote social integration in which people with disabilities are encouraged to interact with coworkers, supervisors, and others at work during lunch times or breaks and during nonwork hours as a result of wages earned. Lastly, supported employment programs promote flexibility in which people with disabilities are provided with various work options consistent with the wide range of job opportunities available in the community.

Benefits Counseling

Obtaining and maintaining competitive employment may have a significant impact on the benefits that individuals with disabilities receive. The provision of **benefits counseling** focuses on reviewing with the individual and RC what can be earned through work without jeopardizing or losing existing benefits if this is a concern for the individual with a disability. The goal of benefits counseling would be to develop a plan for achieving self-sufficiency or a work-related expense plan, so that the individual can maximize workplace participation while retaining important benefits (Fraser & Johnson, 2010).

Assistive Technology

Assistive technology is a class of interventions in which people with disabilities use technology to facilitate the performance of functional tasks (Kirsch & Scherer, 2010). Assistive technology not only includes mobility devices such as walkers and wheelchairs, but also includes computerized devices, software, and peripherals that assist people with disabilities in accessing and using computers or other information technologies. Various service delivery models regarding the application of assistive technology for people with disabilities have been developed in state rehabilitation agencies. Some of these services are provided by a vendor who is an RC who has special responsibility for providing assistive technology services; some others are offered by pertinent health care providers, such as an occupational therapist or an assistive technologist. Evidence also showed that assistive technology can be used to enhance the employment opportunities for people with disabilities (Noll, Owens, Smith, & Schwanke, 2006). Thus, it is important that RCs should be knowledgeable and competent in assistive technology services. RCs should identify the need for assistive technology services or devices for people with disabilities, provide information regarding assistive technology to people with disabilities, and coordinate assistive technology services.

CONCLUSION

Career development, vocational behavior, and employment of individuals with disabilities is a complex and dynamic process that is developmental in nature; it involves the person interacting with the environment and is moderated by social cognitive factors. In this chapter, we attempted to provide RCs with an overview of information that is important to understanding career and vocational behavior and ultimately to enhancing the career and employment outcomes of individuals with disabilities. In discussing the centrality of work and discussing how work is critical in meeting human needs, RCs gain an understanding that work plays an important role in the individual's level of mental health and social integration. Theories of career development were reviewed briefly in an effort to provide RCs with a model to understand the complex nature of vocational behavior. The INCOME Model was introduced as a mechanism that RCs can use in conceptualizing and strategizing the delivery of rehabilitation services. Finally, we briefly described various interventions that can be used by RCs in facilitating vocational behavior change.

Overall, much work is still needed to gain a better understanding of work and disability. There is a very significant need to conduct studies that evaluate the impact of career counseling and vocational interventions for individuals with disabilities. To date, most of the research in this area has focused on supported employment and related interventions. These types of interventions appear to be very robust for those with severe disabilities. However, little, if any, research has been done to examine the development and efficacy of interventions directed at those without severe disabilities. Expanding research beyond those with severe disabilities is a needed priority over the next 10 to 15 years.

CONTENT REVIEW QUESTIONS

- What are the assessment methods that RCs can use to evaluate clients' needs? Use Table 15.1 as a guide.
- For each of the five career theories presented, describe how each theory accounts for the following: individual development, career development, vocational behavior, the person–environment interaction, and important social cognitive variables.
- Explain the relationship between the three primary domains of the Illinois Work and Well-Being model.

- Identify how the Illinois Work and Well-Being model conceptualizes participation and the relevance of work in maximizing participation of people with disabilities.
- Explain how RCs can implement the Illinois Work and Well-Being model to guide career development and employment services for people with disabilities.

REFERENCES

Armstrong, P. I., Hubert, L., & Rounds, J. (2003). Circular unidimensional scaling: A new look at group differences in interest structure. *Journal of Counseling Psychology, 51,* 299–313.

Bandura, A. (1986). Social foundations of thought and action: A social-cognitive theory. Englewood Cliffs, NJ: Prentice Hall.

Baron, R. A., & Greenberg, J. (1990). *Behavior in organizations: Understanding and managing the human side of work.* Boston, MA: Allyn & Bacon.

Blustein, D. L. (1994). "Who am I?": The question of self and identity in career development. In M. L. Savickas & R. W. Lent (Eds.), *Convergence in career development theories: Implications for science and practice* (pp. 139–154). Palo Alto, CA: Consulting Psychologists Press.

Blustein, D. L. (2006). *The psychology of working: A new perspective for career development, counseling, and public policy.* Mahwah, NJ: Lawrence Erlbaum.

Blustein, D. L. (2008). The role of work in psychological health and well-being. *American Psychologist, 63*(4), 228–240. doi:10.1037/0003-66X.63.4.228

Blustein, D. L., Kenna, A. C., Gill, N., & DeVoy, J. E. (2008). The psychology of working: A new model for counseling practice and public policy. *Career Development Quarterly, 56,* 294–308.

Bond, G. R., Resnick, S. G., Drake, R. E., Xie, H., McHugo, G. J., & Bebout, R. R. (2001). Does competitive employment improve nonvocational outcomes for people with severe mental illness? *Journal of Consulting and Clinical Psychology, 69*(3), 489–501.

Bowlby, J. (1982). Attachment and loss: Retrospect and prospect. *American Journal of Orthopsychiatry, 52,* 664–678.

Bureau of Labor Statistics. (2016, June 21). Persons with a disability: Labor force characteristics—2015 (News Release, USDL-16-1248). Retrieved from https://www.bls.gov/news.release/archives/disabl_06212016.pdf

Conte, L. (1983). Vocational development theories and the disabled person: Oversight or deliberate omission. *Rehabilitation Counseling Bulletin, 26,* 316–328.

Crites, J. O. (1978). *Career maturity inventory.* Monterery, CA: McGraw-Hill.

Curnow, T. C. (1989). Vocational development of persons with disability. *Vocational Guidance Quarterly, 37,* 269–278.

Dawis, R. V. (2000). The person-environment tradition in counseling psychology. In W. E. Martin Jr. & J. L. Swartz-Kulstad (Eds.), *Person-environment psychology and mental health* (pp. 91–111). Mahwah, NJ: Lawrence Erlbaum.

Dawis, R. V. (2005). The Minnesota theory of work adjustment. In S. D. Brown & R. W. Lent (Eds.), *Career development and counseling: Putting theory and research to work* (pp. 3–23). Hoboken, NJ: Wiley.

Day, S. X., Rounds, J., & Swaney, K. (1998). The structure of vocational interests for diverse racial-ethnic groups. *Psychological Science, 9,* 40–44.

Deng, C.-P., Armstrong, P. I., & Rounds, J. (2007). The fit of Holland's RIASEC model to US occupations. *Journal of Vocational Behavior, 71,* 1–22. doi:10.1016/j.jvb.2007.04.002

Edgell, P. (2006). *Religion and family in a changing society.* Princeton, NJ: Princeton University Press.

Fogg, N. R., Harrington, P. E., & McMahon, B. T. (2010). Impact of the great recession upon the unemployment of adults with disabilities. *Journal of Vocational Rehabilitation, 33,* 193–202.

Fouad, N. A., Harmon, L. W., & Borgen, F. H. (1997). Structure of interests in employed male and female members of US racial-ethnic minority and non-minority groups. *Journal of Counseling Psychology, 44,* 339–345.

Fraser, R. T., & Johnson, K. (2010). Vocational rehabilitation. In R. G. Frank, M. Rosenthal, & B. Caplan (Eds.), *Handbook of rehabilitation psychology* (pp. 357–363). Washington, DC: American Psychological Association.

Gottfredson, L. (2002). Gottfredson's theory of circumscription, compromise, and self-creation. In D. Brown & Associates (Eds.), *Career choice and development* (pp. 85–148). San Francisco, CA: Jossey-Bass.

Hagner, D., & Salomone, P. (1989). Issues in career decision making for workers with developmental disabilities. *Career Development Quarterly, 38,* 148–159.

Herr, E. L., & Cramer, S. H. (1996). *Career guidance and counseling through the lifespan: Systematic approaches.* New York, NY: HarperCollins College.

Hershenson, D. B. (1981). Work adjustment, disability, and the three R's of vocational rehabilitation: A conceptual model. *Rehabilitation Counseling Bulletin, 25,* 91–97.

Hershenson, D. B. (1996a). A systems reformulation of a developmental model of work adjustment. *Rehabilitation Counseling Bulletin, 40,* 2–10.

Hershenson, D. B. (1996b). Work adjustment: A neglected area in career counseling. *Journal of Counseling and Development, 74,* 442–446.

Hershenson, D. B., & Szymanski, E. M. (1992). Career development of people with disabilities. In R. M. Parker & E. M. Szymanski (Eds.), *Rehabilitation counseling: Basics and beyond* (pp. 273–303). Austin, TX: Pro-Ed.

Holland, J. L. (1985). *The self-directed search professional manual.* Odessa, FL: Psychological Assessment Resources.

Holland, J. L. (1997). *Making vocational choices: A theory of vocational personalities and work environments.* Odessa, FL: Psychological Assessment Resources.

Holland, J. L., Daiger, D. C., & Power, P. G. (1980). *My vocational situation.* Palo Alto, CA: Consulting Psychologists Press.

Kahn, R. L., & Byosiere, P. (1990). Stress in organizations. In M. Dunnette (Ed.), *Handbook of industrial and organizational psychology* (2nd ed., Vol. 3, pp. 571–650). Chicago, IL: Rand-McNally.

Kirsch, N. L., & Scherer, M. J. (2010). Assistive technology for cognition and behavior. In R. G. Frank, M. Rosenthal, & B. Caplan (Eds.), *Handbook of rehabilitation psychology* (pp. 273–284). Washington, DC: American Psychological Association.

Larson, J. E., Barr, L. K., Corrigan, P. W., Kuwabara, S. A., Boyle, M. G., & Glenn, T. L. (2007). Perspectives on benefits and costs of work from individuals with psychiatric disabilities. *Journal of Vocational Rehabilitation, 26*(2), 71–77.

Lent, R. W. (2005). A social cognitive view of career development and counseling. In S. D. Brown & R. W. Lent (Eds.), *Career development and counseling: Putting theory and research to work* (pp. 101–127). Hoboken, NJ: Wiley.

Lent, R. W., Brown, S. D., & Hackett, G. (1996). Career development from a social cognitive perspective. In D. Brown & L. Brooks (Eds.), *Career choice and development* (pp. 373–421). San Francisco, CA: Jossey-Bass.

Lent, R. W., Brown, S. D., & Hackett, G. (2002). Contextual supports and barriers to career choice: A social cognitive analysis. *Journal of Counseling Psychology, 47,* 36–49.

Lofquist, L. H., & Dawis, R. V. (1969). *Adjustment to work: A psychological view of man's problems in a work-oriented society.* New York, NY: Appleton-Century-Crofts.

Lui, J. W., Chan, F., Fried, J. H., Lin, C. P., Anderson, C. A., & Patterson, M. (2010). Roles and functions of benefits counseling specialists: A multi-trait analysis. *Journal of Vocational Rehabilitation, 32,* 163–173.

Lustig, D. C., & Strauser, D. R. (2007). Causal relationships between poverty and disability. *Rehabilitation Counseling Bulletin, 50*(4), 194–202.

Lustig, D. C., Strauser, D. R., Weems, G. H., Donnell, C., & Smith, L. D. (2003). Traumatic brain injury and rehabilitation outcomes: Does working alliance make a difference? *Journal of Applied Rehabilitation Counseling, 34*(4), 30–37.

Neff, W. S. (1985). *Work and human behavior.* New York, NY: Aldine.

Noll, A., Owens, L., Smith, R. O., & Schwanke, T. (2006). Survey of state vocational rehabilitation counselor roles and competencies in assistive technology. *Work: A Journal of Prevention, Assessment and Rehabilitation, 27*(4), 413–419.

O'Sullivan, D., & Strauser, D. (2010). Validation of the developmental work personality model and scale. *Rehabilitation Counseling Bulletin, 54*(1), 46–56. doi:10.1177/0034355210378045

Patterson, J. B., Szymanski, E. M., & Parker, R. M. (2005). Rehabilitation counseling: The profession. In R. M. Parker, E. M. Szymanski, & J. B. Patterson (Eds.), *Rehabilitation counseling: Basics and beyond* (pp. 1–25). Austin, TX: Pro-Ed.

Pope, M. (1999). Applications of group career counseling techniques in Asian cultures. *Journal of Multicultural Counseling and Development, 27,* 18–31.

Quick, J. C., Quick, J. D., Nelsom, D. L., & Hurrell, J. J. Jr. (1997). *Preventative stress management in organizations.* Washington, DC: American Psychological Association.

Rounds, J., & Tracey, T. J. (1996). Cross-cultural structure equivalence of RIASEC models and measures. *Journal of Counseling Psychology, 43,* 310–329.

Ryan, R. M., & Deci, E. L. (2000). Self-determination theory and the facilitation of intrinsic motivation, social development, and well-being. *American Psychologist, 55,* 68–78.

Schein, E. (1990). Organizational culture. *American Psychologist, 45,* 109–119.

Strauser, D. R., Ketz, K., & Keim, J. (2002). The relationship between self-efficacy, locus of control and work personality. *Journal of Rehabilitation, 68*(1), 20–26.

Strauser, D. R., Lustig, D. C., & Donnell, C. (2004). The impact of the working alliance on therapeutic outcomes for individuals with mental retardation. *Rehabilitation Counseling Bulletin, 47,* 215–223.

Strauser, D. R., O'Sullivan, D., & Wong, A. W. K. (2010). The relationship between contextual work behaviors, self-efficacy, and work personality: An exploratory analysis. *Disability and Rehabilitation, 32*(24), 1999–2008. doi:10.3109/09638281003797380

Super, D. E. (1969). The development of vocational potential. In D. Malikin & H. Rusalem (Eds.), *Vocational rehabilitation of the disabled: An overview* (pp. 75–90). New York: New York University Press.

Super, D. E. (1990). A life-span, life-space approach to career development. In D. Brown & L. Brooks (Eds.), *Career choices and development: Applying contemporary theories to practice* (pp. 197–261). San Francisco, CA: Jossey-Bass.

Super, D. E. (1994). A life span, life space perspectives on convergence. In M. L. Savickas & R. W. Lent (Eds.), *Convergence in career development theories: Implications for science and practice* (pp. 63–74). Palo Alto, CA: Consulting Psychologists Press.

Szymanski, E. M., Enright, M. S., Hershenson, D. B., & Ettinger, J. M. (2010). Career development theories and constructs: Implications for people with disabilities. In E. M. Szymanski & R. M. Parker (Eds.), *Work and disability: Contexts, issues, and strategies for enhancing employment outcomes for people with disabilities* (pp. 87–131). Austin, TX: Pro-Ed.

Szymanski, E. M., & Hershenson, D. B. (1998). Career development of people with disabilities: An ecological model. In R. M. Parker & E. M. Szymanski (Eds.), *Rehabilitation counseling: Basics and beyond* (pp. 327–378). Austin, TX: Pro-Ed.

Szymanski, E. M., & Hershenson, D. B. (2005). An ecological approach to vocational behavior and career development of people with disabilities. In R. M. Parker, E. M. Szymanski, & J. B. Patterson (Eds.), *Rehabilitation counseling: Basics and beyond* (pp. 225–280). Austin, TX: Pro-Ed.

Szymanski, E. M., Hershenson, D. B., Enright, M. S., & Ettinger, J. M. (1996). Career development theories, constructs, and research: Implications for people with disabilities. In E. M. Szymanski & R. M. Parker (Eds.), *Work and disability: Issues and strategies in career development and job placement* (pp. 79–126). Austin, TX: Pro-Ed.

Szymanski, E. M., & Parker, R. M. (2010). Work and disability: Basic concepts. In E. M. Szymanski & R. M. Parker (Eds.), *Work and disability: Contexts, issues, and strategies for enhancing employment outcomes for people with disabilities* (pp. 1–15). Austin, TX: Pro-Ed.

Thomas, K. T., & Berven, N. (1990). Providing career counseling for individuals with handicapping conditions. In N. Gysbers & Associates (Eds.), *Designing careers* (pp. 403–432). San Francisco, CA: Josssey-Bass.

Thomas, K. T., & Parker, R. M. (1992). Application of theory to rehabilitation counseling practice. In S. E. Robertson & R. I. Brown (Eds.), *Rehabilitation counseling: Approaches in the field of disability* (pp. 34–78). London, UK: Chapman & Hall.

Thompson, A. S., & Linderman, R. H. (1984). *Career development inventory: Technical manual.* Palo Alto, CA: Consulting Psychologists Press.

Tracey, T. J., & Rounds, J. (1993). Evaluating Holland's and Gati's vocational-interest models: A structural meta-analysis. *Psychological Bulletin, 113,* 229–246.

Tracey, T. J., & Rounds, J. (1995). The arbitrary nature of Holland's RIASEC types: A concentric-circles structure. *Journal of Counseling Psychology, 42,* 431–439.

Turner, K. D., & Szymanski, E. M. (1990). Work adjustment of people with congenital disabilities: A longitudinal perspective from birth to adulthood. *Journal of Rehabilitation, 56*(3), 19–24.

Wehman, P. (1996). Supported employment: Inclusion for all in the workplace. In W. Stainback & S. Stainback (Eds.), *Controversial issues confronting special education: Divergent perspectives* (pp. 293–304). Boston, MA: Allyn & Bacon.

Wilson, W. J. (1996). *When work disappears: The world of the new urban poor.* New York, NY: Knopf.

Wolfensberger, W. (2002). Social role valorization and, or versus, "empowerment." *Mental Retardation, 40*(3), 252–258.

Wright, G. N. (1980). *Total rehabilitation.* Boston, MA: Little, Brown.

SIXTEEN

Forensic and Indirect Services

MARY BARROS-BAILEY

LEARNING OBJECTIVES

After reading this chapter, you should be able to:

- Identify the purpose and origins of forensic rehabilitation counseling and indirect service provision practice.
- Understand the difference between forensic rehabilitation and indirect service provision.
- Distinguish the settings within which forensic rehabilitation and indirect services are used.
- Understand the main methods and techniques applied in forensic and indirect service provision.
- Recognize the use of teams in forensic and indirect rehabilitation practice.
- Describe the main ethical issues for the forensic rehabilitation and indirect service practitioner.

Nearly two decades after *CSI*, the popular American police drama television series that started in 2000, made its debut, the effect on pop culture's understanding of forensic disciplines is evident. When forensic rehabilitation counselors (FRCs) are asked what they do and mention they are in forensic practice, the inquirer typically summons images of the FRC in a lab coat examining DNA samples or at a crime scene. The inquirer's interest is piqued, and it affords the FRC an opportunity not only to explain forensic practice from the rehabilitation perspective, but also to introduce the discipline of rehabilitation counseling itself.

Forensic and indirect service practice is a fast-growing specialty of rehabilitation counseling, and is the best paid. The specialty has much to contribute to general counseling. Scant literature exists regarding forensic practice in other counseling specialties (mental health, marriage and family, school, career, and so forth). The vast majority of the literature in general counseling uses the term *forensic* as a synonym in corrections or criminal justice practice settings where mental health, addictions, or other counseling practitioners may assess or treat a client (Cherner, Nandlal, Ecker, Aubry, & Pettey, 2013; Cianciulli, 1993; Dickens, Sugarman, & Walker, 2007; Gardner-Elahi & Zamiri, 2015; Glassmire, Welsh, & Clevenger, 2007; Jasper, Smith, & Bailey, 1998; Larson, DiCataldo, & Kinscherff, 2013; Livingston, Nijdam-Jones, & Team P.E.E.R., 2013; Pinter, 1999; Ryan, 1999, 2003; Sakdalan, Shaw, & Collier, 2010; Suarez, Weston, & Hartstein, 1978; Thurman, Wortzel, & Martinez, 2011; Travis & Sturmey, 2013). Even the National Association of Forensic Counselors (NAFC, 2009) states that its purpose is to "enhance delivery of safe and effective treatment of offenders in both civil and criminal cases" (para. 4). In this chapter, and within rehabilitation counseling, *forensics* describes those counselors performing evaluations and giving recommendations that inform the trier of fact about liability/damages in civil cases. The different specialties within the counseling profession have existing or untapped opportunities to contribute to the forensic and indirect service practice in civil and criminal legal systems within their respective scopes of practice.

To clarify the role of an FRC, the Commission on Rehabilitation Counselor Certification (CRCC, 2010) defined **forensic** as providing "expertise involving the application of professional knowledge and the use of scientific, technical, or other specialized knowledge for the resolution of legal or administrative issues, proceedings, or decisions" (p. 36). More recently, CRCC (2017) described practitioners in this practice setting as "conducting evaluations and/or reviews of records and conduct[ing] research for the purpose of providing unbiased and objective expert opinions via case consultation or testimony" (p. 18). The American Counseling Association (ACA, 2014) further defines one of the tasks performed by practitioners in this practice setting, describing the forensic evaluation as "the process of forming professional opinions for court or other legal proceedings, based on professional knowledge and expertise, and supported by appropriate data" (p. 20).

Although the CRCC (2010) does not provide a glossary definition for **indirect service practice**, it alludes to the practice as when "rehabilitation counselors [are] . . . employed by third parties as case consultants [and] . . . when there is no intent to provide rehabilitation counseling services directly to clients or evaluees" (p. 15). What is important about forensic and indirect practice is that "file review, second-opinion services, and other indirect services are not considered an ongoing professional relationship" (p. 8). Indeed, in forensic or indirect service practice, there is no client–counselor relationship, but the person for whom the services are being provided is called an **evaluee** (Barros-Bailey et al., 2008/2009).

Forensic and indirect service provision in rehabilitation counseling started long before the modern generation of RCs believe, and the need for those with RC training in these practice settings continues to grow. In its first practice-wide salary survey of rehabilitation counseling, the CRCC (2008) documented that FRCs are paid at a higher rate than any other RC specialty. The average salary for an RC in any setting was $50,000 annually; for those in forensic practice, the average annual salary was $93,000; for those RCs employed in settings such as workers' compensation agencies, private/proprietary rehabilitation, or private practice, average earnings ranged from $58,000 to $74,000 annually (2008). This chapter identifies the origins of forensic and indirect service provision at the very start of the rehabilitation counseling profession nearly a century ago, and traces its growth and trajectory to its continued spread and growth today. The settings, methods, techniques, resources, and ethics of FRC practice are also identified.

HISTORY OF FORENSIC AND INDIRECT SERVICES

The history of forensic rehabilitation and indirect service provision in rehabilitation counseling has often been assumed to be a modern phenomenon emerging with the current generation of practitioners. This impression is incorrect. In fact, the need for practitioners answering the kinds of questions and providing the kinds of services typically addressed today by forensic practitioners can be traced back as far as the mid to late

1800s. At that time, issues of just compensation for loss of the ability to work due to personal injuries were being addressed by juries in cases involving workers and injuries in railroad transportation during the Industrial Revolution (Barros-Bailey, 2014).

By the first decade of the 1900s when the first known counselor, Frank Parsons, was writing *Choosing a Vocation* (1909), states began enacting legislation for no-fault coverage of injuries at work, called **workers' compensation laws**. These laws produced questions that could not be determined just by the administrative rules enacted by such legislation, but were argued in hearings before administrative law bodies and appealed into higher courts by the interested parties. The trier of fact attempted to establish precedent of how the law should be applied in practice. For example, in 1919 the Supreme Court of Illinois ruled on *The Peabody Coal Company v. The Industrial Commission et al.* (1919) case, appealed from lower courts, about fair compensation for an injured worker. This is also the first case in which an expert witness is found to testify on identical issues addressed by FRCs today. Specifically, the case states that "the employer contended that the testimony of the employee's expert witnesses that his partial disability permanently impaired his earning capacity 25 percent was inadmissible because it was an ultimate issue of fact before the arbitrator and the Commission" (Sec. Case Summary, para. 2). From references in case law, it appears that early expert witnesses providing testimony in these kinds of compensation cases were physicians.

The Illinois Supreme Court ruled on the *Peabody* case (1919) the year before the Smith-Fess Act (1920) was enacted that provided counseling, training, prosthetic appliances, and job placement for people with physical disabilities from work injuries. In the Smith-Fess Act, the initial definition of who qualified for services was expanded. Thus, that Act subsequently created the need and structure for what would become the federal-state rehabilitation program of today. In this process, Tracy Copp and William Faulkes from the Wisconsin industrial rehabilitation system brought their expertise of working in the rehabilitation of injured workers to the national capital to spread the philosophy and practice of rehabilitation to all people with disabilities across the nation. Workers' compensation legislation in the civilian sector was concurrent with similar legislation for World War I veterans from 1914 through 1918 (War Risk Act [1914]; Smith-Hughes Act [1917]; and the Smith-Sears Act or Social Rehabilitation Act [1918]).

These developments created the need for a new kind of professional. This practitioner would understand function resulting from physical, mental, and cognitive conditions within the context of the major functions of living (e.g., employment) and develop interventions (e.g., training, physical aids) to help bridge and maximize opportunities for that individual with a disability. RCs were uniquely qualified not only to work in the delivery of services cross-functionally across silos of other disciplines such as medicine and psychology, but also to apply that knowledge base to questions addressed in the courts by physicians.

The intermarriage between the industrial rehabilitation system and the public rehabilitation system and the application to forensic practice is evident in historical records documenting such relationship beginning in the late 1920s (Barros-Bailey, 2014). Indeed, by the mid-1930s, RCs from the federal-state rehabilitation system were being used as expert witnesses on lump-sum settlement decisions involving injured workers (Dawson, 1936).

Although the inception of RCs used as expert witnesses is documented in the literature and cases from the late 1920s, such use expanded slowly for 30 years. The boom in the practice of forensic rehabilitation started in the early 1960s, as a result of two acts by Congress a half decade earlier. The first legislation enacted was the Vocational

Rehabilitation Act of 1954, which professionalized rehabilitation counseling through graduate education and research. The second was the U.S. Social Security Act Amendments of 1956, which integrated disability into its covered benefits. In 1960, the Second Circuit Court of Appeals decided, in *Kerner v. Fleming*, that the U.S. Social Security Administration had the burden of proof as to a claimant's disability. The source for such expert witness testimony was readily found in a well-educated and prepared professional: the RC. By 1962, the *Kerner* criteria swelled the need for vocational expert testimony to 10,000 instances per month and the U.S. Social Security Administration established a formal program for using vocational expert witness testimony in the disability adjudication process.

Attorneys representing clients attempting to qualify for U.S. Social Security disability benefits were suddenly exposed to RCs in a forensic arena in substantial numbers. The legal representatives recognized the usefulness of the FRC's skill set for cases in other jurisdictions. This recognition began the expansion of FRC usage outside the historical workers' compensation and U.S. Social Security social insurance settings, to a larger continuum of cases: bankruptcy law; civil injury; employment law (e.g., Age Discrimination in Employment Act, Americans with Disabilities Act [ADA] and Amendments, Federal and Medical Leave Act, Individuals with Disabilities Education Act); insurance (credit disability, life, liability, no-fault automobile, short/long-term disability); marital dissolution; pension funds; student loan default; tort (Jones Act, Longshore Act, Railroad Retirement Board/Federal Employees Liability Act); trust fund management; and more (Barros-Bailey, 2014).

Those vocational experts filling the ranks of need by the U.S. Social Security Administration and other sources came primarily from rehabilitation counseling. However, the vast demand for the number of experts outstripped the number of RCs available to provide services. As a result, others were recruited to provide vocational expert witness testimony, such as psychologists (particularly from vocational and rehabilitation specialties), counselors (e.g., career), nurses (e.g., rehabilitation), and other adjunct professions. Some of these professionals were already in private practice in clinical specialties. Others were practicing in government or industry and were drawn to a different application of their skill set.

As the forensic rehabilitation and indirect service sector expanded in the 1970s and 1980s, FRCs sought opportunities to connect and discuss issues particular to the growing practice setting. New organizations were formed such as the American Board of Vocational Experts (ABVE) and the National Association of Rehabilitation Professionals in the Private Sector (NARPPS, now called the International Association of Rehabilitation Professionals, IARP), or sections of existing organizations were formed (e.g., National Association of Service Providers in Private Rehabilitation [NASPPR] with the National Rehabilitation Association [NRA]). The organizations within the specialty created a platform where FRCs could connect not only about the business mechanics of practice, such as marketing, insurance, and paraprofessional staffing, but also about advocacy, training, and self-regulation (e.g., ethics, standards of practice).

THE LEGAL AND SYSTEMIC CONTEXT

A detailed review of the legal and systemic context in which an FCR or indirect service provider may practice is beyond the scope of this chapter. The reader is directed to the "Introduction to the American Legal System and Rules of Civil Procedure: A Primer for

Vocational Experts" by Patrick Dunn (2014) or any contemporary survey of the legal context of practice within the RC's country. Generally, an understanding of how the courts are structured and the jurisdiction is delineated at various local, regional, or national levels; the venue; procedural rules; and the FRC's place with the structure, jurisdiction, or system is recommended (Dunn, 2014).

In any case, the FRC can be asked to be a testifying expert, where the FRC's involvement is disclosed as an **expert retained for litigation** to offer opinions; or as an **expert not retained for litigation**, such as an RC who provides direct service, but who will not be providing expert opinions but testifying about factual knowledge. The FRC could be asked to serve as a **consulting expert**; in this instance his or her involvement in the case is never divulged to anyone outside of the retaining party. As a consulting expert, the FRC provides nondirect services that may involve a review of the data and evidence in the case to assist the retaining party to prepare or deliver a strategy. In some circumstances, the FRC could be hired for indirect services that are not specifically related to forensic issues or do not involve direct contact with the evaluee. Examples are performing a labor market analysis given the evaluee's specific residual functional capacity in a particular national or international labor market, providing second opinions as to rates of disability or interventions, assisting the retaining party to identify the merits of a case based on a review of the evidence, or any other related service that may be within the FRC's general or individual scope of practice.

Vocational Expert Testimony

RCs in forensic and indirect service practice are typically hired to provide opinions as to the vocational losses, capacities, or potential interventions for an individual given an acquired condition anywhere along the life span from birth (e.g., wrongful birth cases) to natural or traumatic death (e.g., wrongful death cases). Each system or jurisdiction where FRCs work has separate rules. Knowing the rules in each system is important so FRCs are not using standards or criteria for the development of an opinion that do not correspond to the system in which they are providing services. For example, because someone is found to be qualified for disability benefits under the criteria of the U.S. Social Security Disability Insurance (SSDI) program does not mean that, given the same exact factors, the individual would likewise be considered equally qualified as disabled under a state's workers' compensation program or by a jury in a personal injury case, because the decision-making criteria for each jurisdiction is different. In U.S. Social Security disability adjudication, the vocational expert generally cannot take into consideration issues of accommodation or training capacity or an intervention plan, but these plans can be part of the opinions provided in other systems and may even be expected if the plaintiff has a duty to mitigate damages. Knowing the difference between systems is imperative if the FRC is to provide the appropriate services to the evaluee. A few of the most prominent jurisdictions employing FRCs are covered in this chapter.

Civil Injury Litigation

Civil injury litigation is based on a concept that citizens have basic rights as proclaimed through guiding societal documents as the Bill of Rights or the Massachusetts Body of Liberties (Robinson & Drew, 2014a). The basic principles of civil injury litigation come from these fundamental principles of common law to protect individuals from unjustified harm (Robinson & Drew, 2014a).

The practice areas in civil injury litigation include personal injury, product liability, and professional malpractice. The common vocational issues to be addressed by the FRC include loss of earning capacity, interventions (rehabilitation plan covering services and products to restore the evaluee to maximum vocational capacity based on his or her residual functional capacities), and damage mitigation efforts (Robinson & Drew, 2014a). Where preexisting or other confounding factors exist in a case, the FRC may be asked to apportion any opinion as to capacity of losses or costs of interventions between incident-specific and nonincident factors—the proverbial splitting of hairs in forensic practice.

FRCs practicing in civil injury law have very little probability of going to trial. The American Bar Association estimated in 1962 that 11.5% of cases made it to trial (Refo, 2004). By 2002, the rate of cases going to trial had dropped to 1.8% (Refo, 2004). In some states, such as Florida, by 2010–2011, less than 0.2% of cases went to trial (Williams, 2013).

Employment Law

Over the last century, employment law legislation has followed a trajectory starting with the rise of labor regulation, wage and hour laws, antidiscrimination laws, and protected leave and whistleblower protection at the state and national levels (Heitzman, Amundsen, Gann, & Christensen, 2014). The role of the FRC in this type of case is to "evaluate mitigation of damages and issues such as reasonableness of job search, duration of unemployment, existence of career damage, impact on earning capacity, and job accommodations" (Heitzman et al., 2014, p. 377).

In this setting, it is likely that the FRC may be asked to testify on both liability and damages sides of a case. **Liability issues** in a case involve *what happened* that was purportedly negligent, or what is often referred to as the "incident" that resulted in assumed injuries. **Damages issues** in a case do not worry about the cause of the incident, but attempt to measure the *impact* of the losses created by the assumed incident. For example, in a case asserting ADA violations, the FRC may opine on liability questions such as what kinds of procedures or accommodations the employer could have put in place to allow the individual to obtain or maintain employment; likewise, the FRC could evaluate damages such as the person's ability to engage in the labor market, the capacity to do so, and any plan and related cost to try to remediate any losses.

Marital Dissolution

When a couple agrees to legally separate their lives and their assets, sometimes issues of compensation or support of a spouse arise and must be evaluated. Kohlenberg (2014) outlines the essential services in the marital dissolution analysis performed by an FRC as involving (a) an earning capacity evaluation; (b) labor market research; and (c) vocational planning, which would be this system's version of the intervention or rehabilitation plan. The four areas of further consideration by an FRC as outlined by Kohlenberg (2014) are reentry problems, such as when the spouse has not worked in years and does not know what she or he could or wants to do; disability concerns that affect vocational functioning and choice; motivation questions that may be inconsistent with the evaluee's capacities; and possessing unrealistic expectations of support through prolonged training. Kohlenberg (2014) also identified other factors that could affect the evaluation, such as someone's ability to participate in the labor market and self-employment tax returns that suggest actual profits lower than someone's earning capacity. Special evaluation issues in marital dissolution cases may involve health, accommodations, location, language/culture, age, and child care or related costs (Kohlenberg, 2014).

U.S. Social Security Disability

Vercillo (2014) outlined the factors the FRC considers when presented with hypothetical questions at a hearing. Under U.S. Social Security disability law, the vocational factors considered in decisions regarding someone's capacity to work include age, education, and work experience as well as the claimant's level of skill within the context of strength or exertional levels and nonexertional physical and mental requirements (Vercillo, 2014).

These factors are adjudicated within the **Five-Step Sequential Evaluation Process**. The first three steps of the process include whether the claimant (1) is working or engaged in substantial gainful activity (SGA); (2) has a severe medically determinable impairment; and (3) the impairment meets or equals a medical listing (U.S. Social Security Administration, 2012). The FRC's input is relevant at the last two steps of that process, which are whether the individual can do his or her past work as he or she performed and as it is generally performed in the labor market (Step 4), or whether the individual could perform other work in the labor market (Step 5). Sometimes, this two-step process, which is also evident in short- and long-term disability systems, is call the **own occ** (own occupation) or **other occ** (other occupation) decision.

Workers' Compensation

Workers' compensation cases are the first cases found in the literature where FRC involvement became evident. However, because workers' compensation laws are different on the state, territory, and national levels, the variability between the jurisdictional requirements is the most difficult to generalize.

Broadly, the process of returning someone to work falls into an **order and priority model** that has been associated with the shortest and most effective means using the most accessible resources, skills, and conditions and the lowest risk and cost to the least accessible or newest resources, skills, and conditions that contain the highest risk and costs. Although the origins of the following model have been lost to history, and the detail and depth of the model may change between systems or countries, the general components of a workers' compensation return-to-work model include:

- Same job, same employer (with or without accommodation)
- Different job, same employer (transferability of skill and/or with or without accommodation)
- Different job, different employer (transferability of skill, with or without accommodation, and/or new skill acquisition)
- Retraining (new short- or long-term skill acquisition)
- Self-employment (transferability of skill, with or without accommodation, with or without short- or long-term skill acquisition, with financial and consultative or other supports)

In some jurisdictions, participation in vocational services is mandatory (e.g., federal Office of Workers' Compensation Programs). In most systems, participation is voluntary, or perhaps is not offered at all. In some states, there is little room for forensic expert services, but great demand for direct or indirect service provisions. Although in other systems, the greatest demand may be for forensic and indirect services, other systems may have little demand for direct service provision. It is important to understand the idiosyncrasies of any jurisdiction where an FRC practices. What is standard across all workers' compensation systems internationally, however, is that the evaluee has an acquired physical, mental, and/or cognitive condition based in part or in total due to his or her engagement in work.

Life Care Planning

A subspecialty in forensic rehabilitation counseling is life care planning, which merits mention in any discussion of forensic rehabilitation practice. **Life care planning** is best described as an extension of the intervention or care plan commonly found in traditional rehabilitation counseling and nursing, but expanded to cover probable future needs in the areas of evaluation, therapies, diagnostics, medications, mobility, equipment, supplies, nutrition, transportation, attendant services, adapted recreation, invasive procedures, retrofitting, or other areas of need. Deutsch and Sawyer (2005) are often credited for formalizing the method and practice of modern-day life care planning. Along with colleagues in the nursing profession (Riddick-Grisham, 2011), they have professionalized the subspecialty and developed it to its contemporary form.

Life care planners come mainly from the fields of rehabilitation counseling and rehabilitation nursing; however, a minority are from related rehabilitation fields such as occupational or physical therapy, speech and language pathology, psychology, or rehabilitation medicine. A variety of postsecondary or graduate certificate programs have existed in this subspecialty since the mid-1990s. These programs provide further training, mentoring, and supervision to develop this individual scope of practice.

COMPONENTS OF FORENSIC OR INDIRECT SERVICE PRACTICE METHODS

Beyond the history and context of forensic and indirect service practice and the role of the FRC within that practice, the process of how the FRC performs these services merits discussion.

Evidence-Based Practice

Elaborating on a typology of evidence in case study research introduced by Yin (2012, 2014), Barros-Bailey & Neulicht (2017a) refined the evidence model as it applies to clinical or forensic practice in any setting where a single individual ($n = 1$) is the subject of service provision or an evaluation. The model has two main components falling into **primary data** (collected by the FRC) and **secondary data** (collected by someone other than the FRC). Each domain has three subdomains:

- Primary
  - *Interviews* (structured, semistructured, unstructured, informal, focus)
  - *Observation* (psychometric assessment [Robinson & Drew, 2014b]; experimentation)
  - *Participant observation* (FRC as part of the observation, such as performing the tasks of a job while collecting data for a job analysis; Paquette & Heitzman, 2014)
- Secondary
  - *Documents* (medical, psychological, school, employment, legal, peer-reviewed articles, standards of care or practice, and so forth)

- *Archival* (raw data not interpreted by any source, such as databases from government agencies)
- *Physical artifacts* (e.g., durable medical equipment, artwork, or other work product)

Thomas (2011) explained that **data** are individual units of information, whereas **evidence** is the use of the data in support of a proposition, a position, or an opinion. Through content analysis using the Yin model of evidence, evidence was found to include any data source used in an individualized assessment in clinical or forensic practice (Barros-Bailey & Neulicht, 2017a, 2017b). The evidence model may be useful for any FRC, indirect service, or clinical practitioner to consider when determining the depth or breadth of evidence contained or needed for an assessment. With some aspects of document and archival evidence, understanding and interpreting rehabilitation research is a pivotal part of evidence-based practice (Reid, 2014).

Models

One of the predominant questions that an FRC or indirect service provider is asked to answer revolves around vocational capacity along some timeline spanning birth to death. Robinson (2014) documented the 20 models published since the early 1980s that provide structural frameworks to help guide such an analysis. A review of the models (Barros-Bailey & Neulicht, 2017c) suggested that they fall into three categories. **Content models** indicate what constructs or elements should be contained in the analysis, such as social, vocational, and educational histories, and physical, mental, or cognitive abilities and function. **Process models** may imply the content, but never directly note or reference it, instead focusing on the processes of the evaluation, such as performing a transferable skills analysis (Field & Dunn, 2014), including occupational information (Barros-Bailey & Karman, 2014; Barros-Bailey & Robinson, 2012), or performing labor market research (Barros-Bailey & Heitzman, 2014). However, most are **hybrid models** that include both content and process elements.

In clinical analysis, such as for clinical RCs, it is important to understand and articulate a personal counseling approach. In forensic and indirect service provision, it is also important to review the different models of analysis, determine the model that fits the jurisdiction or system or approach by the FRC, and consciously study and adopt the use of such a model. At some point in an FRC's career, he or she may have his or her testimony challenged as inadmissible (called a **motion in limine**); therefore, careful research, selection, and application of the model are recommended. Variations from any published model based on either systemic or specific case needs should be carefully thought out and justified.

Residual Functional Capacity and the Forensic Analysis

A diagnosis does not necessarily result in a prescribed functional outcome, but may be associated with a series of outcomes that may or may not apply to a specific evaluee. Therefore, understanding medical evidence and residual functional capacity is an essential component of a forensic analysis (Paquette & Lacerte, 2014). For example, someone with a traumatic brain injury could have single or multiple functional outcomes that are physical (e.g., loss of vision or olfactory senses), mental (e.g., adjustment issues, disinhibition), or cognitive (e.g., attention, distraction, memory, executive functioning, social cognition). The FRC may rely on those professionals who are trained to measure and opine on specific functions to provide the foundation upon which the FRC depends for his or her projective vocational or disability opinion. Diagnoses alone are likely insufficient information to obtain from the qualified professionals, such as therapists, neuropsychologists, or physicians, if those diagnoses do not also describe the diagnoses in functional terms or there are no documented limitations or restrictions. The difference between **limitations** and **restrictions** is not always understood. For example, let us assume that I wear prism glasses for double vision (diplopia). Although my ophthalmologist may not restrict my vision, I have an obvious limitation in that function. Therefore, someone may have a limitation in a function although no medical, psychological, or other specialist provides a specific restriction to engage in the activity.

How these functional outcomes relate to a forensic or indirect service analysis rests upon the conceptual principles and standards that underlie such an analysis. Many of these principles relate to concepts, measures, or proxies of vocational functioning adopted by the U.S. Department of Labor (DOL; *Dictionary of Occupational Titles*, 1991a and *Revised Handbook for Analyzing Jobs*, 1991b) and the U.S. Social Security Administration, with the following as the core concepts:

- *Cognitive ability:* Aptitudes to perform work activity have often been used as a proxy for cognitive function or in types of intelligence (U.S. DOL, 1991a, 1991b).
- *Reasoning development:* Levels of mathematical, language, and reasoning development based on academic curricula (U.S. DOL, 1991a, 1991b).
- *Skill:* How long it takes for an individual to acquire the skill through training, experience, or other means to perform a work activity; this is often referred to as Specific Vocational Preparation (U.S. DOL, 1991a, 1991b) and is clustered into descriptors called unskilled, semiskilled, and skilled work activity (U.S. Social Security Administration, 1978).

A host of other factors may be relevant, depending on the individual analysis, such as dexterity, values, personality, or interests.

Temporal aspects of the analysis are often a consideration. These are typically tied to timelines of when (frequency and duration estimates) someone is engaged in the labor market over his or her life, called **worklife expectancy** (Barrett, Jayne, & Robinson, 2014) and levels of tenure. Someone who may have had an average level of labor market participation pre incident may have functional or treatment issues resulting in altered rates of participation post incident, leading to a reduced ability to participate in the labor market with more turnover in jobs and more periods of unemployment between jobs.

Clinical Judgment

Clinical judgment in forensics is not a subjective distal inference, guess, or opinion. Faust and Nurcombe (1989) stated that clinical judgment is not specific to the decision-making process, but rather to a method of judgment. Clinical judgment is not a belief that is devoid of evidence that can be skewed by biases and errors (Barros-Bailey & Beveridge, 2015). Rather, it starts with a knowledge base of qualitative and quantitative data (Barros-Bailey & Neulicht, 2005). It is a process that takes the qualitative and quantitative data, evaluates its relevance, determines if it is a factor for the individual, and whether it provides evidence leading to a conclusion. There is no preconception of the outcome; rather, the clinical judgment process involves data integration using inherent validity and reliability criteria (e.g., data saturation, member checking) to arrive at findings, conclusions, opinions, and/or recommendations (Barros-Bailey & Neulicht, 2005; Choppa et al., 2004; Choppa, Johnson, & Neulicht, 2014; Field, Choppa, & Weed, 2009; Strohmer & Leirer, 2000).

TEAMS IN FORENSIC AND INDIRECT SERVICES

Much like FRCs in clinical and primary care practice are accustomed to working as members of a team, so, too, do FRCs belong to a team in forensic and indirect services. The determination of who is included on the team is entirely contingent on a multitude of decisions that could revolve around the system or jurisdiction and the scopes of practice of those retained by the referral source. The FRC's ultimate conclusions are projective based on assumptions of physical, mental, and cognitive function in vocational and related areas of capacity. Therefore, unless the FRC has an individual scope of practice that allows him or her to give opinions about function (e.g., holds dual credentials as physical therapist and RC, a neuropsychologist and RC), a person who is a qualified professional providing those underlying functional opinions is an important addition to the team. In some systems, such as in civil injury litigation, a **forensic economist** may be another team member. This professional takes the FRC's opinions and applies growth and discount rates to arrive at present-value calculations of projected losses (Brookshire, 2014).

ETHICS IN FORENSICS

A discussion regarding forensic and indirect services in rehabilitation counseling would be incomplete without addressing the ethical issues inherent in the practice. The first known reference included in rehabilitation counseling codes of ethics specific to forensics was in the 1981 IARP *Standards and Ethics* (Barros-Bailey & Carlisle, 2014). This mention called for FRCs to remain within their scopes of practice and set standards for the permissibility of providing opinions on individuals who have been examined in person or hypothetically. This initial reference evolved in the mid-1980s to an expectation that FRCs will provide objective opinions regardless of who retains the FRC's services and avoid conflicts of interest that may introduce bias, such as accepting a case on a contingency basis (Barros-Bailey, 2014).

In 2010, the CRCC created a stand-alone section to its code of ethics for forensic and indirect services (Section F). The section was slightly modified in the recently revised code. Forensic ethics standards in the 2017 code are classified in the following categories:

- *Client and evaluee rights* (primary obligations, informed consent, role changes, consultation)
- *Forensic competency and conduct* (objectivity, qualification to provide expert testimony, avoiding potentially harmful relationships, conflict of interest, validity of resources consulted, foundation of knowledge, duty to confirm information, and review/critique of opposing work product)
- *Forensic practices* (case acceptance and independent opinion, and termination of assignment transfer)
- *Forensic business practices* (payments and outcome, and fee disputes)

The first significant change in the recent revision includes the removal of the term *indirect services* and the inclusion of a standard on consultation. The similarity between indirect services and FRC practice is that in either instance there exists no client–counselor relationship. However, indirect services are not necessarily performed in a forensic setting. When an FRC is hired to perform services on a forensic case, but the FRC's presence will not be disclosed and there is no expectation of the FRC providing testimony, the practice is considered forensic consultation.

The second significant change to Section F in the 2017 code is the removal of the confidentiality standard. Privilege exists between the client and the attorney, but not between the FRC and the evaluee. However, the CRCC's action is not to be construed as confidentiality not existing in forensic practice. Counselors just need to understand the limits of confidentiality, as they would in any other practice setting, and be able to explain such limits through disclosure and informed consent. Indeed, the Section of Litigation of the American Bar Association cleared any doubts on the issue of confidentiality with expert witnesses in 2011 with the *Standards of Conduct for Experts Retained by Lawyers*; this document states, "The expert shall treat any information received or work product produced by the expert during an engagement as confidential, and shall not disclose any such information except as required by law, as retaining counsel shall determine and advise, or with the consent of the client" (2011, p. 4).

In their review of CRCC complaints, Hartley and Cartwright (2015) noted that 10.4% of these between 2006 and 2013 were related to forensic and indirect services. The violations reported by the authors involved primary obligations; unbiased opinions; objective opinions; assessment instrument selection and interpretation; critique of the opposing FRC's work product; conflicts of interest; and failure to disclose role and role limitations. Additional research performed by Hartley and Cartwright (2016) among certified rehabilitation counselors (CRCs) found that 9.1% of identified dilemmas fell into forensics and evaluation, which is fairly consistent with the rate of actual complaints over the previous decade. Given the continued expansion of forensics and indirect service provision and the adversarial nature of many systems in which FRCs practice, continued attention to and training in ethics for current and emerging professionals are advised.

The CRCC's treatment of forensic and indirect service ethics is the most comprehensive in any counseling specialty. The ACA's *Code of Ethics* (2014), by comparison, has five standards where forensic practice is mentioned, four of these within the "Forensic Evaluation: Evaluation for Legal Proceedings" section. The section covers primary obligations, consent for evaluation, evaluation prohibited with current or former clients or their partners or family members, and avoiding potentially harmful relationships. The fifth standard involves the purpose of information gathering in assessment.

CONCLUSION

Forensic and indirect service delivery in rehabilitation counseling has existed for nearly a century and uses traditional vocational rehabilitation counseling principles. The practice started in workers' compensation adjudication and expanded within social insurance to the U.S. Social Security disability system in 1960. Since the 1960s, forensic rehabilitation has spread further to a variety of other jurisdictions and systems, such as civil injury litigation, employment law, marital dissolution, and life care planning.

Because FRCs provide expertise based on their specialized knowledge in rehabilitation and disability in legal settings, their services are expected to involve evidence-based procedures through collected primary and reviewed secondary data. These specialists discern and use case conceptualization models appropriate to the analysis and integrate qualitative and quantitative data through clinical judgment processes to arrive at opinions and/or offer recommendations. Forensic rehabilitation professionals may work in teams with other forensic disciplines and are expected to have strong analytical and research skills. Forensic ethics expectations involve evaluee rights, strong competencies, disclosed conflicts, and appropriate business practices, and can be a challenge for those working in often adversarial systems.

CONTENT REVIEW QUESTIONS

- As the Council on Rehabilitation Education (CORE) merges with the Council for Accreditation of Counseling and Related Educational Programs (CACREP), how can the century of experiences in forensic rehabilitation contribute to other counseling specialties' development of respective forensic applications within their scopes of practice?
- What would be some decision-making criteria that an FRC could use when deciding what earning capacity model to adopt in a civil litigation matter? In a workers' compensation matter? If the existing models do not fit the needed application precisely, how should the FRC proceed?
- An FRC begins work on a case as a consulting expert not retained for litigation and is not disclosed to the opposing parties. After some initial work, the opposing party contacts the FRC to retain him or her as a testifying expert on the same case. How should the FRC handle the situation?
- As a newcomer to the rehabilitation counseling specialty, what resources might you explore in considering entry into the forensic or indirect service practice settings?
- What do you anticipate might be the greatest challenges or opportunities for those working in forensic rehabilitation and indirect service provision in the future?

REFERENCES

American Bar Association, Section of Litigation. (2011). *Standards of conduct for experts retained by lawyers*. Chicago, IL: Author.

American Counseling Association. (2014). *Code of ethics*. Alexandria, VA: Author.

Barrett, G., Jayne, K. A., & Robinson, R. H. (2014). Worklife expectancy models and concepts. In R. Robinson (Ed.), *Foundations of forensic vocational rehabilitation* (pp. 401–428). New York, NY: Springer Publishing.

Barros-Bailey, M. (2014). History of forensic vocational consulting. In R. Robinson (Ed.), *Foundations of forensic vocational rehabilitation* (pp. 13–31). New York, NY: Springer Publishing.

Barros-Bailey, M., & Beveridge, S. (2015, October). *What is and is not clinical judgment in forensics?* IARP Annual Conference on Unmask Your Potential: Connect, Grow, Learn—an Opportunity Jambalaya, New Orleans, LA.

Barros-Bailey, M., & Carlisle, J. (2014). Professional identity, standards, and ethical issues. In R. Robinson (Ed.), *Foundations of forensic vocational rehabilitation* (pp. 443–466). New York, NY: Springer Publishing.

Barros-Bailey, M., Carlisle, J., Graham, M., Neulicht, A. T., Taylor, R., & Wallace, A. (2008/2009). Who is the client in forensics? [White paper].

Barros-Bailey, M., & Heitzman, A. M. (2014). Labor market survey. In R. Robinson (Ed.), *Foundations of forensic vocational rehabilitation* (pp. 167–202). New York, NY: Springer Publishing.

Barros-Bailey, M., & Karman, S. (2014). Occupational and labor market information. In R. Robinson (Ed.), *Foundations of forensic vocational rehabilitation* (pp. 13–31). New York, NY: Springer Publishing.

Barros-Bailey, M., & Neulicht, A. (2005). Opinion validity: An integration of quantitative and qualitative data. *Rehabilitation Professional, 13*(2), 32–41.

Barros-Bailey, M., & Neulicht, A. T. (2017a). *A content analysis of the Federal Rules of Evidence using a case study research evidence typology.* Manuscript submitted for publication.

Barros-Bailey, M., & Neulicht, A. T. (2017b). *Evidence classification and practice in forensic rehabilitation: A content analysis of earning capacity models.* Manuscript submitted for publication.

Barros-Bailey, M., & Neulicht, A. T. (2017c). *What's in an earning capacity model? A content analysis of all published models in forensic rehabilitation practice.* Manuscript submitted for publication.

Barros-Bailey, M., & Robinson, R. (2012). 30 years of rehabilitation forensics: Inclusion of occupational and labor market information competencies in earning capacity models. *Rehabilitation Professional, 20*(3), 157–166.

Brookshire, M. (2014). Issues in the handoff to a forensic economist. In R. Robinson (Ed.), *Foundations of forensic vocational rehabilitation* (pp. 429–442). New York, NY: Springer Publishing.

Cherner, R., Nandlal, J., Ecker, J., Aubry, T., & Pettey, D. (2013). Findings of a formative evaluation of a transitional housing program for forensic patients discharged into the community. *Journal of Offender Rehabilitation, 52*, 157–180. doi:10.1080/10509674.2012.754826

Choppa, A., Johnson, C. B., Fountaine, J., Shafer, K., Jayne, K., Grimes, J. W., & Field, T. F. (2004). The efficacy of professional clinical judgment: Developing expert testimony in cases involving vocational rehabilitation and care planning issues. *Journal of Life Care Planning, 3*(3), 131–150.

Choppa, A., Johnson, C. B., & Neulicht, A. T. (2014). Case conceptualization: Achieving opinion validity through the lens of clinical judgment. In R. Robinson (Ed.), *Foundations of forensic vocational rehabilitation* (pp. 261–278). New York, NY: Springer Publishing.

Cianciulli, J. M. (1993). The outpatient forensic substance abuse profile. *International Journal of Offender Therapy and Comparative Criminology, 37*(3), 231–237.

Commission on Rehabilitation Counselor Certification. (2008). *2008 salary report: An update on salaries in the rehabilitation counseling profession.* Retrieved from https://www.crccertification.com/filebin/pdf/careercenter/CRCcareers_SalaryReport.pdf

Commission on Rehabilitation Counselor Certification. (2010). *Code of professional ethics for rehabilitation counselors.* Schaumburg, IL: Author.

Commission on Rehabilitation Counselor Certification. (2017). *Code of professional ethics for rehabilitation counselors.* Schaumburg, IL: Author.

Dawson, M. (1936). Cooperation of workmen's compensation administrators with rehabilitation agencies. *Monthly Labor Review, 42*, 300–312.

Deutsch, P. M., & Sawyer, H. W. (2005). *Guide to rehabilitation.* New York, NY: AHAB Press.

Dickens, G., Sugarman, P., & Walker, L. (2007). HoNOS-secure: A reliable outcome measure for users of secure and forensic mental health services. *Journal of Forensic Psychiatry and Psychology, 18*(4), 507–514.

Dunn, P. (2014). Introduction to the American legal system and rules of civil procedure: A primer for vocational experts. In R. Robinson (Ed.), *Foundations of forensic vocational rehabilitation* (pp. 239–260). New York, NY: Springer Publishing.

Faust, D., & Nurcombe, B. (1989). Improving the accuracy of clinical judgment. *Psychiatry, 52*, 197–208.

Field, T. F., Choppa, A. J., & Weed, R. O. (2009). Clinical judgment: A working definition for the rehabilitation professional. *Rehabilitation Professional, 17*(4), 185–194.

Field, T. F., & Dunn, P. L. (2014). Transferability of skills: Historical foundations and development. In R. Robinson (Ed.), *Foundations of forensic vocational rehabilitation* (pp. 133–144). New York, NY: Springer Publishing.

Gardner-Elahi, C., & Zamiri, S. (2015). Collective narrative practice in forensic mental health. *Journal of Forensic Practice, 17*(3), 204–218. doi:10.1108/JFP-10-2014-0034

Glassmire, D. M., Welsh, R. K., & Clevenger, J. K. (2007). The development of a substance abuse treatment program for forensic patients with cognitive impairment. *Journal of Addictions and Offender Counseling, 27*, 66–81.

Hartley, M. T., & Cartwright, B. Y. (2015). Analysis of the reported ethical complaints and violations to the Commission on Rehabilitation Counselor Certification, 2006–2013. *Rehabilitation Counseling Bulletin, 58*(3), 154–164.

Hartley, M. T., & Cartwright, B. Y. (2016). A survey of current and projected ethical dilemmas of rehabilitation counselors. *Rehabilitation Research, Policy, and Education, 30*(1), 32–47.

Heitzman, A. M., Amundsen, C., Gann, C., & Christensen, D. R. (2014). Consultation in employment law. In R. Robinson (Ed.), *Foundations of forensic vocational rehabilitation* (pp. 363–378). New York, NY: Springer Publishing.

Jasper, A., Smith, C., & Bailey, S. (1998). One hundred girls in care referred to an adolescent forensic mental health service. *Journal of Adolescence, 21,* 555–568.

Kerner v. Fleming, 283 F.2d 916 (2d Cir. 1960).

Kohlenberg, B. (2014). Consultation in marital dissolution and family law. In R. Robinson (Ed.), *Foundations of forensic vocational rehabilitation* (pp. 341–361). New York, NY: Springer Publishing.

Larson, K., DiCataldo, F., & Kinscherff, R. (2013). *Miller v. Alabama*: Implications for forensic mental health assessment at the intersection of social science and the law. *Criminal and Civil Confinement, 39,* 319–345.

Livingston, J. D., Nijdam-Jones, A., & Team P.E.E.R. (2013). Perceptions of treatment planning in a forensic mental health hospital: A qualitative participatory action research study. *International Journal of Forensic Mental Health, 12,* 42–52. doi:10.1080/14999013.2013.763390

National Association of Forensic Counselors. (2009). The origination of the forensic counselor and criminal justice specialist. Retrieved October 4, 2016 from http://www.forensiccounselor.org/?About_NAFC_and_the_Origination_of_the_Forensic_Counselor

Paquette, S., & Heitzman, A. M. (2014). Job analysis. In R. Robinson (Ed.), *Foundations of forensic vocational rehabilitation* (pp. 145–166). New York, NY: Springer Publishing.

Paquette, S., & Lacerte, M. (2014). Medical evidence and residual functional capacity. In R. Robinson (Ed.), *Foundations of forensic vocational rehabilitation* (pp. 63–87). New York, NY: Springer Publishing.

Parsons, F. (1909). *Choosing a vocation.* Boston, MA: Houghton Mifflin.

Peabody Coal Co. v. Industrial Commission et al., 289 Ill. 353, 124 N.E. 552 (1919).

Pinter, D. (1999). Forensic counseling: Collection of data and effective counseling. *Forensic Examiner, 9*(5-6), 39.

Refo, P. L. (2004). Opening statement: The vanishing trial. *Litigation, 30*(2), 2–4. Retrieved from http://www.americanbar.org/publications/litigation_journal/2016-17/winter.html

Reid, C. (2014). Interpreting rehabilitation research. In R. Robinson (Ed.), *Foundations of forensic vocational rehabilitation* (pp. 279–296). New York, NY: Springer Publishing.

Riddick-Grisham, S. (2011). *Pediatric life care planning and case management* (2nd ed.). Boca Raton, FL: CRC Press.

Robinson, R. H. (2014). Forensic rehabilitation and vocational earning capacity models. In R. Robinson (Ed.), *Foundations of forensic vocational rehabilitation* (pp. 33–62). New York, NY: Springer Publishing.

Robinson, R. H., & Drew, J. L. (2014a). Consultation in civil injury litigation. In R. Robinson (Ed.), *Foundations of forensic vocational rehabilitation* (pp. 325–339). New York, NY: Springer Publishing.

Robinson, R. H., & Drew, J. L. (2014b). Psychometric assessment in forensic vocational rehabilitation. In R. Robinson (Ed.), *Foundations of forensic vocational rehabilitation* (pp. 87–132). New York, NY: Springer Publishing.

Ryan, E. S. (1999). Forensic counseling: To be or not to be. *Forensic Examiner, 8*(11–12), 34.

Ryan, E. S. (2003). Forensic counseling: A new approach to school crime. *Education, 124*(2), 219–222.

Sakdalan, J. A., Shaw, J., & Collier, V. (2010). Staying in the here-and-now: A pilot study on the use of dialectical behaviour therapy group skills training for forensic clients with intellectual disability. *Journal of Intellectual Disability Research, 54*(6), 568–572. doi:10.11111/j.1365-2788.2010.01274.x

Smith-Fess Act, Pub. L. No. 66-236 (1920).

Smith-Hughes Act, Pub. L. No. 64-347 (1917).

Smith-Sears Act, Pub. L. No. 65-178 (1918).

Strohmer, D. C., & Leirer, S. J. (2000). Modeling rehabilitation counselor clinical judgment. *Rehabilitation Counseling Bulletin, 44*(1), 3.

Suarez, J. M., Weston, N. L., & Hartstein, N. B. (1978). Mental health interventions in divorce proceedings. *American Journal of Orthopsychiatry, 48*(2), 273–283.

Thomas, G. (2011). *How to do your case study: A guide for students and researchers.* Thousand Oaks, CA: Sage.

Thurman, M. T., Wortzel, H. S., & Martinez, R. (2011). Mental health evaluation/counseling as a special condition of supervised release. *Journal of the American Academy of Psychiatry and the Law, 39*(3), 432–434.

Travis, R. W., & Sturmey, P. (2013). Using behavioural skills training to treat aggression in adults with mild intellectual disability in a forensic setting. *Journal of Applied Research in Intellectual Disabilities, 26,* 481–488.

U.S. Department of Labor, Employment and Training Administration. (1991a). *Dictionary of occupational titles.* Washington, DC: Author.

U.S. Department of Labor, Employment and Training Administration. (1991b). *Revised handbook for analyzing jobs.* Washington, DC: Author.

U.S. Social Security Administration. (1978). SSR 83-10: Titles II and XVI: Determining capability to do other work—the medical-vocational rules of Appendix 2. Retrieved from https://www.ssa.gov/OP_Home/rulings/di/02/SSR83-10-di-02.html

U.S. Social Security Administration. (2012). SSR 86-8: Titles II and XVI: The sequential evaluation process effective August 20, 1980. Retrieved from https://www.socialsecurity.gov/OP_Home/rulings/di/01/SSR86-08-di-01.html

Vercillo, A. E. (2014). Consultation in Social Security disability law. In R. Robinson (Ed.), *Foundations of forensic vocational rehabilitation* (pp. 311–323). New York, NY: Springer Publishing.

War Risk Insurance Act, Pub. L. No. 65-90 (1914).

Williams, J. M. (2013). What are the odds a case is going to trial? Retrieved from https://legalteamusa.net/civillaw/2013/01/03/what-are-the-odds-a-case-is-going-to-trial

Yin, R. K. (2012). *Applications of case study research* (3rd ed.). Thousand Oaks, CA: Sage.

Yin, R. K. (2014). *Case study research: Design and methods* (5th ed.). Thousand Oaks, CA: Sage.

PART V: PROFESSIONAL COMPETENCIES

SEVENTEEN

Ethics and Ethical Decision Making

VILIA M. TARVYDAS AND SARA P. JOHNSTON

LEARNING OBJECTIVES

After reading this chapter, you should be able to:

- Summarize the major characteristics of the three components of professional standards.
- Discuss the elements and processes of ethics governance.
- Explain the decision-making process as a value-laden, but rational, process.
- Summarize and apply an integrative model of ethical decision making.

Increased quality of life for clients with disabilities depends on professional counselors heeding the caution embodied in the words of Samuel Johnson (n.d.): "Integrity without knowledge is weak and useless, and knowledge without integrity is dangerous and dreadful." The development of a strong professional identity rests on clear professional standards of practice. Clients need solution-focused, respectful, nonexploitative, and empowering—and, therefore, ethical—relationships with their counselors.

Clearly, clients require the services of professionals who are grounded firmly in the awareness of their value-laden mission and who are willing and able to assist people through appropriate knowledge and competencies (Gatens-Robinson & Rubin, 1995). The unusually strong tradition of explicit philosophical foundations is critical to the profession of rehabilitation and led to an early recognition of the value-based nature of rehabilitation counseling (Wright, 1983). This treasured legacy provides a strong basis for understanding the ethical principles at the heart of the ethical decision-making skills needed within the practice of rehabilitation counseling.

COMPONENTS OF PROFESSIONAL STANDARDS

The practice of counseling is both an art and a science, requiring the practitioner to make both value-laden and rational decisions. Rather than being incompatible stances, both facts and values must be considered in juxtaposition to one another to arrive at rational decisions (Gatens-Robinson & Rubin, 1995). Within ethical deliberation, the practitioner blends such elements as personal moral sensitivities and philosophies of practice with clinical behavioral objectivity and the quest for efficient care of clients.

The nature and complexity of standards of practice for all of the professions have changed and grown over the last several decades. The term **professional standards** no longer simply means specifically the ethical standards of the profession. This term is a general term meaning professional criteria indicating acceptable professional performance (Powell & Wekell, 1996), and may encompass ethical and/or clinical care standards. There are three types of standards relevant to describing professional practice: (1) the *internal standards* of the profession; (2) *clinical standards* for the individual practitioners within a profession; and (3) *external regulatory standards*. Taken together, these professional standards increase the status of the profession and its ability for self-governance, as well as enhancing the external representation of and accountability for the profession's competence with clients, the general public, employers, other professionals, external regulators, and payers (Rinas & Clyne-Jackson, 1988). These types of standards, their major characteristics, and principal components are depicted in Figure 17.1.

Internal Standards

First, the internal standards of the profession form the underpinnings of the appropriate role and functions of the profession. **Internal standards** are characterized by being focused on advancing the professionalism of the group in question, having the intent of setting a profession-wide standard of practice, and assisting individual practitioners through defining their professional identity and obligations. Prominent examples of mechanisms in this category are the profession's code of ethics and any guidelines for specialty practice relevant to the discipline.

Clinical Standards

The **clinical standards** for professional practitioners are close to the internal standards, as both are directly relevant to services delivered to the individual client or patient. Additional characteristics of clinical standards include focusing on single professional or interprofessional standards of clinical care. These standards may be specific to a particular setting or client population: they evaluate the competency of individual professionals based on the specific care rendered, and they have a client or patient care outcome measurement focus. Peer review processes and standards, as well as clinical care pathways, are examples of these standards.

Standards of External Regulatory Bodies

The last component of the professional standards is the **standards of external regulatory bodies** of diverse sorts. These standards are focused on regulatory- or institutional-level concerns. They usually involve legal or risk management questions and deal with funding or institutional fiduciary perspectives. There is a judicial type of component in which legal or quasi-legal processes are at play; for example, community standards of a professional group being used in a malpractice suit or a code of ethics adopted by a licensure board to discipline licensees. General social values typically underlie both law and the values of the profession, making them generally compatible. The society would not long tolerate a profession that is routinely operated in a manner significantly at variance with its core value structure. Corey, Corey, and Callanan (2010) noted that law and ethics are similar, because they both constitute guidelines for practice and, in some sense, are regulatory in nature. However, law can be seen as representing the minimum standards that society will tolerate, and ethics involves the ideal standards set by the profession itself. The law also informs the counselor of what is likely to happen if a professional is caught committing a prohibited act, such as sanctions or restrictions to a

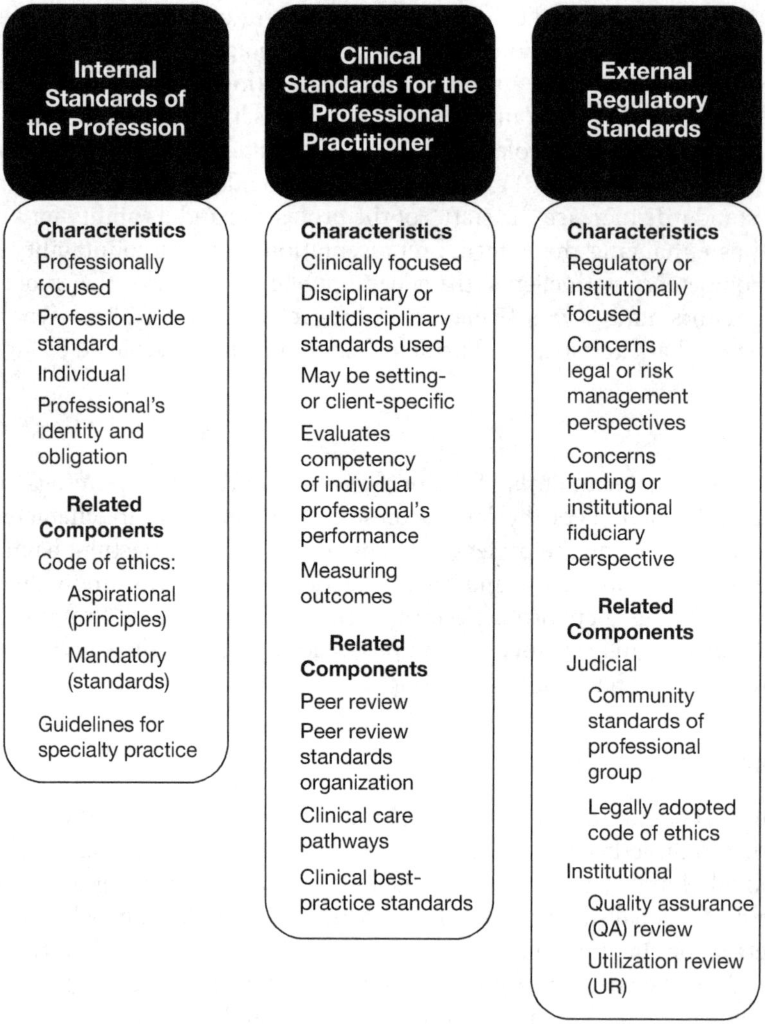

Internal Standards of the Profession	Clinical Standards for the Professional Practitioner	External Regulatory Standards
Characteristics Professionally focused Profession-wide standard Individual Professional's identity and obligation	**Characteristics** Clinically focused Disciplinary or multidisciplinary standards used May be setting- or client-specific Evaluates competency of individual professional's performance Measuring outcomes	**Characteristics** Regulatory or institutionally focused Concerns legal or risk management perspectives Concerns funding or institutional fiduciary perspective
Related Components Code of ethics: Aspirational (principles) Mandatory (standards) Guidelines for specialty practice	**Related Components** Peer review Peer review standards organization Clinical care pathways Clinical best-practice standards	**Related Components** Judicial Community standards of professional group Legally adopted code of ethics Institutional Quality assurance (QA) review Utilization review (UR)

Figure 17.1 The structure of professional standards.

professional license to practice as a counselor. The other component of external regulatory standards involves institutional standards used to judge the effectiveness and efficiency of an entire agency or institutional unit, as is typically done in quality assurance or utilization review. Such strategies have been common in medical settings and are becoming increasingly common in counseling—as the influence of managed care on the profession accelerates—through increasing demands for outcome-based treatment planning. An emphasis on evidence-based practices (such as those discussed in Chapter 19) is increasingly reflected in such standards of care.

This chapter is concerned with the ethical standards of rehabilitation counseling, but it is important to note the synergistic relationship among these three types of professional standards. *Ethics* are the moral principles that are adopted by a group to provide rules for right conduct (Corey et al., 2010). The code of ethics for a professional organization is a specific document formally adopted by the organization, which is an attempt to capture the profession's current consensus regarding what types of professional conduct are appropriate or inappropriate. However, they are normative statements, rather than absolute dictates of situational guidance.

ETHICS GOVERNANCE

Effective processes to govern ethics practice are necessary to give meaning to professional standards of practice and to enhance the societal stature of the profession. These governance processes guide the profession's practitioners through education and socialization into the professional role, and subsequently discipline them if they do not practice within the standards established. Ethical components of the standards of practice can be thought of as being either mandatory or aspirational in the level of direction they provide to the practitioner (Corey et al., 2010). The most basic level of ethical functioning is guided by mandatory ethics. At this level, individuals focus on compliance with the law and the dictates of the professional codes of ethics that apply to their practice. They are concerned with remaining safe from legal action and professional censure. The more ethically sophisticated level is the aspirational level. At this level, individuals additionally reflect on the effects of the situation on the welfare of their clients, and the effects of their actions on the profession as a whole.

These same concepts of mandatory and aspirational ethics can be applied to the overall structure of governance for a profession's ethical standards of practice as a whole. Codes of ethics are binding only on people who hold that particular credential (e.g., certification through the Commission on Rehabilitation Counselor Certification [CRCC]), or have membership in that organization (e.g., member of the American Counseling Association [ACA]). Those professionals so governed must adhere to this ethical guidance, and sanctions may be applied based on the specific ethical codes and disciplinary process of this specific professional entity. The disciplinary process of CRCC is an example of such a process applicable to rehabilitation counseling practice. If a credential holder or member of a particular professional entity violates its code of ethics, the entity has the responsibility to provide a disciplinary procedure to enforce its standards. After due process, the entity applies an appropriate sanction to the violator. In the case of a professional organization, the ultimate sanction would typically be removal from membership, with possible referral of the findings to other professional or legal jurisdictions. For a credentialing entity such as CRCC or a counselor licensure board, the violator could face the more serious option of certificate or license revocation, thus possibly removing an individual's ability to practice. Less serious levels of sanction, such as reprimand or probation, are also available. Often these statuses are coupled with significant educational or rehabilitative conditions, such as taking an ethics course or treatment of an addiction and supervised practice, to assist practitioners in regaining appropriate ethical standards of practice, while protecting their clients. A letter of instruction may be used when no ethical violation is found, but the disciplinary body determines that information could be provided to the practitioner about the best ethical practices that might improve the future provision of services to clients. Once the individual is adjudicated as being in violation of the code of ethics, the assessment of the level of seriousness of the ethical violation will affect the actual choice of sanction. Factors often considered include intentionality, degree of risk or actual harm to the client, motivation or ability of the violator to change, and recidivism of the violator (Koocher & Keith-Spiegel, 2007).

Responsible practitioners supplement this basic mandatory level of practitioner ethics with advanced knowledge of the clinical wisdom and scholarly literature on best practices in ethics. In addition, they will gain guidance from other codes of ethics and specialty guidelines for ethical practice that are relevant to their practices. These sources should be sought to supplement the required mandatory ethical standards with the more aspirational principles and ethical concepts to which the more sophisticated practitioner should aspire. In fact, for certain situations, the course of action suggested by the aspirational ethics perspective may contradict that required by the dictates of mandatory ethics. Such a situation leaves the practitioner in the stressful position of needing to responsibly reconcile the two directions.

The contemporary structure of ethics governance for counselors is presented in Figure 17.2. This representation depicts types of professional organizational entities in counseling—organized hierarchically in the shape of a pyramid. The levels of ethical governance are represented by the vertical arrow to the side of the pyramid, depicting the entities as existing roughly on a continuum from a primarily aspirational to a primarily mandatory level of function.

Colleges and universities provide professional education and research services, doing so under the review of credentialing bodies such as the Council for Accreditation of Counseling and Related Educational Programs (CACREP). As such, they are entities that have the broadest function to provide aspirational education and guidance in ethics, and that represent the foundation of the structure of ethics governance. In addition, they build the theoretical and research base for understanding ethical issues, decision-making processes, and ethics educational methods. These aspects of the aspirational

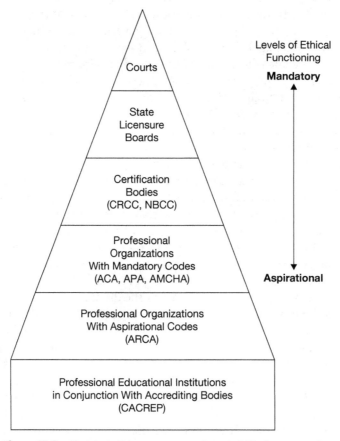

Figure 17.2 Model of ethics governance for rehabilitation counselors.

ACA, American Counseling Association; AMCHA, American Mental Health Counselors Association; APA, American Psychological Association; ARCA, American Rehabilitation Counseling Association; CACREP, Council for Accreditation of Counseling and Related Educational Programs; CRCC, Commission on Rehabilitation Counselor Certification; NBCC, National Board for Certified Counselors.

knowledge base are needed to support the ethical development of the profession. Colleges and universities also ensure that proper preservice education and professional socialization occur to inculcate future practitioners and educators with a proper ethics base from which to conduct their future practice of counseling. This obligation includes active role modeling and supporting ethical analysis and ethical behavior in teaching, supervision, and actual clinical practice. Educational institutions also serve as a resource to other professional organizations and regulatory bodies to provide teaching, research, and service, supporting aspirational and mandatory ethical practice in the community.

At the next level sit the professional organizations with aspirational codes of ethics, but with no internal mandatory enforcement mechanisms for them. For example, the Association for Specialists in Group Work and the American Rehabilitation Counseling Association (ARCA), as divisions of ACA, occupy this position. For such organizations, the primary task is to encourage aspirational ethical levels of function in their members. Mandatory enforcement tasks are not undertaken by such professional organizations because of such factors as lack of appropriate consumer access and protection in the disciplinary process; appropriate remedies for serious infractions; and the substantial financial, staff, and professional resources necessary for responsible enforcement. In some cases, the mandatory enforcement function of the organization is referred to a parent organization (e.g., to ACA, in the case of ARCA members who are ACA members), or the complainant is referred to another appropriate jurisdiction to initiate a disciplinary process.

Nonetheless, professional organizations with aspirational codes perform several significant functions within the ethics governance structure. They may provide supplemental, complementary codes of ethics for their members, which extend and explicate other more general codes of ethics. Such a document provides guidelines for ethical practice for special issues frequently encountered or of particular concern to these professionals. For rehabilitation counselors, examples of such issues might include assessment of people with functional limitations caused by disability, interprofessional team practice relationship issues, managed care practice, and the responsibility of advocacy for people with disabilities. A supplementary code may take the form of specialty guidelines for practice, which address specialty setting or function-specific issues. One example of this type of guideline is the American Psychological Association's (2009) *Revised Guidelines for Child Custody Evaluations in Family Law Proceedings*.

In addition to maintaining supplementary, specialty ethical standards for practice, some professional organizations, with an aspirational ethical level of function, collect information regarding ethical trends and needs for revision of either the specialty or the generalist ethics codes. Their leadership should also participate in the code revision and writing processes for both types of codes. These organizations should identify and supply qualified professionals to serve on the various mandatory enforcement bodies. They provide educational programs to further knowledge and the quality of ethical practice by performing significant educational and socialization functions. An innovative role— yet one that is potentially most meaningful—is the provision of mechanisms and expertise to offer remediation or rehabilitation programs for impaired professionals who have been found in violation (or are at risk of violation) of ethical standards.

At the third level of ethical governance are professional organizations that maintain and enforce a mandatory code of ethics, such as ACA and the International Association of Rehabilitation Professionals (IARP). These organizations provide an entry-level mandatory code of ethics and enforcement process for their members, and, in the case of

ACA, the enforcement for referred complaints of its specialty memberships. This level of organization consults with certification and licensing bodies and the specialty professional organizations to ensure active participation of all parties in the ethics enforcement process, and attempts to incorporate specialty viewpoints into a compatible and continually revised code of ethics. They provide referral to other jurisdictions for complaints against accused parties, as appropriate. They may provide important educational programs to increase practitioner expertise in ethical practice, and may issue advisory opinions to members who inquire to assist in proactively guiding ethical practice.

At the next two levels of ethics governance are professional regulatory bodies that either certify or license professionals, and that constitute the preeminent enforcers of the mandatory code. National certification bodies, such as CRCC and the National Board for Certified Counselors (NBCC), as well as the state counselor licensure boards, operate at this level. They perform a pivotal role in the promulgation and enforcement of ethical standards. However, they draw their specific codes of ethical standards from the professional organizations, because they do not constitute the profession, but rather regulate it, based on the profession's own internal standards. They may provide information and consultation to professional organizations in revising and maintaining the current codes of ethics. Beyond the ethical regulatory function, the regulatory bodies encourage ethical proficiency of their licensees and certificants through requiring preservice education and continuing education in the area of ethics.

As a practical matter, many states that license professional counselors adopt the ACA *Code of Ethics* and Standards of Practice, and a counselor licensed in a state that has adopted the ACA code would be governed by that code or one very closely related to it. In addition, the 2017 CRCC *Code of Professional Ethics for Rehabilitation Counselors* is very similar to the ACA *Code of Ethics* (Tarvydas & Cottone, 2000). In essence, this consistency provides rehabilitation counselors with a unified code of ethics within the profession, which is highly compatible with ethical standards of ACA and most counseling licensure boards.

At the pinnacle of the ethics governance hierarchy are found the civil and criminal courts and other legal jurisdictions that impact the ethical practice of counselors. For example, engaging in sexual intimacy with a client is a criminal offense in many states, and may even result in arrest and incarceration if a practitioner is found guilty of this offense (Corey et al., 2010). However, one of the primary mechanisms of legal governance of ethics is still through the use of malpractice suits in civil courts. In malpractice actions, one of the central points is to establish a violation of duty, requiring determination of the standard of what constitutes "good professional practice" as applied to the matter at hand. This issue is difficult to determine because it is often ill-defined and requires many types of considerations. It is not unusual for various expert witnesses to be called to testify regarding such practices. In addition, there might be an attempt to establish that a blatant violation of the general rules of the profession occurred, by reference to the profession's ethical standards (Thompson, 1990).

Another standard of practice that might be applied would be consideration of whether the action or service in question was both within the scope of practice of the profession and within the individual's personal scope of practice (see Appendix B of this book for the CRCC Scope of Practice). The profession of rehabilitation counseling has established its scope of practice, with which its practitioners must be familiar, to appropriately and ethically establish their personal scopes of practice. In addition, state licensed professional counselors are governed by the scope of practice described for counselors within their state's licensure regulatory language, and may be required to declare their personal scopes of practice at the time they are licensed and to revise them as appropriate. Practitioners are ethically bound to limit their own scopes of practice to areas within the profession's scope, in which they are personally competent to practice, by virtue of appropriate types and levels of education, supervision, and professional experience.

Through these six levels, the various professional governance entities interact to provide a network of mandatory and aspirational ethics functions. Concern for the protection of clients is very strong among these professional governance structures, and they have cooperated to share information about the most serious ethical infractions that are adjudicated within their organizations. In their totality, they are an interactive system of research, educational, and enforcement services to shape and regulate the ethical practice of counselors. Taken together, these systems of knowledge, traditions, rules, and laws form the regulatory content, but they do not provide the practitioner with possibly the most crucial tool for ethical practice: knowledge and experience in application of a decision-making process that can be applied to this form and content.

ETHICAL DECISION-MAKING PROCESSES

The intent of a code of ethics is to provide rehabilitation counselors with guidance for specific situations they experience in their practices. However, authorities have long recognized that codes of ethics must be written in general enough terms that they apply across a wide range of practice settings. They also are reactive in nature; that is, they address situations that have already been part of the profession's experience (Kitchener, 1984; Mabe & Rollin, 1986). As a result, even with knowledge of the profession's code of ethics, rehabilitation counselors may find that they do not have sufficient guidance to resolve the dilemma in question. They may find that the particular situation with which they are faced is not addressed in their code; that their practice is governed by more than one code, providing conflicting direction in the situation; or that conflicting provisions within any one code appear to apply to the situation. For that reason, the rehabilitation counselor must be prepared to exercise his or her professional judgment in ethics responsibly. This type of occurrence is not so much a failure of ethical codes, but rather a natural and appropriate juncture recognizing the importance and role of professional judgment. In other words, it is affirmation that one is involved in practice of a profession, rather than doing a job, however skilled. In order to exercise professional judgment, the rehabilitation counselor must be prepared to recognize underlying ethical principles or conflicts between competing interests, and to apply appropriate ethical decision-making skills to resolve the dilemma and act in an ethical manner (Cottone & Tarvydas, 2007; Francouer, 1983; Kitchener, 1984). In fact, expanding upon the expectation stated in the 2014 ACA *Code of Ethics* for use of an ethical decision-making model, CRCC's *Code of Professional Ethics* charges counselors with the responsibility to "be familiar with and apply a credible model of decision making that can bear public scrutiny of its application" (CRCC, 2017, p. 3) through inclusion of an ethical standard to apply. In addition, counselors must be able to "recognize underlying ethical principles and conflicts among competing interests" (p. 35). This trend is in keeping with the growing recognition that counselors must be prepared to go well beyond the simple knowledge of codes of ethics to know how to reason about complex and sometimes seemingly conflicting types of information through application of a formal ethical decision-making model (Cottone, 2012). Fortunately, professionals are assisted in this task by examination and refinement of their ordinary moral sense, as well as by the availability of thoughtful models for the ethical decision-making process. Many components of ethical decision making involve teachable, learnable skills to supplement the professional's developing intuitive professional judgment.

Several types of models exist, which seek to explain and structure the process of ethical decision making (Cottone, 2012; Cottone & Claus, 2000). Some prominent examples view the ethical decision-making process as professional self-exploration (Corey et al., 2010); a moral reasoning discourse (Kitchener, 1984); the result of a moral developmental process (Van Hoose & Kottler, 1985); a multidimensional, integrative psychological process (Rest, 1984); and involving a hierarchy of four contextual levels that affect the process of decision making (Tarvydas & Cottone, 1991). Generally, ethical decision-making models can be thought of as having the characteristics of either principle or virtue ethics (Corey et al., 2010). *Principle* ethics focus on the objective, rational, cognitive aspects of the process. Practitioners who adhere to this perspective tend to view the application of universal, impartial ethical principles, rules, codes, and laws as being the core elements of ethics. *Virtue* ethics consider the characteristics of the counselors themselves as the critical element for responsible practice. Thus, proponents of virtue ethics approaches would tend to concern themselves more with counselors reflecting on and clarifying their moral and value positions. In addition, they would examine other personal issues that might impact their ethical practice, such as unresolved emotional needs, which might negatively affect their work with their clients. Preferred approaches to ethical decision making should include both aspects (Corey et al., 2010; Meara, Schmidt, & Day, 1996). Among other positive contributions of such a synergistic approach, Vasquez (1996) has speculated that the addition of virtue ethical perspectives may improve ethical conduct in multicultural and diverse interactions and settings. Cottone (2012) has identified multicultural sensitivity as a major theme in the evolution of ethical decision-making models, and Garcia, Cartwright, Winston, and Borzuchowska (2003) have addressed it through infusing multicultural elements into the Tarvydas integrative decision-making model of ethical behavior discussed in the following section.

THE TARVYDAS INTEGRATIVE DECISION-MAKING MODEL OF ETHICAL BEHAVIOR

The Tarvydas integrative decision-making model of ethical behavior builds on several well-known decision-making models widely used by professionals in the mental health and counseling communities. It incorporates the most prominent principle and virtue aspects of several decision-making approaches and introduces some contextual considerations into the process. The Tarvydas integrative model emphasizes the constant process of interaction between the principle and the virtue elements, and places a reflective attitude at the heart of the process. The model also focuses on the actual production of ethical behavior within a specified context, rather than prematurely terminating analysis by merely selecting the best ethical course of action. The model is shown in Box 17.1. This approach considers the importance of setting and environmental factors, which are crucial in counseling. Indeed, in reviewing the various approaches to ethical decision making, Garcia et al. (2003) observed that this model uses virtue ethics and behavioral strategies that are consistent with a multicultural approach to counseling and ethical decision making, and have proposed an integrative transcultural ethical decision-making model that is based primarily on the Tarvydas integrative model.

BOX 17.1 The Tarvydas Integrative Decision-Making Model of Ethical Behavior

Themes or Attitudes in the Integrative Model
Maintain an attitude of *reflection*.
Address *balance* between issues and parties to the ethical dilemma.
Pay close attention to the *context(s)* of the situation.
Utilize a process of *collaboration* with all rightful parties to the situation.

Stage I. Interpreting the Situation
Component 1. Enhance *sensitivity* and *awareness*.
Component 2. Determine the major *stakeholders* and their ethical claims in the situation.
Component 3. Engage in the *fact-finding* process.

Stage II. Formulating an Ethical Decision
Component 1. Review the problem or dilemma.
Component 2. Determine what *ethical codes, laws, ethical principles*, and *institutional policies and procedures* exist that apply to the dilemma.
Component 3. Generate possible and probable courses of action, and consider potential positive and negative *consequences* for each course of action.
Component 4. Consult with supervisors and other knowledgeable professionals.
Component 5. Select the best *ethical course* of action.

Stage III. Selecting an Action by Weighing Competing, Nonmoral Values
Component 1. Engage in reflective recognition and analysis of *competing nonmoral values, personal blind spots*, or *prejudices*.
Component 2. Consider *contextual influences* on values selection at the counselor–client, interprofessional team, institutional, and societal levels.
Component 3. Select *preferred course* of action.

Stage IV. Planning and Executing the Selected Course of Action
Component 1. Figure out a reasonable *sequence of concrete actions* to be taken.
Component 2. Anticipate and work out *personal and contextual barriers* to effective execution of the plan of action, and effective *countermeasures* for them.
Component 3. Carry out, document, and *evaluate* the course of action as planned.

Themes and Attitudes

In addition to the specific elements or steps of the Tarvydas integrative model, there are four underlying themes or attitudes that are necessary for the professional counselor to enact. These attitudes involve mindfully attending to the tasks of:

1. Maintaining a stance of *reflection* concerning one's own conscious awareness of personal issues, values, and decision-making skills, as well as extending an effort to understand those of all others concerned with the situation, and their relationship to the decision maker

2. Addressing the *balance* among various issues, people, and perspectives within the process
3. Maintaining an appropriate level of attention to the *context* of the situation in question, allowing awareness of the counselor–client, treatment team, organizational, and societal implications of the ethical elements
4. Seeking to use a process of *collaboration* with all rightful parties to the decision, but most especially the client

Under a social justice model of counseling practice, counselor–client collaboration is encouraged throughout the counseling relationship to encourage client self-advocacy and empowerment (Ratts, Toporek, & Lewis, 2010). However, traditionally, ethics and ethical decision making have been the "sole province of the counselor" (Tarvydas, Vazquez-Ramos, & Estrada-Hernandez, 2015, p. 230). Prilleltensky, Rossiter, and Walsh-Bowers (1996) termed this counselor-focused approach to ethical decision making the **restrictive orientation**. Under the restrictive orientation, the counselor does not consult or collaborate with the client in the ethical decision-making process, which stands in stark contrast to the recommendation for more client involvement in other stages of the counseling relationship. To address the lack of client involvement in the ethical decision-making process, Tarvydas and colleagues (2015) suggested that counselors use a **participatory orientation**, which infuses the client into the ethical decision-making process. By including rather than excluding the client from ethical decisions that affect the client's therapeutic goals, well-being, and quality of life, counselors can strengthen the counselor–client working alliance and increase client empowerment, which leads to better decision making. The participatory orientation is the basis for the **Applied Participatory Ethics Model**, which places the counselor's ethical decision-making knowledge and skills on a continuum from profession-centered (exclusive) to client-centered (inclusive; Tarvydas et al., 2015).

By adopting these background attitudes of reflection, balance, context, and collaboration, and by working toward a participatory orientation in ethical decision making, counselors engage in a more thorough process that will help preserve the integrity and dignity of all parties involved. This will be the case even when outcomes are not considered equally positive for all participants in the process, as is often true in a serious dilemma when such attitudes can be particularly meaningful. Indeed, Betan and Stanton (1999) studied students' responses to ethical dilemmas, analyzing how emotions and concerns influence willingness to implement ethical knowledge. They concluded that "subjectivity and emotional involvement are essential tools for determining ethical action, but they must be integrated with rational analysis" (p. 295).

Reflection is the overriding attitude of importance throughout the enactment of the specific elements of stages and components that constitute the steps of the Tarvydas integrative model. Many complex decision-making processes easily become overwhelming, either in their innate complexity or in the real-life pressure of the speed or intensity of events. In the current approach, the counselor is urged always to "Stop and think!" at each point in the process. The order of operations is not critical or absolute, nor is it more important than being reflective and invested in a calm, dignified, respectful, and thorough analysis of the situation. Not until we recognize that we are involved in the process and appreciate its critical aspects can we call forth other resources to assist the process and people within it. Such an attitude of reflection will serve the counselor well at all stages of this process.

Elements

The specific elements that constitute the operations within the Tarvydas integrative model have four main stages with several components, including the steps to be taken within each stage. The concepts summarized are drawn, in the main, from the work of Kitchener (1984), Rest (1984), and Tarvydas and Cottone (1991).

Stage I: Interpreting the Situation Through Awareness and Fact-Finding

At this stage, the primary task of counselors is to be sensitive to and aware of the needs and welfare of the people around them, and of the ethical implications of these situations. This level of awareness allows counselors to imagine and investigate the effects of the situation on the parties involved and the possible effects of various actions and conditions. The sense of this state is somewhat like the idea of "situational awareness" as used in military parlance, through which the agents scan the circumstances for potential threats and resources that are relevant to addressing the conflict at hand. This research and awareness must also include emotional as well as cognitive and fact-based considerations. Three components constitute the counselor's operations in this stage.

Component 1 involves enhancing one's sensitivity and awareness. In *Component 2,* the counselor takes an inventory of the people who are major stakeholders in the outcome of the situation. It is important to reflect on any parties who will be affected and who play a major role in the client's life, as well as considering what their exact relationship is—ethically and legally—to the person at the center of the issue, which is the client. Imagine dropping a rock into a pond: the point of impact is where the central figure, the client, is situated; however, the client is surrounded by people at varying levels of closeness, such as parents, foster parents, intimate partners, spouse, children, employer, friends, and neighbors, all radiating out from the client in decreasing levels of intimacy and responsibility to the client.

Figure 17.3 depicts how the spheres of influence of these stakeholders in the client's life, as well as the stakeholders at each of the four levels in the professional world of the counselor, may be seen as intersecting. This way of thinking about the relationships among the different stakeholders in the situation allows for a fuller appreciation of the specific people and contexts of the counselor's practice and the client's situation.

A number of people and levels of the professional service hierarchy will (or should) play a part in any ethical decision. These social forces will create both positive and negative influences in the ethical situation, and should be taken into account in the ethical analysis. The ethical claims of these parties on the counselor's level of duty are not uniform. Almost all codes of ethics in counseling make it clear that the client is the person to whom the first duty is owed, but there are others to whom the counselor has lesser, but important, levels of duty. It is always important to determine whether any surrogate decision makers for the client exist, such as a foster parent, guardian, or person with power of attorney, so that they may be brought into the central circle of duty early in the process. Sensitivity and proactivity are useful in working through situations in which the legal relationships involved do not coincide with the social and emotional bonds between the client and other people involved in the dilemma.

The final element in Stage I is *Component 3,* in which the counselor undertakes an extensive fact-finding investigation, with a scope appropriate to the situation. The nature of the fact-finding process should be carefully considered and is not intended to be a formal investigative or quasi-legal process. The intent is that the counselor should carefully

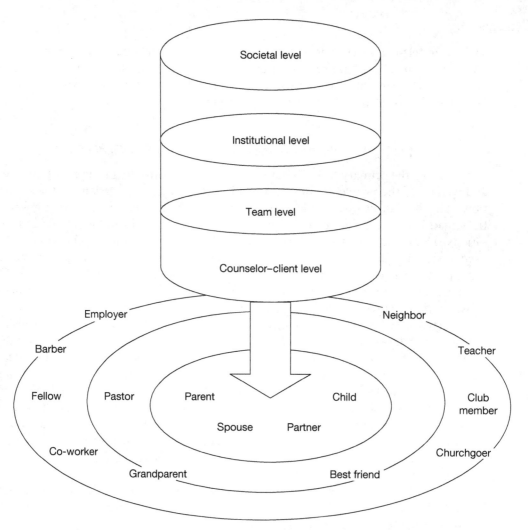

Figure 17.3 The intersection of the client's personal world with the counselor's professional hierarchical contexts.

review and understand the information at hand, and then seek out new information. Only information that is appropriately available to a counselor should be involved. The scope and depth of information that would be rightfully available to the counselor is surprising, but it is often not fully utilized. For example, information might be gained from such sources as further discussion with the client, contacts with family (with appropriate permission of the client), case records, expert consultation and reports, legal resources, or agency policy and procedures.

Stage II: Formulating an Ethical Decision

This aspect of the process is most widely known by professionals, and many may erroneously think it is the end of the process. The central task in this stage is to identify which of the possible ethical courses of action appears to come closest to the moral ideal in the situation under consideration (Rest, 1984). Many decision-making models in other areas of counseling can be applied as a template at this stage, but the following components are drawn from the work of Van Hoose and Kottler (1985).

Component 1 suggests that the counselor review the problem or dilemma to be sure that it is clearly understood in light of any new information obtained in Stage I. In *Component 2,* the counselor researches the standards of law and practice applicable to the situation. This component includes Kitchener's (1984) attention to ethical codes, laws, and ethical principles, and Tarvydas and Cottone's (1991) concern for the team and organizational context in the examination of institutional policies and procedures, to make mention of other useful areas for consideration. The counselor would also analyze which of the six core ethical principles (autonomy, beneficence, nonmaleficence, justice, fidelity, and veracity) may be either supported or compromised by the types of actions that are being contemplated in the situation (see Table 17.1 for brief description of these ethical principles and examples of common counseling practices that are based on them). This operation is formally known as principle analysis and is one of the most challenging, yet critical, aspects of the ethical analysis of a dilemma. The core, or main, principle analysis concerns the ethical obligations owed to the client, rather than to other parties to the situation.

Component 3 initiates the process of formally envisioning and generating possible and probable courses of action. As with all decision-making processes, it is important not to truncate this exploratory process by prematurely censoring the possibilities, or succumbing to a sense of being too overwhelmed, or too limited, in options. After the list of possible and probable courses of action is generated, positive and negative consequences are identified and assessed in relation to risks, as well as to material and personal resources available. In *Component 4,* the counselor is reminded to consult with supervisors and trusted and knowledgeable colleagues for guidance, if this has not been

TABLE 17.1 Ethical Principles and Related Practices

Principle	Brief Definition	Related Counseling Practice
Autonomy	To respect the rights of clients to be self-governing within their social and cultural framework	Obtaining informed consent Keeping confidentiality
Beneficence	To do good to others; to promote the well-being of clients	Hospitalizing a suicidal client Providing high-quality counseling services
Nonmaleficence	To do no harm to others	Avoiding a potentially detrimental dual relationship with a client Referring or not providing counseling services when not fully qualified
Fidelity	To be faithful; to keep promises and honor the trust placed in one	Keeping promises to clients Respecting clients' privacy
Justice	To be fair in the treatment of all clients; to provide appropriate services to all	Advocating on behalf of clients Ensuring that services are fully accessible to all Providing fair access to services to all, even difficult clients
Veracity	To be honest	Providing detailed professional disclosure Describing completely who will have access to clients' files

done before this point. Professional standards of practice emphasize the importance of appropriate collegial consultation to resolve difficult clinical and ethical dilemmas. Research has also demonstrated that such consultations can have a significant influence on those seeking such consultation (Butterfield, Trevino, & Weaver, 2000; Cottone, Tarvydas, & House, 1994). There is value in reviewing the reasoning employed in working through the ethical dilemma to this point, and the solutions and consequences envisioned to be sure that all potentially useful and appropriate considerations have been taken into account. Finally, the best ethical course of action is determined and articulated in *Component 5*. The ethical decision at this stage of the model should be contrasted with the decision about what the counselor actually decided to do, which is the product of Stage III.

Stage III: Selecting an Action by Weighing Competing, Nonmoral Values, Personal Blind Spots, and Prejudices

Many people would think that the ethical decision-making process is concluded at the end of Stage II. This impression is limited in its realization of the many additional forces that may affect the counselor and result in the counselor not actually executing the selected ethical course of action. *Component 1* of Stage III interjects a period of reflection and active processing of what the counselor intends to do, in view of competing, nonmoral values (Rest, 1984). At this point, the counselor considers any personal factors that might intervene to pull him or her away from choosing the ethical action or cause that action to be substantially modified. Nonmoral values involve anything that the counselor may prize or desire, which is not in and of itself a moral value, such as justice. Such values may include such things as valuing social harmony, spending time with friends or working on one's hobby, desiring control or power, or having personal wealth. In this component, counselors are also called upon to examine themselves to determine if they have some personal blind spots or prejudices that might affect their judgment or resolve to do the ethical thing, such as a fear of HIV infection, or the conviction that gay men are also likely to molest children. This portion of the model provides an excellent opportunity for counselors to carefully evaluate whether they have adequately incorporated multicultural considerations and competencies in their work on this ethical dilemma and to be sure that they are not operating from a culturally encapsulated frame of reference.

Counselors must allow themselves to become aware of the strength and attractiveness of other values they hold, which may influence whether they will discharge their ethical obligations. If they are self-aware, they may more effectively and honestly compensate for their conflicted impulses at this point. Counselors may have strong needs for acceptance by peers or supervisors, for prestige and influence, to avoid controversy, or to be financially successful. These value orientations may come into conflict with the course of action necessary to proceed ethically, and must be reconciled with ethical requirements if the client is to be ethically served. In contrast, counselors may place a high value on being moral or ethical and on being accepted as respected professionals with high ethical standards, or they may value the esteem of colleagues who place a high value on ethical professional behavior. Those forces should enhance the tendency to select ethical behavioral options (the influence of the ethical climate on the ethical behavior of the counselor is more fully explored in Tarvydas, O'Rourke, and Urish, 2007). Therefore, the importance of selecting and maintaining ethically sensitized and positive professional and personal cultures should be recognized as critical to full professional functioning, as the next component would suggest.

In *Component 2*, counselors systematically inventory the contextual influences on their choices at the counselor–client, team, institutional, and societal levels. This is not a simple process of weighing influences, but it should serve as an inventory of influences, which may be either dysfunctional or constructive, for selecting the ethical course over other types of values present in these other interactions. Counselors may also use this type of information to think strategically about the influences they will need to overcome to provide ethical service in the situation. Beyond the immediate situation, counselors should control their exposure to contexts that consistently reinforce values that run counter to the dictates of good ethical practices. For example, rehabilitation counselors working in private practices where their employers consistently pressure them to favor the attorneys that hire them in their forensic evaluations run the risk of eventually succumbing to these pressures.

Component 3 is the final aspect of Stage III, in which the counselor selects the preferred course of action or the behavior that he or she plans to undertake.

This decision may be a reaffirmation of the intention to take the ethical course of action, as determined at the conclusion of Stage II, but augmented to deal with some contextual barriers discovered in Stage III. However, it may be some other course of action that may even not be ethical, or a modified version of the ethical course of action selected in Stage II. Whatever the choice, the counselor has selected it after this more extensive reflection on his or her own competing values and personal blind spots, as well as the contextual influences in the situation in question.

Stage IV: Planning and Executing the Selected Course of Action

Rest (1984) described the essential tasks of this stage as planning to implement and executing what one plans to do. This operation includes *Component 1,* in which the counselor figures out a reasonable sequence of concrete actions to be taken. In *Component 2,* the task is to anticipate and work out all personal and contextual barriers to effective execution of the plan. Preparing countermeasures for barriers that may arise is useful. Here, the earlier attention to other stakeholders and their concerns may suggest problems or allies to the process. In addition, earlier consideration of the contextual influences in Stage III assists the counselor in this type of strategic planning. *Component 3* is the final step of this model, in that it provides for the execution, documentation, and evaluation of the course of action as planned. Rest noted that the actual behavioral execution of ethics is often not a simple task, frequently drawing heavily on the personal, emotional qualities and professional and interpersonal skills of the counselor. He mentions such qualities as firmness of resolve, ego strength, and social assertiveness. To this list could be added countless skills, such as persistence, tact, time management, assertiveness skills, team collaboration, and conflict resolution skills. Considerations are limited only by the characteristics and requirements of the counselor and specific situation involved. Clear and thorough documentation of the entire plan and the rationale behind it, and ethical decision-making steps taken in responding to the ethical dilemma as the process unfolds, are critical to protect the interests of both the counselor and the client. The information gained in this documentation process will prove critical in evaluating the effectiveness of the entire ethical decision-making process.

Practicing the Tarvydas Integrative Model

Just like the basic counseling microskills, the skills of ethical decision making as described do not come automatically, or even easily, after merely reading about the concepts in a book. Practice in solving mock ethical dilemmas—working to address actual ethical dilemmas under the supervision of an ethically knowledgeable instructor, clinical supervisor, master counselor, or mentor—and incorporating ethical analysis into clinical training process are all essential to gradual progression in gaining practical skills and sensitive, accurate ethical knowledge. A complex ethical scenario, with a full ethical analysis using the Tarvydas integrative model and all its stages and components, is presented in the following case study. This enables readers to begin an exploration of how to use this rich approach to ethical decision making.

The following analysis does not represent the only answer to this dilemma. Sometimes, information discovered, or concerns raised by other reasonable people, can lead to important shifts in the elements of a case. Also, because reasonable professionals can judge and weigh even the same ideas or risks differently, there may be other valid conclusions to the same case. This process is not so much about getting the hidden, correct answer, but rather is about going through the process of decision making thoroughly and carefully, and exercising due care and good, reasonable professional judgment throughout. If this is done, in the end, the counselor is more likely to have arrived at an explicable judgment that minimizes risk to the client, the counselor, and others. The counselor will also benefit from increased confidence and peace of mind, assured that he or she has done the best in the situation, having used a thorough, thoughtful approach to solving a dilemma that may not have a solution that is satisfying to the parties involved.

CASE STUDY

Case Study Illustration of the Tarvydas Integrative Decision-Making Model of Ethical Behavior

CASE NARRATIVE

John is a 43-year-old man who is meeting with a counselor at the Department of Correctional Services (DCS). He has recently been released from prison on parole, and is meeting with a counselor voluntarily to deal with some issues of depression. He is currently on medication for depression, and has made previous suicide attempts. He was married to a woman for 9 years, and they had two children together, now 7 and 5 years old. She also had two children from a previous relationship, now 12 and 8 years old, whom John also considers to be his children. He and his wife are recently divorced. Before their divorce, John and his former wife met with a family therapist for several sessions; their children continue to meet with the therapist. At first, his ex-wife would not allow the children to visit their dad, but just recently John says they have been talking again, and his ex-wife has started to trust him again and let the children visit whenever they wanted. Just recently, his youngest girl confided in him that their mom and her new friends are still using drugs, and are also selling them from the house. She had found a syringe at the home, which her mom had thought was hidden. John is very adamant that he does not want to contact the Department of Human Services (DHS) or any other similar agency about this. He had contacted DHS for a similar situation a few years ago, and had a bad experience. The caseworker he met with initially was helpful; however, in the end DHS

(*continued*)

CASE STUDY (*continued*)

had "done nothing," and his ex-wife had found out that he had made the report. She did not let him see the kids for a long time after the incident. He feels that, at this point, he can do the most good by keeping a close relationship with his children and a civil relationship with his ex-wife. He is living a clean and drug-free life, and feels that he is his ex-wife's best hope right now to straighten out. He says that if a report is made, the only thing he is sure of is that his ex-wife would not let him see the children, and he does not know if he could live without being part of his children's lives. In this case, the client has his reasons for not wanting to contact DHS, and client autonomy must be respected. The client also raises the issue that maybe contacting the authorities really is not in the best interest of the children. He also made some statements regarding not being able to live without being a part of his children's lives, which has to be taken seriously given the client's suicidal history and current state of depression. However, young children are involved in a dangerous situation. There is no report of physical or sexual abuse occurring, yet drug use in the home and young children coming across needles is dangerous and could be considered abuse. At this point, the counselor feels there may be a potential dilemma that should be explored further.

STAGE I: INTERPRETING THE SITUATION THROUGH AWARENESS AND FACT-FINDING

The primary task of counselors in Stage I is to be sensitive to and aware of the needs and welfare of the people around them, and of the ethical implications of these situations. This level of awareness allows counselors to imagine and investigate the effects of the situation on the parties involved and the possible effects of various actions and conditions. This research and awareness must also include emotional as well as cognitive and fact-based considerations. At this stage, the counselor considers the benefits of including the client in the ethical decision-making process by using a participatory ethics appoach.

Component 1: Sensitivity and Awareness

At this point, the counselor talks to John and gets his impression of who will be affected by this situation, and how they will be affected. John clearly cares about his children, but firmly believes that the best chance they have is if he continues to be a part of their lives. He has no guarantee what would happen if he did contact DHS, and he does not want to take that risk. Given what happened the last time he called, John is very distrustful of the system. He also expressed some concerns for his ex-wife and, even though they parted on unfriendly terms, he still seems to care about her and wants what is best for her also. He says that they are just starting to talk again, and he feels that he may be the only one who truly understands what she is going through with the drugs and might be able to help her kick the habit. Although he admits that he worries what kind of environment his children are living in, John feels that this is the best chance they have.

The counselor also notes that there are four children of varying ages in the house. An 18-year-old might understand how dangerous finding a needle in the house really is, but a 5-year-old most likely would not. Even aside from needles being in the house, there

(*continued*)

CASE STUDY (*continued*)

is also the potential for danger with what kind of people are around the children. If their mother is dealing drugs from the home, many of those she sells to are probably in the house also, and around the children.

The client says he understands all of this, but still feels that he is making progress with his ex-wife, and that he is the best chance for his children. John acknowledges that he is taking on a lot of responsibility, but says that he would do anything for his children and truly believes that he is doing the best for them in the long run.

Component 2: Major Stakeholders and Their Ethical Claims

The counselor identifies the parties who will be affected and what their exact relationship is—ethically and legally—to the person at the center of the issue. There are often others to whom the counselor has lesser, but important, levels of duty, such as parents, intimate partners, spouse, children, employer, friends, neighbors, guardian, or persons with power of attorney. All important parties with an ethical or legal claim in the situation are listed in the following table.

Parties	Ethical Claim
The client, John	He does not want to contact any authorities.
The children	They may be in danger, may not know all of their options or how they could get help.
DCS	They are responsible for their counselors, and could be held liable for mistakes made by their employees.
The counselor	May be held liable for any harm that befalls the children or the client.
The ex-wife	She could face an abuse investigation and the subsequent consequences.
Grandparents	If DHS did find abuse, they would most likely get custody of the children.
The family therapist	The therapist may have information about conditions in the home, which she is required to report to the authorities.
DHS	DHS is responsible for its employees, and could be held liable for mistakes made by those employees.

Component 3: Fact-Finding Process

The counselor undertakes an extensive fact-finding investigation, of a scope appropriate to the situation, by reviewing and understanding current information and seeking out new information. This investigation involves gathering information appropriately available to the counselor, either through professional records and channels (with appropriately obtained releases of information) or through part of public domain information. Sources might include further discussion with the client, contacts with family or other professionals working with the family (with client's permission), current and old client

(*continued*)

CASE STUDY (*continued*)

records in one's own or another agency, expert consultation and reports, legal resources, or agency policy and procedures. There are all the facts or factual questions the counselor should reasonably be able to research or answer.

A call was made to the DHS confidential hotline to find out if the situation in general fell under the guidelines for mandatory reporting, which it did not. DHS stated that it did not fall under mandatory guidelines because it was third-party information.

The counselor talked to the supervisor and found out DCS has an unwritten rule or policy. This policy is to convince the client to call authorities and report the situation.

John stated that if DHS was contacted, an investigation was conducted, and action was taken to remove the children from their mother, her parents would probably receive custody. The client stated that he has a good relationship with his ex-wife's parents. He thought that they would allow him to see the children if they did get custody of the children.

The counselor was informed by a supervisor that one reason DHS may not have done anything the last time John reported was that there may have been some type of drug investigation going on. If there is a current investigation into drug trafficking or selling, they can postpone going into the house for a child abuse charge, because the house is under supervision as part of a larger investigation.

STAGE II: FORMULATING AN ETHICAL DECISION

The counselor's task in this stage is to identify which of the possible ethical courses of action appears to come closest to the ethical ideal in the situation under consideration. If the counselor is following a participatory ethics orientation, the client would be included in the process of formulating an ethical decision.

Component 1: Review Problem or Dilemma

Review the problem or dilemma to be sure that it is clearly understood in relation to any new information.

Because this situation does not fall into the category of mandatory reporting, the counselor is not legally bound to break the client's confidence. However, we now know that the unwritten policy of the institution (DCS) is to try to convince or coerce the client to call DHS on his own. Thus, the counselor must decide whether to respect the client's wishes not to call DHS or to try to coerce the client to call, in accordance with the institution's unwritten policy. If the counselor is following a participatory ethics orientation, the client may be informed of the informal policy and his input sought on how to proceed in light of the informal policy.

Component 2: Determine Ethical Codes, Laws, Principles, and Institutional Policies and Procedures

The counselor must determine and research the standards of law (in any and all applicable local jurisdictions) and professional practices applicable to the situation. The latter material includes ethical codes and related standards of care, laws, ethical principles, and institutional policies and procedures.

(*continued*)

CASE STUDY (*continued*)

ETHICAL CODES

List any rules or canons from applicable code(s) of ethics and provide a summary of their dictates. For counselors, the ACA *Code of Ethics* and any applicable specialty standards, such as the CRCC *Code of Professional Ethics for Rehabilitation Counselors*, are recommended. If the counselor is licensed or holds national certification, the codes of ethics that apply to that credential must also be consulted.

ACA Code of Ethics

Section A. Introduction. Counselors facilitate client growth and development in ways that foster the interest and welfare of clients and promote formation of healthy relationships. Trust is the cornerstone of the counseling relationship, and counselors have the responsibility to respect and safeguard the client's right to privacy and confidentiality. Counselors actively attempt to understand the diverse cultural backgrounds of the clients they serve. Counselors also explore their own cultural identities and how these affect their values and beliefs about the counseling process. Additionally, counselors are encouraged to contribute to society by devoting a portion of their professional activities for little or no financial return (pro bono publico).

Section A.1.a. Primary Responsibility. The primary responsibility of counselors is to respect the dignity and promote the welfare of the clients.

Section A.4.a. Avoiding Harm. Counselors act to avoid harming their clients, trainees, and research participants and to minimize or to remedy unavoidable or unanticipated harm.

Section A.4.b. Personal Values. Counselors are aware of—and avoid imposing—their own values, attitudes, beliefs, and behaviors. Counselors respect the diversity of clients, trainees, and research participants and seek training in areas in which they are at risk of imposing their values onto clients, especially when the counselor's values are inconsistent with the client's goals or are discriminatory in nature.

Section B.2.a. Serious and Foreseeable Harm and Legal Requirements. The general requirement that counselors keep information confidential does not apply when disclosure is required to protect clients or identified others from serious and foreseeable harm or when legal requirements demand that confidential information must be revealed. Counselors consult with other professionals when in doubt as to the validity of an exception. Additional considerations apply when addressing end-of-life issues.

Section D.1.h. Negative Conditions. Counselors alert their employers of inappropriate policies and practices. They attempt to effect changes in such policies or procedures through constructive action within the organization. When such policies are potentially disruptive or damaging to clients or may limit the effectiveness of services provided and change cannot be affected [*sic*], counselors take appropriate further action. Such action may include referral to appropriate certification, accreditation, or state licensure organizations, or voluntary termination of employment.

Section D.1.g. Employer Policies. The acceptance of employment in an agency or institution implies that counselors are in agreement with its general policies and principles. Counselors strive to reach agreement with employers—regarding acceptable

(*continued*)

CASE STUDY (*continued*)

standards of client care and professional conduct that allow for changes in institutional policy conducive to the growth and development of clients.

LAWS/LEGAL CONSIDERATIONS

List any laws or legal considerations that may apply. Research those relevant to your own jurisdiction. The example provided is based on Iowa law, circa 2009. This example is not to be considered a legal opinion, only an example. For further information, consult legal counsel and resources in your own area.

Iowa Code

Section 232.69 Mandatory and permissive reporters—training required. [A counselor is considered to be a mandatory reporter] "1.b . . . who, in the scope of professional practice or in their employment responsibilities, examines, counsels, or treats a child and reasonably believes a child has suffered abuse". [Note: This section includes a list of professionals, e.g., (7) An employee of a department of human services institution listed in section 218.1; and (12) A counselor or mental health professional.]

Section 232.68(2)(a)(6) [Included in the definitions of child abuse] An illegal drug is present in a child's body as a direct and foreseeable consequence of the acts or omissions of the person responsible for the care of the child.

ETHICAL PRINCIPLES

List all ethical principles that describe relevant obligations. Describe the courses of action, the principles upheld, the principles compromised, and the obligations. Sometimes, this process is referred to as *principle analysis,* a process wherein ethical principles are specified and subjected to balancing considerations.

Each of the two courses of action can be supported by one or more ethical principles. Contacting authorities could fall under the category of beneficence toward the children. Keeping John's confidence could fall under the category of autonomy, for honoring the right to individual decisions. There is also the possibility that both scenarios could fit into the category of nonmaleficence. Not telling anyone could lead to harm for the children, in some way. Also, by telling, it is possible that John's fears could materialize and the ex-wife could keep the children away from him. In this way, it may be harmful to the client and also for the children if they are not allowed to see their father.

The ethical principles supporting the other course of action will be compromised. If the authorities are told, the counselor is not respecting the client's autonomy. If authorities are not told, the counselor may be compromising the principles of nonmaleficence toward the children and the concept of beneficence, in the same way.

This situation is an ethical dilemma, not just an ethical issue. An ethical issue has a fairly identifiable course of action that is appropriate, even if taking that action is not necessarily easy in practice (i.e., as in the case of involuntarily committing a seriously suicidal individual).

(*continued*)

CASE STUDY *(continued)*

Action A. Pressuring the Client

Principles Upheld
Beneficence (to children)

Principles Compromised
Beneficence (to client)
Nonmaleficence (to client)
Autonomy (of client)
Fidelity (to client)
Veracity (to client)

Resultant Obligations: Work with client?*

Action B. Not Pressuring the Client

Principles Upheld
Beneficence (to client)
Nonmaleficence (to client)

Principles Compromised
Beneficence (to children)
Nonmaleficence (to children)
Autonomy (of client)
Fidelity (to client)
Veracity (to client)

Resultant Obligations: Work with client?*

*Note: In principle analysis, the obligations owed to the client normally outweigh those to others. Therefore, frequently they are the only ones considered; if obligations to others are considered, those owed to the client generally supersede them, because the counselor incurs these primary obligations by virtue of entering into a professional relationship with the client. The exception to this case would involve obligations to vulnerable others (e.g., small children), and/or those situations in which there a high degree of serious danger or risk. This reasoning is why this case presents a particularly troublesome dilemma.

INSTITUTIONAL/AGENCY RULES OR POLICIES

List any institutional/agency rules or policies that may apply.

In the experience of the counselor, the unwritten policy of DCS is to try to coerce the client into reporting the possible child abuse to DHS. Despite the unwritten policy, other counselors at DCS may know of situations where this unwritten policy was not followed, and why the policy was not followed. Alternatively, if the counselor is following a participatory ethics orientation, the client may be informed of the informal policy and his input sought on how to proceed in light of the informal policy.

Component 3: Courses of Action and Positive and Negative Consequences

List all possible and probable courses of action. If you can boil this selection down to two opposing options, this strategy is recommended.

Action A: Attempt to coerce the client into reporting.
Action B: Do not try to coerce the client into reporting.

(continued)

CASE STUDY (*continued*)

Action B could be expanded to include a variety of actions under a participatory ethics approach.

Consider potential positive and negative consequences for each course of action, in light of the risks.

Action A: Pressure the Client	
Positive Consequences	**Negative Consequences**
May protect the children from abuse	Does not respect the client's autonomy or confidentiality
Follows unwritten DCS policy	
DCS would not step in to coerce the client	Hurts the client's trust of counselor
Protects DCS from liability	Ex-wife may cut off child visitation
	Negative relationship with ex-wife
	May evoke suicidal thoughts
	Less time for other pressing issues of the client

Action B: Do Not Pressure the Client	
Positive Consequences	**Negative Consequences**
Respects the client's autonomy and confidentiality	Does not protect children from possible abuse
Time for the other client issues	Counselor is defying employer (DCS)
Does not evoke suicidal thoughts	DCS might step in and coerce the client anyway
Child visitation is preserved	DCS might be liable (if the child is harmed)
Positive relationship with ex-wife	

Component 4: Consult With Others

Consult with supervisors and other knowledgeable professionals. Review the reasoning employed so far in working through the ethical dilemma in consulting with others.

Individual	Type of Consultation
1. ACA Ethics Committee	Review situation, obtain suggestions and opinion
2. Counselors from other corrections professional organizations	
3. Other colleagues at DCS, and other professionals involved in the case (e.g., the family therapist)	
4. DHS confidential hotline again; DHS caseworker that the client believed was helpful	
5. Attorney	

(*continued*)

CASE STUDY (*continued*)

Component 5: Determine Best Ethical Action

Select the best ethical course of action.

The best ethical course of action would be not to pressure the client to report to DHS, for the following reasons:

1. More ethical principles support this course of action, especially for the client.
2. More positive than negative consequences are likely to result.
3. The Iowa Code does not consider this a situation of mandatory child abuse reporting, because the counselor is not working directly with the children, and the only information is "hearsay."

STAGE III: SELECTING AN ACTION BY WEIGHING COMPETING, NONMORAL VALUES, PERSONAL BLIND SPOTS, OR PREJUDICES

The counselor, in this stage, must realize the many additional forces that may affect the counselor and tempt the counselor to not actually execute the selected ethical course of action.

Component 1: Competing Values or Concerns

The counselor engages in a period of reflection and active processing of personal competing values (e.g., need to be liked by coworkers or the supervisor, or a desire to be seen as a team player, so as to be promoted by the supervisor), personal blind spots, or prejudices that may influence whether or not the counselor will discharge his or her ethical obligations. These value orientations may either come into conflict with the course of action necessary to proceed ethically or enhance the tendency to select ethical professional behavior.

Conflicting Concern	Potential Effects
1. Fear of a negative evaluation by DCS, if unwritten policy is not followed	Loss of job, license, respect, financial consequences
2. Feel the need to protect the children at all costs, no matter what the situation	Loss of reputation and seen as a confidentiality risk
3. Fear of legal repercussions if abuse situation is not reported to DHS	Children are harmed Loss of license and/or job
4. Fear of harm to DCS	Personal mental health Financial impact on agency/self
5. Fear of losing respect of colleagues	Personal mental health Future relationships
6. Feeling that the client should not be pressured and have autonomy in the decision	Harm to children Increased client confidence

(continued)

CASE STUDY (*continued*)

Conflicting Concern	Potential Effects
7. Feeling that counseling session should be used to work on the client's problems (e.g., depression), rather than using all of the time trying to convince the client to call DHS	DHS not contacted and children are harmed Clients benefit from counseling
8. Feelings of disgust and anger related to possible drug abuse on the part of a mother of young children	Loss of professional judgment Harm to the client

Component 2: Contextual Influences

Counselors systematically inventory the contextual influences on their choices at the collegial, team, institutional, and societal levels. These influences might be either dysfunctional or constructive for selecting the ethical course over other types of values.

Level 1: Clinical (Counselor–Client)

1. Counselor's professors/supervisors have recommended advocating for clients' autonomy in the past.

Level 2: Team

1. A few coworkers note that DHS said that the counselor is not required to report the situation to DHS, because it is third-party information.
2. Other professionals are involved in this case, and may be operating under different policies and procedures, and different codes of ethics.

Level 3: Institutional/Agency

1. DCS has an unwritten policy of convincing clients to report abuse on their own.
2. Counselor's supervisor and most colleagues support the institution's policy and feel that all counselors at DCS should adhere to both written and unwritten policies.

Level 4: Social Policy/General Cultural

1. Society values children and children's welfare.
2. Society has little tolerance for drug abuse or the selling of drugs, especially when children are involved.
3. There is a fear of transmitted diseases in society, especially HIV and AIDS, which can be passed through intravenous drug use.
4. Society has a prejudiced attitude toward ex-cons on parole, and makes little distinction between those who are successfully recovering and those who are not.

(continued)

CASE STUDY (*continued*)

Component 3: Select Preferred Action

The counselor selects the preferred course of action.

This course of action is to attempt to convince the client to call DHS anonymously. Yet, the counselor still respects the client's autonomy and will not coerce John to report the situation to DHS.

STAGE IV: PLANNING AND EXECUTING THE SELECTED COURSE OF ACTION

The counselor in this stage plans to implement and execute the selected course of action.

Component 1: Possible Sequences of Actions

The counselor figures out a reasonable, practical sequence of concrete actions to be taken. Following is the list of action steps to be taken.

1. Talk with the client about the consequences of his reporting versus not reporting the situation (using the "hotline" at least) to DHS. (This action is consistent with a participatory ethics orientation.)
2. Attempt to convince the client to call DHS anonymously for information about what would happen if the situation were reported.
3. If the client does not call, do not continue to try to convince him any further.
4. If the client does call and receives the information, give support for what he decides to do next.

Component 2: Contextual Barriers and Countermeasures

The counselor will need to anticipate and work out all personal and contextual barriers to effective execution of the plan. It is useful to prepare countermeasures for any contextual barriers that may arise.

Possible Barriers	*Possible Countermeasures*
1. The client does not wish to call.	Document the attempts to get him to call and do not press the issue any further.
2. Supervisor may want the counselor to continue to coerce the client to call.	Counselor could let the supervisor know what he or she is not comfortable doing and apprise someone in authority above the supervisor of the situation.
3. DCS may assign the case to someone else.	No countermeasure unless the client insists upon seeing the current counselor.
4. John's ex-wife may refuse to let him see the children, if he reports the situation to DHS.	Counselor could encourage the client to speak with an attorney about his rights with the children.

(*continued*)

CASE STUDY (*continued*)

Component 3: Carry Out, Document, and Evaluate

This step provides for the execution, documentation, and evaluation of the course of action as planned. Describe here the planned goal(s) and potential types of measurements of plan effectiveness and sources of information.

The counselor would carry out the plan by talking to the client about the consequences of reporting versus not reporting the abusive situation to DHS and attempt to get the client to call for information. Or, alternatively, under a participatory ethics orientation, discuss with the client the pros and cons of contacting DHS in a way that empowers the client to make the final decision about whether or not to call. If the client decides to call, the counselor would support his next step. The counselor would document the ethical decision-making steps taken. Finally, the counselor would evaluate the effectiveness of the plan of action and the entire ethical decision-making process.

Goal	Measure
1. Review consequences of reporting or not reporting and attempt to get the client to call DHS for information.	Weigh benefits and costs of the client's decision; assess the client's level of comfort with either decision.
2. Support the client if he decides to call.	Assess what the client needs from the counselor.
3. Prevent harm to children and help mother.	Follow up with treatment referrals for mother and on the children's welfare.

Note: This case study was developed by Vilia Tarvydas, PhD, CRC, and uses the Tarvydas Integrative Decision-Making Model of Ethical Behavior.

CONCLUSION

Rehabilitation counseling continues to grow in stature and visibility, as a specialty practice within the counseling profession. As a result, contemporary rehabilitation counselors should anticipate the need to demonstrate high levels of competency in the ethical aspects of their practices. The professional practice as a whole has provided substantial tools to inform this process, including the revised 2017 Ethical Standards of Practice provided by CRCC, mechanisms to educate and govern the practice of these ethical standards, and knowledge and wisdom for individual counselors, embodied within models of ethical decision making and behavior. With responsible utilization of these sizable assets for ethical practice, rehabilitation counseling should continue its leadership in the counseling professionalization movement.

CONTENT REVIEW QUESTIONS

- What are the three components of professional standards? Provide examples of each, and describe how they contribute to the quality of care in the profession.

- What are the major levels of ethics governance, and what role does each play in the enforcement of ethical standards? What bodies represent counseling and rehabilitation counseling at each level?
- What is the difference between mandatory and aspirational ethics? Provide an illustration of a set of ethical standards that represents each type of ethical standard and discuss why, as well as how they serve complementary roles.
- What themes or attitudes must one consider when using the Tarvydas Integrative Decision-Making Model of Ethical Behavior? Why do you think these are important in the process?
- What are the major stages of the Tarvydas Integrative Decision-Making Model of Ethical Behavior? What main processes and goals are characteristic of each one?
- Describe the concepts of participatory and restrictive ethics that may affect the ethical decision-making process. Provide an example of a situation in which a client may benefit from a participatory ethics approach.

REFERENCES

American Counseling Association. (2014). *Code of ethics.* Alexandria, VA: Author.

American Psychological Association. (2009). *Revised guidelines for child custody evaluations in family law proceedings.* Washington, DC: Author.

Betan, E. J., & Stanton, A. L. (1999). Fostering ethical willingness: Integrating emotional and contextual awareness with rational analysis. *Professional Psychology: Research and Practice, 30,* 295–301.

Butterfield, K., Trevino, L., & Weaver, G. (2000). Moral awareness in business organizations: Influences of issue-related and social context factors. *Human Relations, 53,* 981–1018.

Commission on Rehabilitation Counselor Certification. (2017). *Code of professional ethics for rehabilitation counselors.* Schaumburg, IL: Author.

Corey, G., Corey, M. S., & Callanan, P. (2010). *Issues and ethics in the helping professions* (8th ed.). Pacific Grove, CA: Brooks/Cole.

Cottone, R. R. (2012). Ethical decision making in mental health contexts: Representative-models and an organizational framework. In S. Knapp (Ed.), *The handbook on ethics in psychology.* (pp. 99–121). Washington, DC: American Psychological Association.

Cottone, R. R., & Claus, R. E. (2000). Ethical decision-making models: A review of the literature. *Journal of Counseling and Development, 78,* 275–283.

Cottone, R. R., & Tarvydas, V. M. (2007). *Counseling ethics and decision making* (3rd ed.). Upper Saddle River, NJ: Merrill/Prentice Hall.

Cottone, R. R., Tarvydas, V., & House, G. (1994). The effect of number and type of consulted relationships on the ethical decision making of graduate students in counseling. *Counseling and Values, 39,* 56–68.

Francouer, R. T. (1983). Teaching decision making in biomedical ethics for the allied health-student. *Journal of Allied Health, 12,* 202–209.

Garcia, J., Cartwright, B., Winston, S. M., & Borzuchowska, B. (2003). A transcultural integrative ethical decision-making model in counseling. *Journal of Counseling and Development, 81,* 268–277.

Gatens-Robinson, E., & Rubin, S. E. (1995). Societal values and ethical commitments that influence rehabilitation service delivery behavior. In S. E. Rubin & R. T. Roessler (Eds.), *Foundations of the vocational rehabilitation process* (pp. 157–174). Austin, TX: Pro-Ed.

Johnson, S. (n.d.) Samuel Johnson Quotes. Retrieved from http://quotes.yourdictionary.com/author/samule-johnson/168000

Kitchener, K. S. (1984). Intuition, critical evaluation and ethical principles: The foundation for ethical decisions in counseling psychology. *The Counseling Psychologist, 12*(3), 43–55.

Koocher, G. P., & Keith-Spiegel, P. (2007). *Ethics in psychology and the mental health professions: Standards and cases* (2nd ed.). New York, NY: Oxford University Press.

Mabe, A. R., & Rollin, S. A. (1986). The role of a code of ethical standards in counseling. *Journal of Counseling and Development, 64,* 294–297.

Meara, N. M., Schmidt, L. D., & Day, J. D. (1996). Principles and virtue: A foundation for ethical decisions, policies, and character. *The Counseling Psychologist, 24*(1), 4–77.

Powell, S. K., & Wekell, P. M. (1996). *Nursing case management*. Philadelphia, PA: Lippincott.

Prilleltensky, I., Rossiter, A., & Walsh-Bowers, R. (1996). Preventing harm and promoting ethical discourse in the helping professions: Conceptual, research, analytical, and action frameworks. *Ethics and Behavior, 6*, 287–306.

Ratts, M. J., Toporek, R. L., & Lewis, J. A. (2010). *ACA Advocacy Competencies. A social justice framework for counselors*. Alexandria, VA: American Counseling Association.

Rest, J. R. (1984). Research on moral development: Implications for training psychologists. *The Counseling Psychologist, 12*(3), 19–29.

Rinas, J., & Clyne-Jackson, S. (1988). *Professional conduct and legal concerns in mental health practice*. Norwalk, CT: Appleton & Lange.

Tarvydas, V. M., & Cottone, R. R. (1991). Ethical responses to legislative, organizational and economic dynamics: A four-level model of ethical practice. *Journal of Applied Rehabilitation Counseling, 22*(4), 11–18.

Tarvydas, V. M., & Cottone, R. R. (2000). The code of ethics for rehabilitation counselors: What we have and what we need. *Rehabilitation Counseling Bulletin, 43*, 188–196.

Tarvydas, V. M., O'Rourke, B. J., & Urish C. (2007). Ethical climate. In R. R. Cottone & V. M. Tarvydas (Eds.), *Counseling ethics and decision making* (3rd ed., pp. 116–137). Upper Saddle River, NJ: Merrill/Prentice Hall.

Tarvydas, V. M., Vazquez-Ramos, R., & Estrada-Hernandez, N. (2015). Applied participatory ethics: Bridging the social justice chasm between the counselor and the client. *Counseling and Values, 60*, 218–233.

Thompson, A. (1990). *Guide to ethical practice in psychotherapy*. New York, NY: Wiley.

Van Hoose, W. H., & Kottler, J. A. (1985). *Ethical and legal issues in counseling and psychotherapy*. San Francisco, CA: Jossey-Bass.

Vasquez, M. J. T. (1996). Will virtue ethics improve ethical conduct in multicultural settings and interactions? *The Counseling Psychologist, 24*(1), 98–104.

Wright, B. A. (1983). *Physical disability—A psychosocial approach*. New York, NY: Harper & Row.

EIGHTEEN

Cultural Competence and Social Justice

BRENDA Y. CARTWRIGHT, DEBRA A. HARLEY, AND KEISHA G. ROGERS

LEARNING OBJECTIVES

After reading this chapter, you should be able to:

- Understand how a multicultural and social justice framework may be used to assist in working toward equity in the context of changing demographics in American society.
- Understand how individual and group racial/cultural and identity development may impact the counseling process.
- Integrate multicultural and social justice counseling competencies (MSJCCs) in providing services to individuals from historically marginalized groups in society.

We anticipate that this chapter will offer practical utility to help expand rehabilitation counselors' (RCs') and other mental health professionals' thinking about the various considerations that underlie a culturally competent social justice approach to rehabilitation counseling practice. We also recognize that this overview does not represent an exhaustive listing of all the factors affecting individual and group social identity; therefore, we expect that counselors and researchers will work collaboratively in the future and continue adding to a better understanding of working in a culturally diverse society.

Our nation is undergoing numerous demographic transitions and trends, as noted by Hempel (2013). Most striking is the projection that in the near future there will be no numerically dominant racial or ethnic group. In fact, census estimates predict that by 2043, non-Hispanic Whites will cease to be the majority group. In roughly that same time span, the number of multiracial individuals in the United States will triple. By 2040, aging trends will also make history: the number of Americans aged 65 and older will more than double. The quality of the nation's health trends also shows rising adult obesity rates. These rates will have serious repercussions for America's health, considering that obesity is linked with increased rates of hypertension, type 2 diabetes, and other illnesses. Another demographic change is in religious affiliation. Protestants will no longer be the majority. Almost since the inception of time, religious and faith communities have occupied important roles in society. Yet millions are leaving the religious affiliation of their childhood to join different religious denominations or abandoning organized religion altogether. Family structures and socioeconomic statuses have also been affected by shifting trends. The number of multigenerational households has reached 7.1 million, with adult children moving back in with their parents and aging adults moving in with their children. At the same time, America is also becoming increasingly economically stratified, with even greater differences between those who are financially sufficient and those who are not. In 2010, the average number of families receiving government benefits (e.g., Temporary Assistance for Needy Families [TANF]) increased across 47 states. Our nation's shifting demographic profile has major implications for RCs addressing and adapting to these changes.

Rehabilitation counseling has demonstrated its commitment to the importance of cultural competency in improving the quality and availability of counseling and rehabilitation services to clients from traditionally underrepresented racial/ethnic groups. In fact, federal legislation (i.e., Section 21 of the U.S. Rehabilitation Act Amendments) mandated that rehabilitation counseling professionals in the state-federal system develop and maintain culturally competent services to individuals with disabilities from these groups. In a recent study, Whitfield, Venable, and Broussard (2010) found evidence that client–counselor matches based on race (i.e., minority–minority) resulted in a significantly higher (7.3%) rehabilitation rate than did client–counselor mismatches (i.e., minority–majority), supporting the notion that larger numbers of RCs who are minorities may be an effective method of mitigating disparities documented in previous research.

The new MSJCCs, endorsed in 2015 by both the Association for Multicultural Counseling and Development (AMCD) and the American Counseling Association (ACA), demonstrate a strong commitment to social change and remedying social injustices in the field of counseling. These competencies provide guidelines for the counseling profession to offer a more inclusive and broader understanding of culture and diversity and address the expanding role of counselors and other mental health professionals to include social justice and activism (Ratts, Singh, Nassar-McMillan, Butler, & McCullough, 2016). In its mission statement, the National Association of Multicultural Rehabilitation Concerns (NAMRC) and its forerunner, the National Association of Non-White Workers (NANRW), also advocate for quality and equitable services to individuals with disabilities from culturally diverse populations.

Finally, the call for cultural competence is formalized in program accreditation standards. Even before the merger of the Council on Rehabilitation Education (CORE; the historical accrediting body for rehabilitation counseling programs) with the Council for Accreditation of Counseling and Related Educational Programs (CACREP; the accrediting body for general counseling programs), both entities emphasized in their standards the need for practitioners to guard the individual rights and personal dignity of all clients, including those from protected groups, as a result of antidiscrimination laws (e.g., race, color, religion, age, disability status, and gender identity). Justice on ethical grounds has also propelled cultural competency (Whaley & Davis, 2007). In fact, the Commission on Rehabilitation Counselor Certification (CRCC) *Code of Professional Ethics for Rehabilitation Counselors* (2017) articulates the RC's ethical responsibilities for recognizing the needs of diverse client populations. Likewise, the ACA's 2014 *Code of Ethics* emphasized the vital importance of cultural competency when working with diverse client populations.

Although the field of rehabilitation counseling has made progress in understanding the need for cultural competence, the gap between theory, research, and application remains. Evidence suggests that beginning with the Atkins and Wright (1980) seminal study, an ongoing struggle continues among rehabilitation professionals to provide quality and equitable services to individuals from traditionally underrepresented groups. These groups include those from non-White populations, as well as people from specific disability groups, such as spinal cord injuries, stroke, Deaf, late-deafened, hard of hearing, and individuals with mental illnesses (Boutin & Wilson, 2009; Bradley, Ebener, & Geyer, 2013; Ellis et al., 2014; Gao, Gill, Schmidt, & Pratt, 2010; Hasnain & Balcazar, 2009; Houston, Lammers, & Svorny, 2010; Kennedy, Kilvert, & Hasson, 2015; Moore, 2001; Patterson, Allen, Parnell, Crawford, & Beardall, 2000; Rimmerman, Botuck, & Levy, 1995; Wilson, 2002). Although rehabilitation counseling professionals have acknowledged awareness of some of the ways in which diverse cultural contexts impact their clients' lives, many of these professionals fail to effectively implement this knowledge in ways that result in maximized employment, economic self-sufficiency, independence, inclusion, and integration.

This chapter is designed to increase the awareness and knowledge of a broad range of diversity issues that must be addressed by RCs and clinical mental health professionals when serving clients from historically marginalized groups and backgrounds. First, the MSJCCs are described, with particular attention directed to the social justice framework and how it may be used to assist in working toward equity in the context of changing demographics in American society. Second, a discussion follows describing how individual and group racial, sexual identity, cultural, and identity development may impact the counseling process.

MULTICULTURAL AND SOCIAL JUSTICE COUNSELING COMPETENCIES

The most updated description of the MSJCCs for counselors comprises a constellation of four dimensions in the new MSJCCs (Ratts et al., 2016). The **self-awareness** dimension involves taking inventory of one's own assumptions about human behavior, values, preconceived notions, limitations, and biases regarding race, ethnicity, and culture. It also includes one's awareness of the sociopolitical relevance of one's cultural group membership to cultural power, privilege, discrimination, and oppression. Self-awareness is not a concept at which one arrives, but more a process that is lifelong and ever-evolving. The **knowledge** dimension refers to one's understanding of the worldviews of clients who are culturally different, without imposing negative judgments, pathologizing, blaming, or invalidating others' experiences. This dimension also includes information about how culture-specific values, social power, privilege, discrimination, and oppression influence the lived, subjective, and collective experiences of clients from historically marginalized groups and backgrounds, as well as the counseling relationship. The **skills** dimension refers to one's ability to develop and practice appropriate, culturally relevant, sensitive intervention strategies in working with clients from historically marginalized groups and backgrounds. The new **action** dimension requires RCs and other mental health professionals to extend their roles beyond the traditional office setting, using advocacy interventions and strategies to remedy social injustices by partnering and collaborating with community allies. In addition to these four dimensions, the new MSJCCs acknowledge the following principles of practice:

- Understanding the complexities of diversity and multiculturalism on the counseling relationship
- Recognizing the negative influence of oppression on mental health and well-being
- Understanding individuals in the context of their social environment

- Integrating social justice advocacy into various modalities of counseling (e.g., individual, family, partners, groups; Ratts et al., 2016, pp. 30–31)

Based on these principles, Table 18.1 provides a set of guidelines for culturally competent care to assist RCs and other mental health professionals across the nation in tailoring services to the needs of a growing culturally diverse population.

To assist RCs to use the MSJCCs for culturally competent care, a discussion follows on several important considerations needed to increase understanding on how counselors' and clients' privileged and marginalized statuses may influence the counseling relationship.

INDIVIDUAL AND GROUP IDENTITY ON THE COUNSELING PROCESS

As people, we all belong to groups and subgroups that help to form our personal identity and perceptions of who we are and where we belong. By this we mean that group membership or social identity theory is focused on characteristics that define group behavior and intergroup relations. Social identity theory is focused primarily on the roles we perform and role relationships within groups. At a minimum, people universally belong to two groups (i.e., ethnic and gender/transgender) of which we often assume the expected or associated behavior. Thus, what we call ourselves and how we behave is in response to internal and external perceptions. Theories of identity development include *racial/ethnic minority identity* (Cross, 1971, 1991; Jackson, 1975; Kim, 1981; Ruiz, 1990; S. Sue & Sue, 1971; Thomas, 1971), *white racial identity* (Helms, 1984, 1990, 1994, 1995), *gender (based on social learning theory)*, *sexual orientation* (Cass, 1979; Horowitz, 2012; Marszalek, Cashwell, Dunn, & Heard, 2004), *religious/spiritual* (Erikson, 1968; Marcia, 1966; Moulin, 2013), *disability* (Gibson, 2006; Murugami, 2009), *age/stages of psychosocial development* (Erikson, 1968), *class/socioeconomic* status (Tajfel & Turner, 1979), and *language as culture and as communication about groups of people, and racial/cultural* (Atkinson, Morten, & Sue, 1979, 1989, 1998). These identity theories describe stages of development in which individuals progress toward a positive identity of self and group identity.

Research suggests that counselors identify representative characteristics of groups that influence their conceptualizations of working with and understanding culturally diverse groups. These characteristics include racial (Chao, Wei, Good, & Flores, 2011; Ferguson, Leach, Levy, Nicholson, & Johnson, 2008; Han, West-Olatunji, & Thomas, 2010), gender (Artkoski & Saarnio, 2013; Chao, 2012; Maldonado, 2008), sexual orientation (Cox, 2013), and religious identities (Elliott, 2011; Walker, Gorsuch, & Tan, 2004) and are evident among counselors, educators, and other practitioners (Freeman & Kaylee, 2012; Schneider, Zaslavsky, & Epstein, 2002). In their study on race/ethnicity, color-blind racial attitudes, and multicultural counseling competence, Chao et al. (2011) found a significant interaction effect of race/ethnicity (i.e., White versus ethnic minority) and multicultural training on multicultural awareness, but not on multicultural knowledge. Chao et al. (2011) also found that for racial/ethnic minority RCs who had lower levels of multicultural training, their multicultural awareness was significantly higher than that of their White counterparts; however, at higher levels of training no significant difference was found between the two groups. In other words, more training significantly enhanced Whites' multicultural awareness, but not that of racial/ethnic minority trainees. In addition, the effect of training on enhancing knowledge was stronger for those with lower color-blindness than those with higher color-blindness. Because we do not

TABLE 18.1 Guidelines for Culturally Competent and Social Justice Counseling

Guideline	Description
Guideline 1 Self-Awareness	Culturally competent and social justice competent counselors engage in critical self-reflection on their own values, beliefs, and biases, to gain insight on how these contextual factors may affect the provision of culturally responsive services.
	Culturally competent and social justice competent counselors assess how their membership in marginalized and privileged groups, social identity status, and communication style may impact culturally responsive services.
	Culturally competent and social justice competent counselors use reflective and critical thinking skills to understand the extent to which their membership in marginalized and privileged groups may influence the provision of culturally responsive services.
	Culturally competent and social justice competent counselors actively seek opportunities to learn how their membership in marginalized and privileged groups influences their professional experiences and impact culturally responsive care.
	Culturally competent and social justice competent counselors seek to understand how power and privilege impact the growth and development of marginalized and privileged clients.
Guideline 2 Client Worldview	Culturally competent and social justice competent counselors seek to become knowledgeable of the complex variables (e.g., within- and between-group differences) that affect marginalized and privileged clients.
	Culturally competent and social justice competent counselors seek to understand how family systems and the dynamics of cultural privilege, discrimination, and oppression affect marginalized and privileged clients.
	Culturally competent and social justice competent counselors seek ongoing opportunities to partner and consult with other members in the community to learn about the lived experiences of marginalized and privileged clients.
Guideline 3 Counseling Relationship	Culturally competent and social justice competent counselors are mindful of how their self-awareness, acknowledgment of, and respect for their clients' worldviews influence the counseling relationship.
	Culturally competent and social justice competent counselors seek to understand how the interfaces between social identity development status and social justice issues influence the counseling relationship.
	Culturally competent and social justice competent counselors use effective, culturally sensitive, and competent communication skills to interpret how social identity development status, worldviews, and lived experiences influence the counseling relationship.
	Culturally competent and social justice competent counselors expand the concept of individual practice to include nontraditional roles and helping models to offer relevant, ethically, and culturally responsive services.
Guideline 4 Counseling and Advocacy Interventions	Culturally competent and social justice competent counselors, aware of the effect of policies, delivery systems, and resources on members of historically marginalized groups, empower clients who are members of these groups.
	Culturally competent and social justice competent counselors collaborate with other individuals and organizations within the community to share ideas and resources to meet the needs of clients who are members of historically marginalized groups.
	Culturally competent and social justice competent counselors use relevant, linguistically appropriate interventions and strategies.
	Culturally competent and social justice competent counselors advocate for socially just policies and procedures to promote access and equity for all.

exist in a vacuum, as counselors we are influenced by things we have learned from our familial and social networks. Thus, we must reconcile our individual and group identities in such a way that the challenges of one are complemented by the features of the other in order to move toward multicultural counseling competence. That is, counselors need to be able to move from being more focused on their own group identity to becoming aware, knowledgeable, and skilled in working with diverse racial/ethnic, sexual orientation, religious, age, gender, and social class groups and individuals.

For example, look at an African American heterosexual male counselor who is working with an African American gay male client. In this case, the counselor's belief system tells him that homosexuality is a sin. The counselor is aware of his ethical obligation to be respectful of difference and not to impose his beliefs on clients. Although the counselor can identify with the client on the basis of shared racial identity, he is unable to do the same regarding sexual orientation. The client ultimately expresses concern to the counselor about feelings of rejection from and negative labeling by the "Black community" regarding his sexual orientation. In this example, several important points are illustrated. First, although the counselor is aware of his ethical responsibility in working with the client, he may still exhibit both unconscious bias and stereotyping. Second, the counselor's attempt to separate the various aspects of the client's identities into mutually exclusive categories (i.e., accepting racial identity, but rejecting sexual orientation) may end up marginalizing the client. The remaining question is whether the counselor's lack of knowledge and skills in working with sexual minorities further prohibits him from accurately addressing the intersecting relationship of the client's identities. According to Lewis and Marshall (2012), "conceptualizing these identities as additive assumes that they are independent and separate, and that together they cumulatively make up the Black LGBTQ persons' experiences" (p. 11). In other words, the totality of the person is more representative of the person's experiences than his or her individual parts. When these identities intersect, they form a unique experience that is different than what is expected by simply adding separate characteristics into the mix.

Individuals from the same ethnic background may share common cultural attributes that make them part of that group and distinguish them from other groups. According to S. Sue and Sue (2013), however, when counselors use culturally specific characteristics of a group and imply that all individuals with membership in that group are alike, such a monolithic view of culturally diverse group attitudes and behaviors leads to therapeutic problems. The erroneous beliefs held by counselors may often lead them to respond to culturally diverse clients in a very stereotypical manner. It should be noted that counselors across the diversity spectrum have preconceived notions about themselves and others. Thus, a counselor may be comfortable within his or her own skin when communicating with clients of the same racial/ethnic group, but he or she may be uncomfortable when dealing with a client of a different racial/ethnic group. Also, a counselor can be comfortable with a client of a different racial/ethnic group but be uncomfortable with a client with whom he or she shares the same ethnic group, but different sexual orientation. The convergence of a counselor's identity formation and cultural values and beliefs can easily advantage a client in one aspect and disadvantage him or her in another.

Understanding the impact of individual and group identity on the counseling process involves incorporation and examination of the counselor and client from multidimensional perspectives. It is the counselor's own culture, attitudes, and theoretical perspectives; the client's culture; and the multiplicity of components comprising an individual identity (Pederson, 1986) that usher into counseling both the challenge and need for cultural competence. The example mentioned earlier about the African American counselor and client demonstrates that the multiple and intersecting identities of both the counselor and client are at play in the counseling relationship.

SOCIAL IDENTITY COMPLEXITY MODEL

In this chapter, we advocate for consideration of the social identity complexity model (Roccas & Brewer, 2002) so that RCs can better recognize the complexities of themselves (self-identity complexity) and, eventually, of others (other-identity complexity) in the quest for multicultural competence (Martin-Adkins, 2013). The social identity complexity model builds upon the multiple identities included in the RESPECTFUL model (D'Andrea & Daniels, 2001) and the ADDRESSING model (Hays, 2008). Martin-Adkins suggested, however, that although the RESPECTFUL and ADDRESSING models "provide expanded considerations for counselors to use in conceptualizing clients, they do not effectively address how to explore identity categories as interacting, intersecting entities within an ideally unified individual's sense of self" (2013, p. 11). Similarly, Bodenhausen (2010) argues that some research on racism, sexism, ageism, and other forms of identity-based prejudice has taken a single identity dimension, ignoring the inherently multifaceted nature of social identity. In contrast, the social identity complexity model addresses the way in which individuals subjectively represent the relationships among their multiple in-group memberships.

In the development of the social identity complexity model, Roccas and Brewer (2002) proposed the following logic: (a) it is not only how many social groups an individual identifies with that matters, but more importantly, (b) how those different identities are subjectively combined to determine the overall inclusiveness of the individual's in-group memberships. Brewer and Pierce (2005) explain that "social identities can be represented along a continuum of complexity and inclusiveness, reflecting the degree to which different identities are both differentiated and integrated in the individual's cognitive representation of his or her group memberships" (p. 428). Bodenhausen (2010) emphasizes that identity complexity has led to more research examining both when and how particular identities become a focal point and how they function in relation to one another. In other words, individuals with low social identity complexity view their in-group as highly overlapping and convergent. Conversely, those with high complexity view their different in-group identities as distinct and traverse membership across groups (Brewer & Pierce, 2005).

Three approaches have emerged to address the complexities of diversity in the person and diversity in the group: dominance, compartmentalization, and integration. **Dominance** occurs when one identity overrides other potential identities, remaining salient in most circumstances while other identities disappear. For example, an individual may voluntarily assume as the primary identity the one that serves him or her best in a given situation. That is, a White, middle-aged, gay man may conveniently identify as White, and not engage any of his other identities because being White is more advantageous. **Compartmentalization** occurs when various identities exist in an encapsulated form, with nonoverlapping that alternates dominating social perception and self-definition. No one identity has lasting dominance, and any of them can be momentarily primary while the other remains dormant. For example, a White, middle-aged, gay man may alternate between being a middle-aged, White male in the workplace and being gay in his social circles as his primary identity. **Integration** involves utilization of more than one identity membership and in some simultaneous fashion. The identities can be used additively or alternatively in such a manner that the impact of one is modified by the presence of the other(s) (Bodenhausen, 2010). For example, a middle-aged, gay White man may identify as all of these in the workplace because of issues of advocacy and role model/mentorship. Integration is a continuing theme in human development, reflecting a struggle to resolve opposing forces toward separation and unity (Gill, 1997). Josselson (1996) summarized identity and intersections in the following:

> Living our identities is much like breathing. We don't have to ask ourselves each morning who we are. We simply are. . . . Identity is never fixed; it continually evolves. But something in it stays constant; even when we change, we are recognizably who we have always been. Identity links the past, the present and the social world into a narrative that makes sense. It embodies both change and continuity. (p. 29)

Social categories of an individual vary considerably, with overlaps between those categories of which he or she is simultaneously a member, called **cross-categorization** (D. Meyer, 2014). Categorization of people into "us" and "them" or "the other" is a basic characteristic of how we perceive social groups. Because such a simple dichotomization is insufficient to fully capture the complexity of intergroup relations, cross-categorization takes this intricacy into account (Crisp, 2010). Thus, an individual may have other people's group membership in common in one group, but simultaneously belong to another group according to another categorization (D. Meyer, 2014).

When social identity complexity is applied to cultural competence, the counselor is coming to terms with how he or she integrates the concept of the **idealized self** (supposed to be) and the **actual self** (lived experiences). In addition, the counselor must contend with the influence of cross-categorization, which is intended to reduce real-world bias and discrimination (D. Meyer, 2014). Often, counselors oscillate between their private/personal identity and public/professional identity in which they may also have contradicting sets of attitudes and beliefs about people ("the other") who are different from them. Although there is fluidity within identity categories, social structures and norms restrict individuals not only to be one and only one, but also to view others as one and only one. Thus, this imposes upon self and others the expectations of stereotypes that inadvertently impact the counseling process. Within these private and public identities of self, counselors make choices, alter or sustain beliefs, and assume roles within these contexts that make sense to them. In other words, the counselor is seeking congruence between the personal and professional worldviews. The remainder of this section focuses on several key issues in which the confluence of counselor social identity complexity, attitudes, awareness, knowledge, and skills impacts the counseling process for culturally diverse clients.

The Working Alliance

The **working alliance** (Bordin, 1979) is also referred to as the therapeutic, counseling, ego, and helping alliance. It is defined as a collaboration between the client and the counselor based on the development of a bond and shared commitment to the goals and tasks of counseling. A good attitude of the counselor and a good rapport with the client are the foundation for development of the working alliance. The working alliance consists of a collaborative effort, equal contributions, and active participation between the client and the counselor in meeting the three interdependent components of the working alliance: **goals** (agreed-upon objectives), **tasks** (agreed-upon behaviors), and **bonds** (level of empathy; Lustig, Strauser, Rice, & Rucker, 2002). The working alliance consists of both the quality and strength of the reciprocal relationship between the client and the counselor (Bedi, Davis, & Arvay, 2005). In general, the working alliance is important for successful counseling outcomes (Couture et al., 2006; Langhoff, Baer, Zubraegel, & Linden, 2008; Leibert, Smith, & Agaskar, 2011; Lustig et al., 2002; Slone & Owen, 2015); is a salient therapeutic or counseling factor across cultures (Asnaani & Hofmann, 2012; Assouad, 2014; Vasquez, 2007; Yoo, Hong, Sohn, & O'Brien, 2014), gender and age (Wintersteen, Mensinger, & Diamond, 2005), sexual minorities (Alderson, 2004; Ali & Barden, 2015); and in developing counselors' alliance formation competence (Bedi et al., 2005). In fact, Zhang and Burkard (2008) found that White counselors who discussed racial and ethnic differences with their clients of color were rated as more credible and as having stronger working alliances than those who did not discuss such differences. Leibert et al. (2011) also found that higher-rated alliances predicted greater change for clients over time. Clearly, client outcome is positively affected by the working alliance.

In an exploratory study of multicultural competence and the working alliance, Gonzalez (2015) found that the perceptions of counselors-in-training regarding their multicultural competence was a predictor of client outcomes. At the same time, other research has found no relationship between multicultural competence and the working alliance (Hayes, Owen, & Bieschke, 2014; Norcross, 2011; Nyman, Nafziger, & Smith, 2010; Owen, Leach, Wampold, & Rodolfa, 2011) or impact on client outcomes at times and not at others (Drisko, 2013). A potential reason may be related to the methodologies used in these studies. Nevertheless, moving beyond the varied results of studies, multicultural competence in the working alliance may be critically important because of the potential either to reduce early termination of services or to increase service utilization by clients from racial, ethnic, and sexual minority populations and other diverse backgrounds.

Moving beyond the mixed, and at times contradictory, findings of various studies, the counselor who is able not only to recognize, but also to bring cultural capital (i.e., knowledge about a culture because of membership within that group) to the working alliance may be able to increase relationship efficacy because of commonly identified experiences with the client. In addition, the use of cultural capital may assist the counselor and client to use integrated identities of each other to enhance communication and work toward goals. It should be noted that cultural capital does not lead to an automatic identification and understanding of another merely because of shared group membership.

LGBTQ Clients

Individuals who identify as Lesbian, Gay, Bisexual, Transsexual, Questioning (LGBTQ) are included in this chapter for several reasons. First, LGBTQ individuals represent a growing number of people among those with physical, psychological, mental health, dual diagnoses, and sensory disorders (Fredriksen-Goldsen, Kim, & Barkan, 2012; Harley, 2016). Second, LGBTQ individuals lack access to health care and human services that are culturally sensitive and appropriate, even though they have higher rates of health disparities (Baker & Krehely, 2011). Third, LGBTQ individuals are at high risk of victimization and discrimination in health care and human services delivery (Rosenthal, 2009). Finally, the field of rehabilitation counseling has not readily included LGBTQ individuals with disabilities in the literature. These individuals are members of multiple groups along the diversity spectrum, including race/ethnicity, gender, age, religion, geographic location, and disability.

Ali and Barden (2015) emphasized that counselors' competence in working with LGBTQ clients requires counselors to be affirmative, open, and supportive and to utilize holistic approaches in assisting clients. Moreover, counselors' preparedness to work with the LGBTQ population includes, but is not limited to, understanding ethical issues, knowing terminology, being aware of current issues, and being willing to advocate. The role of the counselor is to facilitate the counseling process. The counselor must refrain from categorizing the sexual minority client into only one identity and be aware that the client may be experiencing stressors related to multiple identities, individual and group identities, and to developmental issues. In addition, the counselor will need to understand his or her own perceptions about sexual minorities and identities and how he or she may attempt to categorize sexual minority clients. Explicitly, it is unethical for the counselor to attempt to change clients' views and beliefs or to impose decisions (ACA, 2014). Although counseling programs have increased coursework related to multiculturalism, a substantial need exists for preservice and in-service counselors to learn counseling techniques and issues related to the LGBTQ population.

It is important for counselors not only to be aware of, but also to understand how their own attitudes, beliefs, and values about sexual minorities can impact the working alliance. The need for awareness and the adverse impact of lack of awareness and inclusion of diverse groups on the working alliance were summarized by Fassinger and Richie (1997). They stated, "when prevailing ideologies are rooted in oppression and advantage one cultural group over another, the negative effects of those ideologies become the 'isms' (e.g., sexism, heterosexism/homophobia) that a multicultural perspective seeks to eradicate" (p. 85). Similar sentiments for the inclusion of multicultural counseling competencies on sexual minorities were echoed by Dworkin and Pope (2012); Harley, Alston, and Reid (2006); Harley, Feist-Price, and Alston (1996); Paniagua, 2014); D. W. Sue, Arredondo, and McDavis (1992); and D. W. Sue and Sue (2013).

The counseling literature recognizes LGBTQ individuals as inclusive under the umbrella of multicultural populations, as well as intersecting with other groups because of multiple identities. Troutman and Packer-Williams (2014) recommended moving beyond what is minimally required by the 2009 CACREP standards in training counselors to work competently with LGBTQ clients, because these standards do not include specificity. The intent is to increase the probability "that culturally competent training for working with the LGBTQ population will be both acknowledged and comprehensively addressed" (Troutman & Packer-Williams, 2014, pp. 6–7). A review of the 2016 CACREP standards on social and cultural diversity reveals that they still lack specificity for the LGBTQ population. Yet, according to Alderson (2004), professional counseling associations require their members to be knowledgeable about sexual orientation and to be competent in providing counseling services to diverse clientele. The only specificity added to the new standards is regarding spiritual beliefs. The lack of specificity regarding the LGBTQ population leaves it to individual training programs to decide whether or not to acknowledge LGBTQ clients as included in the term "diverse groups" (language used in the 2016 standards) used by CACREP (Troutman & Packer-Williams, 2014). Troutman and Packer-Williams suggest that counselor education programs may take a similar absent or ambiguous stance in preparing students to work with the LGBTQ population. Among the 12 recommendations by Troutman and Packer-Williams, one in particular is made to "incorporate faculty and student accountability by adopting the ALGBTIC (Association for Lesbian, Gay, Bisexual, and Transgender Issues in Counseling) competencies for counseling lesbian, gay, bisexual, queer, questioning, intersex, and ally individuals (LGBQIQA) and other informal and formal assessments to assess student skills" (p. 8).

Minority Stress

Individuals who are members of minority groups live their lives from several introspections: (a) at the intersection of multiple identities experienced over the life span; (b) in a culture steeped in racism, sexism, ageism, heterosexism and homophobia, religious bigotry, and other "isms"; (c) at the margins of social location; (d) in condemnation and skepticism, and in dependence on the institutions within society that discriminate against them (Hall & Fine, 2005; Woody, 2001). Any of these intersections can contribute to minority stress. **Minority stress** (I. H. Meyer, 2003) refers to chronically high levels of tension experienced by individuals of stigmatized minority groups. Overwhelmingly, individuals with minority group membership experience discrimination, which can be stressful. Research suggests that minority stress has a direct negative impact on minority groups' psychological and physical well-being. Minority stressors include stigma, expectations of rejection, acute events and chronic everyday discrimination and mistreatment, internalized negative beliefs about one's social identities, and stressors related to concealment or management of stigmatized identity (Frost, 2011; I. H. Meyer, 2003). In the delivery of multicultural counseling, counselors must be able to identify presenting symptoms of minority stress in clients with membership in diverse and marginalized groups and identify coping resources and/or refer for culturally appropriate interventions.

Microaggressions

Microaggressions are "brief and commonplace daily verbal or behavioral indignities, whether intentional or unintentional, that communicate hostile, derogatory, or negative racial slights and insults that potentially have harmful or unpleasant psychological impact on the target person or group" (D. W. Sue, Bucceri, Lin, Nadal, & Torino, 2007, p. 72). The intent is to make the person or group feel unwelcomed, unsafe, isolated, and alienated. Counselors must be aware of what microaggressions look/sound like and the messages they transmit. For example, when a counselor asks a Latino American person, "Where are you from?," the implication is that the client is not American. Another example is the counselor saying, "You speak good English," anticipating that the client does not speak standard English. A counselor may make a statement such as, "I don't see color," denying a Person of Color his or her racial/ethnic experiences (D. W. Sue & Sue, 2013). These examples illustrate that words have meaning and that inaccurate statements or microaggressions such as these not only create problems, but also reinforce the notion of "us" and "them." D. W. Sue and Sue postulate that the subtle and insidious nature of microaggressions is outside the level of awareness of perpetrators, but nevertheless causes the targeted individuals to question the intent of the perpetrators and themselves as well. Culturally competent counselors are aware of unconscious biases and prejudices and proactively work to prevent them from becoming a part of the working alliance. Failure to do so results in counselors becoming, intentionally or unintentionally, contributors to the oppressive experiences of culturally diverse clients (D. W. Sue & Sue, 2013). As agents of inclusivity, counselors should be able to integrate and apply the concepts of MSJCCs.

CONCLUSION

The need for culturally competent counselors and mental health professionals continues to be critically important as society becomes increasingly diverse. In many ways, the effectiveness of the working alliance between the client and the counselor may rest on the counselor's ability to recognize how the client's individual and group identity is interpreted. As we move forward as a society and as a profession, it is incumbent upon practitioners not only to understand cultural competence, but to demonstrate it as well.

CONTENT REVIEW QUESTIONS

- In the process of building mutuality with the consumer/client, what factors can influence consumer/client perceptions of counselor cultural competence? Why is it important for rehabilitation professionals to attend to this process?
- How can rehabilitation professionals utilize the social identity complexity model to deepen their own understanding of the contextual influences they bring to the counselor–consumer/client alliance (relationship)?
- What actions can you take as a counselor when you become aware of the need to further engage the process of cultural competence development?

REFERENCES

Alderson, K. G. (2004). A different kind of outing: Training counselors to work with sexual minority clients. *Canadian Journal of Counseling, 38*(3), 193–210.

Ali, S., & Barden, S. (2015). Considering the cycle of coming out: Sexual minority identity development. *The Professional Counselor, 5*(4), 501–515.

American Counseling Association. (2014). *Code of ethics*. Alexandria, VA: Author.

Artkoski, T., & Saarnio, P. (2013). Therapist's gender and gender roles: Impact on attitudes toward clients in substance abuse treatment. *Journal of Addiction, 2013*, Article ID591521, doi:10.1155/2013/591521

Asnaani, A., & Hofmann, S. G. (2012). Collaboration in culturally responsive therapy: Establishing a strong therapeutic alliance across cultural lines. *Journal of Clinical Psychology, 68*(2), 187–197.

Assouad, J.-P. (2014). *The effects of acknowledging cultural differences on therapeutic alliance in cross-cultural therapy* (Doctoral dissertation). Philadelphia College of Osteopathic Medicine. Retrieved from http://digitalcommons.pcom.edu/cgi/viewcontent.cgi?article=1306&context=psychology_dissertations

Atkins, B. J., & Wright, G. N. (1980). Three views: Vocational rehabilitation of blacks. The statement, the response, the comment. *Journal of Rehabilitation, 46*(2), 40–49.

Atkinson, D. R., Morten, G., & Sue, D. W. (1979). *Counseling American minorities: A cross-cultural perspective*. Dubuque, IA: Brown.

Atkinson, D. R., Morten, G., & Sue, D. W. (1989). A minority identity development model. In D. R. Atkinson, G. Morten, & D. W. Sue (Eds.), *Counseling American minorities* (pp. 35–52). Dubuque, IA: W. C. Brown.

Atkinson, D. R., Morten, G., & Sue, D. W. (1998). *Counseling American minorities* (3rd ed.), Boston, MA: McGraw-Hill.

Baker, K., & Krehely, J. (2011). *Changing the game: What health care reform means for gay, lesbian, bisexual, and transgender Americans*. Washington, DC: Center for American Progress. Retrieved from http://www.americanprogress.org/issues/2011/03/aca_lgbt.html

Bedi, R. P., Davis, M. D., & Arvay, M. J. (2005). The client's perspective on forming a counseling alliance and implications for research on counselor training. *Canadian Journal of Counseling, 39*(2), 71–85.

Bodenhausen, G. V. (2010). Diversity in the person, diversity in the group: Challenges of identity complexity for social perception and social integration. *European Journal of Social Psychology, 40*, 1–16.

Bordin, E. (1979). The generalizability of the psychoanalytic concept of the working alliance. *Psychotherapy: Theory, Research, and Practice, 16*, 252–260.

Boutin, D. L., & Wilson, K. B. (2009). Professional jobs and hearing loss: A comparison of deaf and hard of hearing consumers. *Journal of Rehabilitation, 75*(1), 36–40.

Bradley, C. F., Ebener, D. J., & Geyer, P. D. (2013). Contributors to successful VR outcomes among non-Latino (Caucasian) and Latino consumers with hearing loss. *Journal of Rehabilitation, 79*(2), 24–33.

Brewer, M. B., & Pierce, K. P. (2005). Social identity complexity and outgroup tolerance. *Personality and Social Psychology Bulletin, 31*(3), 428–437.

Cass, V. C. (1979). Homosexual identity formation: A theoretical model. *Journal of Homosexuality, 4*, 219–235.

Chao, R. C. (2012). Racial/ethnic identity, gender-role attitudes, and multicultural counseling competence: The role of multicultural counseling training. *Journal of Counseling and Development, 90*, 35–44.

Chao, R. C., Wei, M., Good, G. E., & Flores, L. Y. (2011). Race/ethnicity, color-blind racial attitudes, and multicultural counseling competence: The moderating effects of multicultural counseling training. *Journal of Counseling Psychology, 58*(1), 72–82.

Commission on Rehabilitation Counselor Certification. (2017). *Code of professional ethics for rehabilitation counselors*. Schaumburg, IL: Author.

Couture, S. M., Roberts, D. L., Peen, D. L., Cather, C., Otto, M. W., & Goff, D. (2006). Do baseline client characteristics predict the therapeutic alliance in the treatment of schizophrenia? *Journal of Nervous and Mental Disease, 194*(1), 10–14.

Cox, M. R. (2013, May). When religion and sexual orientation collide. *Counseling Today*. Retrieved from http://ct.counseling.org/2013/05/when-religion-and-sexual-orientation-collide

Crisp, R. J. (2010). Cross-categorization. In J. M. Levine & M. A. Hogg (Eds.), *Encyclopedia of group processes and intergroup relations* (Vol. 1, pp. 163–166). Thousand Oaks, CA: Sage.

Cross, W. E. (1971). The negro-to-Black conversion experience: Towards a psychology of Black liberation. *Black World, 30*, 13–27.

Cross, W. E. (1991). *Shades of Black: Diversity in African American identity*. Philadelphia, PA: Temple University Press.

D'Andrea, M., & Daniels, J. (2001). RESPECTFUL counseling: An integrated model for counselors. In D. Pope-Davis & H. Coleman (Eds.), *The interface of class, culture and gender in counseling* (pp. 417–466). Thousand Oaks, CA: Sage.

Drisko, J. (2013). The common factors model: Its place in clinical practice and research. *Smith College Studies in Social Work (Haworth), 83*(4), 398–413.

Dworkin, S. H., & Pope, M. (Eds.). (2012). *Casebook for counseling lesbian gay, bisexual, and transgender persons and their families*. Alexandria, VA: American Counseling Association.

Elliott, G. R. (2011). When values and ethics conflict: The counselor's role and responsibility. *Alabama Counseling Association Journal, 37*(1), 39–45.

Ellis, C., Hyacinth, H. I., Beckett, J., Feng, W., Chimowitz, M., Ovbiagele, B., . . . Adams, R. (2014). Racial/ethnic differences in post-stroke rehabilitation outcomes. *Stroke Research and Treatment*, 1–12. doi:10.1155/2014/950746

Erikson, E. (1968). *Identity, youth and crisis*. New York, NY: W. W. Norton.

Fassinger, R. E., & Richie, B. S. (1997). Sex matters: Gender and sexual orientation in training for multicultural counseling competency. In D. B. Pope-Davis & H. L. K. Coleman (Eds.), *Multicultural counseling competencies: Assessment, education and training, and supervision (Multicultural Aspects of Counseling Series,* Vol. 7, pp. 83–110). Thousand Oaks, CA: Sage.

Ferguson, T. M., Leach, M. M., Levy, J. J., Nicholson, B. C., & Johnson, J. D. (2008). Influences on counselor race preferences: Distinguishing Black racial attitudes from Black racial identity. *Journal of Multicultural Counseling and Development, 36*(2), 66–76.

Fredriksen-Goldman, K. I., Kim, H.-J., & Barkan, S. E. (2012). Disability among lesbian, gay, and bisexual adults: Disparities in prevalence and risk. *American Journal of Public Health, 102*, e16–e21. doi:10.2105/AJPH.2011.300379

Freeman, J., & Kaylee, K. (2012). Sex vs. gender: Cultural competence in health education research. *American Journal of Health Studies, 27*(2), 122–125. Retrieved from http://www.biomedsearch.com/article/Sex-vs-gender-cultural-competence/308741508.html

Frost, D. M. (2011). Social stigma and its consequences for the socially stigmatized. *Social and Personality Psychology Compass, 5,* 824–839.

Gao, N., Gill, K. J., Schmidt, L. T., & Pratt, C. W. (2010). The application of human capital theory in vocational rehabilitation for individuals with mental illness. *Journal of Vocational Rehabilitation, 32*(1), 25–33.

Gibson, J. (2006). Disability and clinical competency: An introduction. *The California Psychologist, 39,* 6–10.

Gill, C. J. (1997). Four types of integration in disability identity development. *Journal of Vocational Rehabilitation, 9,* 39–46.

Gonzalez, J. (2015). *Client outcome: An exploratory investigation of multicultural competence and the working alliance* (Doctoral dissertation). University of Central Florida. Retrieved from http://stars.library.ucf.edu.cgi/viewcontent.cgi?article=2130&context=etd

Hall, R. L., & Fine, M. (2005). The stories we tell: The lives and friendship of two older black lesbians. *Psychology of Women Quarterly, 29,* 177–187.

Han, H. S., West-Olatunji, C., & Thomas, M. S. (2010). Use of racial identity development theory to explore cultural competence among early childhood educators. *Journal of Southeastern Regional Association for Teacher Educators, 20*(1), 1–11. Retrieved from http://apbrwww5.apsu.edu/SRATE/Journaleditions/201/Han.pdf

Harley, D. A. (2016). Disabilities among LGBTQ elders. In A. E. Goldberg (Ed.), *The Sage encyclopedia of LGBTQ studies* (pp. 303–306). Thousand Oaks, CA: Sage.

Harley, D. A., Alston, R. J., & Reid, C. (2006). Working with sexual minorities of color in rural areas: Counseling and ethical issues. In J. Bethea & E. G. Bryant (Eds.), *Reinventing rehabilitation in a diverse world: Achieving professional excellence* (pp. 126–138). 14th Annual Summer Training Conference Proceedings of the National Association of Multicultural Rehabilitation Concerns.

Harley, D. A., Feist-Price, S., & Alston, R. J. (1996). Cultural diversity and ethics: Expanding the definition to be inclusive. *Rehabilitation Education, 10*(2), 201–210.

Hasnain, R., & Balcazar, F. (2009). Predicting community versus facility-based employment for transition-aged young adults with disabilities: The role of race, ethnicity, and support services. *Journal of Vocational Rehabilitation, 31*(3), 175–188.

Hayes, J. A., Owen, J., & Bieschke, K. J. (2014). Therapist differences in symptom change with racial/ethnic minority clients. *Psychotherapy.* doi:10.1037/a0037957

Hays, P. A. (2008). *Addressing cultural complexities in practice: Assessment, diagnosis, and therapy.* Washington, DC: American Psychological Association.

Helms, J. E. (1984). Toward a theoretical model of the effects of race on counseling: A Black and White model. *The Counseling Psychologist, 12,* 153–165.

Helms, J. E. (1990). An overview of Black racial identity theory. In J. E. Helms (Ed.), *Black and White racial identity: Theory, research, and practice* (pp. 9–47). New York, NY: Greenwood Press.

Helms, J. E. (1994). The conceptualization of racial identity and "other" racial constructs. In E. J. Trickett, R. J. Watts, & D. Birman (Eds.), *Human diversity: Perspectives on people in context* (pp. 285–311). San Francisco, CA: Jossey-Bass.

Helms, J. E. (1995). An update on the Helms' White and people of color racial identity models. In J. G. Ponterotto, J. M. Casas, L. A. Suzuki, & C. M. Alexander (Eds.), *Handbook of multicultural counseling* (pp. 181–198). Thousand Oaks, CA: Sage.

Hempel, M. (2013). The United States of changing demographics. *Policy and Practice, 71*(2), 24–27.

Horowitz, M. J. (2012). Self-identity theory and research methods. *Journal of Research Practice, 8*(2), M14. Retrieved from http://jrp.icaap.org/index.php/jrp/article/view/296/261

Houston, K., Lammers, H. B., & Svorny, S. (2010). Perceptions of the effect of public policy on employment opportunities for individuals who are deaf or hard of hearing. *Journal of Disability Policy Studies, 21*(1), 9–21. doi:10.1177/1044207309357428

Jackson, B. (1975). Black identity development. *Journal of Educational Diversity, 2,* 19–25.

Josselson, R. E. (1996). *Revising herself: The story of women's identity from college to midlife.* New York, NY: Oxford University Press.

Kennedy, P., Kilvert, A., & Hasson, L. (2015). Ethnicity and rehabilitation outcomes: The needs assessment checklist. *Spinal Cord, 53*(5), 334–339. doi:10.1038/sc.2015.14

Kim, J. (1981). Processes of Asian American identity development: A study of Japanese American women's perceptions of their struggle to achieve positive identities as Americans of Asian ancestry. *Dissertation Abstracts International 42,* 155 1A (University Microfilms No. 81-18080).

Langhoff, C., Baer, T., Zubraegel, D., & Linden, M. (2008). Therapist-patient alliance, patient-therapist alliance, mutual therapeutic alliance, therapist-patient concordance, and outcome of CBT and GAD. *Journal of Cognitive Psychotherapy: An International Quarterly, 22*(1), 68–79.

Leibert, T. W., Smith, J. B., & Agaskar, V. R. (2011). Relationship between the working alliance and social support on counseling. *Journal of Clinical Psychology, 67*(7), 709–719.

Lewis, M. K., & Marshall, I. (2012). *LBGT psychology: Research perspectives and people of African descent.* New York, NY: Springer + Business Media.

Lustig, D. C., Strauser, D. R., Rice, N. D., & Rucker, T. F. (2002). The relationship between working alliance and rehabilitation outcomes. *Rehabilitation Counseling Bulletin, 46,* 24–32.

Maldonado, J. (2008). The influence of gender identification and self-efficacy on counseling students: A multicultural approach. *Journal of Multicultural, Gender and Minority Studies, 2*(1), 1–15.

Marcia, J. (1966). Development and validation of ego-identity status. *Journal of Personality and Social Psychology, 3,* 551–558.

Marszalek, J. F., Cashwell, C. S., Dunn, M. S., & Heard, K. (2004). Comparing gay identity development theory to cognitive development: An empirical study. *Journal of Homosexuality, 48,* 103–123.

Martin-Adkins, M. E. (2013). *Exploring relationships between self-identity complexity, other-identity complexity, and multicultural counseling competence in counselors* (Doctoral dissertation). The University of North Carolina at Greensboro. Retrieved from http://libres.uncg.edu/ir/uncg/f/MartinAdkins_uncg_0154D_11260.pdf.

Meyer, D. (2014, November 10). *Social identity complexity and sports fans* (Unpublished master's thesis). University of Pretoria, Gordon Institute of Business Science, Hatfield, South Africa.

Meyer, I. H. (2003). Prejudice, social stress, and mental health in lesbian, gay, and bisexual populations: Conceptual issues and research evidence. *Psychological Bulletin, 129,* 674–697.

Moore, C. L. (2001). Disparities in job placement outcomes among deaf, late-deafened, and hard of hearing consumers. *Rehabilitation Counseling Bulletin, 44*(3), 144. doi:10.1177/003435520104400304

Moulin, D. (2013, November 8–10). *Negotiating and constructing religious identities.* Paper presented at REA Annual Meeting. Retrieved from http://www.religiouseducation.net/rea2013/files/2013/07/Moulin.pdf

Murugami, M. W. (2009). Disability and identity. *Disability Studies Quarterly, 29*(4). Retrieved from http://www.dsq-sds.org/article/view/979/1173

Norcross, J. C. (Ed.). (2011). *Psychotherapy relationships that work: Evidence-based responsiveness.* New York, NY: Oxford University Press.

Nyman, S., Nafziger, M., & Smith, T. (2010). Client outcomes across counselor training level within a multi-tiered supervision model. *Journal of Counseling and Development, 88,* 204–209.

Owen, J., Leach, M. M., Wampold, B., & Rodolfa, E. (2011). Client and therapist variability in clients' perceptions of their therapists' multicultural competencies. *Journal of Counseling Psychology, 58* (1), 1–9.

Paniagua, F. A. (2014). *Assessing and treating culturally diverse clients: A practical guide* (4th ed.). Thousand Oaks, CA: Sage.

Patterson, J. B., Allen, T. B., Parnell, L., Crawford, R., & Beardall, R. L. (2000). Equitable treatment in the rehabilitation process: Implications for future investigations related to ethnicity. *Journal of Rehabilitation, 66*(2), 14.

Pederson, P. (1986). The cultural role of conceptual and contextual support systems in counseling. *American Mental Health Counselors Association Journal, 8,* 35–42.

Ratts, M. J., Singh, A. A., Nassar-McMillan, S., Butler, S. K., & McCullough, J. R. (2016). Multicultural and social justice counseling competencies: Guidelines for the counseling profession. *Journal of Multicultural Counseling and Development, 44*(1), 28–48. doi:10.1002/jmcd.12035

Rimmerman, A., Botuck, S., & Levy, J. M. (1995). Job placement for individuals with psychiatric disabilities and supported employment. *Psychiatric Rehabilitation Journal, 19,* 37–43.

Roccas, S., & Brewer, M. B. (2002). Social identity complexity. *Personality and Social Psychology Review, 6* (2), 88–106.

Rosenthal, J. (2009). *LGBT issues in health reform: Issues brief on making health reform work for all Americans.* Retrieved from https://cdn.americanprogress.org/wp-content/uploads/issues/2009/07/pdf/lgbthealth.pdf

Ruiz, A. S. (1990). Ethnic identity: Crisis and resolution. *Journal of Multicultural Counseling and Development, 18,* 29–40.

Schneider, E. C., Zaslavsky, A. M., & Epstein, A. M. (2002). Racial disparities in the quality of care for enrollees in Medicare managed care. *Journal of the American Medical Association, 287,* 1288–1294.

Slone, N., & Owen, J. (2015). Therapist alliance, activity comfort, and systemic alliance on individual psychotherapy outcome. *Journal of Psychotherapy Integration, 25*(4), 275–288.

Sue, D. W., Arredondo, P., & McDavis, R. J. (1992). Multicultural counseling competencies and standards: A call to the profession. *Journal of Multicultural Counseling and Development, 20,* 64–89.

Sue, D. W., Bucceri, J., Lin, A. I., Nadal, K. L., & Torino, G. C. (2007). Racial microaggressions and the Asian American experience. *Cultural Diversity and Ethnic Minority Psychology, 13,* 72–81.

Sue, D. W., & Sue, D. (2013). *Counseling the culturally diverse: Theory and practice* (6th ed.). Hoboken, NJ: Wiley.

Sue, S., & Sue, D. W. (1971). Chinese-American personality and mental health. *American Journal, 1,* 36–49.

Tajfel, H., & Turner, J. C. (1979). An integrative theory of intergroup conflict. *The Social Psychology of Intergroup Relations, 33,* 47.

Thomas, C. W. (1971). *Boys no more.* Beverly Hills, CA: Glencoe Press.

Troutman, O., & Packer-Williams, C. (2014). Moving beyond CACREP standards: Training counselors to work competently with LGBT clients. *Journal of Counselor Preparation and Supervision, 6*(1), 1–15.

Vasquez, M. J. T. (2007). Cultural difference and the therapeutic alliance: An evidence-based analysis. *American Psychologist, 62,* 878–885.

Walker, D. F., Gorsuch, R. L., & Tan, S.-Y. (2004). Therapists' integration of religion and spirituality in counseling: A meta-analysis. *Counseling and Values, 49*(1), 69–80.

Whaley, A., & Davis, K. (2007). Cultural competence and evidence-based practice in mental health services: A complementary perspective. *American Psychologist, 62,* 563–574. doi:10.1037/0003-066X.62.6.563

Whitfield, H. W., Venable, R., & Broussard, S. (2010). Are client-counselor ethnic/racial matches associated with successful rehabilitation outcomes? *Rehabilitation Counseling Bulletin, 53*(2), 96–105. doi:10.1177/0034355209338526

Wilson, K. B. (2002). Exploration of VR acceptance and ethnicity: A national investigation. *Rehabilitation Counseling Bulletin, 45*(3), 168–169. doi:10.1177/003435520204500306

Wintersteen, M. B., Mensinger, J. L., & Diamond, G. S. (2005). Do gender and racial differences between patient and therapist affect therapeutic alliance and treatment retention in adolescents? *Professional Psychology: Research and Practice, 36*(4), 400–408.

Woody, I. (2001). *Lift every voice: A qualitative exploration of ageism and heterosexism as experienced by older African American lesbian women and gay men when addressing social service needs* (Unpublished doctoral dissertation). Capella University, Minneapolis, MN.

Yoo, S.-K., Hong, S., Sohn, N., & O'Brien, K. M. (2014). Working alliance as a mediator and moderator between expectations for counseling success and counseling outcomes among Korean clients. *Asia Pacific Education Review, 15*(2), 271–281.

Zhang, N., & Burkard, A. W. (2008). Client and counselor discussion of racial and ethnic differences in counseling: An exploratory investigation. *Journal of Multicultural Counseling and Development, 36,* 77–87.

NINETEEN

Evidence-Based Practice and Research Utilization

FONG CHAN, KANAKO IWANAGA, EMRE UMUCU, RANA YAGHMAIAN,
JIA-RUNG WU, KEVIN BENGTSON, AND XIANGLI CHEN

LEARNING OBJECTIVES

After reading this chapter, you should be able to:

- Understand how the transformation of the health care system in the United States has impacted service delivery of health care disciplines, including rehabilitation counseling, in providing the most effective clinical services.
- Understand how research has provided an evidence-based foundation for the discipline in relation to role, function, and knowledge requirements.
- Understand how rehabilitation professionals can become more effective evidence-based practitioners through enhancing their knowledge in evidence-based methodologies, research utilization, and effective vocational rehabilitation (VR) service delivery practices.
- Understand the concepts of systematic reviews, meta-analysis, effect size, and knowledge translation.
- Understand how the mechanisms of theory development, empirical evidence, and clinical application inform practice in VR service delivery, improving evidence-based practice to enhance outcomes and quality of life (QOL) of people with disabilities.
- Recognize the value of continually assessing the way clinical services are provided to increase effectiveness of intervention strategies.

According to the World Health Organization (WHO, 1995, 2005), one of the main root causes of human suffering in this world is poverty. It is well documented that lack of access to health care, poor nutrition, and other stressors associated with poverty frequently lead to deteriorating health and high mortality over time (Dutta, Gervey, Chan, Chou, & Ditchman, 2008; Krause, Carter, Pickelsimer, & Wilson, 2008; Murali & Oyebode, 2014). Poverty and income inequality also negatively impact the social and mental well-being of individuals with and without disabilities (Diette, Goldsmith, Hamilton, & Darity, 2012). Unfortunately, the labor force participation rate for people with chronic illness and disability in the United States is unacceptably low, at 20.4%, compared to 68.3% of people without disabilities (U.S. Department of Labor [DOL], 2016). Because of unemployment and underemployment, people with chronic illness and disability constitute a disproportionate number of the poor (Atkins & Giusti, 2005), with a poverty rate of 28.5% compared to the rate of 12.3% for people without disabilities (Federal Safety Net, 2015). Lack of employment opportunities prevents many people with chronic illness and disability from community inclusion and participation, delays upward mobility, and greatly affects their health and well-being. As such, participation in competitive employment and other meaningful work activities is considered crucial to the health-related QOL and subjective well-being of people with chronic illness and disability (Dutta et al., 2008; Leahy, Chan, Lui, Rosenthal, et al., 2014; United Nations [UN], 2006).

Rehabilitation counselors (RCs) play a vital role in assisting people with chronic illness and disability to achieve their independent living and employment goals, leading to better health and QOL (Dean, Pepper, Schmidt, & Stern, 2014; Dutta et al., 2008; Leahy, Chan, Lui, Rosenthal, et al., 2014; Martin, West-Evans, & Connelly, 2010; U.S. Government Accountability Office [GAO], 2005). The success rate for individuals with chronic illness and disability receiving employment services from state VR agencies is over 50% (Dutta et al., 2008). However, there is still substantial room to improve the quality of VR services, which will lead to better employment outcomes and employment quality for people with chronic illness and disability. In this era of slow economic growth and constrained budgets, rehabilitation agency administrators need to transform their business models by adopting organizational innovations and harnessing advances in information and communication technologies to deliver outcomes expected by people with chronic illness and disability, communities, and the society at large (Leahy, Chan, Lui, Rosenthal, et al., 2014; Technology and Entrepreneurship Center at Harvard, 2010). Similarly, RCs must provide the most effective psychosocial and vocational interventions possible, by integrating scientific evidence with clinical expertise and client perspectives to help people with chronic illness and disability to find career pathways to the middle class (Chan, Wang, Muller, & Fitzgerald, 2011). The development of theory-driven or model-driven research to inform best practices in rehabilitation counseling will undoubtedly be important as professionals in the field strive to improve the effectiveness of VR service delivery practices, especially for subpopulations of VR consumers with the poorest employment outcomes (Chan et al., 2011; Leahy, Chan, Lui, Rosenthal, et al., 2014).

The **evidence-based practice** movement has significant influence on the professional practice of rehabilitation counseling (Chan et al., 2016; Leahy, Chan, & Lui, 2014). Evidence-based practice advocates that RCs deliver the best possible services to people with chronic illness and disability, based whenever possible on research evidence (Chan et al., 2016; Chan, Tarvydas, Blalock, Strauser, & Atkins, 2009). As a result, the Rehabilitation Services Administration (RSA) has begun to encourage state VR agencies to integrate scientific evidence with clinical expertise and client perspectives (Thirty-Third Institute for Rehabilitation Issues, 2008). RSA has recently funded six national technical assistance centers to help state VR agencies and their counselors to provide empirically supported VR services. The National Institute on Disability, Independent Living, and Rehabilitation Research (NIDILRR) has also underscored the need for its sponsored research studies to meet standards for inclusion in systematic reviews (Schlosser, 2006), and emphasized the importance of knowledge translation to facilitate research utilization in clinical rehabilitation counseling practices. The agency also funded a research and training center on evidence-based practice in VR and several knowledge translation centers. The U.S. Department of Education's Institute of Educational Sciences (IES) has created a *What Works Clearinghouse* to provide information on scientific evidence on what works in education, including secondary, transition, and postsecondary education interventions for youth with disabilities.

VR agency administrators and RCs are increasingly being asked to use empirically supported interventions to improve the effectiveness of rehabilitation service delivery practices (Chan et al., 2016; Leahy, Chan, Lui, Rosenthal, et al., 2014b; Rubin, Chan, & Thomas, 2003). According to Chan, Tarvydas, et al. (2009), the use of high-quality research evidence to guide clinical rehabilitation practices helps RCs fulfill their ethical obligations to consumers by protecting consumers from harm (nonmaleficence), improving efficiency in utilization of scarce resources (justice), and empowering consumers to exercise self-determination and informed choice (autonomy). Not surprisingly, several quantitative and qualitative studies found that RCs generally hold positive attitudes toward the use of evidence-based practice to improve their service and counseling outcomes (Fitzgerald, Leahy, Kang, Chan, & Bezyak, in press; Graham et al., 2006; Pfaller et al., 2016; Tansey, Bezyak, Chan, Leahy, & Lui, 2014; Yaeda, Iwanaga, Fujikawa, Chan, & Bezyak, 2015). However, these studies also identified several major barriers to employing evidence-based practice, including a lack of knowledge, academic preparation, organizational support, and empirically validated psychosocial and VR interventions.

To be an effective evidence-based practitioner in rehabilitation counseling, knowledge of basic concepts of rehabilitation research methods acquired from a traditional master's level course is insufficient. Rehabilitation counseling professionals must become more knowledgeable about evidence-based practices, knowledge translation, and research utilization. The purpose of this chapter is to provide a review of key evidence-based practice, knowledge translation, and research utilization concepts. The chapter further discusses how evidence-based practice can be utilized to improve the professional practice of clinical rehabilitation counseling.

CONCEPTS RELATED TO EVIDENCE-BASED PRACTICE

Sackett, Straus, Richardson, Rosenberg, and Haynes (2000) defined *evidence-based medicine* as the integration of best research evidence with clinical expertise and patient values; this definition is easily translated into rehabilitation counseling practice. DePalma (2002) provided a comprehensive description of evidence-based practice, describing evidence-based practice as a process beginning with knowing what clinical questions to ask, how to find the best practice, and how to critically appraise the evidence for validity and applicability to the particular care situation. The best evidence then must be applied by a clinician with expertise in considering the patient's unique values and needs. The final aspect of the process is evaluation of the effectiveness of care and the continual improvement of the process (DePalma, 2002). Consistent with the philosophy of rehabilitation counseling practice, both definitions emphasize the importance of considering the unique needs and values of people with chronic illness and disability.

Steps for Evidence-Based Practice

Formulating a clear clinical question from a client's presenting problem is the first step in effective evidence-based practice. The ability to ask appropriate background and foreground questions is crucial in this step of the clinical decision-making process. Specifically, background questions (or general questions) ask about a setting or context, whereas foreground questions ask about a specific case within that context (Walker, Seay, Solomon, & Spring, 2006). Examples of typical background questions include:

- What are the most effective treatments for presenting problem A?
- Is treatment X an effective treatment for presenting problem A?
- Are there any significant risks associated with treatment X?

Foreground questions should be asked using the patient group (P), intervention (I), comparison group (C), and outcome measures (O) format. The following is an example of a foreground PICO question: For an African American woman with schizophrenia (patient group), is there any evidence that the Individual Placement and Support (IPS) Model of supported employment (intervention) is superior to job placement services, assertive community treatment, and the clubhouse approach (comparison groups), in improving her employment outcome and the quality of her employment (outcome)? A set of well-built background and foreground questions provides direction for determining what evidence to look for and where to search for the best scientific evidence.

To search for strong research evidence, an evidence-based practitioner in rehabilitation counseling must be knowledgeable about specific methods and resources for locating research evidence to guide the selection and implementation of empirically supported intervention as the treatment of choice for the client's presenting problem. The most reliable and scholarly approach to searching for scientific research papers and systematic reviews documents is through academic databases, such as ABI/INFORM Complete, Academic Search Premier, CINAHL, Cochrane Library, Campbell Library, MEDLINE, PsycINFO, PubMed, and Web of Science.

After formulating well-defined, answerable clinical questions and seeking the best evidence available to answer these questions, RCs must critically appraise the scientific evidence. Chambless and Hollon (1998) indicated that best evidence for psychosocial treatments should be evaluated in terms of **efficacy** (statistical and clinical significance), **effectiveness** (clinical utility), and **efficiency** (cost-effectiveness). In evidence-based medicine, the gold standard for best evidence is randomized controlled trials. A five-level hierarchical framework emphasizing the importance of randomized controlled trials offers RCs a format for determining the strength of the evidence based on methodological rigor (Holm, 2000; Nathan & Gorman, 1998). This **hierarchy of levels of evidence** includes:

1. *Level 1* evidence, defined as strong evidence from at least one systematic review of multiple well-designed randomized controlled trials.
2. *Level 2* evidence, defined as strong evidence from at least one or more properly designed randomized controlled trials of appropriate size.
3. *Level 3* evidence, defined as evidence from well-designed trials without randomization, single-group pre–post, cohort, time series, or matched case-control studies.
4. *Level 4* evidence, defined as evidence from well-designed nonexperimental studies from more than one center or research group.
5. *Level 5* evidence, defined as opinions of respected authorities, based on clinical evidence, descriptive studies, or reports of expert committees.

Although randomized controlled trials are useful in medicine, the emphasis on experimental studies may be too restrictive for the behavioral and social sciences. This judgment is because randomized controlled trials do not always take into account the full complexity of human behavior and clinical condition (Wampold, 2001). The complex nature of VR makes it impossible to rely solely on experimental research to determine the effectiveness of treatment contributing to successful outcomes. Tucker and Reed (2008) suggested that evidentiary pluralism, including qualitative research and mixed-methods research designs, should be considered as valid strategies for evidence-based practice research in rehabilitation. In addition, although randomized controlled trials are vital for establishing treatment efficacy, other multivariate approaches used to test mediator and moderator effects (e.g., hierarchical regression analysis), person–environment interactions (e.g., multilevel analysis), and complex theoretical models (e.g., structural equation modeling) in the natural environment can provide invaluable information about contextual, psychological, social, and treatment determinants of functioning, disability, community participation, employment status, and QOL in people with disabilities (Chwalisz & Chan, 2008; Tucker & Reed, 2008). Chwalisz, Shah, and Hand (2008) also articulated that rigorous qualitative research methods have much to contribute to theoretical and applied knowledge in rehabilitation. When considered together with experimental studies, nonexperimental quantitative and qualitative studies can expand the scope and impact of rehabilitation counseling research focusing on interventions intended to improve the health and well-being status of people with chronic illness and disability.

After finding, evaluating, and integrating the research evidence, the next step is to select empirically supported interventions by taking into account the significance of the evidence, the professional expertise and judgment of the counselor, and characteristics, values, needs, and context of the individual client. The American Psychological Association (APA) defines **best evidence** as "evidence based on systematic reviews, reasonable effect sizes, statistical and clinical significance, and a body of supporting evidence" (APA, 2005, p. 1). Professional judgment is used to identify each client's unique disability and health status and to integrate the best evidence with the rehabilitation context. Client characteristics, values, and context are the preferences, values, strengths, weaknesses, personality factors, sociocultural and environmental factors, and expectations that a client brings to the rehabilitation counseling process. Consistent with the expectations of the Rehabilitation Act of 1973, in evidence-based practice, decisions should be collaborative in nature, with both clients and counselors as active members of the counseling process.

The use of current best evidence to guide clinical decision making and the provision of interventions has the potential to improve the effectiveness of psychosocial and VR intervention outcomes for people with chronic illness and disability. Although research utilization in rehabilitation counseling is indeed important, there are many individual and organizational barriers to the use of research in professional practice. Bezyak, Kubota, and Rosenthal (2010) identified a lack of knowledge and insufficient academic preparation in evidence-based practice as major barriers to research utilization. Other challenges can be attributed to negative perceptions about rehabilitation research. RCs may perceive rehabilitation research to have a weak theoretical foundation and to lack practical relevance for practitioners and clients. Furthermore, there exists a dearth of well-designed experimental design studies aimed at validating the efficacy of rehabilitation counseling interventions, and qualitative and mixed-methods research methodologies have been underutilized in rehabilitation counseling research (Berkowitz, Englander, Rubin, & Worrall, 1975, 1976; Chan, Miller, Pruett, Lee, & Chou, 2003; Chan, Keegan, et al., 2009; Chan et al., 2016; Parker & Hansen, 1981; Rubin & Rice, 1986). To train master's level rehabilitation counseling students and professional counselors to be intelligent consumers of research, it is important, though not sufficient, to teach them the basic concepts of research designs and statistical methods. They also need to be knowledgeable about evidence-based practice methodologies and concepts, including research databases, systematic reviews/meta-analyses, knowledge translation, and implementation science. Finally, they need to be able to appreciate the extent to which research evidence and utilization can be a practical and integral part of their professional practice. A brief review of systematic reviews, scoping reviews, meta-analysis, and related databases is presented next.

SYSTEMATIC REVIEWS AND META-ANALYSIS

Systematic Reviews

Cochrane Collaboration defines **systematic reviews** as a transparent and systematic process used to define a research question, search for studies, assess their quality, and synthesize findings qualitatively or quantitatively (Armstrong, Hall, Doyle, & Waters, 2011). Campbell Collaboration (2015) indicated that the purpose of systematic reviews is to summarize the best available scientific evidence on a specific clinical question using transparent procedures to locate, evaluate, and integrate the findings of relevant research. Hence, a systematic review answers a specific clinical question by using pre-determined rules for capturing the evidence, appraising it, and synthesizing it in a manner that is easily accessible to clinicians. Systematic reviews are conducted by scholars with expertise in a substantive area who review and critique the available data in the field using the following steps: (a) asking an answerable clinical question; (b) identifying one or more databases to search; (c) developing an explicit search strategy; (d) selecting titles, abstracts, and manuscripts based on explicit inclusion and exclusion criteria; and (e) abstracting data in a standardized format (Schlosser, 2006). As mentioned, strong evidence from at least one systematic review of multiple well-designed randomized controlled trials is considered the highest level of best evidence (Level 1) and is frequently labeled a *meta-analytic review*. Meta-analysis is a particular type of systematic review that uses quantitative methods to determine the effect of a treatment by combining the results from a number of studies.

Scoping Reviews

In recent years, the term **scoping review** has also emerged in the literature (Dijkers, 2015). Mays, Roberts, and Popay (2001) contend that scoping reviews can be used to map the key concepts for a research area and the types of evidence available. Scoping reviews can be undertaken as stand-alone projects in their own right, especially where an area is complex or has not been reviewed comprehensively before. Although a systematic review might typically focus on a well-defined question where appropriate study designs can be identified in advance, a scoping review study tends to address broader topics where many different study designs might be applicable (Arksey & O'Malley, 2005). Unlike systematic reviews, a scoping study is less concerned about addressing very specific research questions or assessing the quality of the primary studies. A scoping review usually involves several steps: (a) identify the research questions (i.e., the domain has to be explored); (b) find the relevant studies through electronic databases, reference lists (ancestor searching), websites of organizations, and conference proceedings; (c) select the studies that are relevant to the question(s); (d) chart the data; and (e) collate, summarize, and report the results (Arksey & O'Malley, 2005). As an option, scoping review researchers may also consult stakeholders (e.g., RCs, policy makers, and consumers and families) to obtain more references and gain insight on information that the literature fails to highlight.

Meta-Analysis

The goal of science is the production of cumulative knowledge. However, the small-sample studies and overreliance on statistical tests in social and behavioral science research can produce seemingly conflicting results (Borenstein, Hedges, Higgins, &

Rothstein, 2009; Schmidt & Hunter, 2003). **Meta-analytic studies** review the results of a collection of empirical studies in a specific research domain through statistical integration and analysis, and synthesize the results to reveal simpler patterns of relationships, providing a basis for theory development and clinical decision making (Durlak, 1995; Schmidt & Hunter, 2003; Wampold & Imel, 2015). Importantly, meta-analyses can correct for the distorting effects of sampling error, measurement error, and other artifacts that produce the false impression of contradicting findings. Similar to an individual experiment, a meta-analysis contains both independent and dependent variables, with the independent variables being such characteristics as participants, interventions, and outcome measures; and the dependent variable being the effect size, or the outcome of the results of each study selected for review, transformed into a common metric across studies.

In systematic reviews, the focus of meta-analysis is on treatment effectiveness (e.g., "Is cognitive-behavioral therapy more effective than psychodynamic therapy in treating depression?"). The advantages of meta-analysis are its ability to (a) synthesize the results from many studies succinctly and intuitively for nonscientific communities, (b) illustrate the amount and relative impact of different programs on different criteria for policy decision-making purposes, and (c) identify the most effective programs and highlight gaps or limitations in the literature to suggest directions for future research (Durlak, 1995). A meta-analysis is conducted by following six major steps, which include: (a) formulating research questions; (b) identifying relevant studies through a comprehensive review of the literature (computer searches, manual searches, and examination of the reference lists of each identified study); (c) coding the studies (e.g., participants, research designs, therapist qualifications, control group, treatment type, presenting problem, number of sessions, and method of administration); (d) computing the index of effect; (e) conducting the statistical analysis of effects; and (f) offering conclusions and interpretations (Durlak, 1995).

A common index representing the size of the effect produced by each experimental study is Cohen's d, which is the standardized difference between the sample mean of the treatment group and the sample mean of the control group (Borenstein et al., 2009). It should be noted that the population estimator δ for describing the size of effects for statistical power analysis is also sometimes called d, creating some confusion in the literature. Borenstein et al. (2009) recommend the use of the symbol δ to represent the effect size parameter and d for the sample estimate of the parameter. However, d tends to overestimate the absolute value of δ in small samples. This bias can be corrected using Hedges' g (Hedges & Olkin, 1985). As a result, both d and g can be considered unbiased effect-size indexes. In general, Hedges' g provides a better estimate for studies with small sample sizes (Grissom & Kim, 2005).

A positive score indicates that the treatment group outperformed the control group, and a negative score has the reverse meaning. A typical way to interpret the size of an effect is to compare the d or g index with the standards set by Cohen (1988), with small, medium, and large effect represented by .20, .50, and .80, respectively. To examine the overlap of the control and treatment distributions, the effect size index (d or g) is converted to the value of the standard normal cumulative distribution. For example, if $d = 0.85$, and compared to the normal distribution curve, a z-score of 0.85 covers 80% of the normal curve, this would indicate that the average client receiving treatment will be better off than 80% of untreated clients. Other related mean difference effect-size indexes include the proportion of variability (PV) and eta-squared (η^2). For correlational studies, the effect size is reported as r; for multiple regression analysis, the effect size is f^2; and for

TABLE 19.1 Effect Size Measures

Effect Size	PV	r	d/g	η^2	ω	f^2
Small effects	.01	.10	.20	.01	.10	.02
Medium effects	.10	.30	.50	.06	.30	.15
Large effects	.25	.50	.80	.14	.50	.35

a Pearson chi-square test, the effect size is reported as ω. A typical way to interpret the size is to use the standards established by Cohen (1988), as presented in Table 19.1.

Several factors can influence effect size, including sample size, sensitivity of measurement instruments, design characteristics, and clinical significance. Of particular importance for meta-analytic studies are issues of homogeneity and power. The power of a statistical test is the probability that it will yield statistically significant results. Kosciulek and Szymanski (1993) analyzed empirical articles from five rehabilitation counseling-related journals and concluded that due to low statistical power, RC researchers had little chance of finding small but significant relationships that exist in the population of interest. In terms of homogeneity, it is possible that studies included in a meta-analysis may have an array of different independent or dependent variables, and may not have a common population parameter. Hedges and Olkin (1985) developed the Q statistics as a statistical test of homogeneity; if the null hypothesis of homogeneity is rejected (i.e., the Q statistic is significant), the studies should be partitioned based on meaningful categories. Specifically, a meta-analysis may include studies that differ in categorically predictable ways. For example, a well-designed study would produce a larger effect than a poorly designed study; therefore, to control for this difference, the independent variable "quality of research design" can be used to partition studies into two groups (well-designed studies and poorly designed studies). The between-group differences can then be tested using QB, a goodness-of-fit statistic developed by Hedges and Olkin (1985). If a significant difference between groups (QB) and no difference within groups (Q) are determined, then d+ can be computed to estimate the effect size for each group of studies. If there is significant difference within groups, then the groups should be further partitioned.

Systematic Reviews Databases

To critically evaluate research evidence from a single properly designed randomized controlled trial requires a relatively strong background in research methods and a working knowledge of concepts related to internal and external validity (Schlosser, 2006). Given the potential for a vast number of research articles with contradictory findings, the most efficient way for master's level students and RCs to learn how to find best evidence may be to use databases and/or specific evidence-based intervention websites to search for high-quality systematic reviews and scoping reviews. The most useful websites for systematic reviews related to evidence-based medical, rehabilitation, and behavioral science intervention information include the Cochrane Collaboration (www.cochrane.org), Campbell Collaboration (www.campbellcollaboration.org), Agency for Healthcare Research and Quality (www.ahrq.gov/research/findings/evidence-based-reports/index.html), American Congress of Rehabilitation Medicine (www.acrm.org/resources/evidence-and-practice), the U.S. Department of Education, Institute of Educational Sciences' What Works Clearinghouse (www.ies.ed.gov/ncee/wwc), and the Substance Abuse Mental

Health and Services Administration's National Registry of Evidence-based Programs and Practices (www.samhsa.gov/nrepp). In addition, the Rehabilitation Research and Training Center on Evidence-Based Practice in Vocational Rehabilitation (www .research2vrpractice.org) is a useful resource for evidence-based VR practices, and the National Technical Assistance Center on Transition (www.transitionta.org/evidenceprac- tices) provides information on evidence-based practice related to secondary transition and postsecondary education interventions. Rehabilitation counseling professionals and students can also search for systematic reviews, scoping reviews, and meta-analytic studies through Academic Search Elite, CINAHL Plus with Full Text, MEDLINE, and PsycINFO databases.

EMPIRICALLY VALIDATED INTERVENTIONS IN REHABILITATION AND MENTAL HEALTH COUNSELING

Ample research evidence suggests that the provision of rehabilitation counseling and related services can produce significantly positive outcomes in the lives of people with chronic illness and disability. Several frequently used empirically supported rehabilita- tion counseling interventions are described next.

Counseling and Psychotherapy

Counseling and psychotherapy represent some of the strongest evidence-based prac- tices in health care (Norcross & Lambert, 2011). It is also one of the most important job functions and knowledge areas for the professional practice of rehabilitation counseling (Leahy, Chan, Sung, & Kim, 2013). The efficacy of counseling/psychotherapy is well documented (Wampold & Imel, 2015). Specifically, Wampold (2001) analyzed several major meta-analytic reviews and concluded that a reasonable and defensible point estimate for the efficacy of counseling/ psychotherapy is $d=0.79$ (a large effect size), meaning that the average treated person does better than 78.5% of average untreated people. Thus, in order to help people with chronic illness and disability achieve positive behav- ioral change for optimal psychosocial adaptation and vocational adjustment, it is impor- tant that RCs be competent in providing counseling and psychotherapeutic interventions for people with chronic illness and disability.

Working Alliance

An effective therapeutic relationship is essential in helping people with chronic illness and disability actively engage in VR. **Working alliance** can be defined as (a) the client's affective relationship with the therapist; (b) the client's motivation and ability to accom- plish work collaboratively with the therapist; (c) the therapist's empathic responding to and involvement with the client; and (d) client and therapist agreement about the goals and tasks of therapy (Horvath & Symonds, 1991). Wampold (2001) indicated that the **common factors** (e.g., alliance, empathy, expectations, cultural adaptation of evidence- based treatments, and therapist effects) are what affect counseling/psychotherapy out- comes the most, not the techniques associated with specific theoretical orientations. He indicated that up to 70% of the benefits of psychotherapy were due to common factors, 8% were due to specific factors (i.e., different theoretical orientations and techniques), and the remaining 22% were partially attributed to individual client differences.

Horvath, Del Re, Flückiger, and Symonds (2011) analyzed 190 studies representing more than 14,000 clients and found a relatively robust relationship between working alliance and positive counseling outcomes ($r = .27$), which is equivalent to a Cohen's d of 0.57, surpassing the threshold for a medium effect size. Working alliance is especially conducive to promoting active participation between clients and counselors in the rehabilitation process (Chan, Shaw, McMahon, Koch, & Strauser, 1997; McMahon, Shaw, Chan, & Danczyk-Hawley, 2004; Shaw, McMahon, Chan, & Hannold, 2004; Strauser, Lustig, Chan, & O'Sullivan, 2010). Lustig, Strauser, Rice, and Rucker (2002) examined survey data of 2,732 VR clients during fiscal year 2000 and found that (a) employed clients had a stronger working alliance than unemployed clients ($d = 0.73$; large effect); (b) a stronger working alliance was related to a more positive client perception of future employment prospects ($r = .51$; large effect); and (c) a stronger working alliance was related to employed rehabilitation clients' satisfaction with their current jobs ($r = .15$; small effect). Tansey, Bezyak, Iwanaga, Anderson, and Ditchman (2016) also reported a robust relationship between working alliance and outcome expectancy, VR engagement, and readiness for employment.

Motivational Interviewing

Clients' self-determined motivation to work can have a positive influence on VR treatment engagement and compliance (Wagner & McMahon, 2004). Enhancing client motivation is therefore an important factor to consider in counseling people with chronic illness and disability (Chan et al., 1997; Cook, 2004; Manthey, Brooks, Chan, Hedenblad, & Ditchman, 2015). Wagner and McMahon (2004) identified several rehabilitation contexts where **motivational interviewing** might be appropriate, including managing medical issues and adjusting to physical disability, adjusting to cognitive impairment, improving psychosocial functioning, and returning to work. Motivational interviewing is an empirically supported, client-centered, and directive counseling approach designed to promote client motivation and reduce motivational conflicts and barriers to change (Manthey et al., 2015). Most importantly, motivational interviewing plays an important role in changing counselors' attitudes and beliefs about clients' change processes. Rather than negatively attributing poor rehabilitation outcomes to the low motivation levels of their clients, the use of motivational interviewing helps counselors to focus on the processes that help keep clients motivated and engaged in rehabilitation services, thus improving counselors' perceptions of their clients, improving the working alliance, and contributing to positive psychosocial and employment outcomes (Manthey et al., 2015).

Lundahl, Kunz, Brownell, Tollefson, and Burke (2010) conducted a meta-analysis based on 25 years of motivational interviewing empirical studies with substance use (tobacco, alcohol, drugs, and marijuana), health-related behaviors (diet, exercise, and safe sex), engagement in treatment, and gambling addiction as targeted outcomes. They found a small overall effect size of $g = 0.22$ (95% CI [0.17, 0.27]). Although motivational interviewing did not perform better than other strong substance abuse treatments such as cognitive behavior therapy and 12-step programs, motivational interviewing interventions on average require significantly less time (over 100 fewer minutes) to produce equal effects. Motivational interviewing is effective for increasing clients' engagement in treatment and their intention to change. It works relatively well for individuals with all range of distress levels. The effect of motivational interviewing was also found to be durable at the 2-year mark and beyond.

Skills Training

Promoting **self-efficacy** through **skills training** in the areas of social skills, coping skills, general life skills, and specific job skills is an important intervention focus in rehabilitation counseling. *Self-efficacy* is defined as one's belief in one's ability to succeed in specific situations or accomplish a task (Bandura, 1982). Dilk and Bond (1996) conducted a meta-analysis of 68 studies, including 59 between-group studies and 9 within-group studies (i.e., one-group, pretest–posttest), to determine the effectiveness of skills training for individuals with serious mental illness and the influence of such factors as methodological rigor, choice of outcome measures, and service settings. For between-group studies, the overall effect size was medium at posttest ($d = 0.40$) and at follow-up ($d = 0.56$). For the within-group studies, the overall effect size was also medium at posttest ($d = 0.48$), but small at follow-up ($d = 0.30$). Dilk and Bond concluded that behavioral skills training for people with serious mental illness can be effective for teaching inpatients interpersonal and assertiveness skills, as indicated by measures of skill acquisition and symptom reduction. Kurtz and Mueser (2008) conducted a meta-analysis to examine the efficacy of social skills training interventions for people with schizophrenia. A total of 22 studies were included and they reported a moderate mean weighted effect size for performance-based measures of social and daily living skills ($d = 0.52$), and moderate mean weighted effect sizes for community functioning ($d = 0.52$) and negative symptoms ($d = 0.40$). Bolton and Akridge (1995) conducted a meta-analysis of skills training interventions for people with disabilities in VR and found that outcome measures resulted in an aggregate effect size of $d = 0.82$, suggesting that skills training substantially benefits the typical VR participant.

Postsecondary Education

It is well documented that college graduates have higher incomes and lower unemployment rates than those with only a high school diploma or less than a diploma (U.S. DOL, 2014). In addition, studies have demonstrated that educational attainment is more strongly associated with employment for people with disabilities than for people without disabilities, confirming that education can be used as a means to improve employability and income (Carnevale, Rose, & Cheah, 2011; Flannery, Yovanoff, Benz, & Kato, 2008; Jones, Latreille, & Sloane, 2006; Kidd, Sloane, & Ferko, 2000; Smith, Grigal, & Sulewski, 2012; Yamamoto, Stodden, & Folk, 2014). As a result, postsecondary education has gained attention as a VR intervention for people with chronic illness and disability (Gilmore & Bose, 2005). Postsecondary education is also emphasized in the Workforce Innovation and Opportunity Act (WIOA) and the Amendments to the Rehabilitation Act of 1973 as a way to help people with disabilities develop meaningful careers to facilitate entry to the middle class (U.S. Department of Education, 2014).

O'Neill et al. (2015) conducted a case-control study to examine the effect of postsecondary education on earnings for people with chronic illness and disability, using data extracted from the Rehabilitation Services Administration Case Service Report (RSA-911) database. Their study included 178,290 individuals with chronic illness and disability whose cases were closed as "successfully rehabilitated" by the state-federal vocational rehabilitation (VR) program during fiscal year 2011. Propensity scores to receive college or university training were estimated based on demographic variables using the classification and regression tree (CART) method. The CART analysis yielded six homogeneous subgroups, ranging from high propensity to receive college or university training as a VR intervention to low propensity to receive such a service. Individuals who received college/university training had higher weekly earnings than those who did not, and postsecondary education had the greatest benefit for young adults, White, Asian, and Native American women with physical impairments, and people with mental impairments (O'Neill et al., 2015). The effect of postsecondary education training on weekly earnings was reported to have a medium effect size (O'Neill et al., 2015). Similarly, Migliore, Timmoms, Butterworth, and Lugas (2012) found that the receipt of college/university training through VR was the strongest predictor of higher earnings for youth with autism.

Supported Employment

Supported employment is identified as one of the strongest evidence-based practices in VR and mental health services (Drake, Merrens, & Lynde, 2005; Leahy, Chan, Lui, Rosenthal, et al., 2014; Wehman, Chan, Ditchman, & Kang, 2014). **Supported employment** is defined as competitive employment in an integrated setting with ongoing support services for individuals with the most severe disabilities (Wehman et al., 2014). Specifically, Wehman et al. (2014) conducted a case-control study to examine the effect of supported employment intervention on the employment outcomes of transition-age youth with intellectual and developmental disabilities. They found a moderate effect size on employment outcomes for people who received special education in high school and for individuals with intellectual disabilities/developmental disabilities, particularly those who were Social Security beneficiaries. Similarly, Campbell, Bond, and Drake (2011) conducted a meta-analysis to compare the effect of the Individual Placement and Support (IPS) model of supported employment with traditional vocational interventions for people with severe mental illness. They found large effect sizes favoring the use of IPS in job acquisition ($d = 0.90$), total weeks worked ($d = 0.79$), and job tenure ($d = 0.74$).

Vocational Rehabilitation Services

Although it is not possible to conduct experimental studies for state VR services as an independent variable, the Rehabilitation Act Amendments have required the state-federal VR program to conduct ongoing research to demonstrate the effectiveness of rehabilitation interventions on employment rates and quality of employment outcomes of people with disabilities. Research evidence from nonexperimental studies supports the association between VR services and successful employment outcomes. For example, O'Neill, Mamun, Potamites, Chan, and Cardoso (2014) conducted a case-control study to examine the effect of VR services on return-to-work outcomes of Social Security Disability Insurance (SSDI) beneficiaries using two administrative data sets that were matched prospectively: the longitudinal Disability Analysis File (DAF), formerly known as the Ticket Research File (TRF), from the Social Security Administration, and the RSA-911 data file. SSDI beneficiaries ($N = 17,369$) who accessed state VR agency services in 2000 were matched with SSDI beneficiaries who had never applied for state VR services based on 36 demographic covariates. Propensity score matching led to balance between the treatment and control groups on 34 of the 36 variables. Logistic regression analysis results revealed the treatment groups completing the trial work period at significantly greater rates than the control groups in the 10-year period of the study. Dean et al. (2014) examined the association between the receipt of VR services and Supplemental Security Income (SSI)/Social Security Disability Insurance (SSDI) using a special panel data set on Virginians with disabilities who applied for state VR services in 2000. They found that VR services are associated with lower rates of participation in disability insurance programs (a two-point drop in SSDI receipt and one-point drop in SSI receipt); VR service receipt is associated with lower take-up rates of SSI/SSDI; and social security beneficiaries receiving substantive VR services are more likely to be employed.

Dutta et al. (2008) analyzed RSA-911 data for fiscal year 2005 using logistic regression analysis and found job placement, on-the-job support, maintenance, and other services (e.g., medical care for acute conditions) to be significant predictors of employment success across all impairment groups. They found that job placement and support services could improve the odds for obtaining competitive employment: job search assistance (odds ratio [OR] = 1.24; 95% CI [1.08, 1.43]), job placement assistance (OR = 1.89; 95% CI [1.66, 2.16]), and on-the-job support (OR 2.20; 95% CI [1.90, 2.55]). In addition, diagnostic and treatment (D&T) services (OR = 1.57; 95% CI [1.35, 1.82]) and rehabilitation technology (RT) services (OR = 1.97; 95% CI [1.67, 2.33]) were found to uniquely contribute to employment outcomes for the sensory impairments group as well as the physical impairments group (D&T services: OR = 1.31; 95% CI [1.15, 1.48]; RT services: OR = 1.41; 95% CI [1.13, 1.75]), but not the mental impairments group. Substantial counseling was associated with employment outcomes for the physical (OR = 1.16; 95% CI [1.02, 1.32]) and mental impairments groups (OR = 1.18; 95% CI [1.03, 1.35]). Miscellaneous training (OR = 1.31; 95% CI [1.09, 1.49]) was associated specifically with employment outcomes of the mental impairments group.

KNOWLEDGE TRANSLATION

RCs face the challenge of translating the best available evidence into effective and time-sensitive psychosocial and VR interventions. The National Center for the Dissemination of Disability Research (2006) defined **knowledge translation** as the collaborative and systematic review, assessment, identification, aggregation, and practical application of high-quality disability and rehabilitation research by key stakeholders (i.e., consumers, employers, researchers, practitioners, and policy makers), for the purpose of improving the lives of individuals with chronic illness and disability. In the context of evidence-based practice, knowledge translation is the process of connecting research knowledge to the actual applications of such knowledge in a variety of practice settings and circumstances. Sudsawad (2007) suggested that, essentially, knowledge translation is an interactive process underpinned by effective exchanges between researchers who create new knowledge and clinicians who use the information. Continuing dialogues, interactions, and partnerships within and between groups of knowledge creators and users for all stages of the research process are integral parts of knowledge translation. To be effective, conceptual frameworks are recommended to apply theory and enhance implementation efforts (Field, Booth, Ilott, & Gerrish, 2014).

The **Knowledge-to-Action** (KTA) Framework, widely used in practice, provides a useful model for knowledge translation in rehabilitation (Field et al., 2014; Graham et al., 2006; Lui, Anderson, Matthews, Nierenhausen, & Schlegelmilch, 2014). It is composed of two distinct but related components: (a) knowledge creation, and (b) the action cycle. Each component involves multiple dynamic and mutually influencing phases. Action phases may be carried out sequentially or simultaneously, and knowledge phases may impact on the action phases. The action cycle outlines a process, representing the activities needed for knowledge to be applied in practice. Knowledge is then adapted to the local context, and barriers and facilitators to its use are explicitly assessed. Involvement of stakeholders, as well as tailoring knowledge to the needs of rehabilitation professionals, is crucial. The structural relationships among knowledge creation and the associated action steps in the KTA Framework are graphically depicted in Figure 19.1.

Specifically, knowledge creation is composed of three phases: (1) knowledge inquiry, (2) synthesis of knowledge, and (3) creation of knowledge tools. Knowledge inquiry involves the completion of primary research. The synthesis stage requires appropriate research findings (i.e., systematic reviews) to identify common patterns. In the development of tools and products, the best-quality knowledge is further synthesized and distilled into decision-making tools such as practice guidelines, aids for patient decisions, or algorithms (Straus, Tetroe, & Graham, 2009). In rehabilitation counseling, tool kits including empirically validated assessments, planning tools, and interventions can be developed and distributed to practicing counselors.

The action cycle is composed of seven phases based on theories of planned action. These actions can occur sequentially or simultaneously and are influenced by activities of the knowledge phases at any point in the cycle. Included are the processes needed to use knowledge in health care and rehabilitation settings. Specifically, these processes are (a) identifying the problem; (b) identifying, reviewing, and selecting the knowledge to implement; (c) adapting or customizing the knowledge to the local context; (d) assessing

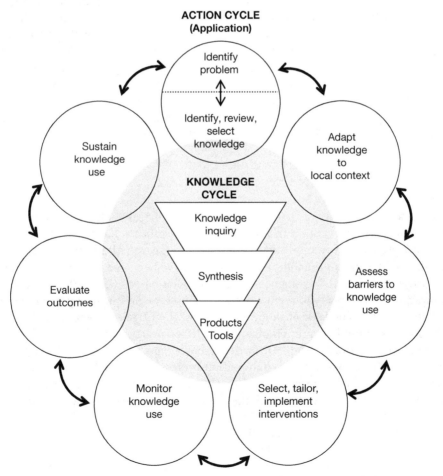

Figure 19.1 Knowledge-to-Action Framework of knowledge translation.

the determinants (barriers) of knowledge use; (e) selecting, tailoring, implementing, and monitoring interventions related to knowledge translation; (f) evaluating outcomes or impacts of using the knowledge; and (g) determining strategies for ensuring sustained use of knowledge. Salient to this knowledge translation framework is its emphasis on the need to incorporate input from the various stakeholders (including patients, clinicians, managers, or policy makers) who are the end users of the knowledge that is being implemented. Inclusion of the end users of the knowledge will ensure that the knowledge and its subsequent implementation are relevant to their needs, promoting the applications of research and the process of knowledge translation. NIDILRR has made knowledge translation a high priority in all of its funded research projects. It has funded the Center on Knowledge Translation for Disability and Rehabilitation Research (KTDRR: www.air.org/center/center-knowledge-translation-disability-and-rehabilitation-research-ktdrr) to provide integrated training, dissemination, utilization, and technical assistance activities to (a) increase use of valid and relevant evidence-based research findings that inform decision making, and (b) increase the understanding and application of knowledge translation principles. It also funded the Knowledge Translation for Employment Research Center (KTER: www.air.org/center/knowledge-translation-employment-research-center-kter) to develop and test knowledge translation strategies designed to help VR agencies and businesses find, understand, and use research related to employing people with disabilities. In addition, all NIDILRR-funded Rehabilitation Research and Training Centers (RRTCs), Disability and Rehabilitation Research Programs (DRRPs), Disability and Business Technical Assistance Centers (DBTACs), Traumatic Brian Injury Model Systems, and Spinal Cord Injury Model Systems are required to conduct research that meets the highest standards for inclusion in evidence-based systematic reviews, and knowledge translation must be an integral component of their systematic research program. These centers are excellent resources for best-evidence information related to psychosocial and vocational interventions for people with disabilities. Information about these knowledge translation–related centers can also be found in the National Rehabilitation Information Center (www.naric.com/?q=en/home).

FUTURE RESEARCH DIRECTIONS

The lack of strong theory-driven research and empirical evidence to inform assessment, planning, and intervention in the rehabilitation process has been one of the most frequent criticisms of rehabilitation counseling research (Berkowitz et al., 1975; Chan et al., 2003). Current rehabilitation practices have been characterized by some scholars as "experience-based," "eminence-based," or "habit-based" (Law, 2002). In addition, rehabilitation research is frequently nonexperimental or quasi-experimental in nature (Bolton, 2004). The lack of randomized controlled trials is seen as a major barrier to the successful implementation of evidence-based practice in rehabilitation (Chwalisz & Chan, 2008). To fully adopt an evidence-based approach in rehabilitation, Dunn and Elliott (2008) proposed that rehabilitation professionals need to (a) embrace a comprehensive theory-driven research agenda; (b) validate effective interventions based on this research agenda; and (c) facilitate the provision of empirically supported interventions based on the research evidence.

Chan et al. (2016) suggested that the evidence-based practice movement may present a window of opportunity for the rehabilitation counseling profession to promote and support a systematic agenda for theory-driven rehabilitation research. The use of scientific evidence derived from theory-driven research could improve independent living and employment outcomes of people with chronic illness and disability, leading to overall happiness and well-being. However, the complex nature of VR makes process and outcome research challenging (Bolton, 2004; Johnston, Stineman, & Velozo, 1997). Specifically, rehabilitation encompasses a broad scope of services, spans the entire medical-VR continuum from hospital care to community-based services, and is provided through an array of disciplines (e.g., occupational therapy, physical therapy, and rehabilitation counseling) for individuals with diverse and complex impairments and disabilities. The process typically involves a range of personal and environmental processes and the interactions thereof, making it difficult to determine what aspects of service delivery contribute to what outcome. Chan, Tarvydas, et al. (2009) advocated that the WHO *International Classification of Functioning, Disability and Health* (ICF) model can be used as a VR framework for conceptualizing and determining medical and VR assessment, planning, and service needs and to provide evidence-based services for people with chronic illness and disability. They also underscored the use of the *ICF* model to develop a systematic research agenda to develop and validate evidence-based practices for VR.

Specifically, the *ICF* paradigm is structured around the following broad components: (a) body functions and structure, (b) activities (related to tasks and actions by an individual) and participation (involvement in a life situation), and (c) severity of disability and environmental factors (Chan & Ditchman, 2013). Functioning and disability are viewed as a complex interaction between the health condition of the individual and the contextual factors of the environment, as well as personal factors. The *ICF* model is consistent with the holistic philosophy of rehabilitation counseling and can be an invaluable framework for case conceptualization purposes by counselors to determine the need for medical, psychosocial, and VR assessment; plan the consumer's rehabilitation program, and select empirically supported VR interventions. Using the *ICF* model to develop a systematic rehabilitation research agenda may allow researchers to quickly identify and validate several universal best practices (e.g., supported employment for ID/DD, IPS model of supported employment for people with severe mental illness, secondary transition, postsecondary life adjustment interventions, motivational interviewing, positive psychology interventions, self-determination interventions, benefits and work incentives counseling, demand-side employment interventions, health promotion interventions, and mobile apps interventions) that can be integrated into RCs' repertoire of best practices.

Importantly, testing mediator and moderator effects should be a high priority in the rehabilitation counseling research agenda, which will further promote the use of evidence-based practice in the field. Research questions involving moderators address when or for whom a variable most strongly predicts or causes an outcome variable, whereas mediators establish how or why one variable predicts or causes an outcome variable (Frazier, Tix, & Barron, 2004; Hoyt, Imel, & Chan, 2008). A mediator provides information about the underlying mechanisms for change, whereas a moderator effect is basically an interaction whereby the effect of an independent variable (e.g., treatment) differs at different levels of another independent variable (e.g., severity). Similar to health care research, the study of moderator effects in VR research is important, as what works for European American clients may not work for individuals from diverse racial and ethnic minority backgrounds; what works for men may not work for women; and what works for individuals with sensory impairments may not work for people with psychiatric disabilities (Chan, Tarvydas, et al., 2009).

Similarly, moderators are extremely important in other key areas of VR research. For example, in studying the role of resiliency factors in psychosocial adjustment to disability, future research can examine whether the adjustment process is similar or different for people with sudden onset versus chronic conditions. Therefore, it is very important for rehabilitation researchers to expend more research efforts to test moderator effects of race, gender, disability type, health status, and immunity (e.g., social support, coping skills, and resilience) and vulnerability factors (e.g., stress). For theory and model building, it is equally important to study the mediator effect (i.e., the underlying mechanisms of change) in order to better design effective interventions (Hoyt et al., 2008). An increased emphasis on testing mediator and moderator variables in the VR research paradigm is needed in order to develop effective model-driven, culturally sensitive, and evidence-based VR interventions for individuals with disabilities in the 21st century (Chan, Tarvydas, et al., 2009).

CONCLUSION

Incorporating research-based knowledge into rehabilitation counseling practice is particularly relevant in today's era of accountability, research utilization, and evidence-based practice (Chan et al., 2016; Chronister, Chan, Cardoso, Lynch, & Rosenthal, 2008; Law, 2002). As a conceptual framework or philosophy, evidence-based practice advocates that every rehabilitation and health professional should have an interest in delivering the best possible services to clients, based whenever possible on the best clinical practices available from the strongest research evidence. Rehabilitation counseling researchers and practitioners must develop a strong focus on theory development, empirical evidence, and clinical application. Within the context of evidence-based practice, Dunn and Elliott (2008) argue for the primacy of theory and its place in rehabilitation research. Advocacy for the development of theory-driven research programs that embrace methodological pluralism will advance new theory and produce meaningful research programs that inform practice in VR service delivery. The development of a systematic research agenda and conduction of meaningful theory-driven research and intervention research will generate new knowledge and accumulate high-quality evidence, enhancing the ability of RCs to truly engage in evidence-based practice to improve employment outcomes and QOL of people with disabilities.

ACKNOWLEDGMENTS

The contents of this chapter were developed with support from the Rehabilitation Research and Training Center on Effective Vocational Rehabilitation Service Delivery Practices at the University of Wisconsin–Madison and the University of Wisconsin–Stout and with funding provided by the U.S. Department of Education, National Institute on Disability and Rehabilitation Research (Grant H133B100034). The ideas, opinions, and conclusions expressed, however, are those of the authors and do not represent recommendations, endorsements, or policies of the U.S. Department of Education.

CONTENT REVIEW QUESTIONS

- How did the evidence-based practice approach to health care service delivery evolve within the United States?
- What are the main conceptual bases of evidence-based practice?

- How can RCs become more effective practitioners within the framework of evidence-based practice?
- Which evidence-based methodologies and concepts are crucial in improving RCs' knowledge of evidence-based practice and research utilization?
- How can the evidence-based decision-making process be illustrated?
- Describe a hierarchical framework that emphasizes the importance of randomized controlled trials/experimental studies.
- What is the gold standard for best scientific evidence in evidence-based medicine? How does it apply to rehabilitation counseling?
- Which elements can be considered as barriers to promoting the application of evidence based in rehabilitation counseling?
- Describe empirically supported strategy interventions in rehabilitation counseling.
- How can the field of rehabilitation counseling apply, support, and advance theory-driven research?
- Discuss how the WHO *ICF* can be used to guide the development of a systematic research agenda in rehabilitation counseling.

REFERENCES

American Psychological Association. (2005). Policy statement on evidence-based practice in psychology. Retrieved from http://www.apa.org/practice/ebpstatement.pdf

Arksey, H., & O'Malley, L. (2005). Scoping studies: Towards a methodological framework. *International Journal of Social Research Methodology, 8*(1), 19–32.

Armstrong, R., Hall, B., Doyle, J., & Waters, E. (2011). Cochrane update: "Scoping the scope" of a Cochrane review. *Journal of Public Health, 33*(1), 147–150.

Atkins, D., & Giusti, C. (2005). The confluence of poverty and disability. In C. Armbrister & K. Smith (Eds.), *The realities of poverty in Delaware 2003–2004* (pp. 6–8). Dover, DE: Delaware Housing Coalition.

Bandura, A. (1982). Self-efficacy mechanism in human agency. *American Psychologist, 37*, 122–147.

Berkowitz, M., Englander, V., Rubin, J., & Worrall, J. D. (1975). *An evaluation of policy-related research.* New York, NY: Praeger.

Berkowitz, M., Englander, V., Rubin, J., & Worrall, J. D. (1976). A summary of "An evaluation of policy-related research." *Rehabilitation Counseling Bulletin, 20*, 29–45.

Bezyak, J. L., Kubota, C., & Rosenthal, D. (2010). Evidence-based practice in rehabilitation counseling: Perceptions and practices. *Rehabilitation Education, 24*, 85–96.

Bolton, B. (2004). Counseling and rehabilitation outcomes. In F. Chan, N. L. Berven, & K. R. Thomas (Eds.), *Counseling theories and techniques for rehabilitation health professionals* (pp. 444–465). New York, NY: Springer Publishing.

Bolton, B., & Akridge, R. L. (1995). A meta-analysis of skills training programs for rehabilitation clients. *Rehabilitation Counseling Bulletin, 38*, 262–273.

Borenstein, M., Hedges, L. V., Higgins, J. P. T., & Rothstein, H. R. (2009). *Introduction to meta-analysis.* New York, NY: Wiley.

Campbell, K., Bond, G. R., & Drake, R. E. (2011). Who benefits from supported employment: A meta-analytic study. *Schizophrenia Bulletin, 37*(2), 370–380.

Campbell Collaboration. (2015). *Campbell Collaboration systematic reviews: Policies and guidelines (version 1.1).* Oslo: Authors. Retrieved from https://campbellcollaboration.org/images/C2_Policies_and_Guidelines_Doc_Version_1_1.pdf

Carnevale, A. P., Rose, S. J., & Cheah, B. (2011, August). *The college payoff: Education, occupations, and lifetime earnings.* Washington, DC: Georgetown University Center on Education and the Workforce.

Chambless, D. L., & Hollon, S. D. (1998). Defining empirically supported therapies. *Journal of Consulting and Clinical Psychology, 66*(1), 7.

Chan, F., & Ditchman, N. (2013). Applying the International Classification of Functioning, Disability and Health to psychology practice [Review of the book *ICF core sets: Manual for clinical practice*], *PsycCRITIQUES, 58*(13), Article 7. Retrieved from http://www.apa.org/psyccritiques

Chan, F., Keegan, J., Muller, V., Kaya, C., Flowers, S., & Iwanaga, K. (2016). Evidence-based practice and research in rehabilitation counseling. In I. Marini & M. A. Stebnicki (Eds.), *The professional counselor's desk reference* (2nd ed., pp. 605–610). New York, NY: Springer Publishing.

Chan, F., Keegan, J., Sung, C., Drout, M., Pai, C. H., Anderson, E., & McLain, N. (2009). The World Health Organization *ICF* model as a framework for assessing vocational rehabilitation outcomes. *Journal of Rehabilitation Administration, 33*, 91–112.

Chan, F., Miller, S., Pruett, S., Lee, G., & Chou, C. (2003). Research. In D. Maki & T. Riggar (Eds.), *Handbook of rehabilitation counseling* (pp. 159–170). New York, NY: Springer Publishing.

Chan, F., Shaw, L., McMahon, B. T., Koch, L., & Strauser, D. (1997). A model for enhancing consumer-counselor working relationships in rehabilitation. *Rehabilitation Counseling Bulletin, 41*, 122–137.

Chan, F., Tarvydas, V., Blalock, K., Strauser, D., & Atkins, B. J. (2009). Unifying and elevating rehabilitation counseling through model-driven, diversity-sensitive evidence-based practice. *Rehabilitation Counseling Bulletin, 52*, 114–119.

Chan, F., Wang, C. C., Muller, V., & Fitzgerald, S. (2011). Vocational rehabilitation outcomes: A multilevel analysis of economic indicators, VR agency characteristics, and RSA-911 data (Phase 1 report). Madison, WI: Rehabilitation Research and Training Center on Effective VR Service Delivery Practices.

Chronister, J. A., Chan, F., Cardoso, E., Lynch, R. T., & Rosenthal, D. A. (2008). The evidence-based practice movement in healthcare: Implications for rehabilitation. *Journal of Rehabilitation, 74*(2), 6–15.

Chwalisz, K., & Chan, F. (2008). Methodological advances and issues in rehabilitation psychology: Moving forward on the cutting edge. *Rehabilitation Psychology, 53*, 251–253.

Chwalisz, K., Shah, S. R., & Hand, K. M. (2008). Facilitating rigorous qualitative research in rehabilitation psychology. *Rehabilitation Psychology, 53*(3), 387–399. doi:10.1037/a0012998

Cohen, J. (1988). *Statistical power analysis for the behavioral sciences* (2nd ed.). Hillsdale, NJ: Lawrence Erlbaum.

Cook, D. W. (2004). Counseling people with physical disabilities. In F. Chan, N. L. Berven, & K. R. Thomas (Eds.), *Counseling theories and techniques for rehabilitation health professionals* (pp. 328–341). New York, NY: Springer Publishing.

Dean, D., Pepper, J. V., Schmidt, R. M., & Stern, S. (2014). State vocational rehabilitation programs and federal disability insurance: An analysis of Virginia's vocational rehabilitation program. *IZA Journal of Labor Policy, 3*(1), 1–19.

DePalma, J. A. (2002). Proposing an evidence-based policy process. *Nursing Administration Quarterly, 26*(4), 55–61.

Diette, T. M., Goldsmith, A. H., Hamilton, D., & Darity, W. D. (2012). Causality in the relationship between mental health and unemployment. In L. D. Appelbaum (Ed.), *Reconnecting to work: Policies to mitigate long-term unemployment and its consequences* (pp. 63–94). Kalamazoo, MI: W. E. Upjohn Institute for Employment Research. Retrieved from http://research.upjohn.org/cgi/viewcontent.cgi?article=1828&context=up_bookchapters

Dijkers, M. (2015). What is a scoping review? *KT Update, 4*(1). Retrieved from http://ktdrr.org/products/update/v4n1/dijkers_ktupdate_v4n1_12-15.pdf

Dilk, M. N., & Bond, G. R. (1996). Meta-analytic evaluation of skills training research for individuals with severe mental illness. *Journal of Consulting and Clinical Psychology, 64*, 1337–1346.

Drake, R., Merrens, M., & Lynde, D. (Eds.). (2005). *Evidence-based mental health practice: A textbook.* New York, NY: W. W. Norton.

Dunn, D. S., & Elliott, T. R. (2008). The place and promise of theory in rehabilitation psychology. *Rehabilitation Psychology, 53*, 254–267.

Durlak, J. A. (1995). *School-based prevention programs for children and adolescents.* Thousand Oaks, CA: Sage.

Dutta, A., Gervey, R., Chan, F., Chou, C., & Ditchman, N. (2008). Vocational rehabilitation services and employment outcomes for people with disabilities: A United States study. *Journal of Occupational Rehabilitation, 18*(4), 326–334.

Federal Safety Net. (2015). U.S. poverty statistics. Retrieved from http://federalsafetynet.com/us-poverty-statistics.html

Field, B., Booth, A., Ilott, I., & Gerrish, K. (2014). Using the Knowledge to Action Framework in practice: A citation analysis and systematic review. *Implementation Science, 9*(1), 1–14.

Fitzgerald, S., Leahy, M. J., Kang, H. J., Chan, F., & Bezyak, J. (2016). A content analysis of practitioner perspective on the implementation of evidence-based practice in rehabilitation counseling. *Rehabilitation Counseling Bulletin.* Advance online publication. doi:10.1177/0034355216659233

Flannery, K. B., Yovanoff, P., Benz, M. R., & Kato, M. M. (2008). Improving employment outcomes of individuals with disabilities through short-term postsecondary training. *Career Development for Exceptional Individuals, 31*(1), 26–36.

Frazier, P. A., Tix, A. P., & Barron, K. E. (2004). Testing moderator and mediator effects in counseling psychology research. *Journal of Counseling Psychology, 51*, 115–134.

Gilmore, D. S., & Bose, J. (2005). Trends in postsecondary education: Participation within the vocational rehabilitation system. *Journal of Vocational Rehabilitation, 22*(1), 33–40.

Graham, I., Logan, J., Harrison, M., Straus, S., Tetroe, J., Caswell, W., & Robinson, N. (2006). Lost in knowledge translation: Time for a map? *Journal of Continuing Education in the Health Professions, 26*(1), 13–24.

Grissom, R. J., & Kim, J. J. (2005). *Effect sizes for research: A broad practical approach*. Mahwah, NJ: Lawrence Erlbaum.

Hedges, L. V., & Olkin, I. (1985). *Statistical methods for meta-analysis*. London, UK: Academic Press.

Holm, M. (2000). Our mandate for the new millennium: Evidence-based practice—the 2000 Eleanor Clarke Slagle Lecture. *American Journal of Occupational Therapy, 54*(6), 575–585.

Horvath, A. O., Del Re, A. C., Flückiger, C., & Symonds, D. (2011). Alliance in individual psychotherapy. *Psychotherapy, 48*(1), 9–16.

Horvath, A. O., & Symonds, B. D. (1991). Relation between working alliance and outcome in psychotherapy: A meta-analysis. *Journal of Counseling Psychology, 38*(2), 139–149.

Hoyt, W. T., Imel, Z. E., & Chan, F. (2008). Multiple regression and correlation techniques: Recent controversies and best practices. *Rehabilitation Psychology, 53*(3), 321–339.

Johnston, M. V., Stineman, M., & Velozo, C. A. (1997). Outcome research in medical rehabilitation: Foundations from the past and directions for the future. In M. J. Fuhrer (Ed.), *Assessing medical rehabilitation practices: The promise of outcomes research*. Baltimore, MD: Paul H. Brookes.

Jones, M. K., Latreille, P. L., & Sloane, P. J. (2006). Disability, gender and the British labour market. *Oxford Economic Papers, 58*(3), 407–449. doi:10.1093/oep/gpl004

Kidd, M. P., Sloane, P. J., & Ferko, I. (2000). Disability and the labour market: An analysis of British males. *Journal of Health Economics, 19*(6), 961–981.

Kosciulek, J. F., & Szymanski, E. M. (1993). Statistical power analysis of rehabilitation counseling research. *Rehabilitation Counseling Bulletin, 36*, 212–219.

Krause, J. S., Carter, R., Pickelsimer, E., & Wilson, D. (2008). A prospective study of health and risk of mortality after spinal cord injury. *Archives of Physical Medicine and Rehabilitation, 89*, 1482–1491.

Kurtz, M. M., & Mueser, K. T. (2008). A meta-analysis of controlled research on social skills training for schizophrenia. *Journal of Consulting and Clinical Psychology, 76*(3), 491–504.

Law, M. (2002). *Evidence-based rehabilitation: A guide to practice*. Thorofare, NJ: SLACK Incorporated.

Leahy, M. J., Chan, F., & Lui, J. (2014). Evidence-based best practices in the public vocational rehabilitation program that lead to employment outcomes. *Journal of Vocational Rehabilitation, 41*, 83–86.

Leahy, M. J., Chan, F., Lui, J., Rosenthal, D., Tansey, T. N., Wehman, P., . . ., Menz, F. E. (2014). An analysis of evidence-based best practices in the public vocational rehabilitation program: Gaps, future directions, and recommended steps to move forward. *Journal of Vocational Rehabilitation, 41*, 147–163.

Leahy, M. J., Chan, F., Sung, C., & Kim, M. (2013). Empirically derived test specifications for the certified rehabilitation counselor examination. *Rehabilitation Counseling Bulletin, 56*, 199–214.

Lui, J., Anderson, C. A., Matthews, P., Nierenhausen, E., & Schlegelmilch, A. (2014). Knowledge translation strategies to improve the resources for rehabilitation counselors to employ best practices in the delivery of vocational rehabilitation services. *Journal of Vocational Rehabilitation, 41*(2), 137–145.

Lundahl, B., Kunz, C., Brownell, C., Tollefson, D., & Burke, B. (2010). A meta-analysis of motivational interviewing: Twenty-five years of empirical studies. *Research on Social Work Practice, 20*(2), 137–160.

Lustig, D. C., Strauser, D. R., Rice, N. D., & Rucker, T. F. (2002). The relationship between working alliance and rehabilitation outcomes. *Rehabilitation Counseling Bulletin, 46*, 24–32.

Manthey, T., Brooks, J., Chan, F., Hedenblad, L., & Ditchman, N. (2015). Motivational interviewing in rehabilitation health settings. In F. Chan, N. Berven, & K. Thomas (Eds.), *Counseling theories and techniques for rehabilitation health professionals* (2nd ed., pp. 247–278). New York, NY: Springer Publishing.

Martin, R., West-Evans, K., & Connelly, J. (2010). Vocational rehabilitation: Celebrating 90 years of careers and independence. *American Rehabilitation, Special Edition*, 15–18.

Mays, N., Roberts, E., & Popay, J. (2001). Synthesising research evidence. In N. Fulop, P. Allen, A. Clarke, & N. Black (Eds.), *Studying the organisation and delivery of health services: Research methods* (pp. 188–219). London, UK: Routledge.

McMahon, B. T., Shaw, L. R., Chan, F., & Danczyk-Hawley, C. (2004). Expectations and the working alliance in rehabilitation counseling. *Journal of Vocational Rehabilitation, 20*, 101–106.

Migliore, A., Timmons, J., Butterworth, J., & Lugas, J. (2012). Predictors of employment and postsecondary education of youth with autism. *Rehabilitation Counseling Bulletin, 55*(3), 176–184.

Murali, V., & Oyebode, F. (2014). Poverty, social inequality and mental health. *Advances in Psychiatric Treatment, 10*, 216–224.

Nathan, P., & Gorman, J. (Eds.). (1998). *A guide to treatments that work.* New York, NY: Oxford University Press.

National Center for the Dissemination of Disability Research. (2006). Overview of international literature on knowledge translation. *FOCUS: A Technical Brief, 14*, 1–6.

Norcross, J. C., & Lambert, M. J. (2011). Psychotherapy relationships that work. *Psychotherapy, 48*, 4–8.

O'Neill, J., Kang, H.-J., Aldrich, H., Pfaller, J., Chan, F., Sánchez, J., & Muller, V. (2015). Effect of college or university training on earnings of people with disabilities: A case control study. *Journal of Vocational Rehabilitation, 43*(2), 93–102.

O'Neill, J., Mamun, A., Potamites, E., Chan, F., & Cardoso, E. (2014). Return to work of SSDI beneficiaries who do and don't access state vocational rehabilitation agency services: Case control study. West Orange, NJ: Kessler Foundation, Rehabilitation Research and Training Center on Individual Characteristics.

Parker, R. M., & Hansen, C. E. (1981). *Rehabilitation counseling: Foundations, consumers, and service delivery.* Boston, MA: Allyn & Bacon.

Pfaller, J., Tu, W. M., Morrison, B., Chan, F., Anderson, C., Owens, L., . . . Menz, F. (2016). Social-cognitive predictors of readiness to use evidence-based practice: A survey of community-based rehabilitation practitioners. *Rehabilitation Counseling Bulletin, 60*, 7–15. doi:10.1177/0034355215591779

Rubin, S., Chan, F., & Thomas, D. (2003). Assessing changes in life skills and quality of life resulting from rehabilitation services. *Journal of Rehabilitation, 69*(3), 4–9.

Rubin, S., & Rice, J. M. (1986). Quality and relevance of rehabilitation research: A critique and recommendations. *Rehabilitation Counseling Bulletin, 30*, 33–42.

Sackett, D. L., Straus, S. E., Richardson, W. S., Rosenberg, W., & Haynes, R. B. (2000). *Evidence-based medicine: How to practice and teach EBM* (2nd ed.). New York, NY: Churchill Livingstone.

Schlosser, R. W. (2006). The role of systematic reviews in evidence-based practice, research, and development. *FOCUS: A Technical Brief, 15*, 1–4.

Schmidt, F. L., & Hunter, J. E. (2003). History, development, evolution, and impact of validity generalization and meta-analysis methods, 1975–2001. In K. R. Murphy (Vol. Ed.), *Validity generalization: A critical review* (*Applied psychology* series, pp. 31–66). Mahwah, NJ: Lawrence Earlbaum.

Shaw, L. R., McMahon, B. T., Chan, F., & Hannold, E. (2004). Enhancement of the working alliance: A training program to align counselor and consumer expectations. *Journal of Vocational Rehabilitation, 20*, 107–126.

Smith, F. A., Grigal, M., & Sulewski, J. (2012). *The impact of postsecondary education on employment outcomes for transition-aged youth with and without disabilities: A secondary analysis of American Community Survey Data* (Think College Insight Brief, Issue No. 15). Boston: Institute for Community Inclusion, University of Massachusetts Boston.

Straus, S. E., Tetroe, J., & Graham, I. D. (2009). Knowledge to action: What is and what it isn't. In S. E. Straus, J. Tetroe, & I. D. Graham (Eds.), *Knowledge translation in health care: Moving from evidence to practice* (pp. 3–12). Chichester, UK: Wiley-Blackwell.

Strauser, D, Lustig, D. C., Chan, F., & O'Sullivan, D. (2010). Working alliance and vocational outcomes for cancer survivors: An initial analysis. *International Journal of Rehabilitation Research, 33*, 271–274.

Sudsawad, P. (2007). *Knowledge translation: Introduction to models, strategies, and measures.* Austin, TX: Southwest Educational Development Laboratory, National Center for the Dissemination of Disability Research.

Tansey, T. N., Bezyak, J. L., Chan, F., Leahy, M., & Lui, J. (2014). Social-cognitive predictors of readiness to use evidence-based practice: A survey of state vocational rehabilitation counselors. *Journal of Vocational Rehabilitation, 41*, 127–136.

Tansey, T. N., Bezyak, J. L., Iwanaga, K., Anderson, C., & Ditchman, N. (2016, April). *Path analysis of a self-determination model of work motivation in vocational rehabilitation.* Paper presented at the 2016 National Council on Rehabilitation Education Spring Conference, Newport Beach, CA.

Technology and Entrepreneurship Center at Harvard. (2010). *The next generation of human services: Realizing the vision* (Report from the 2010 Human Services Summit at Harvard University). Retrieved from http://community.lnwprogram.org/sites/default/files/Realizing_the_Vision.pdf

Thirty-Third Institute for Rehabilitation Issues. (2008). *Evidence based practices: Improving employment outcomes for people with significant disabilities.* Hot Springs, AR: Rehabilitation Continuing Education Center.

Tucker, J., & Reed, G. (2008). Evidentiary pluralism as a strategy for research and evidence-based practice in rehabilitation psychology. *Rehabilitation Psychology, 53*(3), 279–293.

United Nations. (2006). Convention on the rights of persons with disabilities. Retrieved from http://www.un.org/disabilities/convention/conventionfull.shtml.

U.S. Department of Education. (2014). The Workforce Innovation and Opportunity Act overview of Title IV: Amendments to the Rehabilitation Act of 1973. Retrieved from https://www2.ed.gov/about/offices/list/osers/rsa/publications/wioa-changes-to-rehab-act.pdf

U.S. Department of Labor. (2014). Earnings and unemployment rates by educational attainment. Retrieved from http://data.bls.gov/cgi-bin/print.pl/emp/ep_chart_001.htm

U.S. Department of Labor. (2016). Disability employment statistics. Retrieved from https://www.dol.gov/odep/topics/disabilityemploymentstatistics.htm

U.S. Government Accountability Office. (2005). *Vocational rehabilitation: Better measures and monitoring could improve the performance of the VR program* (GAO-05–865). Washington, DC: Author.

Wagner, C. C., & McMahon, B. T. (2004). Motivational interviewing and rehabilitation counseling practice. *Rehabilitation Counseling Bulletin, 47,* 152–161.

Walker, B. B., Seay, S. J., Solomon, A. C., & Spring, B. (2006). Treating chronic migraine headaches: An evidence-based practice approach. *Journal of Clinical Psychology, 62*(11), 1367–1378.

Wampold, B. E. (2001). *The great psychotherapy debate.* Mahwah, NJ: Lawrence Erlbaum.

Wampold, B. E., & Imel, Z. E. (2015). *The great psychotherapy debate: Research evidence for what works in psychotherapy* (2nd ed.). New York, NY: Routledge.

Wehman, P., Chan, F., Ditchman, N., & Kang, H. J. (2014). Effect of supported employment on vocational rehabilitation outcomes of transition-age youth with intellectual and developmental disabilities: A case control study. *Intellectual and Developmental Disabilities, 52*(4), 296–310.

World Health Organization. (1995). *Bridging the gaps.* Geneva, Switzerland: Author.

World Health Organization. (2005). Bridging the "Know-Do" gap: Meeting on knowledge translation in global health. Retrieved from http://www.who.int/kms/WHO_EIP_KMS_2006_2.pdf

Yaeda, J., Iwanaga, K., Fujikawa, M., Chan, F., & Bezyak, J. (2015). The use of evidence-based practice among Japanese vocational rehabilitation professionals. *Rehabilitation Counseling Bulletin, 58,* 70–79.

Yamamoto, K. K., Stodden, R. A., & Folk, E. D. (2014). Inclusive postsecondary education: Reimagining the transition trajectories of vocational rehabilitation clients with intellectual disabilities. *Journal of Vocational Rehabilitation, 40*(1), 59–71.

TWENTY

Psychiatric Rehabilitation

AMANDA B. EASTON AND PATRICK CORRIGAN

LEARNING OBJECTIVES

After reading this chapter, you should be able to:

- Define psychiatric rehabilitation as an approach to assist individuals with psychiatric disabilities to pursue important life goals.
- Understand the principles of recovery, self-determination, and hope as facilitative conditions underlying the practice of psychiatric rehabilitation.
- Explain practices related to psychiatric rehabilitation that have been proven effective, including illness and wellness management, medications, family interventions, and treatments for co-occurring disorders.

Many people are disabled by psychiatric illnesses. What we mean by this is that psychiatric illness can inhibit and limit a person's ability to engage in major life activities. Rehabilitation counselors (RCs) have developed a set of skills to work with individuals who experience psychiatric disabilities. Many RCs have developed specialized skills in either psychiatric rehabilitation programs or in general rehabilitation programs that serve the large number of clients who have a psychiatric disability. In this chapter, we summarize the extensive literature on psychiatric rehabilitation, focusing especially on key principles and interventions addressed in more detail in the most recent edition of Corrigan's (2016) *Principles and Practice of Psychiatric Rehabilitation*. We begin by defining psychiatric disabilities, followed by an overview of psychiatric rehabilitation. Later, we discuss specific psychiatric rehabilitation interventions, including illness and wellness management, medications, family interventions, and treatments for co-occurring disorders. Our goal is to describe psychiatric rehabilitation as an approach to promote hope and recovery so that RCs can better assist people with psychiatric disabilities to pursue their personal, vocational, and independent living goals. A keen understanding of the psychiatric rehabilitation principles and practices contained in this chapter is crucial for all RCs, but particularly for those who seek to provide services in clinical mental health or clinical rehabilitation counseling practices.

WHO ARE PEOPLE WITH PSYCHIATRIC DISABILITIES?

Individuals with psychiatric disabilities are as multifaceted and diverse as the population in general. Henceforth, we have to understand who the person with a psychiatric disability is. People with psychiatric disabilities are individuals who, because of their illness, are unable to attain culturally and age-appropriate goals for extended periods of time. This definition of *people with psychiatric disabilities* contains three parts. First, psychiatric disability is based on a diagnosable mental illness. Second, the person is not able to pursue significant life goals because of the mental illness. The "appropriateness" of goals may vary by culture (e.g., Latino cultures may view familial involvement differently than European families) and age (e.g., education, employment status). Examples of important life goals relate to vocational status, relationships, physical and mental health, and recreation and spirituality. Rehabilitation providers need to be vigilant to context. Third, both the mental illness and its interference with the attainment of goals persist for significant periods of time, often for years. For some, there is an adaptation to the experience of mental illness, but for others there is a greater struggle. Mental health disorders impact people at varying levels and because of this it is helpful to understand the domains of psychiatric disabilities.

Four conceptual domains aid in our understanding of psychiatric rehabilitation:

1. *Diagnoses:* These represent the collections of symptoms and dysfunctions that cohere to form a psychiatric syndrome. Diagnoses that are typically the focus of psychiatric rehabilitation include schizophrenia, the mood disorders (such as major depression and bipolar disorder), some anxiety disorders (such as posttraumatic stress disorder [PTSD]) and obsessive compulsive disorder), and some personality disorders.
2. *Course:* Psychiatric syndromes are not stable phenomena. Psychiatric disorders vary among individuals in terms of onset and trajectory of the illness. They also vary within the individual over time in terms of the severity of symptoms and dysfunctions, such as mood disorders that may cycle over time.
3. *Co-occurring disorders:* Psychiatric disorders rarely occur in isolation. Instead, many people with psychiatric disabilities experience diagnoses that interact to significantly impede their life goals. Substance use disorders, in particular, frequently co-occur with serious mental illness to worsen disease course.
4. *Disabilities:* Disabilities are defined as the inability of people to meet life goals that are appropriate for their age and culture. These goals tend to be macro-level goals that include obtaining a satisfactory job, living independently, developing intimate and mature relationships, managing one's physical and mental health needs, and participating in recreational and spiritual activities. It is important to note that it is disability per se that defines a person as being in need of psychiatric rehabilitation. People can have psychiatric diagnoses that do not interfere with their life goals. The characteristic that distinguishes psychiatric rehabilitation from other forms of psychiatric care is the focus on helping people achieve life goals that are blocked by symptoms, dysfunctions, and environmental barriers.

WHAT IS PSYCHIATRIC REHABILITATION?

Psychiatric rehabilitation is the systematic effort to help adults with psychiatric disabilities attain their personal goals. Within rehabilitation counseling, psychiatric rehabilitation is a framework that RCs can use to assist individuals with psychiatric disabilities to "achieve their personal, career, and independent living goals in the most integrated setting possible" (retrieved from www.crccertification.com). Psychiatric rehabilitation is bidirectional in focus, seeking to influence an individual's strengths and challenges related to these goals *and* the community in which the person will live them out. Many different classifications of the core principles of psychiatric rehabilitation have been proposed over the years (Anthony, Cohen, Farkas, & Gagne, 2002; Bond & Resnick, 2000; Cnaan, Blankertz, Messinger, & Gardner, 1988; Cook & Hoffschmidt, 1993; Dincin, 1995; Hughes & Weinstein, 1997; Pratt, Gill, Barrett, & Roberts, 1999). Hence, Anthony et al. (2002) list eclecticism as one of the core principles, and Dincin (1995) refers to the pragmatism of psychiatric rehabilitation because many of its most widely practiced approaches have been developed through a trial-and-error process. In recent years, Corrigan (2013) has proposed an integrated model resting on the key structures of rehabilitation: principles (the moral imperatives that guide people and society in dealing with disabilities), strategies (the tools that rehabilitation providers might avail to help the person), settings (places where rehabilitation occurs), and roles (people who do rehabilitation).

Central to Corrigan's (2013) integrated theory are the two guiding principles of recovery and self-determination. **Recovery** has been hailed as the primary principle of mental health services for people with psychiatric disabilities in Surgeon General David Satcher's report (U.S. Department of Health and Human Services [DHHS], 1999) to the nation, as well as President George Bush's New Freedom Commission on Mental Health (2003). Specifically, most people learn to live with psychiatric disabilities, even if they do not erase the challenges altogether. By this we mean that the symptoms of illness and barriers of disability diminish or disappear. At the same time, recovery is also a process in which, regardless of a person's current symptoms and disabilities, **hope** is the rule, not the exception. This belief does not mean that RCs ignore a person's worries about the future or questions of doubt and self-worth. To do so would be to ignore essential experiences. Instead, these experiences are framed in terms of hope. With a sense of recovery and hope, success in the community rests on **self-determination** (Corrigan et al., 2012). Self-determination fosters the notion that people with disabilities have final say on the goals they wish to seek, and the supports that they might use to obtain them—supports that include the array of rehabilitation services in their community.

With recovery and self-determination in mind, the remainder of this chapter articulates specific psychiatric rehabilitation *practices* that have been proven effective or, when the evidence is lacking, practices that represent our best understanding of how to help in that process.

ILLNESS AND WELLNESS SELF-MANAGEMENT

An important goal of psychiatric rehabilitation is to help people learn how to manage their psychiatric disability, including understanding the nature and treatment of their mental illness and developing strategies for minimizing its impact on their lives. There are two components to this goal: *illness* self-management, so the person is better able to manage symptoms and disabilities that undermine aims; and *wellness* self-management, so the person is better able to promote health and well-being. Illness self-management includes making informed decisions about treatment, reducing the impact of distressing or problematic symptoms, and lessening relapses and rehospitalizations. Absence of illness is not enough, however. Wellness self-management centers on lifestyle choices that encourage the fullest experience of one's physical and mental capabilities. Quality of life (QOL) requires illness management as well as wellness promotion. Together, illness and wellness self-management help people with psychiatric disabilities identify and pursue personal goals to develop a physically and psychologically healthy lifestyle characterized by hope, optimism, and a sense of purpose.

Illness Self-Management

Psychiatric syndromes are sometimes similar to lifelong illnesses such as diabetes, heart disease, and asthma because they require ongoing care to minimize disruptive effects on daily living and prevent premature mortality. Although increased understanding of the causes of disease and determinants of outcomes have improved long-term prognosis of some psychiatric syndromes, gains from these advances are realized only by teaching people the principles of managing their illness and helping them incorporate critical changes into their lifestyle. This means teaching individuals about the nature and course of those diseases, providing information about lifestyle choices that may promote better disease management, teaching them how to monitor their illness and self-administer treatments, and knowing when to contact treatment providers and others in order to address emergent concerns prior to them becoming more serious (Hanson, 1986). Promoting illness self-management is a critical part of helping professions that attempt to minimize the impact of a chronic disease on functioning and QOL. Further, self-management has become a core concept that is taught to people with psychiatric disabilities in efforts to promote management of the psychiatric disorder (Mueser et al., 2002). Rehabilitation providers help people with a psychiatric disability learn about their mental illness and how to deal with both the illness and wellness self-management more effectively.

Wellness Self-Management

The notion of wellness is often credited to Halbert Dunn (1961), who highlighted the importance of fitness, environment, and self-responsibility in fully understanding health. Dunn claims that the absence of illness does not make for a fully lived life. Recently, scholars have begun to apply wellness to the experiences and goals of people with mental illness (O'Brien et al., 2014; Sterling, von Esenwein, Tucker, Fricks, & Druss, 2010). The goal of wellness in mental health is to integrate education, prevention, and health, while focusing on modifiable health risks such as smoking, poor diet, and little physical activity. Recently, there has been a collaborative effort between researchers and providers as a means to develop programs to remedy these health risks (Kane, 2009).

Wellness management and illness management have fundamental similarities (Salerno et al., 2011). They both use structured curricula that address coping, recovery, relapse, and social supports. These goals are furthered by attention to other factors affecting mental health problems, medication and other treatments, and personal goals development. Wellness management differs by including a focus on instruction and skill for managing practical issues associated with diet, exercise, relationships, and leisure. Positive psychology has an important role, and is consistent with a long-standing philosophical perspective of asset-based focus in the rehabilitation counseling tradition; positive psychology is the study of what is "right" about people. Researchers in this area seek to understand what helps people and their communities flourish. Researchers have identified principles and practices that promote positive psychology (Kobau et al., 2011), which are consistent with the goals of psychiatric rehabilitation and recovery, including shared decision making.

Shared Decision Making

Shared decision making is critical to effective and ethical illness and wellness self-management. At all times, individuals with psychiatric disabilities are active agents in their wellness and recovery plan, having the support and guidance of professionals and anyone else who might be closely involved with the person. Shared decision making is thus the process by which important decisions are made in active collaboration with the person, the treatment provider, and anyone else who may be closely involved with the person, such as family members.

Shared decision making is a movement that has been embraced by modern medicine (Campbell, Donaldson, Roberts, & Smith, 1996; Wennberg, 1991) and rapidly adopted by psychiatry (Fenton, 2003; Hamann, Leucht, & Kissling, 2003). The rationale for shared decision making is twofold. First, as medical technology grows, treatment decisions are less straightforward, and often depend on the personal values and preferences of the individual with the disease. The larger point is that decisions not to pursue treatments may be a source of empowerment if made for personal reasons. Shared decision making requires an individual to learn basic information about the nature of the disorder, the treatment options, and their likely effects, both positive and negative.

Second, choosing not to follow prescriptions of recommended treatments is a problem common to modern medicine (Blackwell, 1973), including psychiatry (Coldham, Addington, & Addington, 2002). *Psychological reactance* is a concept that refers to an individual's sensitivity to others' efforts to control the individual's behavior (Brehm, 1966). Authoritarian-based treatment recommendations may undermine some decisions because of psychological reactance (Fogarty, 1997; Moore, Sellwood, & Stirling, 2000). People may, however, be more open to some treatment recommendations when those recommendations are posed collaboratively, respecting their right to choose which treatments they want. In order to improve adherence to recommended and effective treatments, shared decision making involves providing people with the information they need in order to make informed decisions about treatment.

Peer Support

The historical roots of the mental health peer movement can be traced back to the Alleged Lunatic's Friend Society in England in 1845 and the later publication of Clifford Beer's (1923) book, *A Mind That Found Itself*, which chronicled abuses in the name of treatment for psychiatric disabilities (Frese & Davis, 1997). In the 1970s, several influences contributed to the rise of peer services, including deinstitutionalization, widespread dissatisfaction with traditional psychiatric care, and the growth of self-help approaches for personal problems. Peer services and supports now permeate much of the formal mental health system, not as a substitute for, but as an adjunct to, the more traditional mental health services. Furthering this, the Surgeon General's report on mental health (U.S. Department of Health and Human Services [DHHS], 1999) hailed the importance of self-help groups and consumer-operated services. In 2003, the President's New Freedom Commission on Mental Health (2003) acknowledged consumer-operated services as an "emerging best practice." Peer services emphasize the importance of people managing services for themselves in an environment where all aspects of intervention are self-determined.

The momentum of support coming from federal initiatives has driven the increase in peer services and supports. Results of a Substance Abuse and Mental Health Services Administration (SAMHSA) survey suggested that there were about 7,500 peer support groups and organizations nationally, with 3,315 being mutual support groups (primarily providing support), 3,019 self-help organizations (which are education and advocacy groups that evolve from local support groups into a single network, and may sponsor and/or support mutual support groups), and 1,133 consumer-operated services (included programs, businesses, or services managed and operated by recipients of mental health services; Goldstrom et al., 2006). The number of these peer and support groups surpassed the number of traditional mental health organizations (4,546). Mutual self-help groups reported that 41,363 individuals had attended their last meeting, self-help organizations reported having a membership of 1,005,400, and consumer-operated services noted serving 534,551 individuals in the past year. This suggests not only the importance of peer support within the psychiatric rehabilitation framework, but also the emphasis on efficacious practices that align with recovery.

MEDICATIONS

Psychiatric medication is integral for addressing the challenges of acute episodes of severe mental illness as well as for decreasing relapses. Medications or psychosocial treatment are never one-or-the-other. Statements such as the following examples reflect flawed clinical thinking that does not reflect evidence-based best practices: "No point in providing supported employment to Mary because she is on antipsychotics." "Don't consider antidepressants because Bobby is receiving dialectical behavior therapy." The best rehabilitation plans assist the person in integrating approaches: many people need both medication and psychosocial treatment. Although RCs do not prescribe medications, they can help people with psychiatric disabilities get proper referrals and assist in ongoing decisions about their medication with an accurate understanding of medication effects.

In recent years, there has been a steady proliferation of medications for the major psychiatric disorders of schizophrenia, bipolar disorder, depression, and anxiety (Ferrando, Owen, & Levenson, 2014). Numerous effective medications are now available to alleviate the symptoms of severe mental illnesses (New Freedom Commission on Mental Health, 2003; U.S. DHHS, 1999). To be marketed in the United States, medications must be approved by the federal Food and Drug Administration (FDA). FDA approval requires that a medication be more effective than placebo ("a sugar pill") for a specific condition in at least two independent randomized controlled trials. To give a rough idea of the magnitude of the efficacy of current medications, consider that about 70% of people with symptoms of major depression respond to an efficacious antidepressant, compared to about 40% in a control group who respond to placebo (Rappa & Viola, 2013). Similarly, in 1-year follow-up, about twice as many people with schizophrenia will experience a psychotic relapse if they are taking placebo (70%) as compared to those taking an antipsychotic medication (35%). These figures vary from study to study and with regard to specific medications and situations, but findings are often in the range of a two-to-one or three-to-two for medication versus placebo.

Finding current and accurate information on specific medications and guidelines for use is often a critical, everyday task for RCs. There are widely available sources, but they must be used with caution. Online resources include the *Physicians' Desk Reference* (PDR Staff, 2017; www.PDR.net) and webdMD (www.webmd.com). Using the World Wide Web can also be misleading because the rapidly proliferating health information sites are not regulated and screened for accuracy. Thus, although the Internet has become a vast source of information, much of that information is anecdotal and misleading. The person's doctor and medical team are a vital resource regarding medication. We do not believe that people should just give up decisions to medical doctors; instead, they join with their doctors in coming up with the best plan. Table 20.1 summarizes the major classes of psychiatric medications, common subgroups, clinical benefits, and side effects.

TABLE 20.1   The Seven Major Classes of Medications Grouped by Indications and Clinical Effects*

Indications and Clinical Effects	Subgroups	Side Effects
ANTIPSYCHOTIC MEDICATION		
Antipsychotic medication may be prescribed for disorders in the schizophrenia spectrum (e.g., schizophrenia, schizoaffective disorder) or psychoses related to affective disorders. They may relieve some of the positive symptoms of psychosis, such as hallucinations, delusions, and formal thought disorder. Some second-generation antipsychotics may relieve negative symptoms.	**Conventional** chlorpromazine (Thorazine), chlorprothixene (Taractan), droperidol (Inapsine), fluphenazine (Permitil, Prolixin), haloperidol (Haldol), mesoridazine (Serentil), molindone (Moban), perphenazine (Trilafon), pimozide (Orap), prochlorperazine (Compazine), thioridazine (Mellaril), thiothixene (Navane), trifluoperazine (Stelazine)	Wakefulness: sedation, fatigue. Cardiovascular: low blood pressure. Hormonal (endocrine): breast enlargement and increased milk production. Skin: skin rashes, skin photosensitivity. Neurological (sometimes known as extrapyramidal side effects [EPSs]): dystonia (severe muscle spasms), pseudoparkinsonism (tremor, muscle stiffness, rigidity, stooped posture, mask-like face), akinesia (reduction in spontaneous movements), akathisia (internal restlessness), tardive dyskinesia (involuntary movements, often in mouth, tongue, or fingers).
	Second Generation ("Atypical") aripiprazole (Abilify), clozapine (Clozaril), olanzapine (Zyprexa), risperidone (Risperdal), ziprasidone (Geodon)	Sedation, hypersalivation, constipation, dry mouth, obesity, metabolic changes (lipids and glucose), type 2 diabetes mellitus, pseudoparkinsonism at higher doses, agranulocytosis (sudden drop in white blood cells).
MEDICATION FOR ANTIPSYCHOTIC SIDE EFFECTS		
Medication for the side effects of antipsychotics may be prescribed for the EPSs that often result from conventional antipsychotic medication use. They relieve the various movement disorders that result from EPSs.	amantadine (Symmetrel), benztropine (Cogentin), diphenhydramine (Benadryl), propranolol (Inderal), trihexiphenidyl (Artane)	Dry mouth, blurred vision, memory problems, constipation, rapid heartbeat, loss of appetite.
ANTIDEPRESSANT MEDICATION		
Antidepressant medication may be prescribed for depression and also for some anxiety disorders. They may relieve biological (e.g., insomnia and low energy), psychological (e.g., low mood and hopelessness), and behavioral (e.g., suicide) symptoms of depression.	**Tricyclic and Tetracyclic** amitriptyline (Elavil), clomipramine (Anafranil), desipramine (Norpramin, Pertofrane), doxepin (Adapin, Sinequan), imipramine (Tofranil, Janimine, SK-Pramine), nortriptyline (Aventyl, Pamelor), protriptyline (Vivactil), trimipramine (Surmontil), amoxapine (Asendin), maprotiline (Ludiomil)	Cardiovascular: orthostatic hypotension, palpitations, conduction slowing, hypertension. Central nervous system: tremor, sedation, stimulation, twitches, seizure, EPSs. Other: perspiration, weight gain, sexual dysfunction, impotence, dry mouth, constipation, urinary hesitance, esophageal reflux.

(continued)

TABLE 20.1 **The Seven Major Classes of Medications Grouped by Indications and Clinical Effects*** (*continued*)

Indications and Clinical Effects	Subgroups	Side Effects
	Monoamine Oxidase Inhibitors phenelzine (Nardil), selegiline (Eldepryl), tranylcypromine (Parnate), isocarboxazid (Marplan)	Low blood pressure, high blood pressure crises (interactions with foods or medications), sexual dysfunction, insomnia, sedation, stimulation, muscle cramps, urinary hesitancy, constipation, dry mouth, weight gain, twitches.
	Selective Serotonin Reuptake Inhibitors fluoxetine (Prozac), fluvoxamine (Luvox), paroxetine (Paxil), sertraline (Zoloft)	Gastrointestinal: nausea, indigestion, diarrhea, vomiting, cramping. Neurological: insomnia, jitteriness, agitation, restlessness, headache, tremor. Other: excessive perspiration, decreased libido, delayed orgasm.

MOOD STABILIZERS

Indications and Clinical Effects	Subgroups	Side Effects
Mood stabilizers may be prescribed for bipolar or schizoaffective disorder. They may relieve expansive mood (euphoria) and behaviors (unusual trouble with buying, sexual relations, or the police).	lithium carbonate (Eskalith, Lithane, Lithotabs, Eskalith CR, Lithobid), lithium citrate (Cibalith-S), carbamazepine (Tegretol), valproic acid (Depakene, Depakote), lamotrigine (Lamictal), gabapentin (Neurontin)	Neurological: tremor, ataxia (balance problems), sedation. Gastrointestinal: indigestion, weight gain, diarrhea. Skin: rash, hair loss. Cardiac: arrhythmia. Hematological: low blood count.

ANTIANXIETY MEDICATION (ANXIOLYTICS)

Indications and Clinical Effects	Subgroups	Side Effects
Anxiolytics may be prescribed for anxiety disorders (including panic) and major depression. They may relieve distress as well as related autonomic symptoms such as shortness of breath, rapid heartbeat, and profuse sweating. They may also relieve insomnia.	**Anxiolytics: Benzodiazepines** alprazolam (Xanax), chlordiazepoxide (Librium), clonazepam (Klonopin), clorazepate (Tranxene), diazepam (Valium), lorazepam (Ativan), oxazepam (Serax)	Sedation. Impaired cognitive function and judgment, amnesia. Respiratory suppression. May lead to withdrawal if terminated precipitously.
	Anxiolytics: Nonbenzodiazepines buspirone (BuSpar)	Nausea, headache, nervousness, and insomnia.

SEDATIVES/HYPNOTICS

Indications and Clinical Effects	Subgroups	Side Effects
Sedatives and hypnotics may relieve symptoms related to insomnia.	**Hypnotics—Benzodiazepines** estazolam (Prosom), flurazepam (Dalmane), quazepam (Doral), temazepam (Restoral), triazolam (Halcion)	Sedation. Impaired cognitive function and judgment, amnesia. Respiratory suppression. May lead to withdrawal if terminated precipitously.
	Hypnotics: Nonbenzodiazepines eszopiclone (Lunesta), zalepon (Sonata), zolpidem (Ambien), zopiclone (Imovane), ramelteon (Rozerem)	Similar to benzodiazepines.

(*continued*)

TABLE 20.1 The Seven Major Classes of Medications Grouped by Indications and Clinical Effects* (*continued*)		
Indications and Clinical Effects	**Subgroups**	**Side Effects**
PSYCHOSTIMULANTS		
Psychostimulants may be prescribed for attention deficit hyperactivity disorder (ADHD) or narcolepsy. For ADHD, they may relieve impulsivity, promote attentiveness, and be calming. For narcolepsy, they may reduce sleepiness.	**Stimulants** amphetamine (Adderall), detroamphetamine (Dexedrine), dexmethylphenidate (Focalin), methylphenidate (Concerta, Ritalin), lisdexamfetamine (Prodrug)	Central nervous system: insomnia, headaches, nervousness, and social withdrawal. Gastrointestinal: stomach ache and appetite loss. Cardiac: elevated heart rate and blood pressure. Exacerbate psychotic symptoms.
	Nonstimulants atomextrine (Strattera), clonidine (Kapvay), guanfacine (Intuniv), armodafinil (Nuvigil), modafinil (Alertec, Provigil)	Nausea, decreased appetite, fatigue, abdominal pain, increased heart rate and blood pressure. Insomnia, irritability, and urinary retention.

*Common examples of generic and trade names (written parenthetically) are subgrouped. Significant side effects are summarized.

FAMILY INTERVENTIONS

When a member of a family has a psychiatric disability, it affects not only the person with the disability, but the family members as well. Although reactions differ by individuals as well as by their relationship to the relative with a psychiatric disability, effects of the illness are felt by parents, spouses, siblings, and children (Morey & Mueser, 2007; Tessler & Gamache, 2000). No less than three-quarters of people with psychiatric disabilities have some sort of continuous contact with their families (Lehman & Steinwachs, 1998; Manderscheid & Sonnenschein, 1997) and 30% to 65% are estimated to live with their families (Beeler, Rosenthal, & Cohler, 1999: Goldman, 1982; Guarnaccia, 1998; Miklowitz, 2010). Relatives, particularly parents or guardians, assume the role of caregiver for which they are neither trained nor psychologically prepared (Doornbos, 2001; Hatfield, 1987; Lefley, 1996). Families must learn to manage the symptoms and dysfunctions of the illness as well as the challenges and complexities of the various service delivery systems: mental health, social well-being, social security, vocational rehabilitation systems, substance abuse services, and, in some cases, the criminal justice system.

Psychoeducation

Psychoeducation has both educational and psychotherapeutic components, as the name implies. Psychoeducation has two primary objectives: to provide information regarding the disorder and its treatment; and to teach strategies to cope with the illness, including problem-solving skills, coping and communication skills, and crisis management. Psychoeducation services are often provided in structured programs that last at least 9 months, but may go as long as 5 years and are often diagnosis specific. These programs focus primarily on information dissemination specific to the psychiatric diagnosis of the family member, and less so on the well-being of family members who are partaking in the psychoeducation process (Dixon et al., 2001; Solomon, 1996, 2000).

Psychoeducational interventions may be provided to an individual family member, to a family unit, or to multiple families, typically with the person with psychiatric disability included in all, or part, of the intervention. Psychoeducational services can be facilitated in the family's home, a clinical setting, or another location. Generally, these intervention have concentrated on families with a relative with schizophrenia (Mueser & Gingerich, 2006), yet have additionally been intended for the individuals who have relatives with major depression, bipolar disorder, schizophrenia, and substance abuse, alcohol abuse, and PTSD (McFarlane, Dixon, Lukens, & Lucksted, 2003; Miklowitz, 2010). Current versions of psychoeducational interventions view family members as competent therapeutic agents from a strengths-based perspective. Psychoeducational interventions support collaborative relationships between the family and the practitioner (Lam, 1991).

Three prominent examples of these interventions are behavioral family management by Falloon, Boyd, and McGill (1984), family psychoeducation by Anderson, Reiss, and Hogarty (1986), and McFarlane et al. (2003) multifamily groups. In at least two randomized studies, these interventions have been determined to be effective.

Falloon's et al. treatment has a sequential approach that starts with assessment, then follows to intervention strategies (including communication and problem-solving training) and ends with ongoing review. The intervention encompasses illness management strategies that employ behavior modification techniques. A behavioral analysis of the family unit and each family member is conducted in order to assess for strengths. The purpose of this is to aid each family member in functioning at their best given the challenges associated with having a family member with a psychiatric disability (Falloon et al., 1984)

Anderson's et al. intervention is based on a family system's orientation and starts by establishing an alliance with the family at the point of the relative's admission to the hospital. Once a relationship is established, the provider will step in as a liaison with the hospital system. From there, a day-long workshop is provided to the family discussing information about the psychiatric disorder. The format of this intervention is meant to reduce isolation and stigmatization. Once the relative is discharged from the hospital, individual family sessions begin and contact is made between the family and the relative with the mental illness. Regularly scheduled sessions, phone consultations, and crisis contacts are provided as well. The duration of this type of program is open-ended and contingent on needs and negotiations among family members and the relative with a psychiatric disability. Ongoing sessions apply information from the workshop to deal with the ongoing process of social adjustment and employment for the relative with a psychiatric disability (Anderson, Reiss, & Hogarty, 1986).

McFarlane's intervention is a second-generation treatment because it combines aspects of two family psychoeducation interventions, family behavioral management, and multiple family approaches. The first stage is for practitioners to meet individually with the family to build an alliance. The second stage is a workshop, similar to Anderson's intervention. The difference between Anderson's model and McFarlane's is that this approach employs problem-solving groups for both families and the relative with the mental illness. McFarlane proposes a long-term intervention with a closed format membership, where families receive support and problem-solving suggestions from other families. In addition, this intervention has the advantage of a social support group. The multifamily group, for the first year, focuses on social stabilization of the relative with a psychiatric disability; in the second year, the group shifts to accentuate social and vocational rehabilitation (VR) for relatives with psychiatric disabilities (McFarlane, 2002).

CO-OCCURRING MENTAL ILLNESS AND SUBSTANCE ABUSE

Numerous people struggle with co-occurring or coexisting mental illness and substance abuse or dependence on alcohol or other drugs. First, substance use disorder is common among people with serious mental illness. There have been a number of clinical studies, along with population surveys such as the Epidemiologic Catchment Area Study (Regier et al., 1990), the National Comorbidity Study (Kessler et al., 1996), and the National Comorbidity Study Replication (Kenneson, Funderburk, & Maisto, 2013), that suggest approximately half of people with psychiatric disability report adequate symptoms for diagnosis of substance use disorder. This number is likely to be higher because people tend to underreport substance abuse. Second, people with co-occurring disorders have a much greater rate of adverse outcomes than individuals who have mental illness alone (Drake & Brunette, 1998a). Common adverse outcomes can include higher rates of relapse (Swofford, Kasckow, Scheller-Gilkey, & Inderbitzin, 1996), victimization (Goodman, Rosenberg, Mueser, & Drake, 1997), violence (Steadman et al., 1998), incarceration (Abram & Teplin, 1991), hospitalization (Haywood et al., 1995), homelessness (Caton et al., 1994), and serious infections such as hepatitis and HIV (Rosenberg et al., 2001).

In the past, two uncoordinated systems—mental health and substance abuse—have failed to provide effective interventions for individuals with co-occurring mental illness and substance abuse. Today, integrated care has become the standard of effective programs for people with co-occurring disorders, and interventions are often incorporated into an integrated master plan. A research literature examining the impact of interventions for people with co-occurring disorders is growing (Cleary, Hunt, Matheson, & Walter, 2008; Drake, O'Neal, & Wallach, 2008; Dumaine, 2003; Pawsey, Logan, & Castle, 2011) and have led to consensus guidelines (Ziedonis et al., 2005) summarized in the following sections.

Integrated Treatment

Interventions must be tailored to integrate both mental health and substance abuse interventions at the clinical interface (Drake, Mueser, Brunette, & McHugo, 2004). In spite of this definition of integration differing from administrative, financial, organizational, and physical integration, it often incorporates other concepts. *Clinical integration* refers to the same provider (or provider team) offering comprehensive mental health and substance abuse interventions that are coordinated and allow for the individual to learn about his or her coexisting illnesses (Bellack & DiClemente, 1999; Carey, 1996; Minkoff, 1989; Mueser, Drake, & Noordsy, 1998; Tsai, Salyers, Rollins, McKasson, & Litmer, 2009). It is the responsibility of the provider or providing team to successfully blend interventions that are suitable for the individual. Interventions should seem holistic and specific for the individual with dual disorders, while maintaining a consistent approach, philosophy, and set of recommendations.

Clinical integration functions on the notion that interventions should be modified and combined to meet the person's needs. The components of treatment help people to manage their dual disorders by acknowledging their inseparability. For example, social skills training not only addresses appropriateness of relationships, but also aids in the process of finding beneficial support from individuals who are not substance users and learning to avoid social situations that are associated with substance use (Mueser, Noordsy, Drake, & Fox, 2003). Relapse prevention, which is often a part of integrated treatment, addresses coping strategies and risk situations related to preventing episodes of substance abuse and/or mental illness (Drake, Wallach, & McGovern, 2005). Further, VR focuses on employment (Becker, Drake, & Naughton, 2005), and family psychoeducation emphasizes the need to understand and cope with two (or more) co-occurring disorders (Mueser & Fox, 2002).

Stage-Wise Treatments

Programs with the greatest efficacy tailor interventions to the person's stage of treatment or recovery. Stage-wise treatment is based on the concept of stages of change (Freeman & Dolan, 2001; Osher & Kofoed, 1989; Prochaska & Diclemente, 1984). Although there are differing ways of conceptualizing progress within recovery, commonly used stages of treatment for people with co-occurring disorders include (a) the engagement stage, where the person engages in a collaborative and trusting relationship; (b) the persuasion or motivation stage, where the professional helps the engaged person to build motivation toward recovery-oriented interventions; (c) the active treatment stage, where the person is now motivated toward acquiring new skills and supports to help manage the illness and pursue goals; and (d) the relapse prevention stage, where the person who is stable is helped to remain in remission and develop strategies for preventing relapse.

Long-Term Retention

Co-occurring disorders can lead to significant disabilities that require interventions that last for months or even years with adequate community support, as opposed to short-term intensive treatment programs (Drake et al., 1998b; Xie, Drake, & McHugo, 2006). Learning how to lead a satisfying and sustainable life, free from substances of abuse, often requires changing many aspects of one's life: for example, recreation, hobbies, stress management, relationships, and housing (Alverson, Alverson, & Drake, 2000). One 10-year prospective study indicates that this process takes time and often involves relapses as a part of the recovery process (Drake, McHugo, et al., 2006; Xie, McHugo, Fox, & Drake, 2005). Most research implies that longer treatment intervals are associated with better outcomes. Of course, this finding could be explained by self-selection, since people who are more motivated may elect to stay in treatment longer; or by circularity, because people who relapse are dismissed from treatment programs and therefore have shorter treatment intervals. To date, no studies have systematically varied the length of participation in long-term retention programs.

Comprehensive Services

Programs that are effective for those with co-occurring disorders provide varying individualized interventions according to the person's needs. Services include individual and group counseling, family interventions, peer group supports, vocational services, medication management, money management, housing supports, and acute trauma interventions (Mueser et al., 2003). Comprehensive programs address substances of abuse and mental illnesses broadly as opposed to narrowly as a discrete treatment intervention (Torrey et al., 2002). For example, during acute episodes that lead to hospitalization, opportunities for accurate diagnosis, stabilization, medication changes, and linkages to other outpatient supports and services can ensue (Greenfield, Weiss, & Tohen, 1995). Similarly, social, housing, and vocational programs can support people with dual diagnosis in acquiring skills and supports needed for recovery. Generally, comprehensive programs are difficult to evaluate because the interventions they provide are not discrete.

Motivational Interviewing

Many people who abuse alcohol and other drugs do not believe that the benefits of giving up the addiction outweigh the costs. Motivational interviewing originally was developed to help people make decisions about substance use (Apodaca & Longabaugh, 2009; Barnett, Sussman, Smith, Rohrbach, & Spruijt-Metz, 2012). Motivational interviewing helps people identify advantages and disadvantages of using drugs and alcohol (Miller & Rollnick, 2013). Someone might list advantages of alcohol use to include managing stress better and feeling more outgoing. Costs for the same person might include dealing with my angry husband and a boss who thinks partying at night gets in the way of my job performance. Note that costs and benefits for using alcohol are likely to be different for the same person using a different drug, such as cocaine. Providers rely on listening skills to help people understand the costs and benefits of a decision. This is not as simple as it seems: It extends much beyond a simple task of just adding up costs and benefits and moving forward when there are more benefits. Dialogue is central, creating an interactive process where people hear for themselves what underlies specific decisions. In addition, costs and benefits of giving up drugs or any other substances are not the same as cost and benefits of actively participating in a treatment program. For example, just because an individual wants to stop using alcohol or cocaine does not mean he or she wants to spend 2 hours every day travelling across town on public transportation to get to the treatment program.

Cognitive Behavioral Therapy

Motivational counseling is often followed by cognitive behavioral counseling strategies, which entails helping people recognize their motives and risk factors for substance use; develop alternative strategies for dealing with motives and risk factors; and practice, and then use, these new strategies (Mueser et al., 2003). Cognitive therapy employs a series of interactive strategies in which people learn to identify and challenge beliefs that are problematic to their functioning. For example, a person might believe he or she can only cope with job stress by drinking eight glasses of wine each night. Cognitive therapy would help him or her challenge this belief and develop a counterargument so he or she is less likely to feel an urge to drink in the future. A set of studies have emerged examining the impact of cognitive therapies. One careful review, based on eight studies in the peer-reviewed literature (Cleary et al., 2008), seemed unable to find significant positive results of cognitive therapy on substance use habits of participants with co-occurring disorders. However, research in this review did suggest that the affective symptoms of participants improved. Another study that combined cognitive behavioral therapy with motivational interviewing suggested positive benefits in psychiatric symptoms and substance use at 9, 12, and 18 months (Barrowclough et al., 2001).

Twelve-Step Programs

Twelve-step programs are commonly used to help people address goals undermined by substance abuse. These programs are peer led, with participants benefiting from peer support in the light of 12 principles. The 12-step approach was originally embodied in

Alcoholics Anonymous but has evolved to include Narcotics Anonymous and Cocaine Anonymous. For people with co-occurring disorders, 12-steps programs include Dual Recovery Anonymous (Hamilton & Sample, 1994) and Double Trouble (Vogel, Knight, Laudet, & Magura, 1998).

There has been significant research literature documenting the effects of 12-step programs on people with co-occurring disorders (Aase, Jason, & Robinson, 2008; Bogenschutz, 2007; Bogenschutz, Geppert, & George, 2006). Most of these studies seem to be one-group longitudinal designs showing positive benefits for people who participated in 12-step programs. Only one randomized controlled trial was found: a study with veterans challenged by major depression and substance use problems (Brown et al., 2006). In this study, participants were assigned randomly to cognitive therapy or 12-step facilitation. Results suggest that positive effects were experienced in the cognitive therapy group, whereas such benefits were not shown in the 12-step group. Though research is lacking regarding 12-step services for people with dual disorders, a comprehensive review of the research literature indicates that 12-step programs have significant and positive effects for people with alcohol abuse problems (Kelly, Magill, & Stout, 2009). Further research should be extended to the needs of people with co-occurring disorders with regard to 12-step programs and their efficacy.

Harm Reduction

In some ways, the 12-step programs reviewed suggest that personal goals are facilitated by eliminating, or at least controlling and reducing, substance use. Recent perspectives that emerge from advocates and public health specialists suggest that substance abuse is a life choice that is not necessarily erased by abstinence. The circumstances of a person's life make specific patterns of substance abuse appealing to them, such that they are unlikely to engage in treatments that challenge these preferences (Marlatt, Larimer, & Witkiewitz, 2011). The goal changes for these individuals to reduce harm that results from the use of certain substances. Several programs have emerged to promote harm reduction. Needle exchange programs align with this notion and provide on-the-streets opportunities for people who use IV drugs to replace dirty needles with sterile ones for no charge or recrimination (Duplessy & Reynaud, 2014). Like needle exchange programs, safe injection sites or drug consumption rooms provide crime and abuse-free sites for people to use street drugs (Patel, 2007). Opioid replacement therapy provides people who use heroin with methadone legally (Harlow, Roman, Happell, & Browne, 2013). Methadone is a less risky version of opium, which does not require criminal behavior to obtain. Safe sex programs might also be helpful for some people with psychiatric disabilities. Ready provision of condoms for free has decreased the spread of HIV/AIDS, especially among people with low incomes (Adam et al., 2009; O'Reilly, Fonner, Kennedy, & Sweat, 2014).

Rehabilitation providers involved in harm reduction programs need to be fully aware of laws and statutes that may be relevant to these kinds of programs (Elliott, 2012). Providers are not at liberty to violate laws in promoting harm reduction; for example, they cannot purchase heroin or any other illegal drug for program participants in order to keep them from being victimized by crime. The legality of needle exchange and safe injection sites varies by jurisdiction (they also may vary by federal, state, and local city municipalities) and time period. It is crucial that providers of harm reduction remain up-to-date on the variety of statutes when implementing this kind of approach.

There is evidence that harm reduction is being incorporated into services for people with co-occurring disorders (Laker, 2007), but the quality of this research is limited. Many of the studies found in a comprehensive review suggested that harm reduction interventions were being combined with motivational interviewing. Moreover, research has yet to address how harm reduction should be adapted for people with co-occurring disorders.

Care Coordination

Care coordination is essential to increasing the intensity and integration of community-based services; assertive community treatment (ACT) is one example well studied in the literature. Briefly, ACT for people with co-occurring disorders would include a multidisciplinary team with a relatively small caseload providing comprehensive and time-unlimited services covering the entire scope of challenges, including those reflecting psychiatric disabilities and substance abuse problems. Numerous studies have examined ACT for this group in controlled studies (Carmichael, Tackett-Gibson, & Dell, 1998; Chandler & Spicer, 2006; Drake et al., 1998b; Drake, Yovetich, Bebout, Harris, & McHugo, 1997; Essock et al., 2006; Godley, Hoewing-Roberson, & Godley, 1994; Ho et al., 1999; Jerrell & Ridgely, 1995; Morse et al., 2006). Findings suggest that more intensive and integrated services had superior outcomes in some areas, but not all. However, studies differed from one another in design, clinical model, implementation, measures, and positive outcomes, making conclusions somewhat unclear. The most consistently positive outcomes are increased residential stability, decreased hospitalization, and decreased homelessness. Substance abuse outcomes are sometimes, but not consistently, improved. Substance abuse is difficult to assess, but at least two recent and well-done studies show that substance abuse treatment can be successful within various case management approaches (Essock et al., 2006; Morse et al., 2006). Substance abuse outcomes are likely related to quality rather than structure or quantity of substance abuse services (Jerrell & Ridgely, 1997; McHugo, Drake, Teague, & Xie, 1999). None of the studies showed positive effects on incarceration outcomes, similar to other studies of ACT for people in the criminal justice field (Drake, Morrissey, & Mueser, 2006).

Pharmacological Interventions

Many studies have been done examining the effects of antipsychotic medication on co-occurring disorders (Smelson et al., 2008). Results imply that second-generation antipsychotic medication may have beneficial effects on the psychotic symptoms of people with dual disorders. Second-generation antipsychotic medication is also referred to as *atypical antipsychotic medication*. These medications, developed in the 1980s, have fewer motor and movement side effects compared to the first generation antipsychotic medications (Seida et al., 2012). They may also decrease craving (as found in research on people with cocaine addiction) and decrease substance use. Benzodiazepine use is controversial in people with primary substance use disorders, but the practice appears to be common for people with dual disorders. One prospective study of people with dual disorders showed that prescribed benzodiazepines do not appear to improve outcomes and are associated with the development of benzodiazepine abuse (Brunette, Noordsy, Xie, & Drake, 2003).

Several medications have also been examined to help people with co-occurring disorders. Anticonvulsants, like valproic acid, are often prescribed for people with seizure disorders, but these drugs also have mood-stabilizing capacities. Multiple studies show that valproic acid in combination with lithium is associated with improvement of alcohol disorders in people with bipolar disorders (Brady, Sonnes, & Ballenger, 1995). With regard to other anticonvulsant medications, little is known about their impact on people with dual diagnosis. The antidepressant bupropion has helped with smoking cessation in two small studies of people with schizophrenia (Evins & Mayes, 2001; Weiner & Ball, 2001). To date, however, there is no experimental evidence that antidepressants affect use of alcohol or other drugs of abuse in people with dual diagnosis.

Disulfiram, commonly known as Antabuse, is sometimes prescribed for people who abuse alcohol, as a way to dissuade them from using in the future. Disulfiram intensifies the "hangover effects" of alcohol consumption. As a result, people may want to avoid disulfiram in order to avoid these symptoms; usually, it is only prescribed when the person is fully informed about its effects and consents to take it. The drug has been safely evaluated in open clinical trials and was shown to decrease alcohol use in people with dual disorders (Mueser et al., 2003). Additional studies show that naltrexone, another drug, may be associated with decreased alcohol use in comorbid people with schizophrenia (Dougherty, 1997; Maxwell & Shinderman, 1997, 2000). Naltrexone has been shown to reduce alcohol cravings. In a randomized clinical trial, both disulfiram and/or naltrexone demonstrated positive effects on alcohol abuse for people with dual diagnosis (Petrakis, Nich, & Ralevski, 2006). Finally, methadone replacement therapy has been used for people with schizophrenia, concurrent with psychosocial and psychiatric treatments (Miotto, Preti, & Frezza, 2001). Methadone reduces cravings related to heroin and other opioid addictions; however, methadone therapies have not been experimentally studied in people with dual disorders.

Legal Interventions

It is not uncommon to see interventions used that involve the criminal justice system for people with co-occurring disorders; many are involved with the court system and are under some sort of legal control or supervision. Legal directives may include, but are not limited to, incarceration, conditions of probation and parole, outpatient commitment, involuntary hospitalization, coercive medications, and guardianships for finances. In addition, more subtle but coercive techniques are also used to shunt people into hospitals, group homes, and other supervised situations. Though many individuals experience mandatory intervention, remarkably few studies have addressed them. A small number of controlled studies of outpatient commitment, which include large proportions of people with dual diagnoses, do not show evidence of efficacy (Swanson et al., 2000).

Ancillary Interventions

Several ancillary interventions may be helpful to individuals who do not respond well to the basic approaches mentioned earlier; these may include money management (Ries & Comtois, 1997; Ries et al., 2004), intensive family interventions (Mueser & Fox, 2002), trauma interventions (Harris, 1998; Rosenberg et al., 2001), contingency management (Shaner et al., 1997; Sigmon, Steingard, Badger, Anthony, & Higgins, 2000), conditional discharges (O'Keefe, Potenza, & Mueser, 1997), and medications (Brunette, Noordsy, Buckley, & Green, 2005). Some of these interventions might be instituted at the beginning of treatment. For example, early inclusion of family psychoeducation, which addresses mental illness and substance abuse, seems warranted for those individuals who live with their families. Long-term residential treatment is expensive but may be an effective approach for people who have cognitive problems or impulsive behavior and who have failed to respond to outpatient treatment. Little research has been done on these ancillary approaches to treatment, other than the previously reviewed studies of residential treatment.

CONCLUSION

We have defined psychiatric rehabilitation as systematic efforts to help adults with psychiatric disabilities move forward in their recovery process. In its evolution, the field has moved away from early assumptions related to the concepts of asylum (people are best served in enclaves apart from mainstream community life), separation of rehabilitation and medical models (psychiatric rehabilitation programs should distance themselves from mental health treatment), and transitionalism (people are best helped through gradual, stepwise programs of preparation for community living). Rather, rehabilitation has promoted an emphasis on hope, recovery, and self-determination in efforts to provide individuals with psychiatric disabilities the tools needed to accomplish the goals and pursuits they desire.

CONTENT REVIEW QUESTIONS

- How is psychiatric rehabilitation defined?
- What are the core principles of psychiatric rehabilitation?
- What are some of the inventions and approaches used to promote psychiatric rehabilitation?
- What are some of the complexities of co-occurring disorders, and how are they treated?
- What are the roles of a rehabilitation provider with regard to psychiatric disorders and the principles of recovery and illness management?

REFERENCES

Aase, D. M., Jason, L. A., & Robinson, L. (2008). 12-step participation among dually-diagnosed individuals: A review of individual and contextual factors. *Clinical Psychology Review, 28,* 1235–1248.

Abram, K., & Teplin, L. (1991). Co-occurring disorders among mentally ill jail detainees: Implications for public policy. *American Psychologist, 46,* 1036–1044.

Adam, P. C., de Wit, J. B., Toskin, I, Mathers, B. M., Nashkhoev, M., Zablotska, I., . . . Rugg, D. (2009). Estimating levels of HIV testing, HIV prevention coverage, HIV knowledge, and condom use among men who have sex with men (MSM) in low-income and middle-income countries. *Journal of Acquired Immune Deficiency Syndromes, 52,* S143–S151.

Alverson, H., Alverson, M., & Drake, R. E. (2000). An ethnographic study of the longitudinal course of substance abuse among people with severe mental illness. *Community Mental Health Journal, 36,* 557–569.

Anderson, C., Reiss, D., & Hogarty, G. (1986). *Schizophrenia and the family.* New York, NY: Guilford Press.

Anthony, W. A., Cohen, M., Farkas, M. D., & Gagne, C. (2002). *Psychiatric rehabilitation* (2nd ed.). Boston, MA: Center for Psychiatric Rehabilitation.

Apodaca, T. R., & Longabaugh, R. (2009). Mechanisms of change in motivational interviewing: A review and preliminary evaluation of evidence. *Addiction, 104,* 705–715.

Barnett, E., Sussman, S., Smith, C., Rohrbach, L. A., & Spruijt-Metz, D. (2012). Motivational interviewing for adolescent substance use: A review of the literature. *Addictive Behaviors, 37,* 1325–1334.

Barrowclough, C., Haddock, G., Tarrier, N., Lewis, S. W., Moring, J., O'Brien, R., . . . McGovern, J. (2001). Randomized controlled trial of motivational interviewing, cognitive behavioral therapy, and family intervention for patients with comorbid schizophrenia and substance use disorders. *American Journal of Psychiatry, 158,* 1706–1713.

Becker, D. R., Drake, R. E., & Naughton, W. (2005). Supported employment for people with co-occurring disorders. *Psychiatric Rehabilitation Journal, 28,* 332–338.

Beeler, J., Rosenthal, A., & Cohler, B. (1999). Patterns of family caregiving and support provided to older psychiatric patients in long-term care. *Psychiatric Services, 50,* 1222–1224.

Bellack, A. S., & DiClemente, C. C. (1999). Treating substance abuse among patients with schizophrenia. *Psychiatric Services, 50,* 75–80.

Blackwell, B. (1973). Drug therapy—patient compliance. *New England Journal of Medicine, 289*(5), 249–252.

Bogenschutz, M. P. (2007). 12-step approaches for the dually diagnosed: Mechanisms of change. *Alcoholism: Clinical and Experimental Research, 31,* 64S–66S.

Bogenschutz, M. P., Geppert, C. M. A., & George, J. (2006). The role of twelve-step approaches in dual diagnosis treatment and recovery. *American Journal on Addictions, 15,* 50–60.

Bond, G. R., & Resnick, S. G. (2000). Psychiatric rehabilitation. In R. G. Frank & T. Elliott (Eds.), *Handbook of rehabilitation psychology* (pp. 235–258). Washington, DC: American Psychological Association.

Brady, K. T., Sonnes, A. R., & Ballenger, J. C. (1995). Valproate in the treatment of acute bipolar affective episodes complicated by substance abuse: A pilot study. *Journal of Clinical Psychology, 56,* 118–121.

Brehm, J. W. (1966). *A theory of psychological reactance.* New York, NY: Academic Press.

Brown, S. A., Glasner-Edwards, S. V., Tate, S. R., McQuaid, J. R., Chalekian, J., & Granholm, E. (2006). Integrated cognitive behavioral therapy versus twelve-step facilitation therapy for substance-dependent adults with depressive disorders. *Journal of Psychoactive Drugs, 38,* 449–460.

Brunette, M. F., Noordsy, D. L., Buckley, P., & Green, A. I. (2005). Pharmacologic treatments for co-occurring substance use disorders in patients with schizophrenia: A research review. *Journal of Dual Diagnosis, 1,* 41–55.

Brunette, M. F., Noordsy, D. L., Xie, H., & Drake, R. E. (2003). Benzodiazepine use and abuse among patients with severe mental illness and co-occurring substance use disorders. *Psychiatric Services, 54,* 1395–1401.

Campbell, M., Donaldson, L., Roberts, S., & Smith, J. (1996). A prescribing incentive scheme for non-fundholdng general practices: An observational study. *British Medical Journal, 313,* 535–538.

Carey, K. (1996). Substance use reduction in the context of outpatient psychiatric treatment: A collaborative, motivational, harm reduction approach. *Community Mental Health Journal, 32,* 291–306.

Carmichael, D., Tackett-Gibson, M., & Dell, O. (1998). Texas dual diagnosis project evaluation report 1997–1998. College Station, TX: Texas A&M University, Public Policy Research Institute.

Caton, C., Shrout, P., Eagle, P., Opler, L., Felix, A., & Dominguez, B. (1994). Risk factors for homelessness among schizophrenic men: A case-control study. *American Journal of Public Health, 84,* 265–270.

Chandler, D. W., & Spicer, G. (2006). Integrated treatment for jail recidivists with co-occurring psychiatric and substance use disorders. *Community Mental Health Journal, 42*(4), 405–425.

Cleary, M., Hunt, G. E., Matheson, S., & Walter, G. (2008). Psychosocial treatments for people with co-occurring severe mental illness and substance misuse: Systematic review. *Journal of Advanced Nursing, 65,* 238–258.

Cnaan, R. A., Blankertz, L., Messinger, K. W., & Gardner, J. R. (1988). Psychosocial rehabilitation: Toward a definition. *Psychosocial Rehabilitation Journal, 11*(4), 61–77.

Coldham, E. L., Addington, J., & Addington, D. (2002). Medication adherence of individuals with a first episode of psychosis. *Acta Psychiatrica Scandinavica, 106,* 286–290.

Cook, J. A., & Hoffschmidt, S. J. (1993). Comprehensive models of psychosocial rehabilitation. In R. W. Flexer & P. L. Solomon (Eds.), *Psychiatric rehabilitation in practice* (pp. 81–97). Boston, MA: Andover.

Corrigan, P. W. (2013). The risk of prognostication. *Psychiatric Services, 8,* 719.

Corrigan, P. W. (2016). *Principles and practice of psychiatric rehabilitation: An empirical approach* (2nd ed.). New York, NY: Guilford Press.

Corrigan, P. W., Angell, B., Davidson, L., Marcus, S., Salzer, M., Kottsieper, P., . . . Stanhope, V. (2012). From adherence to self-determination: Evolution of a treatment paradigm for people with serious mental illness. *Psychiatric Services, 63,* 169–173.

Dincin, J. (1995). Core programs in the thresholds approach. *New Directions for Mental Health Services, 68,* 33–54.

Dixon, L., McFarlane, W., Lefley, H., Lucksted, A., Cohen, M., Falloon, I., . . . Sondheimer, D. (2001). Evidence-based practices for services to families of people with psychiatric disabilities. *Psychiatric Services, 52,* 903–910.

Doornbos, M. (2001). The 24-7-52 job: Family caregiving for young adults with serious and persistent mental illness. *Journal of Family Nursing, 7,* 328–344.

Dougherty, R. J. (1997). Naltrexone in the treatment of alcohol dependent dual diagnosed patients (abstract). *Journal of Addictive Diseases*, 16, 107.

Drake, R. E., & Brunette, M. F. (1998a). Complications of severe mental illness related to alcohol and other drug use disorders. In *Recent developments in alcoholism* (Vol. 14, *Consequences of Alcoholism*, pp. 285–299). New York, NY: Plenum.

Drake, R. E., McHugo, G. J., Clark, R. E., Teague, G. B., Xie, H., Miles, K., & Ackerson, T. H. (1998b). Assertive community treatment for patients with co-occurring severe mental illness and substance use disorder: A clinical trial. *American Journal of Orthopsychiatry*, 68, 201–215.

Drake, R. E., McHugo, G. J., Xie, H., Fox, M., Packard, J., & Helmstetter, B. (2006). Ten-year recovery outcomes for clients with co-occurring schizophrenic and substance use disorders. *Schizophrenia Bulletin*, 32(3), 464–473.

Drake, R. E., Morrissey, J., & Mueser, K. T. (2006). The challenge of treating forensic dual diagnosis clients. *Community Mental Health Journal*, 42(4), 427–432.

Drake, R. E., Mueser, K. T., Brunette, M., & McHugo, G. J. (2004). A review of treatments for people with severe mental illness and co-occurring substance use disorder. *Psychiatric Rehabilitation Journal*, 27, 360–374.

Drake, R. E., O'Neal, E. L., & Wallach, M. A. (2008). A systematic review of psychosocial research on psychosocial interventions for people with co-occurring severe mental and substance use disorders. *Journal of Substance Abuse Treatment*, 34, 123–138.

Drake, R. E., Wallach, M. A., & McGovern, M. P. (2005). Preventing relapses to substance use disorder among clients with severe mental illnesses: What do we know and what do we do next? *Psychiatric Services*, 56, 1297–1302.

Drake, R. E., Yovetich, N. A., Bebout, R. R., Harris, M., & McHugo, G. J. (1997). Integrated treatment for dually diagnosed homeless adults. *Journal of Nervous and Mental Disease*, 185, 298–305.

Dumaine, M. L. (2003). Meta-analysis of interventions with co-occurring disorders of severe mental illness and substance abuse: Implications for social work practice. *Research on Social Work Practice*, 13, 142–165.

Dunn, H. (1961). *High level wellness*. Washington, DC: Mt. Vernon Publishing.

Duplessy, C., & Reynaud, E. G. (2014). Long-term survey of syringe-dispensing machine needle exchange program: Answering public concerns. *Harm Reduction Journal*, 11(1), 1.

Elliott, R. (2012). Harm reduction and international law: Drug control vs. human rights. In R. Pates & D. Riley (Eds.), *Harm reduction in substance use and high-risk behaviour: International policy and practice.* (pp. 33–48). Chichester, West Sussex, UK: Wiley-Blackwell.

Essock, S., Mueser, K. T., Drake, R. E., Covell, N., McHugo, G. J., Frisman, L., . . . Swain, K. (2006). Assertive community treatment versus standard case management for clients receiving integrated treatment for co-occurring severe mental illness and substance use disorders. *Psychiatric Services*, 57, 185–196.

Evins, A. E., & Mayes, V. K. (2001). A pilot trial of bupropion added to cognitive behavioral therapy for smoking cessation in schizophrenia. *Nicotine and Tobacco Research*, 3, 397–403.

Falloon, I., Boyd, J., & McGill, C. (1984). *Family care of schizophrenia*. New York, NY: Guilford Press.

Fenton, W. S. (2003). Shared decision making: A model for the physician-patient relationship in the 21st century? *Acta Psychiatrica Scandinavica*, 107, 401–402.

Ferrando, S. J., Owen, J. A., & Levenson, J. L. (2014). Psychopharmacology. In R. E. Hales, S. C. Yudofsky, & L. W. Roberts (Eds.), *The American psychiatric publishing textbook of psychiatry* (pp. 929–1004). Arlington, VA: American Psychiatric Publishing.

Fogarty, J. S. (1997). Reactance theory and patient noncompliance. *Social Science and Medicine*, 45, 1277–1288.

Freeman, A., & Dolan, M. (2001). Revisiting Prochaska and DiClemente's stages of change theory: An expansion and specification to aid in treatment planning and outcome evaluation. *Cognitive and Behavioral Practice*, 8, 224–234.

Frese, F. J., & Davis, W. W. (1997). The consumer-survivor movement, recovery, and consumer professionals. *Professional Psychology: Research and Practice*, 28, 243–245.

Godley, S. H., Hoewing-Roberson, R., & Godley, M. D. (1994). *Final MISA report*. Bloomington, IL: Lighthouse Institute.

Goldman, H. (1982). Mental illness and family burden: A public health perspective. *Hospital and Community Psychiatry*, 33, 557–559.

Goldstrom, I. D., Campbell, J., Rogers, J. A., Lambert, D. B., Blacklow, B., Henderson, M. J., & Manderscheid, R. W. (2006). National estimates for mental health mutual support groups, self-help organizations, and consumer-operated services. *Administration and Policy in Mental Health and Mental Health Services Research*, 33(1), 92–103.

Goodman, L. A., Rosenberg, S. D., Mueser, K. T., & Drake, R. E. (1997). Physical and sexual assault history in women with serious mental illness: Prevalence, correlates, treatment, and future research directions. *Schizophrenia Bulletin, 23*, 685–696.

Greenfield, S. F., Weiss, R. D., & Tohen, M. (1995). Substance abuse and the chronically mentally ill: A description of dual diagnosis treatment services in a psychiatric hospital. *Community Mental Health Journal, 31*, 265–278.

Guarnaccia, P. (1998). Multicultural experiences in family caregiving: A study of African American, European American, and Hispanic American families. *New Directions for Mental Health Services, 77*, 45–61.

Hamann, J., Leucht, S., & Kissling, W. (2003). Shared decision making in psychiatry. *Acta Psychiatrica Scandinavica, 107*, 403–409.

Hamilton, T., & Sample, P. (1994). *The twelve steps and dual recovery: A framework of recovery for those of us with addiction and an emotional or psychiatric illness.* Center City, MN: Hazelden.

Hanson, R. W. (1986). Physician-patient communication and compliance. In K. E. Gerber & A. M. Nehemkis (Eds.), *Compliance: The dilemma of the chronically ill* (pp. 182–212). New York, NY: Springer Publishing.

Harris, M. (1998). *Trauma recovery and empowerment.* New York, NY: Free Press.

Harlow, W., Roman, M. W., Happell, B., & Browne, G. (2013). Accessibility versus quality of care plus retention: The formula for service delivery in Australian opioid replacement therapy? *Issues in Mental Health Nursing, 34*, 706–714.

Hatfield, A. (1987). Coping and adaptation: A conceptual framework for understanding families. In A. Hatfield & H. Lefley (Eds.), *Families of the mentally ill.* (pp. 60–84). New York, NY: Guilford Press.

Haywood, T. W., Kravitz, H. M., Grossman, L. S., Cavanaugh, J. L., Davis, J. M., & Lewis, D. A. (1995). Predicting the "revolving door" phenomenon among patients with schizophrenic, schizoaffective, and affective disorders. *American Journal of Psychiatry, 152*, 856–861.

Ho, A. P., Tsuang, J. W., Liberman, R. P., Wang, R., Wilkins, J. N., Eckman, T. A., & Shaner, A. L. (1999). Achieving effective treatment of patients with chronic psychotic illness and comorbid substance dependence. *American Journal of Psychiatry, 156*, 1765–1770.

Hughes, R., & Weinstein, D. (1997). Introduction. In R. Hughes & D. Weinstein (Eds.), *Best practices in psychosocial rehabilitation* (pp. vi–xvi). Columbia, MD: International Association of Psychosocial Rehabilitation.

Jerrell, J. M., & Ridgely, S. (1995). Comparative effectiveness of three approaches to serving people with severe mental illness and substance abuse disorders. *Journal of Nervous and Mental Disease, 183*, 566–576.

Jerrell, J. M., & Ridgely, M. S. (1997). Dual diagnosis care for severe and persistent disorders. A comparison of three methods. *Behavioral Healthcare Tomorrow, 6*, 26–33.

Kane, J. M. (2009). Creating a health care team to manage chronic medical illnesses in patients with severe mental illness: The public policy perspective. *Journal of Clinical Psychiatry, 70*, 37–42.

Kelly, J. F., Magill, M., & Stout, R. L. (2009). How do people recover from alcohol dependence? A systematic review of the research on mechanisms of behavior change in Alcoholics Anonymous. *Addiction Research and Theory, 17*, 236–259.

Kenneson, A., Funderburk, J. S., & Maisto, S. A. (2013). Substance use disorders increase the odds of subsequent mood disorders. *Drug and Alcohol Dependence, 133*, 338–343.

Kessler, R. C., Nelson, C. B., McGonagle, K. A., Edlund, M. J., Frank, R. G., & Leaf, P. J. (1996). The epidemiology of co-occurring addictive and mental disorders: Implications for prevention and service utilization. *American Journal of Orthopsychiatry, 66*, 17–31.

Kobau, R., Seligman, M. E. P., Peterson, C., Diener, E., Zack, M. M., Chapman, D., & Thompson, W. (2011). Mental health promotion in public health: Perspectives and strategies from positive psychology. *American Journal of Public Health, 101*, e1–e9.

Laker, C. J. (2007). How reliable is the current evidence looking at the efficacy of harm reduction and motivational interviewing interventions in the treatment of patients with dual diagnosis? *Journal of Psychiatric and Mental Health Nursing, 14*, 720–726.

Lam, D. (1991). Psychosocial family intervention in schizophrenia: A review of empirical studies. *Psychological Medicine, 21*, 423–441.

Lefley, H. (1996). *Family caregiving in mental illness.* Thousand Oaks, CA: Sage.

Lehman, A. F., & Steinwachs, D. M. (1998). Patterns of usual care for schizophrenia: Initial results from the schizophrenia patient outcomes research team (PORT) client survey. *Schizophrenia Bulletin, 24*, 11–20.

Manderscheid, R., & Sonnenschein, M. (1997). *Mental health, United States, 1996.* Washington, DC: Substance Abuse and Mental Health Services Administration, U.S. Department of Health and Human Services.

Marlatt, G. A., Larimer, M., & Witkiewitz, K. (Eds.). (2011). *Harm reduction* (2nd ed.). New York: NY: Guilford Press.

Maxwell, S., & Shinderman, M. S. (1997). Use of naltrexone in the treatment of dually diagnosed patients. *Journal of Addictive Diseases, 16,* 125.

Maxwell, S., & Shinderman, M. S. (2000). Use of naltrexone in the treatment of alcohol use disorders in patients with concomitant major mental illness. *Journal of Addictive Diseases, 19,* 61–69.

McFarlane, W. (2002). *Multifamily groups in the treatment of severe psychiatric disorders.* New York, NY: Guilford Press.

McFarlane, W., Dixon, L., Lukens, E., & Lucksted, A. (2003). Family psychoeducation and schizophrenia: A review of the literature. *Journal of Marital and Family Therapy, 29,* 223–245.

McHugo, G. J., Drake, R. E., Teague, G. B., & Xie, H. (1999). Fidelity to assertive community treatment and client outcomes in the New Hampshire dual disorders study. *Psychiatric Services, 50,* 818–824.

Miklowitz, D. J. (2010). *Bipolar disorder: A family-focused treatment approach* (2nd ed.). New York, NY: Guilford Press.

Miller, W. R., & Rollnick, S. (2013). *Motivational interviewing: Helping people change* (3rd ed.). New York, NY: Guilford Press.

Minkoff, K. (1989). An integrated treatment model for dual diagnosis of psychosis and addiction. *Hospital and Community Psychiatry, 40,* 1031–1036.

Miotto, P., Preti, A., & Frezza, M. (2001). Heroin and schizophrenia: Subjective responses to abused drugs in dually diagnosed patients. *Journal of Clinical Psychopharmacology, 21,* 111–113.

Moore, A., Sellwood, W., & Stirling, J. (2000). Compliance and psychological reactance in schizophrenia. *British Journal of Clinical Psychology, 39,* 287–296.

Morey, B., & Mueser, K. T. (2007). *The family intervention guide to mental illness: Recognizing symptoms and getting treatment.* Oakland, CA: New Harbinger.

Morse, G. A., Calsyn, R. J., Klinkenberg, W. D., Helminiak, T. W., Wolff, N., Drake, R. E., . . . McCudden, S. (2006). Treating homeless clients with severe mental illness and substance use disorder: Costs and outcomes. *Community Mental Health Journal, 42,* 377–404.

Mueser, K. T., Corrigan, P. W., Hilton, D., Tanzman, B., Schaub, A., Gingerich, S., . . . Herz, M. I. (2002). Illness management and recovery for severe mental illness: A review of the research. *Psychiatric Services, 53,* 1272–1284.

Mueser, K. T., Drake, R. E., & Noordsy, D. L. (1998). Integrated mental health and substance abuse treatment for severe psychiatric disorders. *Journal of Practical Psychiatry and Behavioral Health, 4,* 129–139.

Mueser, K. T., & Fox, L. (2002). A family intervention program for dual disorders. *Community Mental Health Journal, 38,* 253–270.

Mueser, K. T., & Gingerich, S. (2006). *The complete family guide to schizophrenia: Helping your loved one get the most out of life.* New York, NY: Guilford Press.

Mueser, K. T., Noordsy, D. L., Drake, R. E., & Fox, M. (2003). *Integrated treatment for dual disorders: A guide to effective practice.* New York, NY: Guilford Press.

New Freedom Commission on Mental Health. (2003). *Achieving the promise: Transforming mental health care in America.* Washington, DC: Department of Health and Human Services.

O'Brien, C., Gardner-Sood, P., Corlett, S. K., Ismail, K., Smith, S., Atakan, Z., . . . Gaughran, F. (2014). Provision of health promotion programmes to people with serious mental illness: A mapping exercise of four South London boroughs. *Journal of Psychiatric and Mental Health Nursing, 21,* 121–127.

O'Keefe, C., Potenza, D. P., & Mueser, K. T. (1997). Treatment outcomes for severely mentally ill patients on conditional discharge to community-based treatment. *Journal of Nervous and Mental Disease, 185,* 409–411.

O'Reilly, K. R., Fonner, V. A., Kennedy, C. E., & Sweat, M. D. (2014). Free condom distribution: What we don't know may hurt us. *Aids Behavior, 18,* 2169–2171.

Osher, F. C., & Kofoed, L. L. (1989). Treatment of patients with psychiatric and psychoactive substance use disorders. *Hospital and Community Psychiatry, 40,* 1025–1030.

Patel, K. (2007). Research note: Drug consumption rooms and needle and syringe exchange programs. *Journal of Drug Issues, 37,* 737–748.

Pawsey, B., Logan, G., & Castle, D. (2011). Psychological treatments for comorbidity across the life course. *Mental Health and Substance Abuse, 4,* 72–82.

Petrakis, I. L., Nich, C., & Ralevski, E. (2006). Schizophrenia and alcohol abuse: A review of pharmacotherapeutic strategies and a report on the effectiveness of naltrexone and disulfiram. *Schizophrenia Bulletin, 32*(4), 644–654.

PDR Staff. *Prescribers' digital reference (Physician's desk reference* online). Retrived from http://www.pdr.net

Pratt, C. W., Gill, K. J., Barrett, N. M., & Roberts, M. M. (1999). *Psychiatric rehabilitation.* New York, NY: Academic Press.

Prochaska, J. O., & Diclemente, C. C. (1984). *The transtheoretical approach: Crossing the traditional boundaries of therapy.* Homewood, IL: Dow-Jones/Irwin.

Rappa, L., & Viola, J. (2013). *Condensed psychopharmacology 2013: A pocket reference for psychiatry and psychotropic medications.* Ft. Lauderdale, FL: RXPSYCH.

Regier, D. A., Farmer, M. E., Rae, D. S., Locke, B. Z., Keith, S. J., Judd, L. L., & Goodwin, F. K. (1990). Comorbidity of mental disorders with alcohol and other drug abuse. *Journal of the American Medical Association, 264,* 2511–2518.

Ries, R. K., & Comtois, K. A. (1997). Managing disability benefits as part of treatment for persons with severe mental illness and comorbid drug/alcohol disorders. *American Journal of Addictions, 6,* 330–337.

Ries, R. K., Dyck, D. G., Short, R., Srebnik, D., Fisher, A., & Comtois, K. A. (2004). Outcomes of managing disability benefits among patients with substance dependence and severe mental illness. *Psychiatric Services, 55,* 445–447.

Rosenberg, S. D., Goodman, L. A., Osher, F. C., Swartz, M., Essock, S. M., Butterfield, M. I., . . . Salyers, M. P. (2001). Prevalence of HIV, hepatitis B and hepatitis C in people with severe mental illness. *American Journal of Public Health, 91,* 31–37.

Salerno, A., Margolies, P., Cleek, A., Pollock, M., Gopalan, G., & Jackson, C. (2011). Wellness self-management: An adaptation of the illness management and recovery program in New York state. *Psychiatric Services, 62,* 456–458.

Seida, J. C., Schouten, J. R., Boylan, K., Newton, A. S., Mousavi, S. S., Beaith, A., . . . & Carrey, N. (2012). Antipsychotics for children and young adults: A comparative effectiveness review. *Pediatrics, 129*(3), e771–e784.

Shaner, A., Roberts, L. J., Eckman, T. A., Tucker, D. E., Tsuang, J. W., Wilkins, J. N., & Mintz, J. (1997). Monetary reinforcement of abstinence from cocaine among mentally ill patients with cocaine dependence. *Psychiatric Services, 48*(6), 807–810.

Sigmon, S., Steingard, S., Badger, G. J., Anthony, S. L., & Higgins, S. T. (2000). Contingent reinforcement of marijuana abstinence among individuals with serious mental illness: A feasibility study. *Experimental and Clinical Psychopharmacology, 8,* 509–517.

Smelson, D. A., Dixon, L., Craig, T., Remolina, S., Batki, S. L., Niv, N., & Owen, R. (2008). Pharmacological treatment of schizophrenia and co-occurring substance use disorders. *CNS Drugs, 22,* 903–916.

Solomon, P. (1996). Moving from psychoeducation to family education for families of adults with severe mental illness. *Psychiatric Services, 47,* 1364–1370.

Solomon, P. (2000). Interventions for families of individuals with schizophrenia: Maximizing outcomes for their relatives. *Disease Management and Health Outcomes, 8,* 211–221.

Steadman, H. J., Mulvey, E. P., Monahan, J., Robbins, P. C., Appelbaum, P. S., Grisso, T., . . . Silver, E. (1998). Violence by people discharged from acute psychiatric inpatient facilities and by others in the same neighborhoods. *Archives General Psychiatry, 55,* 393–401.

Sterling, E. W., von Esenwein, S. A., Tucker, S., Fricks, L., & Druss, B. G. (2010). Integrating wellness, recovery, and self-management for mental health consumers. *Community Mental Health Journal, 46,* 130–138.

Swanson, J. W., Swartz, M. S., Borum, R., Hiday, V. A., Wagner, H. R., & Burns, B. J. (2000). Involuntary out-patient commitment and reduction of violent behavior in persons with severe mental illness. *British Journal of Psychiatry, 176,* 324–331.

Swofford, C. D., Kasckow, J. W., Scheller-Gilkey, G., & Inderbitzin, L. B. (1996). Substance use: A powerful predictor of relapse in schizophrenia. *Schizophrenia Research, 20,* 145–151.

Tessler, R. E., & Gamache, A. (2000). *Family experiences with mental illness.* Westport, CT: Auburn House.

Torrey, W. C., Drake, R. E., Cohen, M., Fox, L. B., Lynde, D., Gorman, P., & Wyzik, P. (2002). The challenge of implementing and sustaining integrated dual disorders treatment programs. *Community Mental Health Journal, 38,* 507–521.

Tsai, J., Salyers, M. P., Rollins, A. L., McKasson, M., & Litmer, M. L. (2009). Integrated dual disorders treatment. *Journal of Community Psychology, 37,* 781–788.

U.S. Department of Health and Human Services. (1999). *A report of the Surgeon General.* Washington, DC: Author.

Vogel, H. W., Knight, E., Laudet, A. B., & Magura, S. (1998). Double trouble in recovery: Self-help for people with dual diagnoses. *Psychiatric Rehabilitation Journal, 21,* 356–364.

Weiner, E., & Ball, M. P. (2001). Effects of sustained-release bupropion and supportive group therapy on cigarette consumption in patients with schizophrenia. *American Journal of Psychiatry, 158,* 635–637.

Wennberg, J. E. (1991). Outcomes research, patient preference, and the primary care physician. *Journal of the American Board of Family Practice, 4,* 365–367.

Xie, H., Drake, R., & McHugo, G. (2006). Are there distinctive trajectory groups in substance abuse remission over 10 years? An application of the group-based modeling approach. *Administration and Policy in Mental Health and Mental Health Services Research, 33*(4), 423–432.

Xie, H., McHugo, G. J., Fox, L., & Drake, R. E. (2005). Substance abuse relapse in a ten-year prospective follow-up of clients with mental and substance use disorders. *Psychiatric Services, 56,* 1282–1287.

Ziedonis, D. M., Smelson, D., Rosenthal, R. N., Batki, S. L., Green, A. I., Henry, R. J., . . . Weiss, R. D. (2005). Improving the care of individuals with schizophrenia and substance use disorders: Consensus recommendations. *Journal of Psychiatric Practice, 11,* 315–339.

TWENTY-ONE

Technology

MARY BARROS-BAILEY AND KEITH SOFKA

LEARNING OBJECTIVES

After reading this chapter, you should be able to:

- Have a broad understanding of important areas to consider in the use of technology within and in support of the client–counselor relationship.
- Discuss technology behavioral and competency issues.
- Describe assistive technology and its use in evaluating and meeting the needs of clients.
- Understand the role of distance education in rehabilitation.

Since the Rehabilitation Counseling Consortium (RCC) established definitions for what constitutes rehabilitation counseling and a rehabilitation counselor (RC) in 2005, there have been many changes to the profession and the role of the professional within the context of counseling and the helping professions. The metamorphosis now acknowledges rehabilitation counseling's presence squarely within other specialties of counseling with a slightly modified definition:

> Counseling is a professional relationship that empowers diverse individuals, families, and groups to accomplish mental health, wellness, education, and career goals. The profession of rehabilitation counseling builds upon the general definition of counseling and consists of a group of professionally prepared and credentialed counselors with specialized knowledge, skills, and attitudes who work collaboratively in a professional relationship with people with disabilities to achieve their personal, social, psychological, and vocational goals. These professionals adhere to the rehabilitation counseling code of ethics and practice within the rehabilitation counseling scope of practice in order to ensure the provision of qualified services to consumers. (C. Chapman, personal communication, December 18, 2015)

Today, technology can play a role in the manner in which the client–counselor relationship is established, and every aspect of the relationship and delivery of service. The prevalence of technology in rehabilitation counseling is impossible to encapsulate into a single chapter; thus, an attempt has been made to address the most significant areas of knowledge for RC competencies: general scope of use of technology, counselor and client competencies, assistive technology, distance education, and the future role of technology in the field.

TECHNOLOGY USAGE IN THE UNITED STATES

As soon as a percentage describing the use of any kind of technology by any group is published, the numbers are obsolete given the spread, depth, and emergence of low or high technology that continues to transform our lives. The snapshot of technology use nationally in the United States and internationally by the general public and people with disabilities serves as a temporary mirror to reflect on technology's pervasiveness and trajectories. It should be understood in the context of the ever-changing waves of creation and obsolescence that mark technology's existence in all our lives.

The General Public

Surveys done by the Pew Research Center (2016) have provided a window into the use of technology by the general public and demographic slices of other groups nationally and internationally. Communication is central to the client–counselor relationship. The devices with which people communicate have placed the power of a supercomputer, television, camera, and other devices into our palms. Indeed, the Pew Research Center places the cell phone—and most commonly now the smartphone—at the center of continued growth internationally. In the United States, the growth of past years has reached a point of saturation, with 68% of the population owning smartphones and 45% having tablet computers (Anderson, 2015). Globally, particularly in emerging economies, the use of smartphones and usage of the Internet continues to soar. In advanced economies, the use of the Internet and smartphone ownership in 2015 stood at a median rate of 87% and 68%, respectively (Poushter, 2016). The relative growth of technology in emerging economies has gone from 45% to 54% usage of the Internet from 2013 to 2015, and smartphone usage has almost doubled from 21% to 37% over the same period (Poushter, 2016). The promise of the platforms that technology provides has yet to meet its capacity. Generally, the geographic areas with the most comprehensive coverage include the United States, Canada, Australia, and pockets in Europe; areas of moderate coverage include China, Central and Eastern Europe, some larger countries in South America (Argentina, Brazil, and Chile); and areas of low to very low coverage include Central America, the vast majority of Africa, and much of Asia (Poushter, 2016). Such density in the use of technology nationally and capacity for growth globally permeates what we do in our personal and professional roles and lives. Areas affected include professional and family relationships, recreation, communication, transportation, identity, knowledge, safety and security, and belief systems. Indeed, since the previous version of this chapter, we have seen the use of technology become instrumental in toppling governments, telling us much more about ourselves through wireless wearable sensors, simplifying existing technologies (e.g., miniature leadless pacemakers), increasing precision (e.g., robotic surgery), and inciting new areas of government regulation, such as applications (commonly referred to as apps) that are federally approved (Federal Government Mobile Apps Directory, 2016).

People With Disabilities

Although high and low technology advances hold the potential of a better quality of life (QOL) for people with disabilities, technological access to those individuals with physical, mental, and cognitive functional differences continues to lag behind that of the general population (Fox, 2011). In the United States, the U.S. Department of Commerce's

National Telecommunications and Information Administration (NTIA) regularly reports on the use of computer and Internet technology for people with disabilities. In 2014, it noted that:

- Mobile phone usage increased 4 percentage points each among individuals with family incomes below $25,000 (73 to 77 percent) and among people with disabilities (68 percent to 72 percent). (p. v)
- Popular with the general public, smartphones are also important to people with disabilities for reasons beyond convenience. . . . To help people with vision disabilities, researchers in Pakistan have developed a smartphone app that monitors a user's location and distance walked from a destination to warn of imminent nightfall. The application is geo-aware and so knows the time of sunset around the world. . . . (p. 2)
- Among people with disabilities, 10 percent expressed dissatisfaction with their computer's adequacy or stated they had no computer to use for Internet access at home in 2012. (p. 35)
- In 2012, households led by people with disabilities [that cited] lack of interest or need for home Internet use increased to 56 percent of non-users, compared to 51 percent in 2011. (p. vii)

Perhaps one of the reasons for the increased lack of interest in Internet use at home for people with disabilities is the increased use of smartphone technology that uses mobile phone antennas rather than Wi-Fi or Internet connection for connectivity. Regardless, technological access by people with disabilities continues to lag behind that of the general population for a myriad of reasons.

TECHNOLOGY AND BEHAVIOR

Behavior, and awareness of it as a control in the use of technology, is the most important factor in technology use. Early in the study of behavior and technology, Shechtman and Horowitz (2003) tested the assumption that people interact the same with computers as in live communication. They found that when people thought they were interacting with a computer, they used less effort in the communication process. That is, people act differently when they are using technology, particularly in the online environment, than when they are in face-to-face or telephonic interactions. The immediacy of Internet communications draws upon people's impulsivity (Caplan, 2002; Davis, Flett, & Besser, 2002; Suler, 2004). Goleman (2007) explained that in the interaction with a computer, there is an absence of cues from body language and other sensory stimuli to assist in decoding communications. He stated,

> the absence of information on how the other person is responding makes the prefrontal circuitry . . . more likely to fail. Our emotional impulses disinhibited, we type [a] message and hit "send" before . . . [we] hit "discard." (Para. 12)

As social media platforms capture and remit short messages (e.g., Twitter, SnapChat), the tendency not to control for impulsive actions that one may regret later is accentuated.

Knowing that communication may be constructed socially through the influence of technology among different demographic groups making up a counselor's caseload is an important insight. This information contributes to an understanding of how or why people communicate differently through the use of various platforms. Beyond the lack of cues, the immediacy of the decoding process when information is received through a particular gadget or platform and the resulting response fails to allow time to mitigate impulsivity.

When it comes to the use of existing and emerging technology, impulsive responses often become the norm rather than the exception. Understanding the occurrence of such behaviors is vital in the client–counselor relationship so that communication can be understood better and improved. In short, less communication effort coupled with impulsivity through the use of technology may lead to a kind of mindless communication. This type of communication may result in behaviors that otherwise would be considered improper in the more traditional forms of communication used in counseling.

If technology is a medium used in the client–counselor relationship, it should be evaluated so that the technological medium is a facilitator rather than an inhibitor of that communication. The awareness and discussion of technological options also puts a check against misinterpretation of the intent, tone, or other content of a message. The recipient's reaction to the message also may fuel the flames of the communication in a direction that the sender never intended originally. Because technology automatically creates a record of the communication that may be saved on one or multiple servers, there is documentation of the interaction to which either or both parties, or others, may have access. It may be further interpreted or remitted in the future.

For more than two decades, Shea (1994) have promoted netiquette rules. These rules are as relevant today for today's social media, texting, and other platforms operating on a variety of mobile or wireless technologies as they were when the platform was a bulletin board accessed through expensive long-distance dial-up connections. Their 10 rules are:

Rule 1: Remember the human
Rule 2: Behave in the same way online as in real life
Rule 3: Know where you are in cyberspace
Rule 4: Respect other people's time and bandwidth
Rule 5: Make yourself look good online
Rule 6: Share expert knowledge
Rule 7: Help keep flame wars under control
Rule 8: Respect other people's privacy
Rule 9: Don't abuse your power
Rule 10: Be forgiving of other people's mistakes

(Shea, 1994, p. 1)

RCs may find that some clients disclose more about themselves and their circumstances through their use of technology than they do in face-to-face interactions. There might be expectations as to how immediately or when the counselor or client should respond. These kinds of issues, and others that may arise in the client–counselor relationship, all become points for awareness and discussion, clarification, and boundary setting between both parties. Examples of common boundaries may include agreement about what kinds of interactions are allowable with the use of any medium, when or how often it is to be used, response times, or other expectations.

TECHNOLOGICAL COMPETENCY

Measuring technological competency—a dynamic, moving target—is not always easy. Someone's subjective concept of being "good" or "bad" at the use of technology sometimes has to be measured against an objective standard. This assessment is difficult to capture in an interview process. Therefore, computer and Internet assessment tools and questionnaires based on standard competencies supplement the interview process with additional information for the client and the practitioner (Brasley, 2006; Hobbs, 2002; Jiang, Chan, & Chen, 2004). These instruments could assist in understanding the level of technological competencies and provide better screening when the counselor makes such decisions about whether to use a psychometric instrument administered through paper-and-pencil format or through technology, the need for computer literacy classes in a prevocational or training program, or other similar services or needs.

Barros-Bailey (2007) found that RCs had difficulty with the expectation that they might be ethically responsible for assessing their client's level of technological competence, given that counselors themselves may feel inadequate in their own technological competencies. Some existing assessments, such as the *Technology and Internet Assessment* (H & H Publishing, 2016), have scales measuring the use of technology, specific computer skills, acquisition of technical knowledge, basic Internet knowledge, Internet information skills, adapting to technological change, impact of technology, and ethics in technology (Barros-Bailey & Saunders, 2010). This assessment may help counselors understand the need for continued education for themselves and their clients. Many government and educational entities have basic computer literacy and competency criteria that cover knowledge areas such as keyboard, mouse, computer concepts, file management, Internet and security, and e-mail knowledge and use. The RC can use these criteria as a source in developing short questionnaires or interview questions to help determine the client's knowledge and competencies in the context of these regional and local standards.

ASSISTIVE TECHNOLOGY

What Is Assistive Technology?

The first legal mention of assistive technology devices or services is found in the Individuals with Disabilities Education Act (IDEA; 1990) often referred to as IDEA 1990. However, it is clear that as early as 1973, in the Rehabilitation Act of 1973 (Section 504), there was an understanding that the use of assistive technology should be considered for eligible individuals with disabilities. Several other laws related to disability and technology have recognized the need for the application of specific assistive technology devices and services for people with disabilities since that first effort.

Currently, the definition of **assistive technology** in common use comes to us from the IDEA of 2004. The definition has been refined over the years to mean:

> Any item, piece of equipment or product system, whether acquired commercially off the shelf, modified, or customized, that is used to increase, maintain, or improve the functional capabilities of children with disabilities. The term does not include a medical device that is surgically implanted, or the replacement of such device. (20 U.S.C. §1401(1)(a)(B))

Although the definition is widely accepted, it was developed specifically for an educational setting and so may have some limitations when considering the entire constellation of assistive technology devices and services used in the home or community. This definition also lacks specific examples of assistive technology. The definition found at the Assistive Technology Industry Association (ATIA) is much more comprehensive and includes clarity and examples of technologies: "Assistive technology helps people who have difficulty speaking, typing, writing, remembering, pointing, seeing, hearing, learning, walking, and many other things. People with different abilities require different assistive technologies" (Assistive Technology Industry Association [ATIA], 2017, para. 5). For examples of high, low, and other assistive technologies and an expanded definition, the reader is directed to the ATIA website (atia.org).

When considering this definition, it must be stressed that appropriate assistive devices will likely be different for each person. This observation will be true even if those individuals have the same disabilities, experience the same obstacles, and have the same presenting need for modification. Just as each of us has our own way of completing a task, so too the tools used to modify a task must fit the temperament, outlook, personality, desired degree of independence, and abilities of the individual who will be using the modification.

Who Provides Assistive Technology Services?

The individuals involved in the provision of assistive technology are considered to be from a multidisciplinary profession. The individual who will be using the technology is seen as the central team member. Typically, he or she is surrounded by a team of professionals with skills most related to the obstacle to be modified. Members of these teams should be changed as needed, but may include family doctors, speech–language pathologists, rehabilitation engineers, occupational therapists, physical therapists, RCs, regular and special education teachers, and even representatives from manufacturers of assistive technology devices. Many individuals who hold degrees in one of these professions have also received training in assistive technology. There are numerous programs based in universities internationally where interested students may participate in short certificate programs, and/or receive focused graduate training in assistive technology.

What Is the Process for Recommending Assistive Technology?

Before the process of identifying assistive technology devices can begin, the need for assistive technology must be identified. Sometimes this can be the most difficult part of the process. Many people do not understand technology and how it might be used to assist an individual in accomplishing a task. Here are some questions that may be considered to help identify the likelihood that technology may be of assistance:

- Has this individual had prior experience using technology?
- How comfortable is this person using technology?
- Can the individual accomplish the task that is presenting the obstacle if another person helps with parts of the task?
- Has this individual tried different ways to accomplish the task in question?

Once the need for assistive technology has been identified, the modification process may begin. An appropriate team should be identified and convened. This team should include all of the individuals who might have information regarding the modifications to be made. The pivotal member of the team should be the individual who will ultimately be using the accommodations identified. When considering modifications for this individual, consideration must be given to how this device or accommodation will fit within the context of the individual's entire life. In other words, when planning modifications for employment, the team must be careful not to ignore housing access needs, transportation requisites, and community access requirements.

Clearly defined goals describing the intended results should be created and agreed upon. Next, the abilities of the individual who will be using the modifications should be fully described across all activities of daily living and instrumental activities of daily living.

Care should be taken by all team members to identify an adaptation that is unique to that individual and best suited to his or her needs. The focus of the accommodation process should be on function, simplicity, and safety. It is important to anticipate that some modifications may achieve access but create new obstacles. The need for training, repair, maintenance, and function of the device or devices in the future should also be described. Consideration should be given, when appropriate, to how this device will function in all aspects of the individual's life, as well as any caregiver training requirements attendant to proper use of the device.

To achieve simplicity, the process of modification should be iterative in nature. The team begins by trying the simplest, least technological solution first. Next, more complex solutions may be explored using readily available consumer technologies. After that, modifications using technologies developed specifically for individuals with disabilities should be considered. Ultimately, the team may consider custom-built modifications if none of the previous examples suffice. Depending upon the complexity of the task or tasks to be modified, some combination of solutions may be utilized. The most exciting part about assistive technology is being able to move someone from having an obstacle in a major life area he or she formerly enjoyed to being able to accomplish that task, sometimes almost immediately.

The Three-Step Assessment Process

Barros-Bailey (2010) identified a three-step assessment process for the consideration of accommodation and the use of assistive technology in the workplace.

Step 1: Assess Work, Home, or Demands

RCs need to know what the demands of the work entail. That is, what are the physical, mental, and/or cognitive demands of work against which the individual's residual function could be mapped? The best tool to assess work demands is the **job analysis**, or **position analysis**, whereas a tool for home-based accommodation may contain information about household services or **instrumental activities of daily living**. Many job analysis formats use constructs derived from the *Revised Handbook for Analyzing Jobs* (U.S. Department of Labor [DOL], 1991b) that were the job rating standards upon which the *Dictionary of Occupational Titles* (*DOT*; U.S. DOL, 1991a) occupations were classified. However, these standards are often insufficient to measure the demands of work within the disability context, and do not contain constructs regarding the mental and cognitive demands of work (Occupational Information Development Advisory Panel [OIDAP], 2009, 2010). O*NET is the database developed by the U.S. Department of Labor in 1998 to replace the *DOT* (U.S. DOL, Employment and Training Administration, 2017). The database was developed for workforce development purposes, not for disability assessment. The *O*NET* does not use constructs, descriptors, scales, and measures to capture work demands that are well suited to map against human function, as is needed in working with people with disabilities (OIDAP, 2009, 2010). Therefore, *DOT* constructs such as those defining strength demands (e.g., sedentary, light, medium, heavy, and very heavy) continue to be used in many public and private disability systems until an alternative occupational information system is developed that could be more appropriately applied in disability assessment, such as what the U.S. Department of Labor, Bureau of Labor Statistics (BLS, 2017) is attempting to develop through the Occupational Requirements Survey.

Step 2: Evaluate Physical, Mental, and Cognitive Function

Evaluating the capacities of the individual is the part of the three-step analysis corresponding to that of the requirements of work, household, or other activities. This information is triangulated from a variety of different sources: the diagnostic vocational interview and the functional capacities information obtained from qualified professionals (e.g., rehabilitation audiology, neuroophthalmology, or orthopedics) using a variety of assessment tools (e.g., functional capacity evaluations, neuropsychological batteries, or audiology exams).

Step 3: Perform a Gap Analysis

A **gap analysis** involves assessing the difference between the requirements of work, home, or other activities and the person's physical, cognitive, or mental function. For example, if the client sustained a dominant arm amputation and is required to change a diaper for a toddler (either as an essential function of the job or home requirement as a single parent), a gap analysis would assess the difference between the requirements of the task and the function of the client to then determine what equipment, environment, technique, or other accommodation could best allow the task to be completed. Many assistive technology checklists provide ideas and resources to consider tailoring the assistive technology assessment vis-à-vis the needs of an individual. Care should be taken to understand if any attempts have already been made to accommodate activities in any setting and the outcomes of those attempts. Becoming familiar with these areas provides a rubric for RCs when interviewing a client, structuring an assessment, and developing a rehabilitation plan to meet the client's needs. Ultimately, the assessment of work, home, or other demands and of the individual's residual functions should be based on human function so that the terminology and constructs are more readily matched and an assessment of the gaps between the person's needs and work, home, recreational, or other activity are determined.

The development of a rehabilitation plan using appropriate assistive technology is best served by a common language. There are multiple resources available to clients, counselors, and the public to identify sources of assistive technology. The U.S. DOL's (2016a) Office of Disability Employment Policy provides the **Job Accommodations Network (JAN)** and access to free consultation, assessment tools, and a databank of resources, such as product lists organized by disability type. The **Searchable Online Accommodation Resource (SOAR;** U.S. DOL, 2016b) is a database that contains thousands of potential low and high technology solutions. Locally, assistive technology projects provide directed assessments and services, professional expertise, training, lending libraries, computer laboratories, and more to help identify the best interventions to include in the rehabilitation plan to facilitate access and inclusion of people with disabilities in the workplace. These federally funded programs by the Technology-Related Assistance for Individuals with Disabilities Act of 1988 (Public Law 100-407) provide local communities with free or low-cost access to technical specialists who could assist with the evaluation and accommodation alternatives to meet the needs of people with disabilities.

What Are Some Examples of Assistive Technology?

When thinking about assistive technology, it is often easier to consider it in terms of the functional obstacle rather than the name of a particular disability. Using this method, general categories of obstacles can be created, such as mobility, sensory, speech and language, hearing, or cognitively based obstacles. Although some individuals with disabilities may experience obstacles across more than one of these categories, other individuals may experience an obstacle in only one category. Some examples of assistive technology in each of these categories follow.

Mobility

Most people may have experience with this category. Examples of assistive technology used to reduce or eliminate mobility obstacles include a cane, a walker, and wheelchairs of various varieties, both manual and powered, as well as the control systems to operate them. These devices range in complexity from low to middle to high technology. An example of new high-tech technology just coming to market is the exoskeleton mobility system, which is a microprocessor-controlled system that the user straps onto his or her body to support the body in walking movements. A **prosthetic** is a constructed body part. Examples include cosmetic fingers, an ocular implant prosthesis that may fit over an ocular implant, or artificial limbs. The field of prosthetics is also making tremendous gains using similar kinds of technology and actuators that can detect minute muscle, nerve, and electromyography (EMG) activity.

Sensory

Many assistive devices can be used to address sensory obstacles. Eyeglasses may be the simplest and most common type of sensory aid. Hearing aids of various types may be the second most common. Beyond those two examples, a whole world of assistive technology exists that permits access to computers using speech output or Braille, small special purpose speech-output note takers, and FM listening systems for students or audience members with hearing. Systems that enlarge text either on a computer or from print may assist individuals who have low vision.

Speech and Language

A range of devices exist for improving the ability to communicate face-to-face. This type of device is often referred to as an **augmentative and alternative communication (AAC) device**. These devices can be as simple as a picture board with images representing important things the individual wants to communicate. More sophisticated versions may include a touch screen with pictures or symbols that may be touched in sequence to create new and unique sentences that are then spoken using synthesized speech. Apps are available for tablets that can convert a simple tablet into a very sophisticated communication device.

Cognitive

Some simple devices that can be used to address obstacles with cognition are pillboxes, where a week's worth of pills can be laid out and readily monitored to see if they have been taken. More complex applications are pillboxes with alarms. Also available are timers that not only remind the individual when it is time to take the pill, but also, with proper setup, presents the appropriate pill. Smartphones and tablets contain so much processing power that, if coupled with the appropriate applications, they can assist an individual to organize the day, help with memory problems, assist with meal preparation, and other aspects of daily living, as well as in the employment setting. These kinds of devices require very careful use and must be customized to suit the particular individual as closely as possible. Training in use of the device should stress the precautions to be taken regarding issues of safety.

ASSISTIVE TECHNOLOGY OF THE FUTURE

There are a number of technologies holding promise for the future that may have profound effects on the field of assistive technology. Self-driving vehicles may be the most dramatic of these developments. Once in common use, transportation for individuals who are blind or have low vision and others who are currently unable to drive a vehicle independently will suddenly have independent access to their communities. Three-dimensional printers are already changing many aspects of assistive technology especially in situations that require a one-of-a-kind device. For instance, prosthetists can rapidly develop and test new devices that otherwise might be too time-consuming and costly to produce. What once used to be costly and somewhat temperamental **environment control units** have become readily available consumer products now called **home automation**. Most commonly, these devices are voice controlled, but other methods of operation can be added. They are typically used to control all manner of devices in the home, such as lighting, heating and air conditioning, opening and closing drapes, and operating the television and other home entertainment systems.

Another area of promise is the use of apps, particularly with the use of the fast-growing acquisition of smartphones and tablets. We have seen a variety of apps being increasingly recommended in intervention plans in rehabilitation. In an attempt to bring some level of credibility and standardization to the value of these apps, the federal government in the United States has established guidelines and standards for such apps as they apply to medicine (Food and Drug Administration, 2015). The emergence, usefulness, and regulation of such apps will likely be an area for RCs to be aware of in the future.

DISTANCE EDUCATION AND REHABILITATION

The misconception that distance education is a new phenomenon brought on by high technology in the current generation is false. Indeed, the Distance Education Accrediting Commission (DEAC, 2016) was established in 1926 and accredits programs "from the secondary school level through professional doctoral degree-granting institutions" (para. 1). It was established about four decades after the University of Chicago developed the first-known correspondence program (Association for Educational Communications and Technology, 2016).

Distance education can take on a variety of formats beyond the correspondence education that started the field. Depending on the institution or the profession, courses could be open-schedule, fixed-time, modular, mostly at a distance with some level of intense short-term residency, or a variety of formats in between.

Distance education in rehabilitation counseling has been around for nearly a generation of students (Leech & Holcomb, 2004). Today, traditional and clinical rehabilitation counseling programs are like any other type of training available for many professions and vary in the delivery of their accredited curriculum through a variety of synchronous and asynchronous methods. Some programs are completely at a distance. Some programs are completely face-to-face. Some programs are a hybrid of the two points on the education continuum (Main & Dziekan, 2012).

Technology in general, and instructional performance technology in particular, has enhanced the ability of faculty to tailor instruction specific to the needs of each student's learning style. It has also presented the opportunity to expand practice settings for internship and practicum opportunities, monitoring, and supervision (Byrne & Hartley, 2010; Kampfe, Smith, & Manyibe, 2009; Lund & Schultz, 2015; Morissette, Bezyak, & Ososkie, 2012). Distance education also allows educators to test the efficacy of traditional counseling techniques that were once just taught in the classroom between traditional and distance education settings (Degiorgio, Moore, Kampfe, & Downey, 2011; Meyer, 2015).

Distance learning is not without its challenges. Access to some of the platforms may be particularly difficult for some people with disabilities, particularly those with sensory, cognitive, or learning disabilities (Ting-Feng, Ming-Chung, Yao-Ming, Hwa-Pey, & Chang, 2014) and **universal design** for learning should be considered to enhance knowledge acquisition for all learners. Whether the RC or the client is considering the use of distance counseling for professional development or a rehabilitation plan, careful consideration about the delivery system and supports for the individual should occur in the decision-making process, in addition to determining whether assistive technology or educational supports exist to build the bridge for effective learning.

CONCLUSION

Technology always has been part of the client–counselor relationship, whether when the first-known counselor Frank Parsons used quills and paper to collect data during an interview more than 100 years ago, or today using paper and pen(cil) or audio, video, or other digital means for face-to-face or distance sessions. Low and high technology media are important tools to support the building and maintenance of the relationship, and for the provision of services to our clients. Current and emerging low and high technologies should be a continued source of support and efficiency and not create barriers to any parts of the process.

This chapter examined technology use in the United States and internationally as it pertains to the general public and the digital divide for people with disabilities. The evolution of technology that facilitates synchronous and asynchronous communication, education, storage, and other functions has created a dynamic means through which people communicate and affect behavior. RCs and the programs educating these professionals need to integrate awareness and understanding of not only low and high, software and hardware, technologies into the curriculum, but also the behavior differences in the use of any technology. A variety of sources of technological assessment were discussed to help measure competencies of clients and counselors, and to help with the evaluation and planning of employment and training needs.

Literature regarding technology in rehabilitation counseling would be deficient if it did not include a discussion about assistive technology. Here, an introduction as to the range of content, methodologies, content, procedures, resources, and future advances provided the reader with preliminary understanding of this vital resource to the rehabilitation counseling process.

Finally, a brief history of distance education, its continuum, and application was added to this edition of the chapter. The efficacy of such a form of education and training was tempered by the advice to carefully consider convenience along with any other issues of access that may emerge.

The challenge of writing any chapter about technology is that as soon as the words hit the press, new forms of technology make some lexicon seem dated or make it obsolete. It is imperative that the reader focus on the essential concepts of technology use and misuse, assets and challenges, while constantly seeking information to enhance services to the client being served and to the profession.

CONTENT REVIEW QUESTIONS

- When using technology in the client–counselor relationship, why is awareness of how technology can affect the relationship important? What considerations and expected behaviors or boundaries should be set within the relationship so that technology can assist and not inhibit it?
- How can RCs assess technological competencies? Why is such assessment important? Where in the rehabilitation process can such assessment be most effective?
- Discuss how you would assess your own technological competencies. How would you find standards specific to your practice setting or location? Would the competency standards for clients be different from those for an RC?
- Identify a hypothetical case and outline an assistive technology plan to address the needs of the individual. How do you determine what might be the best assistive technology given the physical, mental, or cognitive functional abilities and the needs of the client?
- What resources exist to help professionals and client with assistive technology in your community? How can you empower clients to access assistive technology resources over their work lives or life spans when they are no longer receiving services from you?

REFERENCES

Anderson, M. (2015). Technology device ownership: 2015. Retrieved from http://www.pewinternet.org/2015/10/29/technology-device-ownership-2015

Assistive Technology Industry Association. (2017). What is AT? Retrieved from https://www.atia.org/at-resources/what-is-at

Association for Educational Communications and Technology. (2001). History of distance education. Retrieved from http://www.aect.org/edtech/ed1/13/13-02.html

Barros-Bailey, M. (2007). *Internet and computer ethics for public sector rehabilitation counselors: A mixed methods study* (Doctoral dissertation). Available from ProQuest Dissertations and Theses database. (UMI No. 3265569)

Barros-Bailey, M. (2010, October 15). *Assistive technology in the accommodations process.* Idaho Business Leadership Network 2010 Conference, Boise, ID.

Barros-Bailey, M., & Saunders, J. L. (2010). Ethics and the use of technology in rehabilitation counseling. *Rehabilitation Counseling Bulletin, 53*(4), 255–259.

Brasley, S. S. (2006, May). Building and using a tool to assess info and tech literacy. *Computers in Libraries,* 6–7, 44–48.

Byrne, A. M., & Hartley, M. T. (2010). Digital technology in the 21st century: Considerations for clinical supervision in rehabilitation education. *Rehabilitation Education, 24*(1–2), 57–68.

Caplan, S. E. (2002). Problematic Internet use and psychosocial well-being: Development of a theory-based cognitive-behavioral measurement instrument. *Computers in Human Behavior, 18,* 553–575.

Davis, R. A., Flett, G. L., & Besser, A. (2002). Validation of a new scale for measuring problematic Internet use: Implications for pre-employment screening. *CyberPsychology and Behavior, 5*(4), 331–345.

Degiorgio, L., Moore, S., Kampfe, C. M., & Downey, B. O. (2011). Teaching counseling skills using interactive television: Observations from a rehabilitation counseling classroom. *Journal of Applied Rehabilitation Counseling, 42*(3), 32–38.

Distance Education Accrediting Commission. (2016). *Welcome to DEAC.* Retrieved from http://www.deac.org

Federal Government Mobile Apps Directory. (2016). Retrieved from https://www.usa.gov/mobile-apps

Food and Drug Administration. (2015). Mobile medical applications: Guidance for industry and Food and Drug Administration staff. Retrieved from http://www.fda.gov/downloads/MedicalDevices/ . . . / UCM263366.pdf

Fox, S. (2011). Americans living with disability and their technology profile. Retrieved from http://www.pewinternet.org/2011/01/21/americans-living-with-disability-and-their-technology-profile

Goleman, D. (2007, February 20). Flame first, think later: New clues to e-mail misbehavior. *New York Times.* Retrieved from www.nytimes.com

H & H Publishing. (n.d.). *Technology and internet assessment.* Clearwater, FL: Author.

Hobbs, S. D. (2002). Measuring nurses' computer competency: An analysis of published instruments. *Computers, Informatics, Nursing, 20*(2), 63–73.

Individuals with Disabilities Education Act, 20 U.S.C. § 1400 (1990).

Jiang, W. W., Chan, W., & Chen, Y. C. (2004). Important computer competencies for the nursing professional. *Journal of Nursing Research, 12*(3), 213–225.

Kampfe, C. M., Smith, M. S., & Manyibe, E. O. (2009). Coping strategies used by distance rehabilitation counseling interns. *Rehabilitation Education, 23*(2), 77–86.

Leech, L. L., & Holcomb, J. M. (2004). Leveling the playing field: The development of a distance education program in rehabilitation counseling. *Assistive Technology, 16*(2), 135–143.

Lund, E. M., & Schultz, J. C. (2015). Distance supervision in rehabilitation counseling: Ethical and clinical considerations. *Rehabilitation Research, Policy, and Education, 29*(1), 88–95.

Main, D., & Dziekan, K. (2012). Distance education: Linking traditional classroom rehabilitation counseling students with their colleagues using hybrid learning models. *Rehabilitation Research, Policy, and Education, 26*(4), 315–320.

Meyer, J. M. (2015). Counseling self-efficacy: On-campus and distance education students. *Rehabilitation Counseling Bulletin, 58*(3), 165–172.

Morissette, S., Bezyak, J. L., & Ososkie, J. N. (2012). A closer look at distance-based supervisory relationships in master's level rehabilitation counseling programs. *Journal of Applied Rehabilitation Counseling, 43*(2), 3–7.

Occupational Information Development Advisory Panel. (2009). *Content model and classification recommendations for the Social Security occupational information system.* Baltimore, MD: Social Security Administration.

Occupational Information Development Advisory Panel. (2010). *OIDAP findings report: A review of the National Academy of Sciences report entitled a database for a changing economy: Review of the occupational information network (O*NET).* Baltimore, MD: Social Security Administration.

Pew Research Center. (2016). Mobile fact sheet. Retrieved from http://www.pewinternet.org/fact-sheet/mobile

Poushter, J. (2016). Smartphone ownership and Internet usage continues to climb in emerging economies but advanced economies still have higher rates of technology use. Retrieved from http://www.pewglobal.org/2016/02/22/smartphone-ownership-and-internet-usage-continues-to-climb-in-emerging-economies

Rehabilitation Act, 29 U.S.C. § 701 (1973).

Shea, V. (1994). Netiquette. *Albion.com.* Retrieved from http://www.albion.com/netiquette/book/index.html

Shechtman, N., & Horowitz, L. M. (2003). *Media inequality in conversation: How people behave differently when interacting with computers and people.* Conference on Human Factors in Computing Systems, Ft. Lauderdale, FL. Retrieved from https://www.sri.com/sites/default/files/publications/mediainequality.pdf

Suler, J. (2004). The online disinhibition effect. *CyberPsychology and Behavior, 7*(3), 321–326.

Technology-Related Assistance for Individuals with Disabilities Act, 29 U.S.C. 2201 (1988).

Ting-Feng, W., Ming-Chung, C., Yao-Ming, Y., Hwa-Pey, W., & Chang, S. C. H. (2014). Is digital divide an issue for students with learning disabilities? *Computers in Human Behavior, 39,* 112–117.

U.S. Department of Commerce, National Telecommunications and Information Administration. (2014). *Exploring the digital nation: Embracing the mobile Internet.* Washington, DC: Author. Retrieved from https://www.ntia.doc.gov/files/ntia/publications/exploring_the_digital_nation_embracing_the_mobile _internet_10162014.pdf

U.S. Department of Labor. (1991a). *Dictionary of occupational titles.* Washington, DC: Author.

U.S. Department of Labor. (1991b). *Revised handbook for analyzing jobs.* Washington, DC: Author.

U.S. Department of Labor. (2016a). Job accommodations network. Retrieved from https://askjan.org

U.S. Department of Labor. (2016b). Searchable online accommodations resource. Retrieved from https:// askjan.org/soar

U.S. Department of Labor, Bureau of Labor Statistics. (2017). Occupational requirements survey. Retrieved from http://www.bls.gov/ors

U.S. Department of Labor, Employment and Training Administration. (2017). Occupational information network (O*NET). Retrieved from https://www.onetonline.org

TWENTY-TWO

Rehabilitation Counselor Supervision

JAMES T. HERBERT

LEARNING OBJECTIVES

After reading this chapter, you should be able to:

- Provide an operational definition of clinical supervision.
- Examine initial considerations when seeking or providing clinical supervision.
- Describe a framework that exemplifies good clinical supervision and, in particular, one consistent with multicultural practice.

Recent narratives on the topic of rehabilitation counselor (RC) supervision have described (a) barriers to effective supervision, the transitional process from working as a counselor to becoming a supervisor, and a developmental model when providing supervision to a diverse workforce (Herbert & Caldwell, 2015); (b) evidence-based information to inform effective practice and multicultural aspects when providing group supervision (Herbert, 2016a); and (c) supervision behaviors characteristic of effective, ineffective, and possibly harmful supervision (Herbert, 2016b). Using this material as well as additional resources as a foundation for this chapter, this narrative provides readers with an overview of important considerations when seeking and providing clinical supervision consistent with accepted ethical and professional standards within rehabilitation counseling.

Before describing a framework of clinical supervision, it is important to clarify this term, as it supports a rationale for training methods used in RC supervision practice. **Clinical supervision** is an evaluative process characterized by a supportive relationship that is developmental in nature in which supervisors use consultant, counselor, and teacher roles to develop and enhance counselor skills and case management decisions. This process may involve individual, **triadic** (supervision of another supervisor who is supervising the counselor), and group supervision formats that involve **direct** (e.g., observing client–counselor interactions in the field) or **indirect methods** (e.g., conducting discussions of specific clients and their rehabilitation needs). As part of the clinical supervision process, RC supervisors demonstrate appropriate ethical practices to promote counselor awareness, knowledge, and skills directed toward achieving successful rehabilitation outcomes. Although the term *clinical supervision* may conjure associations with pathology that are often used in medical training models, in actual practice, it is applied synonymously with the term *counselor supervision*, which has been used historically in various human service and counseling professions (Herbert, 2012). Clinical supervision complements another and perhaps the more commonly cited form of administrative supervision, which is designed to maintain organizational policies and procedures that rehabilitation personnel must follow to monitor quality and timeliness of services as well as ensure that funding to support services is being used appropriately (Herbert & Trusty, 2006). Thus, within clinical supervision, there are administrative components that basically attend to the mechanics of how supervision is provided and monitored when providing rehabilitation counseling and related services.

STATUS OF CLINICAL SUPERVISION IN REHABILITATION COUNSELING PRACTICE

Although clinical supervision is a process that occurs as a part of graduate training, here we focus more on postgraduate supervision practices, as coverage of this area has been noticeably lacking within the literature. Supervision standards pertaining to preprofessional training as part of practicum and internship can be found in those approved by the Council on Rehabilitation Education (CORE, 2010; see Section D) and the Council for Accreditation of Counseling and Related Educational Programs (CACREP, 2016; see Section 3). It should be noted that although these standards provide parameters regarding supervision, they are largely geared toward administrative aspects (e.g., number of clinical hours required in practicum and internship, frequency and format of supervision, and qualifications needed to supervise). In fact, these standards have very little to say on the nature of clinical supervision and offer limited guidance on what constitutes best practice.

In considering the preparation needed to procure and provide effective clinical supervision, as it applies to state-federal vocational rehabilitation (VR) programs and proprietary rehabilitation systems, it is something that seems largely ignored and misunderstood. Data from studies that have investigated clinical supervision practice indicate that the time devoted to individual supervision ranges between 20 minutes per month to 45 minutes per week; and, as far as group supervision, most counselors and supervisors indicate that it is rarely used (see Herbert, 2004a; King, 2008; Schultz, Ososkie, Fried, Nelson, & Bardos, 2002). More recently, a study by Landon (2016) examined clinical supervision practices from a broader national sample of certified rehabilitation counselors (CRCs) who worked in private for-profit and private not-for-profit service settings. They found that in terms of frequency and duration, supervisors reported providing individual supervision about four times per month, with each session lasting nearly 50 minutes. As far as group supervision, these biweekly sessions lasted almost an hour for each session. Interestingly, counselors reported that clinical supervision occurred less frequently and with less duration for both individual and group supervision formats. Counselors also reported that individual supervision occurred about 2.5 times each month, lasting an average of 30 minutes per session, whereas group supervision occurred about 1.43 times per month lasting 30 minutes per session. In addition, more than half of counselors reported never meeting at all for group supervision, supporting a similar observation found in earlier studies (e.g., Herbert & Trusty, 2006; Schultz et al., 2002). However, Landon noted that a subset of counselors and supervisors who worked in the proprietary sector were, by the nature of their work, more likely to be independent. For this reason, they are less likely to have opportunities for either individual or group supervision. Furthermore, it is also important to note that differences reported by counselors and supervisors were from independent samples and not from the same counselor–supervisor dyad. Finally, when looking at perceptions of clinical supervision satisfaction, the Landon study corroborated an earlier finding noted in the Herbert and Trusty study that despite the limited frequency of clinical supervision, counselors and supervisors (particularly those in the private not-for-profit sector) still remain "slightly satisfied" with how clinical supervision occurs.

As a comparable benchmark, the effort devoted to clinical supervision across rehabilitation settings seems less than what is espoused in psychological treatment settings where the minimum guideline is 60 minutes per week (individual or group supervision; Ellis et al., 2014). The investment difference in supervision between rehabilitation counseling and psychological settings may be attributable to the centrality of how counseling comprises one's professional identity. Nonetheless, on the basis of nearly 60 years of research that has examined professional roles and functions, it is clear that RCs continue to perceive this task as a central part of their professional work (e.g., Jacques, 1959; Leahy, Chan, & Saunders, 2003; Leahy, Chan, Sung, & Kim, 2013; Muthard & Salamone, 1969). It would follow, then, that providing ongoing supervision as part of promoting counselor skill development constitutes an important activity among rehabilitation professionals, and is something they believe they are adequately prepared to perform. In terms of CRC knowledge of theories and techniques of clinical supervision, the survey by Leahy et al. (2013) suggested this belief is the case. With regard to the frequency with which clinical supervision is provided and in what formats, the Leahy et al. study only addressed supervising "new counselors and/or practicum or internship students in rehabilitation counseling activities" (p. 204). As such, respondents indicated that this job function was something performed "very infrequently." Thus, our understanding of the frequency of providing or receiving clinical supervision remains unknown, outside of counselors-in-training completing university programs. Related to the frequency of clinical supervision, an interested finding was noted in the study by Herbert and Trusty (2006), which showed that among state vocational RCs from one state, counselors with 2 or more years experience reported greater satisfaction with clinical supervision when *fewer* supervisory sessions were provided. If this finding generalizes to other states and other practice settings, it suggests that clinical supervision is something that experienced counselors do not perceive as relevant to their continued development as professional counselors. Taken collectively, it seems paradoxical that RCs are required to provide competent and ethical services; but as a professional group, they are largely unchecked by people responsible for supervising them (Herbert, 2016a). For this reason, counselors seeking clinical supervision need to take an active role in selecting an appropriate supervisor and how services are provided. Also, as a parallel, supervisors should evaluate their own competence in order to ensure that supervision is consistent with evidence-based practice.

USING THE PROFESSIONAL ETHICAL CODE AS A FRAMEWORK FOR CLINICAL SUPERVISION

One of the most important considerations that counselors and supervisors address pertains to the basic understanding that supervision is provided in an ethical manner consistent with accepted standards of practice (American Counseling Association [ACA], 2014). Within the field of rehabilitation counseling, these standards are described in Section H within the recently revised *Code of Professional Ethics for Rehabilitation Counselors* (Commission on Rehabilitation Counselor Certification [CRCC], 2016; herein referred to as the Code). Within this general section, there are eight subsections, each attending to some aspect of supervision, training, and teaching; of these, four subsections address a specific component of clinical supervision: H.1. Clinical Supervisor Responsibilities, H.2

Clinical Supervisor Competence, H.3 Roles and Relationships Between Clinical Supervisor and Supervisees, and H.4 Supervision Evaluation, Remediation, and Endorsement. Although these standards offer a sound guideline in preparing for supervision, they are not always presented in a format that may be easily interpreted as it applies directly to clinical supervision in helping professionals identify behavioral indicators of good practice. With this consideration in mind, each of the applicable standards is examined from counselor and supervisor perspectives that may help clarify what is meant by "good supervision." In this process, they help establish certain benchmarks that counselors may consider when seeking clinical supervision.

CREATING THE PROPER ATMOSPHERE

Clinical supervision involves an evaluation process, which, by its nature, means that an unequal partnership exists, with the supervisor usually having greater power. As a result, it can introduce anxiety, defensiveness, and tension for the supervisee. In order to minimize the impact of this dynamic, Bernard and Goodyear (2009) recommended that supervisors acknowledge this process during supervision. In the process of supervisee evaluation, supervisors should (a) recognize when conflict arises and be able to effectively address it within supervision, (b) provide continual and consistent feedback, (c) avoid making premature evaluations without sufficient information, (d) invite and receive supervisee feedback, and (e) understand that everything that happens within supervision is a function of the working alliance between counselors and supervisors; if this relationship is weak, then the supervisee is less likely to disclose mistakes. An **effective working alliance** is characterized by a mutual agreement of proposed goals, the extent of and clarity about the identified goals, and the level of trust or bond that exists between individuals (Bordin, 1983). The importance of having a solid working alliance between counselors and supervisors is paramount because it affects both whether counselors feel supported and their willingness to examine the intra- and interpersonal dynamics that exist not only between clients and counselors but between counselors and supervisors as well. In addition, there is evidence that this working alliance can affect VR outcome for clients assigned to newer counselors who participate in clinical supervision (McCarthy, 2013).

Ensuring Client Welfare

Perhaps it comes as no surprise that as applied to Standard H, client welfare is the first standard articulated in the Code, given the fact that above all else, it represents the principal concern of the supervisor; in fact, it constitutes a legal responsibility of supervisors who share in the responsibility for maintaining client welfare (Herbert, 2004b). As part of ensuring client welfare, supervisors have an obligation to monitor services provided by RCs through regular communication that involves a review of their work in meeting the needs of a diverse clientele (Standard H.1.a.). As part of ensuring client welfare, supervisees should communicate to their clients information about their supervisors' qualifications (Standard H.1.b). Although not specified in the new Code, information about the supervisor's education, training, and competence in the area(s) for which the client is seeking service might be discussed during the initial session. Furthermore, in order to provide additional protection of client rights and promote informed consent, supervisors must make supervisees aware of applicable policies and procedures in place to protect client rights, including those pertaining to privacy and confidentiality (Standard

H.1.c.). Goodwin (2016) provided an excellent example of a professional disclosure statement that could be used in counseling practice that readers may want to review; as applicable to supervision, it noted: "Periodically, I may seek consultation from a professional colleague to better serve my clients. I keep my clients' identity anonymous and share information on a need-to-know basis" (p. 72). Depending on individual circumstances, counselors may also wish to disclose to the client the name of the supervisor, what and how information is being disclosed (e.g., written case notes and related client reports, digital recordings of counseling sessions), and mechanisms and procedures used to ensure client confidentiality (e.g., password-protected access to any electronic file, written documents secured in a locked file cabinet). In instances where the client may not have capacity of being fully informed including any ramifications of allowing or not allowing consent (e.g., minors, court-mandated referrals, people with severe cognitive disabilities), as Goodwin noted, the counselor is obligated to secure written consent from the appropriate legal guardian before any services are given.

Developing and Maintaining Supervisor Competence

There are two aspects within the Code that address supervision competence. The first aspect ensures that supervisors participate in ongoing training to enhance their own skills (Standard H.2.a), whereas the second aspect, which is addressed in more detail in this chapter, specifically focuses on cultural diversity competence as it applies to the delivery of supervision services and counselor development (Standard H.2.b). Embedded in both standards is the idea that maintaining the CRC credential is insufficient if it is not accompanied by ongoing continual education to further develop competence in specific practice areas and consistent with existing state licensure requirements, if applicable. Clearly, professional counselors must maintain whatever credentials are needed for licensure and/or certification within their scope of practice (Tarvydas, Hartley, & Gerald, 2016). For example, in 1998, the National Board for Certified Counselors (NBCC) and the Association for Counselor Education and Supervision (ACES) established an approved clinical supervisor designation (NBCC, 1998), which is now under the auspices of the Center for Credentialing and Education (CCE, 2016). A similar credential as a certified clinical supervisor is available through the International Certification & Reciprocity Consortium (IC & RC) for supervisors who work in the addiction and prevention field (IC & RC, 2016). Interestingly, at one time the CRCC offered a credential RC-clinical supervisor designation (CRCC, 1999). There was insufficient professional interest to continue offering this credential and, in a few years, it was discontinued. On the basis of studies that have inquired about professional credentials of RC supervisors (e.g., Herbert & Trusty, 2006; Landon, 2016), it seems that few supervisors within rehabilitation counseling practice have any type of specialized certification in supervision. Although these credentials may provide one indication of competence in providing clinical supervision, as noted earlier, the professional ethics code for RCs provides a context in establishing criteria when contracting for supervision services. For those who receive internal supervision as part of their place of employment, these criteria may also help inform best practices. Using the Code as context and general guideline, counselors may wish to consider the following questions:

- Does the supervisor have the necessary experience and training and participated in ongoing continued education to address clinical concerns, counseling and case management skills as it applies to professional areas needing improvement or further development? (Standard H.2.a)

- Does the supervisor possess awareness, knowledge and skills needed to promote cultural diversity within the supervisory relationship and, by extension, help supervisees in their development to become a multiculturally competent RC? (Standard H.2.b)
- Whenever technology is used in supervision, how will the supervisor ensure that confidentiality is maintained when using electronic transmissions? (Standard H.2.c)

Given the complexity of the clinical supervisor relationship, the Code outlines a number of interpersonal boundary concerns that can sometimes emerge. Primarily, as has been noted in the literature (e.g., Schultz et al., 2002), there is an inherent power differential that exists between supervisors and supervisees and, as a result, supervisors must make every effort to minimize any harm to supervisees (Standard H.3.a). Extreme cases where this may occur are those that are sexual or romantic (Standard H.3.b) or exploitative in nature, where a supervisor may have authority or control (Standard H.3.c), or those that promote sexual harassment (Standard H.3.d). As it applies to former supervisees or trainees, supervisors recognize the power differential that exists within the clinical supervision relationship. In such cases, it is incumbent on the supervisor to talk openly about potential risks when considering any "romantic, sexual or other intimate relationships" (Standard H.3.e). Finally, supervisors have an ethical responsibility to avoid situations where they may be supervising close relatives, romantic partners, or friends and, should these instances be unavoidable, then they must use a formal review mechanism (Standard H.3.f).

Evaluating and Endorsing Supervisees

Inherent in the definition provided in this chapter is the recognition that clinical supervision, by its very nature, involves an evaluation process of supervisee competence and, in recognition of this process, the important role supervisors play to ensure that services are provided by competent personnel. Recognizing that client welfare represents the most important function of a clinical supervisor, in order to make certain that supervisees are competent, ongoing assessment and feedback by their supervisors are needed (Standard H.4.a). As they pertain to the assessment process, RCs and supervisors may wish to consider:

- What criteria will be used to evaluate counselor competence? How often and what methods will be used as part of the assessment (case review, live observation, digital recording of prior counseling sessions; Standard H.4.a)? Will this information be shared with anyone else besides the counselor being supervised? The Code stipulates that rehabilitation counselor supervisors document and provide supervisees with "ongoing feedback regarding their performance." Unfortunately, there are no guidelines as to what constitutes "ongoing performance appraisal." As we have read, surveys have examined the frequency of individual supervision and its duration and found a wide range of practices (Herbert & Trusty, 2006; Schultz et al., 2002). These studies indicated that within the state-federal VR program as well as other private not-for-profit and private for-profit settings (Landon, 2016), the average time devoted to an individual supervision session is about 45 minutes. Interestingly, self-reports of duration and frequency of individual supervision in these studies reveal that supervisors report duration and frequency as longer and more often than what counselors report. Given the large caseloads assigned to counselors of approximately 100 or more clients (e.g., Cumming-McCann & Accordino, 2005; McCarthy, 2013), one could question the effectiveness of individual clinical supervision. One solution may be to implement group supervision, but this approach is almost nonexistent within the state VR program (Herbert & Trusty, 2006; Schultz et al., 2002). In contrast, within other private not-for-profit and private for-profit settings, group supervision occurs biweekly, lasting about 1 hour each time on average (Landon, 2016). It also seems clear that if clinical supervision occurs, it is something generated more often by the counselor rather than something that is supervisor initiated (e.g., Herbert & Trusty, 2006; Landon, 2016; Schultz et al., 2002). In terms of focus, there is a tendency to structure supervision along more administrative rather than clinical lines (McCarthy, 2013).

- Is there a written agreement that describes individual supervision goals, what will occur during supervision, methods used to assess and address counselor competence, and an explanation of due process should any disputes arise as part of supervision? As noted by Schultz et al. (2002), **supervision contracts** contribute to an effective working relationship because they clarify expectations and goals, and establish parameters with in which responsibilities are outlined and negotiated. Despite this benefit, the research of Schultz et al. on state VR counselors from two states indicates that only one in three counselors reported using them. Using a larger sample, McCarthy (2013) found that only 15% of rehabilitation counselors from five state VR programs used supervisory contracts. It was also reported that counselors who had a supervision contract and regular contact with their supervisors were more likely to have a stronger working alliance.

- In the event that the supervisor becomes unavailable to provide supervision due to temporary absences or emergencies, are there policies and procedures in place for backup supervision should the counselor require it? (Standard H.1.e)

- In the event that supervision disputes arise and cannot be resolved satisfactorily, will the supervisee receive adequate notice that supervision will be terminated and, where possible, the current supervisor will make provisions for referral to another supervisor? (Standard H.1.f)

- Should the supervisor determine that the counselor is not qualified to perform job duties expected as part of professional service, what measures (remedial assistance, referral to another consultant, dismissal) will be taken to address deficiencies (Standard H.4.b)? Furthermore, if the supervisee is a counselor-in-training and there is a recommendation that this person be dismissed from the training program or supervision setting, this standard requires that efforts to seek consultation and outline options available to supervisees be pursued. Although the Code does not provide any suggestions as to what a supervisee should do in these situations, as a general strategy, consultation with another supervisor of equal status may be prudent, particularly if there is fear that retribution may occur (Herbert, 2004b).

- If one of the remediation strategies for the counselor is to participate in counseling for herself or himself, in order to avoid any dual relationship issues, does the supervisor have other referral contacts to assist the counselor? (Standard H.4.c)

- At the successful completion of supervision, will the supervisor provide verbal and/or written endorsement of the counselor as it relates to competency areas required of academic completion training, certification, employment, or licensure? (Standard H.4.d)

- Conversely, in the event the supervisor determines that the counselor is **impaired** (i.e., at one time the counselor demonstrated the required skill set but, at present, does so in a reduced capacity; see Muratori, 2001), will the supervisor refrain from any endorsement? (Standard H.4.d)

Implementing Multicultural Aspects in Supervision

As noted earlier, in addition to requiring that supervisors be sufficiently prepared when providing clinical supervision, the Code draws particular attention to supervisors having awareness and ability of how cultural diversity impacts the supervisory relationship (Standard H.2.b). Although studies are limited, in terms of multicultural awareness, knowledge, relationship, and skills, an earlier study by Matrone and Leahy (2005) found that multicultural awareness was the area where RCs demonstrated the least competence. As used in this study, the term **awareness** refers to a person's life experiences, sensitivity, responsiveness, and enjoyment of multicultural aspects. According to the authors, their findings suggested that counselors should be more introspective and reflective through self-evaluation and monitoring. Racial attitudes as well as other demographics impact self-perception of multicultural counseling competence among RCs (Cumming-McCann & Accordino, 2005). Because improved multicultural counseling competence constitutes a perceived training need (Beveridge, Karpen, Chan, & Penrod, 2016), it also is an important area to explore as part of clinical supervision.

Even though professional codes such as those within rehabilitation counseling espouse the importance of being multiculturally competent, one of the challenges confronting our profession is that specific competencies have not been validated and, as noted in the counseling and psychology field, it constitutes a neglected area of study (Falender, Burnes, & Ellis, 2013). Within the clinical supervision process, discussion of cross-cultural issues between counselors and supervisors is a dynamic that often induces anxiety (Burkard, Knox, Hess, & Schultz, 2009). In these situations, even the manner in which cross-cultural discussions occur is different when the supervisor is someone who is White v. non-White. For example, an analysis of structured interview comments of psychology supervisors from varying races/ethnicities found that cultural differences within the supervisory dyad influence how supervision feedback is provided. For example, European American supervisors were more likely to discuss cross-cultural issues through questioning of specific counseling skills, including active listening, restatements, questions, and reflection of feelings. In contrast, supervisors of color were more likely to address these issues in terms of cultural insensitivity. However, both supervisory groups expressed concerns about imposing their cultural worldviews on those of their supervisees and how that may be appropriate or inappropriate for practice (see Mintz & Bieschke, 2009).

The success of introducing and addressing multicultural aspects among client, counselor, and supervisor viewpoints seems largely predicated on the working alliance that exists in each of these dyads. Several studies and summaries found in the counseling literature have examined desired supervisory behaviors (e.g., Herbert & Caldwell, 2015; Ladany, Mori, & Mehr, 2013; McCarthy, 2013; Schultz et al., 2002). Findings from these studies suggested that effective supervisory alliances are those where clinical supervisors demonstrate (a) sensitivity to individual learning needs, (b) commitment to professional development through regular ongoing contact, (c) knowledge of counselor performance that includes direct observation of counselor skills, (d) listening skills that offer constructive and specific feedback, (e) appropriate use of self-disclosure and humor, and (f) willingness to explore alternative views when problems arise. Perhaps not surprisingly, many of these attributes are the same ones associated with promoting cross-cultural discussions in supervision. For example, Wong, Wong, and Ishiyama (2013) asked 25 graduate-level psychology students what they perceived as being helpful or to hinder cross-cultural supervision. The major themes of helpful indicators were those associated with the supervisor perceived as accepting, encouraging, and supportive; who provided clear, constructive, and timely feedback within a safe and trusting environment; and facilitated appropriate risk taking in order to grow professionally. Conversely, supervisors perceived as having less sensitivity to cross-cultural incidents were those viewed as being too controlling, insulting, intimidating, or judgmental; not providing adequate feedback or creating a trusting environment; or responding in an irresponsible, unprofessional, or unethical manner. In terms of specific cross-cultural incidents, positive aspects included supervisors having cross-cultural competence and, in certain training settings, counselors with minority status were viewed as an asset as it was believed that "they could better meet the needs of minority clients" (p. 76). Negative incidents included supervisors who lacked multicultural competence and, in particular, encountered difficulty in working with a visible ethnic minority. In these instances, supervision problems were associated with language and cultural barriers or the occurrence of stereotyping.

One of the unique aspects about supervision as it applies particularly to examining multicultural aspects is that given the unequal status that exists between counselors or trainees and supervisors, it is incumbent upon supervisors to initiate such discussions. For counselors with less developed awareness regarding multicultural issues, these initial discussions are likely to promote defensiveness and avoidance when attempting to explore this topic (Wilcoxon, Norem, & Magnuson, 2005). As a general strategy in promoting discussion of multicultural issues, Hays (2008) recommended that counselors ask questions regarding: (a) how they came to their understanding of people who are different from themselves, (b) how they know these differences are true, (c) whether there alternative explanations or opinions that might be equally valid in explaining differences, and (d) how perceptions about a client might be influenced by the counselor's age, generational experiences, ethnic background, and socioeconomic status. Engaging in these inquiries may allow counselors and supervisors to better understand each other and what they think they know about themselves and people who are different.

Further Examination of the Clinical Supervision Process

The guidelines described in the Code provide a context for providing effective and ethical supervision, but in an effort to provide additional pragmatic suggestions, we are going to examine other strategies that can be used as part of clinical supervision practice. These suggestions are consistent with research summaries that describe effective clinical supervisor behavior found in both the general counselor supervision (e.g., Ladany et al., 2013) and the RC literature (e.g., Herbert, 2016a). Early in the process, procedural or administrative aspects should be explored and agreed upon by the counselor and supervisor, in a way that results in a written agreement to which both parties have agreed. The first session that occurs after this activity is particularly important because it "sets the stage" for how this process unfolds.

Getting to Know the Supervisee

One of the first tasks in supervision is to ascertain what the counselor or supervisee wants to get accomplished as a result of supervision. It may be that the supervisee wants to know more about a specific counseling model, technique, or different way to conceptualize a counseling problem or specific clinical situation. In these situations, some type of assessment is usually required that involves either using an informal or standardized assessment of counselor skills. The Comprehensive Counseling Skills Rubric by Flynn and Hays (2015) is an example of a standardized assessment that can be applied across settings and counseling orientations. Comprised of five domains, this rubric assesses the supervisee's invitational skills (e.g., nonverbal communication, encouragers, use of silence), attending skills (e.g., goal setting and open-/closed-ended questioning, paraphrasing, summarizing), and influencing skills (e.g., advocacy, immediacy, reframing), as well as competencies required in different counseling phases (opening, working, and closing phase) and aspects of the counseling relationship (intake, assessment, and termination). Having the supervisee complete this assessment or other similar instrument at the beginning of supervision not only serves as an indication of where the counselor perceives relative strengths and areas needing further development, but also serves as a benchmark for subsequent evaluation to assess the impact of supervision. It may be that in later evaluations, both counselors and supervisors may wish to complete the assessment independently and then discuss areas where there are differences in appraisals with regard to specific items on the assessment instrument used. Although this rubric is particularly designed to assess the competence of counselors-in-training, the authors recommended that additional measures be supplemented in the event supervisors wish to assess related situational concerns such as multicultural competence or ethical decision making. A useful review of 40 other self-report inventories can be found in a review by Tate, Bloom, Tassara, and Caperton (2014). There is a good availability of formal assessment methods to assess counselor skill competence. However, it is interesting to note that in terms of actual employment settings, their use is almost nonexistent (Herbert, 2004a). It may be that RC supervisors simply see no need to conduct any formalized assessment approach and instead prefer more informal methods of determining counselor competence. A description of assessment procedures and what questions are used to assess counseling skill competence seems to be absent from the rehabilitation counseling literature. As a general framework based on the author's own work, some useful questions might include:

- What experiences have you had as far as clinical supervision? If you received supervision, what did you gain from this experience? As a result of supervision, what aspects of yourself have grown most as a counselor? Where do you think you need to grow?
- What counseling theory or theories do you use in practice? What is it about those theories that make sense to you? Are there aspects of these theories when implementing them that are challenging for you? Are there other approaches that you have considered and want to learn more about?
- What types of supervision methods have you used in the past (e.g., case review method, live supervision, digital recording reviews)? Are there some methods that you prefer more than others?
- If I were to talk with a sample of clients with whom you have worked during the past year, what would they tell me about your strengths as a counselor and what would they say are areas that you need to continue to work on?

Additionally, it is important to examine counseling theory at the beginning and throughout supervision. It is this author's belief that although discussion about counseling approaches is an important aspect of preprofessional training, it is seems largely ignored once students start to work as professional RCs. This lack of attention is perplexing, as existing accreditation standards provide ample emphasis on where programs must demonstrate how their curricula address counseling approaches and principles, group work, and family dynamics (Standard C) and provide clinical experiences as part of supervised practica and internships (Standard D; CORE, 2010). However, once graduated, examination of counseling theory seems largely forgotten as part of supervision discourse. The basis of this belief comes as a result of doing numerous training sessions for the past 30 years on the topic of clinical supervision when audience members are asked questions such as: "What counseling theory do you subscribe to as a counselor?," "How did this theory change (or not) throughout your professional work as a rehabilitation counselor?," "How does the way you work with clients complement your current counseling theory beliefs?" and, in terms of supervision, "How do your supervision methods and style complement your counseling theory?" When answering these questions, audience members often indicate something to the effect that while "all of that counseling theory stuff was important in graduate school but in the 'real world,' we do not really spend too much time talking about counseling theory." This reaction is not only unfortunate but also misguided. It is reminiscent of a quote attributed to Kurt Lewin, a noted social psychologist, who indicated: "There is nothing so practical as a good theory" (Cherry, 2016). This statement is not only very insightful, but also reminds us that the beliefs that we have regarding how to improve the quality of life (QOL) for people with disabilities largely depend on our individual theoretical orientation on how to help people. Our theoretical perspective helps inform our ideas about the reasons clients are coming for help through guiding the answers to such questions as: How do we interact with clients; what assessments are used to determine the nature of a problem; what tools are available to address these problems, and on what system level (personal, couples, family, societal) can we can work that addresses the reasons clients are coming for help. Stated succinctly, examining counseling theory helps each of us answer the question: "What I am doing and why am I doing it?" For this reason, supervision has to operate from this understanding in order to make the process sensible to the counselor and the supervisor.

Before leaving the topic of theory, although many counselors and supervisors have some understanding of specific counseling theories, there are also specific supervision theories. They include those that are person centered (e.g., cognitive behavioral), developmental (e.g., stage models such as the Integrated Developmental Model), or focus on social role (e.g., Discrimination Model) as ways of viewing the supervision process. Having some understanding of these theories is considered a topic of "moderate importance" as reported by CRCs in a study (Thielsen & Leahy, 2001). At the same time, even though the empirical evidence to support these theories is lacking, the theories provide a structure and a language for supervisees and supervisors to work together and build a solid working relationship (Ellis, 2010). Given the limits and focus of this chapter, interested readers may wish to review supervision theories and models as presented by Bernard and Goodyear (2009) to gain a broader understanding.

Checking In With the Supervisee

Before exploring new material at the start of a supervision session, time should be devoted to processing what transpired in the prior supervision session to solicit any further reactions or thoughts. Supervisees might be asked questions such as:

- "Tell me one thing that you took away from supervision the last time we met."
- "Was there anything that happened last week that was troubling for you?" [and in a similar manner,] "Was there anything that was reaffirming or perhaps provided insight for you?"

- "Now that you have had time to think about our last session, was there anything that we did not discuss that you wanted to start with today?"

These inquiries not only address residual aspects from the prior session but, in many cases, also serve as a continuing or transitional point that could be addressed in the current session. Similarly, prior to the end of the supervision session, time should be set aside to review what occurred during the current supervision session and whether there was anything not discussed that should be reviewed in the subsequent session. For example, questions such as, "Is there anything that we have not addressed in this session that you want to bring up for our next session?" or "Could you describe in a few sentences what you take away from today's session?" These kinds of inquiries provide the supervisor with some understanding of how supervision was received and, if needed, to make any adjustments for the next supervision session. Most importantly, questions that not only focus on the content of the session but also the process of what occurred should be a part of every supervision session. Ultimately, the most important question is: "Was the supervisee heard?" As noted in this chapter, the relationship between supervisors and counselors often determines whether clinical supervision results in an effective learning experience. Without this foundation in place, it is highly doubtful that professional growth is likely to occur.

Reviewing Client–Counselor Interactions

Supervisors have several options to review client–counselor interactions. They may use delayed methods that are either direct (watching digital recording of an earlier session) or indirect (conducting a case review discussion) or live methods that are also either direct (participating as a cocounselor) or indirect (observing a counseling session via a two-way mirror; see Herbert, 2004c). Each of these methods has inherent advantages and disadvantages that should be taken into consideration as part of how clinical supervision is provided. Of course, the advantage of using digital recordings is that supervisors have the opportunity to observe counseling session interactions and can form their own opinions about the session. However, unless live cosupervision is used, whereby the supervisor and counselor are both present in the counseling session with the client, reviewing previously recorded material may not offer the benefit of providing timely feedback. Although the benefit of live supervision allows the supervisor to model specific behaviors for the counselor, it requires careful preparation with the counselor and client. As a general strategy, Campbell (2006) suggested that supervisors explain why their presence is required and what their role will be during the session, and place themselves in such a way that is the least physically distracting to both client and counselor. It is also important that supervisors not simply inform clients as to what will happen, but also obtain their permission allowing the supervisor to observe or, if needed, participate directly in the session. Some initial time should be allowed for processing this request, and it must be built into the session as well. For these reasons, many supervisors prefer using case method analysis when providing supervision. In this instance, the counselor provides relevant background information about the client as well as counselor impressions, presenting questions and reasons for seeking consultation. Although this method has the advantage of requiring very little preparation time, the major drawback is that information presented is viewed only from the counselor's perspective. Thus, the opportunity for the supervisor to form an independent evaluation is not available.

It is important to engage supervisees to better understand their thoughts and perceptions during the counseling process, whether supervisees are asked to review digital recordings of client–counselor counseling interactions or recount specific situations using a case review method. One method often used in clinical supervision is **interpersonal process recall** (IPR), developed by Kagan (1980). IPR involves having supervisees review audio/video-recorded material of client–counselor interactions with the supervisor and then being asked to describe feelings, thoughts, and reactions that occurred during this interaction. By doing so, supervisees become more sensitive to and aware of their own internal processes during counseling sessions. Because of recency effects, it is suggested that IPR interviews occur within 48 hours of the recorded session and when doing so, that the supervisor focus on process and not the content of the session (Larsen, Flesaker, & Stege, 2008). Examples of process questions that a supervisor might ask are: "When the client was telling you this story, how did it impact you?" "What was it like being in the room with the client at that point?" "You remained silent during these last several minutes in the session—what was going on with you?" "How would you complete this sentence: My client reminds me of _____." "If you could replay the last segment that we listened to, what would you have liked to have done differently?" or "If you had to paint a picture of your relationship with the client at this point, what would it look like?" There are any numbers of questions that can be directed to the supervisee. As these examples (it is hoped) demonstrate, they are intended to elicit internal reactions so that the relevance of these reactions can be explored in supervision.

The manner in which supervision material is explored and specifically how feedback is provided has to be considered within the context of the unique relationship between the counselor and the supervisor. Chief among these considerations is the counselor's developmental level. For example, as a general guideline when working with novice counselors (those with 2 years or less experience), supervisors should offer greater structure and support, as there is considerable energy invested in performance anxiety among new professionals. At this initial point in their development, new trainees are what Stoltenberg and Delworth (1987) characterized as Level I supervisees, and gravitate to supervision that offers structure, support, and clear and consistent feedback. Accordingly, **Level I supervisees** have strong motivation to learn and, by extension, a desire to perform in a way that demonstrates competence. Because of intrapersonal counselor dynamics associated with performance, having access to client–counselor interactions using digital recording or live supervision is particularly useful given the unreliability of counselor self-report of clinical events that have occurred. Clinical supervision at this level has a tendency to focus on counselor thoughts, perceptions, and feelings, and less on what may be going on with the client. In other words, supervision efforts are devoted to helping the counselors/supervisees understand what may be going on for them individually, and how internal dynamics help to build or interfere with a good working alliance with the client. As a result of this dynamic, Huhra, Yamokoski-Maynhart, and Prieto (2008) recommended that supervisors continually use recording or observing of counseling sessions to monitor the accuracy of supervisee perceptions regarding events that occur during the session.

In the case of more experienced and competent counselors, who are **Level II supervisees**, Huhra et al. (2008) contended that these counselors are less anxious, as they have formed a clearer understanding of their competencies. However, at this level supervisors need to help counselor/supervisees differentiate between their needs and client needs. Unlike Level I supervisees, where the focus is more on counselor worldview, at this point in the counselor's professional development, there is greater focus on helping the counselor explore and focus on client needs. Using recording technology, supervisors can focus on specific client–counselor interactions to help counselor/supervisees process their thinking and emotional reactions. This focus leads to more effective self-evaluation. Huhra et al. contended that "the goal is to (a) facilitate communication about trainees' underlying thoughts and feelings and (b) increase their awareness of (and discrimination among) issues of concern to them and the client and the interactions between the two parties" (p. 416).

Finally, in instances where supervision is provided to more experienced counselors who have a clear understanding of their competencies, the focus is on areas needing improvement, and continuing to work on increasing skill levels (**Levels III and IIIa**; see Stoltenberg, McNeill, & Delworth, 1998). At this level, the supervisor may work more in a consultant rather than a mentor or teacher role. In this capacity, the supervisee may lead the discussion and conduct an analysis of recorded sessions with the supervisor, as opposed to earlier counselor levels that were more supervisor-directed. In situations where a supervisor has had the opportunity to work with the same counselor/supervisee throughout the initial stages to a more developed skill level, Huhra et al. (2008) noted that recorded sessions allow for a longitudinal perspective. Supervisors may wish to review recorded segments of issues that were personally and professionally challenging earlier, but now provide a completely different perspective and understanding. Supervisees, in turn, may want to continually monitor the supervision process to make sure that this experience is professionally rewarding and there are clear indications that their competence in providing rehabilitation counseling services is improving.

CONCLUSION

The review of clinical supervision research and what we can learn from it, presented in this chapter, may leave the reader wondering about the empirical basis that informs evidence-based practice. As a field of study, rehabilitation counseling supervision research is in an exploratory phase. We are only starting to learn how this process occurs in different settings and its perceived value to counselors and supervisors. We operate on the basis of a rudimentary but largely untested assumption that counselors who receive supervision will ultimately become better in providing counseling services; and, in turn, impact their clients in positive ways. Yet we know virtually nothing about how supervisors actually impact counselor behavior and case management decisions, and whether counselors or supervisors see any inherent value in clinical supervision and its connection to successful rehabilitation outcomes. We have a vague understanding of what the process involves from earlier graduate training but, once completed, continued efforts to build on this foundational work gradually fade away (Herbert & Caldwell, 2015). For whatever reason, clinical supervision seems to be something designed for the "newer professional." After a few years, there seems to be an unspoken acknowledgment that experienced counselors no longer have a need for it, as evident by the lack of participation in this process. We have not yet explored whether supervision has intended positive effects in counselor skill development, or perhaps impacts practice in a negative or even harmful way. One could reasonably expect that postgraduate supervision experiences that were not helpful would lead the counselor to refrain from any subsequent supervision. This outcome is coupled with the predicament that supervisors may also find clinical supervision something that they are not trained to provide. These factors contribute to the status quo of a process practiced widely, but not understood (Herbert, 2004a). For the most part, training interventions to enhance clinical supervision have been absent from the literature, with few exceptions (e.g., Herbert, Byun, Schultz, Tamez, & Atkinson, 2014). Until we can offer the profession successful training models and interventions that have empirical support, we will continue to operate more as art than science. In the meantime, counselors will have to advocate for supervision. As they become more experienced, counselors also may engage in peer supervision as a way to evolve as a master counselor. Supervisors also may engage in peer supervision to increase their awareness of facilitating counselor skill development and, when available, pursue formal training in clinical training. Finally, RC educators need to remind students that being a professional RC is an ongoing process that continues throughout one's career. Obtaining a graduate degree, certification as an RC, and counselor licensure are only the first steps in becoming a professional. In essence, these accomplishments provide us with professional benchmarks. Counselors may fail at some aspects initially, but through clinical supervision efforts, they may learn from mistakes so that they can continue to improve the QOL for people with disabilities. Operating within a vacuum without the benefit of having someone else review our work is not only unprofessional, but also unethical.

CONTENT REVIEW QUESTIONS

- What is the definition of clinical supervision and how is it different from administrative supervision?
- How often do RCs engage in clinical supervision and what methods do they typically use? Do they participate in the same way when they are newer counselors as opposed to when they have become more experienced counselors?
- How can the *Code of Professional Ethics for Rehabilitation Counselors* help in providing a framework when seeking clinical supervision services?
- What supervisor qualities and practices are indicative of good clinical supervision?
- What questions can I ask myself regarding multicultural competence?
- What parameters would I want to include when developing an individualized clinical supervision contract?
- What counseling theory do I subscribe to and how would that be relevant in clinical supervision?
- What are some things that I would look for in a clinical supervisor in order "to be heard?"
- Are there any preferences that I have regarding supervision methods to improve my skills (case review, live supervision, digital recordings) and what contributes to these preferences?
- If clinical supervision is important to my professional development, how will I ensure that I participate in this process once I begin my career as a professional counselor?

REFERENCES

American Counseling Association. (2014). *Code of ethics*. Alexandria, VA: Author. Retrieved from http://www .counseling.org/Resources/aca-code-of-ethics.pdf

Bernard, J. M., & Goodyear, R. K. (2009). *Fundamentals of clinical supervision* (4th ed.). Boston, MA: Allyn & Bacon.

Beveridge, S., Karpen, S., Chan, C., & Penrod, J. (2016). Application of the KVI-R to assess current training needs of private rehabilitation counselors. *Rehabilitation Counseling Bulletin, 59*, 213–223.

Bordin, E. S. (1983). A working alliance based model of supervision. *The Counseling Psychologist, 11*(1), 35–42.

Burkard, A. W., Knox, S., Hess, S., & Schultz, J. (2009). Lesbian, gay and bisexual affirmative and non-affirmative supervision. *Journal of Counseling Psychology, 56,* 176–188.

Campbell, J. M. (2006). *Essentials of clinical supervision.* Hoboken, NJ: Wiley.

Center for Credentialing and Education. (2016). ACS-approved clinical supervisor. Retrieved from http://www.cce-global.org

Cherry, K. (2016). Kurt Lewin quotes: Some of psychologist Kurt Lewin's best sayings. Retrieved from https://www.verywell.com/kurt-lewin-biography-1890-1947-2795540

Commission on Rehabilitation Counselor Certification. (1999). *CRC-CS certified rehabilitation counselor-clinical supervisor: An adjunct designation for specialized practice within rehabilitation counseling.* Rolling Meadows, IL: Author.

Commission on Rehabilitation Counselor Certification. (2016). *Code of professional ethics for rehabilitation counselors.* Schaumburg, IL: Author. Retrieved from https://www.crccertification.com/filebin/pdf/CRCC_Code_Eff_20170101.pdf

Council for Accreditation of Counseling and Related Educational Programs. (2016). *2016 CACREP Standards.* Alexandria, VA: Author. Retrieved from http://www.cacrep.org/section-3-professional-practice

Council on Rehabilitation Education. (2010). *Accreditation manual for masters level rehabilitation counselor education programs.* Schaumburg, IL: Author. Retrieved from http://www.core-rehab.org/Files/Doc/PDF/CORE%20ACCREDITATION%20%20MANUAL%20Revised%2005_21_2012.pdf

Cumming-McCann, A., & Accordino, M. P. (2005). Counselor characteristics, white racial attitudes, and self-reported multicultural counseling competencies. *Rehabilitation Counseling Bulletin, 48,* 167–176.

Ellis, M. V. (2010). Bridging the science and practice of clinical supervision: Some discoveries, some misconceptions. *The Clinical Supervisor, 29,* 95–116. Retrieved from http://www.tandfonline.com/doi/full/10.1080/07325221003741910

Ellis, M. V., Berger, L., Hanus, A. E., Ayala, E. E., Swords, B. A., & Siembor, M. (2014). Inadequate and harmful clinical supervision: Testing a revised framework and assessing occurrence. *The Counseling Psychologist, 42,* 434–472.

Falender, C. A., Burnes, T. R., & Ellis, M. V. (2013). Multicultural clinical supervision and benchmarks: Empirical support informing practice and supervisor training. *The Counseling Psychologist, 41,* 8–27.

Flynn, S. V., & Hays, D. C. (2015). Development and validation of the Comprehensive Counseling Skills Rubric. *Counseling Outcome Research and Evaluation, 6*(2), 87–99.

Goodwin, L. R., Jr. (2016). Professional disclosure in counseling. In I. Marini & M. Stebnicki (Eds.), *The professional counselor's desk reference* (2nd ed., pp. 69–74). New York, NY: Springer Publishing.

Hays, P. A. (2008). *Addressing cultural complexities in practice: Assessment, diagnosis, and therapy* (2nd ed.). Washington, DC: American Psychological Association.

Herbert, J. T. (2004a). Qualitative analysis of clinical supervision within the public vocational rehabilitation program. *Journal of Rehabilitation Administration, 28,* 51–74.

Herbert, J. T. (2004b). Clinical supervision. In D. R. Maki & T. F. Riggar (Eds.), *Handbook of rehabilitation counseling* (2nd ed., pp. 305–317). New York, NY: Springer Publishing.

Herbert, J. T. (2004c). Clinical supervision in rehabilitation counseling settings. In F. Chan, N. L. Berven, & K. R. Thomas (Eds.), *Counseling theories and techniques for rehabilitation health professionals* (pp. 510–533). New York, NY: Springer Publishing.

Herbert, J. T. (2012). Clinical supervision. In D. R. Maki & V. Tarvydas (Eds.), *The professional practice of rehabilitation counseling* (pp. 427–446). New York, NY: Springer Publishing.

Herbert, J. T. (2016a). Clinical supervision within counseling practice. In I. Marini & M. Stebnicki (Eds.), *The professional counselor's desk reference* (2nd ed., pp. 23–30). New York, NY: Springer Publishing.

Herbert, J. T. (2016b). Clinical supervision of rehabilitation counselors. In I. Marini & M. Stebnicki (Eds.), *The professional counselor's desk reference* (2nd ed., pp. 75–79). New York, NY: Springer Publishing.

Herbert, J. T., Byun, S., Schultz, J. C., Tamez, M., & Atkinson, H. A. (2014). Evaluation of a training program to enhance clinical supervision of state vocational rehabilitation supervisors. *Journal of Rehabilitation Administration, 38*(1), 19–34.

Herbert, J. T., & Caldwell, T. A. (2015). Clinical supervision in rehabilitation counseling practice. In F. Chan, N. L. Berven, & K. R. Thomas (Eds.), *Counseling theories and techniques for rehabilitation health professionals* (pp. 443–461). New York, NY: Springer Publishing.

Herbert, J. T., & Trusty, J. (2006). Clinical supervision practices and satisfaction within the public vocational rehabilitation program. *Rehabilitation Counseling Bulletin, 49,* 66–80.

Huhra, R., Yamokoski-Maynhart, C. A., & Prieto, L. R. (2008). Reviewing videotape in supervision: A developmental approach. *Journal of Counseling and Development, 86,* 412–418.

International Certification & Reciprocity Consortium. (2016). About IC & RC's credential. Retrieved from http://www.internationalcredentialing.org/creds

Jacques, M. E. (1959). *Critical counseling behavior in rehabilitation behavior in rehabilitation settings*. Iowa City, IA: State University of Iowa, College of Education.

Kagan, N. (1980). Influencing human interaction—Eighteen years with IPR. In A. K. Hess (Ed.), *Psychotherapy supervision: Theory, research and practice* (pp. 262–283). New York, NY: Wiley.

King, C. L. (2008). *Rehabilitation counselor supervision in the private sector: An examination of the long term disability system* (Unpublished doctoral dissertation). Boston University, Boston, MA.

Ladany, N., Mori, Y., & Mehr, K. E. (2013). Effective and ineffective supervision. *The Counseling Psychologist, 41*, 28–47.

Landon, T. J. (2016). *Perceptions of supervisory knowledge, behavior, and self-efficacy: Supervisor effectiveness in performing clinical supervision and developing the supervisory relationship* (Unpublished doctoral dissertation). East Lansing: Michigan State University.

Larsen, D., Flesaker, K., & Stege, R. (2008). Qualitative interviewing using interpersonal process recall: Investigating internal experiences during professional–client conversations. *International Journal of Qualitative Methods, 7*(1), 18–37.

Leahy, M. J., Chan, F., & Saunders, J. L. (2003). Job functions and knowledge requirements of certified rehabilitation counselors in the 21st century. *Rehabilitation Counseling Bulletin, 46*, 66–81.

Leahy, M. J., Chan, F., Sung, C., & Kim, M. (2013). Empirically derived test specifications for the certified rehabilitation counselor examination. *Rehabilitation Counseling Bulletin, 56*, 199–214.

Matrone, K., & Leahy, M. (2005). The relationship between vocational rehabilitation client outcomes and rehabilitation counselor multicultural counseling competencies. *Rehabilitation Counseling Bulletin, 48*, 233–244.

McCarthy, A. K. (2013). Relationship between supervisory working alliance and client outcomes in state vocational rehabilitation counseling. *Rehabilitation Counseling Bulletin, 57*, 23–30.

Mintz, L. B., & Bieschke, K. J. (2009). Counseling psychology model training values statement addressing diversity: Development and introduction to the major contribution. *The Counseling Psychologist, 37*, 634–640.

Muratori, M. C. (2001). Examining supervisor impairment from the counselor trainee's perspective. *Counselor Education and Supervision, 41*(1), 41–56.

Muthard, J. E., & Salamone, P. R. (1969). The roles and functions of the rehabilitation counselor. *Rehabilitation Counseling Bulletin, 13*, 81–168.

National Board for Certified Counselors. (1998). NBCC news notes. Retrieved from http://www.nbcc.org/Assets/Newsletter/Issues/spring98.pdf

Schultz, J. C., Ososkie, J. N., Fried, J. H., Nelson, R. E., & Bardos, A. N. (2002). Clinical supervision in public rehabilitation counseling settings. *Rehabilitation Counseling Bulletin, 45*, 213–322.

Stoltenberg, C. D., & Delworth, C. (1987). *Supervising counselors and therapists: A developmental approach*. San Francisco, CA: Jossey-Bass.

Stoltenberg, C. D., McNeill, B., & Delworth, U. (1998). *IDM supervision: An integrated developmental model for supervising counselors and therapists*. San Francisco, CA: Jossey-Bass.

Tarvydas, V. M., Hartley, M. T., & Gerald, M. (2016). What practitioners need to know about professional credentialing. In I. Marini & M. Stebnicki (Eds.), *The professional counselor's desk reference* (2nd ed., pp. 17–22). New York, NY: Springer Publishing.

Tate, K. A., Bloom, M., Tassara, M., & Caperton, W. (2014). Counselor competence, performance assessment, and program evaluation: Using psychometric instruments. *Measurement and Evaluation in Counseling and Development, 47*, 291–306.

Thielsen, V. A., & Leahy, M. J. (2001). Essential knowledge and skills for effective clinical supervision in rehabilitation counseling. *Rehabilitation Counseling Bulletin, 44*, 196–208.

Wilcoxon, S. A., Norem, K., & Magnuson, S. (2005). Supervisees' contributions to lousy supervision outcomes. *Journal of Professional Counseling, Practice, Theory, and Research, 33*(2), 31–49.

Wong, L. C. J., Wong, P. T. P., & Ishiyama, F. I. (2013). What helps and what hinders in cross-cultural clinical supervision: A critical incident study. *The Counseling Psychologist, 41*, 66–85.

Acronyms for Common Terms in Rehabilitation Counseling

BY CATEGORIES

SELECTED ORGANIZATIONS

ACA	American Counseling Association

Subdivisions of the ACA

ARCA	American Rehabilitation Counseling Association
IAMFC	International Association for Marriage and Family Counseling
NRA	National Rehabilitation Association

Subdivisions of the NRA

NAMRC	National Association of Multicultural Rehabilitation Concerns (formerly National Association of Non-White Workers [NANRW])
NRCA	National Rehabilitation Counseling Association
RCEA	Rehabilitation Counselors and Educators Association

OTHER ORGANIZATIONS

AAMFT	American Association for Marriage and Family Therapy
ACCD	American Coalition of Citizens with Disabilities
ADAPT	American Disabled for Adaptive Public Transportation
ADARA	Professionals Networking for Excellence in Service Delivery with Individuals who are Deaf or Hard of Hearing (formerly American Deafness and Rehabilitation Association)
AERA	American Educational Research Association
AMCHA	American Mental Health Counselors Association
APA	American Psychological Association
ARC	Alliance for Rehabilitation Counseling
IARP	International Association of Rehabilitation Professionals
IRI	Institute on Rehabilitation Issues

NCME	National Council on Measurement in Education
NCRE	National Council on Rehabilitation Education
PNHP	Physicians for a National Health Program
RESNA	Rehabilitation Engineering and Assistive Technology Society of North America
UN	United Nations

Specialized Agencies of the UN/Acronyms

CRPD	Convention on the Rights of Persons with Disabilities
CSDH	Commission on Social Determinants of Health
ICD	*International Classification of Diseases and Related Health Problems*
ICF	International Classification of Functioning, Disability and Health
ICF-CY	Children and Youth Version of the International Classification of Functioning, Disability and Health
ICFDH-2	International Classification of Functioning, Disability and Health; Beta-2
ICIDH	International Classification of Impairments, Disabilities and Handicaps
ILO	International Labour Organization
MDG	Millennium Development Goals
UNDP	United Nations Development Programme
UNESCO	United Nations Educational, Scientific and Cultural Organization
UNICEF	United Nations International Children's Emergency Fund
WHO	World Health Organization

CERTIFICATION BODIES/CREDENTIALS

AASCB	American Association of State Counseling Boards
APCB	Addiction Professionals Certification Board
CFT	Certified Family Therapist
CRC	Certified Rehabilitation Counselor
CRCC	Commission on Rehabilitation Counselor Certification
LPC	Licensed Professional Counselor
NBCC	National Board for Certified Counselors
NCA	National Credentialing Academy

ACCREDITATION BODIES

CACREP	Council for Accreditation of Counseling and Related Educational Programs
CHEA	Council for Higher Education Accreditation
COPA	Council on Postsecondary Accreditation
CORE	Council on Rehabilitation Education
CORPA	Commission on Recognition of Postsecondary Accreditation (formerly Council on Postsecondary Accreditation [COPA])

GOVERNMENTAL/LEGISLATIVE

ACTKIT	Assertive Community Treatment Knowledge Informing Transformation
ADA	Americans with Disabilities Act
CAP	Client Assistance Program
CFR	Code of Federal Regulations

CIL or ILC	Center for Independent Living
DBTAC	Disability and Business Technical Assistance Center
DCS	Department of Correctional Services
DHS	Department of Human Services
DOL	Department of Labor
DOT	Dictionary of Occupational Titles
DRRP	Disability and Rehabilitation Research Program
EEOC	Equal Employment Opportunity Commission
EN	Employment Network
FMLA	Family and Medical Leave Act
GAO	Government Accountability Office
GINA	Genetic Information Nondiscrimination Act
HIPAA	Health Insurance Portability and Accountability Act
HITECH	Health Information Technology for Economic and Clinical Health Act
HUD	Housing and Urban Development
IPE	Individual Plan of Employment (formerly Individualized Written Rehabilitation Plan [IWRP])
JAN	Job Accommodation Network
NCD	National Council on Disability
NCDDR	National Center for the Dissemination of Disability Research
NIDRR	National Institute on Disability and Rehabilitation Research
NTIA	National Telecommunications and Information Administration
OCR	Office of Civil Rights
OIDAP	Occupational Information Development Advisory Panel
OIS	Occupational Information System
OSERS	Office of Special Education and Rehabilitative Services
PHI	Protected Health Information
RRTC	Rehabilitation Research and Training Center
RSA	Rehabilitation Services Administration
SAMHSA	Substance Abuse and Mental Health Services Administration
SSA	Social Security Administration
SSDI	Social Security Disability Insurance
SSI	Supplemental Security Income
TWWIIA	Ticket to Work and Work Incentives Improvement Act
USERRA	Uniformed Services Employment and Reemployment Rights Act
VOIP	Voice Over the Internet Protocol
WIA	Workforce Investment Act

CANADIAN ACRONYMS

CARP	Canadian Association of Rehabilitation Professionals
CCRC	Canadian Certified Rehabilitation Counselor

MISCELLANEOUS

AT	Assistive Technology
CBR	Community-Based Rehabilitation
DALY	Disability-Adjusted Life Year
DPO	Disabled Peoples' Organization
DSM	*Diagnostic and Statistical Manual of Mental Disorders*
GATB	General Aptitude Test Battery
GDP	Gross Domestic Product
GRE	Graduate Record Examination

HMO	Health Maintenance Organization
HRQOL	Health-Related Quality of Life
IDM	Integrated Development Model
INCOME	Imaging, iNforming, Choosing, Obtaining, Maintaining, and Exiting
IPS	Individual Placement and Support
IRT	Item Response Theory
JTI	Job Task Inventory
MHID	Multiple Heritage Identity Development
MID	Minority Identity Development
MVS	My Vocational Situation
NGO	Nongovernmental Organization
PDO	People with Disability Organization
POS	Point of Service
PPO	Preferred Provider Organization
PSR	Psychosocial Rehabilitation
PUI	Problematic Use of the Internet
PWD	People with Disability
QOL	Quality of Life
RC	Rehabilitation Counselor
RCE	Rehabilitation Counselor Education
R/CID	Racial/Cultural Identity Development
RIASEC	Realistic, Investigate, Artistic, Social, Enterprising, and Conventional
SAT	Scholastic Aptitude Test
SCID-I	Structured Clinical Interview for DSM-IV Axis I Disorders
SDS	Self-Directed Search
SSN	Social Safety Net
TSA	Transferable Skills Assessment
VR	Vocational Rehabilitation
W3C WAI	World Wide Web Consortium Web Accessibility Initiative

ALPHABETICALLY

AAMFT	American Association for Marriage and Family Therapy
AASCB	American Association of State Counseling Boards
ACA	American Counseling Association
ACCD	American Coalition of Citizens with Disabilities
ACTKIT	Assertive Community Treatment Knowledge Informing Transformation
ADA	Americans with Disabilities Act
ADAPT	American Disabled for Adaptive Public Transportation
ADARA	Professionals Networking for Excellence in Service Delivery with Individuals who are Deaf or Hard of Hearing (formerly American Deafness And Rehabilitation Association)
AERA	American Educational Research Association
AMCHA	American Mental Health Counselors Association
APA	American Psychological Association
APCB	Addiction Professionals Certification Board
ARC	Alliance for Rehabilitation Counseling
ARCA	American Rehabilitation Counseling Association
AT	Assistive Technology
CACREP	Council for Accreditation of Counseling and Related Educational Programs

CAP	Client Assistance Program
CARP	Canadian Association of Rehabilitation Professionals
CBR	Community-Based Rehabilitation
CCRC	Canadian Certified Rehabilitation Counselor
CFR	Code of Federal Regulations
CFT	Certified Family Therapist
CHEA	Council for Higher Education Accreditation
CIL or ILC	Center for Independent Living
COPA	Council on Postsecondary Accreditation
CORE	Council on Rehabilitation Education
CORPA	Commission on Recognition of Postsecondary Accreditation (formerly Council on Postsecondary Accreditation [COPA])
CRC	Certified Rehabilitation Counselor
CRCC	Commission on Rehabilitation Counselor Certification
CRPD	Convention on the Rights of Persons with Disabilities
CSDH	Commission on Social Determinants of Health
DALY	Disability-Adjusted Life Year
DBTAC	Disability and Business Technical Assistance Center
DCS	Department of Correctional Services
DHS	Department of Human Services
DOL	Department of Labor
DOT	Dictionary of Occupational Titles
DPO	Disabled Peoples' Organization
DRRP	Disability and Rehabilitation Research Program
DSM	*Diagnostic and Statistical Manual of Mental Disorders*
EEOC	Equal Employment Opportunity Commission
EN	Employment Network
FMLA	Family and Medical Leave Act
GAO	Government Accountability Office
GATB	General Aptitude Test Battery
GDP	Gross Domestic Product
GINA	Genetic Information Nondiscrimination Act
GRE	Graduate Record Examination
HIPAA	Health Insurance Portability and Accountability Act
HITECH	Health Information Technology for Economic and Clinical Health Act
HMO	Health Maintenance Organization
HRQOL	Health-Related Quality of Life
HUD	Housing and Urban Development
IAMFC	International Association for Marriage and Family Counseling
IARP	International Association of Rehabilitation Professionals
ICD	*International Classification of Diseases and Related Health Problems*
ICF	International Classification of Functioning, Disability and Health
ICF-CY	Children and Youth Version of the International Classification of Functioning, Disability and Health
ICFDH-2	International Classification of Functioning, Disability and Health; Beta-2
ICIDH	International Classification of Impairments, Disabilities and Handicaps
IDM	Integrated Development Model
ILO	International Labour Organization
INCOME	Imaging, iNforming, Choosing, Obtaining, Maintaining, and Exiting
IPE	Individual Plan of Employment (formerly Individualized Written Rehabilitation Plan [IWRP])
IPS	Individual Placement and Support
IRI	Institute on Rehabilitation Issues

IRT	Item Response Theory
JAN	Job Accommodation Network
JTI	Job Task Inventory
LPC	Licensed Professional Counselor
MDG	Millennium Development Goals
MHID	Multiple Heritage Identity Development
MID	Minority Identity Development
MVS	My Vocational Situation
NAMRC	National Association of Multicultural Rehabilitation Concerns (formerly National Association of Non-White Workers [NANRW])
NBCC	National Board for Certified Counselors
NCA	National Credentialing Academy
NCD	National Council on Disability
NCDDR	National Center for the Dissemination of Disability Research
NCME	National Council on Measurement in Education
NCRE	National Council on Rehabilitation Education
NGO	Nongovernmental Organization
NIDRR	National Institute on Disability and Rehabilitation Research
NRA	National Rehabilitation Association
NRCA	National Rehabilitation Counseling Association
NTIA	National Telecommunications and Information Administration
OCR	Office of Civil Rights
OIDAP	Occupational Information Development Advisory Panel
OIS	Occupational Information System
OSERS	Office of Special Education and Rehabilitative Services
PDO	People with Disability Organization
PHI	Protected Health Information
PNHP	Physicians for a National Health Program
POS	Point of Service
PPO	Preferred Provider Organization
PSR	Psychosocial Rehabilitation
PUI	Problematic Use of the Internet
PWD	People with Disability
QOL	Quality of Life
RC	Rehabilitation Counselor
RCE	Rehabilitation Counselor Education
RCEA	Rehabilitation Counselors and Educators Association
R/CID	Racial/Cultural Identity Development
RESNA	Rehabilitation Engineering and Assistive Technology Society of North America
RIASEC	Realistic, Investigate, Artistic, Social, Enterprising, and Conventional
RRTC	Rehabilitation Research and Training Center
RSA	Rehabilitation Services Administration
SAMHSA	Substance Abuse and Mental Health Services Administration
SAT	Scholastic Aptitude Test
SCID-I	Structured Clinical Interview for DSM-IV Axis I Disorders
SDS	Self-Directed Search
SSA	Social Security Administration
SSDI	Social Security Disability Insurance
SSI	Supplemental Security Income
SSN	Social Safety Net
TSA	Transferable Skills Assessment
TWWIIA	Ticket to Work and Work Incentives Improvement Act

UN	United Nations
UNDP	United Nations Development Programme
UNESCO	United Nations Educational, Scientific and Cultural Organization
UNICEF	United Nations International Children's Emergency Fund
USERRA	Uniformed Services Employment and Reemployment Rights Act
VOIP	Voice Over the Internet Protocol
VR	Vocational Rehabilitation
W3C WAI	World Wide Web Consortium Web Accessibility Initiative
WHO	World Health Organization
WIA	Workforce Investment Act

Scope of Practice for Rehabilitation Counseling

ASSUMPTIONS

- The Scope of Practice Statement identifies knowledge and skills required for the provision of effective rehabilitation counseling services to persons with physical, mental, developmental, cognitive, and emotional disabilities as embodied in the standards of the profession's credentialing organizations.
- Several rehabilitation disciplines and related processes (e.g., vocational evaluation, job development and job placement, work adjustment, and case management) are tied to the central field of rehabilitation counseling. The field of rehabilitation counseling is a specialty within the rehabilitation profession with counseling at its core, and is differentiated from other related counseling fields.
- The professional scope of rehabilitation counseling practice is also differentiated from an individual scope of practice, which may overlap, but is more specialized than the professional scope. An individual scope of practice is based on one's own knowledge of the abilities and skills that have been gained through a program of education and professional experience. A person is ethically bound to limit his or her practice to that individual scope of practice.

UNDERLYING VALUES

- Facilitation of independence, integration, and inclusion of people with disabilities in employment and the community.
- Belief in the dignity and worth of all people.
- Commitment to a sense of equal justice based on a model of accommodation to provide and equalize the opportunities to participate in all rights and privileges available to all people and a commitment to supporting persons with disabilities in advocacy activities to achieve this status and empower themselves.
- Emphasis on the holistic nature of human function, which is procedurally facilitated by the utilization of techniques such as:
  - interdisciplinary teamwork;
  - counseling to assist in maintaining a holistic perspective; and

- a commitment to considering individuals within the context of their family systems and communities.
- Recognition of the importance of focusing on the assets of the person.
- Commitment to models of service delivery that emphasize integrated, comprehensive services, which are mutually planned by the consumer and the rehabilitation counselor.

Scope of Practice Statement

Rehabilitation counseling is a systematic process that assists persons with physical, mental, developmental, cognitive, and emotional disabilities to achieve their personal, career, and independent living goals in the most integrated setting possible through the application of the counseling process. The counseling process involves communication, goal setting, and beneficial growth or change through self-advocacy, psychological, vocational, social, and behavioral interventions. The specific techniques and modalities utilized within this rehabilitation counseling process may include, but are not limited to:

- assessment and appraisal;
- diagnosis and treatment planning;
- career (vocational) counseling;
- individual and group counseling treatment interventions focused on facilitating adjustments to the medical and psychosocial impact of disability;
- case management, referral, and service coordination;
- program evaluation and research;
- interventions to remove environmental, employment, and attitudinal barriers;
- consultation services among multiple parties and regulatory systems;
- job analysis, job development, and placement services, including assistance with employment and job accommodations; and
- the provision of consultation about and access to rehabilitation technology.

Selected Definitions

The following definitions are provided to increase the understanding of certain key terms and concepts used in the Scope of Practice Statement for Rehabilitation Counseling.

Appraisal

Selecting, administering, scoring, and interpreting instruments designed to assess an individual's aptitudes, abilities, achievements, interests, personal characteristics, disabilities, and mental, emotional, or behavioral disorders, as well as the use of methods and techniques for understanding human behavior in relation to coping with, adapting to, or changing life situations.

Diagnosis and Treatment Planning

Assessing, analyzing, and providing diagnostic descriptions of mental, emotional, or behavioral conditions or disabilities; exploring possible solutions; and developing and implementing a treatment plan for mental, emotional, and psychosocial adjustment or development. Diagnosis and treatment planning shall not be construed to permit the performance of any act that rehabilitation counselors are not educated and trained to perform.

Counseling Treatment Intervention

The application of cognitive, affective, behavioral, and systemic counseling strategies includes developmental, wellness, pathologic, and multicultural principles of human behavior. Such interventions are specifically implemented in the context of a professional counseling relationship and may include, but are not limited to: appraisal; individual, group, marriage, and family counseling and psychotherapy; the diagnostic description and treatment of persons with mental, emotional, and behavioral disorders or disabilities; guidance and consulting to facilitate normal growth and development, including educational and career development; the utilization of functional assessments and career counseling for persons requesting assistance in adjusting to a disability or handicapping condition; referrals; consulting; and research.

Referral

Evaluating and identifying the needs of a client to determine the advisability of referrals to other specialists, advising the client of such judgments, and communicating as requested or deemed appropriate to such referral sources.

Case Management

A systematic process merging counseling and managerial concepts and skills through the application of techniques derived from intuitive and researched methods, thereby advancing efficient and effective decision making for functional control of self, client, setting, and other relevant factors for anchoring a proactive practice. In case management, the counselor's role is focused on interviewing, counseling, planning rehabilitation programs, coordinating services, interacting with significant others, placing clients and following up with them, monitoring progress, and solving problems.

Program Evaluation

The effort to determine what changes occur as a result of a planned program by comparing actual changes (results) with desired changes (stated goals), and by identifying the degree to which the activity (planned program) is responsible for those changes.

Research

A systematic effort to collect, analyze, and interpret quantitative or qualitative data that describe how social characteristics, behavior, emotions, cognition, disabilities, mental disorders, and interpersonal transactions among individuals and organizations interact.

Consultation

The application of scientific principles and procedures in counseling and human development to provide assistance in understanding and solving current or potential problems that the consultee may have in relation to a third party, be it an individual, group, or organization.

Index

CPSIA information can be obtained
at www.ICGtesting.com
Printed in the USA
BVHW010931180621
609835BV00018B/70